POLITICAL ECONOMY

POLITICAL ECONOMY

The Contest of Economic Ideas

Frank Stilwell

OXFORD

UNIVERSITY PRESS

OXFORD

UNIVERSITY PRESS

253 Normanby Road, South Melbourne, Victoria 3205, Australia

Oxford University Press is a department of the University of Oxford.
It furthers the University's objective of excellence in research, scholarship,
and education by publishing worldwide in

Oxford New York

Auckland Bangkok Buenos Aires Cape Town Chennai
Dar es Salaam Delhi Hong Kong Istanbul Karachi Kolkata
Kuala Lumpur Madrid Melbourne Mexico City Mumbai Nairobi
São Paulo Shanghai Taipei Tokyo Toronto

OXFORD is a trade mark of Oxford University Press
in the UK and in certain other countries

National Library of Australia
Cataloguing-in-Publication data:

Stilwell, Frank J. B.
  Political economy: the contest of economic ideas.

  Bibliography.
  Includes index.
  ISBN 0 19 551458 0.

  1. Economics. I. Title.

  330

Typeset by OUPANZS
Printed through Bookpac Production Services, Singapore

CONTENTS

PREFACE

This book seeks to provide an overview of political economy and a scholarly contribution to its further development. It has been written in the conviction that economic issues are fundamentally important to our well-being, individually and collectively. How wealth is created and used, the inequalities between rich and poor, and the tensions between economic growth and the environment are important concerns. However, the capacity of conventional economics to illuminate these issues is limited; and it is therefore necessary to forge a more coherent and constructive political economic alternative.

The book has also been written from a particular pedagogic perspective. This emphasises the desirability of seeing the 'big picture' right from the outset, of coming to grips with the economic system as a whole and its connection with social and political concerns. It focuses on the diversity of viewpoints on economic issues, thereby providing an invitation to controversy. It emphasises the necessity of looking carefully at the principal analytical tools and value judgments associated with each school of economic thought. Subsequent and more sophisticated study can build on this basis.

It is quite a big book. A short cut through it is possible, if you are seeking only a broad overview of political economy and some application to contemporary issues. You could achieve this by reading the chapters in the first two parts, the first chapter only in each of the next five parts, and then all chapters in the last two parts. That would mean twenty chapters rather than the full forty. You could also skip some of the 'boxes', which deal with more technical and specialist issues or provide biographical information about prominent figures in political economy. You would miss out on the details of the competing schools of thought, but you would nevertheless gain an overview of the major contributions and controversies. You would also be introduced to the ideas of leading personalities in the historical development of economic analysis: Adam Smith, Karl Marx, Alfred Marshall, Thorstein Veblen, and John Maynard Keynes. You might then feel inclined to go back and 'flesh out' your understanding of political economy—and the contributions of some other outstanding scholars—by reading the remaining twenty chapters. Either way, whether you tackle the book as a whole or take the short cut, I hope it leads you to delve deeper into this fascinating field of enquiry.

For stimulation in developing the book, I would like to thank my colleagues in the Political Economy discipline at the University of Sydney: Tim Anderson, Dick Bryan, Gavan Butler, Pamela Cawthorne, Joseph Halevi, Liz Hill, Evan Jones, Andrew Mack, Gabrielle Meagher and Stuart Rosewarne. To Eleanor Armstrong goes my deep gratitude for her technical skill in typing the manuscript and dealing with multiple revisions thereto. Chris Williams also helped at an early stage in this word processing. Thanks are also due to Jill Henry, formerly of Oxford University Press, for her enthusiasm about producing this book and to Cathryn Game, Chris Wyness, Racheal Stines, Heather Fawcett and Carol Aikman for their roles in bringing it physically to fruition. To Ann Grealis goes my loving appreciation for her continuous encouragement.

The book is dedicated to my students—past, present, and future.

Frank Stilwell

PART I

Economic Processes and Problems

The current context

CHAPTER 1

What is Political Economy?

What problems does political economy address?
What questions does it ask?
On what analytic foundations does it build?

As a discipline, modern political economy provides an accessible approach to the study of economic issues. It seeks to 'illuminate the world in which we live so that we may act in it intelligently and effectively'.[1] This introductory chapter explains how this ambition can be achieved. It suggests three ways of defining political economy: (1) in terms of the practical, 'real-world' problems on which it focuses; (2) in terms of how these problems are analysed; and (3) in terms of the currents of economic thought from which it draws. It also proposes that the pedagogy of modern political economy can counteract the dwindling interest in the formal study of economics.

RELEVANCE TO REAL ECONOMIC PROBLEMS

The relevance of economic issues in the real world is obvious. Economic concerns beset us individually in our everyday lives—the problems of earning a living, managing an income, and making decisions about consumption and saving. They also beset us collectively, necessitating political decisions on difficult issues, such as how to balance economic growth against environmental concerns, how much to redistribute income through taxes and government expenditure, and how to deal with imbalances in international trade.

The way in which these issues have been addressed in economic analysis and policy has been strongly influenced by one particular economic theory—neoclassical economics. This emerged in the late nineteenth century and is still the dominant economic orthodoxy today. It stresses the beneficial effects of competitive markets as a means of allocating economic resources. From the neoclassical viewpoint, the role of government is, at most, that of an adjunct to the 'free-market' economy. The underlying view is that the capitalist economy is a stable, self-equilibrating system.

A frequently recurring charge against this economic orthodoxy is that it is 'unrealistic'. Models of market exchange under competitive conditions fail to illuminate the world in which we live. Such models, it is commonly said, prioritise elegance over relevance. There is much in that criticism. However, the theoretical models have a strong influence on economic policies in practice; and they therefore have an awesome relevance—for better or worse. This has been particularly evident in the last two decades, which have seen the ascendancy of neo-liberalism. Orthodox economic reasoning has given rise to particular policy prescriptions, such as the liberalisation of trade, the deregulation of capital and labour markets, the privatisation of public enterprises, and the extension of 'user-pays' principles to the public services that have not been privatised. The proponents of these policies seem relatively untroubled by the failure of the real world to exhibit the features assumed in the abstract theories. It is as if the real world is being reconstructed in the image of a particular theory. Either way—as a rarefied theoretical exercise or as a vulgarised version used for political purposes—conventional economics has deep problems.[2]

A more refreshing alternative—and one that makes for more interesting study—is to directly confront *current political economic problems and policy issues*. There is no shortage of such concerns: the challenge for governments posed by the power of multinational corporations; the tension between economic growth and ecological sustainability; the intensification of economic insecurity and economic inequality driven by contemporary structural economic changes; the proliferation of speculative financial activities and their adverse consequences for economic stability and productivity; and the continuing problems of promoting balanced economic and social development, especially in poorer nations.

The immediate appeal of the political economic approach is its direct confrontation of these issues. A link is thereby established between studies in economics and what is reported in the daily newspapers, and on radio and television current affairs programs. Simultaneously, links are created with other areas of study, such as geography, history, social studies, political science, and industrial relations. Indeed, this *interdisciplinary* character of political economy is one of its strengths. Real-world phenomena do not fit neatly into boxes labelled 'economic', 'social', 'political', or 'cultural'. These categories have been constructed for academic convenience. The disciplinary divisions—between economics, sociology, and political science, for example—can be useful for the organisation of research and study, but they can impede a full understanding. Certainly, economic analysis is the richer if it draws from these other disciplines. Concurrently, the interdisciplinary inclination of political economy poses considerable challenges.

THE POLITICAL ECONOMIC QUESTIONS

Major explorations require an orderly procedure. In the case of political economy, this means systematically 'interrogating' each issue under investigation by posing questions such as:
- What is happening?
- Why?
- Who gains; who loses?
- Does it matter?
- If so, what can be done about it, and by whom?

Take the issue of globalisation, for example. It is commonly said that we are living at a time when our lives are being radically changed by the integration of economic activities on a global scale. Globalisation is said to be breaking down the territorial boundaries limiting the opportunities (and threats) that confront us. Technological and economic changes are said to be transforming society and culture. Is this really so?

A systematic, political economic analysis of these processes can be aided by asking the above questions.

First, to answer '*what is happening?*' requires a careful definition of the process. It requires important distinctions to be made between the globalisation of finance and trade, of culture, of environmental concerns, and of human rights. Each of these is affected by globalisation in different ways. Focusing on the globalisation of business activities provides the most distinct political economic perspective. It requires careful consideration of the extent to which 'globalising' economic processes involve international trade in goods and services, international investment, or international finance (including the proliferation of speculative activities).

The question '*why?*' draws attention to the causal factors. So, for each of these aspects of globalistion, we have to explore the relative significance of, for example, technological change, consumerism, and government policies in driving the changes. It is a process of enquiry that takes nothing as given. In the case of globalisation, it seeks to illuminate the complex interactions between forces external to nation states and forces nurtured within them. The goal is nothing short of understanding the political economic forces reshaping modern society.

The question '*who gains; who loses?*' is equally complex. This can be illustrated by looking at a specific aspect of globalisation, such as the changing international distribution of jobs. Large multinational companies, seeking to take advantage of differential labour costs, have often relocated parts of their routine manufacturing activities to Third World nations. This helps the companies maximise their rates of profit. Their employees in more affluent nations face pressures for wage reduction in order to try to keep the local manufacturing businesses 'competitive', or face unemployment if the firms go under. Whether these workers are losers in the longer term depends on whether there are alternative employment opportunities. That depends on the regional distribution of jobs in the manufacturing industries shedding labour and the regional pattern of jobs in other sectors, such as the service industries, which may be expanding. It also depends on the impediments to occupational and geographical mobility.

Meanwhile, the same processes of globalisation produce winners and losers among people in the more economically peripheral nations. Significant numbers of Third World workers, for example, have gained industrial employment previously unavailable to them. However, although usually better paying than the traditional occupations in those countries, these jobs are frequently associated with particular health or environmental risks. Whether the industrialisation, often localised in enclaves called 'export-processing zones', has 'trickle-down' benefits for the rest of the society is also uncertain and depends on how and where the extra income is spent, and on whether the companies pay significant amounts of money in local taxes. The close linking of national economies can also create problems if political or economic instability develops in a country. These circumstances of international economic interdependence remove the 'shock absorbers' that domestic economic policy instruments have previously provided. Taking stock of winners and losers in a situation like this is evidently very difficult. It illustrates the interdependence of economic, social, and political considerations, which is one of the hallmarks of political economy.

An evaluative approach is also necessarily part of political economy, for the link between analysis of problems and consideration of policy responses is inescapably normative. Hence the question '*does it matter?*' Unless this issue is confronted, remedial policies and strategic responses cannot be systematically developed. It requires specification of the *criteria* by which evaluation occurs. Such criteria may include *efficiency* (in achieving what?), *equity* (according to what standards of fairness?), *sustainability* (economic, social, or ecological?), and *consistency with other social and political goals* (which themselves need to be clearly specified). Establishing acceptable trade-offs between different goals is equally problematic. For example, would we be willing to accept a lower average standard of living in order to reduce the gulf between rich and poor? Or, how much short-term production might we be willing to sacrifice in order to achieve an economy that is sustainable in the long term? Political economy emphasises that a 'positive', or 'value-free', economics is not possible without setting aside all the important and interesting questions. The task for political economy is to confront the evaluative issues systematically and openly.

Finally, in considering '*what can be done?*', the role of government—and the state generally—comes under scrutiny. On the issue of globalisation, a key question is whether the state's capacity for national economic management is undermined by the greater mobility of capital. If it is, by how much is it undermined? To what extent, and in which policy fields, has the state the ability to shape the 'terms of engagement' with the global economy? If the state is indeed losing its managerial capacity, to which other institutions—local, non-governmental, or supranational—can we instead look to control the processes of change? Can labour, environmental, or consumer movements, for example, 'go global' in order to counteract the globalisation of business and finance? These are the kinds of big, strategic questions that modern political economy explores.

We are not simply passive observers of political economic change: we are active participants, and our effectiveness depends on how systematically we address the strategic question of what can be done.

CONTRIBUTORY CONCEPTUAL CURRENTS

Describing the concerns of political economy in terms of the major challenges in a changing world is a down-to-earth beginning to our explorations. Analysis of these contemporary challenges requires us to draw on the rich heritage of concepts that have been developed to aid understanding of how the economy works. The focus on the big, 'real-world' questions does not deny the value of economic theories, but it does require us to make selective use of the competing currents of economic analysis.

Among the different schools of economic thought that have developed during the last two and a half centuries, four have obvious relevance in the construction of modern political economy. One is *classical political economy*. Eighteenth-century scholars like Adam Smith and David Ricardo wrote about economic affairs when capitalism was emerging from feudalism to become the dominant economic system in Western Europe. Although the economy then looked very different from today's—with less sophisticated production and transport technologies, and smaller businesses that usually served only local markets—Smith's and Ricardo's insights into economic interests and political processes are of enduring relevance. The notion that the economic system produces goods and services surplus to what is required for social reproduction remains valuable. Understanding how that surplus may be expanded—whether through trade and an increasingly complex division of labour, for example—is central to the analysis of economic growth. Understanding how the surplus is generated also leads to explaining how the fruits of economic activity are distributed—among capitalists, workers, and landowners, for example. Classical political economy is generally held to have markedly conservative political implications, but the underlying conceptions of economic production, distribution and economic growth can be given a progressive, modern twist. The emphasis on the troublesome issue of land and land ownership, ignored by much economic theorising over the last century, is particularly important.

Marxist economics also warrants careful consideration. Having its roots in classical political economy, it provides a quite different, more critical, interpretation of capitalism. It emphasises the basis of the capitalist economy in particular property relations, the associated class structure and economic inequalities, and the relentless drive for capital accumulation. It posits the exploitation of labour as the source of the economic surplus. From that springs class conflict and, according to Marxists, the potential for radical political economic change. The tenets of Marxist economic analysis that underlie this view (such as the labour theory of value, the theory of surplus value, and the explanation of recurrent economic crises in terms of overproduction and underconsumption) need to be critically re-evaluated to test their applicability to the modern economy. These are, quite properly, focal points for debate about the relevance of Marxism today. Generally, though, the holistic character of this approach to capitalism has evident appeal in the current context. Globalisation, for example, can be interpreted from this perspective as the drive by capitalist business interests to break through the constraints on their expansion imposed by national boundaries.[3]

Institutional economics also has much to offer. This rather more eclectic tradition, which emerged from the German historical school of the nineteenth century, flourished in the twentieth century, partly as a reaction to the 'unrealistic' abstractions of orthodox economic theory. Its leading exponents, from Thorstein Veblen to J.K. Galbraith, have persistently emphasised the need to come to terms with the changes in institutional form associated with the ongoing development of capitalist economies. Distinctive themes are the growth of big business, transnational corporations, the influence of trade unions, and the character of governmental economic activities in different nations. Although coming from politically diverse positions, the institutional economists have provided a number of powerful ideas for shaping economic reform.[4] The potential for more extensive interventions by the state to alleviate the inequality and instability of free-market capitalism is a particular focus.

Keynesian economic analysis also has continuing importance in this context. John Maynard Keynes explained the persistence of involuntary unemployment, and identified the necessary remedial policies, at a time when more conventional economic prescriptions had demonstrably failed. He showed that the 'macro' economy did not function simply as the aggregation of 'micro' economic markets and that, without enlightened government intervention, the capitalist economy would not ensure full employment. The force of these ideas was reflected in the subsequent attempt by orthodox economists to graft a mechanistic interpretation of Keynes on to their economic theory of markets in order to produce a 'neoclassical synthesis'.[5] However, splicing together a microeconomics emphasising market freedoms and a macroeconomics emphasising the necessity of government intervention was bound to lack coherence, both analytically and politically. In that sense, the assault by monetarists and other neo-liberals on Keynesian economic 'interventionism' during the last quarter of a century has produced a more consistent capitalist free-market ideology. But it takes us back to pre-Keynesian economics and spurns the valuable, practical insights that Keynes made. As post-Keynesians remind us, there is much in the original work of Keynes about the inherent instability of a monetary economy and about policies conducive to long-run expansion of productive capacity that is worth rescuing.[6] Here is another important analytical current flowing into modern political economy.

The role of *neoclassical economic theory* is more problematic. One approach is to consider it pragmatically, as a possible source of contributions to the modern political economist's tool kit. Some elements within neoclassical economics—such as the analysis of 'externalities' and the measurement of demand and supply 'elasticities'—can be salvaged for this purpose. However, as indicated earlier, modern political economy is generally critical of the deficiencies of neoclassicism, both in theory and in policy practice. The view reflected in this book is that these orthodox economic ideas *do* need to be systematically studied, but that their strengths and weaknesses are better understood when treated comparatively with classical, Marxist, institutional, and Keynesian views. This is the essence of the liberal educational principle applied to the study of economic issues.

Looked at in this light, *modern political economy* is not a return to the situation before the dominance of neoclassical economics; it is not simply a revival of the concerns of classical political economy as reflected in the writings of Smith and Ricardo and in the more radical analysis of Marx. Certainly, there is a strong echo of classical political economy in the breadth of issues considered in modern political economy. Studying the conditions for the broad progress of the economy and society is more in tune with that classical tradition than with the narrow, neoclassical focus on market equilibrium conditions. However, the analytical construction of modern political economy also draws on vigorous currents of economic thought that have been developed by subsequent scholars, including Joseph Schumpeter, Joan Robinson, Nicholas Kaldor, Michal Kalecki, Paul Sweezy, and Gunnar Myrdal, as well as Veblen, Galbraith and Keynes. A common theme is the rejection of the pseudo-scientific 'positive economics' in favour of a more down-to-earth approach that addresses real problems and makes values explicit.

At present, there is also a pressing need to extend the definition of the subject of political economy to embrace *environmental concerns*. Perhaps the greatest challenge for us in the twenty-first century is to reconcile the economic with the ecological. There are some relevant concepts that can be drawn from existing economic analyses for this purpose. Neoclassical economists, for example, commonly concede that external diseconomies of production and consumption ('externalities') are sources of recurrent market failure. This leads to the advocacy of policies of 'environmental fine-tuning' through the extension of private property rights to environmental goods, the use of pollution taxes, and so forth. Whether this is an adequate conceptualisation of the problem is a contentious point; other social scientists reject this 'environmental economics' add-on to market theory, arguing instead for a fundamental reconstruction to create an 'ecological economics'.[7] Either way, the point is that the environmental issue must necessarily be central to modern political economy. In effect, that means seeking to build on, but also to *transcend*, the legacy of existing currents of economic analysis.

Box 1.1

Studying economics or political economy?

It appears paradoxical that, at a time when economic issues are of such importance in the real world, there has been widespread decline in student enthusiasm for studying economics. Reorienting the discipline towards modern political economy, as suggested here, does not necessarily arrest or reverse that decline. At the secondary school level, the fall in enrolments in Economics courses, and the corresponding growth in subject areas like Business Studies, has a complex explanation that goes beyond the concerns of this introductory chapter. However, to the extent that the aversion to studying conventional economics is partly the product of its 'dry' subject matter, the political economic approach offers a potentially engaging alternative. It is capable of stimulating more interest and enthusiasm than the more conventional economics syllabus. Studying political economy is not easy: indeed, the emphasis on competing currents of economic thought and their association with rival political philosophies adds complexity to the subject. But this engagement with controversial issues creates more intellectual excitement than a narrow, seemingly 'technical', treatment of orthodox economic analysis.

The link between political economy and topical events, as discussed in newspapers, and on radio and television, is also more explicit. There is less requirement than in orthodox economics courses and textbooks for the 'suspension of disbelief'. The students do not have to 'switch off' from the world around them as they watch elaborate theories being constructed with little evident connection with observable phenomena. In political economy, the point of the analysis can usually be seen more clearly and directly. There are theories to be studied, of course, but their relative plausibility can be discussed with reference to real-world observations. Moreover, there is plenty of scope for students to develop links between their own personal experiences and the broader concerns of political economy. Case studies (of particular firms or industries, of cities and regions, of industrial disputes, of unemployment problems, or of the winners and losers under different types of taxes, for example) can be a useful vehicle for this. For all these reasons, the approach of political economy has substantial appeal for students who are interested in how they fit into the world around them, and how they might contribute to changing it for the better.

CONCLUSION

In the real world there is considerable continuity in how the economy works—using natural, human, and manufactured resources to produce goods and services, and distributing the fruits of those endeavours according to the relative economic power of the participants. There is also considerable change, particularly in the present period of rapid technological innovation, globalisation, and structural economic adjustment. In political economic *analysis* a similar dualism exists: there is continuity in building on the existing corpus of economic knowledge, but change comes through adapting and extending the analysis to deal with the evolving character of real political economic problems. The present time is one in which the need for such creative political economic thinking is imperative.

CHAPTER 2

The Personal is the Political Economic

Who makes economic decisions?
What is the current political economic context in which those decisions are made?
What are the principal political economic challenges we face?

Many people come to the study of economics expecting that it will offer guidelines for 'making money'. They are sometimes disappointed to find that it is about how the economic system works rather than how the system can be worked! The former may help the latter, of course. People are likely to make more astute business and financial decisions if they know about the economic, social and political forces shaping the business and financial environment.

Generally, it is not an unreasonable expectation that the study of economics should serve the needs of intelligent citizens who wish to make sense of the world around them. At the present time, it is an expectation that is both in sharp focus and difficult to satisfy. This is because it is a time of economic uncertainty, when individuals are forced to cope with major changes to their material circumstances, often with little understanding of what is driving those changes and the potential for a change of direction.

Taking this personal perspective helps focus attention on how individuals are affected by broader political economic forces. It provides a way of understanding the connections between the individual's economic circumstances and the functioning of the economy as a whole. It makes the link between 'micro' personal choices and 'macro' social choices.

ECONOMIC DECISIONS

Our day-to-day lives involve many economic decisions. Most of these are fairly small-scale and short-term and of no apparent significance beyond our immediate family and friends. In the aggregate, they shape the economic environment in which we live. Some such decisions, illustrating our various social and economic roles, are described below.

- As *students*, we are, in effect, investing in our economic future as well as (hopefully) pursuing personal development. How much education we undertake and how many qualifications we acquire are likely to have a bearing on our future economic opportunities. Here are important strategic choices about investment in 'human capital'.
- As *consumers*, we are faced with daily decisions about which of the sometimes baffling array of products we will spend our disposable income on. We also make

decisions, if only by default, about how prepared we are to forgo the immediate gratification of consumption in order to accumulate personal savings.

- As *workers*, we are faced with constrained choices about the jobs we seek and the hours we work. We also have to make periodic strategic decisions, individually or collectively, about the stance to take in negotiations with our employers about wages and conditions of work.
- Meanwhile, *business decision-makers* make their own strategic decisions about employment and wages payments. They also periodically review the methods they use for producing goods and services, decide how much they will invest in new production facilities, decide on the prices they will charge for their products, and review their sales promotion practices.
- *Speculators* continually review their portfolio of assets, deciding what to buy and sell according to their judgments about future price movements and the possibility of making capital gains. When media commentators refer to how 'the markets' respond to breaking economic news or government policy initiatives, it is the behaviour of these speculators to which they are referring.
- *Bank managers* decide about making loans to their clients, usually according to guidelines set by their head office. The head office also makes decisions about the interest rates offered to depositors and charged to borrowers. The margins between these borrowing and lending rates are the principal source of banks' profits, and they are kept under continual review.
- *Government ministers*, especially those in key departments like Treasury and Finance, also make frequent adjustments to economic policies. They do so in response to changing economic conditions in national and global markets, and to political pressures (including the speculative sentiments of 'the markets') to modify their policy settings. As we will see in later chapters, these public policy positions are also significantly influenced by the prevailing economic ideas of the day.

It is reasonable, as a first approximation, to see what is happening in the economy as a whole as the outcome of these decisions. So, whether the economy is functioning well or not—whether the overall conditions are buoyant or stagnant, for example—is the result of numerous interdependent decisions. Whether the decisions 'mesh' effectively is, according to this way of viewing the economy, the key issue in determining the overall health of the economy. There is, of course, much scope for inconsistency, conflicts of interest, and contradictory elements in such arrangements.

As political economists, we can step back from the minutiae of these individual choices and short-term decisions to see the bigger picture. This can help us understand the political economic structures that shape and constrain our options. It can also—albeit with more difficulty—help to reveal the forces operating to change the context within which individual economic decisions are made. It can thereby help us see the distinctive political economic characteristics of the present.

AN ENVIRONMENT OF ECONOMIC UNCERTAINTY

We live in exciting but unsettling times. Dramatic changes in technology are transforming the way goods and services are produced and, particularly, the way information is transmitted. The barriers to economic intercourse imposed by the 'tyranny of distance' and national boundaries, though still very significant, are being eroded. This process of globalisation has cultural and political, as well as economic, dimensions; but its most notable feature is perhaps the growing economic power of transnational corporations. Some of these companies are larger than national economies.[1] Understandably, many individuals feel dwarfed and powerless in these circumstances. The capacity of the democratic institutions within nation states to exercise control over the enormously powerful private corporations is under challenge; in many cases, the state does not even seem to have the will to exercise such control.

Meanwhile, the nature of work is rapidly changing. A significant proportion of the potential workforce seems to be permanently excluded from making a direct, productive contribution. Solving this problem of persistent unemployment is one of the great contemporary challenges. For those who are in work, the emphasis is increasingly on casual, part-time, or contract employment. The number of manufacturing jobs relative to service-sector jobs continues to shrink in the advanced industrial nations. More women are in the waged workforce, but it is commonly observed that the allocation of household tasks according to gender has not changed correspondingly. The proportion of older people in the population continues to grow, albeit slowly, posing a challenge to develop appropriate mechanisms for intergenerational income transfers. The capacity of governments to manage those processes—or any other income redistributions—seems to be regularly threatened by the difficulties of maintaining systems of taxation to generate the necessary revenue.

Increased income inequalities, both within and between nations, are a predictable feature of these circumstances. These repeatedly undermine the conditions for effective cooperation in seeking solutions. The presence of glaring economic inequalities between individuals is not conducive to the cooperative behaviour necessary for the simultaneous achievement of higher productivity and social cohesion. Similar problems exist on an international scale. Imbalances of trade and debt between rich and poor countries accentuate the long-established problem of economic inequality. Some of the poorer nations were achieving impressive economic growth rates in the 1980s and 1990s; but that growth was cut short, especially in South-East Asia, with the financial crisis at the end of the 1990s.

The slowdown in economic growth rates in the wealthier nations that began in 2000 and accelerated in 2001 also showed the vulnerability of economic trends to sudden reversals. The economic exuberance of the 1990s was replaced with a more troubled economic outlook at the start of the twenty-first century. It is a reminder that the capitalist system has always been prone to a cyclical pattern of boom and bust. Even more worrying for the long term is the recognition that the pursuit of economic growth on a global scale, as the principal means of addressing problems of continuing poverty, may be unsustainable because of the constraints imposed by the physical environment. How to most effectively harmonise economy, society, and ecology is a question to which there is, as yet, no agreed answer.

It is not surprising that many individuals feel overwhelmed by these developments and problems. Therein lies the twin challenge for political economy: to analyse the underlying forces and to posit some effective solutions.

THREE TRILOGIES

A simple device for constructing a political economic perspective on these contemporary concerns is shown in figure 2.1. It is taxonomic in character—emphasising classification rather than explanation. It draws attention to some broad social choices and to some tensions that arise at the interfaces between various types of economic arrangement[2].

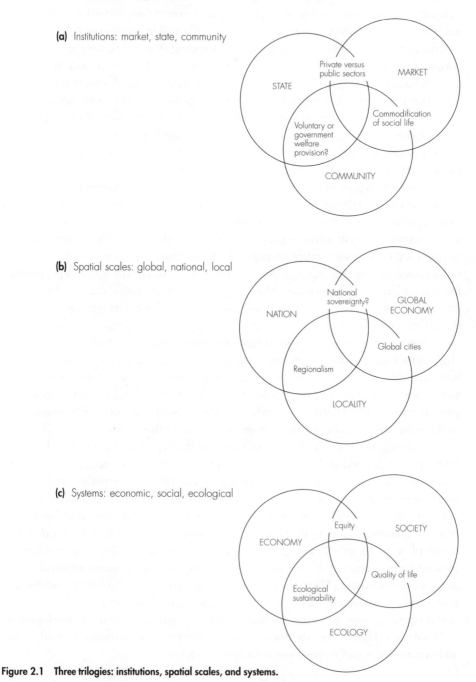

(a) Institutions: market, state, community

Private versus
public sectors
MARKET
STATE
Commodification
of social life
Voluntary or
government
welfare
provision?
COMMUNITY

(b) Spatial scales: global, national, local

National
sovereignty?
GLOBAL
ECONOMY
NATION
Global cities
Regionalism
LOCALITY

(c) Systems: economic, social, ecological

Equity
SOCIETY
ECONOMY
Quality of life
Ecological
sustainability
ECOLOGY

Figure 2.1   Three trilogies: institutions, spatial scales, and systems.

The first consideration is the relationship between *market, state,* and *community.* The first diagram in figure 2.1 draws attention to the different ways in which economic activity can be organised. Goods and services may be produced for exchange in the market. Many are. Alternatively, the production of goods and services, and their distribution, may be organised by a central coordinating agency. The state then usually becomes the economic manager. As such, it may be responsive to the wishes of the society through democratic processes, or it may be authoritarian in character. The third possibility is that production and distribution could occur directly in the community, to serve community needs. The community may be quite small—perhaps just a household—or it may comprise a larger group of people whose voluntary cooperation results in purposeful economic activity without the need for markets or a state. Community provision involves people producing goods and services for themselves and their neighbours and benefiting from reciprocal relationships.[3]

Here are three quite different systems for economic 'provisioning', three different ways of providing for our material needs and wants. All three normally coexist in any society, but the relative weight can vary enormously.[4] Illustrative tensions concern the balance between public and private sectors of the economy, voluntary and government welfare provision, and the extent to which social life is structured by market processes.

The second trilogy concerns the *spatial scales* at which economic activities can be organised and coordinated. Local production can be for local consumption. Much is. National coordination of productive activity is also commonly attempted; the markets for some products are nationwide, and governments usually attempt, more or less successfully, to manage national economies. The global dimension is becoming increasingly important, however—as noted already. Global markets, even some embryonic forms of a global state, are striking features of the present time. How these three spatial scales are articulated and how best to strike a balance between them are key issues. From a political perspective, these concerns manifest in the challenges to national sovereignty, the development of global cities and regionalist responses. From an analytical perspective, this means that the spatial dimension is an important aspect of political economy. All economic activity—all of life—takes place in both time and space, so we need analytical structures that pay due attention to these coordinates of our behaviour.[5]

The third trilogy depicts the relationship between *economy, society,* and *ecology.* Economic activities do not take place in a vacuum. They depend on certain social and ecological preconditions—the availability of labour and natural resources, for example—and they have major social and environmental consequences. Political economy must necessarily focus on these connections. What determines the relative priority given to economic, social, and ecological concerns? In part, it is the outcome of the balance struck between market, state, and community, and between local, national, and global scales of economic organisation. It also depends on the personal priorities of the participants in all aspects of economic life, particularly those with the greatest power to shape the outcomes. The tensions affect distributional equity, ecological sustainability, and the quality of life.

What should be the balance between these three sets of concerns—market, state, and community; locality, nation and global economy; economy, society and ecology? From this perspective, the significance of the three trilogies is in drawing attention to *social choices*. Do we want our economic arrangements to be mainly market-oriented, increasingly global in character, and with the concern for economic growth dominating social and environmental concerns? Or, would we prefer a greater emphasis on the role of the state, on planning national economic development with a greater focus on social and/or environmental goals? Or some other combination emphasising a stronger focus on community and more localised forms of political economic organisation? What balance of arrangements would be most desirable? And how can we seek to achieve those different outcomes, whether through individual and collective action? What political processes facilitate making systematic social choices? These are fundamental questions facing us all as citizens. They are issues which political economy seeks to illuminate.

CONCLUSION

As individuals, we all participate in the political economic drama. The personal is the political economic. However, our roles in the drama are not predetermined. As actors, we can improvise, even tear up the script. So, it helps to know what is going on and what our options are, individually and collectively. We need an understanding of the political economic possibilities open to us. At the present time, this is especially important because of the structural economic changes that are creating conditions of considerable uncertainty—locally, nationally, and globally.

So, what are the major challenges facing us as political economists now? We must try to understand the economic institutions and the structures of political economic power that shape our lives, for better or worse. We have to understand the forces driving the economic changes and shaping the political priorities and possibilities. More than that, we have to identify what can be done to produce political economic futures more in keeping with our individual and collective needs and aspirations.

Examples of such practical concerns include the following:
- understanding the capabilities and limitations of markets as means of organising and integrating economic activities
- exploring appropriate roles for community and/or government economic policy that are desirable and feasible in an increasingly 'globalised' context
- devising ways of determining the most effective means for securing economic progress
- considering how best to balance concerns about economic efficiency with social justice and ecological sustainability
- evaluating alternative strategies for the pursuit of greater economic security, stability, and equity.

Addressing these issues requires us to step back from the short-term, day-to-day economic decisions we make as consumers, workers, investors, or business managers. It requires us to deepen our understanding of the political economic forces reshaping our lives. It requires us to take the 'broader view'.

CHAPTER 3

Structural Economic Change
The broader view

What major political economic changes have taken place in the last two decades?
To what extent do they have common purposes?
Do they have contradictory characteristics?

It is sometimes difficult to see patterns in the complex array of political economic changes taking place in the world around us. This has been particularly true in the last couple of decades, when the changes have been particularly rapid and diverse. Business organisations and governments have been energetically reorganising their activities in order to develop new opportunities for profit and to establish the conditions for faster economic growth. Businesses, of course, have a direct interest in higher profitability. Governments have broader concerns, but they too have an interest in creating profitable conditions, not least because their prospects of re-election are likely to be enhanced in buoyant economic conditions.

Somewhat schematically, we can identify six interlocking elements in the processes of structural economic change: (1) the application of new technologies, (2) the reorganisation of businesses through mergers and takeovers, (3) the globalisation of production, (4) the reorganisation of employment conditions, (5) changes in the economic role of governments, and (6) significant changes in prevailing economic ideologies. This chapter considers each in turn.

THE APPLICATION OF NEW TECHNOLOGIES

It is usually in the interest of businesses to implement new technologies that cut the costs of production. This often involves labour displacement, producing more outputs of goods and services with fewer workers. Such has been the case throughout the history of industrial society when particular sectors of economic production have been transformed through technological innovation. The 'microelectronic revolution' that began in the 1970s heralded a particularly dramatic wave of change in technologies of production and information dissemination. Computer-assisted design (CAD) and computer-assisted manufacturing (CAM) became widely applied in industry. The increasing use of robotics is perhaps the ultimate illustration of this transformation.

Structural unemployment is a recurrent concern in these circumstances. Unemployment arising from technological change is a contentious claim because this type of unemployment has not previously been a major long-term problem. Of course, workers have frequently lost their jobs as a result of technological change; workers employed in making wagons, carts, and stagecoaches, for instance, lost their jobs when the technology for making motor cars arrived. However, new technologies have opened up many more markets and avenues for economic growth. Jobs for car workers exceeded the number of jobs displaced in the manufacture of horse-drawn vehicles. For the most part, unemployment has therefore been only a problem of transition between the old and new structures. Hence, there are good reasons to be sceptical about the notion of technological unemployment.

What is different now is that the new technologies are affecting the very sectors that have absorbed the labour displaced by technological change in the past. We can visualise the process of technological change as a series of overlapping waves. The first wave affected farming. The workers displaced by the mechanisation of agriculture moved to the cities, where they found jobs in manufacturing industries. Then technological change in manufacturing displaced these workers. This second wave saw the major job growth occurring in the growing services sector. One wit coined the term 'McDonald's law' to describe this situation, positing that, for every job lost in the manufacturing industry, a new job opened up in 'fast food' provision. But the technological changes associated with computerisation and information technologies are now impacting on the service industries, too. The interesting question arises: where is there left to go? Some argue that technology will continue to be job-creating as the 'information economy' sector expands. Others are expressing growing concern about the possibility of 'jobless growth', that is, growth in the output of goods and services unmatched by growth in employment.[1]

So, while the application of new technologies has a strong logic—even constituting an imperative—from the business perspective, there is a potential significant social fallout. A similar dualism is evident in the other dimensions of contemporary structural economic change.

MERGERS AND TAKEOVERS

The reorganisation of businesses through mergers and takeovers has been a notable feature of the last two decades. Like the introduction of new technology, there is nothing particularly novel about this. The voluntary combination of firms into larger units (a merger) or the acquisition of one firm by another (a takeover) is commonly driven by the pursuit of higher profitability. If the larger business unit can achieve *economies of scale* in the production and/or distribution of its products, it may be able to reduce costs. Indeed, political economists have noted that this type of business reorganisation is a predictable, perhaps necessary, response to a period of economic difficulties. Inefficient production units are 'weeded out' in order to enhance the overall efficiency with which capital is used. Such processes of corporate 'rationalisation' and 'downsizing' usually follow successful mergers or takeovers.[2] The social costs of dislocation are painful for those who lose their jobs or their businesses, but, on this reasoning, the process may be functional for the capitalist economic system as a whole.

The tension between private interests and social costs is yet more striking when mergers or takeovers are undertaken primarily to secure *market dominance*. This would normally be conducive to higher business revenues or wider profit margins. But there is a strong likelihood that broader community interests—consumers' interests, in particular—will be violated if the outcome is greater corporate monopoly power. How that power is used or abused becomes a matter of key political concern. The traditional assertion that 'what is good for General Motors is good for the USA' has a decidedly hollow ring in these circumstances. Business interests are not synonymous with social interests. Not surprisingly, herein lies one of the most frequently recurring economic policy debates: whether to regulate the processes leading to the growth of big business or to permit freedom of the market place. Traditionally, economists have usually seen competition as preferable to monopoly and have argued the case for public policies to defend and promote it. However, another view, which is being increasingly heard, favours the use of public policy to foster the growth of large businesses as 'national champions' in a world of competitive, international trade. This last view is the direct consequence of growing concerns about how to be a 'winner' in the global economy.

THE GLOBALISATION OF PRODUCTION

Globalisation opens up wider economic opportunities but poses particular threats. This, indeed, is one of the key issues of the present time—coming to terms with the global economic forces that have been unleashed by technological change, neo-liberal economic ideology, and the drive by transnational corporations for higher profitability and greater economic power.

These are multifaceted processes. In its basic form, globalisation involves the breaking down of the impediments to economic interaction arising from distance and/or regulations imposed by nation states (impeding the movement of goods, labour, or capital across national boundaries, for example). With the economic integration of nations (the breakdown of the coherence of national economies, some would say) comes social and cultural integration.[3]

Focusing on simply the globalisation of production, it is not difficult to discern the basic logic behind the viewpoint of international business. If corporations can 'shop around' the globe for the cheapest raw materials and cheapest labour, they can minimise their costs of producing goods and services. If they can find, or create, new markets for their products in distant lands, that will increase their revenue. If they can locate their activities in the nations with the lowest tax rates—or at least make it *appear* that their profits are generated there—that helps them maximise after-tax profits. Similarly, they may 'shop around' for the countries with the least restrictive environmental regulations applying to their activities. Through all these means, globalisation serves business interests. The outcome is the dramatic geographical reorganisation of the activities of transnational corporations, which has proceeded apace over the last few decades.

However, the *politics* of globalisation is contestable. The very changes that have served business interests have been associated with significant economic and social problems. There is commonly said to be a 'race to the bottom' in wage rates, tax rates, and environmental standards as nations compete to attract investment by transnational corporations. Living standards for workers, the capacity of governments to finance infrastructure and social services, and our collective ability to achieve more ecologically sustainable development can be casualties in the process. How to balance the potentially progressive aspects of globalisation against these real dangers is one of the key issues of the present time.

Box 3.1

Contesting globalisation

The twentieth century ended and the twenty-first century began with widely publicised 'anti-globalisation' protests. Thousands of demonstrators took to the streets in various cities around the world where meetings were being held by the World Trade Organization, the World Economic Forum, and the G8 (comprising the political leaders of the eight most powerful nations). Among the most widely publicised of these protests were those in Seattle, Davos, Prague, Melbourne, Quebec City, Gothenburg and Genoa. The demonstrators were protesting about the concentration of power in the hands of transnational corporations; about the trend towards greater economic inequality on a global scale; and about consumerism, environmental decay, and the undermining of working conditions, human rights, and the rights of indigenous peoples.

Struggle in the streets is only the visible face of a broad and persistent social movement. It can be interpreted as a global movement with diverse local and national focal points. Targeting the anti-social behaviour of particular corporations is one strategy being pursued. The 'Sweating for Nike' campaign, which exposed the exploitation of low-wage workers in Third World nations, is an example of this. Contesting intergovernmentalism is another strategy. This means intervening in the processes by which international agreements are made, and insisting on the insertion of labour and human rights clauses in trade agreements, for example. Building a progressive transnational consciousness is a yet more ambitious theme. It requires linkage between indigenous peoples, environmental groups, and other activists in different nations so that they can learn from one another about the most effective forms of resistance and discuss feasible alternatives to the current form of global capitalism.

In some respects, the 'anti-globalisation' label is inappropriate for this movement. What it stands in opposition to is the globalisation of capital. It seeks to combat corporate globalisation with a more progressive 'grass-roots' globalisation, taking advantage of modern technologies, such as email and the Internet, to exchange information among activist groups. It has had significant successes, perhaps most notably in helping to thwart the introduction of the Multilateral Agreement of Investment in the late 1990s, which would have further restricted the capacity of governments to regulate the activities of transnationals operating in their nations.[4] The struggles continue …

THE REORGANISATION OF EMPLOYMENT CONDITIONS

The way in which work is organised within individual workplaces has also been subject to dramatic changes in the last couple of decades. In part, this is a consequence of changes in production and information technologies that require different types of labour, with different skills. In part, it is a consequence of the reassertion of managerial prerogatives, reflecting an ongoing power struggle between employers and employees as classes with competing interests. In part, it is also the product of the drive for more 'flexibility' in the workplace as a means of achieving higher rates of profit.

These pressures are manifest in the greater emphasis on casual, part-time, and contract labour. This gives firms more flexibility in varying the number of workers they employ, to respond to fluctuations in the level of economic activity. Such arrangements also open up opportunities for increasing the *intensity* of labour—in the extreme, a simple speeding-up of the work required. Their potential to raise labour *productivity* opens up some more attractive prospects for the nature of work—working smarter rather than simply harder. However, the realisation of that potential for higher productivity depends on workers' commitment to employers, which may be undermined by the erosion of job security. Indeed, greater economic insecurity is the most obvious social fallout of these changes in economic conditions, which place the costs of adjustment squarely on the shoulders of the workforce.[5]

Some contend that these changes in the organisation of work are transforming a Fordist economic system to a *post-Fordist* one. Fordism, named after Henry Ford (who pioneered the mass production of motor vehicles), has required large numbers of workers to engage in routinised tasks to produce standardised products for mass markets. According to the proponents of post-Fordism, we are seeing those arrangements being increasingly replaced by smaller workforce teams with relative autonomy, producing more diverse products for niche markets. This is what flexibility at work means, according to the post-Fordist interpretation. Whether a shift to post-Fordism is indeed taking place, and, if so, whether it is more beneficial for employers or employees is a matter of ongoing debate.[6] Could it comprise a win–win situation? The employers' aim is clear: to reorganise workplaces and introduce 'world's best practice' procedures in order to advance business competitiveness and enhance profitability. The consequences for the workforce are largely a by-product of this drive.

CHANGES IN THE ECONOMIC ROLE OF GOVERNMENTS

Governments have played an active role in facilitating the four dimensions of structural economic change already described in this chapter. They have set the 'rules of the game' for businesses, prescribing particular structures and conduct and proscribing others. However, the rules have been changing. Increasingly, governments have asserted the need for more emphasis on market processes rather than 'interventionist' planning. At least that is the declared aim of *neo-liberalism* (sometimes called 'economic fundamentalism' or 'economic rationalism').[7] The core belief is that giving freer reign to market forces will produce more efficient economic outcomes. Hence, the push, evident in most of the major industrial nations in the last couple of decades, for dereg-ulation, privatisation, and the liberalisation of trade and capital movements. The declared goal is to create the conditions for the reinvigoration of free-enterprise capitalism.

Deregulation involves the removal of government regulations on businesses—regulations to control their pricing policies, environmental impacts, or employment practices, for example. Privatisation involves the transfer of businesses from public ownership to private ownership, usually through the sale of shares in these former public enterprises. Trade liberalisation involves the reduction of tariffs on imported goods and other impediments to international commerce. Other related policies (anti-policies, one might say) are the removal of government controls over financial institutions and over the flow of capital into and out of countries, and the lowering of business tax rates as means of increasing the material incentive for economic activity. The common theme is the restoration of the vitality of the capitalist econ-omy, which is thought (by neo-liberals) to have been curtailed by excessive government 'intervention' in economic matters.

In practice, the outcomes have been much less clear-cut. The rhetoric about 'small government' commonly masks a process that actually involves 'different government'. The economic activities of government are not reduced, only reoriented towards directly serving the interests of business; they become less concerned with progressive income redistribution and the amelioration of social problems arising from the oper-ations of the market economy. The policies certainly create winners and losers, whatever their effectiveness in relation to the dynamism of the economy as a whole: the removal of regulations protecting employment conditions predictably leads to more unevenness of employment practices and greater wage disparities; the relaxation of environmental controls leads to more environmentally degrading activities; and the withdrawal of redistributive policies leads to growing problems of economic inequality and poverty. Not surprisingly, 'neo-liberalism', 'economic rationalism', and 'economic fundamentalism' have become pejorative terms for many people.

CHANGES IN PREVAILING ECONOMIC IDEOLOGIES

The viability of any institution depends on the widespread acceptance of its 'legiti-macy'. So it is with whole economic systems. They depend on the dissemination of acceptable economic ideologies. Such ideologies are structures of belief about how the economy operates and the social values that it serves. Neo-liberalism as a political practice is closely linked to, arguably dependent on, the ideology of free-market economics. At its core is the emphasis on *individualism*, the belief in the primacy of the individual as the basic unit of society. As Margaret Thatcher, Conservative prime minister of the United Kingdom 1979–90, once put it: 'There is no such thing as society; there are only individuals …'.[8] Those individuals are assumed to be self-interested, rational, and acquisitive, and it is through their interaction in a free-market economy that economic progress is assured. So the argument runs. In the extreme, 'greed is good' appears to be the central tenet.

Such economic ideologies have been vigorously disseminated in the last couple of decades, effectively countering and undermining the beliefs (such as those associated with Keynesian economics) about the need for a more extensive role for government in the pursuit of social goals. Vigorously promoted by New Right 'think-tanks', they have also provided a head-on challenge to socialist and social democratic beliefs about the desirability of collective provisioning to satisfy collective needs.[9]

As with the policies of neo-liberalism, the associated ideologies have many variations. They are also plagued by the recurrent possibility of internal contradiction. Even the neoclassical economists, from whose theories the general claims about the efficiency of the market economy derive, have substantial reservations. The more punctilious among them stress the gulf between theoretical propositions based on restrictive assumptions and the messy conditions prevailing in the real world. However, the test of an ideology is not its sophistication, rather its effectiveness in conveying a simple and seemingly persuasive story. According to that test, the neo-liberal ideologies associated with free-market economics continue to be a major force with which to be reckoned.

Ideological struggles are seldom, if ever, concluded. Rival beliefs stressing social justice, communitarian values, and ecological sustainability continue to vie with the dominant orthodox economic ideologies. Indeed, because the other dimensions of structural economic change reviewed in this chapter—new technologies, business reorganisation, globalisation, and changing employment conditions—have unsettling and contradictory consequences, these rival ideologies are continually reinvigorated. To the extent that ideologies based on competitive individualism undermine social cohesion, they create fuel for a collectivist alternative. To the extent that they pave the way for environmental decay, they stimulate the development of more ecologically based viewpoints. Therein lies much of the source of the social dynamic underpinning the ongoing public contest of economic ideas.

CONCLUSION

Economic organisation is constantly changing. This is why a historical, rather than mechanistic, approach is necessary in studying how the economy works. 'History versus equilibrium' is Joan Robinson's characterisation of the two types of approach to studying economics, the former being less elegant but more realistic and useful.[10] History in this context does not simply mean the past: it also means the continuous unfolding of events in real historical time. As political economists, we need a *dynamic* approach to analysing the world around us, an approach that shows the forces provoking and steering the processes of change. This is particularly the case in a time of dramatic and profound political economic change. A static view of the economy, in which the economy functions according to eternal 'laws of motion', sits too uncomfortably with these conditions in the real world.

This reasoning also indicates why seeking 'quick-fix' solutions to economic problems is likely to be unsuccessful. In so far as economic problems—such as periodic recessions, economic insecurity, or economic inequality—have complex and changing roots, they are not amenable to resolution through simple remedies. Indeed, as some of the reasoning in this chapter has foreshadowed, governments as well as businesses may pursue strategies that are themselves at the root of our individual and collective economic difficulties. Posited solutions can themselves compound the problems. Our principal task as political economists is to try to make sense of this complexity.

CHAPTER 4

A New Political Economic Order?

Continuing challenges

Have the structural economic changes produced beneficial outcomes?
What are the principal political economic problems to be addressed now?
Are solutions possible?

Do recent structural economic changes provide the basis for a coherent new political economic order? In the broad sweep of historical change one might surmise that this is their common purpose. The origin of the structural changes described in the preceding chapter can be traced to the end of the 'long boom' experienced by the capitalist economies during the 1950s and 1960s. The 1970s saw the problem of unemployment re-emerge on a scale unknown since the years of the Great Depression in the 1930s. The situation was made more difficult by the simultaneous appearance of substantial inflation. Economic growth slowed and became more erratic. These were conditions in which significant structural change seemed necessary in order to establish conditions for renewed economic expansion and prosperity. The structural changes that have taken place throughout the world economy since then have indeed been wide-ranging and dramatic. Have they produced the desired outcome?

Certainly there has been economic growth. However, growth continued to be punctuated by significant periods of recession. The early 1980s and early 1990s were periods of economic downturn in most of the major capitalist economies. In the late 1990s, major financial and economic crises pervaded nations as diverse as the Russian Federation, Brazil and the developing economies of South-East Asia. Japan, the former focal point of the East Asian 'miracle', faced relatively stagnant economic conditions in the 1990s and entered the new century in particularly difficult conditions. In the United States, growth was already slowing, even before the terrorist attacks in New York and Washington DC on 11 September 2001 accentuated the shift from boom to recession.

What are the future prospects? Apologists for capitalism in the 1990s proclaimed its 'triumph'. Even more boldly, they posited the 'end of ideology' following the collapse of the principal rival to the capitalist economy, the communist bloc of countries in Eastern Europe, which comprised the former Union of Soviet Socialist Republics (USSR) and its 'communist state' satellites.[1] The prospect of perpetual progress towards prosperity, albeit subject to temporary interruptions, was also trumpeted in the wake of a US-led process of globalisation. The US president talked of establishing a 'new world order'. A more sober assessment of the obstacles to establishing any such 'new order'—with all that phrase implies about prosperity and stability—is needed. This chapter identifies six pervasive political economic difficulties that need to be confronted.

UNEVEN DEVELOPMENT

Economic development on a global scale continues to be remarkably lop-sided. The most obvious dimension of this is the gulf in economic prosperity between the affluent and the poor nations. Of course, there are significant inequalities within all countries, so it is not altogether helpful to talk about whole nations being either rich or poor. However, looking at *per capita* income (total national income divided by the total population), some striking disparities exist. They are of long standing. This is the essence of what is commonly called the 'North–South problem' (although this terminology is problematic in that there are some poor nations in the northern hemisphere and some rich ones in the southern).[2]

Which are the most affluent nations, and which are the poorest? Table 4.1 shows a selection of them ranked according to two different economic and social indicators for the year 2000. The first indicator is gross domestic product (GDP) per head. This is the conventional measure of the value of goods and services produced in each year, divided by the number of people in the country. For the countries shown in this table, it is highest for the United States, then Norway, Switzerland, and Canada. The other indicator is a human development index (HDI), which takes account of national standards in health, housing, education, environmental quality, and equity in income distribution. This measure shows Norway topping the chart, with Sweden, Canada, Belgium, and Australia. The United States ranks significantly lower on this measure.

The poorer, Third World nations are not in this league. A number of formerly poor countries have certainly experienced significant industrialisation and economic modernisation over the last couple of decades. South Korea, Singapore, Hong Kong, and Taiwan—the so called 'four Asian tigers'—achieved particularly rapid growth in *per capita* incomes in the last two decades of the twentieth century, while others, such as Malaysia and Thailand, also had rapid increases in national prosperity (although, as the regional economic crisis of the late 1990s reminded us, what goes up can come down, too). India and the People's Republic of China, the world's two most populous nations, have also recorded significant increases in overall economic performance, although major socioeconomic problems remain. Elsewhere, particularly in the poor nations of Africa, the achievement of economic development seems as elusive as ever. The bottom of table 4.1 shows a selection of some of these poorer nations' GDP and HDI performance indicators. Brazil and South Africa are rather different from other countries in this group because their GDP *per capita* figures are middle-ranking—the effect of averaging the living standards of rich and poor in vastly unequal societies. In the nations towards the bottom of the table, even allowing for the exclusion of the value of their non-marketed production, the general living standards are very poor. Overall, the gulf between the rich and poor nations is glaringly wide.

The persistence of such entrenched economic inequalities on a global scale is not conducive to a stable world economic order. At the very least, the credibility of any such order would depend on the laggards catching up. Some are: some are not. According to the United Nations Human Development Report 2002, 'the level of inequality worldwide is grotesque. But trends over recent decades are ambiguous. The range of

Table 4.1   Economic performance and human development 2000: selected countries

	GDP Per capita (US$)	GDP Index	Human Development Index
Rich countries:			
Norway	29 918	0.95	0.942
Sweden	24 277	0.92	0.941
Canada	27 840	0.94	0.940
Belgium	27 178	0.94	0.939
Australia	25 693	0.93	0.939
United States	34 142	0.97	0.939
Netherlands	25 657	0.93	0.935
Japan	26 755	0.93	0.933
Finland	24 996	0.92	0.930
Switzerland	28 769	0.94	0.928
France	24 223	0.92	0.928
United Kingdom	23 509	0.91	0.928
Denmark	27 627	0.94	0.926
Austria	26 765	0.93	0.926
Germany	25 103	0.92	0.925
Ireland	29 866	0.95	0.925
New Zealand	20 070	0.88	0.917
Italy	23 626	0.91	0.913
Some poorer countries:			
Brazil	7 625	0.72	0.757
China	3 976	0.61	0.726
South Africa	9 401	0.76	0.695
Indonesia	3 043	0.57	0.684
India	2 358	0.53	0.577
Papua New Guinea	2 280	0.52	0.535
Pakistan	1 928	0.49	0.499
Nigeria	896	0.37	0.462
Ethiopia	668	0.32	0.327
Burkina Faso	976	0.38	0.325
Burundi	591	0.30	0.313
Niger	746	0.34	0.277

Source: United Nations, Human Development Report, UNDP, Geneva, 2002.

economic performance across countries and regions has increased between some regions and decreased between others'.[3] The challenge for the proponents of a new world order is to establish more effective mechanisms to narrow the gap. Indeed, to the extent that economic disparities—and the perception that they are the product of imperialism and exploitation—underpin international conflict, including terrorism, then the systematic reduction of those disparities has to become the top priority.

TRADE IMBALANCES AND DEBT

In practice, trade imbalances and cumulative debt generally entrench uneven development. Trade deficits are understandably the norm among the poorer nations. Their exports are typically primary products—the produce of farming, forestry, fishing, and mineral extraction—while their imports are characteristically manufactured goods. The relative prices of these exported and imported goods—the 'terms of trade'—have tended to move adversely, as manufactured goods have become relatively more expensive in relation to primary products. Trade deficits result.

Such trade deficits can be financed by the inflow of foreign investment or by the accumulation of debt. Both have the effect of accentuating economic dependency. The latter often has particularly pernicious effects. Debt, of course, *can* be economically advantageous. A carpenter who borrows money to buy some tools may then be able to earn sufficient income to pay the interest on the debt and eventually repay the principal of the loan. Debt aids economic development, on a personal scale, in such a case. However, if the income generated is insufficient to repay the interest on the loan, and if the carpenter then has to borrow more in order to meet those interest payments (or, in the extreme, sell the tools in order to do so), then disaster looms. This is the 'debt trap'. It is the sort of situation into which many of the poorer nations have slipped. Paying a quarter, or even more, of their earnings from exports to meet their interest payments is not uncommon among these nations. Such debt impedes economic development.

The central role played by the International Monetary Fund and the World Bank in these processes has led to growing demands for their reform, even for their abolition. These institutions were set up by the richer nations at the Bretton Woods conference in 1944, ostensibly to facilitate economic security and development. However, their critics note that more has been taken out of the poorer nations in debt repayments than has been put in to promote economic development. Drawing on World Bank data, a recent book on globalisation notes that most of the increase in the debt of the poorer nations during the 1990s was generated to pay interest on existing loans, rather than to tackle poverty or to finance productive investment: 'In six of the eight years from 1990 to 1997, developing countries paid out more in debt service (interest plus repayments) than they received in new loans—a total transfer from the poor South to the rich North of US$77 billion'.[4]

SPECULATION AND FINANCIAL INSTABILITY

Within the more affluent nations there is also evidence of a diversion of capital away from productive investment into various forms of speculation. Speculative activities are those that offer the possibility of substantial individual material gain (or loss), depending on future price movements, but add nothing to collective wealth and well-being. There are numerous focal points for speculation, ranging from the buying and selling of tangible assets like works of art, antique furniture, and stamp collections (all of which have inherent scarcity value), to buying and selling real estate, precious metals, national currencies, and financial instruments, including futures and other derivatives. The increases in the volume of speculative transactions in national currencies and financial instruments has been particularly dramatic.

The result is what is sometimes called 'casino capitalism', or the quest for 'profits without production'.[5] Financial speculation may indeed be economically rational for an individual, especially when the rate of return on productive investment is relatively low. Investment in establishing and expanding industrial enterprises takes time and old-fashioned capitalist 'know-how'. Speculation offers the prospect of quicker and more spectacular returns for those with nerve and, preferably, some inside information on factors likely to affect asset price movements. However, for the economy as a whole, the result is counter-productive. An economy in which speculation is rife also tends to be more unstable because speculative markets are renowned for their price volatility. 'Follow-the-leader' swings in speculative behaviour lead to alternating booms and slumps.

A speculation-oriented economy also tends to be less productive in the longer term. Some markets in financial instruments may be a necessary adjunct to productive economic activity, but the proliferation of speculative activities in those markets tends to have a capital-diverting effect. It certainly has a personal energy-diverting effect. Entrepreneurial activities come to be focused more on 'paper games' of speculative trading than on the real economy in which tangible goods and services are made. This tendency, like the problems of uneven development, trade imbalance, and debt, also bodes ill for generalised prosperity within the capitalist economy in the years ahead. At the very least, some ways will need to be found to encourage the redirection of funds from speculative to productive purposes.

UNEMPLOYMENT

Meanwhile, millions are unemployed. Looking at the world economy as a whole, and taking account of underemployment as well as officially recorded unemployment, one estimate is that there are about 800 million people whose potential labour is not effectively utilised.[6] Therein lie massive *personal costs*—the lack of income, the absence of occupationally defined social position and work-related social networks—and major *social costs*, such as the costs of ill-health and crime, which are correlated with the incidence of unemployment. Therein also lies a massive *opportunity cost*—the goods and services that society forgoes because the unemployed or underemployed are not engaged in socially valued productive activities.

The causes and possible remedies for this problem are the focal point of much political debate, as subsequent chapters of this book will indicate. Whether a faster rate of job creation is feasible or desirable is one of the key issues. If that implies a faster rate of economic growth, is that ecologically sustainable? The question of the redistribution of work is also contentious. Is it better to find mechanisms to spread the work around more equitably rather than try to increase the total number of full-time jobs? Or is it more important to redefine socially useful employment in order to include activities not currently valued in capitalist labour markets, and to find some mechanisms for redistributing the pattern of rewards accordingly?

Until such issues have been resolved, it cannot be said that a sound basis for our collective economic future has been established. On the contrary, it seems that the persistence of the unemployment problem, and its concentration in particular localities and among particular minority groups, is giving rise to greater social divisions. Some describe this in terms of the growth of an 'underclass' more or less permanently excluded from the economic mainstream of society.[7] It bodes ill for social cohesion.

ECONOMIC INEQUALITY

Social cohesion within individual countries is also fractured by persistent economic inequalities. Table 4.2 provides some illustrative data on income inequalities in selected nations, based on the latest available United Nations figures. The ratio of the income received by the richest 10 per cent of people to the income of the poorest 10 per cent is a good summary measure. For the United States, this is over 16:1, for Australia it is over 12:1, and for the United Kingdom over 12:1. In the European nations, particularly in Scandinavia, the ratio is typically around 5:1, indicating the egalitarian effects of social democratic policies. At the other extreme, some South American nations, such as Brazil, have ratios of over 60:1. So, too, does South Africa which is over 40:1, partly because of the legacy of racial discrimination from the apartheid era. In some of the other poorer nations (such as Indonesia, Pakistan, and Burundi) there are also wealthy elites, but the data indicates that greater 'equality of poverty' generally prevails.

Generally speaking, these economic inequalities seem to be increasing. The United States is the extreme case, with sharply increased disparities between rich and poor evident in the last couple of decades.[8] Although less dramatic, the dominant trend in most of the other comparatively affluent nations has been in a similar direction. Why this should be so is the subject of ongoing controversy. There is also some evidence of a 'shrinking middle' in the types of jobs available. The number of highly paid professional and executive positions has increased, and a more than corresponding growth in their remuneration has taken place. Executive salaries of over a million dollars a year, sometimes rising to more than five or even ten times that figure, are now commonplace. At the other extreme, there has been growth in the number of jobs in 'secondary' labour markets—usually casual, part-time, and low-paid. Between the two extremes, for the advanced industrial nations at least, there are fewer of the traditional, middle-income positions based on skilled employment in manufacturing industries or the public sector. A British commentator has described this as the development of a '40:30:30' society: about 40 per cent of the people prospering as a result of technological and structural economic changes; 30 per cent hanging on to less secure employment-based incomes; and the other 30 per cent more or less permanently excluded from participation in regularly remunerated productive activity.[9]

Table 4.2   Economic inequalities within nations 2000: selected countries

	Survey year	Share of income (%)		Ratio of richest 10% to poorest 10%
		Poorest 10%	Richest 10%	
Rich countries:				
Norway	1995	4.1	21.8	5.3
Sweden	1992	3.7	20.1	5.4
Canada	1994	2.8	23.8	8.5
Belgium	1996	3.2	23.0	7.3
Australia	1994	2.0	25.4	12.5
United States	1997	1.8	30.5	16.6
Netherlands	1994	2.8	25.1	9.0
Japan	1993	4.8	21.7	4.5
Finland	1991	4.2	21.6	5.1
Switzerland	1992	2.6	25.2	9.9
France	1995	2.8	25.1	9.1
United Kingdom	1995	2.2	27.7	12.3
Denmark	1992	3.6	20.5	5.7
Austria	1995	2.5	22.5	9.1
Germany	1994	3.3	23.7	7.1
Ireland	1987	2.5	27.4	11.0
Italy	1995	3.5	21.8	6.2
Some poorer countries:				
Brazil	1998	0.7	48.0	65.8
China	1998	2.4	30.4	12.7
South Africa	1993–94	1.1	45.9	42.5
Indonesia	1999	4.0	26.7	6.6
India	1997	3.5	33.5	9.5
Papua New Guinea	1996	1.7	40.5	23.8
Pakistan	1996–97	4.1	27.6	6.7
Nigeria	1996–97	1.6	40.8	24.9
Ethiopia	1995	3.0	33.7	11.4
Burkina Faso	1998	2.0	46.8	23.5
Burundi	1998	1.8	32.9	18.3
Niger	1995	0.8	35.4	46.0

Note: Because data comes from surveys covering different years and using different methodologies, comparisons between countries should be made with caution.

For the rich countries, the data is based on surveys of income distribution; for the poorer nations (except Brazil), the data is based on surveys of consumption. The latter data therefore tends to be more equally distributed, for poor people generally consume a greater proportion of their income than rich people do.

Source: United Nations, Human Development Report, UNDP, Geneva, 2002.

Is this the basis for a sustainable economic order? At best, it seems that it would be one that would depend on the enforcement of *social control* to maintain order in the face of polarised interests. Therein lie difficulties which could be expected to become more problematical. If the rich take refuge in security-patrolled, suburban 'gated communities', and if the poor are increasingly policed or incarcerated, as is the case in the United States, then order is maintained at a high social cost. Moreover, in so far as a belief in the equitable sharing of the fruits of cooperation is a necessary precondition for increased productivity, these trends may ultimately prove counter-productive, even from a narrowly economic perspective.

ENVIRONMENTAL STRESS

Whether economic growth is sustainable raises yet more fundamental problems. There has been growing recognition of the ecological constraints. Some resources, such as oil, are, to all intents and purposes, non-renewable, and there is necessarily concern about their exhaustion.[10] Other potentially renewable resources are being used more rapidly than they are being replaced. Meanwhile, pollutants produced as a by-product of economic activities are the source of cumulative, and sometimes irreversible, environmental decay. Global warming and damage to the ozone layer surrounding the earth—although still debated among scientists—may be regarded as manifestations of these problems on a global scale.[11] Locally, in individual cities and regions, environmental problems are manifest in unhealthy atmospheric pollution, loss of arable land, damage to waterways and marine life, loss of habitat, and the extinction of many species of flora and fauna. These are not features of a sustainable economic system.

As with the other difficulties briefly reviewed in this chapter, there is no shortage of posited solutions. Some are reformist, some more radical—even revolutionary—in character. The extension of market principles in limiting the use of scarce environmental goods is favoured by 'free-market environmentalists'. The price mechanism can be adapted to provide incentives for more ecologically sustainable economic practices, according to this viewpoint. Others argue the contrary, that the market economy is the problem rather than the solution because of the expansionary, even rapacious, patterns of economic behaviour it fosters.[12]

Meanwhile, the intensification of environmental stresses interacts with the other problems, such as economic inequality and uneven development. Societies characterised by major economic inequalities are generally less able to collectively control environmentally damaging processes. Their wealthy classes can, to some extent at least, buy their way out by acquiring environmental goods increasingly beyond the reach of the poor. And different countries of markedly uneven economic development have great difficulty in securing collective agreement on the control of further environmental degradation. The poorer nations tend to be resentful of regulatory policies, which they see as impeding their capacity to achieve the material economic conditions already achieved by the wealthier nations. The higher production and consumption levels of those wealthier nations contribute disproportionately to the problems of global environmental stress.[13]

CONCLUSION

Dramatic structural changes have been propelled by businesses and governments intent on creating the conditions for economic expansion and profitability. A political economic perspective can help us to assess whether these conditions lay the foundation for a new era of general prosperity that is stable and sustainable.

Economists are notoriously poor at prediction; however, if we can understand the past and present conditions, we are better able to identify the possibility of repeating the successes and avoiding the problems previously experienced. Of course, some aspects of economic change are historically specific, so the 'lessons of history' may not be readily transferable to other times and places. Understanding the historically contingent character of political economic processes requires sophisticated judgments.

The evidence reviewed in this chapter suggests that optimism about the 'triumph of capitalism' on a global scale must be tempered, to say the least, with a recognition of some deeply entrenched problems. It is debatable whether these problems can be resolved within the framework of a capitalist economy, or whether they require fundamental socioeconomic and political transformations. Our task as political economists is to understand the problems, to analyse their causes, and to contribute towards their resolution. There are both intellectual and practical aspects to this challenge. This is what the rest of this book is about: understanding the economy and the state of economic analysis so that we can change them for the better.

PART II

Economic Systems

What's so special about capitalism?

CHAPTER 5

Understanding and Evaluating Economic Systems

What functions must an economy perform?
How is the economy linked to the society?
How can we judge whether the economy is serving the society well?

We now need to establish some principles on which our subsequent explorations into political economy can be based. Having reviewed in the preceding four chapters the broad sweep of issues with which contemporary political economists are concerned, it is time for a change of gear. We must establish more carefully the nature of the economic enquiry itself. This means discussing what an economy is and does, what forms economic organisation can take, and how economic activity links generally with social structure. It also requires some preliminary consideration of how we can judge the performance of an economy in meeting social goals. It is through looking at these issues that we also start to see some of the sources of conflict in the process of political economic enquiry.

ECONOMIC FUNDAMENTALS

The economy can be understood most simply as *the means whereby goods and services are produced, exchanged, and distributed among the members of a society*. Incomes and wealth are generated through these processes of production, exchange, and distribution. These incomes are more or less evenly shared—creating outcomes that can be egalitarian or markedly inegalitarian. The wealth can be more or less wisely used—for immediate consumption, for reinvestment in increasing the productive capacity of the economy, or for wasteful purposes associated with military or environmental destruction, for example. Over time, the volume and value of the income-generating economic activities may either expand or contract—this means either economic growth or stagnation and slump.

Looking at the economy in this way draws attention, first and foremost, to *the system by which we provide for our needs, individually and collectively*. The most basic need is for food, then for clothing and shelter. Providing for those needs is the most basic economic activity; thus, farmers and fishermen are more fundamental to economic activity than financiers. By similar reasoning, clothing manufacture and housebuilding are also basic economic activities, although many of the products now made—fancy clothes and suburban palaces—go far beyond the satisfaction of our basic needs. Indeed, a vast array of products is made in modern economies, which satisfy desires that are psychological rather than physiological and, arguably, are created through the functioning of the economic institutions themselves. Notwithstanding the difficulty of distinguishing needs from wants in practice, the point remains: the basic function of the economy is the practical task of 'provisioning'.[1] The processes by which those produced goods and services are exchanged, and how the resulting incomes and wealth are distributed, may involve complex financial arrangements. Certainly this is true of capitalism, and may explain the common perception that economics is 'all about money'. However, as defined here, the basic and universal feature of all economic systems is the use of tangible resources—natural, human, and manufactured—for making goods and services.

Economics is the *discipline* that studies these issues. It analyses the production and exchange of goods and services, the distribution of income and wealth, the disposition of that income and wealth, and the material factors shaping social progress or social regress. Economists have always claimed that, by casting light on these concerns, they can help us gain more control over the economic factors that shape our existence. This is not to claim the capacity to illuminate *all* the factors that influence our happiness or well-being—spiritual considerations and the quality of social life are excluded from such a material calculus—but it is indicative of the essentially *social purpose of studying economics*. The social purpose is to contribute to human betterment. By understanding the causes of poverty, recessions, and low productivity, for example, economists can contribute to pushing back at least some of the constraints on our well-being, individually and collectively.

So, wherein lies the distinction between economics and political economy? It rests largely on the claim by contemporary political economists that mainstream economists have, in practice, abandoned this social mission in favour of a narrowly constructed set of abstract theories that reveal little about how the economy actually operates. Political economy is distinguished by its emphasis on the broader view of economic enquiry—its social purpose and its political application. Two different aspects of this interpretation of political economy can be identified:

- Political economy emphasises that economic issues cannot properly be studied independently of their social context. It adopts a broader definition of the subject than mainstream economics, seeking links with insights drawn from other fields, such as sociology, political science, industrial relations, history, and geography. This gives a distinctively *interdisciplinary* character to political economy—albeit with material economic concerns as the central focus.
- Political economy emphasises that the way in which economic issues are analysed cannot be wholly value-free. The selection of issues for study, the distinctive assumptions made, and the form of investigation are all pervaded by judgments. So, a value-free analysis is unattainable. The important thing is to make the values *explicit*, rather than leave them implicit, masked by claims about the scientific status of the discipline. Better blatant than latent.

From these two fundamental propositions, many other features of political economy emerge: the emphasis on evolutionary processes rather than equilibrium states; the emphasis on equity and sustainability, as well as efficiency; and the emphasis on the role of the state, as well as the market in shaping economic outcomes, for example.

These are central themes to be developed in subsequent chapters. Their common concern is understanding the social character of economic activity.

ECONOMY AND SOCIETY

What shapes the relationship between economy and society? The functioning of the economy does not take place separately from the functioning of other aspects of social life. Political economists have repeatedly stressed the need to study the 'social embeddedness' of the economic system to analyse how it is related to the construction and reproduction of social order.[2]

Five dimensions of the interaction between the economy and society can be distinguished.

Markets

Production for exchange is a pervasive feature of economic activity. Markets, as the processes and places where those exchanges occur, are therefore of central importance, both economically and socially. Market interactions impose discipline on the participants in the economic system: sellers cannot sell whatever they want for whatever price they like, nor can consumers buy whatever they want for whatever they would like to pay. Exchanges will only occur when they are expected to be mutually advantageous. An effective market mechanism creates the conditions for such outcomes, but it cannot thereby resolve all economic problems. For example, there may be circumstances in which no goods and services are available because of interruptions to the production process, or because maldistribution of income causes buyers to come to the market with markedly uneven purchasing power. An economy in which markets play a central role depends on certain social underpinnings—an acceptance of commercial contractual obligations as a legitimate and enforceable foundation for personal interactions, for example. In turn, it also tends to leave its clear stamp on the prevailing social structures and attitudes—emphasising market values and material acquisition as the key indicators of social worth and social position.

State

Economic processes of production, exchange, and distribution can be organised by the state rather than left to the operation of market forces. The state in this respect can be considered as comprising all the institutions of national and regional administration, including the government, the public service, and the judiciary. Its most direct economic role in production is through public-sector business enterprises—hence the importance of political decisions about the balance between nationalisation and privatisation. Its other regulatory activities and its tax revenue-raising and expenditure functions are also fundamentally important in shaping economic activity in the private sector of the economy. How these aspects of state involvement in the economic system are constructed and blended is an intensely *political* issue. A society in which economic provision is state-centred can be expected to be more collectivist in character than one in which private enterprise dominates. But how the state is controlled then becomes the key issue.

Class

Class relationships are another central feature of the interaction between economy and society. If, for example, some people own the means of production (factories, tools, machines, etc.), while others have only their labour to sell, that gives rise to a distinct class divide. It is likely to be associated with sharp differences in income, wealth, and power. It is the source of potential social conflict—although some degree of cooperation between classes is essential if the economic system is to continue to function. Indeed, it is this uneasy blend of *conflict and cooperation* that is the hallmark of a class society. It should also be noted that, while class differences are rooted in economic conditions, their social manifestations—differences in social status and social behaviour, for instance—are often very complex and cannot be simply 'read' from class position.

Gender and ethnicity

Gender and ethnicity also shape economic functions and social standing. A 'sexual division of labour' is said to characterise economic arrangements in which men and women characteristically do different jobs. Likewise, people of different ethnic background are often located in different segments of the labour market. In both cases, this can be seen as the result of *discrimination*—although it may be deeply rooted in economic and social institutional procedures and not be merely the result of personal prejudice by individual employers. Sexism and racism are pervasive ideologies, and sexist and racist practices can be institutionally embedded. They cause inequalities of economic opportunities and economic rewards, which are systemically structured according to gender and ethnicity. How such inequalities interact with one another, with class relationships, and with the balance between market and state in economic organisation is complex and changeable.

Ideology

Ideologies can be understood as systems of belief that shape behaviour, individually and collectively. In general, one would expect such ideologies to reflect the existing material economic conditions—hence the association between consumerist values and an economic system geared to the production of ever more goods and services, for example. However, dominant ideologies are continually challenged by rival, dissident beliefs. Therein lies an important impetus for change in economic and social organisation.

These five dimensions of the relationship between the economy and society can be regarded as the 'glue' holding the political economic system together and determining how it works.[3] How the elements are constructed varies considerably from country to country, and over time. The relative importance of market, state, class, gender, ethnicity, and ideology in shaping economic and social order varies enormously. How well these different arrangements work is also the focus of endless debate in political economy. The 'glue' can sometimes fail and the system come unstuck.

EVALUATING ECONOMIC PERFORMANCE

Understanding economic organisation—its different forms, diverse interpretations, and social implications—is the first task of political economy. The second is to *evaluate* economic performance. If political economy is to contribute to social progress, this essentially normative dimension is necessary in our deliberations. We need to know what works well and what does not. For this purpose, we need reasonably clear *criteria* of evaluation. The following four are suggested.

Efficiency

Any economic system should make efficient use of the available resources—natural, human, and manufactured. However, what efficiency really means in this context remains open to debate. The *avoidance of waste* is certainly implied, but what constitutes waste may itself be a matter of judgment. In practice, efficiency has multiple dimensions. There is efficiency of resource *utilisation*—not leaving resources unused, as occurs, for example, whenever there is a significant incidence of unemployment in a region or nation. There is efficiency of resource *allocation*—ensuring that the goods and services produced are those that the members of the society actually want to consume, for example. There is efficiency of resource *creation*—fostering the most productive development of the workforce, for example, or of new production technologies through innovation. In respect of these three dimensions, we need to remember that efficiency implies a *means* to a particular end or ends: it is not an end in itself.

Equity

The economic system should distribute its fruits in accordance with our social standards of equity. Equity implies fairness. Therein, of course, lies plenty of scope for different interpretation. Some people interpret equity as requiring equality of economic *outcomes*, such as equal incomes for all members of the population. Others stress the more modest goal of equality of *opportunity*, accepting major income inequalities as long as all have an equal opportunity to succeed. On either reading, inequalities associated with systemic patterns of social differentiation according to class, gender, or ethnicity violate the equity ideal. For practical purposes, the degree of inequality in the overall distribution of income or wealth is usually taken as a rough primary indicator of the extent of equity in different types of economy.

Sustainability

We also require of an economic system that it be sustainable. In other words, it must be capable of reproducing itself. That means not using non-renewable natural resources, or using renewable resources at a faster rate than that at which they are replenished. The extent of harmony between the economy and the physical environment is obviously crucial here. Economic growth based on a rapacious attitude to the environment clearly fails this sustainability test. Sustainability has its *economic* and *social* dimensions, too. Economically, it is crucial that productive equipment subject to wear and tear through its use in producing goods and services be maintained and/or periodically replaced; consequently, a sustainable economy must involve foregoing some current consumption in order to ensure sufficient productive investment in capital goods. Socially, sustainability also requires that the relationships between classes, genders, and ethnicities be sufficiently stable for people to continue cooperating in economic activity. For this to happen, those relationships must be perceived as legitimate and acceptable; otherwise, social turmoil, even revolution, may eventuate.

Compatibility with social goals

The ultimate test of an economic system is whether it serves society well. Does it generate the necessary goods—the food, clothing, housing, and other material requisites for a contented society? Does it produce the quality health and educational services necessary for a healthy and well-informed citizenry? Generally, is it conducive to personal and community development, to personal freedom, to cultural enrichment, or to the realisation of spiritual as well as material goals? These are the higher social purposes against which the mundane contributions of the economy need to be judged. Therein lies a host of difficulties—identifying the relevant social goals and their relative importance, deciding how they can be measured or otherwise assessed, and learning how political judgments can be made about trade-offs between them. On such contentious matters there can never be unanimous agreement. There are also good reasons to expect that the character of the prevailing economic system will itself have a major bearing on the pattern of prevailing social aspirations—so an objective test is elusive. However, if nothing else, such considerations are a reminder of the need to take a broader view of the economy and of economic progress than that based on the conventional economic indicators.

WHAT MEASURE OF PROGRESS?

The overall performance of a national economy is conventionally measured according to gross domestic product (GDP), which is the sum of the market value of all goods and services produced in a country during a year, irrespective of whether they are produced by individuals, private business enterprises, or government institutions. If this sum is greater than the preceding year's, then economic growth is said to have occurred—which indicates effective performance. Conversely, no growth or, worse, a decline is held to be indicative of relative economic failure. League tables are commonly constructed on GDP *per capita* to indicate the ranking of the different countries of the world in any one year according to this performance measure. In principle, the measure can also apply to subnational areas (gross regional product or gross city product) and to the world as a whole (gross planetary product).

(a) GDP and GPI per capita, USA, 1950–94

(b) GDP and GPI per capita, UK, 1950–96

(c) GDP and GPI per capita, Australia, 1950–2000

Figure 5.1   Growth or progress? GDP and GPI indicators.

Adapted from: (a) The Genuine Progress Indicator: Summary of Data and Methodology, Redefining Progress, *September 1995;*
(b) H. Daly and J. Cobb, For the Common Good, Beacon Press, Boston, *1994; New Economics Foundation;*
(c) C. Hamilton and R. Denniss, Tracking Well Being in Australia, *Australia Institute, Canberra, December 2000.*

Notwithstanding its widespread application, this conventional measure of economic performance is subject to numerous problems.[4] For example:

- It excludes many useful goods and services that are produced directly for personal consumption rather than for sale. Much domestic household production—disproportionately performed by women—is of this character.
- It includes expenditure on goods and services whose production is only necessary because of the damage done in the process of producing or consuming other goods and services. Expenditures on pollution control devices and vehicle smash-repair are obvious examples. These 'defensive expenditures' add to GDP, but there is no *net* contribution to community well-being.
- No account is taken of the rundown in the stocks of environmental resources that may occur in the process of producing marketed goods and services.
- The time and effort involved in producing goods and services does not enter into the calculations. By inference, leisure is economically worthless.
- The distribution of the products is not considered. So, the production of frivolous, luxury consumption items for the wealthy counts equally with the production of basic necessities for the poor.

Reflecting on these problems, one economist has described conventional national measures, 'the crown jewels of economic statistics', as 'almost trivial indicators of anything worth measuring'.[5] The need to construct better indices of progress is being increasingly widely recognised. For example, attempts have been made to construct a genuine progress indicator (GPI).[6] This deals with the above problems by adding estimates for the value of non-marketed production, subtracting 'defensive expenditures' and the costs of environmental decay, adding the value of leisure, and weighting the index according to the degree of inequality in the income distribution. Such GPI estimates may be 'rough and ready', but the results often provide a striking contrast to the conventional GDP indicators. Illustrative outcomes (based on somewhat different calculations of the GPI) are shown in figure 5.1 for the United States, the United Kingdom, and Australia. In each case there is a striking contrast between GNP and GPI measures of national performance. The inference is clear—that increasing the volume and value of marketed economic products does not reliably constitute progress.

CONCLUSION

There are various ways in which economic activity can be organised. Identifying market, state, class, gender, ethnicity, and ideology as dimensions of economic and social order draws attention to the array of organising principles and institutions. It draws attention to the complexity of the interrelationships between the economy and society. There are also various ways in which economic performance can be evaluated. Identifying efficiency, equity, sustainability, and compatibility with social goals indicates the most important dimensions. It also draws attention to some of the deficiencies of narrowly constructed conventional economic indicators, such as GDP.

These considerations make necessary the exercise of judgment in political economic analysis. Indeed, the scope of political economic enquiry itself is a matter of judgment. While the economy and economics can be reasonably clearly defined—in terms of production, exchange, and distribution—there is no line clearly dividing the economy from society, or economics from the other social sciences. There are also inescapably normative elements involved in analysing and evaluating economic systems. The delineation of the discipline is made yet more complex by the recognition that capitalism is only one among many types of possible economic organisation.

CHAPTER 6

The Distinctive Features of Capitalism

What different systems of economic organisation are possible?
What is special about capitalism?
What are the common features of capitalist economies, and what are the differences?

Economic activity can be organised in various ways in the attempt to satisfy the social purposes we have identified. Communal, slave, feudal, capitalist, and socialist systems are usually distinguished as the principal alternatives. Capitalism is evidently the predominant system at the present time. A careful definition of this system is required before theories about how it works are studied and judgments about how well it works are made. This is attempted in this chapter, first by contrasting capitalism with other ways in which economic activity can be organised, and second by looking in more detail at its distinctive features.

ALTERNATIVE ECONOMIC SYSTEMS

Economic activity can be organised *communally*. In small social clusters, for example, members of the society can gather to decide what they will produce, how the tasks will be shared, and how the fruits of their economic effort will be distributed and used. These decisions may be strongly influenced by custom and convention. Such has been the case in many tribal societies, a traditional focus in anthropological studies. The term *primitive communalism* is often applied in this context, although the structure of economic and social processes may actually be highly sophisticated. Whether such communal organisation constitutes a viable basis for a large-scale, industrial economy is a moot point.

Socialism may be regarded as the application of collectivist principles in the context of a modern advanced economy. The central organising principle is *collective decision-making*. The nature of the economic activity performed, who performs it, how it is performed, and where and when it is performed are determined by a planning process. Therein lies much of the appeal of socialism, in principle at least, as a rational, democratic, and egalitarian set of socioeconomic arrangements. Whether these principles can be implemented in practice is one of the major debates of contemporary political economy. There were some controversial twentieth-century experiments—in the former Soviet Union, for example—but whether these embodied socialist principles in practice is a contentious matter. There is no single model of socialism: 'market socialism', for example, strikes a different balance between planning and markets from a command economy, in which the allocation of economic resources is determined by the state. Similarly, socialism may be based on either centralised or relatively decentralised decision-making processes—although the attractive latter variant has to deal with the seemingly pervasive tendency to centralisation and authoritarianism, which violate the 'ideal' principles. Rethinking socialism as a viable basis for economic organisation in the twenty-first century is a big challenge.[1]

A third possible means of economic organisation is *slavery*. Historically, this has been an economic system of considerable significance. Explicit use of *force or coercion* by one class (slave-owners) over another (slaves) is the central organising principle. Violence (or the threat of it) is the driver of economic activity, determining what gets done, by whom, how, where, and when. Slavery was commonplace in the Mediterranean lands, which were the cradle of modern Western civilisation, but it has also been crucially important in the recent economic development of a number of countries. No analysis of the United States, for example, could sensibly ignore the role of slavery in its economic development: slaves from Africa were the principal source of plantation labour and, after emancipation, became a major source of labour in industrial cities like Chicago and New York. A significant part of Great Britain's wealth in the eighteenth century derived from slavery, too. Coerced labour was also important in Australia, where convict labour was used to build infrastructure, laying the foundations for subsequent economic development. 'Indentured labour' from the islands of the South Pacific also provided a sizeable workforce, especially on the Queensland sugar plantations. Residual elements of slavery persist today in other nations—the use of child labour and prison labour to produce cheap products is very similar to slavery.

Feudalism is a fourth means of economic organisation. It, too, is of considerable historical and contemporary significance. Like slavery, it has coercive elements, but the core differentiating principle is *mutual obligation*. Under feudalism, the different social classes are linked by a system of mutual rights and obligations, usually based on traditional roles and beliefs. Serfs work on the land of landowners in exchange for social 'protection'. This was the norm during the Middle Ages in England and much of Western Europe. Derivatives of this system continue to shape the economic development in many of the poorer nations today. The control of any economic surplus over and above the requirements for social reproduction is in the hands of a landowning class. Social conventions and religious ideologies are usually woven into the structures of reciprocal obligation, ensuring at least some degree of social acceptance of what might otherwise be deemed unacceptable inequalities of class, social position, and power. The demand for 'land reform' is the usual signal of a move to challenge and change these residual feudal arrangements. Even in modern industrial societies, control over land—both access to it and the use of it—continues to be a significant factor determining the distribution of the economic surplus. However, what most clearly distinguishes feudalism from capitalism is the switch from an economic and social organisation based on mutual obligation to one based on monetary relationships.

Capitalism, broadly speaking, is the economic system in which *financial* considerations dominate. It is a system in which the quest for financial reward is the driving force shaping what is done, by whom, how, where, and when. It also determines 'who gets what' in the distribution of rewards. Work is done for wages; business activity is undertaken for profit. The primacy of these *pecuniary* relationships is the basic defining feature of capitalism. The pecuniary character does not preclude some collective decision-making, coercion, or mutual obligation, but it does pervade the economy and society.[2]

THE DISTINCTIVE FEATURES OF CAPITALISM

Capitalism cannot be defined as easily as we may define 'chair' or 'elephant': we do not so readily know it when we see it. A definition that is to serve as the basis for political economic analysis, showing capitalism as a cluster of interconnected characteristics, has to be set out more fully. The following eight features, summarised in figure 6.1, identify what is special about the system. Each is not unique to capitalism, but together they convey its distinctive character.

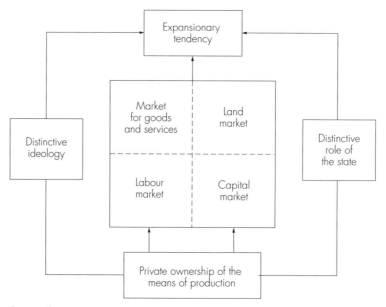

Figure 6.1   Elements in the capitalist system.

Private ownership of the means of production

Capitalism is based on a distinctive system of property rights. Economic resources are characteristically owned by private individuals and institutions. Some economic resources—land and other natural resources, or public utilities supplying such things as electricity, gas, water, and public transport—may be owned by society as a whole. However, this is an aberration, at odds with the basic capitalist principle of economic activity being in the hands of private businesses. These businesses may be run by individuals, such as sole proprietors of small firms, or by institutions legally recognised as entities, such as corporations owned by shareholders with limited liability.

The capacity of these property owners to derive income from their control over the means of production—the factories, offices, plant, and equipment with which goods and services are produced—identifies them as a distinct class. How that capitalist class is constituted depends on how numerous the small businesses are and how widespread the shareholdings in the larger firms are. Its existence as a class does not mean that internal conflicts of interests cannot occur—indeed, the owners of rival business enterprises are usually pitted against each other—but its defining feature is a common interest in the pursuit of profit.

The labour market

Under capitalism, those who do *not* own the means of production depend for their economic livelihood on the sale of their capacity to work. That requires the existence of a labour market (or, more usually, a set of labour markets, segmented according to region and occupation). The buyers of labour—those who own and control the means of production—interact there with the sellers of labour. Sometimes there is direct negotiation of wages and employment conditions between individual buyers and sellers, but the negotiation process is usually mediated by trade unions, employer associations, and regulatory institutions that set the 'rules of the game'. However, the dependence of the bulk of the population on the sale of their capacity to work (in either manual or mental labour)—that is, the existence of a working class—is the common feature.

Workers under capitalism are free in that, unlike slaves or serfs, they are not tied to a particular employer by force or convention. However, their freedom is a constrained freedom—the freedom, and the necessity, to sell their capacity to work. This is why capitalism is sometimes said to be a system of 'alienated labour', or a system in which labour is treated as a commodity.

The capital market

Those who establish and run capitalist businesses need funds for that purpose. They need financial capital before they can employ the means of production in order to make goods and services. So, an institution (or group of institutions) is necessary for channelling funds from savers into the hands of businesses or people who can then invest those funds productively. Banks carry out that institutional function by passing on depositors' funds in the form of loans to businesses. Indeed, they can lend much more than they have in deposits—effectively 'creating' money in the process. As such, banks are key capitalist institutions, facilitating the conversion of savings into investment as well as being themselves profit-seeking entities.

However, the most characteristic capital market institution under capitalism is the *stock exchange*. This is where shares in companies are sold to the public, and where the owners of those shares can sell them to others. Not surprisingly, the stock exchange is sometimes held to be the ultimate symbol of capitalism. It is a place where fortunes can be made or lost. However, it is really an adjunct to the productive economy, not in itself a place where wealth is created. Indeed, large companies often make such enormous profits that they can finance and expand their businesses without having recourse to major revenue-raising on the stock exchange. In effect, the capital market has become partly *internal* to capitalist businesses. External capital markets usually continue to exert some discipline on those businesses, though, if only because the threat of takeover becomes more likely when a firm's share price falls.

The land market

Land is of fundamental importance in all types of economic organisation. In a rural context, its fertility and the efficiency of its stewardship determines its capacity to contribute that most basic of human needs—food. In an urban context, its use has a major bearing on the effectiveness of cities as focal points of modern economic life. So, how land is owned, allocated, and regulated has major socioeconomic implications.

Under capitalism, land is characteristically privately owned and is usually allocated through market processes—subject to varying degrees of regulation by the state. Land, like labour and capital, is bought and sold in the market. Arguably, this is not essential for capitalism: land *could* be owned collectively through the state, while labour and capital continued to be subject to market processes and conflictual class relationships. As such, the form of land ownership is not such a fundamentally defining feature of the economic system under capitalism as it is under, say, feudalism. However, the very generality of market processes under capitalism makes land yet another tradeable commodity.

Markets for goods and services

Capitalism is a system of *generalised commodity production*. The production of goods and services for exchange in the market makes those goods and services commodities, that is, items produced for sale rather than for personal use by their producer.

The processes of exchange sometimes involve direct interaction between buyer and seller, but usually they are mediated by the institutions of wholesale and retail trade. Shopping is the name of the game! Indeed, shoppers play a crucial role in the capitalist system as a whole because, if their purchases do not match the volume and array of commodities produced, economic crises may occur. No wonder the emphasis on *consumerism* is so pervasive under contemporary capitalism, and no wonder so many resources are channelled into marketing and sales promotion.[3]

The distinctive role of the state

The fifth characteristic of capitalism is, at first sight, more surprising. Surely, one might think, if capitalism is primarily a market economy, then there is no significant role for the state. Not so. In all economic systems other than anarchism the state has a significant presence. The key point is what *form* the state presence takes. This can be expected to reflect the systemic features we have already discussed.

Thus, under capitalism, the state regulates and enforces the property rights on which the capitalist economy is based. It determines the rules underpinning the operation of markets for labour, capital, land, and commodities. It may act as an umpire in respect of rivalries between businesses that might otherwise be sources of economic instability. It may seek to redistribute 'market' incomes in order to ensure social stability. It may also be directly engaged in the provision of goods and services that are not otherwise provided because of 'market failure'. The market predictably fails to provide some goods and services because people who do not pay for them cannot be excluded from enjoying the benefits of their provision; that is why fire-fighting, law enforcement, and defence, for example, are normally provided by government. The nature and extent of these state activities is the focus of continued political debate, of course. The point here is that capitalism is not synonymous with a pure 'market economy'.

Distinctive ideology

All economic systems have ideologies associated with them. What matters is how the dominant ideologies are shaped by, or reflect, the structure of the economy. Determining the direction of causation is a highly contentious exercise, but some broad correlations are clear enough. For instance, the consumerism mentioned earlier (or, generally, the emphasis on material goods as the source of personal satisfaction and social status) is by no means unique to capitalism, but it seems to reach its zenith in this type of economy. *Homo economicus* is fostered by capitalist economic interests.

An emphasis on 'competitiveness' seems to be a similarly predictable characteristic of an economic system based on competing market interests (although monopoly may be as prevalent as competition in practice). By contrast, ideologies emphasising cooperation can be expected to be prominent where the economic organisation is collectivist in character. Both types of ideology are usually present, in uneasy alliance with each other. However, to the extent that ideology legitimates an economic system, it is not surprising that the predominant capitalist ideology is consumerist and competitive.

Expansionary tendency

Last, it is pertinent to note the *dynamic* character of capitalism. As a system driven by the quest for profit, it is geared for growth. This is not to say that growth is always achieved—indeed, the history of capitalist development worldwide is of alternating periods of boom and slump. However, this particular type of economic system works best when it is growing. It may be said that, like a bicycle, it requires forward motion for its stability. That is why periods of recession or economic stagnation precipitate dramatic processes of economic restructuring, as described in chapter 3.

This dynamism is capitalism's most obvious strength, the source of its capacity to reproduce itself, expand, and adapt. It is also perhaps the source of its most fundamental tensions. There is perpetual conflict between the profit-seeking interests and the broader goals of society, as the former continually challenge the prevailing social structures. There is also a fundamental tension between this growth-oriented economy and the finite character of the planet on which it exists, a tension that is manifest in growing environmental stresses.

CONCLUSION

Defining capitalism in terms of a cluster of key characteristics does not produce a simple picture. Even the above eight-part representation is significantly simplified. It is a description of an 'ideal' model. It is not necessarily ideal in the *normative* sense of being desirable (the pros and cons of that come later), but in the sense of being a simplified *abstraction* of a complex reality. The question remains: do economies in the real world—national economies, for example—approximate this 'ideal' model? In other words, are the economies of the United States, the United Kingdom, Australia, Sweden, Singapore, and other 'capitalist' nations essentially the same? Posed in this blunt manner, the question has to be answered in the negative. The range of economic functions undertaken by the state; the character of the economic institutions that shape the functioning of markets for labour, capital, and land; and the prevailing ideologies in those countries all have significantly different characteristics. In the United States, for example, the state has been more concerned with supporting the interests of capital and the functioning of the capitalist market economy than in Sweden, where the state has played a substantial role in the redistribution of income and in economic and social planning. On the other hand, the United States is highly 'interventionist' on a world scale, much more than Sweden (or any other country), because of its role as self-appointed policeman of international capitalism.[4]

These examples illustrate variations on capitalism in different national contexts. The variations are partly explicable in terms of the historical evolution of the countries concerned. They can also be analysed in terms of the relationships between the economy and society discussed in chapter 5, that is, the character and 'mix' of market, state, class, gender, ethnicity, and ideology in each case. If we are to understand different countries and how their economies work, there is no substitute for detailed historical and institutional study on a case-by-case basis. The distinctive methodological position being argued here—the punchline to this chapter—is that a necessary prelude to those investigations is an analysis of *capitalism in general*. Once we understand its fundamental features, we are then in a better position to 'layer on' the details necessary for a comprehensive understanding of the complexities of the real world in which we live.

CHAPTER 7

Economic Theory in Historical Perspective

Why theorise about the economy?
What has shaped the theorising about capitalism?
How have different analyses of capitalism evolved in the history of economic thought?

Having defined capitalism as a distinctive system of economic organisation, our task now is to understand how it works. For this purpose we must theorise. We have to abstract from the complexity of the economic system in the real world in order to focus on the essential or core elements. But what are these core elements? Which theory is appropriate? This chapter begins the process of exploring the competing economic theories about capitalism.

WHY THEORISE?

For many people, 'theory' is a pejorative term. It is something to be avoided if possible. This understandably wary attitude is encapsulated in the familiar expression 'that is all very well in theory, but in reality …'. The inference is that theory is inferior to the direct study of the reality 'out there'. The problem is that reality is so, so complex. How can we begin to understand it?

To avoid theory, we may elect to undertake a direct, down-to-earth, *empirical* examination of the capitalist economy in practice. So, we sally forth into the real world—or at least our local region of it—armed with clipboard and pencil (or computer 'notepad'), and look around. Where shall we look first? At the shops: their vast array of goods, the relative prices of the goods, and the fluctuations in demand and supply for these goods? At the factories, where those goods are produced: the production technologies, labour relations, wage rates, and other determinants of the costs of production? At the docks and airports, to see which goods are being exported and imported and how their relative prices compare? At the volume and values of transactions on the stock exchange and other financial markets? Or at the array of economic activities undertaken by governments: providing goods and services, redistributing income through taxation and public expenditures, and engaging in myriad regulatory economic functions? The list of possibilities is mind-boggling. The body of evidence we would accumulate would be indigestibly huge. Without guidelines to distinguish between what is important and what is less relevant, the task is unmanageable. We have to rethink our investigative strategy.

In effect, we are forced to accept the need for some simplification. This process of simplification is the essence of *theory construction*. We select particular key variables for study and set aside the rest as not being of fundamental importance. We are then able to investigate the nature of the relationships between the key variables. We try, thereby, to develop a sequential process of analysis to help us understand the complex world around us. As the economist Kenneth Boulding put it: 'Knowledge is always gained by the orderly loss of information, that is by condensing and abstracting and indexing the great buzzing confusion of information that comes from the world around us into a form we can appreciate and comprehend'.[1] To quote another prominent American economist, 'knowing how to simplify one's description of reality without neglecting anything essential is the most important part of an economist's art'.[2] In other words, we cannot avoid theorising. Some degree of abstraction from reality is unavoidable. The question is *how* it can most effectively be done without 'losing touch' with reality altogether (a common criticism of conventional economics). On which aspects of the economic system should the theory focus? Which aspects can be safely neglected? It is because economists are not agreed on these matters that economics as a discipline is pervaded by competing economic theories.

This is where the story starts to get interesting. These questions bring us directly to the central theme of the book: the contest between different 'ways of seeing' the capitalist economy. Of course, the existence of competing theories is not unique to economics: it is characteristic of most academic disciplines. Indeed, some would say it is the hallmark of an open society. However, in economics, the existence of different 'ways of seeing' is particularly problematic. In part, this is because economic ideas have influence on the behaviour of governments and other economic institutions. In part, it is because of the interconnectedness of issues of economic methodology and matters of political philosophy. The different viewpoints in economics reflect different ideas about the nature of knowledge in general and the construction of economic knowledge in particular. The different 'ways of seeing' also partly reflect different political perspectives—conservative, liberal, and radical—about the way in which the economy functions and how it should function. These are the bases of fundamentally different views about capitalism and social progress.

COMPETING 'SCHOOLS OF THOUGHT'

In order to understand the diverse theories about the economy, it is useful to distinguish between competing schools of thought. In effect, this enables us to cluster similar or related theories and make the number of competing theories more manageable. It is a particularly useful means of understanding both the history of economic thought and current political economic debates.

This notion of a school of thought has much in common with the concept of a paradigm. The term 'paradigm' gained particular prominence as a result of a book by Thomas Kuhn called *The Structure of Scientific Revolutions* (1962) in which he described the development, not of economics, but of the physical sciences.[3] The central question is how new theories may overthrow existing orthodoxies. Kuhn argued that such transformations periodically occur, often in a quite dramatic manner. For example, the belief that the Earth was the centre of the solar system was challenged in the sixteenth century by some upstarts who sought to demonstrate that the Earth actually revolved around the Sun. They were ridiculed and persecuted, but eventually their view came to replace the earlier one; it proved to be more consistent with empirical observations and had fewer anomalies requiring explanation. The Sun-as-the-centre-of-the-solar-system paradigm replaced the Earth-as-the-centre-of-the-solar-system paradigm.

We can think of a paradigm as *a framework of analysis that defines the issues to be studied and the methods to be applied in studying them.* Competing paradigms, Kuhn argued, have been common in the physical sciences. At any time, one paradigm tends to predominate. This constitutes a period of 'normal science'. A clear research agenda is set, but at the expense of limiting the questions that the discipline poses. That eventually becomes a hindrance to further significant scientific progress; anomalous observations proliferate, and a period of crisis occurs. A new paradigm emerges, resolving at least some of the anomalies, and new questions are posed and a new research agenda set; thus, science evolves, not in a linear fashion in which the edifice of knowledge is steadily built brick-by-brick, but through periodic revolutions that open the way for surges in scientific advance.

There are some important differences between the physical sciences and the social sciences, including economics. In the social sciences, the object of the enquiry is constantly changing. Evolution is a feature of the physical world, too, of course, but economic and social conditions are subject to rapid change, which makes for particular difficulties in economic and social analysis. Theories that may be appropriate at one time are rendered inappropriate by changed circumstances resulting from the passage of time. Capitalism today is not what it was a century ago: its institutional features have changed dramatically, even if its essential character has some significant elements of continuity.

This problem is further complicated by the interdependence of theories about social phenomena and the behaviour resulting from those the application of those theories. To give an obvious example: how we understand the economy influences the nature of economic policies implemented by governments, which then changes, at least to some degree, how the economy operates. Again, this problem of interdependence of subject and object is not unknown in the physical sciences, but it is particularly prevalent in economics and the social sciences. Even the process of studying people's behaviour can radically change their behaviour: they act differently when being observed or monitored.[4]

Last, it is pertinent to note that the development of economics, and the social sciences in general, is permeated by the influence of *material interests*. Particular theories may suit the requirements of particular individuals, classes, or nations. Because they serve a useful function for the vested interests they support, they can hold out against competing arguments and contradictory evidence. The contest of economic ideas is intertwined with the conflict of economic interests.

This last consideration helps to explain why rival schools of economic thought seem to have such durability. They do not slink away when trounced by superior explanations of economic phenomena. Their persistence is doubly remarkable in light of the first of the above considerations—the changing character of the economy in practice. Economists are continually modifying their theories—the professional journals are full of such adaptations—but the core principles have remarkable tenacity.

The 'conversations' among practitioners of each school of thought and between practitioners of different schools of thought in books and journal articles have a rhetorical character.[5] The emphasis is on a process of persuasion; it is a contest of economic ideas. It should already be clear that this is not a purely academic contest. The *political purposes* that economics serves also have to be taken into account in any serious analysis of the development of schools of economic thought.

AN HISTORICAL OVERVIEW

The essentially political character of economic thought is most obvious when the subject is studied in historical perspective. Over more than two and a quarter centuries, paralleling the development of the capitalist economy, the competing schools of economic thought have argued about how capitalism works. Figure 7.1 provides a simple summary of the evolving currents of economic analysis.

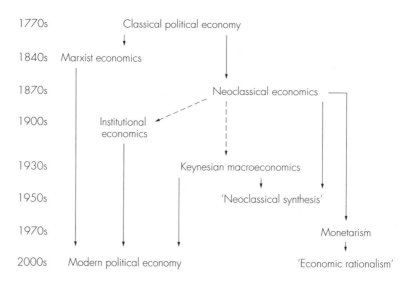

Figure 7.1   The history of economic thought. This chart of the main currents of political economic analysis in historical perspective simplifies the complex history of the subject; however, it does draw attention to the principal avenues of continuity (represented by the continuous vertical lines) and discontinuity (represented by the dotted lines). In the former, the new school of thought is a development from the previous one; in the latter, it is a reaction against it.

Each of these competing schools of thought can be understood in terms of the changing economic conditions of the time, the influence of particular economic interests, the influence of prevailing intellectual fashions, and the innovative ideas of great economic thinkers.

Much of the rest of the book is an illustration of these themes. All that remains for this chapter is to make some prefatory remarks about each of the major schools of thought, setting the scene for the more detailed investigations that follow.

It is sensible to begin in the late eighteenth century, when capitalism was clearly emerging from feudalism in Great Britain and, more haltingly, in other nations in which capitalist economic relationships were eventually to predominate. This was the period when Adam Smith wrote his seminal book *An Inquiry into the Nature and Causes of the Wealth of Nations* (usually shortened to *The Wealth of Nations*) and when what we now call classical political economy became established. Of course, there had been earlier considerations of economic phenomena: the capacity for people to reflect on the economic conditions affecting their lives knows no time limits. However, with classical political economy we can see the emergence of a specifically *capitalist* economics.

The classical political economists were concerned with studying the economic character of the society in which they lived. They reflected on the propensity of an economic system based on market exchange, rather than customary relationships or state management, for increasing national wealth. They believed this because such a system opened up opportunities for individual initiative, increased productivity, and the growth of trade. (Some did have grave reservations about whether the mass of the working population would experience rising living standards, however.) The 'economic liberalism' characteristic of these diagnoses and prognoses has been one of the strong currents in much subsequent economic thought. It continues to have a major influence today.

The theories of neoclassical economics built on the foundations of classical political economy. They have been a consistently strong source of support over more than a century for the view that free markets produce efficient outcomes. Emerging in the late nineteenth century, neoclassical theory provided a formal modelling of equilibrium conditions in competitive markets. This was clearly an attempt to put economics—then newly separated from the study of history and politics—on a more 'scientific' basis. (Whether the result was and is actually more scientific or more ideological, showing capitalism in an unrealistically favourable light, is a seemingly perpetual controversy.)

Meanwhile, Marxist economists, also starting from a basis in classical political economy, have taken a markedly different stance in their interpretation of capitalism. They have argued that the operation of such an economy generates pervasive economic inequality, social conflict, and periodic crisis. This quite different analysis of the capitalist economy also emerged in the nineteenth century, responding to the economic, social, and political transformations then taking place. The pioneering analysis of Karl Marx, and his collaborator Friedrich Engels, continues to lay foundations for radical critiques of the capitalist system, such as those frequently advanced by critics of the corporate globalisation process of the present time. On this reasoning, only a fundamental transformation of the political economic system can reconcile economic concerns with social justice and social progress.

Between these extremes are reformist political economic perspectives, such as those associated with John Maynard Keynes and with the institutional tradition of analysis. These also warrant careful consideration, for they particularly focus on what governments can do—given the political will—to eradicate unemployment, redistribute incomes more equitably, and promote more balanced economic and social development.

The institutional economics tradition had its roots in the 'historical school' of the nineteenth century and was propelled by the critical social analysis of the dissident American economist Thorstein Veblen. Veblen was deeply critical of capitalism, but his critique was quite different from Marx's, emphasising the social manifestations of business behaviour and economic inequalities rather than the forces for change generated by class conflict. The political tenor of the institutional economics tradition after Veblen has usually been more concerned with the amelioration of the problems of capitalism than with a revolutionary challenge to the system. It can be argued that the development of the welfare state in the twentieth century was due to the thinking of these institutional economists, as well as the work of other social reformers.

Keynes, writing between World War I and World War II when unemployment was particularly pervasive and persistent, also saw economic analysis as a means towards reform. He considered the capitalist system 'morally objectionable' but thought it better than the possible alternatives: communism and fascism, support for which was then growing internationally. Understanding the causes of unemployment, and positing solutions for it through enlightened economic policy, would, on this reasoning, make a particularly valuable social contribution. As with institutional economics, this was a perspective in which the state was necessarily central. As historian Eric Hobsbawm put it, Keynes 'wished to save the essentials of a capitalist system but realised that this could be done only within the framework of a strong and systematically interventionist state'.[6] It was in contributing to such reforms, Keynes said, that economists can be the trustees of 'the possibilities of civilisation'.[7]

The ideas of Keynes, reinterpreted in a mechanistic form in an effort to make them compatible with neoclassical theory, became the basis for a new orthodoxy during the three decades after World War II. This was the age of 'neoclassical synthesis': an uneasy blend of the 'interventionist' ideas of Keynes with the 'free-market' theory of the neoclassical economists. It coincided with the years of the long boom when, for the advanced industrial capitalist nations at least, there indeed did seem to be continuous economic growth and full employment. The collapse of that long boom in the 1970s ushered in a major assault on Keynesian economics, both in theory and in policy practice. Western capitalism saw the impact of a resurgent pre-Keynesianism, known as monetarism, which argued that capitalism would work best when government 'interfered' least.

Monetarism has been associated with a general revival in the last three decades of various forms of 'free-market' economics. The ideas of Adam Smith are blended with propositions from neoclassical theory and other contemporary 'New Right' theorists (in the process setting aside Smith's reservations about markets and businessmen, and overlooking the fundamental differences between capitalism in his time and ours) to show the benefits of releasing capitalism from the constraints imposed by trade unions and states.

Modern political economists usually express profound reservations about the ascendancy of this neo-liberal 'free-market' economics. They argue that it fails to provide a coherent means of understanding contemporary capitalism, and that its policy prescriptions accentuate economic inequality, instability, and insecurity in practice. They put the case for drawing on the dissident traditions of Marxist economics, institutional economics, and the political economics of Keynes, and for building a more critical analysis of capitalism that takes account of contemporary economic problems (as reviewed in chapter 4).

This, in a nutshell, is the story of the competing schools of economic thought. It is the story of ongoing rivalry—partly methodological and partly political in character—within this contested but highly influential discipline. It illustrates the controversial character of economic ideas about capitalism over more than two centuries.

Have we come a long way? Or are there elements of circularity, repetition, and regress in the development of economic thought? Has the inherently political nature of economics impeded our understanding of capitalism? And, on what basis can future progress be made, both in understanding the economic system and in changing it for the better? A prerequisite for such progress is understanding how we reached this point. That, essentially, is the rationale for studying political economic analysis in historical perspective. It is the rationale for much of what follows in the rest of this book. This is not a matter of studying the history of economic thought for its own sake, but of doing so in a selective, illustrative manner in order to tease out what is of continuing relevance to understanding and resolving economic problems today.[8]

CONCLUSION

Identifying the key processes that shape the functioning of the capitalist economic system, for better or worse, is the key concern of political economy. Even the interpretation of the economy as a 'system' implies some such analytical stance: 'system' implies regularities of behaviour, forces that impose order on the outcomes, and systemic features that, in principle at least, can be understood and then controlled.

However, there is no unanimity on how to fashion this understanding. Rather, it is evident that an economic system like capitalism can be understood in various ways. Those different 'ways of seeing' exist partly because of methodological differences regarding theory-construction and partly because of differences in value judgments associated with rival political philosophies. Moreover, as a historical analysis of the discipline reveals, there is a strong connection between the contest of economic ideas and the conflict of economic interests.

PART III

Back to Basics

Classical political economy

CHAPTER 8

Capitalism Emerging
A 'natural' order?

Do the concerns of the classical political economists still matter?
What processes produced the economic system that the classical political
economists sought to understand?
Why did they see the emerging capitalist system as progressive?

Classical political economy spanned the period from the mid eighteenth century to the late nineteenth century. During this period significant contributions to economic theory were made by Adam Smith, David Ricardo, Thomas Malthus, Jean-Baptiste Say, James Mill, John Stuart Mill and many others. Most of these scholars came from relatively privileged backgrounds: the conditions of ordinary working men and women permitted no comparable opportunities for leisured study, publication, and social influence.

Why should we be interested now in the ideas of these dead white males? Surely, theirs was a different society, with different economic characteristics and problems. It would be unreasonable to claim that their analyses can simply be applied today without substantial revision. However, some familiarity with their contributions is useful for at least three reasons. First, it is interesting in its own right to see how these practical scholars grappled with the workings of the emerging capitalist economy. Second, their work has had a major influence on subsequent economic thought; it is no exaggeration to say that the major traditions of economic analysis, both conservative and radical, are largely developments of, or reactions against, classical political economy. Modern political economy is, in important respects, an extension of this classical tradition. Third, the prescriptions of the classical political economists are of continuing influence on economic policies in the real world, notwithstanding the major economic changes that have taken place since the end of the nineteenth century.

THE CURRENT INFLUENCE OF CLASSICAL IDEAS

Many modern economic viewpoints are traceable to classical political economy. Adam Smith (1723–90) is often cited in support of the arguments for 'free-market' capitalism, for example. The belief that *freedom of exchange* and a *self-regulating market* are the preconditions for social progress is one of the hallmarks of 'New Right' ideology today. Promoted vigorously by so-called 'think-tanks', operating both nationally and internationally, this particular economic ideology has had widespread influence. It has had a direct connection with the policies of influential politicians in the late twentieth century, such as former British prime minister Margaret Thatcher, former US presidents Ronald Reagan and George Bush, and contemporary Australian political leaders, such as John Howard. Their economic advisers, if not actually tie-wearing members of the 'Adam Smith Club', have been imbued with a preference for the 'invisible hand' of the market over the 'visible hand' of the state. This preference is revealed in the political rhetoric, if not in the economic policies actually implemented.

The ideas of David Ricardo (1772–1823), another of the leading classical political economists, are also of enduring significance. In his own day, Ricardo was a strong advocate of breaking down the barriers to international trade, arguing that, if each nation specialised in the production of the goods and services for which it was best suited and traded its surplus with other nations, all would benefit. This is the basis of his famous doctrine of *comparative advantage*. Proponents of globalisation today generally mount similar arguments—although the term 'competitive advantage' has replaced the Ricardian 'comparative advantage'. A careful assessment of the case for and against tariff protection or other impediments to trade can usefully begin with a reconsideration of Ricardo's reasoning.

Or take the case of Thomas Malthus (1766–1834), the 'gloomy parson' famous for his views on *population growth*. Malthus argued that there would be a persistent tendency for the rate of population growth to outstrip the rate of growth in food production, leading to famines, illness, and wars, and preventing the living standards of the mass of the population from rising substantially above subsistence level. There are strong echoes of such concerns in current debates about Third World poverty and the environmental constraints on economic growth.[1] On a global scale, high birth rates and poverty remain strongly correlated, although there are grounds for believing that poverty causes high fertility, rather than *vice versa*. The distinguished economist Amartya Sen also argues that the Malthusian 'food availability doctrine' pays insufficient attention to the importance of political factors in explaining and resolving poverty; he contends that 'no famine has ever taken place in the history of the world in a functioning democracy'.[2] Most modern environmentalists, stressing the consequences of wasteful production and consumption and the problems arising from the maldistribution between rich and poor nations, do not adopt a Malthusian 'doomsday perspective' either. Some do, however; prominent American environmentalist Paul Ehrlich, for example, continues to argue that excessive population growth underpins the problems of poverty and environmental decay.[3] Moreover, even those who argue that production and consumption levels, rather than population numbers *per se*, are the root problem tend to couch their concerns in terms of the stresses, and ultimate unsustainability, of growth.

A final illustration concerns the views of French classical political economist Jean-Baptiste Say (1767–1832). He is best known for what has come to be called 'Say's Law'. This, in a nutshell, is the proposition that *supply creates its own demand*. Thus, the production of goods and services can be expected to generate the income that is necessary to purchase those commodities. Hence, there need be no general tendency towards economic recession arising from a shortage of demand. Under-consumption need never be a problem, according to this view. Although the modern 'free-market' economists seldom explicitly cite Say's Law in support of their prescriptions, the legacy lives. Milton Friedman, for example, has repeatedly argued that a capitalist economy tends towards its own stable equilibrium, and that government 'intervention' intended to offset recessions by boosting the level of demand is likely to do more harm than good.

Box 8.1

Adam Smith (1723–90)

The outstanding figure in classical political economy was actually a professor of moral philosophy. The study of economic issues was not then separated from the broader study of society—its historical evolution and the political ramifications of change. The ethical aspects of economic behaviour were regarded as being of paramount importance.

Adam Smith was born in Scotland in 1723. He spent six years in England as a student at Oxford University, where, as one biographer notes, he 'was dismayed by the low level of intellectual activity and the immorality of his fellow students'.[4] He had a pretty low opinion of the professors, too, and he reflected on the question of whether they might be more productive if they were paid according to their performance.

After returning to Scotland he secured a teaching position at the University of Glasgow, before being appointed to the chair of Moral Philosophy. In 1759, he published an important treatise entitled *The Theory of Moral Sentiments*. However, it was the publication in 1776 of *An Inquiry into the Nature and Causes of the Wealth of Nations* (usually known simply as *The Wealth of Nations*) that really made his name as the leading political economist of the time. With *The Wealth of Nations*, Smith laid the foundation for the systematic study of political economy. Here, indeed, was an intriguing blend of political judgments, philosophical reflections, and practical observations about commercial activities.

Smith wrote *The Wealth of Nations* after resigning from his professorship to take up a lucrative post as personal tutor to a young nobleman travelling in Europe. (He revealed in *The Wealth of Nations* that he was personally quite sceptical of the educational value of extended continental tours for young men.) Later, he held the office of Comptroller of Customs for Scotland, in which capacity he managed the tariffs on imported goods. Smith, although committed to a belief in the progressive role of markets, was clearly a pragmatist. His support for the principles of a market economy was conditional and hedged by ethical concerns. He may well be 'turning in his grave' at some of the extreme *laissez-faire* ideological positions taken by his modern followers, including some who proudly wear the tie of the 'Adam Smith Club'.

The ideas of classical political economists are strikingly—almost eerily—relevant to current debates about market freedoms, the benefits of trade, population growth, recessions, and the appropriate role of government. But are they helpful? They were developed to understand an economic environment quite different from today's. So, in considering the applicability of this intellectual legacy, it is pertinent to consider the historical context in which the ideas originally developed.

THE EMERGENCE OF CAPITALISM FROM FEUDALISM

The classical political economists were writing at a time when one economic and social order was being replaced by another. Indeed, whether it did actually constitute a new *order* was a fundamental concern. Smith, Ricardo, Malthus, and Say were observing a dramatic historical transformation that was to culminate in capitalism becoming the predominant economic system. It did not occur overnight, nor even over a few decades: it was a process that evolved over many centuries. It was the culmination of changes in patterns of economic production and class relationships that had been taking place in Europe from about the eleventh century onwards. By the sixteenth century, the rate of change had accelerated, making that century in particular the watershed between the old, decaying feudal order and the new, rising capitalist system. From then, up to the nineteenth century, the 'great transformation' occurred.[5]

Many scholarly works have been written about the nature of this transformation.[6] For our purposes, it will suffice to list some of the key elements in this interconnected process of transformation, focusing particularly on the historical conditions in Great Britain, where the capitalist system first took clear shape before it became well developed elsewhere in Europe, was 'exported' to the colonies, and became global in form.[7]

- *Improvements in agricultural technology* were a particularly important foundation. People usually think of capitalism as being an urban, industrial economic system, so it is pertinent to note that its origins were rural. Only when a society can meet its own food requirements without expending all its labour continuously on producing food do other forms of economic development—urban and industrial— become possible. Such potential was already being realised by the eleventh century. A key contributor was crop-rotation (leaving a third of the acreage fallow each year so that the soil's nutrients could be restored), which resulted in higher yields. And horses came to replace oxen as the principal sources of traction, enabling more efficient ploughing. Some degree of *rural and urban specialisation* became possible because of the greater productivity that these changes brought.
- The creation of an agricultural surplus facilitated the *growth of towns*. No longer did all the people need to work on the land in order to subsist. Before the tenth century, there had been only a few small trade centres among the scattering of villages, but significant towns—albeit still tiny by modern metropolitan standards—were well established by the thirteenth century. The towns that developed in this period can be regarded as the cradles of capitalism; however, this was primarily a *merchant capitalism* rather than an industrial capitalism. Craft production was a characteristic economic activity, involving the manufacture of items for both local consumption and, increasingly, trade.
- *The development of long-distance trade* opened up further opportunities for commodity exchange. Even by modern standards, some of this trade involved quite prodigious distances. The Venetian trader Marco Polo traversed Asia in the thirteenth century,

for example. By that time, annual trade-fairs, often lasting several weeks, were flourishing in Europe. From about the fifteenth century, fairs were starting to be replaced by permanent commercial centres located in cities and had increasingly sophisticated systems of currency exchange and credit facilities. These places were, in effect, embryos of modern *financial centres*. They laid the foundations for *commercial law*, gradually supplementing and then replacing the customary laws that formerly prevailed. This is a reminder that capitalism is not a 'natural' order that develops in a vacuum: it depends on certain social preconditions, including legal structures relating to contractual arrangements and property rights.

- These economic and social developments accelerated the *decline of the manorial system*. Feudalism was essentially a *localised* rural economic and social system based on individual manors, each ruled by a lord. This manorial system, the 'bastion of feudalism', was vulnerable to the spread of monetary exchange relationships. The growth of towns and the growth of trade between rural manors and cities began to erode the autonomy and self-sufficiency of the manors. The lords of the manors purchased luxury goods from urban merchants, and peasants supplemented their subsistence livelihood by selling some of their produce at local markets. Production for profit, and monetary relations in general, began to replace the customary relationships on which the manors had traditionally been based.

- Meanwhile, the *putting-out system* was developing. This was a production system in which craftsmen were contracted to manufacture items directly for merchant-capitalists. These merchants typically provided the raw materials and the craftsmen made the products in their own homes, selling them directly to the merchants for a fee. These arrangements, well developed by the sixteenth century, were a forerunner of capitalist industry. The putting-out system was not itself fully capitalist. The workers worked in their own homes, not under the direct supervision of employers, and, significantly, their labour was not wage-labour—they were remunerated for the *products* made. However, the system can be regarded as paving the way for capitalist employment. The putting-out system persists in many sectors of modern industry—as 'outwork' in the clothing industry, for example. Indeed, it has become increasingly widespread in computer-based service industries (such as desktop publishing), which seem to be developing the characteristics of modern 'hi-tech cottage industries'.

- For there to be a fully fledged industrial capitalism, a *working class* had to be created. Peasants and artisans had to be severed from their traditional livelihoods in order to create pools of wage-labour. The *enclosure movement* was a particularly important means to that end—although its immediate motivation was acquiring profits through the privatisation of land. During the eighteenth century, more and more common land—land on which peasants had traditionally grazed their livestock—was fenced off, especially for sheep-grazing to produce wool for the expanding textile industry. This accelerated a process of rural–urban migration that had already started in the fifteenth and sixteenth centuries. Peasants, driven from their villages because they no longer had the means to support themselves, frequently became vagrant and moved to the towns in search of whatever livelihood they could eke out. They were the raw material for the development of an urban industrial working class.

- *Improvements in transportation and production technologies,* culminating in the 'industrial revolution', were the final piece in this jigsaw of forces precipitating social change. Improvements in transportation technologies had been taking place over a long period of time. Bigger and better sailing ships, and improved navigational aids facilitated trade and the establishment of colonies, such as those in the Americas and the Antipodes. A great burst of technological innovation in the eighteenth and nineteenth century led to dramatic advances in the production of textiles, in coal mining, and in the forging of iron and steel. The development of the steam engine was a great leap forward, both for industrial production and rail transport. These industrial changes took place in a socioeconomic context where the foundations for capitalism had already been established. They provided unstoppable momentum.

A DESIRABLE TRANSFORMATION?

The transition from feudalism to capitalism involved changes in class structures, in spatial form, in technological conditions, and in patterns of trade that provided the necessary and sufficient material conditions for the new economic and social order. These dramatic changes in material economic conditions were accompanied—as dramatic economic changes usually are—by corresponding changes in prevailing *ideas.* Indeed, some scholars have argued that it was the widespread acceptance of particular ideas conducive to acquisitiveness and material progress that explains why capitalism first took root in Great Britain and then in Europe. The Protestant strain of Christianity is often described as providing the accommodating ideology, making the pursuit of personal wealth no obstacle to getting to heaven.[8] But the economic changes themselves precipitated further ideological changes. It was in the context of this great transformation that classical political economy emerged.

The transformation was neither smooth nor uncontested. The erosion of feudal arrangements created considerable insecurity and generated much social conflict. Major changes to traditional economic and social structures always create winners and losers: the latter can always be expected to resist. So it was with the changes just described: peasants' revolts were common from the fourteenth to sixteenth centuries; there was bitter resistance to the enclosure movement; some workers, feeling their working conditions threatened by the introduction of new machinery and managerial techniques, formed significant resistance movements, most famously the Luddites; and agricultural workers who sought to form themselves into a union to protect their wages and working conditions were found guilty under the Mutiny Act and 'transported' to Australia (before public protest succeeded in pressuring the authorities to allow them to return from that dreadful place).[9]

Concerns about the *ethical* aspects of the transformation to capitalism were also widespread. Would it be a stable economic system? Would it serve society well? Many churchmen worried about the primacy afforded the quest for profit, and the implications of putting individual self-interest before social responsibility in economic affairs. It was in assuaging such concerns that classical political economy made its great ideological contribution.

CONCLUSION

Classical political economy developed in the context of a great historical transformation. Although the concerns, analyses, and prescriptions of the classical political economists were diverse, we can see them as being essentially concerned with understanding the emerging socioeconomic system that eventually came to be known as capitalism. They did not see it as a blessing for all humankind, but their teachings generally served as a supporting ideology for the new system. By inference, it was a 'natural' order, compared with which previous systems of economic organisation were underdeveloped precursors.

The class relationships, social customs, and moral beliefs of the feudal era persisted into the age of classical political economy. Disquiet about the ethical implications of embracing a capitalist economy was common. So, there is something rather ironic about taking the analyses developed by classical political economists directly into the modern context, particularly when those ideas are used to justify the extension of capitalist, 'free-market' principles. Nevertheless, as this chapter has argued, there are some significant elements of continuity between the age of classical political economy and today, both in the way capitalist development is interpreted and in the associated dilemmas—moral as well as material. The classical political economic concerns have strong contemporary echoes.

CHAPTER 9

Private Vices and Public Virtues

What beliefs about society underpinned classical political economy?
What are the ethics of relying on self-interest as the driver of economic activity?
Do these 'liberal' economic ideas provide a strong case for an unregulated market economy?

Is capitalism a progressive economic system, contributing to our capacity to achieve social progress? From the time of the classical political economists, this has been a contentious issue. Adam Smith and the other leading intellectuals of the day were essentially concerned with ethical issues, seeing dangers in the breakdown of the old social order as well as the opportunities being opened up by the new. They established the basic principles of *economic liberalism*, on which most subsequent pro-capitalist ideology has been constructed. They thereby built a strong case for the market economy, reassuring the dominant classes that it could be an engine for substantial material progress. However, significant reservations were expressed about its social effects and whether it would benefit the mass of the people. Because of the strong influence of these ideas—particularly on neo-liberal views and policies today—they warrant consideration in the context in which they were developed.

CHALLENGING MERCANTILISM

The ideas of the classical political economists were, first and foremost, a challenge to the prevailing practices and beliefs of *mercantilism*. Mercantilist doctrines were influential in the seventeenth and eighteenth centuries. The prevailing view was that national economic progress required a major role for government in managing national economies and regulating trade. A particular focus was on the need for policies to stimulate exports and minimise imports, thereby ensuring an inflow of gold that would increase the supply of money—and by implication the total wealth—in the national economy. The mercantilist regime saw governments granting major monopolistic privileges to the big financial and trading companies in order to promote this goal. Understandably, these state-sponsored businessmen had a vested interest in preserving the existing economic arrangements.

However, mercantilism had its increasingly influential opponents. Small business people and farmers generally resented the monopolistic privileges accorded to the big trading houses. The taxes levied in order to finance the national powers—economic, political, and military—also created resentment, especially in the colonies. The claim for 'no taxation without representation' was one of the central themes of the War of American Independence (1775–83). This resentment against mercantilism, together with the growing interest in liberal economic ideas, such as those promulgated by Smith, began to bode ill for the old order. The classical political economists' call for freedom of the market place had growing appeal, particularly to the emergent capitalist class.

CHALLENGING THE CHRISTIAN CORPORATE ETHIC

There was also a striking clash in the eighteenth and early nineteenth centuries between the new economic ideas and the values and interests associated with the old order. The clash was not only with the elements of the state and the businesses wedded to mercantilism, but also with the medieval social and religious institutions. It was a period of considerable uncertainty and grave disquiet about what the future held in store. It was 'an era in which an outdated economic ideology, the Medieval version of the Christian corporate ethic, came into increasingly sharp conflict with a new social and economic order with which it was incompatible'.[1]

The old order had been based on explicit ethical principles. This 'Christian corporate ethic' accepted private property and enterprise as a basis for economic activity, but saw it as a means of generating wealth to support charitable acts. 'The rich man, if he does not give alms, is a thief' was one common view.[2] A benevolent paternalism was expected of the upper classes. Greed, selfishness, and covetousness were reviled and denounced. Merchants were regarded as being morally bound to trade at a 'just price' (admittedly an ill-defined concept, but one sharply at odds with the temptation to charge 'whatever the market would bear').

By contrast, the new order seemed to require fewer constraints to be imposed on business activity. Altruism was no longer considered necessary for socially beneficial outcomes: self-interest would suffice, indeed would be the key driving force for economic progress. As E.K. Hunt puts it, 'the sins that were most strongly denounced within the context of the Christian paternalistic ethic were to become the behavioural assumptions on which the capitalist market economy was to be based'.[3]

Therein lies a tension that has existed in right-wing politics ever since. On the one hand, the so-called 'Tory' tradition emphasises the paternalistic obligations of the economically well-to-do, the value of charitable works, and the need for the state to engage in economic and social regulation in order to achieve social cohesion; while on the other hand the right-wing 'libertarian' view has a fundamental antipathy towards the state and a greater confidence in the capacity of competitive markets to reconcile conflicting interests and ensure efficient economic outcomes, thereby making social policy less necessary. These are the familiar 'wet' and 'dry' factional positions in modern conservative political parties.

Did the classical political economists have more in common with the 'wets' or the 'dries'? Adam Smith's position shows the tension. He saw social and economic order arising from people's natural desire to better their lot in life and thereby gain social esteem; however, he strongly emphasised the social context in which acquisitiveness occurs. His was not the crude 'greed is good' position sometimes espoused by his modern 'dry' disciples. Indeed, Smith, the moral philosopher, had argued in his first major work, *The Theory of Moral Sentiments*, that society is not held together merely by neutral rules: sympathy for the plight of our neighbours is important because it leads to a sharing of emotions and sensations. Given these preconditions, he argued, self-interest can then be of positive economic benefit. It is a conclusion summed up in his oft-quoted statement in *The Wealth of Nations* that, 'It is not from the benevolence of the butcher, the brewer or the baker that we expect our dinner, but from their regard to their own interest'.[4]

Here is the classical political economist's case for the market as the means by which self-interest can be harnessed for social purposes. Smith's great ideological achievement was to show that a new social order could emerge out of the potential chaos of an individualistic society. In his own words:

> each producer intends only his own security; and by directing that industry in such a manner as its produce may be of the greatest value, he intends only his own gain, and he is in this, as in many other cases, led by an invisible hand to promote an end which was no part of his intention. Nor is it always the worse for the society that it was not a part of it. By pursuing his own interest he frequently promotes that of society more effectually than when he really intends to promote it. I have never known much good done by those who affected to trade for the public good. It is an affectation, indeed, not very common among merchants, and very few words need to be employed in dissuading them from it.[5]

The phrase 'invisible hand' is rather buried in this quotation. However, it has come to symbolise Smith's intellectual legacy, providing *the* classical argument for a free-market economy. If reliance on the 'invisible hand' is sufficient basis for a thriving economy, no further economic planning or political intervention seems warranted. It is pertinent to note, however, that although the notion of an 'invisible hand' implies a general preference for self-regulating markets, Smith saw those markets as requiring social foundations that would shape behaviour in desirable ways. There is an explicitly ethical dimension to the reasoning: there is an inference that the invisible hand may, after all, be the hand of God.

ECONOMIC LIBERALISM

In putting the case for the greater individual freedom of the market place, Smith was in agreement with a number of other leading intellectuals of the eighteenth century. A particularly intriguing contribution to the debate had been published some decades earlier, in 1704. Written by Bernard Mandeville and entitled *The Fable of the Bees*, it was a bestseller. It is a strange book; it begins with a poem and continues with a number of essays and dialogues. The central theme is how 'private vices' (such as self-interest) can lead to 'public benefits' (the better operation of the society as a whole); thus, Mandeville argued, individual human actions spontaneously generate orderly social structures like law, language, the growth of knowledge, and, yes, the market.[6] Selfishness, because of its association with industriousness, would thereby tend to contribute to a thriving economy.

Similar views came from many intellectuals of the age. Collectively, this was a crusade for *liberty*. The emphasis on the freedom of the individual was married to assertions about the need for freedom of trade. It produced an ideology markedly favourable to the ascendancy of capitalist values and practices. It helped sound the death knell of mercantilist doctrines, if not of all mercantilist policies in practice. Moreover, it fitted in with the Protestant theology that emerged from the Reformation—a set of religious beliefs largely free of the moral opprobrium that the Catholic church had heaped on commercial activities. Protestantism held that people would be judged by their faith rather than their works, so a pure heart and faith in God could be quite compatible with acquisitive economic behaviour. Wryly, one might say that a businessman looking into his conscience could readily find 'that God had planted there a deep respect for the principles of private property'.[7]

Economic liberalism draws these ideas together. It is not altogether compatible with liberal philosophy in general, but provides a particular view of the relationship between people's essential nature and their economic activities. Somewhat schematically, we may identify its four interrelated assumptions as follows:

- *individualism*: the individual is regarded as the basic unit of society; consequently, no sound claim can be made about any social interest that purports to be more than, or different from, the aggregation of individual interests
- *hedonism*: individuals are driven by self-interest, seeking pleasure and avoiding pain
- *rationality*: the pursuit of self-interest takes a deliberate form, each individual weighing up the costs and benefits of alternative courses of action and choosing that which promises him or her the most advantageous outcome
- *inertia*: people are basically lazy, remaining inactive unless motivated to action by the prospect of personal gain.[8]

If we regard people in this way, it is not difficult to see why the market is held to be a desirable arrangement for dealing with economic matters. Individual preferences for goods and services can be expressed in the market place, sending signals to the producers about what is wanted and what is not. Sellers compete with one another to supply the products to meet the demand, and that process of competition keeps prices at a minimum. Not all individual aspirations are necessarily met, but the market mediates between all the individuals to achieve effective compromises. Mutually advantageous exchanges occur. Economic resources are efficiently used.

ON THE OTHER HAND ...

Although classical political economy—and the tradition of economic liberalism that it spawned—played a key role in legitimising capitalist market relationships, the classical political economists themselves expressed significant reservations. Adam Smith was certainly no apologist for capitalist business practices in general. Smith's 'ambivalence towards nascent capitalism' is evident from a careful reading of his work.[9] A deep suspicion is evident, for example, in his observation that 'people of the same trade seldom meet together ... but the conversation ends in a conspiracy against the public or in some contrivance to raise prices'.[10] What he favoured was a process of *competition* in the market to limit such anti-social business behaviour.

It is also important to note that, although Smith was unsympathetic to governments wielding great economic power, his was not a simple advocacy of *laissez-faire*. In the lectures on jurisprudence that he delivered at the University of Glasgow he argued that the chief purpose of government is to preserve justice, and that this would require the state to protect the individual's personal rights, property, reputation, and social relations.[11] In *The Wealth of Nations* he argued that government must carry out important functions in providing defence against foreign invaders, maintaining public institutions (such as those providing for transport, education, and religion), and protecting citizens against injustices suffered at the hands of other citizens.

Nor was Smith in favour of greater economic inequality. By the general standards of the time, an egalitarian sentiment can be discerned in his writing. His was a vision of society in which all people would be making their personal contributions to economic advancement. In his own words, economic progress would stem from 'the uniform, constant and uninterrupted effort of every man to better his condition'.[12] It would be from the grass-roots effort of the great mass of people, rather than from particular leaders of business of finance, that economic progress would emanate.

It must be borne in mind that Smith was writing about a very different economy from today's. The businesses were usually tiny by modern standards. What Smith saw as desirable was competition, not capitalism *per se*. He was an opponent, first and foremost, of monopoly. He favoured markets, but saw an important role for government. He emphasised the need to have individual incentives, but did not support increased economic inequality. His views helped to undermine the Christian corporate ethic, but he was deeply concerned about the moral dimension of economic behaviour; as political economist Robert Heilbroner notes, 'Smith was by no means oblivious to the moral costs of acquisitiveness'.[13] These are the reasons why the attempt by modern neo-liberals to claim descent from Adam Smith is so problematic. To quote Heilbroner again: 'In Smith's hands the interplay of market forces and moral decline takes the form of a subtle dialectic that invests his work with its remarkable depths. In the hands of his successors the dialectic disappears, and the evaluation of economic growth emphasises its material aspects without any concern as to untoward moral consequences, in terms of either motives or social outcomes'.[14]

CONCLUSION

Classical political economy provides the basis on which subsequent economic thought has developed. It challenged prevailing mercantilist beliefs about what constituted ordered arrangements of economic activity and social progress. It established economic liberalism as the dominant economic outlook, building on existing views about individualism and acquisitiveness. It flourished in a time when the Christian corporate ethic was starting to be eroded. It seemed to be the 'modern' way of understanding economic activity.

In any period of rapid economic and social change there are always anxieties and tensions. Today, for example, we find a former academic supporter of the 'New Right' warning against further moves towards globalisation and neo-liberalism: 'a deepening international anarchy is the human prospect', says John Gray.[16] Taking a longer-term perspective, another recent reviewer of our experience of economic progress warns that 'the essential balance between the collectivist and individualist traditions that has existed for most of the last two hundred years may have been a historical accident ... only possible during the transitional phase between the religious pre-capitalist era and the secular capitalist age. If that is so, the prospects for continued human progress are bleak indeed'.[17]

Box 9.1

The Irish potato famine

In the period 1845–49, a disaster befell Ireland. The potato crop, the staple of the Irish peasants' diet, failed in many parts of the country. Disease caused the potatoes to rot in the ground before they had ripened. What to do about this appalling situation was a major concern for the political leadership in London. In this context, classical political economy wielded awesome influence. The British leaders had the capacity to resolve, or at least ameliorate, the Irish crisis by arranging for the supply of food from other sources. However, as the historian Cecil Woodham-Smith notes, their actions (or rather, their inactions) were shaped by a belief in an economic theory that almost every politician of the day held to with religious fervour.

> This theory, usually termed *laissez faire*, insisted that individuals should be allowed to pursue their own economic interests, and that governments should interfere as little as possible. Not only were the rights of property sacred; private enterprise was revered and respected and given almost complete liberty, and on this theory, which incidentally gave the employer and the landlord freedom to exploit his fellow men, the prosperity of nineteenth-century England had unquestionably been based.
>
> The influence of *laissez-faire* on the treatment of Ireland during the famine is impossible to exaggerate. Almost without exception, the high officials and politicians responsible for Ireland were fervent believers in non-interference by Government, and the behaviour of the British authorities only becomes explicable when their fanatical belief in private enterprise and their suspicions of any action which might be considered Government intervention are borne in mind.
>
> The loss of the potato crop was therefore to be made good, without Government interference, by the operations of private enterprise and private firms, using the normal channels of commerce. The Government was not to appear in food markets as a buyer, there was to be 'no disturbance of the ordinary course of trade' and 'no complaints from private traders' on account of Government competition.[15]

Shops and organisations for importing foodstuffs and distributing them were generally found only in prosperous districts of Ireland: in Ulster in the northeast, in Dublin, and in some places in eastern Ireland, including the larger towns like Cork. In the places where relief would be most needed, in the west and southwest of Ireland, the means by which it could be distributed rarely existed. It is estimated that over a million people died in the famine, and a further million, emigrated because of it. Some joined the flow of emigrants to Australia; many more went to the United States. It was an tragic result of *laissez-faire* economics.

In Britain during the late eighteenth and nineteenth centuries the ideas of classical political economy were widely influential—for better or for worse. As capitalism developed in other nations and their colonies these ideas became yet more widespread. Classical political economy reassured sceptics of an earlier era that an economy based on individual enterprise and markets would not result in chaos. Here were arguments showing that the greater freedoms of the market place would produce a healthier economy and more progressive society. However, the leading classical political economists, most notably Adam Smith, were well aware of the need to qualify the general case for *laissez-faire* with observations about the dangers of monopoly and the need for good government. While it is important to interpret these views in their historical context, it is also necessary to be wary about their application, *carte blanche*, to modern capitalism.

CHAPTER 10

Value, Distribution, Growth

What, according to the classical political economists, determines the value of goods and services?
What shapes the distribution of income?
What conditions are conducive to economic growth?

As discussed in the previous chapter, classical political economy has had a powerful ideological influence. A vulgarised version of it can be used to support the case for an economic system based on individual initiative and market organisation. Its more sophisticated aspects raise fundamental questions about the ethics, and the social foundations, of commercial enterprise. These ethical and philosophical aspects of classical political economy are of central importance in assessing its role as capitalist ideology. However, the classical political economists were also deeply concerned with the construction of *economic analysis*. It is to this aspect that we now turn.

What were the main analytical concerns of classical political economy that flow through into modern economic analysis? It is difficult to provide a summary because significant points of difference separated the leading scholars, such as Smith, Ricardo, Malthus, and Mill. For our purposes here, it is sufficient to identify three themes: value, distribution, and growth. These are fundamental to the capitalist economy—indeed to understanding any type of economic system. What is the value of a commodity and how is it determined? What economic forces shape the distribution of income among the members of a society? How is economic growth generated and what may sometimes cause it to stall? This trilogy of concerns has been central to economic analysis ever since.

VALUE

What determines the *value of different goods and services*? You may have personally pondered this issue as you survey supermarket shelves or wonder whether you can afford a particular purchase. Why do different brands of car have the prices they do? What determines the relative prices of a cup of coffee and a bar of chocolate? Is the 'value' of something purely a question of its market price? Or, does it reflect some innate characteristic of the product—some personal evaluation of its usefulness or measure of its intrinsic social worth? Philosophical issues mingle with more down-to-earth, empirical issues in such deliberations.

As a broad generalisation, we can identify three contributions to the analysis of value stemming from the works of the classical political economists. First is the distinction between *value in use* and *value in exchange*. The water–diamonds paradox is the standard illustration. Water has more value in use than do diamonds: it is an essential item, necessary for life itself; diamonds, however, are a luxury item with much more limited uses. But diamonds have the higher value in exchange: their market price by weight or volume is far higher than water's. The obvious explanation for this divergence between usefulness and market price is the differences in supply conditions between the two goods: water is plentiful and needs little labour to make it available for consumption, while diamonds are scarce and take a great deal of effort (prospecting, mining, cutting, and polishing) to make them available. According to classical political economy, these supply conditions are crucial in shaping exchange values.

The second proposition follows from this. Broadly speaking, the value of a commodity reflects its cost of production. Where labour is the sole or principal cost this meas that exchange values depend on the amount of labour expended. As Adam Smith said, 'if, among a nation of hunters, it usually costs twice the labour to kill a beaver which it does to kill a deer, one beaver should naturally exchange for, or be worth, two deer'.[1] It seems natural that what is usually the produce of two days' labour should be worth double the produce of one day's labour. This is the essence of the *labour theory of value*, which Karl Marx was later to develop into his critique of capitalism. For the classical political economists its more limited role was in explaining the relative prices of different goods and services. It was recognised that scarcity can affect value in exchange, but the main emphasis was on the cost of production of the items in question.

Third, the classical political economists' approach emphasised the '*natural price*' of each product. This is its innate value. It is not necessarily its actual market price at any particular time. It is a sort of long-term equilibrium price around which day-to-day changes in the market price can be expected to fluctuate. If the actual market price is above the 'natural price' for any significant period of time (because of the scarcity of the item in question, for instance), this will induce the entry of new firms into the market to supply the item, and thereby cause the market price to fall. If the actual market price is below the 'natural price' (because of temporary overproduction relative to demand, say), firms will leave the industry, the glut will be eradicated, and the market price will rise; thus, in the longer term, the 'natural price' tends to prevail.

These three propositions—about the distinction between use values and exchange values, the role of labour in the determination of value, and the character of 'natural prices'—have given rise to a wide range of subsequent developments. The radical twist given by Marx to the labour theory of value, for example, stands in striking contrast to the neoclassical economists' attempt to refocus the explanation of prices on scarcity and use values. Thus, a common foundation in classical political economy underpins rival views about capitalist exploitation and price determination according to supply and demand. What has dropped out of the picture along the way is the notion of 'natural price'. Even more striking is the abandonment of any concern with a 'just price'. In this respect, the attempts by classical political economists to develop a theory of value can be considered as marking a transition from traditional concerns with ethical aspects of commodity exchange to modern attempts to refashion economics on a more 'scientific' basis.

DISTRIBUTION

What determines the *distribution of income and wealth* within a society? This second concern may be regarded as even more fundamental than the first. Ever since the classical political economists focused attention on the question, it has commanded constant attention. One should hardly be surprised. The question 'who gets what?' is inherently contentious in any society. Under what circumstances will one individual, or a social class, receive the bulk of the income? Under what circumstances can more equitable outcomes be expected? Is it better to have even or uneven distributional outcomes? According to which criteria? Such questions are among the most politically sensitive issues in economic enquiry.

David Ricardo, who provided perhaps the most notable of the classical political economists' contributions to this topic, considered the distribution of income among the classes to be 'the principal problem in political economy'. 'Among the classes' is a key phrase here. For simplicity, it is useful to distinguish three such classes and the characteristically different type of income each receives: (1) capitalists, who receive profit; (2) landowners, who receive rent; and (3) workers, who receive wages.

These are classes of real people, not inanimate 'factors of production'. What would determine their relative standards of living? Separate explanations of each type of income were proffered.

Profits are identified as the incentive for business activity and the necessary condition for capital accumulation. Material acquisitiveness is an essential element here, driving the accumulation process. However, the capitalists' economic function is not in amassing wealth for its own sake, but in ploughing profits back into further rounds of business activity in order to increase the value of the capital. Thus, making profits is the *raison d'être* of successful business enterprise. As noted in the preceding chapter, this is the positive face of self-interest, whereby the quest for profits contributes to economic prosperity and expansion. However, because profit is a surplus (that which is left over after wages have been paid to workers and rents to landowners), its magnitude crucially depends on the size of those other income claims.

Rent is a payment to landowners, reflecting their capacity to capture part of the surplus. In the agricultural context, it is a type of income dependent on the difference between a piece of fertile land and a piece of land that is just worth cultivating. As Adam Smith wrote, 'as soon as land becomes private property, the landlord demands a share of almost all the produce which the labourer can either raise or collect from it. His rent makes the first deduction from the produce of the labour which is employed by the land'.[2] The land is necessary for production, but the capacity of landlords to charge a rent for all land other than the most marginal means that the income available for workers and capitalists is correspondingly reduced. For capitalists, this means less capacity for capital accumulation; for workers, it means a reduced possibility of earning higher wages, compounding the forces causing their perpetual consignment to a subsistence standard of living.

Wages, according to classical political economists, would tend to be kept at the minimum level necessary for workers to reproduce themselves. Were wage increases to encroach on profits, the capital accumulation process would be impeded. So, if workers could not significantly share in the economic surplus, they would have to remain at subsistence level. It was a gloomy prediction for the mass of society. It had its most depressing form in the famous doctrines of Thomas Malthus.

According to Malthus, population growth would keep the working class poor. If any rise in wage rates occurred, the population would increase, putting pressure on the capacity for food production, and driving living standards down to subsistence level. An equilibrium of sorts would be restored, but it would be a diabolical equilibrium of poverty or near-poverty. Population growth, the inexorable consequence of the 'passion between the sexes', would have the effect of consigning the masses to a life of poverty, despite economic growth. Because 'the power of population is infinitely greater than the power in the earth to produce subsistence for men', any attempt to raise wages would be self-defeating.[3]

Although highly controversial, the Malthusian view about population growth keeping wages to subsistence level formed the bedrock of classical political economic reasoning. By the same reasoning, any attempt to help the poor would also be self-defeating, since charity would encourage faster population growth and discourage productive effort. This was a very austere view, but Malthus evidently felt his austerity and pessimism to be driven by the logic of the situation. It certainly illustrates the 'freedom from extreme sentimentality', as E.R. Canterbury puts it, that characterises classical political economy.[4]

Overall, these reflections on what determined the distribution of income between the major classes reinforced the view of economic inequalities as inexorable. The classical political economists' concern with liberty did not imply equality. On the contrary, it was the existence, even the 'naturalness', of the class system that underpinned the different types of income and the necessary economic inequalities. John Stuart Mill (1806–73) thought that the inequalities could be redressed by political means without violating the economic principles of production. However, then as now, most orthodox economists worried that significantly redistributive policies would impair economic efficiency.

GROWTH

The third issue addressed by classical political economists had more positive connotations. This is the question of what determines *the possibility of economic growth*. Like the questions of value and distribution, it is a conundrum that continues to be central to political economic deliberations to this day.

How are economic systems able to expand the production of goods and services and the total flows of income and wealth generated? What conditions are conducive to that expansion? What circumstances are likely to impede it, causing stagnation or even plunging the economy into depression? Is growth necessary, desirable, and sustainable in the longer term?

As with the theories of value and distribution, summarising the views of the classical political economists on these issues is not easy. There were marked differences between the various contributors. For simplicity, we can identify three main themes: (1) the division of labour, (2) the expansion of trade, and (3) the accumulation of capital.

The *division of labour* is the foundation for growth, according to classical political economy. Smith was particularly emphatic about this, beginning *The Wealth of Nations* with the famous example of a pin factory in which production levels are increased many times over as a result of workers doing more specialised tasks.[5] The higher output made possible by the complex division of labour would lead to higher profit, which could then lead to the purchase of more tools and equipment, further increasing the productive capacity of the enterprise. A virtuous cycle of expansion would ensue. It would not be virtuous in all respects, though; Smith had significant concerns about its implications for the nature of work itself. This is what we might now call the problem of worker *alienation*. In his own words, 'the man whose sole life is spent performing a few simple operations … generally becomes as stupid and ignorant as it is possible for a human creature to become'.[6] There was also the problem of the *demand* for the product. There would be no point in expanding pin production if there were no growth in the demand for pins. In general, Smith noted, the division of labour is limited by the extent of the market.

The *expansion of trade* would create the conditions for that increase in demand. This second element in the analysis of growth is closely linked to the doctrine of *comparative advantage* developed by Ricardo. This doctrine seeks to demonstrate that all countries can benefit economically by specialising in producing those items in which they have a relative cost advantage, and then trading with one another in those items. Consider the situation where two countries, A and B, can produce two commodities, X and Y. Even if country A can produce both X and Y more cheaply than B, the doctrine of comparative advantage says it should specialise in the one in which it has the greater relative cost advantage, leaving the production of the other to B. International trade will then be to mutual advantage.

Ricardo used the theory of comparative advantage to support the repeal of the Corn Laws, which restricted agricultural imports to the United Kingdom. Nowadays, the same doctrine is used to support the case for trade liberalisation, including the removal of tariffs imposed by national governments on imported goods. It warrants critical consideration. What is the situation, for example, if the transport costs involved in international trade substantially offset the benefits of lowered production costs? Or, to put a topical, environmental spin on the issue, what is the situation if scarce, non-renewable energy resources are used in that transportation process? And are there not benefits for a nation from having diversified industries (ensuring greater national self-reliance in wartime, for example, or a wider range of employment opportunities for local citizens) that need to be set against the gains from specialisation and trade? Such concerns are raised here to caution against the extension of comparative advantage theory to more complex modern situations where there may be sound reasons to restrict trade. From the vantage point of the United Kingdom in the nineteenth century, comparative advantage theory constituted a convenient rationale for national self-interest. Its status as a general rationale for free trade, however, is contentious, despite its widespread influence.[7]

What about the possibility of continued *capital accumulation*? As capitalism was establishing itself as the dominant economic system, many people worried that the growth of productive capacity would outstrip the market demand for the products. With workers' wages tending to be kept down to subsistence levels, as the classical political economists predicted, this was presumably an even more likely scenario. Would growth necessarily lead to a slump? The classic reassurance came from the Frenchman Jean-Baptiste Say. His argument (introduced in chapter 8) was that supply creates its own demand, so there was no need to fear any general tendency towards depression, at least not because of overproduction. To be sure, temporary overproduction could occur in any particular industry as a result of miscalculation by the producers, but this would be matched by shortages in another industry. A fall in the price of the product in the industry that overproduced and price rises in the industry that underproduced would quickly correct the imbalance.

Malthus was not so certain that a general glut was impossible, arguing that wages, because they are not the total cost of production, may not be sufficient to purchase all that is produced. If that causes prices to fall, the incentive to invest falls and a prolonged slump may ensue. Excessive savings could have a similar effect, reducing the demand for products and causing stagnation.

Ricardo disagreed, taking basically the same position as Say. He argued that lower wages are a cure for slump, not a cause of it, because businesses will hire the idle workers with the capital created by savings. According to this reasoning, savings are not an end in themselves, but a means of generating capital in order to employ labour in production. The potential imbalance between savings and investment, which Keynes was later to emphasise, was disregarded. According to Galbraith, adherence to Say's Law was 'the prime test by which economists were distinguished from crackpots' until Keynes challenged the classical orthodoxy.[8]

Did these doctrines paint a rosy picture for the prospects of capitalist development? At first sight it may seem so. The classical political economists' emphasis on the benefits arising from the division of labour and the expansion of trade, and the general confidence that there need be no problem of overproduction, seemed to bode well for the future of capitalism, even though the workers in general could not expect a rise in material living standards.

However, the forecast for economic expansion was actually rather more pessimistic. Yes, the division of labour and the growth of trade would create conditions for prosperity, but this would also lead to population growth, requiring land that was less productive to be brought under cultivation. That would cause food prices to rise, and so the general level of wages, in money terms, would have to rise in order to ensure that workers continued to subsist. That rise in wages would reduce profits, slowing capital accumulation and economic growth.

Ricardo expected that this slowing of capital accumulation would result in a 'stationary state'. Such a situation, John Stuart Mill subsequently argued, could be interpreted in a favourable light as the basis for a progressive society, in which people could turn their attention from mundane economic matters to higher cultural and artistic pursuits. In terms of the analysis developed in chapter 5 of this current book, it would presumably mean paying less attention to GDP and more to the social and environmental improvements that would show up in terms of a Genuine Progress Index. For Ricardo, the prospect of a stationary state was an undesirable

Box 10.1

John Stuart Mill (1806–73)

John Stuart Mill was widely regarded as the greatest political economist of his day and the successor to Smith and Ricardo. His magnum opus, *Principles of Political Economy*, was published in 1849 and remained the standard reference on the subject for the best part of half a century until displaced by Alfred Marshall's *Principles of Economics*.

A child prodigy, Mill was said to have made 'a complete survey of all there was to be known in the field of political economy' when only thirteen years old, having already learnt Latin and Ancient Greek; mastered geometry, algebra and the differential calculus; written a Roman history, a history of Holland and an abridged version of the *Ancient Universal History*.[10] His father, the historian and philosopher James Mill, had insisted on this childhood of extreme intellectualism, allowing no holidays 'lest the habit of work should be broken and a taste for idleness acquired'.[11]

The wonder is that Mill not only avoided being emotionally crippled by his upbringing, but also went on to be a notably humane man, combining the principles of political economy with ethical social concerns. He supported democratic reforms, and women's rights in particular.

Mill's political economy synthesised the classical ideas. However, he broke with other classical political economists in one key respect—by emphasising the malleability of income distribution. He argued that economic principles govern production, but that political choices can shape distribution; thus, once wealth has been produced, we can share it as we collectively choose, untrammelled by any absolute 'laws' of political economy. In his own words, 'the distribution of wealth, therefore, depends on the laws and customs of society'.[12] It is a matter of politics, not economics. This was the basis for a much more optimistic view of the prospects for humankind than was to be found in Malthus, in particular, and the work of the 'dismal science' of economics, in general.

Mill thought that reason would prevail in public affairs. Once the working classes understood the Malthusian problem of excessive growth in population causing food shortage, they would voluntarily regulate their numbers. Eventually the economy would reach a 'stationary state', in which there would be no more economic growth but plenty of scope for social betterment. The government would create a more equal society by taxing rents and inheritances.

Mill's mild socialism had little in common with the revolutionary socialism that Marx propounded. As Heilbroner describes it, it was 'a doctrine English to the core: gradualist, optimistic, realistic and devoid of radical overtones'.[13] An echo of Mill's views may be discerned today in the claim by orthodox economists that efficiency is an economic concern and equity a political concern. Unfortunately, this normally leads to the concern with equity being set aside. Mill would have been aghast at this modern tendency.

outcome, a situation in which the dynamics of economic growth were not able to operate. The pessimistic nature of this prognosis is reflected in Thomas Carlyle's famous description of political economy as the 'dismal science'.[9]

CONCLUSION

The classical political economists laid the foundation for understanding capitalist development. Their method of analysis was influenced by the prevailing ideas of the age. Isaac Newton's pathbreaking work in physics is a case in point: the classical political economists were, in effect, seeking to do for the study of social phenomena what Newton had done for the study of the physical world. For this purpose, the economy could be likened to a clock: if one could only understand the mechanism, then one could understand the regularities in its working. Thus, the quest was to discover the *laws of motion* in economic life. In Newton's theory, there was the law of gravity; in classical political economic theory, there was self-interest—the propulsive element in an essentially natural and progressive economic system.

The classical political economists, although constrained by this methodology, were holistic thinkers. Indeed, by the standards of most of their successors, they were indeed 'gentlemen and scholars'. They did not artificially separate the study of economic phenomena from history, geography, politics, and the study of society in general. Modern political economy, as we shall see in later chapters, is partly an attempt to regain this position—to re-establish the discipline as an interdisciplinary mode of analysis concerned with the study of value, distribution, and growth, and the economic dimensions of social progress in general.

The view of the economy as a means of producing an *economic surplus* is central to this story. It was a key element in classical political economy, underpinning much of the theory summarised in this chapter. An economic surplus is the excess of the value of production over and above what is necessary merely to reproduce the economy. How it is generated, how it is distributed, and the purposes for which it is used are the key determinants of how the economy works. The concern to understand this economic surplus constitutes a further element of continuity between classical political economy and modern political economy, and a point of contrast with neoclassical economics, which has no place for any such analytical construct. Focusing on the generation and disposition of an economic surplus draws attention to the importance of the relationship between capital and labour as social classes. It also makes necessary the study of the role of land and rent in the economy.

CHAPTER 11

Capturing the Economic Surplus
The land question

Is land economically important?
Is the rent of land a drain on economic progress?
Should land rent be taxed?

The analysis of land has a rather shadowy presence in modern economics. In agricultural economics and natural resource economics it cannot be ignored, of course; elsewhere it tends to be treated either as a factor of production—on a par with labour and capital—or as part of the backdrop to the real economic action of production, distribution, and exchange. This marginalisation of the analysis of land was not always the case, however. In classical political economy, the analysis of land was a central concern.

Why the change? To some extent it may be explained by the different *material* economic conditions. Economic 'modernisation', particularly over the last century, has caused proportionately fewer people to be directly engaged in farming. Meanwhile, modern technologies have made more and more industries 'footloose', not tied to particular geographical locations. All economic and social activities necessarily involve the use of land in some way, but the modern economy in general seems less place-bound. However, the neglect of the distinctive role that land plays in the economy also has an *ideological* dimension—diverting attention from the economic and social consequences of private land-ownership. Therein lies a significant bias. Its redress requires some reconsideration of what the leading classical political economists had to say about land. It also requires attention be given to the radical variation on the theme of land-ownership in the writings and teaching of Henry George.

THE SIGNIFICANCE OF LAND IN DIFFERENT ECONOMIC SYSTEMS

From an *ecological* perspective, it is particularly important that the use of land be carefully considered—after all, land is fundamentally different from labour and capital because its supply is inherently limited. It is part of our natural resource endowment. Even from a narrowly *economic* perspective, it is clear that the availability, use, and productivity of land (both in rural and urban contexts) has a major bearing on the capacity for economic growth. From a broader *social* perspective, land is also special. Some of us enjoy roaming over publicly accessible tracts of land, while others enjoy exclusive use of small parcels of it. Managing the tension between these public and private perspectives is a key issue for public policy. So, the institutions that shape the use of land are of fundamental economic, environmental, and social significance.

There are enormous differences in the ways in which land is allocated and used. Consider, first, the role of land in traditional *aboriginal* societies, like the Aboriginal peoples of Australia or the Native American peoples of North America. Land is integral to subsistence and to community: indeed, it is usually not seen as something separate from life itself. People exist through being in, and of, nature. The land provides the sustenance that makes life possible. The people may be regarded as its custodians, but it makes little sense to think of them 'owning' the land, either individually or collectively. They no more own the land than it 'owns' them. Land is simultaneously history, geography, and spirituality; it is not a marketable economic asset.

Under *feudalism*, land also has a crucial, but quite different, role. Command over the disposition of land is a defining feature of the economic and social order. A person's relationship to the land significantly defines his or her social standing. The privileged position of the ruling class depends on control of the large areas of land that they possess. They 'call the shots' because they control the key resource that enables them to capture the lion's share of the economic surplus. The mass of the people, on the other hand, are in a position of economic dependency and social subordination because their livelihood depends on their access to the land that they themselves do not own.

For the classical political economists, the emergence of capitalism from this feudal order needed to be understood. The transition involved a significant change in the distribution of economic power. It saw a switch from landowners being the dominant element in the ruling class to capitalists being the ascendant element—economically, if not socially and politically. The landowners still dominated Parliament, of course. Then, as now, the social and political dimensions of the changes in the composition of the ruling class lagged behind the economic changes.

So it was natural that, in order to understand the economic conditions of their age, the classical political economists should pay particular attention to questions about land—its ownership, how income is derived from it, and the size of that income relative to the incomes derived from labour and capital. Indeed, even before the age of classical political economy, the land question had been central to economic discourse. The French physiocrats had argued that land—a gift of nature—was the only real source of wealth because it enabled agriculture to generate a net product in excess of production costs.[1]

RENT AS A BRAKE ON ECONOMIC PROGRESS?

Of the classical political economists, David Ricardo had perhaps the most well-developed analysis of the role of land in economic progress. Himself a landowner, Ricardo was nevertheless no apologist for the interests of the landowning class. On the contrary, he saw the capacity of landowners to obtain a major share in the economic surplus as an obstacle to economic development. According to Ricardo, the income that they derive in the form of rent comes from the incomes that would otherwise go to capitalists and workers. In so far as it comes from the profit share in particular, rent impedes the process of capital accumulation and thus limits economic growth. It is an argument that needs careful consideration. It is of continuing significance, notwithstanding the greater interpenetration of land and capital ownership in modern capitalism.

Rent has to be carefully defined in this context. We are used to thinking of rent as a payment for the use of *housing*. We commonly talk of 'renting' a house or a flat (or, generally, any commodity for hire, such as a car or a floor-sanding machine). In that popular sense, we are talking of a payment for temporary access to, or use of, the property—a payment that buys a flow of services over a specified period of time. It is important to emphasise that, in the current context, rent is being used in a more specific sense. It refers only to a payment for land: in other words, it is a *site rent*. What we normally call the rent for a house can be seen as having two components: the site rent for the land and the payment for hiring the house that stands on the land. Only the first of these two components can properly be called rent for the purposes of the current analysis. Defining rent in this way immediately draws attention to its class character—its association with the wealth and power of landowners.

According to Ricardo, 'the interest of the landlord is always opposed to the interest of every other class in the community'.[2] Why is this so? The Ricardian theory is based on two key assumptions. The first is that land differs in its fertility—so all lands can be ranked from the most fertile to the least fertile. The second is that competition equalises the profit rate among farmers who hire land from landowners. We can then visualise land generating the income flows depicted in box 11.1.

The revenue generated by the economic use of more land has to be shared between landowners, capitalists (the tenant farmers in this model), and workers (the farm employees). The general tendency is for profits to be squeezed because landowners capture a share of the economic surplus generated. Indeed, as more land is brought under cultivation (that is, previously submarginal land becomes marginal), the proportion of the total value of production captured by landowners increases. So, even if wages remain at subsistence levels, the profit share declines.

Therein lies a deeply troubling paradox. According to this analysis, profits are the source of capital accumulation, the driving force in the capitalist system, but they are increasingly hard to sustain as economic expansion occurs. The root problem is that growth is stymied by the diversion of the economic surplus into rent payments. 'Do away with the landowners' is an understandable response. As a member of parliament surrounded by members who typically represented landowners' interests, Ricardo took a more reformist stance. He thought the problem could be significantly reduced by the removal of the impediments to trade that led to less fertile land being brought under cultivation. He argued forcefully that the repeal of the Corn Laws, which protected local agriculture from competition from imports, would counter the tendency for rents to rise at the expense of profits.

Whether more free trade is the appropriate antidote to the power and wealth of landowners remains a contentious point. Restrictions on agricultural trade are still commonly said to be justified by the need to protect the interests of rural landholders and regional communities whose economic prosperity depends on such protection.

Box 11.1

Rent, wages, profit: A Ricardian view

The figure below depicts how the value of the produce from land is shared between landowners, capitalists, and workers. The vertical axis measures the monetary values of the land and its produce, while the horizontal axis measures the amount of land used (the number of hectares, for instance).

The line showing the value of the additional product (for example wheat) from each successive unit of land slopes down to the right as less fertile land is successively brought under cultivation. In other words, the marginal product of land declines as more is used.

The rent is the difference between the value of product generated by each unit of land and the value generated by the marginal unit, that is, the last piece of land brought under cultivation. This is the *differential rent*. It is the upper limit of what landowners can charge farmers for using their superior quality land (the land that is more fertile than the marginal land). If OA units of land are used, the total rent is the shaded triangular area XYZ.

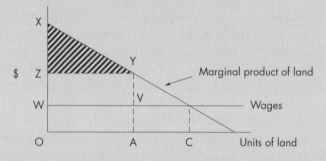

How is the rest of the value (that is, the area OAYZ) shared among farmers and those who work for the farmers as employees? If, as the preceding chapter argued, employees' wages are kept at subsistence level (OW in the graph), then the total wage share is shown by the area OAVW, leaving VWZY as the profit share to go to the farmers as a return on their investment of capital and effort.

Now visualise the situation in which the economy has expanded and more land has been brought under cultivation. The share of rent in the total value produced increases. In the extreme, the profit share disappears (when OC land is used). This illustrates the general tendency for profits to be squeezed out between rents and wages. If wages are raised as more land is brought under cultivation, the squeeze is yet tighter. This may occur when food becomes more expensive because inferior land has to be used and the subsistence wage is consequently increased. In that case, the line showing the wage rate would slope upwards to the right, which would mean that profits would be eliminated even more quickly as additional units of land were cultivated. It would bode ill for the future of economic growth under capitalism.

The protection of agricultural interests has been one of the most controversial political economic issues in the development of the European Community, and also in Japan. The Japanese government imposes restrictions on rice imports, seeking to maintain the viability of the local farming sector, whose importance is social and cultural as well as economic. Although the case for such policies is not normally couched in terms of safeguarding landowners' interests at the expense of capital and labour, that is the usual economic effect. It runs counter to the Ricardian argument for squeezing rents by breaking down the impediments to agricultural trade. The Ricardian view can be considered part of the general case, considered in the preceding chapter, for trade liberalisation based on the principle of comparative advantage. Restrictions like the Corn Laws both boosted rents at the expense of profits and impeded the process of specialisation, which free trade is held to encourage. On this reasoning, it is free trade that is the antidote to the power of landowners to capture the economic surplus as rent. It is a chain of reasoning thoroughly in keeping with the classical political economists' view of the extension of capitalist markets as a progressive force for economic change.

A GENERAL ASSAULT ON LAND RENT

The argument so far has been couched mainly in terms of agricultural land. However, similar principles apply if we consider the use of land in an urban context. Instead of thinking of the land as having a capacity to 'earn' differential rent according to its *fertility*, we can now visualise its capacity to 'earn' differential rent according to its *accessibility* (to and from a city's centre of commercial activity). As a city grows, more land is brought into urban use (for housing, industrial purposes, water storage, waste disposal, and so forth). As in the agricultural model, that more extensive land use raises the capacity of existing urban land to earn even higher levels of rent. So, as towns grow, the landowners are the primary beneficiaries—at the expense of capitalists and workers. Some claim that this process is operating in modern cities, with dramatically adverse economic and social consequences.[3] The ideas of Henry George, as well as David Ricardo, are pertinent to understanding these contemporary processes.

As George emphasised, land is essentially a gift of nature. The problems start to arise when it becomes substantially privately owned. As more of nature's gift is used for income-generating purposes, a greater share of the society's total income goes to those who have acquired property rights in land. In the historical development of the United States, for example, the westward movement of the settlers, and their capture of the land from the indigenous peoples, vastly increased the material wealth of the settler society. With economic growth in general, the increased value of the land is captured for private rather than public purposes. Coupled with the unequal distribution of its ownership, this exacerbates socioeconomic inequalities. Speculation flourishes as land values change with the spatial pattern of development. That speculation then fuels further socioeconomic inequality, as well as diverting funds from productive purposes. Land may often be held idle because it is bought and sold for speculative gain. The general problems of economic inefficiency and social inequality both have their roots in these tendencies.

Box 11.2

Henry George (1839–97)

Henry George was the founder of a social movement that, in its time, rivalled Marxism as a major force for radical political economic change. His focus on the inefficiencies and inequities associated with the private ownership of land, and on the simple remedy of land taxation, inspired many social activists. The ideas he pioneered are still of significant contemporary relevance.

Unlike most of the other intellectual giants in the history of political economy, George had no academic credentials. As a young man in the United States, he had various jobs, eventually turning to journalism, running a struggling little newspaper in San Francisco. He visited New York in 1869 to set up a telegraphic news bureau for the paper (unsuccessfully, as it turned out, because of opposition from larger and more powerful press and telegraph monopolies). While in New York—then the epitome of the modern capitalist city—he was dismayed by the gross inequalities between rich and poor that he witnessed. He asked himself, why, in a country so blessed by nature, with more than enough resources for all, should there be such maldistribution? By all accounts, the answer—and the remedy—came to him in a blinding flash.

He began writing his analysis of how the appropriation of rents by landowners was at the root of all such economic and social problems, and how a single tax on land rent could resolve these problems. His work appeared in a series of pamphlets and then in his major book *Progress and Poverty*, which was published in 1879. *Progress and Poverty* was translated into fifteen languages and sold millions of copies. George travelled internationally, preaching his distinctive gospel. In Australia, his public meetings enjoyed massive attendances. George's diagnosis of the injustices associated with the 'land question' had widespread appeal in a 'frontier' economy like Australia—comparable to the United States in this respect.

The strong social movement that Henry George started is no longer the force it was. Sadly, it seems more people today are concerned with claiming a stake in the 'land racket' than with the reform of public policy regarding land. As a consequence, our cities become more expensive to live in and more socially divided, and most of the economic surplus associated with land price inflation is appropriated for private rather than public use.

It is also important to note that, from a Georgist perspective, the appropriation of the economic surplus in the form of rent is at the expense of ordinary working people. As Henry George said, 'the increase in land values is always at the expense of labour'.[4] In the Ricardian view, rent is at the expense of profits (since wages are destined to remain at a subsistence level anyway). The Georgist perspective has more widespread political appeal because most people, it seems, would benefit from redressing this source of social injustice.

One obvious solution is *public ownership*. The collective land resources could then be used according to whatever development plan the society establishes. However, Henry George did not consider this necessary, sharing, in this respect, the classical political economists' aversion to an extensive role for the state in the direct management of economic resources. He favoured a market-oriented approach, but with *a uniform land tax*. Other classical political economists, notably David Ricardo, favoured substantial land taxes, but George was unique in thinking that a general tax on the site rent of land would be sufficient to finance all the necessary public expenditures of government. A land tax is the best sort of tax, Georgists have consistently argued, because it creates an incentive to use all land for its most productive purpose in order to generate the revenue to pay the tax. By contrast, taxes on labour and capital create disincentives to productive effort. A single tax on land, replacing all personal income taxes, business taxes, inheritance taxes, and taxes on goods and services, is held to be more economically efficient.

Whether a single tax on site rents today could generate sufficient revenue to finance all government expenditures is debatable, given the growth in the array of such expenditures since George's time.[5] But the case for land taxes remains strong. Local property taxation is widely used as a means of taxing land ownership and generating revenue for local governments. As a matter of political pragmatism, some balance between taxation of land, other assets, income, and expenditure seems inescapable. Should land tax play a bigger role in this policy mix? The argument that it should do so is historically grounded in classical political economy. It also addresses contemporary concerns about the diversion of the economic surplus into the hands of people who make no directly productive economic contribution.[6]

CONCLUSION

It is over a century since Henry George noted that the contrast between affluence and poverty was most striking in 'the great cities where the ownership of a little patch of ground is a fortune'.[7] That tendency has been multiplied many times over in the intervening period as cities have grown and land prices escalated. Those land prices are a major element in creating divided cities, and spatial divisions generally. In conjunction with housing markets, land markets commonly lead to a striking spatial segmentation of cities into affluent suburbs and poorer areas, the latter sometimes forming ghettos where socioeconomic disadvantage is perpetuated in a vicious circle. As David Harvey, the leading urban geographer, has argued, the rich command space while the poor are trapped in it.[8]

Real estate, and the intergenerational transmission of its ownership, is a major source of economic and social inequality. This is not a problem of transition between feudalism and capitalism, as it may have been perceived during the age of classical political economy. It is an enduring feature of a society in which income from property ownership commonly outstrips income from productive effort. So, the land question remains at the heart of practical political economy. However, as the ownership of land has become ever more intertwined with the ownership of capital, there is a need for an analysis of unearned incomes in general (from capital as well as land). The study of Marxist economics is inescapable in this context.

PART IV

The Critique of Capitalism

Marxist economics

CHAPTER 12

Contesting Capitalism
The Marxian perspective

Why study Marx? Are Marxist ideas relevant today?
What were the origins of the Marxist critique of capitalism?
What is distinctive about the Marxist method of analysis?

Many different structures have been built on the foundations laid by classical political economy. Indeed, it is not surprising that such a broad-ranging political economic analysis should subsequently have been developed in different ways. The neoclassical economists developed it in a conservative direction, maintaining the focus on the beneficial effects of markets, but narrowing the range of social concerns and purging the theory of its explicitly ethical aspects. We look at their work and its influence a little later. The immediate concern is with the radical traditions developing from classical political economy. We have already seen the important contribution of Henry George. More significant still, and chronologically a little earlier, is the contribution of Karl Marx. Whereas George thought a change to the tax system was the necessary 'remedy' for the ills of capitalism, Marx thought the political economic system would eventually have to be changed in its entirety. Here was, and is, the foundation for a thorough critique of the capitalist system.

WHY STUDY MARX?

There is a common view that Marx is dead—not just the man, but his ideas and their relevance to our lives today. It is a view based largely on the problem of constructing a viable alternative to capitalism in practice. The great experiments of the twentieth century that tried to reconstruct whole nations on 'Marxist' principles ultimately proved disappointing. The 'communist states' in the former Soviet Union and in Eastern Europe collapsed more than a decade ago, having failed, despite major economic and technological transformations, to satisfy the economic and social aspirations of their people.[1] The People's Republic of China has increasingly turned to capitalist modes of economic development, accommodating them within an authoritarian state. Only tiny Cuba remains an outpost of a genuine socialism.[2] Little wonder that it is difficult for 'Marxist' views to get a hearing.

The problem with this negative view is that it ignores Marx's central concerns: interpreting the workings of a capitalist economy, understanding economic change, and considering the principles on which alternatives to capitalism might be based. These aspects of Marxism are not negligible: they are central to political economy.

A more positive view posits three reasons to study Marxist political economy. First, it has a key place in the *history of economic thought*. Marx developed his ideas from a basis in classical political economy. The development of subsequent schools of thought in the economics discipline can be interpreted, in large measure, as either extensions of Marx's analysis or reactions against it, analytically and politically. Orthodox economist Paul Samuelson once denigrated Marx as a 'minor post-Ricardian'.[3] It is more sensible to see Marx standing centre stage, with the other actors in the drama either challenging him or tiptoeing around him and pretending he is not there. An understanding of the development of economic ideas would be markedly deficient without some introduction to Marx and Marxism.

Second, Marxist political economy provides a framework for *understanding capitalism today*. The institutional features of the economy are, of course, different in various ways from the economy Marx analysed in the nineteenth century. But modern Marxists contend that there are elements of continuity in the fundamental nature of the system—the relationship between capital and labour, the process of capital accumulation, and the contradictions that periodically cause economic crises. These claims warrant careful consideration. Does Marxism indeed have the capacity to explain contemporary phenomena, such as the persistence of poverty amid affluence, and the problems of economic inequality, underdevelopment, and recessions? How can the basic Marxist tenets be updated and revised for this purpose?

Third, Marxism warrants our attention because it has had such a great *influence in the real world*. It has inspired numerous struggles for liberation. Marx's insistence that it is people who make history—albeit in circumstances not of their choosing—has given this current of thought an essentially *activist* element. This is where many of the problems with interpreting the experience of socialism and communism in practice begin, for all sorts of political acts have been carried out in the name of Marxism. Some have been progressive, but others have done harm. Similarly, it is necessary to distinguish between the Marxist analysis of capitalism and the experience of trying to construct non-capitalist economies. The former is our immediate concern here. By looking at the analysis of capitalism, we can situate Marx's analysis in relation to the classical political economy that preceded it and the developments in orthodox economics, which were partly a reaction to these 'dangerous doctrines', that followed it.

First and foremost, Marx sought to understand capitalism: its emergence from feudalism, its internal dynamics and contradictions, and the type of economic system that might follow it. He developed a view of the economic process as restless, evolutionary, and potentially revolutionary. Whereas the classical political economists emulated the method of Isaac Newton, Marx, in effect, tried to emulate Charles Darwin, whose ideas about biological evolution were so influential in his day. It was certainly a time when dramatic changes were taking place in Britain and Europe. Capitalism was evolving and reshaping society in its own image.

Box 12.1

Karl Marx (1818–83)

Karl Marx is surely the most controversial figure in the history of political economy. His analysis of capitalism, and his advocacy of a socialist alternative, has had enormous influence.

Marx was born in 1818 in Trier, in what is now Germany. At university he studied law and came to be associated with a group of radical intellectuals called the Young Hegelians, who were followers of the philosophy of G.W.F. Hegel (1770–1831). Marx's increasingly critical social and political views found expression in articles he wrote for newspapers. His growing reputation as a dissident eventually led to the closure of the journal he edited.

He took refuge in France and then, briefly, in Belgium, where the authorities also found his presence unwelcome. In Galbraith's words, 'Germany, France and Belgium would all unite in the view that Marx was an excellent resident of some other country'.[4] Marx eventually settled in London with his wife and family. They lived poorly, dependent on the small income generated by Marx's writing for newspapers and on the financial support of friends.

Marx spent a great deal of time in the reading room of the British Museum, immersing himself in the works of the classical political economists. His critique of them was central to his radical interpretation of the capitalist economy, developed in his own three-volume work *Capital* and in numerous other books and pamphlets. These works stand as the most powerful critique of the capitalist system ever written.

Marx was also concerned with practical matters. He sought to organise the working classes so that they could challenge capitalism. He convened international meetings for that purpose, known as the First and Second Internationals. He did not see the capitalist system overthrown in his own lifetime, although the 1848 uprising in Paris seemed to herald that possibility before it was brutally crushed.

Marx died in 1883 and was buried at Highgate cemetery in North London. The cemetry continues to be visited by his followers and by those who are merely curious about this person who has had so much influence on the world. You now have to pay to get in.

THE HISTORICAL CONTEXT

In the first half of the nineteenth century, the industrial revolution transformed Great Britain, with corresponding transformations following in Europe and the United States. It was in Great Britain, particularly in rapidly growing industrial cities like Manchester, that the face of capitalism was most clearly evident. Marx and his collaborator Friedrich Engels did not think it a pretty sight.

The views of the classical political economists about the generally progressive character of the new economic order seemed out of kilter with observable reality. Capitalism in practice seemed to be a dynamic but rapacious system based on the alienation and exploitation of labour. It produced glaring economic inequalities and led to the commodification of social life.

What were the major changes then taking place? Most obvious was the growth of the *factory system*, which was largely replacing the putting-out system. Instead of workers making products in their own homes and selling them to merchants, they now increasingly went to work at the premises of their employer. They worked in factories, mines, shops, and warehouses for wage payments—usually paid by the hour. *Wage-labour* was not new, of course, but it had now become the norm. It was an arrangement that suited capitalist employers. It gave them more direct control over the workers' time, and more direct control over the quality of the products, than they had under the putting-out system. However, it also raised complex problems, such as the *management* of larger groups of workers. It created an identifiable industrial *working class*.

Many businesses continued to be small-scale operations, owned and managed by individuals and families. However, *joint stock companies* (businesses that were owned by their shareholders) became increasingly common and led to the creation of a class of 'absentee owners' able to derive 'unearned income' (for they had not worked or directly participated in management) from business enterprises. The disposition of this income became crucial for the growth of the economy—whether it was to be ploughed back into investment to expand productive capacity or used for luxury consumption purposes, for example. So the *accumulation of wealth* created some significant tensions for capitalist development.

There is continuing debate about whether the material conditions of ordinary working people improved during the period of the industrial revolution. Living in conditions of urban poverty was probably a step up for some people, compared with the debilitating rural poverty they had previously experienced. But the general *conditions of the labouring masses* in the towns were deplorable: child labour was common, as were working days of anything between fourteen and eighteen hours; terrible industrial accidents were frequent; and living conditions were horrendous. There was chronic overcrowding in the houses of the workers, poor sanitation, and widespread incidence of disease. Life was short and mean.

Capitalism did not seem to be delivering the ordered and progressive outcomes its apologists had promised. Here was a situation crying out for a thorough critique. Of critics there was no shortage. The disruptive social consequences of the rapid economic change were the target of both conservatives and socialists. Some of the latter sought to design utopian alternatives. The Frenchman Henri de Saint-Simon argued that government should actively intervene in production, distribution, and commerce in order to promote the welfare of the masses; the Englishman William Godwin, critical of both capitalism and government, emphasised education and reason as the means of ushering in a socialist alternative; the Welsh humanitarian Robert Owen blended visionary utopian thinking with practical measures to improve the living conditions of the workers in his factory in Scotland; and the Frenchman Charles Fourier promoted the idea of cooperatives as an alternative to the wastes of capitalism.[5]

Karl Marx, working in conjunction with Friedrich Engels, stood head and shoulders above the rest of these socialist theorists and activists because his critique of capitalism was so comprehensive and because it blended analysis of the current economic situation with a political program for systemic change.

Summarising the essential elements of Marxist political economy is not easy because the analysis Marx and Engels pioneered was subsequently developed in different ways. However, there is some unity in the disparate contributions in at least three respects: the *scope* of enquiry, the *method* of analysis, and the key political economic *concepts*. This chapter considers the first and second of these, illustrating the wide range of concerns addressed by Marxism and the distinctive method used in analysing them. The third aspect is developed in the following chapters by examining key concepts such as the mode of production, surplus value, the circuit of capital accumulation and economic crises.

Box 12.2

Friedrich Engels (1820–95)

Engels is mainly remembered for his working partnership with Karl Marx. It was a remarkable partnership, not least because Engels was a capitalist. A German, he managed his family's substantial textile business in Manchester, England.

Three aspects of his partnership with Marx are noteworthy. First, as a relatively wealthy capitalist, Engels was able to give financial assistance to the impecunious Marx. Therein lies a delicious irony. The profits from the Engels family business, extracted through the exploitation of labour, partly financed the production of books and pamphlets exposing the system of exploitation and the organising of its overthrow. Engels shared Marx's revolutionary socialist views, and both knew that the system would not be challenged by individual employers turning their back on the process of capitalist commodity production.

Second, Engels was a creative thinker and a powerful writer in his own right. He wrote perceptively about the terrible living conditions of the working class in Manchester, which was the epitome of a rapidly industrialising capitalist city. He also wrote about the 'housing question', exploring what was at the root of the appalling contemporary housing problems.[6] Many regard him as a clearer expositer than the brilliant, but sometimes obscure and disorganised, Marx. The *Manifesto of the Communist Party* is the best known and most polemic of their joint works, but many of their other works also benefited enormously from Engels's clarity of expression.

Third, Engels outlived Marx by twelve years. During that time he assembled many of Marx's unfinished notes and manuscripts and put them into a form suitable for publication. Only the first volume of *Capital* had been published before Marx's death. Engels arranged for the publication of the other two volumes and thereby contributed mightily to the foundation of the Marxist tradition of radical scholarship.

THE SCOPE OF MARXISM

The following nine themes illustrate the broad range of concerns within Marxist political economy.

- The study of *social classes*: The emphasis is on people, how the economy structures their interests, and how conflicting interests are expressed. The tendency for other currents of economic analysis to focus on things, rather than people, is derided as 'commodity fetishism'.

- The analysis of *exploitation*: A non-symmetrical relationship between classes under capitalism is posited. Because capital hires labour, and not *vice versa*, there is the possibility—indeed the inevitability—of exploitation. Marxist analysis treats this as a systemic feature, dependent not the rapacious inclinations of employers, but rather on the structural imperatives of the capitalist economy.

- The growth of *monopoly power*: Competitive markets are sometimes held to be the essence of capitalism, but Marxists emphasise the tendency for them to be supplanted by monopolistic enterprises. This further accentuates the disparities of economic power—the concentration and centralisation of capital proceeds apace as 'the big fish eat the little fish'.

- The *expansionary nature of capitalism*: Marxist analysis focuses on the reproduction and growth of the economy, emphasising the dynamism of the capital accumulation process. This directs attention to the process of imperialism and, in modern capitalism, to the role of transnational corporations in driving the globalisation of capital.

- The analysis of *uneven development*: Capitalism has always been characterised by great variability—spatially and temporally. Its uneven development over space is manifest in the contrast between rapidly expanding cities and economically stagnant, or declining, regions. Its uneven development over time is manifest in alternating periods of boom and slump. These, too, are focal points of Marxist analysis.

- The *commodification of social life*: Going beyond the purely economic, it is important to understand the systemic forces shaping and reshaping our social activities. According to Marxists, the expansionary character of capitalism tends, little by little, to transform social pursuits into marketable commodities. Sport, popular music, and education are pertinent contemporary examples.

- The problem of *alienation*: Here, too, is a tendency that Marxists see embedded in the economic structures of capitalism. It involves workers having no control over their own labour and the products of their labour. However, alienation is not limited to the workplace; according to contemporary political economists, it may also take other forms—economic, social, political, and environmental.[7]

- The role of *the state*: As stressed in chapter 6, capitalism is not, in practice, a purely free-market economy. What role the state plays, and how its activities are related to competing class interests, warrants careful consideration. In general, Marxists take the view that the state serves capitalist class interests—although there are many variations on that theme.

- Understanding *social change*: The focus on the study of change emphasises the processes of economic and social transformation, sometimes evolutionary and sometimes revolutionary in nature.

THE METHOD OF MARXISM

How are these aspects of capitalism to be analysed? Studying methodology in the abstract is notoriously unpalatable, but some consideration of it helps to reveal what is distinctive about Marxism in comparison to other theories. In general, what you see depends on how you look. Marx looked at capitalism from a perspective that was simultaneously historical, materialist, and dialectical.

To say that the method of Marxism is *historical* means that the principal focus is on historical processes, on change over time. The obvious point of contrast is with the focus in orthodox economic theory on equilibrium conditions at a particular point in time, as we will see in Part V of this book. The Marxian focus on history follows from the concern to study the evolution of economic systems.

To say that the method of Marxism is *materialist* requires a rather fuller explanation. Materialist in this sense needs to be distinguished from its more common usage of referring to a state of being primarily concerned, even obsessed, with the acquisition of wealth and possessions. In the philosophical context, materialist is the opposite of *idealist*. It denotes a primary focus on material conditions, such as the prevailing economic structure, as the key factor shaping society. The German philosopher Hegel, whose ideas strongly influenced Marx in his youth, had propounded an idealist philosophy that saw the 'totality of natural, historical and spiritual aspects of the world represented as a process of constant transformation'.[8] Marx is said to have 'stood Hegel on his head' by emphasising the primary importance of material conditions rather than ideas.[9] In his own words, 'it is not the consciousness of men that determines their existence, on the contrary, their social existence determines their consciousness'.[10] That material and ideological conditions interact is one of the main themes throughout political economy. The distinctive feature of the materialist position is that the material conditions are regarded as the leading factor.

Putting the historical and materialist aspects of Marxist methodology together produces *historical materialism*—the view that material factors, especially economic conditions, drive social change. This is what is sometimes known as *the materialist conception of history*. When Marx hit on this concept he knew he was on to something big—really big. The claim is that the broad sweep of history is not a series of more or less random or independent events, but rather a process that has a structure shaped by the economic conditions and thus, in principle at least, is predictable. It is one of the most controversial claims in the whole of social science.

The third element in the Marxist method—integrated with the historical materialist perspective—is *dialectics*. This also shows the influence of Hegel. To say that the method of Marxism is dialectical means that the focus is on the conflicts and contradictions internal to the economic system that propel change. The model of *thesis, antithesis and synthesis* helps us understand dialectical processes. It helps to show how change arises out of conflict. Take the simple example of a discussion—perhaps in a university tutorial—about something like 'the causes of unemployment'. One person may begin by setting up a 'thesis', for example: 'unemployment exists because some lazy people simply don't want to work'. A second person then proffers an opposite view: that unemployment results from the excess of potential workers over the number of jobs available. The second view is the 'antithesis' of the first. Discussion then ensues, which may (if the tutorial participants are sufficiently open-minded) result in the development of a 'synthesis'. For example, it may be agreed that a deficiency of demand for labour is the root problem, but that, after a period of involuntary unemployment, some unemployed people may begin to rationalise their own situation by saying that they do not want to work, anyway. The synthesis embodies elements of thesis and antithesis, but transcends both. It moves the issue on. It constitutes progress.

This example emphasises the interaction of ideas. In a materialist context, more characteristic of Marxist analysis, the obvious example of a dialectical process is *class struggle*. As Marx and Engels wrote at the very beginning of the *Manifesto of the Communist Party*, 'the history of all hitherto existing society is the history of class struggles'.[11] This puts the focus on the conflict of interests—for example conflict over the organisation of work and its remuneration. It emphasises that it is the *contradictory* elements within an economic system that propel change. It emphasises the progressive character of class struggle. It has given participants countless anti-capitalist political activities and liberation movements the dignity of representing a historical imperatives.

The activist element brings in the final element of the Marxist method—*praxis*. Marxism claims to be not merely a method for the analysis of capitalism: it claims to be simultaneously a tool for changing it and eventually replacing it with socialism. This integration of theory and political practice differentiates Marxism from more detached scholarly activities. Scholarship is important for Marxism—Marx himself was a scholar, studying the work of the classical political economists and developing detailed critiques. However, praxis requires that scholarship be blended with activism.

There are some interesting tensions in all this. If material conditions, rather than ideas, propel economic, social, and political change, why bother with the construction of a *theory* about capitalism, or anything else for that matter? Is not theorising inherently idealist? And, if the structural conflicts and contradictions within capitalism are destined to usher in socialism, why bother to organise a revolutionary movement? Why not just await the inevitable? These seem to be paradoxical aspects of historical and dialectical materialism, considered in the context of Marxist politics. The notion of praxis provides the necessary reconciliation. By emphasising the importance of material interests and ideas—the unity of action and theory—it indicates the holistic character of the Marxist method. As the inscription on Marx's tombstone reads, 'the philosophers have only interpreted the world in various ways: the point however is to change it'.

CONCLUSION

Marxist economics has provided the basis for a comprehensive critique of capitalism. In his own time, Marx addressed the problems of a rapidly industrialising society in which exploitation and class conflict were increasingly blatant. The scope of the analysis he and Engels developed was very broad—in this respect similar to classical political economy, although quite different in its political implications. The method of analysis emphasised the study of contradictory elements in the processes of historical change. That method is married in Marxist analysis to the use of particular analytical concepts, which are developed and discussed in the next few chapters.

Marxist political economy is highly controversial. Its claim to provide an analysis of the 'laws of motion' shaping capitalist development has strong echoes of classical political economy. Its emphasis on the conflictual character of capitalism and capitalism's tendencies to inequality, instability, and insecurity gives it a distinctively radical character. For more than a century it has been a rallying point for anti-capitalist sentiments. In studying Marxism, it is important to keep an open mind about the extent to which the analysis needs to be developed, modified, or rejected in the light of changes to capitalism since the time Marx wrote. Here is an invitation to controversy: to the study of one of the most influential thinkers of the last two centuries and to the assessment of the relevance of his ideas today.

CHAPTER 13

Understanding Capital
The mode of production

Does the economy shape the society?
What is distinctive about capitalism as a mode of production?
How are class relationships structured in such an economy?

Marxism is concerned with understanding society in its entirety, but focuses on the economy as the starting point for that enquiry. How it depicts the economy as a *mode of production* is distinctive. Understanding these issues is the concern of this chapter. The analysis contrasts with subsequent forms of economic enquiry, which delineate economics more sharply from other social sciences. For Marx, and others working in this analytical tradition, an explicitly political economic approach is preferred.

In grappling with a broad array of social, economic, and political concerns, a systematic and sequential approach is needed. The Marxian inclination is to begin with the study of the structures shaping how *production* is organised and how wealth is thereby generated. Understanding the institutions and characteristics of society as a whole, including its political institutions, then follows. The analysis thereby moves from the study of the economic base to the study of the social superstructure. In a famous passage, Marx said: 'The economic structure of society [is] the real foundation on which rise legal and political superstructures and to which correspond definite forms of social consciousness'.[1] Thus Marx began, as Russian revolutionary Lenin put it, 'by selecting from all the social relations the production relations as being the basic and prime relations that determine all other relations'.[2]

PRODUCTION AS THE PRIMARY CONCERN

All societies must produce in order to survive. Food, clothing, and shelter are the basic necessities: once their supply is ensured we can consider producing other goods and services of a luxury character. But how these productive activities are organised can vary quite significantly. Some societies organise production through capital-intensive and highly mechanised or automated processes; others use more labour-intensive methods of production. Land is sometimes used extensively, sometimes intensively, for productive purposes. And the way in which decisions about production are made may be made through institutional processes that are haphazard or coherent, centralised or decentralised, authoritarian or democratic.

Box 13.1

Base and superstructure

Does the economic base shape the social superstructure? A direct link of this kind is not hard to visualise. Take educational institutions, for example. Schools, technical colleges, and universities are an important aspect of the modern social superstructure. Their form is, to a considerable extent, shaped by the needs of the economy. These needs are partly ideological—for a workforce inculcated with values conducive to the acceptance of authority structures in the workplace. The needs are also practical—for a certain number of skilled technicians, for a certain number of semi-skilled process workers, labourers, and so on. Schools, technical colleges, and universities are structured in such a way that they produce these 'outputs' in more or less the required proportions. Indeed, in recent years there have been many calls from political leaders for this link to be an even more explicit policy objective. Rhetoric about the need for the education system to play a more direct role in fostering the development of a 'clever country' or a 'knowledge nation', for example, has a clearly instrumental character. It implies that the education system should be reshaped to meet national economic needs, first and foremost, rather than cater for the personal development or cultural enrichment of the persons involved. The application of economic criteria in evaluating the effectiveness of the education system is ever more pervasive. The educational institutions themselves have become more entrepreneurial in their own behaviour, especially as the politicians' calls for better economic outputs have not been matched by the necessary public funding.[3] Overall, these 'superstructural' institutions are being shaped and remoulded to serve the economic requirements of contemporary capitalism.

If that were the whole of the story, the base–superstructure model would fit neatly. However, other tensions and contradictions exist. Within educational institutions are strong traditions emphasising the pursuit of the truth and the development of critical reasoning. Such traditions may not sit comfortably with short-run capitalist interests—although they are surely important in fostering innovation and social progress in the longer term. So it makes more sense to think of the base–superstructure relationship as a two-way relationship. In other words, the character of the superstructure affects the base as well as *vice versa*. Indeed, if that were not so, changes in the economic base would always be quickly followed by corresponding changes in the social superstructure. Changing the economic system from one based on private ownership to one based on public ownership, for example, would necessarily produce a change in social institutions and dominant ideology. Things are not so simple in practice, for the characteristics of the superstructure, including the prevailing ideologies, are also shaped by broader historical and cultural influences, as well as the prevailing economic arrangements. Political economic transitions are invariably messy.

The focus of Marxist political economy on the organisation of production is distinctive. As we shall see in later chapters, the more orthodox neoclassical economists do not start here: their analytical focus is on *exchange* rather than production relationships—on choices between technically feasible combinations of the factors of production, rather than on the socioeconomic processes by which commodities are actually made. The Keynesian focus is also different, putting more emphasis on the determinants of the overall *demand* for goods and services, rather than on the processes of production *per se*. Institutional economists come closer to the Marxian orientation with their concerns about how *technology* influences, and is influenced by, economic institutions; but the mode of production as the central analytical concept is uniquely Marxist.

What is the mode of production? It is the character of the processes—technical and social—by which goods and services are made. Figure 13. 1 gives the simplest depiction of its essential elements.

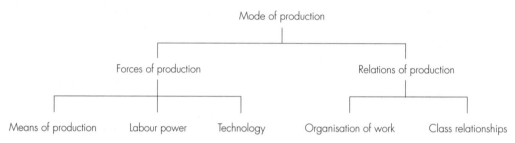

Figure 13.1   The mode of production.

The *forces of production* are the most tangible elements. These are the means of production, the labour power and the technology involved in making goods and services. The *means of production* comprise the raw materials—those useful things, such as minerals, coal, petroleum, wood, and water, that come from natural sources. They also include capital goods—the instruments, machines, and tools that make it possible to extract or harvest useful natural materials, to transport them, and to industrially transform them. *Labour power* is the human effort—whether by muscle or brain—that is necessary in order for these means of production to be put to effective use. How the labour power is combined with the means of production influences the productivity of the processes by which goods and services are made. It depends significantly on the nature of *technology*—the cumulative contributions of scientific and technological innovation—because technology governs the connection between the inputs and the outputs of the production process. In other words, it sets limits on the goods and services that can be produced with the land, labour, and capital available in the economy; it comes to be embodied in the form of the capital goods, and it shapes the form of the production process itself.

The *relations of production* concern the social-organisational aspects of that production process. Whereas the forces of production are tangible and technical, the relations of production concern how *people* are organised for the purpose of making the goods and services. Relations of production can take various forms. Imagine a small isolated community of people, on an island perhaps, deciding how they will cater for their own material needs. They may collectively take stock of their resources (human, natural, and manufactured) and decide how they will allocate them between different types of production (food, housing, clothing, and so on). Who does what, when, and how is determined by a process of collective choice. Quite likely, this sort of decision-making process will lead to the adoption of some egalitarian principles, such as the rotation of the less pleasant tasks. Now, contrast this situation with one in which more hierarchical arrangements prevail. If one person is able to dictate the tasks to the others—perhaps because she or he has acquired monopoly control over the means of production—the nature of interpersonal relationships in the production process is likely to be significantly different. Authoritarian practices will prevail, and egalitarian principles will be less likely to have much influence. Whether the situation is stable will depend on whether the owner of the means of production is able to ensure compliance, either through coercion or legitimising ideologies, and whether the system 'works' well in providing for the material needs of all.

How the forces of production and the relations of production *interact* determines the overall character of the mode of production. Here is the interface of the physical and the social, of technology and class. The relationships are not random. Indeed, according to Marx, a historically significant connection between the development of the two aspects is identifiable. A *slave* mode of production, for example, uses characteristically rudimentary forces of production. The labour performed by slaves, using basic means of production, is the principal input into the production process. The relations of production are correspondingly crude, based on a coercive relationship between slave-owners and slaves. The simple threat 'work harder or I will punish you!' provides the incentive.

Under *feudalism*, the forces of production are usually a little better developed. The means of production comprise crude agricultural implements, and labour is performed by serfs who work on the land of the feudal lords in exchange for social protection. Elements of physical coercion are sometimes present, but the social aspects of production process are based on *mutual obligation* between the feudal lords and the 'lower orders' of society. The relations of production exhibit more sophistication than under slavery.

The connection between the forces and relations of production becomes yet more evident with the development of *capitalism*. The means of production, the quality of labour power, and the nature of technology become increasingly complex. The relations of production centre on the *wage* relationship, based on buying and selling in the market. This pecuniary orientation then shapes all aspects of capitalist society, leading to an increasingly commercialised and commodified world.

Under *socialism* and then *communism*, Marx hoped and anticipated that a new conjunction of the forces and relations of production would prevail. The forces of production, developed under capitalism to the level that makes a materially affluent society possible (but unrealisable because of the problems arising from conflicting class interests), would be carried over and further developed under socialism. Importantly, according to this reasoning, they can then be married to more egalitarian relations of production. Production and distribution can be organised on the principle 'from each according to their ability; to each according to their needs'.[4] A society that is both affluent and democratic becomes achievable for the first time in human history. Affluence is possible because there is no dominant class controlling the economic surplus for its own purposes; while democracy can be extended to the economy (for example through workers' control of the enterprises in which they work) and need not remain restricted to the sphere of parliamentary elections, as it is under capitalism.

This, in bare outline, is how the forces and relations of production can be visualised as interacting through different modes of production. It is a story of the forces and relations of production working in tandem—the development of one making the further development of the other possible. It is a powerful story, providing a strong basis for optimism about economic and social progress. In the extreme, it is the view of history as the unfolding of an sequence of increasingly more sophisticated, and ultimately more liberating, modes of production.

However, Marxism (in its more careful constructions, at least) sees nothing inevitable about the movement through successive modes of production. Yes, the process of technological change (in the forces of production) and the social tensions and contradictions (in the relations of production) do tend to drive change. So, modes of production seemingly well established at a point in time (as capitalism is at the dawn of the twenty-first century) have no claim to permanency. But the form sequential changes take is open-ended. 'Reversals' in the sequence may occur. So, too, may 'jumps' between different modes of production. Obvious examples are Russia and China, which were still predominantly feudal societies with only partial and incomplete elements of capitalist development at the time of their socialist revolutions in the twentieth century. Both made radical breaks in seeking to build a socialist mode of production, but 'leapfrogging' capitalism proved profoundly problematic for the achievement of that socialist goal. Both have experienced policy reversals towards capitalism—albeit in a highly corrupted form in Russia and under the auspices of an authoritarian state in China.

A second qualification to the theory of successive modes of production concerns their impurity. Modes of production may *coexist*. Indeed, different modes of production are normally present in any one country at any one time. Modern societies that we usually think of as capitalist, such as the United States, the United Kingdom, or Australia, commonly have vestigial feudal elements and/or embryonic socialist elements alongside the dominant capitalist mode of production. The organisation of *domestic labour* in those societies, for example, is not characteristically capitalist: some domestic tasks may be done for wages (by hiring a gardener, cleaner, or childcarer, for example), but most are done by household members themselves (usually disproportionately by women). Intra-household transfer of income may be involved (between 'breadwinners' and other members of the household), but this is not synonymous with wage-labour, the hallmark of capitalism.

Outwork is a second example of the 'impurity' of modes of production in modern economies. It is common in industries like the clothing industry, where production involves paying for the products of the workers' labour rather than for the labour time spent. Such an arrangement is historically more characteristic of the 'putting-out' system that developed under feudalism before capitalism became established.

Economic activities that are organised in the form of *cooperatives* are not characteristically capitalist, either. Many business cooperatives exist in the advanced industrial nations, but they do not operate according to purely capitalist principles. 'Counter-culture' communities concurrently seek to practise collectivist forms of production and distribution, their members commonly seeing them as embryonic elements of a society not yet fully developed but perhaps capable ultimately of transcending capitalism.[5] Whether or not such aspirations are achievable is not the key issue here. The point is an analytical one: what we commonly call 'capitalist' societies are not necessarily capitalist in all respects. Different modes of production may coexist in any given society. So, when we talk of a particular society being based on a capitalist economy we are referring only to the *dominant* mode of production in that place at that time.

The effect of these qualifications is to scale down the boldness of the claims arising from Marx's analysis of the modes of production. It is not a simple *stages theory* of historical evolution. Rather, it offers a means of interpreting the interactions between economic and social change. As such, it is an analytic framework rather than a specific prediction about the direction of economic development over the long term. Perhaps its greatest value is in drawing attention to the characteristics of capitalism as a mode of production that differentiate it from other modes of production.

CAPITALISM AS A MODE OF PRODUCTION

The significance of defining capitalism as a mode of production can be brought into sharper focus by comparing it with other ways of defining capitalism, as Maurice Dobbs does in his book *Studies in the Development of Capitalism*.[6] Five possibilities are considered.

First, capitalism may be defined as a system based on 'roundabout' or time-using methods of production. This emphasises the *technological* aspect of the economy. According to this view, what makes an economy 'capitalistic' is the use of capital in complex production processes. The problem is that, beyond the most primitive, all economies have been capitalistic in this sense, varying only in degree. So, the possibility of identifying capitalism with particular epochs of economic development is denied.

Second, capitalism may be defined as a system based on the unfettered operation of the competitive market mechanism. This fits in with commonly held notions about capitalism as the 'free-market' economy. However, it interprets capitalism so narrowly as to make it almost non-existent. In few places, other than the United Kingdom and the United States in the nineteenth century, have economies conformed closely to such a freely competitive regime, and even the UK and US passed quickly into an age of corporate enterprise and monopoly power. The state has always been a significant presence in capitalist development—indeed usually establishing the preconditions for capitalist development. As Dobb says, 'if capitalism is to be so straitly limited in time as this, how are we to characterise the system which preceded it and the system which followed it, both of which resembled it so closely in a number of leading respects?'[7] Making capitalism synonymous with *laissez-faire* is not helpful in understanding this type of economy in practice.

Third, capitalism can be defined as a system in which production occurs for distant markets. This emphasises *trade* as the distinctively capitalist feature. It locates the origins of capitalism in the encroachment of commercial dealings on the localised economic system characteristic of the medieval era. It emphasises the breakdown of the craft guilds, which restricted craftsmen to selling their products only in the local town market. Indeed, the opening-up of regional, national, and international trade was surely an important element in the transition from feudalism to capitalism, as noted in chapter 8. However, production for distant markets was not unknown in the pre-capitalist period. It was characteristic of socialist-based economies in the twentieth century, too. So, Dobb's case for rejecting the attempt to define capitalism in terms of market competition applies equally to this attempted definition in terms of trade relationships: in the former case the definition is too restrictive, in the latter not restrictive enough.

Fourth, we may approach the issue rather differently by emphasising the nature of capitalist *ideology*. Perhaps capitalism can be defined as the economic system resulting from a particular set of attitudes held by society at large—attitudes to rationality and the entrepreneurial spirit, for instance. In the words of sociologist Max Weber, capitalism is 'present whenever the industrial provision of a human group is carried out by the method of enterprise'.[8] The role of ideology in shaping society had been emphasised by the German philosopher Hegel who, as previously noted, was a strong influence on Marx. Hegel envisaged the history of civilisation as a succession of epochs marked by the dominance of successive national cultures. But is ideology more an *effect* than a cause of such historical changes? If it is, it seems inappropriate to *define* economic systems in terms of the ideologies to which they give rise. That is why Marx 'inverted Hegel' by emphasising the driving force of material economic conditions. What people think, especially about political economic issues, is important, but does not constitute a sufficiently fundamental basis for defining the economic system itself.

It is the definition of capitalism as a *mode of production* that most clearly identifies the particular epoch in which capitalism developed and became readily distinguishable from other economic systems. In his own day, witnessing the establishment, expansion, and evolution of the capitalist system, Marx emphasised its three key characteristics:

- the separation of labour from the ownership of the means of production
- the concentration of the ownership of the means of production in the hands of a single class—the *bourgeoisie* or capitalist class
- the appearance of a social class dependent for its subsistence on the sale of its labour power—the *proletariat* or working class.

This economic and social transformation continues to reverberate to this day. Although capitalist institutions have become characteristically—in some cases, enormously—larger, using increasingly sophisticated technologies and interacting with the state in complex ways, the essential feature of capitalism as a mode of production exhibits considerable continuity. The system is distinguishable from others largely because of the *class* relationships associated with how production is organised. Putting the spotlight first and foremost on class, rather than on technology, market structures, trade, or ideology, is the hallmark of this identification of capitalism as a mode of production. This is not to deny the importance of the other elements, interacting as they do with class, but to regard them as attributes of an economic system in which class relationships are fundamental.

CONCLUSION

Defining capitalism as a mode of production puts the focus on the relationship between capital and labour. This relationship has a *technical* economic dimension, emphasising capital and labour as inputs into the production of goods and services. It also has a *social* dimension, emphasising capital and labour as classes, as groups of people with potentially conflicting interests. According to Marxist economics, this tension is the essential dynamic of capitalism as an economic system.

Rather schematically, we can say that capitalism is a *progressive* system, or has been so historically, in facilitating the development of the forces of production. Industrialisation, mechanisation, and the increased complexity of capital goods make possible ever greater levels of material productivity (at least until ecological constraints begin to bite). Concurrently, capitalism has a *reactionary* character, retarding social progress because its relations of production prevent the achievement of a genuinely affluent society in which the wealth is shared by all. Conflict arising from the relations of production—manifest in worker alienation, industrial disputes, and periodic economic crisis—impairs the achievement in practice of the economic prosperity that the forces of production would otherwise make possible.

Understanding these two faces of capitalism is central to Marxist political economy. Capital and labour must cooperate for production to occur and for the system to be reproduced. However, as social classes, capital and labour have conflicting interests regarding economic power (who should take the production decisions, for example) and the distribution of the fruits of cooperation (the extent of inequality in the distribution of income and wealth, for example). Because the relationship between capital and labour is non-symmetrical—capital hires labour and not *vice versa*—the need for cooperation sits uneasily with these recurrent tendencies towards conflict. It is rather like a marriage that is on a permanent knife-edge, where the husband and wife can neither live apart nor live comfortably together. Coping with conflict and contradiction is the name of the game ...

CHAPTER 14

Labour, Value, Exploitation

What is the labour theory of value?
Can this theory be used to explain the values of different commodities?
Can it explain the exploitation of labour as a pervasive, rather than exceptional,
feature of the capitalist economy?

Having defined capitalism as a mode of production, the task now is to understand how it works. How does the capital–labour relationship affect the functioning of the economy? What determines the value of the products that are made? Where do profits come from? These are the questions that Marx sought to answer by adapting the labour theory of value from the classical political economists. Marx took this theory and gave it a radical twist, turning it into a means of understanding the exploitation of labour by capital. To this day, the labour theory of value has been one of the most contentious currents of political economic analysis. It requires careful consideration.

COMMODITIES AND VALUES

The Marxist analysis, like classical political economy, makes an initial distinction between *use values* and *exchange values*. Of course, the production of useful things must occur in every society if it is to sustain itself, let alone prosper economically. Such items range from food, housing, and clothing to a vast array of non-essential goods and services. Each has its own use value, but that use value depends on who consumes it. (You may like hamburgers; I don't. You may not want another pair of shoes; I do. You may like this particular pair of shoes; I don't.) So, use values are inherently *subjective*. They vary from person to person, and a common unit of comparison is hard to find. In other words, it is difficult to establish a general economic theory of use values. It seems to be a matter more in the realm of psychology than of economics.

The problem of comparing the usefulness of one thing with another would not matter much in the simplest society where individuals produce items for their own use. People would allocate their working time according to their own subjective preferences for the things they can hunt, grow, or make. Production would be directly for consumption, not for exchange. But few societies work like that in practice. Even the most rudimentary division of labour makes it possible for people to produce more of some items than they need for their own consumption, and then exchange them in the market for items that they want. This entails the production of commodities—goods and services made for exchange rather than for personal consumption. A world of commodity production is one in which an explanation of exchange values is needed.

So, what determines how much of one commodity will be exchanged for another in the market? Why are shoes more expensive than hamburgers? Why is a silk shirt more expensive than a cotton one? What determines the price of these goods and the countless other commodities available for sale? As we have seen, the classical political economists reasoned that, in general, relative prices reflect the cost of production of each commodity. The greater the labour needed to make the commodity, the higher the value of that commodity. Marx extended this basic insight into a comprehensive explanation of commodity production and capitalist markets.

THE LABOUR THEORY OF VALUE

Formally, the labour theory of value asserts that the value of a commodity is determined by *the amount of labour needed for its production*. This deceptively simple proposition requires three supplementary points of explanation. The first concerns the *efficiency* of the labour process. The word 'needed' appears in the preceding definition because it is not the amount of labour actually performed that determines the value of a commodity. A chair made in three hours by an efficient carpenter is not worth less than a chair made in five hours by a less efficient carpenter. Assuming that both chairs have the same characteristics, they can be expected to sell in the market at the same price. The labour that determines the value is only the 'socially necessary' labour—the labour reflecting the general standards of productivity and the state of technology prevailing in the economy at any particular time.

Second, account must be taken of the variations in the *skill* of the workers. Some occupations require many years of training; others do not. A skilled worker or tradesperson usually produces more value in one hour of work than an unskilled labourer. The concept of *abstract labour* takes this into account. It gives us a common unit of the value-creating capacity of labour. Thus, we can express the value created by a skilled worker in terms of abstract labour as a multiple of that created by an unskilled worker. The size of this multiple will normally depend on the time taken to acquire the extra skills. If a quarter of a skilled worker's time is taken up in the acquisition of skills, for example, we might regard his or her work as contributing 1.25 times as much abstract labour per hour as an unskilled worker's. In this way, the existence of diversity of skills among the workforce can be reconciled with a single labour theory of value.

Third, there is the issue of *unproductive* workers—not those who are inefficient or relatively unskilled, but those who do not directly produce commodities at all. There are frequently many such workers in a capitalist economy. Supervisors, for example, may be *necessary* to ensure that other workers work hard, but they do not themselves produce the commodities. According to a strict interpretation of the labour theory of value, their labour time should not therefore be counted as contributing to the value of the products. This reasoning does not imply that such jobs are unnecessary. Supervisors are normally essential in a capitalist economy because workers work for wages rather than directly for the products of their own labour. Supervisors are necessary, but they are not productive because their labour does not directly add to the value of the products. No normative judgment about social worth is necessarily implied. However, difficult decisions need to be made about the range of jobs that are regarded as unproductive in this sense.

Having made these qualifications to the basic labour theory of value, a workable basis for calculating the value of different commodities is established. One can calculate how much 'socially necessary' time goes into making them, measuring the contribution of workers of different skill levels in terms of abstract labour, and excluding the time expended by unproductive workers. However, a basic question remains: why should *only* labour add to value? How can the fundamental proposition underlying the labour theory of value be justified? Drawing on the reasoning of Ernest Mandel, three possible 'proofs' of the theory can be considered.[1]

First is the demonstration by *disaggregation*. This rests on the proposition that everything that goes into making a commodity can ultimately be traced back to the contribution of labour. Take the example of a wooden chair. What determines its value is not only the time spent by the carpenter in making it, but also the time spent by the timber worker in felling the tree, by the sawmiller in cutting the tree into useable planks, and by the truck driver in transporting the planks to the carpenter's workplace. The workers who made the screws the carpenter uses also have imparted some value to the product, as have, indirectly, the coal and iron ore miners and the foundry workers whose labour made the steel from which the screws were made. And the carpenter's tools—the saw, screwdriver, and chisel—were made by toolmakers using raw materials extracted and transformed by yet other workers. Those tools would not be fully used up in making the chair, but some part of the value embodied in them, which would depend on the degree of wear and tear on them, could be regarded as having been transferred to the chair.

According to this chain of reasoning, everything that adds to the value of the commodity is ultimately traceable to labour. It is a powerful argument. It recognises that capital goods are important in commodity production—indeed increasingly important in an era of ever more sophisticated mechanisation—but it also emphasises that these capital goods themselves are the products of labour. Similarly, it indicates that, although natural resources as well as labour are involved in the production process, those resources acquire economic value only through the application of labour to their extraction and processing as inputs into the production process. Environmentalists should be reassured that this is not to deny that nature has value in its own right. The argument simply asserts that, under capitalism, natural resources only become commodities with *market* value when labour is applied to their conversion for commodity production.

A second attempt to justify the labour theory of value involves more abstract reasoning. This is the so-called *logical proof*. The claim here is that, while commodities may have many common properties (molecular structure, size, weight and colour, for example), the only common property that can serve as a basis for their exchange is that they are products of labour. Weight, for example, cannot be the basis for determining value. If it were, a kilogram of butter would have equal value to a kilogram of gold or a kilogram of electric light globes, which would be a patent absurdity. Only their common property as being products of labour can serve as a systematic basis for the determination of their relative value.

A third chain of reasoning rests on imagining an extreme case: a wholly mechanised society in which no labour is used. Machines produce machines, which produce all the goods and services that everybody needs. In such a society, it is argued, there would be no role for market arrangements since scarcity would have been abolished. It is a world of complete abundance. The elimination of labour has also eradicated exchange value. There could be no wages system in such an economy either, since nobody would need to work. There would have to be some other means of distributing the goods and services produced. In other words, it would not be a capitalist economy, and the value basis of the capitalist system would no longer exist.

Whether these 'proofs' of the labour theory of value are persuasive is a matter of judgment. Theoretical reasoning alone is inherently problematic in this context; the ultimate test is whether a theory actually helps in understanding the world around us. So, the practical question is whether the labour theory of value helps to explain the basis of commodity exchange in real market economies.

VALUES AND PRICES

Marx certainly thought that the relative prices of commodities could be explained by reference to the labour theory of value. In his own words, 'the determination of price by cost of production is equivalent to the determination of price by the labour-time requisite to the production of a commodity'.[2] However, such an attempt to apply the labour theory of value to explaining prices in practice has to deal with some rather tricky problems.

First, prices may be influenced by *fluctuations in consumer demand*. A commodity will not have a high market value unless it is in demand, irrespective of how much labour goes into making it. Producers will not make it if it is not in demand, you may say. Indeed, but producers do make mistakes, and anticipating changes in demand is seldom easy. So, market prices may fluctuate independently of the amount of labour that goes into making the products. A fruitseller may reduce her prices just before packing up for the day, not because of any variation in the amount of labour going into the production of that fruit but because she judges that the fruit might otherwise spoil and therefore become unsaleable.

Second, by similar reasoning, the *state of market competition* also usually has a bearing on actual market prices. Where competition is vigorous, prices will tend to conform more closely to labour values than where elements of monopoly are present. Monopolists can drive up prices by creating artificial scarcity, irrespective of the amount of labour embodied in the products they sell.

Third, where different branches of industry have an *unequal degree of mechanisation* there may also be a tendency for relative market prices to deviate from relative labour values for the products concerned. Firms in the technologically advanced sectors will normally be able to secure higher profit margins than firms in the less technologically advanced sectors. If the rate of profit is not the same in all branches of industry, then the relationship between labour values and market prices will not be uniform. This is the essence of the 'transformation problem'—the problem of transforming values into prices.[3]

These considerations cast doubt on the adequacy of the labour theory of value as a means of explaining relative commodity prices in practice. It is on these grounds that neoclassical economists, among others, reject the theory. However, a more positive interpretation is possible that emphasises its usefulness in explaining *long-run price trends*. Indeed, notwithstanding the above factors, which may cause short-run deviations of market prices from labour values, there are good grounds for thinking that, over long periods of time, prices do broadly reflect the labour that goes into making different commodities.

Consider a simple illustration comparing the prices of haircuts and watches. Thirty years ago, in countries like the United States, the United Kingdom, and Australia, the price of a simple, cheap watch was many times more (perhaps ten in round terms) than the price of a basic haircut for a man. There has been prodigious technological advance in watch production since then, partly as a result of the 'microelectronic revolution', so that much less labour, both direct and indirect, is now needed to make a watch. By contrast, there has been no significant advance in hairdressing technologies: a haircut is still largely a matter of one worker standing beside a person's head with a pair of scissors. Cheap watches now cost less than a professional haircut. Of course, one can spend a prodigious sum on a watch made with more labour-intensive methods and/or more valuable materials. One can also spend more on a haircut if more complex and time-consuming treatments are required. But the differential rate of technological change in watchmaking and hairdressing have clearly influenced the general pattern of relative prices. One example like this does not 'prove' the labour theory of value, of course. Nor would a longer list of examples (which would not be difficult to construct). What it does suggest, if our concern is with understanding long-run trends in commodity prices, is that a labour theory of value can have a significant role.

However, the labour theory of value, according to Marxists, has a more important role than explaining relative prices: it is the key to understanding *exploitation*. The former concern with the price of things may even be regarded as a form of 'commodity fetishism'; the latter takes us to the core of the Marxist concern with the *class* character of capitalism.

VALUE AND SURPLUS VALUE

> There are people in this country who work hard every day;
> Not for fame and fortune do they strive;
> And the fruits of their labour are worth more than their pay.

This is the 'jingle' in a television beer commercial in which sweaty workers are shown enjoying a drink or two after their daily efforts. The advertiser's aim is to present ordinary citizens contributing to the advancement of the nation over and above what they are rewarded in wages (and, hopefully, spending some of those wages on the advertiser's 'liquid gold' as well). Ironically, and no doubt unintentionally, the jingle also summarises the Marxist theory of surplus value—that workers produce value over and above what is returned to them as wages.

Let us build up this theory more systematically. The starting point is the distinction between labour power and labour. *Labour power* is a person's potential to work. In Marx's words, it is 'the aggregate of those mental and physical capabilities existing in a human being which he exercises whenever he produces a use-value of any description'.[4] *Labour*, on the other hand, is work actually undertaken. So, the one is a capacity, the other an actual activity. It is rather like the distinction between the power to digest food and the actual process of digestion, or between nuclear strike capacity and nuclear war.

When an employer hires labour (by the hour, week, or year), it is labour power that is being purchased. Labour power is a commodity and, according to Marx, will normally exchange in the market at its value, like any other commodity. That value—the prevailing wage rate—varies from place to place and from time to time, determined historically through processes of class struggle. The wage rate in Australia for unskilled workers, for example, is currently around $160 for an eight-hour day. Given that prevailing wage rate, employers have to decide whether it is in their interests to hire workers, that is, purchase labour power in the market. The answer is that it is worth them doing so only when the value of the commodities produced by workers exceeds the wages that must be paid. The capitalist employer does not employ workers because of altruism: the goal is profit. As a result, workers will be hired only when they are expected to contribute to the profitability of the enterprise by producing more value than they are paid in wages. Formally, this means that the condition for employment is that the value of the commodities produced by labour exceeds the value of labour power.

A *division of the working day* is implied. For the first part of the working day, the employee is producing just enough commodities to cover his or her own wage. This is called the *necessary labour*—that which is necessary to produce value equivalent to the wage paid. The rest of the day involves *surplus labour*. This is the labour expended by the worker that directly benefits the employer. In value terms, this contribution by the worker to the income of the employer is *surplus value*. It is the amount of value created by the worker that is not returned as wages. It is the primary source of the profit made by the enterprise.

SURPLUS VALUE AS THE SOURCE OF PROFITS

Who shares in the surplus value? The *profits of the capitalist business enterprises* are the most obvious and direct manifestation of surplus value in monetary form. In this regard, Marxist economics is in accord with the most conservative conventional accounting practices. It treats profits as an economic surplus, just as accountants calculate profits as the surplus of revenues over costs. How these profits are then shared between the shareholders (whose interests are in dividend payments and increasing their share prices) and the managers of the capitalist enterprises (whose interests are in their own remuneration packages and the growth of the firms) is a matter of contention. Both have a common interest in maximising the flow of surplus value into profits, however.

There are other claimants to surplus value. *Supervisory workers* have to be paid their wages and, since they do not themselves directly produce value, their wages must come from the surplus value generated by other, productive workers. It is profitable to employ such supervisors to the extent that they help to ensure that surplus value is extracted from productive workers. So, although they are formally unproductive workers, their employment is not 'uneconomic'. Within the logic of the capitalist economy, they have a claim on surplus value. The size of their share depends, like other workers', on their strength in bargaining over their wage or salary levels with their employers.

Other claimants to surplus value include *banks and other financial institutions*. These commonly lend money to businesses, producing income for themselves in the form of interest payments and other charges that are associated with those loans. Those income flows are therefore deductions from the surplus value that would otherwise be retained as profits by industrial enterprises. Banks themselves are capitalist businesses and seek profit; the peculiarity of their position is that this profit largely involves the transfer of surplus value produced in productive enterprises.

Governments may also capture part of the surplus value through taxation. Taxes on businesses reduce corporate post-tax profits. In return, governments usually provide services that are useful for business, such as investing in the basic infrastructure necessary to make commerce possible. So it is not all one-way traffic. It is not as if the presence of government is at the expense of business profits, as some right-wing libertarians imply, for the role played by government may well expand the scope for capitalist development over time. However, at any particular stage in capitalist development, the revenues generated by governments from business taxation (usually a small minority of total tax revenue sources) is a claim on surplus value.

It should be evident that many sections of society have an interest, more or less directly, in surplus value—capitalist firms, their shareholders and managers, supervisors, financial institutions, and governments. They have *divergent* interests in how the surplus value is shared.[5] However, they have a *common* interest in there being a large total pool of surplus value. In Marxist terms, this means a common interest in the process of exploitation.

EXPLOITATION AND CLASS STRUGGLE

In Marxist theory, the term 'exploitation' refers to any situation where *one class of people derives income from the labour of another class*. It is a pervasive process. Indeed, Marx noted that exploitation, in this sense, had characterised all preceding societies. Under slavery, slave-owners lived in relative affluence because of the work done by slaves. Under feudalism, the standard of living of the manorial lords depended on the labour contributed by serfs. What Marx saw as being novel about capitalism was the persistence of exploitation, despite labour becoming 'free'. Indeed, the freedom of workers under capitalism is historically unprecedented. Workers are not tied to a master but are free to work for whomever is willing to hire them. Hence the great puzzle: how can labour be both 'free' and exploited? The characteristically Marxist response emphasises the constrained character of that freedom: it is the freedom to work for employers who are seeking to extract surplus value.

Not surprisingly, herein lies a pervasive conflict of interests. The employers want the highest possible ratio of surplus labour to necessary labour, or (what amounts to the same thing) the highest possible ratio of surplus value to wages. The employees want the reverse: the highest possible ratio of wages to total value produced. The conflict of interests is structurally embedded. The diverse forms of struggle to which it gives rise are broadly distinguishable as struggles over either absolute surplus value or relative surplus value. Increases in *absolute surplus value* arise when workers work longer to produce more value without a corresponding increase in wages. Increases in *relative surplus value* arise whenever the employer is able to capture a larger proportion of the total value produced during a given period of time.

Struggles over *the length of the working day* put the focus on absolute surplus value. Such class struggles have been of great historical significance. In the early stages of capitalist development, working hours were lengthened: in the early nineteenth century, for instance, fourteen-hour workdays were common. Since then, workers, largely through their organisation into trade unions, have been successful in shortening the length of the normal working day, first to twelve hours, then to ten hours, and eventually to eight hours. By the early twentieth century, the eight-hour workday had become the norm in countries like the United Kingdom and Australia. The push for shorter working hours has stalled significantly over the last half century and there has been evidence of some reversals—as shown by the growing trend to unpaid overtime. However, a strong push for further reductions in the length of the working week has resumed in recent years. In France, a maximum working week of thirty-five hours has become mandatory.[6]

Facing these setbacks in respect of their capacity to generate absolute surplus value, capitalist employers have responded by seeking to raise relative surplus value. They have usually done so by increasing the productivity and/or intensity of labour. Raising the *productivity of labour* may be achieved through enhancing the skills of the workforce, equipping the workers with superior tools or machinery, or eliminating waste from the production process. If workers produce more value during a given time period, and if their wages do not rise correspondingly, surplus value is increased.

Raising the *intensity of labour* has a yet more direct effect. It means that workers produce more value during a given time period because they are working harder. How to make workers work harder is, of course, the great challenge for capitalist management. What employers buy is labour power—the capacity to work—but their task is to make sure that the maximum amount of labour—actual work—is undertaken. Box 14.1 summarises some managerial strategies employed for this purpose.

From a Marxist perspective, exploitation is not something imposed by particularly nasty employers, but rather a condition for the *normal* functioning of the capitalist economy. It is a systemic characteristic, not an aberration. Part of the value produced by workers is taken by capitalist employers—there would be no point, from an employer's perspective, in employing the workers otherwise. Capitalism needs exploitation for its normal functioning. Whether a labour theory of value is necessary to make this point is a contentious matter. Some political economists argue that positing a connection between profits, surplus labour, and exploitation does not require a formal basis in value theory.[7] The value theoretic aspect reflects the influence on Marx of the classical political economists. Its grand claim is to provide a bridge between the analysis of production and the analysis of distribution.

Box 14.1

Managerial strategies for increasing the intensity of labour

Many workers take a pride in their jobs and their own productivity. Some perform unpaid overtime. The belief in doing 'a fair day's work for a fair day's pay' is widespread. In various ways, these personal, ethical, and social commitments influence how work is performed. But the basic fact remains: under capitalism, work is done for wages, so the material benefits of harder or faster work usually accrue, in the first instance, to the employer rather than the employee.

An influential book on political economy by Harry Braverman, *Labor and Monopoly Capital*, describes how employers in the twentieth century sought to raise the intensity of labour by using 'scientific management'. This approach to management, which emphasised managerial control over each and every stage of workers' productive activities, changed the nature of work in many industries and occupations.[8] 'Scientific management' has come to be known as 'Taylorism', after its pioneer Frederick Taylor (1856–1917).

Other political economists have pointed out that the quest by managers to increase the intensity of labour has taken more diverse forms in practice. Richard Edwards, for example, distinguishes between three strategies: simple control, technical control, and bureaucratic control.[9] *Simple control* occurs when bosses directly exert their personal authority over workers. 'Work harder or you'll be fired' is the characteristic message. *Technical control* involves the use of technology as a means of increasing the intensity of labour. Setting the pace of work by setting the pace of machinery is the characteristic method here. It is commonplace in many routine factory jobs. *Bureaucratic control* is the more sophisticated alternative, embedding work incentives in the social-organisational aspects of the enterprise. Its hallmarks are career ladders, bonus payments, and the encouragement of personal identification with corporate goals.

Political economists also distinguish between 'lean production' and 'team production' in the organisation of work.[10] The former is the modern form of Taylorism, requiring centralised control over the workforce, usually with an eye to cutting out 'unnecessary labour'. The latter entails more decentralised decision-making, giving some degree of autonomy to groups of workers. Team production is often more conducive to productivity, but managers tend to be cautious about its introduction, fearing that the empowerment of workers may threaten managerial prerogatives.

Modern managers also tend to be coy about explicitly admitting to their primary concern of extracting more work from the workers. 'Human resources management' is the more acceptable face of capitalist businesses today—in effect comprehensively extending the process of bureaucratic control throughout the workplace while encouraging worker compliance. The central economic goal remains the same: a higher intensity of labour and a corresponding increase in surplus value.

CONCLUSION

The twists and turns in the development of Marxist value theory have a dual purpose: to explain the market prices of commodities and to explain the capital–labour relationship. There is an obvious connection. Because labour power is itself a commodity, its price is determined in the market. The difference between that price and the total value of production shapes the overall amount of profit that capitalist firms make. Employers and employees have a fundamental conflict of interest over the relative size of these wage and profit shares (and a yet more fundamental conflict of interest about a system that generates such pervasive conflict). So here we have a theory of the origin of profits in the exploitation of labour and an explanation of the economic drivers of class struggle.

Marxist political economy also draws particular attention to the struggle over the economic surplus. All economic systems need some sort of surplus—an excess of the value of what the workers produce over what is returned to them in the form of wages. That surplus is needed in order to make good the depreciation of machinery, to invest in new infrastructure, and to fund innovation. What is distinctive about capitalism—by comparison with the socialist system that Marxists have always advocated—is not the existence of a surplus, but *the control of that surplus by a particular class*. In this respect, capitalism does indeed have some continuity with slave and feudal modes of production. The size and disposition of the surplus reflects the exercise of the power of the dominant class in each case. Under socialism, Marx anticipated, the size and disposition of the surplus would be a matter for collective determination by the society as a whole.

CHAPTER 15

Capital Accumulation

What drives the capitalist economy?
Is economic growth inexorable?
How does the system change as it grows?

Previous chapters have shown how capitalism can be understood as a mode of production, and how its functioning depends crucially on the character of the capital–labour relationship. But the economy does not stand still while it is being studied. Trying to understand how capitalism works is made more complicated by its restless nature. It reproduces itself. It grows. It changes as it grows. A central focus of Marxist analysis is the process of capital accumulation that shapes these dynamics.

ECONOMIC GROWTH AND CAPITAL ACCUMULATION

The great historical achievement of capitalism is the increase in productive capacity: the ability to produce vast quantities of a bewildering array of goods and services. As noted in chapter 5, it would be simplistic to assume that there is a necessary connection between this achievement and the increase of human happiness. Some of the things produced are of dubious merit. Some are destructive. And the distribution of the goods and services has commonly been so inequitable that more than two centuries of economic growth has not eradicated poverty, even within affluent nations. Still, notwithstanding these reservations, the overall expansion of production and consumption under capitalism has been spectacular in comparison with anything that happened before. The process continues, as new production technologies and new products are developed, and consumerism becomes the predominant culture.[1]

The driving force of growth in a capitalist economy is the *accumulation of capital*. Individual businesses seek profit and, if successful, usually invest at least some of the profits in expanding the firm's output and market share. It is by increasing the amount of capital under their control that individual businesses grow. So it is for the economy as a whole: the overall rate of economic growth depends on the rapidity of the capital accumulation process.

So, what conditions are conducive to the accumulation of capital? The classical political economists pondered this question. Marxist economics offers two different responses. One involves the use of a formal *quantitative* model of the process of reproduction and growth based on a two-sector model of the economy. The other involves an examination of the *qualitative* aspects of the capital accumulation process, emphasising how the system changes as it grows over time.

A model of reproduction and growth

Marx developed a model based on the simple division of the capitalist economy into two sectors: Department 1, comprising the industries producing capital goods; and Department 2, comprising the industries producing consumer goods.

Capital goods are distinctive in that they are usually purchased only by other capitalist businesses. They comprise products like steel, aluminium, heavy engineering products, and machine tools. Consumer goods, on the other hand, are things that you and I might buy, ranging from foodstuffs to clothing, from houses to the sundry consumer durables people put in houses, from cars to watches, and from stereos to cameras. The distinction between capital and consumer goods is not always clear in practice since some products, such as personal computers, may be bought either for business investment or for personal consumption by individuals. However, as a rough-and-ready distinction, it can be quite useful for understanding the reproduction and growth of the economy.

Box 15.1 shows the formal model of how an economy can reproduce itself. The key element is the *necessary balance between the two departments producing capital and consumer goods*. If the economy is to reproduce itself, the output of the capital goods industries must be wholly purchased by the capitalist businesses making capital goods and/or consumer goods; and the capitalists and the workers, together, must have sufficient income to purchase all the output of the consumer goods industries. If not, there will be a glut in one or other of the departments, leading businesses to cut their outputs for the next time period.

For these conditions to hold, it is essential that capitalists *not* spend all their income on luxury consumption. Were they to do so, they would not be buying capital goods, so the capital goods industries would not be able to sell their products. On the other hand, if the capitalists spent *only* on capital goods, there would be a strong likelihood that the capacity of the economy to produce consumer goods would outstrip the demand for them. It is important that capitalists strike the right balance between consumption and investment. Whether they actually do so in practice depends on whether the price system sends the necessary signals to producers in the two main economic sectors to synchronise their production decisions—or on a liberal slab of pure luck.

The necessary condition for the *expansion* of the economy is yet more exacting. Growth requires that capitalists be abstemious, refraining from immediate consumption spending and instead ploughing more of their profits back into the purchase of capital goods. That makes possible the expansion of the industries in Department 1, which in turn makes possible the expansion of industries in Department 2. Remember, though, that the Department 2 industries will only seek to increase their productive capacity if their managers perceive a growing demand for their products. It is rather a 'knife-edge' condition, where either too much or too little investment in expanding productive capacity undermines the requirements for capital accumulation and growth. The periodic failure to meet that condition is one of the causes of economic crisis, as will be discussed in chapter 17.

Box 15.1

A two-sector Marxist economic model

The total value of goods and services produced in each industry in a capitalist economy has three components: constant capital (c), variable capital (v), and surplus value (s). Constant capital is the contribution of capital goods, like plant and machinery. It is 'constant' in the sense that the value created by labour in making those goods flows through to the products they help to make, without any additional value being created. In monetary terms, constant capital is the cost of depreciation of the plant and machinery. The variable capital is the direct contribution of the workforce. It is variable because new labour creates new value. In monetary terms, the variable capital is represented by the wage bill that the employer pays. The third item, surplus value, is that part of the total value created that is appropriated by the employer. In monetary terms, it is represented most directly as profit.

Dividing the industries into two groups according to whether they produce capital goods (Department 1) or consumer goods (Department 2):

$$\text{Department 1: total value} = c_1 + v_1 + s_1$$

$$\text{Department 2: total value} = c_2 + v_2 + s_2$$

Two conditions must be met if the economy is to reproduce itself. The first is that the value of capital goods used up in the production process during any time period ($c_1 + c_2$) must be matched by new expenditures on capital goods ($c_1 + v_1 + s_1$):

$$c_1 + c_2 = c_1 + v_1 + s_1$$

If this condition is met, the productive capacity of industry is maintained.

The second condition is that the total disposable incomes of the workers ($v_1 + v_2$) and the capitalists ($s_1 + s_2$) should equal the value of the output of consumer goods ($c_2 + v_2 + s_2$):

$$v_1 + v_2 + s_1 + s_2 = c_2 + v_2 + s_2$$

If this condition is met, all the commodities made will be sold.

Cancelling terms that appear on both sides of these equations, both conditions reduce to $c_2 = v_1 + s_1$. In words, the constant capital used in making consumer goods is just matched by the variable capital and surplus value in the capital goods industries. If this condition is met, the capacity of the economy to produce goods and services in the next time period will be the same as it was in the preceding one. The economy can reproduce itself.

GROWTH AND CHANGE

The capital accumulation process involves quantitative change: increase in the volume of productive capacity and in the size of the economic surplus. It also involves *qualitative* change: processes of institutional adaptation that make further economic growth possible. From a Marxian perspective, three aspects of qualitative change are particularly significant: (1) the changing form of the reserve army of labour, (2) the concentration and centralisation of capital, and (3) the process of imperialism.

The reserve army of labour

Capital accumulation typically generates an increase in the demand for labour. Larger outputs of goods and services usually require more workers to make them. Whether the rate of increase in the demand for labour is equivalent to the increase in output, or proportionately less, depends on the method of production—whether it is labour-intensive or capital-intensive. Either way, any increase in the demand for labour may cause *rising wage rates*. From a capitalist perspective, any such wage rise creates the unwelcome possibility that it will cut into surplus value and thereby reduce profits.

What can prevent this from happening? Thomas Malthus famously claimed that population growth would do so. The growth in the supply of labour, he thought, would continually outstrip the demand for labour, forcing the prevailing wage rate back to a mere subsistence level. The 'insatiable lusts of the masses' would thereby prevent wages encroaching on the economic surplus. Marx called this a libel on the human race.[2] What keeps wages in check, he argued, is something internal to capitalism itself: the continual recreation of a reserve army of labour.

In general terms, this reserve army of labour comprises those members of the working class who are unemployed or intermittently employed.[3] The existence of this 'relative surplus population', Marx claimed, keeps wages at subsistence level. If the members of the reserve army are willing to work for rock-bottom wages, employed workers cannot easily gain significant wage rises because capitalist employers can always draw from the reserve army to replace their existing employees. So, the existence of the reserve army keeps wages down and profits up.

Herein lies a paradox. Leaving people unemployed is not an altogether rational state of affairs for capitalists: unemployed people, unlike people at work, are not creating surplus value for their employers. However, the Marxist argument is that the unemployed people may make an equally important contribution to capitalist interests—by keeping the brake on other workers' wage rises. No permanent balance exists. A rapid burst of capital accumulation may result from a new technological innovation or from the opening up of a new market. On those occasions, the reserve army is diminished, and wages may indeed rise at the expense of surplus value. However, as Marx pointed out, 'as soon as this diminution touches the point at which the surplus labour that nourishes capital is no longer supplied in normal quantity, a reaction sets in: a smaller part of the revenue is capitalised, accumulation lags and the movement of rise in wages receives a check'.[4] Capitalists in general would prefer this not to happen because it means that the reserve army is replenished at the expense of economic growth. They would rather the normal reduction in the number of unemployed people due to economic growth be offset by new sources of potential workers replenishing the reserve army.

In Marx's own time, the principal sources of the reserve army were *peasants* displaced from their traditional livelihood on the land and *artisans* displaced by mechanisation. These people—victims of what we would now rather politely call 'structural economic change'—swelled the growing ranks of the potential working class. Desperate for employment, they usually moved to the growing industrial towns.

Such social upheavals continue in the poorer developing nations today, as people move from rural areas to the burgeoning cities in quest of whatever work they can find. However, in the more advanced capitalist nations, the potential sources of a reserve army have changed over the last half century. *Women*, previously excluded from many areas of employment and told that their proper place was 'in the home', have increasingly participated in paid work. Indeed, paid work has become the norm, although women's employment remains disproportionately concentrated in casual and part-time jobs, often without employment security. These are distinctive reserve army characteristics. The spectacular growth in the numbers of *immigrant* workers can also be interpreted in similar terms. In Europe, millions of 'guest-workers' have swelled the workforce; while in the United States, millions of illegal immigrants from Central America have been willing to work for much lower wages than those paid to American citizens. The internationalisation of capital has been accompanied by a significant internationalisation of labour supply, notwithstanding the border controls that individual nation states seek to enforce. As a consequence, the 'reserve army' function has been displaced significantly to immigrants.[5]

So, while its character and composition have changed over time, the reserve army of labour has enduring relevance in modern capitalism. Indeed, it seems that we are already witnessing a further wave of change: the development of a youth reserve army. Large numbers of young people, who in an earlier age might have expected 'career' jobs, are now concentrated in casual, low-paid jobs without security. They are increasingly assuming the reserve army characteristics. Generally, the emphasis on 'workforce flexibility' in modern capitalist businesses has strong echoes of the reserve army requirement: workers in an increasingly insecure economic environment are effectively forced into competition for their continued employment. The resulting downward pressure on wages helps businesses keep their production costs down.

Concentration and centralisation of capital

The accumulation of capital also tends to be accompanied by changes in the organisation of capital. Individual capitalist businesses generally grow larger, seeking to increase their scale of production. This is what Marx called the *concentration of capital*. Concurrently, firms often combine through mergers and takeovers, a process that Marx termed the *centralisation of capital*. These are important qualitative changes accompanying the quantitative growth process. They have significant consequences for the nature of work, the rate of technological change, and the growth of monopoly power.

The consequential changes in *the nature of work* are partly a matter of scale. Being employed in big factories rather than small workshops, or in big rather than small offices, often significantly changes working conditions. However, big business does not necessarily mean big workforces in big workplaces: many capitalist enterprises continue to have only a handful of employees. The fundamental point is the rationalisation of the labour process itself. This is not simply a matter of having a more complex division of labour, as in Adam Smith's famous example of the pin factory. It is, in Marx's own words, 'the progressive transformation of isolated processes of production carried on in accustomed ways into socially combined and scientifically managed processes of production'.[6] The adoption of 'scientific management' and of systems of technical and bureaucratic control (as noted in box 14.1) are twentieth-century examples. These practices tend to change the nature of employment experiences and to enhance the capacity of employers to extract surplus value.

The concentration and centralisation of capital also tends to accelerate *technological change*. To quote Marx again, 'centralisation, by thus accelerating and intensifying the effects of accumulation, extends at the same time the revolution in the technical composition of capital which increases its constant part at the expense of its variable part and thereby reduce the relative demand for labour'.[7] This process is not inexorable; experience shows that smaller firms are sometimes more technologically progressive than larger ones. However, the centralisation of capital does generate the resources that make major investments in innovation possible. Historically, the trends towards rapid technological change and the concentration and centralisation of capital have run in tandem.

The growth of *monopoly power* has been a predictable accompaniment. The larger firms usually have more control over the prices of their products because the size of their market share makes them less vulnerable to competitive pressures. Sometimes they collude with one another for these purposes. Their economic power can also be used politically to pressure governments to change business regulations or tax rates in order to advantage particular corporate interests. Thus, the concentration and centralisation of capital has enormous political economic significance. It tends to change the balance of power between capitalist business enterprises answerable to their financial backers and the institutions of government supposedly embodying democratic principles.

Some contemporary Marxists use the term 'monopoly capitalism' to draw attention to these trends.[8] They contend that the process of capital accumulation has fundamentally transformed the nature of capitalism—from an economic system based on competition to one in which the use and abuse of monopoly power is its most pervasive and distinctive characteristic. Others argue the contrary, that global expansion has been associated with the breakdown of local monopolies, leading to greater competition between capitalist enterprises on a world scale.[9] Either way, there is no doubt that the capital accumulation process has wrought significant qualitative change in the institutional character of the capitalist economy.

Imperialism

The process of capital accumulation shapes the nature of the international economy significantly. Herein lies an important connection with the processes of imperialism. Of course, it is possible for capital accumulation to take place within a locality or within a nation, but in practice it tends to break down those spatial constraints on economic activity. Capitalist businesses trawl the globe for the cheapest available labour or raw materials. They also seek out new markets in other regions or nations to provide outlets for their growing production of goods and services. They may also seek to minimise taxes by 'shopping around' for the countries with the lowest tax rates so that they can locate their activities there—or at least to make it appear that their profits are generated there. 'Shopping around' for the locations with the least restrictive environmental regulations has a similar corporate logic. Having a 'global reach'—or having 'the world as your oyster'—thereby increases the range of business options. Not surprisingly, a tendency towards *geographical expansion* is one of the inherent features of the capitalist economy.

Historically, this process of international expansion has been associated with relationships of *domination* that constitute imperialism. Territorial conquest and colonial exploitation have been its hallmarks. Serving the requirements of the dominant classes in the major metropolitan capitalist nations has been the driving force. It is interesting to note that the empire-builders themselves were sometimes not at all coy about this. For example, Cecil Rhodes, a pioneer in the imposition of British imperialism in Africa during the nineteenth century, stated the goals of imperialism as clearly as any Marxist might. In his own words:

> We must find new lands from which we can easily obtain raw materials and at the same time exploit the cheap slave labour that is available from the natives in the colonies; the colonies would also provide a dumping ground for the surplus goods produced in our factories; the Empire, as I have always said, is a bread and butter question. If we want to avoid class struggle in the United Kingdom, we must become imperialists.[10]

Lenin, the father of the Russian revolution, wrote of imperialism as 'the highest stage of capitalism'.[11] He saw it as a process shaped by a number of interconnected features:

- several advanced capitalist nations competing for world markets
- *monopoly capital* being the dominant organisational form of capital
- considerable exporting of *capital*, not just trading in goods and services
- severe *rivalry* occurring in world markets, leading alternately to cut-throat competition and the development of international monopoly combines
- the world economy being *territorially divided*.

This last feature was particularly pronounced at the time Lenin was writing. By the start of the twentieth century, the British, French, Dutch, Spaniards, Portuguese, and Belgians had carved up much of the world among themselves. Africa, less than 10 per cent of which had been under external dominion in 1875, was almost completely partitioned by the European nations over the next quarter of a century. Such imperialist processes were accompanied by ruthless forms of oppression and militarism. It was this situation about which Lenin wrote.

There are both continuities and discontinuities between the situation then and now. The United States effectively took over from the European states as the leading imperialist power, but the US has usually based its dominance, particularly in Latin America, on having compliant satellite states rather than colonies.[12] There are also significant differences between the classical form of imperialism described by Lenin and its characteristic modern forms. Instead of Third World nation states being dominated by individual advanced capitalist nations, the contemporary face of imperialism is of *transnationalised domination by global institutions*. Transnational corporations, supported by international agencies such as the International Monetary Fund and the World Bank, play a dominant role in the economies of the poorer nations in particular, strongly influencing their possibilities of economic development. So, here too we can see that the accumulation of capital has given rise to qualitative change—from classical imperialism to its modern form as 'imperialism without colonies'.[13]

CONCLUSION

Marxist economic analysis emphasises that growth is integral to capitalism. It is not simply a matter of the economy becoming bigger: the capital accumulation process also drives qualitative change. Some of the most important historical changes have been in the form of the reserve army of labour, the concentration and centralisation of capital, and the character of imperialism.

The growth process opens up more and more opportunities for profit. As Humphrey McQueen puts it, 'the essence of capitalism is capital's need to expand'.[14] However, capital accumulation is not unproblematic for capitalist businesses. As illustrated by Marx's two-sector growth model, the necessary conditions for the achievement of coordinated expansion can be quite elusive. There is a permanent tension between capitalists' 'desire for enjoyment and the drive for self-enrichment' manifest in the relationship between luxury consumption and productive investment.[15] Whether the economic system rides out such problems depends substantially on its capacity to meet the requirements for the continued circulation of capital. It is with these matters that the following chapter is concerned.

CHAPTER 16

Reproduction, Growth, Change

What is the circuit of capital?
How can we use this notion to understand how the economy functions and expands?
How has capitalism adapted in practice to meet these conditions?

The task of understanding how the economy works requires stepping back from some of its day-to-day features in order to discern the broader forces shaping its development. We need to see how the various parts of the economic system fit together and how they relate to the social and political institutions characteristic of capitalism.

A distinctive Marxian approach to understanding capitalism in its entirety can be constructed on the basis of a theory of the circuit of capital. This chapter presents a simple version of this model to show how capitalism works as an integrated system.

THE CIRCUIT OF CAPITAL

Think of a young person setting up a small firm (to make surfboards, glove puppets, or jewellery, for example). He or she would normally begin with capital in money form (perhaps the result of past savings, or a loan from friends or a bank). That money can be used to rent business premises, buy raw materials, and hire labour. Production can then be undertaken, at which stage his capital takes the form of some as yet unsold commodities. If all goes well, those commodities can then be sold, thereby transforming the capital back into monetary form—the sales revenue. If that final amount of capital is greater than the initial capital, the business has made a profit.

Successfully completing this 'circuit of capital' makes it possible for the business to undertake another round of production. Indeed, the next round of production can be on a larger scale, if the young person is able to hire the necessary additional means of production and labour power, manage the expanded production process, and find markets for the increased number of commodities produced. That being so, the business has reproduced itself and created the potential for further growth. The circuit of capital has been completed and capital accumulation can proceed apace.

A similar process occurs in the capitalist economy as a whole—looking at it as if it were a single firm writ large. The steps involved in the circuit of capital are formally represented in box 16.1. This way of setting up the issue enables us to see how the necessary conditions for capital accumulation are met in practice.[1] It is a means of drawing together a number of themes from preceding chapters in order to illuminate the working of the economy as an integrated system. It directs our attention to five necessary conditions: (1) minimising production costs, (2) generating surplus value, (3) realising that surplus value in a monetary form as profits, (4) circulating capital rapidly, and (5) ensuring economic and social reproduction. We consider each in turn.

Box 16.1

The circuit of capital

The circuit of capital can be represented as a sequence, as follows:

$$M–C\overset{LP}{\underset{MP}{<}}...[P]...C'–M'$$

M denotes the initial capital in a monetary form.
C denotes capital in the form of commodities used for producing commodities.
LP is labour power.
MP is means of production.
P is production.
C' denotes capital in the form of the output of commodities.
M' denotes capital in a monetary form after the sale of the produced commodities.
M' > M, the difference being the surplus value generated during the production process.
The dashes represent the movement of capital: they are *not* minus signs.

The point of this model is to show how capital expands as a result of the successful completion of the various stages in the production process. The amount of expansion (M' > M) is equivalent to the surplus value generated during production, as described in the preceding chapter.

This model of the circuit of capital can now be used to identify the five necessary conditions for capital accumulation, as follows:

1 minimising costs (in the M—C stage of the circuit of capital)
2 producing surplus value (in the M ... [P] ... C' stage)
3 realising surplus value (in the C' — M' stage)
4 rapid circulation of capital (the 'dashes' between M, C, C' and M')
5 economic and social reproduction (underpinning the whole process).

MINIMISING PRODUCTION COSTS

As every business manager knows, it is important to keep costs of production down by finding the cheapest labour, raw materials, and equipment appropriate for the particular task at hand. The last phrase here is an important reminder that minimising costs is always relative to a given quality and quantity of output. So, it is not necessarily a matter of 'buying cheap' at the expense of product quality (although this is common enough) but of avoiding unnecessary costs and waste. How is this to be done?

Extending the geographical area from which resources are drawn is one means. If firms can shop around the globe for labour, machinery, and raw materials, this can help them to minimise their costs (although it may simultaneously impose other costs on the community). Their capacity to shop around may also intensify the competitive character of the economic environment, causing suppliers to drive their prices downward. The cost of transportation limits this process to some extent, as there may be a trade-off between lower resource costs and higher transport costs. However, in general, increased *internationalisation of production* is conducive to minimising the overall costs of production for capitalist businesses.

Firms may also reduce the costs of labour through hiring people from 'minority' groups at lower wage rates. If women can be employed more cheaply than men to do similar work, if black people can be employed more cheaply than white, or if young workers can be hired at lower wages than adults, it is in the immediate interest of the firms to exploit those inequalities. Historically, *racial and sexual discrimination* in labour markets has been a significant means of keeping wage costs down, although governments have increasingly implemented regulations to limit such practices.

The presence of unemployment is also conducive to keeping costs to a minimum. In the absence of strong trade unions or regulatory mechanisms, competition among workers for jobs tends to drive wage levels downwards. Where there are significant levels of unemployment, this tendency may be accentuated. So, as noted in the preceding chapter, the interest of capitalist employers are served by having a *reserve army of labour*. By the same token, therein lies a significant social and economic waste.

GENERATING SURPLUS VALUE

Firms need to organise their production processes so as to ensure propitious conditions for extracting surplus value. This is the second condition for the viability of capitalist enterprises. Surplus value is the source of profit. How are firms to ensure it is kept at a high level? Clearly, keeping down production costs—wage costs in particular—is an important element. Businesses are understandably concerned to ensure that not all the value created by producing goods and services is returned to workers as wages. It is equally important for capitalist firms to ensure a high volume and value of goods and services produced. The rate of surplus value—the total surplus value divided by total wages—is the indicator of their success in this aspect of the circulation and accumulation process.

Raising the *productivity of labour* is one means by which capitalist businesses can ensure a high rate of surplus value, so long as the labour productivity gains are not matched by fully corresponding wage rises. Employers have a collective interest in training and retraining workers with this goal in mind. However, because there is always the possibility of workers moving to other employers, this collective interest is not always perceived and acted on by individual employers. They may prefer to 'poach' skilled workers from elsewhere rather than undertake the long-term commitment of training. So, governments often act on behalf of the collective interests of capitalist employers, providing the education and training facilities from which capitalists as well as workers collectively benefit.

Policies to raise the *intensity of labour* have an even more direct effect on the rate of surplus value. Prevailing upon workers to work harder, faster, or smarter is a key concern for capitalist employers. It may be achieved through various types of management strategy, as summarised in box 14.1.

Mechanisation of the production process may also contribute to higher surplus value. Equipping workers with more technologically advanced means of production usually raises the volume and/or value of output. Whether it actually raises the rate of surplus value depends on the cost of the machinery and on whether higher wage rates have to be paid to ease the acceptance of the more mechanised production. Mechanisation tends to reduce the relative importance of direct labour in the production process. However, it is pertinent to recall that, from a Marxian perspective, labour is the source of value from which surplus value derives. Therein lies a potential contradiction, suggesting that what is rational for one capitalist enterprise may not be in the interests of capital as a whole.

REALISING SURPLUS VALUE

The immediate problem confronting capitalist businesses is selling the goods and services produced. Surplus value is never realised in a monetary form as profit unless the products are actually sold. Not surprisingly, then, much individual capitalist business activity goes into marketing products as well as making them. For the capitalist economy as a whole, the overall economic conditions must be conducive to the effectiveness of such marketing efforts. This means that there must be a high overall demand for goods and services to match the growing volume of the goods and services produced. How is this requirement met?

Fundamentally, markets must be created. Historically, the development of capitalism as an economic system has done this through the *commercialisation of social life*. Education and health services have been made into saleable items, for instance, and music and sport have become focal points for commercial enterprise, not purely means of personal fulfilment. New avenues for profit-making and capital accumulation are thereby created.

Meanwhile, the *sales effort* by capitalist businesses is undertaken to ensure that demand is maximised in both new and existing markets. For the individual firm, this is usually a matter of maintaining or expanding market share. However, when all firms are simultaneously engaged in such practices, the effect is to intensify the culture of 'consumerism', in which commodity consumption is glamorised and represented as the means to personal satisfaction. The sales effort by individual firms generates, in effect, a demand-creation industry. Advertising becomes increasingly sophisticated, sometimes playing on fears (of lack of personal freshness, of social rejection, or of sexual failure, for example) and then showing the product that will remove that anxiety. Luxury consumption, often involving products that have *built-in obsolescence* or are based on engineered, short-term waves of fashion, is vigorously promoted as markets for basic necessities become saturated. Markets are extended internationally. Tobacco companies, for example, have sought new territories as their principal existing markets come to be increasingly constrained by health regulations, while companies producing baby foods have sought to persuade women in the poorer nations to switch from breastfeeding to more 'modern' formula-feeding. The quest to realise surplus value evidently has enormous social implications.

So does the extension of *credit facilities* that has occurred alongside these marketing efforts. The capacity to consume, as well as the willingness to consume, determines the level of demand. That is why credit is so important: it enables people to consume in excess, or at least in advance, of their income. The market for houses, for example, depends overwhelmingly on such credit facilities, without which few people would ever have the savings to buy such an expensive item outright. A wide range of consumer durables are also based on ready access to loan finance. The introduction of credit cards has been a major factor facilitating this, and commercial institutions are relentless in seeking further avenues for the proliferation of credit facilities. Importantly, while this facilitates the realisation of surplus value, it also adds to the potential instability of the economy. This is linked to the role financial institutions play generally in relation to the circulation of capital.

THE RAPID CIRCULATION OF CAPITAL

The annual rate of return on capital is higher if investments quickly generate profits that can then be reinvested. The rapid circulation of capital is therefore in the interests of those who own and control productive capitalist businesses. What this means, in terms of box 15.1, is that the movements of capital between its successive stages (M, C, C' and M') should be, as far as possible, unimpeded. Blockages on the road to capital accumulation must be removed.

The image of the road in this context is particularly apt because *improvements in transport technologies* have been a major contributor to facilitating the rapid circulation of capital in its physical forms—as raw materials, machinery, labour power, and outputs of finished products. It is not simply a matter of more and better roads to permit faster movement of goods and people. Historically, the construction of canals and railways was crucial to capitalist development; recently, larger freighters, container shipping, and air cargo have also made significant contributions. The common element is the role of transport technology in extending the terrain of capital. Improvements in *information* technology are currently further overcoming the 'tyranny of distance'.

Urbanisation can also be interpreted as speeding the circulation of capital. As such, urbanisation is functional for capitalism. This is not to say that it is unproblematic. On the one hand, it brings different elements in the production and consumption process into greater spatial proximity. This is ongoing, for spatial change continues to produce new forms of regional specialisation. On the other hand, as cities grow and become more congested, impediments to rapid circulation may reassert themselves. So, there are potential contradictions here: overcoming some impediments to the circulation of capital can create new ones.

The role of *banks and other financial institutions* is also relevant in this context since they are a means whereby the rapid circulation of capital is achieved. One effect of their activities is to facilitate the movement of capital between its physical and monetary forms. Think, for example, of a small manufacturer of, say, bicycles. A protracted period of bad weather may temporarily undermine the demand for her product. This will cause a crisis because the cash flow is inadequate to meet the ongoing costs of rent, wages, and so forth. So, she requests a loan from a bank. The bank manager, noting that the manufacturer has a warehouse full of bicycles that can be expected to sell again when the weather improves, accedes to the request. The manufacturer stays in business, pays the interest on the loan, and eventually repays it in full when the stock of bicycles is sold. The bank has helped the firm bypass a bottleneck that might otherwise have caused business failure.

Not all relationships between productive and financial institutions are as harmonious as this. Indeed, as noted in chapter 4, some political economists see the growth of financial capital as partly undermining productive capital, channelling funds into speculative activities and adding to the instability of the system. However, the example presented here is a reminder of the general importance of finance in the capital accumulation process. Financial institutions do not themselves create value, according to Marxist analysis, but are crucial for the capacity of modern capitalism to reproduce the conditions for capital accumulation.

ECONOMIC AND SOCIAL REPRODUCTION

Yet more fundamental are those institutions that underpin and legitimise the capitalist system itself. Like any economic system, capitalism depends on the capacity and willingness of people to make it work. In other words, it has systemic requirements for its own reproduction. The workforce must be continually regenerated. The underlying capital–labour class relationships must either be seen as acceptable by the various participants in the production process or there must be mechanisms for their enforcement. The people as a whole must regard the economic arrangements as tolerable, if not the best of all possible worlds. Herein lie some complex interconnections between the capitalist economy and the institutions of modern capitalist society.

Consider *the family*, for example. The simple biological reproduction of the workforce does not require any particular family structure but, as Marxist feminists have frequently pointed out, the conventional sexual division of labour within households tends to serve the needs of capital. Children are reproduced, nursed, and educated mainly by women and usually at no direct cost to the capitalist employers. Yet, the employers eventually benefit from those 'domestic' processes by having a healthy and appropriately disciplined workforce. We return to this issue in chapter 36. It will suffice to note here that the structure of the household, ostensibly standing 'outside' the marketed production processes of the capitalist economy, may be crucial for the capitalist economy's reproduction.

Similar considerations apply to *the state*. Do the institutions of the modern state constitute a non-capitalist sphere of society? At first, it might seem so. Their presence is commonly justified by the need to have institutions concerned with social goals broader than the ones capitalist businesses normally address. Their rationale and organisation need not be directly geared to the accumulation of capital. However, as Marxists have often emphasised, the state in a capitalist society operates within the constraints of that economic system and may be interpreted as directly serving it. The *ideological state apparatus* is a term sometimes used in this context. It draws attention to the role of the state in the dissemination of ideologies that reinforce the existing economic and social order—ideologies about the importance of private property rights, for example. The ideological state apparatus may be defined very widely to include not only the institutions of government but also the churches, the media, and the education system. Within such institutions, there are many dissident, even anti-capitalist, voices, but the actions of such institutions are usually supportive of the prevailing economic and social order; if they were not, political destabilisation would be a recurrent possibility.

If the ideological state apparatus does not work effectively, the *repressive state apparatus* may be mobilised. This is far from exceptional. Every society, other than an anarchist society based on voluntary cooperation, has some sort of back-up system of a coercive nature. The legal system, the police, the armed forces, the prison system, and the intelligence agencies are its usual key elements. What is distinctive about capitalism, according to Marxist reasoning, is the way in which these institutions serve particular class interests. The legal system may help in the settlement of interpersonal disputes, and the police may provide social protection or facilitate traffic flows, but their broader socioeconomic function is the enforcement of property rights. Is this repressive? This role of the state apparatus is usually relatively uncontentious in liberal capitalist societies, except at times when coercion is used for particular class purposes, such as when police or defence force personnel are used as strike-breakers. However, many capitalist nations have more authoritarian traditions and structures; imprisoning political dissidents and deploying the military against civilians have been commonplace in many nations in the Americas, Asia, and Africa. Therein lies an obvious tension: in so far as the political economic system manifestly depends on its forced imposition, its legitimacy is undermined.

CONCLUSION

Capitalism is an adaptable economic system. It has its own systemic needs, which can be understood in terms of a Marxist model of the circuit of capital. These needs are five-fold: minimising costs, managing production, marketing products, rapidly circulating capital, and reproducing the economic and social order. Capitalism has been remarkably successful in meeting these systemic requirements. It has adapted diverse institutions for these purposes, wreaking massive transformations in technology, the organisation of work, social structure, and ideology.

These adaptations have not generally been the product of a master plan. No assertions about conspiracy are necessary. The adaptations have largely been the product of decisions by the owners and managers of individual capitalist enterprises pursuing their own self-interest. Politicians and bureaucrats have usually played supportive roles, but generally fallen short of providing coherent, long-term economic planning. The adaptations of the capitalist system as a whole have been the outcome of responses to changed historical circumstances and driven mainly by the imperative of profit-seeking. It is somewhat ironic that we can use a Marxist model to understand the 'success' of capitalism in making these adaptations.

If is not a success story in all respects. As noted throughout this chapter, the systemic requirements and the adaptations involve numerous tensions: generating unemployment to restrict the power of labour constitutes a significant economic waste; reducing wages to lower production costs tends to undermine the demand for the commodities produced; developing financial institutions to facilitate the circulation of capital may lead to speculation that steers capital away from productive uses; and heavy-handed measures by the state to ensure social control can undermine the perceived legitimacy of the system. These tensions inhibit the achievement of any comfortable 'equilibrium' outcome. Indeed, the picture painted here is one of an economy beset with internal *contradictions*. The resulting stresses are manifest in uneven development—spatially and temporally. Some areas prosper while others decay; and periods of rapid capital accumulation and economic expansion are interrupted by periods of economic crisis.

CHAPTER 17

Economic Crises
Cycles or breakdown?

Why is economic growth periodically interrupted by economic crises?
Does this imply the breakdown of the system?
Can Marxism explain the survival, and continuing dominance, of capitalism?

Why should there ever be problems in an economic system in which capitalists put so much effort into the pursuit of profits, capital accumulation, and economic growth? The classical political economists were confident that such commercially motivated behaviour would produce generally positive economic outcomes. Marx disagreed, emphasising the distinctive flaws in the capitalist system that he predicted would lead to deepening crises and eventually capitalism's demise. This is not to say that capitalism cannot be a progressive economic order. Marx thought it was progressive in comparison to what had preceded it, helping to eradicate 'the idiocy of rural life'.[1] Capitalism has facilitated the phenomenal development of the forces of production. So, why might it be only a transient phase in human history, eventually yielding to a yet more progressive socioeconomic system?

The most remarkable of all Marxist claims is that capitalism will eventually be replaced by socialism. It is a claim that rests on distinctive views about the combination of structural forces and purposeful political activity capable of effecting that transformation. Elements of both 'structure' and 'agency' are integral to the process.

The structural aspect concerns *economic crises*. These are periods during which capital accumulation slows, the production of goods and services falls, and unemployment rises. 'Economic crisis', 'slump', 'depression', 'recession'—terms of varying emotive impact—all describe essentially the same phenomenon: economic downturn. Marx thought that capitalism would be afflicted with such periodic crises and, indeed, that these crises would likely deepen over time. Why? His reasoning rests on three distinct theories: the theory of disproportionalities, the theory of the tendency of the rate of profit to fall, and the theory of underconsumption.[2] It is useful to look at each of these theoretic explanations of economic crisis first, before asking how they interrelate, whether they do indeed explain economic crises in practice, and, if they do, what political responses might follow.

THE 'ANARCHY OF CAPITALIST PRODUCTION'

There is a recurrent possibility in a capitalist economy that the production decisions of firms in different industries will not be synchronised. Steel producers usually have to decide how much steel to produce before they know how much steel will be bought from them by car manufacturers, engineering firms, and their other customers. Car manufacturers, in turn, have to decide how many vehicles to produce without knowing (unless they engage in illegal industrial espionage) how many their competitors are planning to make. They cannot know for sure what their market share will be. Even the total market demand is uncertain; an unexpected event, such as a sharp rise in petrol prices, may cause consumer demand for cars to deviate from projections based on past trends. So, firms' production decisions, in the absence of industry-wide or economy-wide planning, do not necessarily produce a balance between supply and demand.

This situation has been described as the 'anarchy of capitalist production'. Anarchy in this context denotes an unplanned, quite likely chaotic, situation (not to be confused with 'anarchism', which is a coherent political philosophy emphasising the desirability of basing society on voluntary cooperation rather than state-sponsored coercion). The absence of a centralised planning mechanism in a capitalist economy is the source of the uncertainty, if not chaos. Such central planning mechanisms have their own problems, it should be noted, if only because of the sheer size and complexity of the task of coordination. Further, markets are not altogether chaotic: *the price mechanism* plays a coordinating role. If a steel producer makes too much steel, for example, the market price will fall, which will help sell the surplus steel and also signal the need to scale back production. The price system thereby restores some balance between output and demand. The problem is that it operates *after* the plans for steel production for the coming period have been made. In the interim, the imbalance may spiral into a generalised economic crisis.

Why might this occur? Consider the steel industry example again. If the steel producer makes too much steel, workers at the steel plant are likely to be laid off. Without income, these workers will not be likely to buy cars or washing machines, for instance. This will mean that the producers of such consumer goods will demand less steel from the steel producers. The laid-off workers will also have less income to spend on food or clothing, which will create economic downturn and unemployment in the food and clothing industries. So, a localised structural imbalance becomes a generalised recession. The original 'disproportionality' triggers an economic crisis.

The term *'disproportionality'* formally refers to imbalances between the two sectors in the model Marx developed to examine the necessary conditions for reproduction and growth of the economy (as depicted in box 15.1; see p. 122). Disproportionality implies that the condition for balance identified in that model ($c_2 = v_1 + s_1$) is not attained. It is perhaps remarkable that intersectoral balance is *ever* attained, other than by pure luck, in an economy like capitalism. Without coordinated economic planning, it would seem that disproportionality is likely, if not probable, most of the time. Therein lies a problem with this particular theory of economic crises: it seems too general. It leaves us wondering why capitalism is not usually, if not always, experiencing recession.

The value of disproportionality theory is its insight into the *transmission* process: it shows how a localised problem can trigger an economy-wide downturn. It shows how the price mechanism performs a corrective function when such a downturn does occur. As already noted, discounting unsold stock may help it to be sold. Fundamentally, the cheapening of capital will tend to restore the potential for future profitability. This is what Marxists call the 'devalorisation of capital'. The reduction in the value of capital helps raise the rate of profit because less capital now has to be laid out to achieve those profits. Recessions are painful for capitalists as well as workers: some capitalist enterprises are usually forced out of business altogether. However, Marxists regard the weeding-out of the more inefficient capitals as 'cleansing' the economy as a whole, thereby creating the conditions for renewed capital accumulation process. No gain without pain, it seems. The swelling of the ranks of the 'reserve army' of unemployed labour is also conducive to the enforcement of more discipline on the workforce. For all these reasons, a capitalist economy is likely to 'bounce back' from a recession brought on by structural imbalance or 'disproportionality'. Yet, according to a second strand of Marxist crisis theory, more fundamental problems remain.

THE TENDENCY OF THE RATE OF PROFIT TO FALL

Is the problem of recession deeply embedded in the capital accumulation process itself? This second strand of Marxist crisis theory posits that the more successfully capitalists accumulate capital, the greater the downward pressure on the rate of profit. Seeing their profit rates falling, capitalists will be less inclined to expand the productive capacity of their enterprises. Investment and output falls. An economic crisis occurs. Individual success causes systemic failure.

This paradox can be explained in various ways. Box 17.1 sets out the formal explanation, using some simple algebraic notation. The basic proposition is that the capital accumulation process tends to raise the organic composition of capital, which is the ratio of constant capital to variable capital. Broadly speaking, this means that capitalists install more machinery and equipment in the process of expanding their businesses. If the rate of surplus value remains unchanged, the rate of profits would then tend to decline. This is definitional, but what is the underlying economic logic? Recall that, according to the labour theory of value, labour produces value. So, if the process of capital accumulation causes less labour to be used in production (*relative* to capital goods such as plant, machinery, and equipment), the rate of profit will fall. The total amount of surplus value generated may well continue to rise but, expressed as a ratio of total capital outlaid (constant capital and variable capital), the rate of profit will decline.

One might wonder why capitalists would continue to accumulate capital and expand their businesses if the ultimate effect is to undermine their own rate of profit. It seems self-defeating. The best explanation of this paradox hinges on the tension between individual and collective rationality. It is indeed rational for individual capitalists to invest and expand, perhaps by installing the latest equipment in order to gain an advantage relative to their rivals. If their rivals follow suit, however, the advantage is eradicated. All the firms then face the common tendency for the rate of profit to fall. The source of capitalism's vitality—individual initiative in search of higher profits—becomes its Achilles heel as falling profit rates periodically herald recession.

Explained in this way, one might think that recession would not be an intermittent problem. The tendency for the rate of profit to fall could be expected to be even more persistent than the problem of sectoral 'disproportionality', perhaps destined to sound the death knell of the whole system. Indeed, Marx did expect this tendency of the rate of profit to fall to be manifest in intensifying economic crises over time, but he also conceded that there would be *offsetting forces*. Obviously, the rate of surplus value could rise. That would offset the effect of increases in the organic composition of capital. Of course, capitalists are always concerned to raise the rate of surplus value. If installing new machinery enables capitalist firms to increase the pace of work performed by their workforce, they thereby increase the intensity of labour. If the resulting increase in the rate of surplus value is proportionately larger than the increase in the organic composition of capital, the overall profit rate will actually rise. The crisis tendency is averted.

Other offsetting forces (or 'counteracting causes') noted by Marx included the effect of foreign trade in cheapening raw materials, the depression of wages below the value of labour power, and the cheapening of constant capital. The first of these—foreign trade—may provide a short-run counter to a falling profit rate.

Box 17.1

The mechanics of the falling rate of profit

As shown in box 15.1 (see p. 122), the total value of commodities produced $= c + v + s$

where c is constant capital

v is variable capital

s is surplus value

Three important ratios using these terms can be defined as follows:

s/v is the rate of surplus value (sometimes called the rate of exploitation)

c/v is the organic composition of capital

$s/(c + v)$ is the rate of profit.

This rate of profit can be expressed in terms of the rate of surplus value and the organic composition of capital by dividing each term in the numerator and denominator by v, that is:

$$\frac{s/v}{c/v + 1}$$

This is an alternative expression for the rate of profit, showing its positive relationship with the rate of surplus value (s/v) and its inverse relationship with the organic composition of capital (c/v).

Why does this rate of profit tend to fall as capital accumulation occurs? Consider the effect of a rise in c/v, caused by businesses installing more plant and machinery in their production processes. If s/v remains constant, any such rise in c/v depresses the rate of profit.

The assumption of a constant s/v is crucial to this reasoning. However, the assumption may be relaxed. Then the rate of profit may rise or fall depending on the relative size of changes in c/v and s/v. In other words, the rate of profit may fall (heralding a recession) or rise (heralding a period of expansion) according to the relative movements in the rate of surplus value and the organic composition of capital.

However, by drawing distant lands into the capitalist production process (what we would now call 'globalisation'), it ultimately reproduces the same systemic contradictions, but on a larger scale.

The second offsetting force—depression of wages—looks the most obvious counter to the falling rate of profit. Marx actually placed little stress on it because of the general assumption that all wages and prices are market-determined. Wages in general therefore reflect the value of labour power. However, where employers have particular monopoly power, and where the replenishment of the reserve army of labour weakens the bargaining position of labour, wage-cutting is always an option. That, too, may offset the tendency of the rate of profit to fall.

As for the third factor—cheapening of constant capital—it is important to remember that, in Marxist theory, the organic composition of capital is defined in terms of labour values, not market prices. So, if machinery and other capital goods are becoming relatively cheap in the market, increased mechanisation is possible without raising the organic composition of capital. In such circumstances, the overall rate of profit may be constant or even rising, and there need be no general tendency towards economic crisis.

An apparently weak conclusion beckons. The rate of profit may go up or down according to the relative strength of a rising organic composition of capital and these various offsetting forces. In other words, what starts out as a strong proposition about the inexorable tendency towards economic downturn ends up concluding that the outcome is contingent. Capital accumulation can create the conditions for recession, but, equally, it may create the conditions for yet more accumulation. But is this a weak conclusion? Capitalism does indeed alternate between periods of growth and recession. The Marxist theory suggests this pattern is explicable in terms of the relative movements in the rate of surplus value and the organic composition of capital.[3] The wave-like motion of capitalist development is thereby explained.

UNDERCONSUMPTION

What about consumers? Is the inadequacy of consumer spending relative to the vast growth in output of goods and services an alternative explanation of recurrent economic crises? Here is a third strand of reasoning about the cause of recurrent economic crises. It is not exclusively Marxist, reflecting a long-standing tradition of 'underconsumptionist' thought, and also having some echoes in the rather different types of analysis developed by John Maynard Keynes and Michal Kalecki to explain the problem of inadequacies in effective demand.[4] However, it has a central place in Marxist crisis theory. As Marx himself put it:

> the epochs in which capitalist production exerts all its forces are always periods of overproduction, because the forces of production can never be utilised beyond the point at which surplus value can be not only produced but also realised; but the sale of commodities, the realisation of the commodity capital and hence also of the surplus value, is limited not only by the consumption requirements of society in general, but by the consumption requirements of a society in which the great majority are poor and must always remain poor.[5]

An influential book by American Marxist economists Paul Baran and Paul Sweezy gives the reasoning a contemporary resonance. According to Baran and Sweezy, modern capitalism is *monopoly capitalism*.[6] The large companies that now dominate the economy have the power to simultaneously raise the prices of their products, sometimes colluding to do so. They also have the ability to lower their costs through technical innovation. A widening gap between prices and costs results, making possible an even greater economic surplus. The problem is who is to buy the goods. Capitalists try to keep workers' wages down, but thereby undermine the major source of potential consumer spending. Capitalists' own consumption can partly fill the gap, but the scope for this is limited because (as demonstrated in box 15.1) capitalists must channel a proportion of their funds into business investment if capital accumulation is to continue. Commercial advertising and the 'sales effort' is a major push, and the extension of credit facilities does enable consumers' spending to exceed their incomes, at least in the short run. Governments also 'do their bit' to pump up the aggregate demand through various forms of civilian and military expenditure, thereby helping to absorb the economic surplus. However, to the extent that these expenditures are financed by general taxation, they only divert expenditures from private to public sectors; the general problem of underconsumption remains. The root problem is the restricted purchasing power of the mass of the people, which prevents the growth of productive capacity being easily matched by a corresponding growth of demand.

Setting this underconsumptionist reasoning in the context of Marxist theory, a key conclusion is that it illustrates the *inherent tension between the conditions for the production and realisation of surplus value*. The production of surplus value requires low wages, whereas the realisation of surplus value is facilitated by having high wages. Low wages keep production costs down, but high wages help capitalists sell their products. From the viewpoint of an *individual* capitalist, the ideal solution is obvious enough: keep the wages of your own workers down but encourage other capitalists to pay high wages in order to generate a buoyant market demand for the output. However, if all capitalists seek that outcome, it will not add up. The tension is systemic. From the viewpoint of capitalists as a whole, wages are always simultaneously too high and too low. This is because wages have a *dual role*—as a cost of production and as a source of demand for goods and services. Oscillations in the level of economic activity are the result of capitalist firms, and governments acting on their behalf, wrestling with this contradiction.

ECONOMIC CRISES AND SOCIAL CHANGE

These three strands of Marxist crisis theory—emphasising disproportionalities, the tendency of the rate of profit to fall, and the problem of underconsumption—can all be applied to understanding downturns in the level of economic activity in the real world. While explanations for particular economic crises at specific times and in specific places cannot simply be 'read off' from these theories, they direct attention to key variables for analysis. A fuller understanding of particular crises then requires consideration of the historical context, the monetary factors associated with financial institutions, the role played by governments, the problems of inflation, the impact of international trade, and so forth. The Marxist analysis focuses on basic underlying conditions, rooted in the nature of capitalist production, but does not deny that other factors may play a part.[7]

An economic crisis does not necessarily herald the demise of capitalism. If it results in structural economic changes that foster conditions for renewed capital accumulation, slump turns into boom. It is rather like a crisis in your personal life: if you make the necessary adjustments to cope with it, life goes on—and may even be better than before. In the case of economic crises, the adjustments are often painful, usually involving the closure of businesses and the loss of jobs. However, if that weeding-out of 'inefficient' elements in the system results in a more dynamic economy, then capitalism moves again into an expansionary phase. Looked at from this perspective, a theory of periodic economic crises is not a theory of *system break-down*. It is an explanation of alternating booms and slumps—what orthodox economists more politely call the *business cycle*.

Whether it is sensible to retain an economic system whose structural contradictions cause recurrent recessions—not to mention alienation and class inequality—remains the big question. If enough people think not, and decide to do something about it, alternative political economic arrangements can be fashioned. This is where human 'agency' enters the story—as an instrument for change, operating alongside the 'structural' aspects we have been discussing. This is where the Marxian view turns towards the workers, not as victims of capitalist exploitation, but as the active agents of progressive social change. Marx anticipated that the working class, enlightened by radical intellectuals like himself, would bring about the *revolutionary* transformation from capitalism to socialism. More moderate reformers have anticipated and advocated more incremental changes to the economic system to reduce its tendency to fall into periodic economic crises. This view has been characteristic of Keynesian and institutional economists, as we will see in later chapters.

Marxists are usually sceptical of any such attempts to put 'band-aids' on the structural problems of capitalism. The fundamental flaw in the system that they identify, underlying each of the three strands of Marxist crisis theory, is that *economic crises are a feature of an economic system based on production for profit*. Crises arise whenever the conditions for profit are not present, whether because of structural imbalances, insufficient demand, or any other factor. At such times, unemployment and unfilled social needs coexist. Any genuinely rational economic system would mobilise the unemployed resources to make the goods and services to satisfy those needs. Capitalism does not do this because it is based on production for profit rather than production to directly satisfy human needs.

Therein lies the general Marxist case for moving from capitalism, with its inherent class conflicts and crisis-prone character, to a socialist alternative. Marx anticipated that the problems of recurrent economic crisis would fuel this revolutionary sentiment and bring more converts to the socialist cause. The final chapter in this book returns to the question of why this has not come to pass—or at least not yet—in the advanced capitalist nations.

CONCLUSION

Marxism provides a grand theory of the coexistence of cooperation and conflict within the structure of the capitalist economy. It emphasises the economy's essential dynamic and its fundamentally contradictory character. Workers and capitalists have to cooperate to win their 'daily bread' (and cake); but there is a fundamental conflict of interest, manifest in distributional struggles and crisis tendencies. In seeking to develop an analysis of these conditions, Marxist political economy presents us with some particularly distinctive propositions:

- profits come from the exploitation of labour
- growth comes from the accumulation of capital
- crises come from inherent contradictions in the system of production for profits
- conflict comes from the class structure
- change comes from class struggle.

This interpretation of capitalism is as contentious today as it was when it was first developed. Marx just will not lie down. Although his ideas were formulated in an early phase of capitalist development, they continue to have striking resonance today. Indeed, as long as capitalism exists, Marxism will be bound to be a major reference point for the analysis of its contradictions. Equally predictably, the Marxist interpretation of capitalism is hotly contested by those with a stake in maintaining the existing economic system. In the conventional teaching of economics, Marxism usually has a shadowy presence—if it is considered at all. Usually it is sidelined by the overwhelming emphasis on a quite different theory, that of neoclassical economics.

PART V

The Ideology of the Market

Neoclassical economics

CHAPTER 18

Free-market Economics
The foundations

Why study neoclassical economics?
What were the origins of this influential school of economic thought?
What support does this type of economic theory give to neo-liberalism today?

There is much more to capitalism than markets. There are underlying property rights and class relationships, economic activities by the state, and distinctive ideologies—as emphasised in chapter 6. However, a dominant, if not exclusive, focus on markets is characteristic of orthodox economics. The core of that orthodoxy throughout the last century has been neoclassical theory. Its exponents seldom use the term 'capitalism'. They implicitly represent the economy as a set of interconnected and self-regulating markets in which buyers and sellers freely interact without the need for substantial government regulation—indeed they work better in the absence of such regulation. This is a body of theory that has been particularly influential in the last couple of decades as a means of reshaping the role of government in the economy. It needs to be understood.

THE MARKET RULES

Why are markets held in such high regard by orthodox economists? The short answer is because they are thought to permit *mutually advantageous exchanges* and ensure the *efficient allocation of economic resources*. Markets allow consumers to 'shop around' for what suits them best, at a price they can afford. Producers seek to satisfy those consumer demands—producers whose goods are not favoured by consumers will go out of business. There is no coercion and no intervention by third parties to disrupt or impede the transactions between self-interested buyers and sellers. From this perspective, in the words of one textbook author, 'markets are the most effective as well as the most democratic mode of economic organisation that has yet been developed'.[1]

Underlying this faith in markets are two related assumptions: the *desirability of private property* and the *undesirability of a substantial role for the state* in economic affairs. These are the hallmarks of free-market ideology, most clearly expressed in neoclassical theory. Private property is favoured because it is the basis of the individual interests and incentives that drive a market economy. Collectively owned and managed property is held to be less conducive to the development of markets as the principal means of allocating economic resources. Similarly, a substantial role for the state in the economy is held to constitute an unwarranted 'intervention', likely to 'distort' patterns of resource allocation. The institutions of the state cannot know what serves individuals' interests as well as the individuals do themselves. Because the collective well-being of society is no more than the sum of individual well-beings, it is best to leave the individuals to organise their own transactions in the economic market place.

A variation on this theme emphasises the *dynamic* character of the market as its principal virtue. According to this view, markets encourage innovation and risk-taking, while penalising failure. A world of 'rugged individualism' provides the necessary incentives for economic progress; thus, the strength of the market economy is not that it necessarily produces an efficient allocation of resources at any time, but that it is conducive to change and growth. This view of the market is significantly different from the view of the market as an 'equilibrium' mechanism. It derives from the Austrian school of economic thought, most notably the work of Frederik von Hayek (1899–1992),one of the most controversial winners of the Nobel Prize in Economic Sciences.[2] However, it shares with neoclassical theory a strong belief in the market economy as the best of all possible worlds.

These pro-market economic theories have significant echoes of 'social Darwinism', emphasising the 'struggle for existence' and 'survival of the fittest' in producing a healthy society. Modern economists generally eschew any explicit connection with these principles, which were popular a century ago and were most clearly expounded by Herbert Spencer (1820–1903).[3] The implicit connection is still there, though. Because markets reward enterprise and weed out inefficiency, orthodox economists continue to hold them in high regard. By emphasising those features, neoclassical theory links up with general social beliefs—what Daniel Fusfeld calls 'the folklore of individualism'.[4] It links up with 'New Right' beliefs favouring 'free enterprise' and 'freedom of choice' and opposing 'politically motivated interventions' in economic affairs. As such, neoclassical economics is an intriguing blend of technical analysis and ideology.

THE ORIGINS OF NEOCLASSSICAL ECONOMICS

Neoclassical theory originated in the 1870s, when scholars, working independently in different countries, laid the foundations for a new paradigm of economic analysis. The most prominent among them were the English economist William Stanley Jevons (1835–82), the Austrian economist Carl Menger (1840–1921), and the Swiss economist Leon Walras (1834–1910). Earlier in the century, David Ricardo had steered economic analysis towards more abstract reasoning, paving the way for the theoretical model-building of orthodox economics. The neoclassical economists took this model-building further, narrowing the broad-ranging concerns of classical political economy to a formal analysis of individual economic behaviours and the functioning of markets.

Menger and Jevons simultaneously developed the basic principles of *marginal analysis*, still the essence of the neoclassical method today. Marginalism emphasises small adjustments, such as the adjustments a consumer might make in deciding which combinations of commodities might yield the greatest satisfaction. 'A little more of this and a little less of that', or 'a little more of that and a little less of this'—this incrementalism in individual choices is presented as the essence of economic decision-making. A rational consumer, one may surmise, will shift his or her spending between commodities until the utility, or satisfaction, given by each is equalised 'at the margin'.

Jevons also posited that the utility gained from consuming extra units of each commodity would diminish as more of it were consumed. This is the basic principle of *diminishing marginal utility*. The more you have of something, it is inferred, the less extra satisfaction results from having a little more of it. So, commodities that are abundant in supply generally command lower prices; consumers, experiencing diminishing marginal utility, are reluctant to pay much for additional units. Scarce commodities, on the other hand, are expensive, not necessarily because of the amount of labour that has gone into their production, but because they yield higher utility at the margin. Hence, diamonds are more highly priced than water—notwithstanding the fact that the latter is of greater importance to life. Marginal utility is decisive.

Walras developed a view of the economy as a whole that showed how consumers' decisions interlock with producers' decisions. Changes in consumers' purchasing patterns, it was argued, would change the prices of the goods and thereby change the amount of each that would be supplied in the market. Thus a web of intricate relationships would ensure the pattern of production would continuously adjust to the pattern of demand. Walras represented this interdependence in a mathematical model of the equilibrium conditions for an economy with numerous producers and consumers. It forms the basis of what is known as *general equilibrium theory*.[5]

These contributions constituted powerful theoretical innovations. Classical explanations of value, emphasising the role of labour, were refuted. Utility replaced labour values. As Menger put it, 'the value of goods arises from their relationship to our needs, and is not inherent in the goods themselves. With changes in this relationship, value arises and disappears'.[6] Concern with analysing the total economic surplus is jettisoned, along with the labour theory of value. Only individuals have surpluses, and these are of a psychological kind, such as when the utility derived from a commodity is over and above what the consumer had to pay for the commodity. The social perspective changes accordingly. The previous political economic concerns about classes, their competing interests, and the conditions for social progress—characteristic of both Marx's and the classical political economists' analyses—have no place in these new theories. Instead, the spotlight shifts to the behaviour of individuals and competitive markets, and to how consumers' demand influences prices and the allocation of resources.

A synthesis of these ideas, and further extensions and practical applications, was provided by Alfred Marshall (1842–1924). His *Principles of Economics*, first published in 1890, was the standard economics textbook in the first few decades of the twentieth century. Even today, it is possible to come across economists who claim that pretty much all worthwhile economic reasoning can be found in Marshall's text. It was certainly a significant achievement—blending the central concepts of marginal analysis with enduring ideas from classical political economy, adding some more practical concerns about industry and trade, and introducing (mainly in footnotes) a distinctive form of diagrammatic representation that has been widely used in orthodox economic analysis ever since. Marshall was not blind to the social problems that accompanied capitalist economic development in his time; however, his economic theory was, in essence, a sophisticated exposition of the self-adjusting mechanisms operating in a competitive market economy.

Box 18.1

Alfred Marshall (1842–1924)

Alfred Marshall was Professor of Economics at the University of Cambridge in England during a period when that university was renowned as a citadel of Victorian piety and temperance. In his inaugural lecture in 1885, Marshall set himself three tasks: to strengthen the scientific authority of economics, to align it with the Victorian moral and political mood, and to draw the best Cambridge men to the subject. During the twenty-three years he occupied the chair he energetically pursued these goals, and did so with considerable success.

As a mathematician, Marshall thought that economics would have greater potential for scientific development if it were detached from moral philosophy. He believed that mathematics should only be an adjunct to economic reasoning, however—used as a means of expressing economic ideas in clear writing.[7] Subsequent neoclassical theorists have tended to invert these priorities, defining the concerns of the subject in terms of analytical technique; in Marshall's work the mathematics and diagrams are usually in the footnotes, not in the body of the text.

Marshall's alignment with Victorian sentiments was evident in the way he sought to reconstruct economics to mirror the ethical aspirations of the enlightened middle class of his time. His political inclination was to favour incrementally raising the living standards of ordinary people, but only as part of a process of raising the moral tone of society, 'as capitalists and workers learnt to behave more honourably towards each other'.[8] He had some interest in socialism, but came to strongly oppose it. He was cautious about trade unionism and evidently feared the exercise of union power. Of the engineers' strike of 1887, he said, 'I want these people beaten at all costs: the complete destruction of Unionism would be … not too high a price'.[9]

His lectures did indeed attract able students. Marshall initially supported women's rights to study at the university—a contentious issue in the late nineteenth century—but later opposed the granting of degrees to women.

One of Marshall's biographers describes him as 'the Soaring Eagle',[10] but others regard him as a rather pedestrian figure. He exemplified the Victorian occupation to blend practical concerns with a more 'scientific' method of analysis. His synthesis of economic analysis in the *Principles of Economics* had original elements; however, in trying to make economics more rigorous in its methods, he imposed a *particular* analytical orientation that excluded radical and challenging lines of enquiry. The price of respectability was, and is, a narrowing of vision.

WHY NEOCLASSICAL THEORY?

It is interesting to reflect on why neoclassical theory, pioneered by Menger, Jevons, and Walras and synthesised by Marshall, developed at this particular time and came to be readily accepted as orthodox. At first sight it seems incongruous. Capitalism in the real world was experiencing turbulent times, contrasting vividly with the picture painted by equilibrium theory: a deep, prolonged economic depression had occurred in the 1880s; imperialist adventures were proceeding apace in the late nineteenth and early twentieth centuries; and corporate capitalism was on the rise. As another economist describes the situation:

> Just as competitive capitalism seemed to be achieving its greatest successes, the forces that Marx had predicted would lead to the concentration of capital began to show themselves. Improvements in technology were such that larger-sized plants were necessary to take advantage of the more efficient methods of production. Competition became so aggressive and destructive that small competitors were eliminated. Large competitors, facing mutual destruction, often combined in cartels, trusts, or mergers in order to assure their mutual survival.[11]

For neoclassical economists to be theorising at such a time about free markets, consumer choice, and the stability of equilibrium seems to indicate an enormous gulf between economic theory and actual economic conditions.

How can this be explained? A number of possibilities may be considered. One view emphasises the extension of markets. By the end of the nineteenth century, the spread of market relationships was much in evidence. The proponents of this process needed it to be seen as legitimate and advantageous, particularly because of its links in practice with imperialism. Theoretical developments focusing on the pervasive and generally beneficial character of market relationships fitted well with these developments and attitudes.

Second, an antidote was needed to the 'dangerous doctrines' of Karl Marx.[12] It is not that the leading neoclassical scholars of the time had read Marx, or were consciously attempting refutations—usually that was not the case. But the economic and social elite of the time, fearing the possibility of popular uprisings that might threaten the existing political economic order, were naturally attracted to a body of theorising that showed capitalism in its most favourable light as a market economy in which freedom of exchange would ensure socially beneficial outcomes.

The theorists themselves were more concerned with the extension of ideas and the solution of theoretical puzzles carried over from classical political economy. Therein lies a third explanation, of a purely intellectual character, for the ascendancy of neoclassical economics: the neoclassicals were dissatisfied with the existing theory of value because it seemed to pay insufficient attention to demand-side considerations. Shifting the focus from how labour creates value to how consumers shape the demand for products seemed to address a lacuna in the prevailing economic theory. In other words, the rise of neoclassicism was partly the consequence of novel solutions to some unresolved conceptual problems in classical political economy.

Last, it is pertinent to note that these posited solutions reflected the state of thinking in other disciplines. The growing influence of *utilitarian philosophy*, associated with the ideas of Jeremy Bentham (1748–1832), is particularly noteworthy.[13] The neoclassical economic terminology shows some obvious links with utilitarianism—consumers' utility and disutility, for example. Here are particular economic instances of the pleasures and pains that shape all human conduct, according to utilitarian philosophy. From this perspective, neoclassical theory can be regarded as the application to economics of a prevailing intellectual fashion of the nineteenth century.

All this took place in the context of a general reverence for 'science' in social enquiry. No doubt the pioneering neoclassical economists thought they were applying unprecedented scientific rigour to the study of economic phenomena. The delineation of economics as something separate from other social studies certainly reflected this. The label 'political economy' was beginning to be regarded as value-laden; 'economics' was preferred because it sounded more like 'physics'. The attempt to emulate the scientific method and basic concepts so successfully used in Newton's physics was not altogether novel—it had been evident in classical political economy, too—but it reached its peak in neoclassical theory. One critic has called it 'physics envy'.[14] Hence the emphasis in neoclassical theory on the behaviour of atomistic units (treating firms and consumers as the 'molecules' in the economic system) and on equilibrium conditions (determined by the interaction of those molecules according to the 'laws of economic motion'). In neoclassical economics, the principal 'law of motion' is not gravity, as in Newtonian physics, but economic self-interest. Markets are the natural state in which the equilibrating mechanisms work best.

Some continuity between classical political economy and neoclassical economics can be discerned in all this. An essentially *pro-capitalist ideology* is the common element. 'Economic liberalism' lives on in neoclassical economics. Indeed, it continues to the present day in various extensions of this mainstream current of economic thinking. A preference for the market and a general aversion to state intervention are manifestations of what has come to be known as neo-liberalism, which has shorn away Adam Smith's ethical concerns and subtle reservations about market behaviour.

There is also a significant discontinuity between neoclassical economics and classical political economy. Gone is the classical political economists' quest to understand society in its entirety—the complexity of its economic, social, and political institutions, and the conditions for social progress. In its place is the more limited neoclassical concern to model the price system under conditions of market competition. The focus narrows from production, distribution, growth, capital accumulation, and economic crises to *exchange* relations. We enter a theoretical world of buyers and sellers interacting on a level playing field.

DEMAND AND SUPPLY; PRICES AND EQUILIBRIUM

How are the interactions between buyers and sellers to be understood? Box 18.2 shows the most fundamental of all orthodox economic propositions: the theory of the determination of price by demand and supply, and its depiction as the 'Marshallian cross'. It represents demand and supply as being of equal importance in determining prices. According to Marshall, 'we might as reasonably dispute whether it is the upper or under blade of a pair of scissors that cuts a piece of paper, as whether value is determined by utility or cost of production'.[16]

Box 18.2

The determination of price by supply and demand

If sellers supply more of a commodity when its price rises, and buyers demand more of a commodity when its price falls, supply and demand curves can be constructed with the following characteristics:

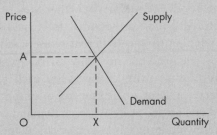

Price OA ensures that supply equals demand. Quantity OX is bought and sold at that price. The market clears.

The market price will respond to any change in consumer demand. The shift in the demand curve from Demand 1 to Demand 2 in the following diagram may be the result, for example, of a sudden surge in consumers' liking for the product. The equilibrium price rises to OB and the amount bought and sold rises to OY.

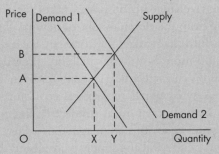

The market price also responds to a change in supply conditions. The shift in the supply curve from Supply 1 to Supply 2 in the following diagram may be caused by a lowering of the costs of production following the implementation of new technology. The equilibrium price falls to OC and the amount bought . and sold rises to OZ.

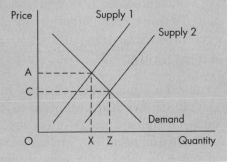

Marshall's dual emphasis on demand and supply was not novel, having been evident in Adam Smith's work, for example. It sought to balance the emphasis of the early neoclassical theorists on utility and demand with some consideration of supply conditions. The role of labour in production, which had been the focus of value theory hitherto, was to be regarded as only one of many factors shaping prices.

Three other points about neoclassical theory are notable. One is its posited *generality*. The theory of demand and supply, as depicted by the 'Marshallian cross', is held to apply to all goods and services, whether they be agricultural products or minerals, manufactured goods or services. It is held to apply equally to factors of production, whether they be different types of labour, or land or capital. For each factor, there is a demand that normally varies inversely to its price, and a supply that responds positively to price changes. For each product or factor of production (except in 'perverse' cases where demand or supply curves bend backwards), there is just one 'market clearing' price at which demand equals supply.

Second, following from this last observation, there is the claim that markets tend towards *stable equilibrium*. A rise in price will cause supply to exceed demand, so sellers will bid against one another for customers, causing the price to go down again. A fall in price will cause demand to exceed supply, so buyers will bid against one another, causing the price to climb again. An analogy may be drawn with the equilibrium of a ball in a saucer. The ball will be disturbed if the saucer shakes, but it will tend to revert to its central position. So it is with market prices, according to this model. The prevailing prices respond to changes in the conditions of demand (resulting from a change in consumers' tastes, for example) or the conditions of supply (resulting from the development of new production technologies or the entry of new firms into the market, for instance). Each response involves a shift to a new equilibrium position. A systemic stability prevails, underpinning the day-to-day price oscillations characteristic of a competitive market economy.[16]

Third, the way in which neoclassical economics accounts for these posited features of the market economy is distinctive. Everything is modelled according to *marginal analysis*. The focus is on incremental adjustments—on how small changes in the conditions of demand and supply bring about the small changes in prices necessary to restore equilibrium. The door is opened to the use of differential calculus. Neoclassical theory becomes, in effect, a means of applying that particular mathematical tool to the study of individual and market behaviour. Alongside this distinctive methodology is a distinctive ideology: only small adjustments are necessary in order to achieve optimal economic outcomes. The 'big picture' concerns characteristic of Marxist economics—class struggle, economic crises, and revolution (or even evolution)—have no place in such an idealised world.

NORMATIVE IMPLICATIONS

Neoclassical economists claim to be concerned with 'positive' economics—with understanding what is, rather than what ought to be. The range of economic matters that are studied is typically market-oriented. Characteristic questions are 'why do peaches cost more than potatoes?', 'why are carpenters' wages higher than those of clerks?', and 'why is the value of the national currency rising or falling relative to the currencies of other nations?' These *relative prices* are held to be the key to under-standing how economic resources are allocated. Their explanation requires analysis of the demand and supply conditions relating to each of the products, factors, or assets in question.

Neoclassical economics also has a normative dimension in practice. Not-withstanding the professed emphasis on 'positive' economics, distinct values intrude into the understanding of the price system. On occasions, neoclassical theory is used overtly in the attempt to show the price system as a means of securing an *optimal* allocation of economic resources. This represents the market economy in its most favourable light, as a mechanism responsive to changes in the conditions of demand and supply, continually reconciling competing interests. Buyers cannot always obtain what they want at the price they want. Sellers cannot charge whatever price they like for their products. But the interaction of buyers and sellers establishes the conditions for mutually acceptable exchanges. The price system resolves conflict.

Is the outcome of such a market process necessarily *efficient*? Subject to some caveats (to be considered in chapter 23), the neoclassical answer is that, in general, it is. The allocation of resources between industries is held to reflect both the pre-vailing technologies of production and the prevailing consumer preferences. No particular claim is made about equity but, in terms of allocative efficiency, the mar-ket exchange system apparently scores well. Showing capitalism in this favourable light is the normative function of neoclassical theory.

CONCLUSION

Box 18.3 draws out the contrasting features of Marxism and neoclassicism. There are significant differences of methodology, significantly different assumptions, and strik-ing contrasts of political interpretation. The neoclassical approach to economic

---

Box 18.3

Comparing neoclassical and Marxist views

Neoclassical economics	*Marxist economics*
Deductive methodology	Study of *historical* processes
Focus on the *individual*	Focus on *classes*
Analysis of *exchange* based on the theory of *utility*	Analysis of *production* based on the labour theory of value
Marginal analysis, substitution, and *equilibrium*	Analysis of major structural political economic changes
Assumption of *competition*	Concentration and *centralisation* of capital
Markets leading to *harmony*	Capitalism characterised by *conflict*

analysis focuses on an abstract world comprising individuals and markets, not classes and power relationships. A connection between that abstract world of 'pure' markets and the real world of capitalism is often implied, though. If the principles of demand and supply can show competitive markets to be efficient allocative mechanisms, one may infer that capitalism, notwithstanding the 'market imperfections' it features in practice, has similar tendencies. But how close is the connection? The foundations of this influential theory warrant careful consideration. The analysis of the individual, particularly the individual consumer, is its most distinctive underpinning.

CHAPTER 19

Consumers
The ultimate power?

What is meant by the term 'consumer rationality'?
How do neoclassical theorists analyse consumer behaviour? Does this give us a useful guide
to the behaviour of consumers in practice?
Do consumers wield the ultimate power in a capitalist economy?

The orthodox economic theory of markets gives considerable attention to consumer behaviour. This should come as little surprise. Markets are focal points for the interaction between buyers and sellers. The sellers normally make the first move, bringing to the market what they have for sale. But they will have wasted their time and effort if consumers do not buy their wares. A recurrence of this pattern would normally cause those sellers to disappear from the market, to be replaced by others whose wares have characteristics and prices more to the consumers' liking. The story becomes a little more complicated when *retail stores* act as intermediate institutions between the buyers and the producers of the goods. It becomes more complicated still when the preferences and behaviour of the consumers are shaped by processes of *commercial advertising* and other forms of demand management.

Neoclassical economists adopt a very distinctive approach to the analysis of consumer behaviour. They build particular models based on assumptions about *utility maximisation, consumer rationality,* and *consumer sovereignty.* This chapter explores this modelling process and these assumptions, raising questions about the relationship between the theory and the practical processes of consumer choice. In what sense, if any, are consumers rational? Is it sensible to regard consumers as the most powerful actors in the economic drama? If they are not the most powerful actors, who is?

CONSUMER RATIONALITY

If you ask yourself if your decisions are rational, can you feel confident about giving a clear answer? Few of us would willingly admit to recurrent irrationality, even if we concede that we sometimes make ill-informed or unwise choices that we subsequently regret. Our consumption decisions are a case in point. They may vary from the impulsive to the habitual, but both extremes may be justified as suiting our personal circumstances, needs, and desires. We do not usually like to admit to being 'pawns' of sales promotion. Of course, we see and hear the commercials, but we generally prefer to feel ourselves sufficiently selective, critical, and maybe just downright cynical about them.

However, the claim to consumer rationality implies a clear yardstick by which we can measure the effectiveness of our actions. Does rationality imply something about the *process* by which we make choices—collecting information about all the available products, for example? *How much* of this information is it rational to collect, given that the information-gathering process itself may be costly or time-consuming? Or does rationality only imply something about the *outcome* of choice—the absence of regret, or a perceptible increase in personal happiness, for example? These are not easy questions to answer.

The neoclassical economists cut through this complexity by positing the universal goal of *utility maximisation*. Consumers have varying personalities and preferences, but they are assumed to pursue a uniform objective: the pursuit of the greatest utility (or satisfaction) that is attainable with their disposable income. Rationality implies seeking and achieving that goal. At first sight, it seems a reasonable, if rather general, proposition. It implies that considerations of self-interest dominate all other influences in the consumption process. It implies that consumers have sufficient self-awareness to know which goods and services best suit their own needs and desires. It implies purposive action.

Box 19.1

The neoclassical theory of consumer choice

The essential features of neoclassical consumer theory, in the simplest case of a consumer facing a choice between two commodities (say, bread and wine), can be summarised as follows:

Assumed objective:
The consumer seeks to maximise his or her utility.

Given knowledge of:
- the consumer's income;
- the prices of the commodities;
- the consumer's utility function which shows how his or utility depends on the quantities of bread and wine consumed.

Deduce:
The consumer selects the optimal commodity combination such that:

$$\frac{\text{marginal utility of bread}}{\text{marginal utility of wine}} = \frac{\text{price of bread}}{\text{price of wine}}$$

The marginal utility of a commodity is the additional utility the consumer derives from consuming one more unit of it. By consuming products so that their relative utilities 'at the margin' are equal to their relative prices, the consumer maximises utility.

The problem is that this assumption of utility maximisation may involve circular reasoning. Anything that consumers do can be held to be consistent with maximising utility. Consuming addictive drugs, for instance, may be deemed to satisfy one person's particular needs. Making impulsive consumer decisions rather than carefully considered ones may be interpreted as utility maximising for someone who places a high premium on the time spent making choices—or on the thrill of a spontaneous and risky decision. Each of us has different preferences. So, it is difficult to establish that any particular patterns of choice are *not* self-interested and rational for the persons concerned. Utility maximisation starts to look like a tautology: a proposition based on circular reasoning that cannot be refuted, and which therefore has no place in any enquiry purporting to be scientific.

What the utility maximisation postulate does for neoclassical theory is establish a common basis for the study of all consumer decisions. It offers a theory of *the* consumer to represent the behaviour of all consumers. In this way, is *Homo economicus*, the universal rational economic person, born.[1]

MODELLING CONSUMER CHOICE

Box 19.1 shows the formal process of modelling the consumption decisions of a utility-maximising individual. It considers the simplest case of a choice between two commodities. The consumer is deemed to be in an imaginary situation where there are just two commodities, bread and wine. It is the sort of (momentary) world depicted in the following stanza from the famous poem *The Rubaiyat* by Persian astronomer–poet Omar Khayyam:

> A book of verses underneath the bough
> A loaf of bread, a jug of wine and thou
> Beside me singing in the wilderness
> Oh wilderness were paradise enow.[2]

Forget paradise for the moment and just concentrate on the bread and wine. What balance between the two commodities will the consumer select? If the consumer's income is limited, he or she will presumably seek a combination depending on their relative prices and their expected contribution to his or her satisfaction. This latter aspect can be represented in terms of a *utility function*, showing the extent to which different quantities of the two commodities contribute to the consumer's total satisfaction. Utility is a function of (or depends upon) consumption; thus, the utility function mentioned in box 19.1 denotes the functional relationship between the consumer's utility and the quantity of bread and wine consumed.

If the consumer has all the relevant information (that is, income, commodity prices, and the characteristics of his or her own utility function), the best selection may be deduced. What is this optimal combination of the two commodities? It is the combination at which the ratio of marginal utilities for bread and wine equals the ratio of their prices. Marginal utility is the additional amount of utility or satisfaction generated by the last unit of the product consumed—that is, by consuming one more loaf of bread or one more bottle of wine. Where the ratio of marginal utilities between any pair of commodities (sometimes known as the marginal rate of substitution) equals the ratio of their prices, the consumer cannot do any better.

Why is this the equilibrium condition for the consumer? Intuitively, it is not difficult to visualise why it should be so. One can think of the consumer juggling the pros and cons of having a little more wine and a little less bread, or a little more bread and a little less wine until the balance is 'just right'. Formally, the conclusion can be established using some diagrammatic analysis, as shown in figure 19.1.

The *budget line* in diagram 1 of figure 19.1 shows how much bread and/or wine the consumer can afford with his or her existing income. The slope of the line

Diagram 1 The budget line

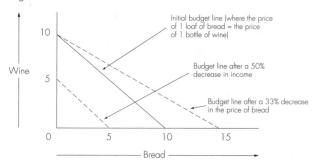

Diagram 2 Indifference curves

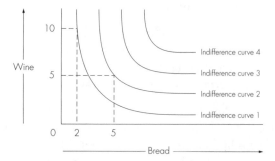

Diagram 3 Consumer equilibrium

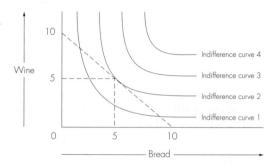

Figure 19.1   **The neoclassical analysis of consumer demand: the case where one consumer is confronted with a choice between two commodities.**

depends on the relative prices of the two commodities; the line's distance from the point of origin depends on the consumer's income.

The *indifference curves* in diagram 2 depict the consumer's utility function. An indifference curve connects the combinations of the two commodities that give equal utility (or satisfaction) to the consumer. The shape of each indifference curve depends on the degree of willingness with which the consumer would substitute one product for the other (which will depend on the characteristics of the products and on the consumer's personal tastes). Higher indifference curves indicate higher levels of utility (or satisfaction). Assuming that more of each commodity is preferred to less, the indifference curves will normally be roughly parallel to each other and will not intersect. They are like the contour lines on a topographic map of a hill, each connecting points of the same height (or, in this case, satisfaction). In effect, they represent contour lines on a hill of pleasure!

Superimposing the budget line (diagram 1) on the indifference curves (diagram 2) enables us to identify the consumer equilibrium (diagram 3). In this case, given the consumer's income, indifference curve 2 is revealed as the highest level of utility attainable. The consumer will spend his or her income on five units of wine and five units of bread. This is better than buying eight units of wine and two of bread, or two of wine and eight of bread—both of which would result in the lower level of utility associated with being on indifference curve 1. On the other hand, the utility levels marked by indifference curves 3 and 4 are unattainable: the consumer's income and the prevailing prices of bread and wine put those levels of happiness beyond reach.

The equilibrium point is where the budget line is at a tangent to the highest attainable indifference curve. At that point, the ratio of the prices of the two commodities is equal to the ratio of their marginal utilities to the consumer. It should not be difficult to see why: the ratio of the prices is given by the slope of the budget line; the ratio of the marginal utilities is given by the slope of the indifference curve at that point; where the two ratios are equal is the equilibrium outcome. This occurs at the point of tangency between the budget line and the indifference curve, as shown in diagram 3. It conforms with—indeed purports to prove—the decision rule posited in box 19.1.

CONSUMER DEMAND

This theorising about the psychological processes involved in consumers' decisions sounds rather complicated. It actually involves a simple linear process—almost ludicrously simple by the standards of modern psychology.[3] Consumers, knowing their own utility functions, weigh up the price of each product against the pleasure they will derive from consuming incremental units of it, and select an optimal combination within their budget. You may wonder if consumers actually do this. Neoclassical economists make no such claim. To them, it does not matter whether consumers *actually* go through this systematic thought sequence before they buy bread and wine, or bars of chocolate, suits of clothes, cars, or houses. What does matter is that consumers act *as if* they do.

All that we can observe in practice are the *outcomes* of the consumers' decision-making processes. One commonly observable outcome is described by the so-called *law of demand.* This states that the demand for a commodity tends to fall when its price rises, if other influences on demand remain unchanged. It is a generally acceptable proposition, although there are exceptions, such as when goods are purchased mainly for their 'snob' appeal.[4] It underpins the depiction of the demand curve introduced in the preceding chapter.

The simplest explanation of this proposition builds on the *principle of diminishing marginal utility.* This holds that the more units of a commodity a person consumes, the less additional satisfaction is derived from each successive unit. The standard example is that of a man who, having been lost in the desert and now dying of thirst, is offered successive glasses of water. The first glass gives enormous satisfaction; it saves his life. The second is delicious, the third very enjoyable, the fourth rather less so, and so on. Eventually, more water adds nothing to the man's well-being. By implication, the amount a consumer would be willing to pay for successive units of the commodity declines, until a point is reached at which the consumer is not willing to pay anything at all for one more unit.

Further reflection suggests two supplementary reasons for a generally inverse relationship between the price of a product and the demand for it. One is the *substitution effect.* A consumer is likely to substitute another commodity for one whose price has risen. If wine is rising in price, a consumer may buy beer or whisky instead. The other influence is the *income effect.* A rise in price of any commodity, particularly if it is one on which the consumer spends a substantial proportion of his or her income, effectively reduces that person's real disposable income. As a result the consumer will be likely to buy less of the commodity—and less of other commodities, too. The two effects together explain the inverse form of the relationship between demand and price.

These kinds of consumer responses to price changes are observable in the market place. The ambition of neoclassical theory is to explain the underlying utility-maximising processes. It is not difficult to envisage the connection, based on the analytical devices introduced in figure 19.1. The effects of a change in the price of a commodity on an individual's demand for it can be interpreted as a series of consumer equilibria, each equilibrium relating to a different budget line. For example, a fall in the price of bread (causing the budget line to 'hinge' outward to the right) enables the consumer to do one of the following: (1) buy more bread, substituting it for wine, which is now relatively more expensive; (2) buy rather more of both bread and wine; or (3) perhaps buy the same amount of bread and take the benefits of low bread prices in the form of more wine. It all depends on the consumer's preferences. In the aggregate, though, one would normally expect that the higher the price of a product, the lower the demand for it will be—and the demand curve will slope down to the right. *Eureka!* The connection between the general 'law of demand' and the theory of individual consumer choice is demonstrated.[5]

This is the grand claim of neoclassical consumer theory: that it links observable empirical phenomena with theorising about the nature of consumer behaviour. Thus, it claims to go 'behind the demand curve' to reveal the fundamental features of rational choice. If individual consumer choices can be understood in this way, the argument runs, we can infer something, maybe quite a lot, about the processes underpinning the swings in the behaviour of consumers in the aggregate.

Box 19.2

Elasticity of demand

Orthodox economics provides a tool of practical value in measuring the responsiveness of consumer demand to changes in price, income, or other relevant variables. This is the elasticity of demand. It shows the responsiveness of demand for a commodity to changes in its own price.

If the proportionate change in demand is less than the proportionate change in price, the demand is said to be *inelastic*. This is typically the case where a product has no readily available substitute, especially if that product accounts for a small proportion of total consumer expenditure. Salt is a classic example. On the other hand, if a change in the price of a commodity brings about a more than proportionate change in the demand for it, the demand is said to be *elastic*. This is the usual case where substitutes are readily available. Whether this is so depends, in part, on the breadth of definition of a commodity. Thus, the overall demand for food or for clothing may be relatively inelastic, but the demand for particular types of food or for particular items of clothing is normally much more elastic.

This notion of elasticity is useful. Among other things, it is an antidote to the popular view that sellers always make more revenue by raising the price of their products. They will do so only when the demand for their products is inelastic. When the demand is elastic, the higher price will cause potential customers to stop buying, so the total sales revenue will fall. So, if you are running a dance party, you do not necessarily make more income by raising the admission price. Similarly, a bookseller does not necessarily make more profits by raising the prices of the books. Evidently, knowing about elasticity is useful for sellers who have the ability to make independent decisions about their pricing policies.

Different measures of elasticity can show the responsiveness to other variables, too. The *income* elasticity of demand, for example, measures the responsiveness of demand to changes in consumer incomes. The *cross price* elasticity of demand measures the responsiveness of the demand for one commodity to changes in the price of others (how much the demand for wine responds to changes in the price of bread, for instance). Elasticity can be applied to *supply*, too: elasticity of supply shows the responsiveness of the supply of a commodity to changes in its price.

Measures of elasticity are useful tools for empirical research. However, their use for such practical purposes is quite independent of any connections with neoclassical economic theory.

CONSUMER SOVEREIGNTY?

There is a normative dimension to consumer demand theory. This is because its primacy in neoclassical economics embodies the *consumer sovereignty* postulate. What does consumer sovereignty mean? To quote Paul Samuelson, the Nobel Prizewinning author who set the standard for all textbooks of orthodox economics in the last half century, it implies that 'the consumer is, so to speak, the king ... each is a voter who uses his money as votes to get the things done he wants done'.[6] (The sexist bias in the language is presumably not meant to deny a similar role for women as sovereigns of the market place.) All consumers, by their purchasing decisions, send signals to the producers as to which goods and services to continue supplying. Thus, the pattern of consumer preferences determines the pattern of production. Shoppers rule.

Were this consumer sovereignty assumption to hold true in practice, it would be a very attractive feature of the market economy. It could be inferred that *laissez-faire* capitalism is conducive to maximum consumer well-being. Indeed, the opponents of government regulation of markets commonly base their arguments on this very presumption.[7] Not surprisingly, the claim has also been subject to regular criticism.

The most obvious challenge is to the underlying assumption of *consumer rationality*. A particular difficulty in this respect concerns the *origin* of consumer preferences. Consumers' tastes are taken as a given for the purposes of constructing neoclassical theory. This is what may be described as the 'immaculate conception of the indifference curve'. The failure to address the formation of preferences means that the theory is inherently incomplete. We need to ask how tastes are formed and how rational those processes are. In practice, consumers' tastes are likely to depend on a number of interconnected social influences—custom, habit, and social emulation, for example.[8] Does this undermine the assumption of the cool, calm, calculating consumer considering the consequences of alternative courses of action? Unless we are happy to accept utility maximisation as a tautology (that is, whatever consumers do, and for whatever reason, maximises their utility), then we are bound to question whether the outcomes of socially conditioned consumer choices are 'rational' in any objective sense. And if they are not rational, then the presumption that their free expression will lead to optimal outcomes looks correspondingly dubious.

A second strand of criticism links these concerns to the *sales effort* by firms seeking to shape consumers' demand. If consumers base their decisions on incomplete information, we cannot automatically assume that the outcome of their choices is utility maximising. If they base their decisions on biased information, the problem is worse. In practice, of course, much of the information that consumers have comes in the form of commercial advertising messages disseminated by the firms trying to sell their products to them. One might try to differentiate the *informational* from the *persuasive* elements in those messages, but this is very difficult in practice. The common aim of the messages is to adjust demand to supply, rather than *vice versa*. Firms usually develop a product first, then launch it. Of course, consumers are not always responsive to the advertising messages: sometimes new products are commercial failures. There are also occasions when the advertising messages of rival producers cancel one another out. Market research may also play a part in product design and modification, providing a 'feedback loop' between supply and demand. However, the general assumption of consumer sovereignty looks significantly less tenable in conditions where 'sales and production efforts interpenetrate to such an extent as to become virtually indistinguishable'.[9]

A third, rather different, reservation about the conventional neoclassical reasoning accepts the assumption of consumer rationality but emphasises the problems arising from consumers' constrained array of choices. In other words, consumers are regarded as doing their best with their restricted incomes and with less-than-perfect information. However, they have to choose from a subset of the fuller range of possibilities, a subset that serves the interests of capitalist businesses, not consumers and society generally. Under capitalism, the only choices offered to consumers are those from which *privately appropriated profits* can be generated, unless governments or other non-profit agencies intervene to supply public goods serving collective social needs, such as a cleaner environment. So, consumers buy flashier cars, for example, seeking to enhance their personal pleasure (by attaining more comfort, increasing their social status, or compensating for their sexual inadequacy, for instance), or four-wheel drives ('urban assault vehicles', as they are sometimes called), which are prodigiously wasteful of fuel. As a consequence, the cities become more congested, the atmosphere becomes more polluted, and our energy resources become more depleted. The aggregation of individually rational choices does not necessarily produce socially rational outcomes.[10]

A variation on this last theme is the problem posed by the presence of 'positional goods'.[11] Some goods that consumers seek are inherently limited in their accessibility. Not everyone can live in a house by the beach or in the most prestigious suburb. Not everyone can own an original Monet or Picasso. With rising incomes, the competition to attain these goods intensifies. This raises their price. Or, if positional goods do become more widely consumed, their value tends to be eroded in the process. Thus, the personal enjoyment of visiting a mountain wilderness area diminishes as more visitors come; those seeking tranquillity and communion with nature now need to spend more money seeking it further afield. There is an even more fundamental tension. This concerns the interdependence between consumers' aspirations and achievements. If, having attained a particular standard of living, consumers aspire to yet higher consumption levels, the utility they derive from current consumption tends to diminish. It is in the interest of capitalist businesses to fuel those aspirations, because it helps to sell their products, but the effect is to perpetuate dissatidfaction. If consumer well-being reflects the relationship between aspirations and achievements (the wish to buy and the capacity to buy), then it is continually frustrated in these circumstances.

CONCLUSION

Neoclassical theory presents us with an elegant theory of consumer demand. In an age when 'consumerism' is pervasive, the emphasis on the primacy of consumers may be regarded as timely and appropriate. However, whether neoclassical theory helps to illuminate consumer behaviour in the real world is a contentious matter.[12] Whether the assumption of consumer sovereignty is justified is yet more so. The reflections above suggest that a fuller consideration of consumer behaviour must consider the social context within which consumers' tastes are formed.

The study of consumer behaviour must also be linked with a study of business behaviour. We cannot reasonably claim *a priori* that consumers have the main power over firms, especially where the firms are giant corporations equipped to promote brand loyalty for their products. From a political economic perspective, it may be inferred that the relative power of the consumers and the firms depends on the resources available to them and the extent to which they are organised to pursue their collective interests. Even from a more narrow, neoclassical perspective, it is important to bring firms into the picture. Interactions in markets always involve two parties, just as 'it takes two to tango'. From this neoclassical economic perspective the relevant questions are: What shapes firms' behaviour? And what are the types of market structures within which firms and consumers interact?

CHAPTER 20

Firms

Engines of efficiency?

What are firms? What do they seek? How do they get it?
How do neoclassical economists analyse firms?
Does this provide a useful guide to business behaviour in practice?

Firms are key players in the capitalist drama. Their behaviour shapes the overall character of the economic system. Whether firms are the drivers of exploitation and class inequality, as Marxists contend, or instruments for serving consumers' interests, as the neoclassical consumer sovereignty model implies, is a crucial question in any assessment of the capitalist economy. This chapter examines how firms are viewed within neoclassical theory, seeking to emphasise the distinctive underlying assumptions and the inferences drawn about business efficiency.

DIVERSE BUSINESSES; SINGLE THEORY

What are firms? Evidently, business organisations come in many shapes and sizes. Some are engaged in agricultural production, some in mining, some in manufacturing, some in finance, and some in the provision of services. Some are big, some small. Some are companies, some partnerships, and some sole traders. Some are transnational corporations, some are corner stores. Neoclassical economics attempts to build a single theory that applies to them all. Alfred Marshall paved the way for this with his notion of the 'representative firm'.[1] Contemporary neoclassical economics textbooks develop this theme by presenting models purporting to show the universal features of business behaviour. This is not to claim that all firms are identical; rather, it is to assert that common principles underlie the differences in scale, organisation, and type of activity. It is a bold claim.[2]

Firms may raise capital in financial markets, they may hire their workers from labour markets, and they may sell their products in markets for goods and services; however, they are not markets. Their *internal* characteristics are based on non-market principles: hierarchy and command. The allocation of resources is determined by managerial fiat. As Stefano Zamagni puts it, 'In general, economic activity can be organised according to two modes, the market and the system of firms: the latter is the antithesis of the former'.[3] Following this reasoning, one might expect the theory of the firm to be based on the study of organisational form and power relationships. There have been some interesting developments along this line.[4]

However, the dominant tradition within neoclassical theory has been to treat firms as single decision-making units operating in a market context. They are atomistic units in an economic environment characterised by equilibrating processes.

What do firms seek? An obvious answer is *profits*. Indeed, if firms do not make an excess of revenue over costs they are likely to have difficulty continuing in business. But do they always seek to *maximise* profits? In practice, some small family businesses may be concerned with attaining only that level of profit necessary for a comfortable material standard of living, especially if making more profit requires greater personal effort or risk-taking. On the other hand, big businesses are commonly concerned with security and long-term growth—the pursuit of which may not be consistent with relentless profit maximisation.[5] Some observers of business behaviour contend that 'satisficing' (attaining a satisfactory, rather than necessarily maximum, rate of return on capital) is more common.[6] Indeed, the notion of a 'firm' that is managed by individuals with multiple personal goals consistently seeking a single objective is itself highly contentious; decisions in large businesses are usually outcomes of group decision-making processes that are not amenable to such simple interpretation. Neoclassical theory attempts to cut through these real-world complexities, indeed to assume them away. Profit maximisation is taken as the universal goal.

How do firms attain such a goal? All kinds of strategic behaviour may be envisaged. Producing goods and services at minimum cost and selling them for the greatest attainable revenue are two obvious dimensions of profit-maximising behaviour.

Box 20.1

The neoclassical theory of a firm's choice of output

The essential features of the neoclassical theory of the firm can be summarised as follows:

Assumed objective:
The firm seeks to maximise its profit.

Given knowledge of:
- the firm's production function, showing the relationship between the physical quantities of inputs (land, labour, and capital) used and the output of the finished product;
- the prices of the factors of production (land, labour, and capital);
- the demand curve, showing the feasible combinations of output and price.

Deduce:
The firm produces the level of output such that:

$$\text{marginal cost} = \text{marginal revenue}.$$

Marginal cost is the additional cost of producing an extra unit of output, and marginal revenue is the additional income that results from selling that extra unit of output. Where marginal revenue equals marginal costs, the firm maximises its profit.

However, these processes may involve quite different patterns of behaviour. On the one hand, firms may simply take the existing production technologies, labour wage rates, raw material prices, and market demand conditions as *given* and seek to optimise their production and sales levels accordingly. On the other hand, firms may pursue more active strategies to *shape their economic environment*—by developing (or suppressing) new technologies, by colluding to drive down the wages of workers or the prices of other inputs, or by fostering new markets for their products, for example. Again, neoclassical theory takes a distinctive stance. Its core model represents the firm as a fundamentally *passive* respondent to existing market conditions. This is not to deny the possibility that firms in practice may indeed seek to shape their economic environments. Nor does it deny the possibility of 'learning by doing'—drawing on past experience to acquire information that helps firms gain or maintain a competitive advantage in their industry.[7] It simply reflects the particular methodological stance of neoclassical theory, which emphasises the construction of a 'theory of the firm' based on a given state of technology, factor prices, and market demand.

MODELLING THE PROFIT-MAXIMISING FIRM

Box 20.1 shows the key steps in constructing the basic neoclassical theory of the firm. It parallels the model of consumer choice set out in box 19.1. This analytical symmetry is one of the most striking features of neoclassical theory—arguably the source of much of its appeal to theoreticians. Having posited the universal goal of profit maximisation and taken three sets of data (about technology, factor prices, and product demand) as given, the quantity of each product the firm should make can be deduced. The firm is assumed to know the array of production possibilities depicted by the *production function*, that is, how much output of each product is attainable from different combinations of the factors of production—land, labour, and capital. It is assumed to know the *prices of the factors of production*, and it can obtain as much of each as it wishes at the prevailing market prices. It is also assumed to know the *market demand* for each of its products, that is, how much output it can sell at different market prices. Given that information, the firm's decision focuses on the *optimal* level of output and sales, this being the quantity for which marginal cost equals marginal revenue for each type of product being made.

This conclusion can be understood intuitively by considering how a profit-maximising firm will decide when to stop expanding its output. It is a decision made incrementally, that is, by reference to marginal adjustments in the volume of output produced. Thus, the firm can be expected to continue making more output if the extra costs of producing it are less than the extra revenues derived from selling it. It makes a profit on each such additional unit in those circumstances. However, when the extra cost of the last item produced (the marginal cost) just equals the extra revenue obtained from selling it (the marginal revenue), the firm can be expected to stop making more output. Indeed, it should be indifferent about whether to produce the last item because it just breaks even at that point, making neither a profit nor loss on that last unit produced and sold. If further units of output then cost more to make than they generate in extra revenues, it is not sensible for the firm to produce them. In other words, the firm should not expand beyond the point at which marginal cost equals marginal revenue. That is where the profit-maximising output is attained.

Figure 20.1 elaborates on this basic model by introducing some diagrams (characteristic of neoclassical reasoning). They relate to the simplest case: a *single-product firm in a competitive market*. It is a *short-run* model in the sense that the firm can vary the quantity of only some of its factors of production (labour in this case); others (like land and capital) are assumed to be fixed in quantity. That is how the short-run

Diagram 1 Relationship between output of finished product and quantity of the variable factor of production (e.g. labour)

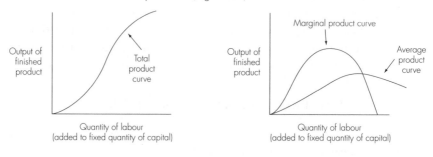

Diagram 2 Relationship between output of finished product and costs of production

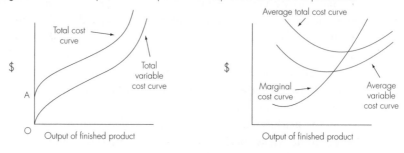

Diagram 3 Determining the equilibrium output for the profit-maximising firm in a perfectly competitive market

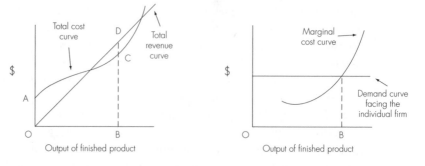

Figure 20.1 The neoclassical theory of the firm: diagrammatic analysis.

is defined, not as a particular time period, like a week or a year, but as the circumstances in which not all factors of production are variable. In the *long run*, all quantities of land, labour, and capital could be adjusted by the individual firm, but in the short run depicted here all the firm can do is vary the amount of labour added to the temporarily fixed factors of production.[8]

Imagine the firm is a wheat farm. In the short run, a hundred hectares of land, one tractor, one combine harvester, and one storage barn are available to the farmer. How many workers should the owner of the farm employ? If only one is hired, that worker will probably produce only a small output of wheat. It is possible that two workers could produce more than twice as much, if there are some benefits arising from cooperation between them in the production process. Perhaps a third worker would also increase the total output of wheat substantially. Eventually, however, extra workers are likely to produce smaller and smaller increments in production. This is because of the *principle of diminishing returns*. Formally, this states that, if additional units of a variable factor of production are combined with a fixed factor of production, after a certain point the additional quantity of output will decline. Refer to the diagram at the top left of figure 20.1. The principle of diminishing returns explains why the *total product* (measured on the vertical axis) rises at a slower rate as more labour is employed (measured along the horizontal axis). In the top-right diagram, the same processes are shown in terms of *average* and *marginal product* curves. The average product is the total product divided by the amount of the variable factor of production used. The marginal product is the addition to total product resulting from the last unit of the variable factor of production used. Both rise and then fall as the initial benefits of cooperation are outweighed by the principle of diminishing returns.[9]

One might infer that this principle of diminishing returns favours small-scale production over large-scale production. This is not so. When all factors of production are variable (in the long run), bigger firms may indeed be able to produce at lower average costs because of *economies of scale*. The point being emphasised here is that, in the restricted, short-run situation, if a firm tries to expand output by adding more of the variable factor of production to the fixed factor of production, it may raise its average costs of production per unit of output made. In the example of the wheat farmer, 501 workers on the 100 hectares, with only one tractor, one combine harvester and one storage barn among them, are unlikely to produce more wheat than 500 workers. By that stage, extra workers would simply be getting in the way of one another. In the extreme case, hiring extra workers would actually cause total production to fall, so the marginal product would be negative.

Another point to note about this analysis is of a technical character. It concerns the relationship between average and marginal product. In the top-right diagram in figure 20.1, the marginal product curve cuts the average product curve at its highest point. Why? It is a matter of simple arithmetic, which any cricketer or baseball player will readily understand. Where a marginal score (in the last innings, for instance) is above the player's average score (for the season so far), the player's average rises; where the marginal score is below the average, the player's average falls. The same reasoning applies to marginal and average products for a firm. So, is the optimal output where the average product is at its highest? One might initially think so, but the identification of the optimum output actually depends on considerations about costs and market demand. The information about the production function needs to be supplemented with information about factor prices and sales revenues for this purpose.

Having information about the *prices* of factors of production enables us to shift from analysing the quantity of product to the *costs* of producing it. In figure 20.1 this is shown in the second pair of diagrams. Note that in those diagrams the horizontal axis now represents the output of the finished product (for example wheat), and the vertical axis the costs of making that product. If we assume that the price of the variable factor of production does not vary with the number of people employed (for example the farmer can hire as many workers as she wants at $160 each per day), then there is a mirror relationship between the total product curve and total variable cost curve. The early benefits of cooperation, which cause the total product curve to rise more steeply, cause the total cost curve to rise more slowly. As the principle of diminishing returns then sets in, the total product curve rises more slowly and the total variable cost curve climbs more sharply. In other words, larger outputs generate more than proportionately greater costs of the variable factor of production. Finally, adding the fixed costs for the land and capital (OA in the diagram) to the total variable costs for each level of output enables us to calculate the *total cost* curve. We can see the total costs incurred in producing different quantities of wheat on the farm.

The second diagram in the middle row shows the same relationships in terms of *average* and *marginal costs*. Marginal cost is the additional cost of producing an extra unit of output (for example one bushel of wheat). Average cost is the total cost of production (including fixed costs) divided by the number of units of output. As output expands, the marginal cost starts to rise as the process of diminishing returns (increasing costs per extra unit of output) sets in. Eventually, the marginal cost curve rises above the average variable cost curve, thereby pulling it upwards (the cricket or baseball scores analogy applies again here). The average total cost curve is also pulled upwards, but, as the fixed costs are spread over a larger and larger volume of output, this curve does not rise as steeply.

The analysis moves towards an interim conclusion when information about *revenues* (in this case, from the sale of the wheat) is introduced. Here, too, the simplest possible assumption is made: that the price of the product is unaffected by the quantity the individual firm offers for sale. The firm's output is assumed to be so small, relative to the total supply of this product, that it has no effect on the prevailing market price. This is characteristic of the extreme situation of *perfect competition*, which we look at more thoroughly in the next chapter. Suffice it to note here that, under these particular market conditions, the individual firm is a 'price-taker' and a 'quantity-maker'. It cannot affect the price of its own product, which is set in the market according to the balance between total consumer demand and the supply of all the firms making that product. The firm's only decision is how much of the product to supply at the prevailing market price.

The third row of diagrams shows the firm's choices. On the left we see the *total revenue* curve sloping up to the right. The more of the product that is produced and sold, the greater the firm's income in direct proportion. Total revenue equals price per unit multiplied by the quantity of units produced. In perfect competition, the total revenue curve is a straight line because the price is fixed, irrespective of the amount that the individual firm produces and sells in the market. So, what level of output should the firm aim for? Superimposing the total cost curve (the same curve shown in the diagram above) enables us to discern at which level of output the total revenues exceed total costs by the greatest amount. In the case illustrated, it is at output OB on the horizontal axis. At that point the profit made is shown by the distance DC, measured in dollars on the vertical axis. This is the profit-maximising situation.

The bottom-right diagram in figure 20.1 shows the same reasoning in terms of *marginal cost* and *marginal revenue*. Marginal cost, remember, is the additional cost of producing an extra unit of output; the marginal cost curve shown here simply reproduces the curve in the diagram above. The marginal revenue, on the other hand, is the extra revenue derived from selling an extra unit of output; the marginal revenue curve shown here is horizontal because the price of the product does not vary with the output for a firm operating in a perfectly competitive market. Optimal output is the point where *marginal cost equals marginal revenue* (output OB in the diagram). Up to that level, a marginal profit is made on each unit of output produced (that is, marginal revenue exceeds marginal cost). For higher levels of output, a marginal loss would be made (that is, marginal costs exceed marginal revenue). An efficient profit maximiser will not expand beyond the optimal output OB.

What would happen if the prevailing market price were to suddenly increase (that is, if the horizontal marginal revenue line in the bottom diagram were to shift upwards)? The profit-maximising firm would now expand output to the point at which the existing marginal cost curve would cut the new marginal revenue curve. In other words, the rising part of *the marginal cost curve is the firm's supply curve* because it shows how much output the firm will supply at different prevailing market prices.

Note the analytical symmetry between this theory of the firm and the theory of consumer demand in the preceding chapter. Here again is a posited link between an empirically observable phenomenon (the amount a firm supplies at different prevailing market prices) and a model of the behaviour of a representative agent (based on assumptions about the firm's motivation and its information requirements for making optimal decisions). As with the consumer theory, the claim is not necessarily that firms actually go through the analytical procedures described here before making their decisions (although this may be intuitively more plausible than in the case of consumers), rather that they are supposed to act *as if* they do.[10]

ECONOMIC EFFICIENCY

As with the theory of consumer sovereignty, there is also a normative dimension to the neoclassical theory of the firm. The point is not purely to model the behaviour of an individual firm in highly restrictive economic conditions (perfect information, perfect competition, continuous small changes in production levels, and so on). It also purports to show the *economic efficiency* of the economic system in which 'free enterprise' prevails.

Why is economic efficiency implied? The neoclassical reasoning posits this as a structural imperative, effectively imposed on firms by the competitive economic

environment in which they operate, whatever their individual inclinations. An efficient allocation of economic resources is the product of four forces:

- Firms must combine the factors of production efficiently, given the existing state
  of technology and the prices of those factors of production. They must be producing at a point *on* the total cost curve rather than producing at a higher cost for the
  same level of output. Failure to do so can be expected to result in the firm being
  driven from the industry by firms who do use efficient production methods.
- Each firm must produce the most efficient level of output. 'Marginal cost equals
  marginal revenue' is the optimising rule. As in the story of Goldilocks, it is a matter of 'not too little, not too much, but just the right amount'. All profit
  opportunities are taken, but respect for the principle of diminishing returns
  ensures that firms do not seek to expand output by using inefficiently large
  amounts of the variable factors of production.
- The total number of firms in each industry also tends to be 'just right' in the long
  run. If existing firms are making substantial profits, new entrants will be attracted to
  the industry. The extra output supplied by those new firms would then add to total
  supply and thereby drive prices down until the excess profits were eliminated. If
  this process were to 'overshoot' and firms started to make losses, the firms would
  leave the industry, thereby reducing supply. This would cause the market price to
  rise and normal profitability levels to be restored. 'Normal' in this context means a
  rate of return on capital that is just sufficient to keep the firms in the industry.
- The consumers obtain the product at the lowest possible cost, given the prevailing state of technology and factor prices. Because firms must combine factors of
  production efficiently and produce optimal output levels, the prevailing market
  price is kept at the minimum. Thus the 'consumer sovereignty' assumption reap-
  pears in a yet more attractive guise: not only do consumers' choices signal what is
  to be produced, but consumers acquire their goods and services at the lowest
  prices consistent with sustaining the necessary levels of production. It seems a
  thoroughly admirable state of affairs.

Whether these attractive features are manifest in reality depends on whether
conditions in the real world approximate those assumed in the theory. There are
pervasive reasons to expect otherwise. In practice, capitalist businesses may use their
power over economic resources to suppress socially beneficial technical innovations,
to limit the freedom of entry of new firms, to otherwise reduce or eliminate market
competition, or to influence government policy to serve their interest at the expense
of other community concerns. Such conduct implies a quite different normative
assessment of the attractiveness of the 'free-enterprise' system. Exploring its significance requires going beyond the view of the firm as an atomistic unit operating in a
competitive economic environment to a more 'realistic' view of firms in practice.

Herein lies an irony concerning neoclassical theory. The theory of the firm is presented by economics textbooks as a means of modelling the behaviour of capitalist
businesses. Yet it is remarkably innocent of the concern by capitalist businesses in practice to re-shape their economic environment in order to loosen the constraints on
their activities imposed by competitive markets. Ironically, the neoclassical theory's

greater value may be for the organisation of a planned non-capitalist economy. In other words, the decision rules for determination of price and output (and the criteria for assessing allocative efficiency) may be more appropriate as socialist planning tools than as means of understanding actual capitalist businesses.

CONCLUSION

The neoclassical theory of the firm—typically taking up many chapters in neoclassical economics textbooks and presented only in brief outline here—is an elegant edifice. As the core of orthodox economic thinking about business behaviour, it warrants careful consideration. Like the theory of the consumer, it is based on some distinctive assumptions about rationality and the nature of the environment within which economic decisions are made. It presents a general view of firms as calculating and competitive, as instruments for making choices conducive to clearly defined goals. Also like consumer theory, it seeks to link behavioural postulates, such as the quest for profit maximisation, with empirically measurable constructs, such as supply curves showing how much firms will produce at different market prices. Elasticity of supply is a measure of the responsiveness of output to price changes—another obvious parallel to demand elasticity in consumer theory.

The theory of the firm is more than an exercise in geometry; it also seems to convey a powerful message about the nature of a 'free-enterprise' capitalist economy. It emphasises the relentless pressures for efficiency and the essential subservience of business interests to those of consumers. As such, it is the basis for a powerful economic ideology. The question is: how much of it starts to unravel as the simplifying assumptions of the theory are relaxed? The assumption of perfect competition is particularly crucial in this respect, as the following chapter reveals.

CHAPTER 21

Market Structures

Competition as a virtue?

What types of market structure are identified by neoclassical theory?
Are competitive markets ideal?
What policies are necessary to deal with imperfectly competitive markets?

Consumer behaviour and business behaviour cannot be understood independently of each other. Consumers buy from business, and firms must have customers for their products. How best to understand those interactions? The neoclassical economic stance is distinctive, using models of different market structures to analyse the interconnections of demand and supply. Particular emphasis is placed on how competitive markets can be distinguished from less competitive ones, and on the economic implications of those differences.

Four categories of market structure are distinguished: perfect competition, monopolistic competition, oligopoly, and monopoly. Almost without exception, neoclassical economics textbooks contain a chapter on each, describing their characteristics in detail and adapting the sort of analysis introduced in the preceding chapter of this book to examine the different equilibrium conditions. We can do that more summarily here, revealing the distinctive character of these neoclassical concerns, examining the implications for public policy, and teasing out the underlying assumptions about the nature of competition and economic power. In this way, a political economic perspective on the neoclassical theory of market structures can be developed.

PERFECT COMPETITION

Table 21.1 shows the three bases on which the four types of market structure are differentiated: the number of sellers and their importance, the nature of the products supplied, and the entry conditions for new firms. *Perfect competition* is the obvious starting point. This theoretical model is at the heart of neoclassical economics. It is the extreme case, where the number of firms is so large and the product each makes so uniform that no single firm can affect the price of its products. Consumers cannot distinguish between the products of the different producers. So, each firm has to accept the prevailing market price and simply decide how much to produce and sell at that price. Since there are no barriers to the entry of new firms, the existing firms cannot make profits over and above the bare minimum needed to maintain the existence of the industry in the long run.

Table 21.1   A general classification of market structures

Type of market situation	Number of sellers and importance of each	Nature of products supplied	Entry conditions
Perfect competition	A large number of sellers, each accounting for a very small proportion of the total output of the industry	Homogeneous (i.e. perfectly substitutable products supplied by each firm)	No restriction on entry of new firms
Monopolistic competition	Normally fewer sellers than under perfect competition, but the proportion of output supplied by each is still relatively small	Although broadly substitutable, the products are differentiated from one another	Usually no restriction on entry
Oligopoly	A few important sellers accounting for a large proportion of the total output	The products are normally differentiated (e.g. according to brand names)	Usually some restriction on entry
Perfect monopoly	One seller	No directly competitive product	Some restriction (otherwise the monopoly will only be temporary)

Is perfect competition an 'ideal' market structure? It is certainly not ideal from the viewpoint of the firms themselves. They must strive continuously to minimise their costs for fear of being driven out of business by more efficient rivals. They have no customers on whose loyalty they can rely. Even if they do stay in business, in the long run their profits will be minimal. This is a business nightmare. On the other hand, from the *consumers'* point of view it seems to be a very attractive scenario. Consumers are well served by a multitude of firms who compete with one another for market share and keep product prices at the lowest possible level, given the current state of technology and the costs of the factors of production.

How is that market price for the product determined? The neoclassical answer is simple—by the principle of demand and supply. As noted in chapter 18, this is the ubiquitous principle said to be continuously reconciling the interests of buyers and sellers in the market place. An equilibrium price is established through the interaction of demand and supply. Figure 21.1 shows the process involved, according to neoclassical theory.

The *aggregate (industry) demand curve* is derived as the sum of all individual consumer demand curves for the product in question. (Only five consumers are shown here because of space constraints, but you are asked to imagine that this may be five thousand or more—a number sufficient to ensure that no single buyer can exercise any significant market power.) To derive the aggregate demand curve, take a particular price (on the vertical axis) and add the demand of each consumer at that price

a) The aggregate demand curve: obtained by horizontal summation of all individual consumers' demand curves

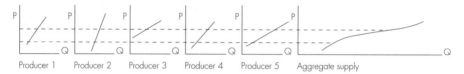

Consumer 1   Consumer 2   Consumer 3   Consumer 4   Consumer 5   Aggregate demand

(b) The aggregate supply curve: obtained by horizontal summation of all producers' supply curves

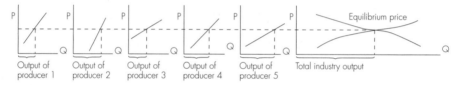

Producer 1   Producer 2   Producer 3   Producer 4   Producer 5   Aggregate supply

(c) Putting (a) and (b) together to find the equilibrium price in the industry (each firm is then faced with a perfectly elastic demand curve and selects its output accordingly)

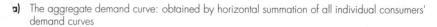

Output of   Output of   Output of   Output of   Output of   Total industry output
producer 1   producer 2   producer 3   producer 4   producer 5

Figure 21.1   **The short-run equilibrium of a competitive industry.**

(on the horizontal axis) to reach a point on the aggregate demand curve. Repeat that process for other prices to arrive at more points on the aggregate demand curve, and finally join those points, as shown in the last diagram on this row.

The *aggregate supply curve* is derived, by similar reasoning, from the sum of individual producers' marginal cost curves. As noted in the preceding chapter, the rising part of each firm's marginal cost curve is its supply curve because it shows how much that firm will vary its production as the market price changes. (Only five firms are shown in figure 21.1, but, again, you are asked to imagine, say, five hundred or more—a number sufficient to ensure that no single seller can exercise significant market power.) To derive the aggregate supply curve, take a particular price, see how much each firm will supply at that price and add those amounts to arrive at the aggregate supply. Repeat the process for other prices, and join the points on the aggregate supply curve, as shown in the last diagram on the second row.

Putting the aggregate demand and supply curves together enables us to identify the equilibrium or market-clearing price. We can then 'read back' to the individual firms' supply curves (as shown in the third row of figure 21.1 reproduced from the line above) to see how much each will supply at that price. By similar reasoning, we could 'read back' to see how much each individual consumer will demand at this prevailing equilibrium market price.

So much for the *mechanics* of the model. What is its relevance to the real world? Perfect competition is not usually found in practice, as neoclassical economists generally concede. Some markets for agricultural products, where there is a large number of small farmers producing an identical crop and where there are low barriers to entry (e.g. just the initial cost of acquiring the necessary land and tools), may approximate it. Some financial markets, where there are numerous buyers and sellers, each too small to influence market prices, may have some of these competitive characteristics, too. But these are exceptional instances.

The centrality of perfect competition theory in neoclassical economics has less to do with its real-world relevance than with its analytical elegance and its posited 'ideal' normative properties. Perfectly competitive markets are held to be 'ideal' because they ensure maximum efficiency in use of factors of production, continuous adjustment of market prices to changes in the conditions of demand and supply, and the elimination of any excess profits that would result from the exercise of monopoly power. Perfect competition is not a common market structure in practice because it is normally in the interest of firms to try to deviate from this 'ideal'—to differentiate their products, to seek to establish customer loyalty, and to erect barriers to the entry of potential competitors. Such business behaviour tends to result in monopolistic competition, oligopoly or monopoly.

MONOPOLISTIC COMPETITION

The smallest deviation from the perfectly competitive extreme takes us into the realm of *monopolistic competition*. In this market situation there is still a large number of firms, but there is some degree of *product differentiation*. This is the essential difference from perfect competition. In monopolistic competition the consumers can tell the difference between the products of the various firms in the industry, although they are usually broadly substitutable in practice. All petrol stations sell essentially the same fuel, but they may be differentiated in the eyes of consumers according to the convenience of their location or the friendliness of their staff. Similarly, all chemist shops sell essentially the same medicines and pharmaceutical products but may differ in the perceived attractiveness of their premises, the helpfulness of the resident pharmacist, or—again—location.

Location is perhaps the most pervasive form of product differentiation leading to monopolistic competition. If convenience of access is relevant to consumer choice (as it usually is), a situation that might otherwise tend towards perfect competition almost invariably becomes monopolistic competition in practice. Indeed, one may reasonably conclude that, because a spatial dimension exists in virtually *all* economic behaviour in the real world, perfect competition is a logical impossibility. Even the development of modern information technologies and increasingly rapid means of transport does not wholly eradicate the 'tyranny of distance'. Goods purchased on the Internet still have to be physically transported to the consumer. In practice, monopolistic competition is about as competitive as markets usually get.

The possibility of persistent economic inefficiency exists in such a market structure, for product differentiation may cause duplication and waste of resources. Do we need petrol stations on each corner at major road intersections? Do we want chemist shops clustered in the high street, while outlying areas are less well served? Are economic resources wasted on product differentiation that is sometimes of a spurious nature? Such deviations from the norm of perfect competition are commonly regarded as drawbacks of monopolistic competition, although neoclassical economists usually regard them as relatively unimportant so long as the barriers to entry of new firms are low. It is the latter aspect—competition from potential new entrants to the industry—that is said to keep existing firms 'on their toes' and to inhibit the tendency to excessive waste.

OLIGOPOLY

Oligopoly involves a major departure from the perfectly competitive norm. This is a market structure in which there are relatively few firms in the industry, and each usually produces differentiated ('brand-named') goods or services, the prices of which are directly under the control of the firms themselves. New firms have difficulty coming into the industry, either because of the inherent difficulties of establishing sufficiently large productive capacity or because the collusive practices of existing firms (sometimes involving government cooperation) impose substantial 'barriers to entry'. This is the world of *big business*, as perceived by neoclassical economists.

Commonly cited examples of industries with these general oligopolistic characteristics are oil production/distribution, steel and aluminium production, car production, the manufacture of computers, food processing, the manufacture of laundry detergents, aircraft production, and airline travel. Oligopoly can also exist in service industries. Some would say that universities—large institutions vigorously competing for students, research funds, and sponsors—now have the characteristics of oligopolistic industries, too. A cynic would add political parties, the biggest of which compete with one another for 'market share', differentiating their offerings to the extent necessary to secure a strategic competitive advantage. In all these cases, the dominant feature is 'competition among the few'. There may be a number of smaller players alongside the bigger ones, but it is the behaviour of the latter that determines how the industry functions.

Such behaviour is shaped by the perceived *interdependence* of the major players. Each seller in an oligopolistic industry recognises that any change in its policies (regarding production technologies, production locations, the range of product lines, prices, and commercial advertising strategies, for instance) is likely to precipitate a changes in its rivals' policies.

This perceived interdependence gives rise to distinctive patterns of behaviour. *Price rigidity* is a predictable outcome. It is a common consequence of interdependent behaviour under conditions of oligopoly, even without explicit collusion in price-fixing. Prices tend to be sticky, remaining fixed for quite long periods of time, despite fluctuations in demand and supply conditions that would cause price fluctuations in more competitive markets.[1] Periodic bouts of vigorous price competition may occur, especially when a new entrant threatens to invade the market territories of existing firms.[2] Typically though, *non-price competition* prevails. Rivalry over market shares, focusing on commercial advertising, for example, may be intense, but it is a very long way from the business behaviour required in the realm of perfect competition.

Box 21.1

Game theory

Many economic decisions involve strategic choices. For example, when setting the prices of their products, individual firms, particularly in oligopolistic market situations, have to try to anticipate the impact of their decision on the pricing policy of their rivals. They weigh up the anticipated advantages and disadvantages of competitive and cooperative strategies, taking into account the likelihood of any cooperative agreements being maintained in practice and the possible consequences of their being dishonoured.

The term 'game theory' implies a sporting analogy. Indeed, the complex and shifting relationship between cooperation and competition is one of the more intriguing aspects of sporting endeavours. Warfare is the yet more obvious arena where strategic choices are important. The development of mathematical models to help decision-making processes was in fact stimulated by World War II and the subsequent Cold War. Its application to economics followed quickly. John Nash, the mathematics professor on whose remarkable life the 2002 Hollywood movie *A Beautiful Mind* was based, was a particularly significant contributor in its development. The 'Nash equilibrium' is a central concept in game theory. Essentially, this is the situation created when the set of strategies that individuals willingly choose as the best response to the predicted strategies of other players produces 'strategically stable' or 'self-enforcing' outcomes in which no single player wants to deviate from his or her predicted strategy.

Consider, for example, the 'dating game', which looks at two players. Chris and Pat will be dining together at Chris's place, but are currently on their separate journeys home from work. Pat has agreed to buy the wine and Chris the food for the main meal. Pat could buy red or white wine, and Chris could buy steak or fish. Both prefer red wine with steak and white wine with fish, but Chris prefers the former combination and Pat the latter. Red wine and steak is a Nash equilibrium—so is white wine and fish—but there is no way to decide between these equilibria. In practice, unless Pat and Chris talk to each other before they meet, it is equally likely that a suboptimal outcome will eventuate.

Applying game theory to the study of economic behaviour is currently in vogue. It has been a focal point in the further development of mathematical economic theory and in some more down-to-earth experimental studies involving putting real people in simulated strategic-choice situations and monitoring their behaviour. Is this merely fun and games? On the one hand, game theory has demonstrated that the focus in mainstream microeconomics on rational individual decision-makers is both internally inconsistent and descriptively inaccurate. As such, it has strengthened the critique of conventional neoclassical theory. On the other hand, it has difficulty producing alternative, well-defined predictions of economic behaviour and therefore remains constrained by a choice-theoretic methodology, even while trying to push against the boundaries of orthodox economics.

Collusion is a strong tendency under conditions of oligopoly. It can take many forms. For example, firms in an oligopoly may agree to a territorial division of the market. A mutual interest in the avoidance of beggar-thy-neighbour competition may also lead firms to collude in pricing their products. They recognise that one firm seeking to increase its market share by lowering its prices is likely to trigger a 'price war', which would eventually cause each firm to suffer reduced profits. Better not let the process start. So, a system of tacit *price leadership,* whereby one firm in the industry (not necessarily the biggest) sets the general industry standard and the others follow suit, is commonly adopted. In effect, collusive oligopoly converges on monopoly.

PERFECT MONOPOLY

As global media magnate Rupert Murdoch says, 'monopoly is a terrible thing until you have it'.[3] Strictly defined, perfect monopoly is the polar extreme of perfect competition. This is where there is only one firm supplying the product in question: *the firm is the industry.* It will maintain its monopoly position by imposing barriers to the entry of new firms. It will also take advantage of its monopoly position by restricting output and raising prices in order to generate maximum profits. So, the prevailing market price will be higher than that under perfect competition—assuming that production costs are the same in either case. That is the basis for neoclassical economists' antipathy towards the presence of monopoly. It fits with the popular presumption that monopolists tend to exploit their economic power by charging higher prices for their products.

Whether markets that are more competitive do actually generate lower prices depends crucially on the level of production costs. The foregoing case against monopoly rests on the assumption that an industry's production costs would be the same irrespective of whether it is organised as a monopoly or as perfect competition. This is not necessarily the case. A monopolist lacks the imperative to minimise costs that firms have in perfectly competitive market situations. However, a monopolist usually has more resources at its disposal to invest in new technologies, and product and process innovations, if it so wishes. Because the costs of production may be either higher or lower for the monopoly in practice, we cannot know for certain how the prevailing price level compares with the perfectly competitive norm. All we can say with confidence is that, whatever the costs of production may be, monopolists have the capacity, unless constrained by government regulations or faced with a highly elastic demand for their products, to seek higher profits by raising prices.

This illustrates a general feature of the neoclassical theory of market structures. Only in the perfectly competitive case does the market structure actually *determine* the conduct and performance of the firms. The further one deviates from this norm, the greater the scope for firms to engage in *strategic action*, which, by its very nature, is harder to model and predict. This is particularly so for oligopoly, where the uncertainties associated with the perceived interdependence of firms are most striking. Neoclassical economists have sought to apply *game theory* in this context in order to 'graft on' some models of strategic behaviour.[4] This helps to inject some realism into the analysis of business behaviour, but at the price of producing more uncertainty about the predicted outcomes. The general problem remains: the greater the departure from the perfectly competitive 'ideal' and the closer the approximation to 'real-world' market situations, the less effective is neoclassical theory as a means of explaining and predicting market behaviour.

In discussing the features of different market structures, the term 'monopoly' is often used interchangeably with 'imperfect competition'.[5] In other words, it is used to refer to any market situation in which firms have the capacity to significantly differentiate their products, command some degree of 'brand loyalty' among their customers, impede the entry of new firms, or otherwise mould the operations of the market to their own interests. This is a much broader use of the term than that of 'pure' or 'perfect' monopoly, where only one seller exists. It is a use of the term associated with the concern to understand business behaviour in all contexts—other than the idealised perfect competition—and to decide what to do about it.

STRUCTURE, CONDUCT, PERFORMANCE

The orthodox economic approach assumes that the structure of a market shapes the conduct and performance of firms operating within it. In a perfectly competitive structure, firms' conduct is necessarily that of the price-taker; therefore, their performance depends on efficient resource use in the process of cost minimisation, and their capacity to make profits is always constrained by the actual or potential entry of new firms into the industry. The structure of monopolistic competition, on the other hand, allows for more competitive conduct through price and product differentiation—although firms' ability to generate high levels of profit is still constrained by the relative ease of entry. In oligopoly, the structure makes strategic conduct a business imperative, and successful performance in these strategic games is usually rewarded with substantial profits. In conditions of pure monopoly, the structure imposes no requirement on the firm to act energetically, other than to continually secure its own monopoly position, and its profit performance can be enhanced by monopoly pricing (subject to the constraint imposed by the elasticity of demand).

This structure–conduct–performance approach to understanding business behaviour embodies a distinctive interpretation of what competition means.[6] It is treated as an *end state*—a consequence of market structure rather than a *process*. A contrast may be made with Adam Smith's conception of competition as a process of *rivalry*, such as that between producers in different locations. This alternative, more dynamic, view of competition has strong echoes in Marx, Marshall, and the Austrian tradition of economic analysis, from Menger through to Schumpeter and Hayek. It puts more emphasis on *entrepreneurship* as an active element in business behaviour. Entrepreneurship is the process by which firms create business opportunities. It is a means by which firms pursue rivalrous business behaviour. It has no equivalent place in the standard neoclassical approach, notwithstanding the common (and confusing) reference to the firm as the 'entrepreneur'. Rather, in neoclassical theory, the extent of competition is understood to be determined by the industry structure, particularly the number of firms in the industry in question. In practice, whether the number of firms is the key determinant of the extent and form of competition is a moot point; even the notion of an 'industry' comprising firms making similar products sits uneasily with the development of businesses that have multiple industrial interests.

The concept of efficiency in neoclassical theory is primarily restricted to considerations of resource *allocation*. The typical concern is whether resources are being properly allocated between industries, given the prevailing state of technology and pattern of consumer demand. Questions about resource *creation* are paid significantly less attention. Yet the issue of whether competitive or oligopolistic industries are more likely to generate technological progress over time (or to improve the quality of 'human capital') may be much more important than the question of which market structure is more conducive to allocative efficiency at any given point in time.

A restricted view of *economic power* is also evident in the neoclassical theory of market structures. Economic power is only market power. The power of oligopolists or monopolists is their ability to charge higher prices than would prevail under perfectly competitive conditions (assuming similar production costs). Firms may also have power to reduce the costs of factors of production—because of their monopolistic position as buyers of labour, for example. However, their power to shape the broader economic environment is not usually considered. Yet therein may lie the major consequences of the general transition from competitive to monopoly capitalism. In so far as giant businesses in the modern economy can influence government policies (on taxes, tariffs, or industry development, for example), or play off national governments against one another through the international movement of capital, they have far greater power than these models of 'imperfect competition' imply. To the extent that their activities foster consumerist behaviour and/or deplete natural resources, the social and environmental consequences of their activities are far-reaching.

TAMING THE TIGERS?

The neoclassical theory of market structures, based on these distinctive views of competition, efficiency, and market power, could be expected to generate clear guidelines for public policy. It presents different types of market structure according to their presumed deviation from the competitive 'ideal'.[7] Its process of formal modelling emphasises key economic variables, setting aside other complexities. It should have something to say about policies towards markets in practice. Indeed, this is a significant focus of the theory as it is presented in the orthodox economics textbooks. In line with the structure–conduct–performance continuum, three policy approaches may be discerned.

First is the emphasis on policies to influence *market structure*. If perfect competition is an 'ideal' in the normative sense, then presumably public policy should seek to achieve it in practice, or at least to approximate it. A case is thereby made for breaking up large firms into smaller ones, or preventing smaller ones from combining into larger ones through mergers and takeovers. This is the characteristic anti-monopoly stance of neoclassical economics. Historically, it has been influential in a number of countries, including the United States. It was the rationale for the decision by the US Supreme Court in 1911 to break up Standard Oil into thirty-four smaller companies. It implicitly underlay the US District Court ruling in 2000 that giant software company Microsoft be divided in two (still giant) companies.[8] It is an approach to economic policy that seems to prioritise consumers' interests relative to those of business (although it should be noted that, in practice, many of the consumers of big businesses are other businesses, big and small). As a general policy approach, it is bedevilled by the tension between the concern to prevent monopoly pricing and the desire to reap the economies of large-scale production. Moreover, especially for governments of smaller nations, it now sits uncomfortably with the strategy of promoting big firms as 'national champions' capable of competing effectively in world markets.

A second approach, focusing on firms' *conduct*, emphasises the case for the regulation of business behaviour. Restrictions on monopoly pricing, on collusive activities, and other restrictive trade practices are implied. Box 21.2 gives some examples of what has come to be generally known as competition policy. It has been a major feature of public policy in practice in many countries, such as the United States, the United Kingdom, and Australia, and is motivated by a liberal reformism supported by neoclassical economic reasoning emphasising the perfectly competitive ideal. It requires a regulatory role for government that sits uncomfortably with the purist strain of economic liberalism ('neo-liberalism'). The latter viewpoint harbours deep distrust of government 'intervention' of any sort. Regulations that may stifle the dynamism of the 'free-enterprise' system are not seen as appropriate from this perspective. In practice, where the provision of essential goods and services is involved, the policy choice is commonly between 'the devil and the deep blue sea'—between public enterprises and strictly regulated private enterprises.

A third approach focuses on *performance*. 'Let the structures of imperfect competition remain; let firms decide what strategic business behaviour and pricing policies are best for them; just focus on dealing with the outcomes,' this argument runs. Profit outcomes are a particular focus. If the fruits of oligopoly or monopoly are 'excessive' levels of profit (however that be defined), then business taxation can cream off whatever portion is deemed necessary in order to finance government expenditures. This deals with the consequences rather than the causes of monopoly power. However, it offers a potentially appealing way of dealing with the lack of adequate competition in industry—appealing to citizens, not to big business, of course.

Note, though, that the victims of monopoly pricing, for example, are not necessarily the same people as the beneficiaries of the government spending financed by taxes on monopoly profits. So complex redistributions between losers and winners may ensue. Yet more troubling is the evident aversion by most governments nowadays to imposing high levels of business taxation. In a world of increasingly mobile capital, there is the frequent fear that such taxes may precipitate capital flight to other nations where tax rates are lower. Faced with this threat, real or imagined, the prevailing tendency is to shy away from tackling the power of big business

So, governments, faced with practical decisions about coping with big business and restrictive trade practices, tend to take a more pragmatic approach, seeking 'workable' competition. It seems that the closer one gets to matters of practical judgment, the cloudier the issues become and the less relevant the principles derived from the neoclassical theory appear. 'Workable competition', in one wry opinion, is 'a vague term meaning simply the degree of competition considered acceptable by the economist calling it workable'[9].

Box 21.2

Competition policy

How much competition among firms supplying goods and services is necessary, desirable, or possible? How concerned should governments be about enforcing competition? Herein lie major dilemmas. The case for a capitalist market economy relies on the posited link between competition, efficient resource allocation, and consumer welfare. Yet, ever since Adam Smith, it has been recognised that the forces of competition are continually confronted, even thwarted, by the forces of monopolisation. Governments have sought to deal with these tensions by having national competition policies.

Legislative restrictions and regulations have generally sought to preclude business practices such as:

- anti-competitive agreements and exclusionary provisions, including primary and secondary boycotts
- misuse of market power, such as charging excessively high prices
- exclusive dealing, such as when a large firm insists that its suppliers do not deal with other firms
- resale price maintenance, whereby manufacturers insist on the price at which retailers sell their products, and
- mergers that have the likely effect of substantially lessening market competition.

In recent years, governments subscribing to neo-liberal principles have extended national competition policies to previously exempt areas such as public utilities. In effect, competition policy thereby becomes linked to the push for privatisation—either directly transferring public enterprises into the private sector through the sale of their assets, or requiring public enterprises to act more like private-sector enterprises. Insisting on 'contestable markets' for the provision of all services is a recurrent theme. The declared aim is to enforce efficiency on the providers of public services. In practice, it usually results in services previously provided by public enterprises (such as electricity and gas suppliers) and local governments being 'contracted out' to private-sector firms, and the relinquishment of community service obligations that previously guided the behaviour of the public enterprises.

The Organization for Economic Cooperation and Development (OECD) has been trying to promote 'convergence' of national competition policies in different nations. It stresses the importance of transparency and non-discrimination in enforcement, and the need for competition laws to be applied uniformly with a minimum of exceptions'. This has the appeal of creating a so-called 'level playing field' for business, but in practice it can mean a level playing field on which transnational corporations can extend their domination. The tension between the principles of competition and the political economy of capitalism in practice becomes ever greater.

CONCLUSION

Competition policies in practice escillate between attempts to influence structure, conduct, and performance. However, closer investigation indicates some fundamental problems with this body of analysis. The models quickly become 'open-ended' in what they have to say about expected business behaviour as soon as the perfect competition model is set aside. The result is that the precision sought by neoclassical theorists cannot be achieved, except by making some truly heroic assumptions (such as costs of production being independent of market structure).

These difficulties also limit the use of the theory of market structures in the formulation of public policies. How best to promote business competition and limit monopoly power? No clear policy prescriptions emerge, despite the strong commitment to the perfectly competitive 'ideal'.

In the end, one has to wonder what the point of the theory is. Is its purpose to *describe* (or at least approximate) real-world market structures? Is it meant to provide a *normative ideal* that can be used as a basis for policy formulation? Or is there a yet more contentious purpose: to provide an *ideology* that diverts attention from the actual structures of economic power, thereby serving as a legitimising device for capitalist interests? These three possibilities apply not only to the theory of market structures, but also to neoclassical economics as a whole, including what it has to say about the distribution of income between land, labour, and capital.

CHAPTER 22

Distribution
Rewards for productivity?

What shapes the distribution of income?
Does it reflect the productive contributions of the various factors of production?
Is the neoclassical explanation of income distribution useful in explaining
economic inequalities in practice?

David Ricardo's claim that understanding the distribution of income among the social classes is 'the principal problem in political economy' is a pertinent reminder that economists have always been concerned to analyse economic inequalities. In popular discussions of economic matters today, the question 'who gets what?' is no less dominant—although many people feel uncomfortable about explicit reference to 'class'.

Explaining economic inequalities has a more shadowy role in neoclassical economics. Early writers in the development of this analytical tradition—notably the American economist J.B. Clark (1847–1938)—explicitly linked explanations of income distribution with propositions about the role of markets in creating social equity. According to Clark, 'the distribution of the income of society is controlled by a natural law ... which assigns to everyone what he has specifically created'.[1] In a similar vein, the Italian economist and social theorist Vilfredo Pareto (1848–1923) claimed that the 'constancy of inequality in the distribution of income reflects inequality of human ability, which is a natural and universal category'.[2] These days, neoclassical economists usually restrict their analysis to attempted explanations of the prices of the different factors of production.

Even that narrower agenda raises some interesting issues. Why are some occupational groups paid more than others? What determines the relative share of income going to labour as a whole, compared with the shares going to the owners of capital and land? Can those patterns of reward be changed without impairing economic efficiency?

DEMAND AND SUPPLY (AGAIN)

Box 22.1 shows the interconnecting influences in an orthodox economic explanation of income distribution. It emphasises the connections between the distribution of income, the distribution of economic resources, and the price that each commands in the market. In other words, 'who gets what' depends on 'who owns what' and 'what prices prevail for those factors of production'.

Box 22.1

Explaining the distribution of income

The principal influences on the distribution of income can be classified as follows:

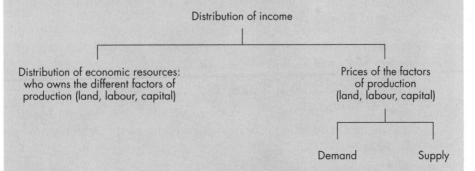

Neoclassical economic theory focuses on the right-hand side of this 'tree' by looking at the roots of income distribution in the demand and supply for capital, labour, and land. For each of these factors of production (and their constituent parts), determination of the market price is represented by the now familiar 'Marshallian cross':

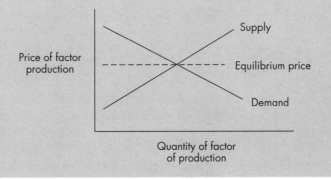

Conventionally, three factors of production are identified: land, labour, and capital. Reference to these as the defining features of three rivalrous social classes—landowners, workers, and capitalists—is muted, if not altogether absent in neoclassical theory. Taking the distribution of economic resources as given (in much the same way the theory of the consumer takes preferences as given, and the theory of the firm takes the state of technology as given), the analytical task narrows to identifying what shapes the pattern of factor prices.

Here, too, there is a fairly predictable neoclassical position. It emphasises the interaction of the supply and demand for each factor of production in determining its market price. The second diagram in box 22.1 illustrates this in terms of the Marshallian cross, now applied to explaining factor prices rather than the prices of goods and services. Note that the roles of buyers and sellers are *reversed* in factor markets: firms are the buyers, and households the sellers, of factors of production.

Looking first at the demand side, a formal statement of the relevant variables is presented in box 22.2. The objective of *cost minimisation* is the assumed starting point; this is a necessary but not sufficient condition for the general goal of profit maximisation (as discussed in chapter 20). To minimise costs, each firm needs to know what volume of output it is aiming to produce, the ways in which it is technically possible to combine the various factors of production, and the prevailing prices of those factors of production.

Box 22.2

The neoclassical theory of the demand for factors of production

The essential features of a firm's demand for factors of production can be set out as follows:

Assumed objective:
The firm seeks to minimise costs.

Given knowledge of:
• the volume of output produced by the firm;
• the production function, showing the relationship between what combinations of factors of production (labour, capital and land) can be used to produce the required output;
• the prices of the factors of production:

Deduce:
The firm employs factors of production such that the ratio of their price to their marginal productivity is equal. So, considering just two factors, labour and capital:

$$\frac{\text{marginal productivity of labour}}{\text{marginal productivity of capital}} = \frac{\text{price of labour}}{\text{price of capital}}$$

The marginal productivity of a factor of production is the extra amount of output generated by employing one more unit of that factor in conjunction with the other fixed factors of production. Where the ratio of the marginal productivities is equal to the ratio of prices of those factors of production, the firm has an optimal capital–labour ratio, according to this theory.

The first of the information requirements listed in box 22.2 is particularly important. Firms do not employ factors of production other than as a means to an end, and the end is producing goods and services for profit. The significance of this is that the demand for a factor of production is a *derived demand*: it derives from the demand for the product that it is made into. To illustrate the point, consider a firm that has already decided on the level of output to produce, following the procedure described in chapter 20 (or, more precisely, acting *as if* it followed those steps). If the firm enjoys a monopoly position, according to the reasoning in chapter 21, its demand for factors of production would be less than that of an equivalent firm in an industry organised on the principle of perfect competition. Because a monopolist can be expected to restrict output and raise the price of its product, its derived demand for factors of production is correspondingly reduced—other things being equal. So, the primary influence on the demand for factors of production is the output of the firms employing them.

The second influence is the state of technology, as shown by the *production function*. These are usually alternative ways of producing a particular output—whether by capital-intensive or labour-intensive methods of production, for example. Selecting from among those options requires a firm to have information on the relative factor prices. At first sight, this is a strange data requirement, since the point of the analysis is to explain how the demand for the factors of production influences their prices. It seems that we need to take as given what we are seeking to explain. The conundrum is resolved by recognising that, according to neoclassical theory, the *aggregate* demand by all the firms for each factor of production determines its market price, but that, once established, the market prices must then be taken as given by individual firms. Essentially the same model-building methodology that was applied to the study of consumer demand (in chapter 19) and the theory of the firm (in chapter 20) is now applied to the study of factors of production.

Finally, given all this data, the coolly calculating, cost-minimising firm selects the particular production method that satisfies the decision rule shown in box 22.2: it employs factors of production in such proportions that the ratio of the marginal products of any pair of them equals the ratio of their market prices. Marginal product is the extra quantity of output generated by hiring one more unit of a factor of production. So if, say, labour costs twice as much per unit as does a unit of capital (setting aside for the moment how those units are measured), then it makes sense to employ labour and capital in the proportion that ensures the productivity of the last man employed is twice that of the last unit of capital. Thus is cost minimisation achieved.

It is pertinent to note in passing that this analysis regards cost minimisation by firms as essentially a matter of making wise choices about *optimal combinations* of land, labour, and capital. There is no concern here with the actual processes of *managing* the factors of production—labour in particular—which are such a concern in Marxist analysis, for example (as discussed in chapter 14). Rather, the efficient management of resources is simply assumed (and class conflict in the workplace is assumed away) for the purpose of building a model to explain how much land, labour, or capital will be employed. The focus here, as elsewhere in neoclassical theory, is on *choice* rather than on conflict or coercion.

If each firm decides on the quantity of each factor of production it would employ at each price, the totals can be added to determine the aggregate demand for each factor of production. Thus, the demand curve, as shown in box 22.1, can be constructed. A downward slope to the right indicates that the higher the price of the factor of production, the less of it will be demanded. The nature of this relationship is shaped by both *substitution* and *output* effects (analogous to the substitution and income effects in the analysis of consumers' demand considered in chapter 19). A high price for a factor of production will encourage firms to adopt production technologies that use little of that factor—so they substitute cheaper factors of production for the high-priced one. This is the *substitution effect*. A high price of a factor of production also increases firms' overall cost levels (assuming that they cannot avoid using that factor of production altogether). Because that reduces the optimum level of output (where marginal cost of production equals marginal revenue), it also reduces the demand for all factors of production. This is the *output effect*. Both substitution and output effects work in the same direction, producing an inverse connection between price and demand.

What about *supply*? Neoclassical economists generally assume, as shown in box 22.1, that the supply of a factor of production and its market price will have a positive association. In other words, a higher market price for a particular factor of production will draw forth a greater supply of it. This sounds generally plausible, particularly for subcategories of factors of production (for example different types of labour, such as professors, electricians, or garbage collectors). In the case of labour, there are possibilities of occupational substitution (professors becoming garbage collectors, for instance), if the relative market rewards change sufficiently. Existing workers in any one occupation may also work for longer hours if the rewards are higher. Other workers may migrate from other geographic regions, attracted by the higher wages.

None of these supply-side responses is inevitable. In practice, there are often substantial *constraints* on occupational and geographical mobility. The number of hours of work may be institutionally fixed. Even when working hours are variable, perverse outcomes may occur; workers may actually work fewer hours when their wage rates are raised, for example, because they need to commit less time to work in order to achieve their target incomes. In this case, the income effect of the wage rise dominates the substitution of work for leisure. For all these reasons, the supply curves for factors of production may be quite inelastic, even backward-bending (indicating a negative association between rewards and the amount of the factor of production supplied). However, as long as there is a unique point of intersection between the aggregate demand and supply curves, a 'market-clearing' equilibrium price can be established, according to this neoclassical theory. Thus, the theory seeks to indicate how factor prices reflect the conditions of demand and supply.

REWARDING PRODUCTIVITY?

This explanation of income distribution—or what should more properly be called *a theory of factor prices*—has, at first sight, a pleasing symmetry with other elements of neoclassical theory. It is very similar to the theory of how prices for goods and services are determined. It also implies a symmetry between the rewards for capital, land, and labour. In this latter respect it stands in striking contrast to Marx's theory of exploitation of labour by capital, and to Henry George's claim that the revenues obtained by landowners are 'always ultimately at the expense of the value of labour'.[3] There is no economic surplus. Rather, everything is rewarded in proportion to its productivity at the margin.

Herein lies the distinctive ideological character of this aspect of neoclassical theory. Orthodox economists today seldom make the sort of explicitly normative claims about the distribution of market incomes that were made by J.B. Clark and Vilfredo Pareto. However, the general inference remains: that reward according to marginal productivity is both efficient and fair. Therein also lies a reason why orthodox economists are commonly reluctant to prescribe substantial income redistributions in order to satisfy broader, social objectives. 'Meddling' with the distribution of income, it is implied, is likely to have economically damaging consequences. Milton Friedman, for example, has argued strongly against 'the attempt to separate this function of the price system—distributing income—from its other functions—transmitting information and providing incentives', claiming that, 'If prices are prevented from affecting the distribution of income, they cannot be used for other purposes'.[4] This sort of reasoning suggests that we must accept substantial economic disparities as a necessary corollary of a capitalist market economy. It is an argument that requires critical re-examination, focusing on the posited connections between rewards and productivity in a market economy.

REWARDING POWER?

One obvious lacuna in the orthodox reasoning is the issue of *resource ownership*. As noted in box 22.1, the overall extent of income inequality depends on both the distribution of reseource ownership and the pattern of fator prices. To adapt Marshall's famous phrase in this different context, these two aspects of income distribution interact like the two blades of a pair of scissors. To neglect 'who owns what' impedes an understanding of 'who gets what'. Formally, any given pattern of factor prices is consistent with an *infinite* array of income distributions, depending on the inequality of resource ownership. If land, labour, and capital resources are widely dispersed among the population, the distribution of income is likely to be more egalitarian than if they are concentrated in the hands of a few—whatever the pattern of factor prices. On a practical level, policies to secure more dispersed patterns of resource ownership can be expected to produce more equitable distributional outcomes. However, on this issue the neoclassical theory is silent; it takes the distribution of resource ownership as given, in the same way that consumers' tastes and technology are taken as given in other aspects of the theory.

Second, the orthodox neoclassical theory ignores the role of *economic power* in shaping the pattern of factor prices. In practice, professional groups, such as lawyers and doctors, use their representative collective bodies to restrict entry (usually in the name of 'maintaining quality') and thereby maintain high rewards. Trade unions seek to push the wage rates of their members above those that would prevail in more perfectly competitive market conditions. Employer organisations concurrently pursue the reverse goal. The actual wage outcomes—and, generally, the relative income shares of labour and capital—depend on the relative power of these organised groups and on the institutional context within which the contest between them occurs. The non-symmetrical nature of the power relationship between capital and labour in a capitalist economy underpins all such processes. Neoclassical theory is sometimes modified to take account of institutional 'rigidities', but it remains fundamentally ill-suited to considering the nature and consequences of the resulting power plays.

The state is not external to the political economic conditions shaping the distribution of income, either. Indeed, in so far as it enforces the underlying property rights and polices in the industrial relations arena, it is a key participant in the power plays. Its effects on income distribution are not only the result of explicit 'intervention' in redistributing 'market incomes' through taxation and public expenditure. The power relationships of capital, labour, and the state intertwine in shaping all aspects of the distribution of pre-tax incomes and wealth in a capitalist society.

Third, there are fundamental *conceptual problems* with the attempt to theorise income distribution in terms of the productivity of labour, land, and capital. What the neoclassical theory must do, if it is to be consistent, is relate the income of each factor of production to an empirical measure of its productivity. Rent must be shown to reflect the measured productivity of land; wages must be shown to reflect the measured productivity of labour; and profits must be shown to reflect the measured productivity of capital. Unfortunately for neoclassical theory, this cannot be done.

Part of the problem is that of *disentangling* the relative productive contributions of land, labour, and capital when all (or even just two) of the factors must be combined in order to produce goods or services. This difficulty may be addressed (in theory) by holding one factor constant and observing the impact on output of variations in other factor(s) at the margin. In practice, the empirical measurement of marginal products is usually difficult, if not impossible, to achieve.

Yet more fundamental is the conceptual problem of finding consistent *units of measurement* for each of the factors of production. This is not a major difficulty in relation to labour: inputs of labour can be measured in terms of person hours of work, so the reward to labour can be expressed as a wage rate per hour and related to the productivity of that hour's labour. It is also possible for land: inputs of land can be measured in terms of hectares, so the reward to land can be expressed as a rental per hectare and related to the productivity of that land. However, no such physical measure exists for *capital*. Capital goods comprise diverse items—machinery, equipment, tools, plant, and buildings—for which the only common measure is their market value. However, that market value is not independent of the profitability of the firms using those capital goods. And there is the rub. Because the 'productivity' of capital goods affects their valuation, measuring a rate of return on capital involves circularity. When business is profitable, capital has a higher market value; when it is unprofitable, capital has a lower market value. So, the estimated rate of return on capital is not independent of the valuation of the capital input.

This last point may seem somewhat esoteric, but its economic significance is substantial.[5] It means that the neoclassical attempt to establish a theory of distribution that treats land, labour, and capital in a symmetrical fashion is ultimately unsuccessful. Profit cannot be treated as a payment for the productivity of capital in the same way that wages reflect the productivity of labour or rent reflects the productivity of land. The root problem here is the attempt to eradicate the notion of an *economic surplus* from economic theory. In the classical and Marxist economic traditions profit is treated as a *surplus*, arising after wages, rent, and other costs have been deducted from revenue. It is the neoclassical economists' attempt to explain profits in terms of the marginal productivity of capital rather than the class power of capital that is so deeply problematic.

Entrepreneurship may be posited as a fourth factor of production, as one means of trying to escape the conceptual problem of defining and measuring a return to capital. Profits can then be regarded as a reward for entrepreneurship, reflecting the skills of capitalist managers in organising the other factors of production, innovating, and taking

Box 22.3

Joan Robinson (1903–83)

At last a famous female economist! The economics profession has been dominated by males, but not exclusively. Joan Robinson is probably the most distinguished female economist, certainly from the political economy perspective. She was a student and, subsequently, a colleague of John Maynard Keynes at Cambridge University. At various stages of her career she made substantial contributions to neoclassical economics, Keynesian economics, Marxist economics, and post-Keynesian economics.

Her early work adapted neoclassical theory in the light of the growth of big business, providing the foundation for a theory of 'imperfect competition'. Her analysis remained constrained by neoclassical assumptions but showed that 'exploitation' could result from firms with market power depressing wage rates below the level that would prevail under perfectly competitive conditions. This gave a slightly radical twist to the orthodox theory.

She became a significant figure in the formulation and teaching of Keynesian ideas. Her *Introduction to the Theory of Employment* (1937) was a point of access. Her subsequent books, particularly *An Essay on Marxian Economics* (1942), took an anti-capitalist turn, although her embrace of Marxism was less than complete. The labour theory of value had no place in her political economy because she thought it unnecessary as a basis for understanding profits and the exploitation of labour. Indeed, she held that any theory of value, by its very nature metaphysical, was an impediment to understanding capitalism in practice.

Her book *The Accumulation of Capital* (1956), which reflected the influence of the Polish political economist Michal Kalecki as well as Marx, developed the analysis of economic growth. Turning her attention to the critique of neoclassical theory, she also wrote important journal articles that demonstrated the incoherence of the orthodox theory of income distribution. She showed that the marginal productivity theory rested on a concept of capital that was theoretically unsound and not amenable to measurement, arguing that this was a reflection of a deeper problem—the ahistorical character of neoclassical economics. She launched many other assaults on orthodoxy, repeatedly stressing the need to tackle the neoclassical theorists on their own terrain by showing the logical flaws in the reasoning.

Joan Robinson took the view that economics should be considered a 'tool kit'. In her judgment, the best introduction for students would be to combine the study of economic history, the history of economic thought, and economic statistics.

risks in the process of running their businesses. In effect, this means distinguishing between entrepreneurial incomes and the more routinely market-determined interest payments that are the reward for capital (in its monetary form). This usefully acknowledges the dynamic element in business management. However, the analytical difficulty remains. There is no measure of the quantity or quality of entrepreneurship other than the profitability of the firm in question. Good entrepreneurship is presumably that which earns high profits; poor entrepreneurship is that which results in low profits or causes losses. The problem of circular reasoning recurs: the link between entrepreneurial quality and profits is either tautological or untestable. Faced with these kinds of problems, some neoclassical theorists have resorted to declaring their 'faith' in the neoclassical analysis,[6] but that is hardly a satisfactory stance for a school of economic thought claiming scientific status for its approach to economic enquiry.

CONCLUSION

The analysis of income distribution is of fundamental importance in political economy. Neoclassical theory evidently makes little contribution in this regard. It draws attention to the role of productivity in shaping the financial rewards going to different factors of production. However, there are substantial difficulties in measuring productivity and in applying the analysis of productivity to land, labour, and capital in anything like a symmetrical manner. The neoclassical theory also omits consideration of the distribution of ownership of economic resources and the power that owners may exercise, individually and collectively, in the pursuit of their sectional interests.

Introducing these considerations into the study of distribution also raises practical questions about the scope for governments to pursue policies of income *re*distribution. If policies were to explicitly target the ownership of economic resources and/or the power that the owners of economic resources exercise in pursuit of their interests, they could presumably produce more equitable distributional outcomes. Whether that would require a 'trade-off' in terms of efficiency is debateable.[7] Whether such forms of government 'intervention' are compatible with the pursuit of enhanced social well-being is also contentious. Further exploration of these issues require more explicit analysis of what determines 'economic welfare'.

CHAPTER 23

Economic Welfare and Neo-Liberalism

Does equilibrium in the economy necessarily imply socially desirable outcomes?
Can neoclassical economics provide a coherent basis for judging the desirability of economic changes?
How does neoclassical theory link to neo-liberal policy prescriptions in practice?

Orthodox economists often claim to be concerned with 'positive' economics. This implies an analysis free of value judgments. As earlier chapters have argued, a value-free economics is difficult, if not impossible, to attain in practice. The values—customarily associated with the tradition of economic liberalism—are implicit. If economic analysis is to be applied to the great tasks of public policy formulation and social betterment, it is necessary to make them explicit. We need clear guidelines for making judgments about what would constitute improved well-being of the community and how economic policy might contribute to serving that goal.

Some neoclassical economists have responded to these concerns by developing an explicitly normative analysis, generally known as *welfare economics*. Its limited achievements are reviewed here. Attention is also given to contemporary arguments about the relative importance of 'market failure' and 'government failure', drawing on the theory of *public choice*. The uncomfortable connection between the 'policy interventionist' and 'free market' currents of thought in orthodox economics today is thereby revealed.

GENERAL EQUILIBRIUM

If we are to evaluate the working of the economy as a whole, there must be some basis for seeing how all the parts fit together. *General equilibrium theory* performs this function in neoclassical economics. General equilibrium is said to exist when a set of prices for goods and factors of production equates supply and demand in all markets simultaneously. It is a purely theoretical situation. No neoclassical theorist would claim that the real world ever achieves this state. There are always some forces bound to cause disequilibrium in particular markets—a change in consumer preferences or in the state of technology affecting the production process in one or more industries, for example. Once one market has been disturbed by such changes, there are bound to be 'knock-on' effects in other markets. An increase in demand for ice cream, for example, due to a long spell of hot weather, will tend to increase the demand for milk (if that is what ice creams are made from), which will increase the demand for workers in the dairy industry, which may affect the prevailing wage rates, which may then affect the demand for products that these workers consume, possibly leading to changes in those commodity prices, consequent changes in the demand for the factors of production used in making them, and so on. A change in one market can cause changes in many others.

The notion of general equilibrium draws attention to this *interdependence* of markets in the economy as a whole. It may readily be conceded that, at any particular time, general *dis*equilibrium is the normal state. However, according to neoclassical theory, market adjustments operate relentlessly in the direction of restoring general equilibrium, even though the system is unlikely to ever reach equilibrium before it is disturbed by other 'shocks'.[1] The analogy of the ball on a saucer, introduced in chapter 18, is pertinent here, too: if the saucer is frequently knocked or shaken, the ball will keep moving, but it will always tend towards the middle of the saucer. A general equilibrium that is unique and stable has a similar character. It may be seldom, if ever, attained, but it is a condition to which the economy continuously tends.

This notion of general equilibrium, though abstract, is an influential way of envisaging the economy as a whole—as a network of interdependent markets producing overall stability. In the hands of neoclassical theorists, working in the tradition pioneered by Leon Walras, general equilibrium theory has been developed into a sophisticated mathematical model. It is a model that typically takes as *given* some key socioeconomic conditions: consumers' tastes, the state of technology, the ownership of economic resources, and workers' preferences between income and leisure. These affect, respectively, the demand and supply for goods and services, the distribution of income, and the supply of labour. Critics argue that the model takes as *given* the key variables that really need to be explained. Mathematical precision evidently comes at a high price in terms of practical relevance.

From a political economic perspective, what is more important than the technical specifications of general equilibrium theory is the vision it presents of a *self-regulating market economy*. This is its normative application—the basis for the belief that markets are the best means of economic organisation. As such, it has a powerful ideological function supporting *laissez-faire* principles.

WELFARE AND OPTIMUM

Whether an equilibrium situation constitutes an *optimum* condition requires more systematic consideration. A market economy *may* or may not have an underlying tendency towards general equilibrium in practice; but, even if it does, this does not necessarily refute the case for economic planning or other forms of state policies. A world of general equilibrium, should it ever exist, would not necessarily be desirable in all respects. The continual flux in the process of adjustment to new equilibria may have undesirable social consequences—instability in employment, for example. The general equilibrium situation itself may have some socially undesirable features, such as a highly inegalitarian distribution of income, or excessively high prices for particular goods that society considers necessary or in some way meritorious. An equilibrium situation is not necessarily an optimum situation.

Explicit normative standards are required if economists are to pronounce systematically on what is optimal. Yardsticks are needed against which progress towards more desirable outcomes can be measured, particularly if economists are concerned to be relevant to *public policy* discussions. It is for these reasons that neoclassical economists developed *welfare economics*—as a bridge between the analysis of what *is* and the discussion of what *ought to be* if the economy is to better serve social goals.

A.C. Pigou, who succeeded Alfred Marshall as Professor of Economics at Cambridge, laid some important foundations in his book *The Economics of Welfare*.[2] He recognised that economic welfare (or well-being) is only one aspect of broader societal goals. Economic welfare is not synonymous with social welfare. Nor is it independent of the distribution of income. If, for example, the principle of diminishing marginal utility applies to *income* in general, a strong case for egalitarian redistribution can be made. The last dollar received by a rich person is likely to add little to his or her economic well-being, whereas an extra dollar received by a poor person is likely to add significantly. The rich person may not even notice that marginal dollar, whereas for the poor person it may be the difference between eating and starving. The obvious prescription is to redistribute income from the rich to the poor in order to increase total economic welfare—indeed, to continue that process of progressive redistribution until the marginal utility of income is equal for all citizens.

This seems to be a rather radical policy prescription, argued from an impeccably orthodox economic stance. Not surprisingly, it is not the sort of economic reasoning universally acceptable to the wealthy. Nor to other neoclassical theorists, who attacked Pigou's underlying logic. *Interpersonal comparisons of utility* are illegitimate, they asserted. We cannot know for sure how much the dollar taken from the rich person will reduce his or her welfare. It may do so substantially if, for example, the rich person is a miser who is deeply distressed at having that dollar taken away. On the other hand, the poor person may be an individual with no economic aspirations, who is quite content with a meagre income and will derive little, if any, pleasure from the extra dollar. So we cannot say *for certain* that the posited income redistribution adds to total economic welfare. Perhaps there is no systematic way of comparing people's subjective well-being. The prohibition on interpersonal comparisons of utility is the apparent conclusion. However, this leaves no obvious basis for making judgments about appropriate public policies.

If interpersonal comparisons of utility cannot be made, orthodox economists conclude, we can only say that a redistribution of income (or any other change) constitutes an improvement if it makes some person (or people) better off without making anyone worse off. This is the *Pareto principle*, named after the Italian economist Vilfredo Pareto. It is much weaker than the principle underlying Pigou's reasoning. Is it a useful guideline? On the one hand, it is unobjectionable in the sense that it seems to have no significant exceptions—if you are better off and no one is worse off as a consequence (or even *feels* worse off), then it seems reasonable to conclude that we are collectively better off. On the other hand, it only rarely applies in the real world—almost every economic change generates both winners and losers, and in such circumstances the Pareto principle cannot tell us if the change constitutes a general improvement. It is a deeply agnostic position.

Responding to these difficulties, other welfare economists in the twentieth century developed supplementary principles based on *compensation payments*. For example, if a person or persons who benefit from an economic change can financially compensate the losers such that the latter feel no net disadvantage as a result, then that change may be deemed socially desirable. Or, to be yet more restrictive, if that compensation principle is met, the compensation is actually paid *and* the income distribution is no more unequal at the end of the process than it was at the start, then the change is deemed desirable. Here are some interesting thought experiments.[3] The problem with their practical application is that there is no general mechanism for making those compensation payments in a market economy. In effect, the chain of reasoning leads towards the advocacy of a much more substantial economic role for the state than economic liberals would normally allow. Detailed government interventions or legal procedures to enforce income redistributions associated with a vast array of otherwise private market transactions are implied.

In practice, the problems of identifying consistent welfare criteria and compensation principles usually lead to a *laissez-faire* response. Since it is very difficult to justify any economic policy 'intervention' by reference to the Pareto test, so the argument runs, it is best to leave resource allocation processes to the market. This is not a matter of logic: the market is no more 'natural' than government and therefore has no innate claim to priority. Rather, the stance reflects the general ideological orientation of neoclassical economists towards a preference for the market.

There is yet one more big fly in the ointment: *the theory of second best*. This theorem shows that, if not all the conditions for an optimal economic outcome are attainable, then a move towards that optimum may not constitute an improvement.[4] In other words, if the 'first best' outcome is not possible for some reason, then the 'second best' may be quite a different situation from the one that approximates the optimum. Take the example of market structures. We might agree in principle, if we were persuaded by neoclassical reasoning, that it would be best if all markets were perfectly competitive. However, if that were not possible (perhaps because of the economies of large-scale production or the existence of 'natural monopoly' in one or more markets), then it might not be desirable to try to move closer to perfect competition in the other markets. The second-best outcome might involve balancing the power of some big businesses, or strengthening the market power of consumer groups or trade unions. We cannot know for sure. We certainly cannot 'read off' the optimal solution purely from theoretical reasoning. So, public policies that make incremental changes—and that is all that normally can be done—have inherently uncertain effects on overall economic welfare. According to the neoclassical economists' own reasoning, it starts to look silly to talk about universal optimum conditions at all.[5]

MARKET FAILURE

A more pragmatic approach to considering economic policy is adopted in practice. Neoclassical economists seek to reconcile their general *laissez-faire* inclinations with selective public policy proposals by emphasising, or at least acknowledging, the problems of 'market failure'. The market is taken as the norm, but some imperfections are recognised, and remedial public policies recommended in specific circumstances. So, what are these circumstances in which markets are likely to fail to produce an optimal allocation of resources?

The first concerns *public goods*. That some goods will not be provided at all in a pure market economy was acknowledged by Adam Smith. Where people cannot readily be excluded from enjoying the benefits of particular goods or services that are inherently collective in character, they cannot be charged individually for consuming them. The market system fails in these circumstances. Public provision of the goods or services is necessary, or they will not be provided at all.

The second type of 'market failure' concerns *externalities*. Some goods are over-provided in a market economy, while others are underprovided because the costs and benefits they confer on society are not adequately taken into account by the market mechanism. 'Environmental goods' like clean air and water, being free to the individual consumer and producer, are used without restraint and are correspondingly degraded. Education, on the other hand, is generally underprovided and underconsumed because its positive externalities are not reflected in a market price. So, the free market produces a lopsided pattern of economic activity. The rationale for government 'intervention' in these circumstances is either to 'correct' the market prices or to otherwise compensate for the resource misallocation.

The next issue concerns *equity* in distribution. As Amartya Sen has noted, an economic situation can be both 'Pareto optimal and ... sickeningly iniquitous'.[6] The neoclassical economists' advocacy of the market economy is based more on considerations of allocative efficiency than on claims of fairness. An economic system, on this reasoning, may be efficient, even though the distribution of incomes—and hence access to the consumption of goods and services—is manifestly inequitable. Indeed, there is a presumption of inequality in a market economy because material incentives drive the system. However, distributional equity may be a precondition for the cooperation needed for superior economic performance. It may be necessary for social cohesion. So a redistributive role for government may be warranted, even from an economic liberal perspective.

The fourth source of 'market failure' is *imperfect competition*. Neoclassical economists are generally uncomfortable about any deviations from the perfectly competitive 'ideal'. Only under conditions of perfect competition are markets held to produce economic efficiency and to ensure the provision of goods and services to consumers at the lowest possible prices. Yet monopolistic competition, oligopoly, and monopoly are more common market structures in the real world. While the orthodox economists have no agreed prescriptions for dealing with these circumstances, as noted in chapter 21, they do concede some role for government in redressing the market 'distortions' resulting from imperfect competition.

Finally, there is the problem of *instability*. As noted earlier, proponents of general equilibrium theory usually represent a free-market economy as basically stable. However, they sometimes concede that the processes of adjustment to changing equilibria are not instantaneous and may impose social costs. Opponents of the theory emphasise more substantial flaws in the 'adjustment mechanisms' of capitalism in practice, such as the tendencies to alternating boom and slump and to recurrent unemployment. These tendencies violate the orthodox economists' own criterion of efficiency, for it is blatantly inefficient for resources to be left idle while social needs for goods and services are simultaneously unfulfilled.

Box 23.1

Cost–benefit analysis

Most economic decisions generate both social costs and social benefits. Cost–benefit analysis is a means of comparing these beneficial and adverse consequences in order to determine whether the expected outcomes are, on balance, in the public interest. It has become a widely used method for evaluation of public investment projects.

The procedure involves five steps:

- *identify* all the relevant consequences of a particular public policy decision
- *evaluate* all the consequences in monetary terms, so as to derive values for the costs and benefits expected to accrue to society as a whole
- *estimate* the net present value of the future costs and benefits
- *compare* the net present value of the costs and the net present value of the benefits, that is, the overall cost–benefit ratio
- *select* all the policy alternatives where the cost–benefit ratio is less than 1; or, in the case of mutually exclusive alternatives, select the policy alternative with the lowest cost–benefit ratio.

Consider the construction of a new urban freeway, for example. The first step would require the analyst to list all the likely effects, such as how travel times for freeway users and for users of existing roads would be affected, the likely incidence and severity of traffic accidents, the expected impact on atmospheric pollution, and the expected loss of flora and fauna resulting from this change in land use. The second step would require putting a dollar value on each item, that is, the value of travel time saved, the value of lives lost or saved, the health cost of air pollution, and the value of the threatened species. The third step would involve expressing these various streams of costs and benefits in terms of their current value equivalent, on the assumption that future costs and benefits would have less weight than immediate costs and benefits. How much less weight depends on the choice of a discount rate. The fourth step would involve comparing the discounted costs of the freeway construction with its estimated benefits, all expressed in terms of these monetary net present values. The freeway is then deemed to be socially desirable only if the benefits exceed the costs. If two or more freeway routes were under consideration, the preferred route would be the one with the lowest cost–benefit ratio.

Proponents of cost–benefit analysis emphasise the advantages of having a method of project evaluation that increases the consistency of decision-making. Its critics challenge the legitimacy of trying to place monetary values on 'intangibles' like environmental quality, even on life itself. Cost–benefit analysis shares with neoclassical welfare economics a distinctive set of assumptions about the nature of the economy and society. It is a monetary calculus of the determinants of community well-being, for better or worse.

This all adds up to a quite considerable indictment of free-market capitalism within a body of analysis predisposed to favour the market. The acknowledgement of the various sources of 'market failure' provides a strong rationale for trying to rectify the recurrent problems of markets by developing appropriate government policies. This is the *liberal-interventionist* position. It has usually been embraced by economists seeking a compromise between their professional adherence to neoclassical theory and their personal commitment to economic reform and social progress. It is associated with the use of techniques like cost–benefit analysis (see box 23.1) to decide the 'what, where, and when' of public expenditure and the appropriate regulation of private-sector developments.

However, the liberal-interventionist position has always had its critics among other neoclassical economists concerned to 'maintain the faith' in the free-enterprise system. They warn of the greater economic, social, and political problems that may result from such attempts at steering or regulation. In the last two decades, this purist position has gained strength. It has become the predominant orthodoxy, variously labelled *'neo-liberalism', 'economic rationalism'*, and *'economic fundamentalism'*.[7] Its conceptual basis is the notion of 'government failure'.

GOVERNMENT FAILURE

Scepticism about government is a long tradition with various manifestations, both popular and academic. Politically, it has a base in anarchist thought as well as right-wing libertarianism. The latter viewpoint derives in part from *social Darwinism*; it sees the 'struggle for existence' and the 'survival of the fittest' as elements in a natural order, which governments should not spoil by attempting to redress economic inequality and other social problems. The aversion to government also has roots in popular 'folklore', particularly in the United States, about the advantages of living in a society that promotes individualism rather than seeking the redress of its problems through collective action. Anyone can make it 'from rags to riches' by individual initiative, according to this view. Governments, however well intentioned, stand in the way of such drives for personal advancement in a 'free society'. Worse, they tend to be parasitic and/or corrupt.

Developments in orthodox economics during the last two decades have given some academic legitimacy to these popular perceptions. *Public-choice theory* is particularly significant in this respect. It has been an increasingly influential current of thought running between neoclassical economics and political science. It represents politicians and bureaucrats as subspecies of *Homo economicus*, self-interested individuals whose actions are calculated responses to vote-maximising processes. They tend to implement policies to satisfy the demands (and secure the votes) of sectional interest groups, systematically violating the broader national interest. Manufacturers win the tariff protection they seek, unions secure minimum wage legislation, housing tenants secure rent control, and so forth. However, the result is not conducive to the economic welfare of society as a whole. On the contrary, the overall effect is an incoherent series of regulations and policy interventions that impede the capacity of the market to ensure an efficient allocation of resources.

Variations on this theme are developed with varying degrees of analytical sophistication. In the words of one of the leading proponents of this modern current of theory, 'in a very real sense, public choice theory offers a theory of government-political failure that is on all fours with the theory of market failure that emerged from the theoretical welfare economics of the 1950s'.[8] Indeed it has become more powerful, since the dominant argument is that 'government failure' is more deeply problematic than 'market failure'.

Critics of public-choice theory have countered by emphasising its neglect of the institutional and sociological factors that cause political processes to work quite differently from economic markets.[9] It is quite bizarre, one might infer, to apply market economic reasoning to the sphere of politics, whose very existence reflects the inadequacies of the market as a means of providing for all our economic needs, still less all our social aspirations. The proponents of public-choice theory have evidently been little perturbed by such criticisms. Their work has been influential as a supporting ideology for systematic assaults on the welfare state and other forms of government intervention developed in previous decades. Its practical consequence is a resurgent 'free-market' economics that supports these pervasive neo-liberal policy prescriptions.

ECONOMIC RATIONALISM IN PRACTICE

'Economic rationalism' involves the extension of neoclassical economic reasoning to the realm of public policy. The terminology conveys a strong inference that subjecting policy issues to a rigorous economic analysis is conducive to rationality. However, economic rationalism is not necessarily rational. The term 'rationalism' is better understood as 'deriving from theory'—in this case, neoclassical economics and its variant, public-choice theory—and is the opposite of empiricism, which is the gaining of knowledge from experience. In practice, economic rationalism has the characteristics of a faith: faith in the 'free market' to deliver superior outcomes to government 'intervention'.

The most obvious manifestations of economic rationalism in practice are policies of privatisation, deregulation, trade liberalisation, reductions in the level and progressivity of income taxation, 'contracting-out' of public services, and the withdrawal of governments from their previous commitment to universal provision of social security and other welfare state entitlements. The provision of public highways is increasingly being contracted to private companies, who construct and manage private tollways. Even health and education services are increasingly financed and provided along market principles. The array of public goods is being scaled back. Defence largely remains a public commitment (although mercenary armies are available for hire), but many other aspects of public provision are being 'corporatised' and 'marketised'. Privatising prisons, for example, would have been considered laughable a couple of decades ago, but it is now common. The speed and comprehensiveness with which this economic rationalist program has been pursued varies from country to country. It has been generally less pronounced in continental Europe than in the United Kingdom, North America, Australia and New Zealand, but it has been quite pervasive in character.

Whether it all adds up to 'slimming the state', as its proponents commonly claim, is a debatable point. The implementation of economic rationalist policies usually involves a change in the functions of the state—a shift from direct service provision to regulation of private providers, for example. So far, there has not been a consistently marked diminution in the public sector's proportion of gross domestic product. From this perspective, what we are witnessing is an attempt to challenge the long-term trend whereby more economic resources are brought under the control or influence of political process rather than being left purely to market forces. We live in a time of uncertainty about the continuation or reversal of that trend. It is a time of contestation between radically different views about markets and states and of major experiments in the application of those competing views. The economic rationalist ideologies and policy experiments are a distinct element in this process. They are a practical extension of neoclassical reasoning, stripped of all its caveats about 'market failure' and problems of 'second best'. They are a vulgarised form of neoclassical economics in action.

CONCLUSION

There is a paradox to confront. It concerns the relationship between economic theory and the practice of economic policy. On the one hand, neoclassical economic theory, particularly its general equilibrium variant, largely ignores the messy complexities of the real world. The centrality of the perfect competition model in the teaching of economics is a symbol of this. As a consequence, neoclassical economics faces the repeated charge of failing to engage with capitalism in practice. The attempts by the neoclassical economists to erect a bridge between their theories and practical concerns about economic policy—through the development of welfare economics—have also been largely unsuccessful. Welfare economics has turned out to be a *cul de sac*[10]. Yet, many of the major political economic changes in the real world in recent decades have reflected the influence of neoclassical economic theory. It seems that the real world is being changed so that it conforms more closely to the orthodox economics textbooks.

There are contrary trends, too. The neo-liberal drive towards 'economic rationalism' is not all one-way traffic. It has strong political opponents, whose opposition connects with other popular beliefs (about egalitarianism, social solidarity, community, and collective action, for example). Some neoclassical economists themselves are less than enthusiastic about 'economic rationalism' because it ignores the restrictive assumptions and strips away the qualifications they attach to their theories about markets. Other neoclassical economists of a liberal-interventionist bent continue to subscribe to the view that 'market failures' are more problematic than 'government failures'. This division among the neoclassical economists themselves gives orthodox economics the appearance of internal diversity, thereby providing some defence against charges that it is monolithic or dogmatic.

Yet stronger bases for opposition to 'economic rationalism' come from other currents of political economic thought—from Marxist economics, of course, but also from the more consistently 'interventionist' Keynesian economics, and the dissident tradition of institutional economics. It is to a consideration of these alternatives that we now turn.

PART VI

Evolution and Reform

Institutional economics

CHAPTER 24

Economy and Society
Institutional foundations

Why focus on economic institutions?
What does an evolutionary approach to economics entail?
What were the main ideas of Thorstein Veblen, the leading light in the
development of institutional economics?

Institutional economists have mounted a strong challenge to the dominance of neoclassical economics, and to its associated 'economic rationalist' prescriptions. These economists argue that the pure market economy is nothing more than a fiction. Market arrangements in practice are socially embedded, dependent on supportive structures for their effective operation—on legal institutions to establish and enforce property rights and contractual principles, on financial institutions that underpin the legitimacy and value of the means of exchange, and on social institutions that reinforce ideologies underlying the existing economic order. As William Lazonick puts it, 'history shows that the driving force of successful capitalist development is not the perfection of the market mechanism but the building of organisational capacities'.[1]

The involvement of the state in the economy is particularly important from an institutional economic perspective. Government economic activity cannot sensibly be regarded as 'intervention', with all that term implies about being external to the normal processes of the market. Rather, it is an important element of a workable economy. Historically, it has been a key driver and manager of capitalist development. International variation in the form of government economic activity today gives capitalism a qualitatively different character in different nations.

According to institutional economists, these are the real political economic phenomena that need to be studied—not the unrealistic abstractions about perfectly competitive markets. In effect, these economists are making a plea for the reintegration of economic enquiry into the group of social sciences—sociology, politics, history, geography, industrial relations, and anthropology. Institutional economics, reflecting this orientation, has sometimes been called *economic sociology*. This is sometimes taken to imply that it is not 'real economics'.[2] However, its proponents argue that it studies economic issues in their *real-world* context, where they are inexorably linked with social and political matters, and nothing could be more real than that.

INSTITUTIONS AND EVOLUTION

Institutional economics takes an *evolutionary* rather than mechanistic view of the economy.[3] The focus is on history rather than equilibrium. It is concerned with studying the interactions between social values, technology, and economic institutions. In this respect, it can be seen as exploring the very things that neoclassical economists take as given in their models—consumers' tastes, the state of technology, and the ownership of economic resources, for example. According to institutional economists, it is through the study of these socially moulded phenomena that a better understanding of the evolution of economic society can be constructed.

This orientation also leads to a focus on the diverse patterns of capitalist development. The economic institutions of countries like the United States, the United Kingdom, Australia, Japan, Germany, Sweden, and Singapore are quite different. We need to understand why. Such understanding can only come from the detailed study of each country in its historical context. Taken to the extreme, this denies the usefulness of a concept such as 'capitalism' and the possibility of a general explanation of its structure and functioning. The quest, common to both Marxist and neoclassical economics, for a unified theory to explain the economic system may be regarded as misplaced in this respect. Perhaps it is more important to look at the variety of economic experience in American capitalism, Australian capitalism, Japanese capitalism, and so on. The result may be less tidy, but, according to its proponents, it is likely to be markedly more realistic.[4]

Still, some structural guidelines are imperative for any political economic enquiry. The *capital–labour–state* framework is useful in this regard. As noted in preceding chapters, these three conceptual categories are used in other currents of economic thought. What is distinctive about the institutional approach is the treatment of them as institutional clusters having internal diversity, particularly in respect of their relative economic power. Capital is not an amorphous factor of production, but rather something that comes in many institutional forms, ranging from large multinational corporations to smaller businesses whose behaviour is moulded by local conditions. The institutional forms of labour also vary significantly, according to whether workers are organised into trade unions and whether they are fragmented by locality, gender, or race. The institutions of the state are yet more varied, ranging from public enterprises concerned with the direct provision of goods and services, to agencies responsible for the provision of infrastructure, central banking, regulation of markets, and arbitration of wages and industrial disputes.

How these institutions of capital, labour, and state interact is not an *equilibrium* process. It is a *power play*. It follows that the study of economic power—its sources, its uses and abuses—is a necessary part of institutional analysis. Of course, power is also part of the Marxist and neoclassical stories—class power in the former, and the market power associated with oligopoly and monopoly in the latter. The conception of power in institutional economics is more broad-ranging and eclectic, as we shall see in the next chapter. As a bridge between economics and sociology, it is not surprising to see in institutionalism the influence of seminal social theorists such as Max Weber and Emile Durkheim.[5] The influence on the institutional economics tradition of the German historical school of the nineteenth century is also significant.[6]

As a distinctive tradition of economic analysis, institutionalism's peak was reached in the United States in the first half of the twentieth century. Indeed, it is no exaggeration to claim that it then rivalled the neoclassical school as the most influential type of economics. It was more evidently in tune with changes taking place in the real world in the late nineteenth and early twentieth centuries: increasingly powerful economic institutions were coming to dominate the economy; corporate power was growing; trade unions were forming; and states were assuming a yet more extensive role in the management of economic affairs, including the orchestration of imperialism on a world scale. The incapacity of neoclassical economics to illuminate these changes was a particular focus of criticism by institutional economists. The most notable of the critics was the dissident American economist, Thorstein Veblen (1857–1929). As we all see, his concerns have strong contemporary resonance.

Box 24.1

Thorstein Veblen (1857–1929)

To call Thorstein Veblen the founder of institutional economics might imply that this tradition of economic thought is more coherent than is really the case. However, Veblen is widely acknowledged as its principal inspiration. An American of Norwegian descent, he had an 'outsider's view' of the society in which he lived. He saw its excesses, its inefficiencies, and its wastes, and he wrote about them with insight and wit. Among his various books, *The Theory of the Leisure Class* (1899), *The Theory of Business Enterprise* (1904), and *Absentee Ownership and Business Enterprise in Recent Times* (1923) are notable.

Veblen held a series of academic appointments, but he did not enjoy the secure tenured status accorded to many lesser scholars. It is difficult to escape the inference that he was discriminated against because of his dissident views—although his reputation of having affairs with the wives of faculty members may also have contributed to his difficulties in securing continuous academic employment.

By all accounts he was an eccentric character, both in his appearance and personal habits. He had an unkempt moustache and a short, straggly beard. His socks were sometimes held up by safety pins attached to his trousers. He is said to have not washed his dishes after meals, preferring to hose down stacks of them periodically. He was taciturn in manner and a notoriously dull teacher, mumbling into his beard and setting long reading lists designed to discourage all but the most conscientious students.

Notwithstanding these personal eccentricities and foibles, Veblen was undoubtedly one of the most outstandingly perceptive social scientists of his era. He was eventually invited to be president of the American Economics Association, but turned the invitation down, saying that the position should have been offered to him earlier in his academic career, when it could have been of some professional value. He died in 1929 in relative poverty and obscurity. His legacy to society was his published work. His books and articles are still frequently referred to, whereas those of his more 'respectable' colleagues have long since been forgotten.

THE SOCIAL NATURE OF CONSUMPTION

Veblen sought to develop a more subtle view of the relationship between the individual and society than in the orthodox conception of 'rational economic man', or *Homo economicus*. An analysis of the social character of consumption is central to this endeavour. People's preferences, shaping their consumption of goods and services, cannot sensibly be taken as given, Veblen thought, because they are largely socially determined. Our tastes are learnt as we grow up, and that learning process can produce quite different patterns of demand between different localities and different social groups. Moreover, those demands themselves commonly have as much to do with the expected *social* consequences of consumption as with its purely physical consequences (eating to stop hunger, wearing clothes to keep warm, and so on). This is particularly so for those who have the greatest disposable income.

Veblen identified this trend-setting affluent social stratum as *the leisure class*, emphasising its tendency to engage in *conspicuous consumption* and *conspicuous leisure*. (All these terms, it may be noted, have since acquired common usage.) In Veblen's day, the leisure class was itself notably conspicuous. The late nineteenth century in America is sometimes known as the era of the 'robber barons'. Families such as the Vanderbilts, Astors, Whitneys, and Rockerfellers became prodigiously rich, often through activities involving the unscrupulous exercise of economic power.[7] Karl Marx would not have been surprised by this, of course, since he foresaw that the concentration and centralisation of capital would make for growing class inequality. Henry George argued that the roots of the prodigious wealth lay in the alienation of land and the 'unearned increment' of incomes deriving from its ownership. Veblen's concern was more with the social consequences of such concentrations of wealth.

Conspicuous consumption means buying things for the purpose of display. The ideal house is not merely one in which it is comfortable to live, but also one whose palatial character impresses the neighbours and passers-by. A motor car has to be not simply a reliable means of transport, but also a status symbol: it must be expensive, and widely perceived as such. Likewise a yacht. Clothing has to be more than functional; it must indicate to all who care to observe that the wearer is a person of economic wealth and social position, if not refinement. If the apparel signals that the wearer does not have to toil for a living, so much the better, for that is the hallmark of the leisure class. White shoes and white gloves are ideal accoutrements for all who want to show their social distance from the world of manual labour. Wives are particularly useful in this process—as objects of display for wealthy men, to be kept 'togged up' in whatever finery most clearly signals that they have no need to work.

Such social pretension is all too familiar to us. Veblen wrote of its development a century ago in a way that was both witty and insightful. His observations in *The Theory of the Leisure Class* are like those of an anthropologist observing a strange tribe, or of an ecologist observing an exotic species of bird. One can almost imagine a nineteenth-century David Attenborough crouching in the shrubbery at a garden party thrown by a member of the leisure class, saying, 'See how the male of the species is inclined to predatory behaviour, but always finds time to display his acquisitions. And look at how the apparel of the women indicates their social position. See how they strut and preen themselves at every occasion. And note how the whole process is reproduced in succeeding generations through careful attention to encouraging the offspring to adopt similar modes of behaviour'. The 'human ape' is under observation, and looks distinctly risible.

But there is a more serious point here. Because the 'leisure class' devotes prodigious economic resources to this conspicuous consumption and conspicuous leisure, there is *social waste*. Can throwing extravagant parties, where champagne flows like water and people light cigars with twenty-dollar bills, be held, by any standard, to be an efficient allocation of resources? The neoclassical economists duck the issue, protesting their reluctance to make value judgments about consumers' preferences. Veblen was more concerned to describe than to judge; but drawing attention to the social excesses invites normative reflection. With the benefit of hindsight, one can infer that Veblen was observing the tendency, not towards efficiency, but towards waste as the central feature of capitalist society. His analysis was a forerunner of modern concerns about *consumerism*—its excesses and its dubious connection with enhanced community well-being.

The problems of ultimately unsatisfying consumption are magnified by the process of *social emulation* (another piece of Veblen's terminology that has since gained widespread currency). It is, of course, difficult for poor people to emulate the sumptuous lifestyles of the rich and famous. They may seek to do the best they can, consuming scaled-down and cheaper versions according to the limits of their incomes (and sometimes beyond), but it is a process fraught with inherent frustration. If our perceived well-being depends on what we have *relative* to what others have, mass consumerism is a recipe for permanent dissatisfaction. The assumption of a correlation between increased consumption and higher utility evaporates.

THE SOCIAL NATURE OF PRODUCTION

Veblen also made major contributions to understanding industry. As with the analysis of consumption, his analysis of the processes of production draws attention to the sources of tension, waste, and inefficiency. Production of goods and services is not treated, as in neoclassical theory, as a technical puzzle involving the selection of the least-cost combination of factors of production and a profit-maximising output. It is treated as a social process. As such, it reflects a fundamental disjuncture between the *instinct of workmanship* and the *predatory instinct*. Veblen posited these two instincts as universal features of human behaviour. They have strong contemporary resonance. Think, for example, of the choices facing a student writing a university essay—whether to do systematic library research, take notes, and compose a synthesis based on thoughtful assessment, or to plagiarise another student's essay or a published article on the topic.

The tension between the instinct of workmanship and the predatory instinct is particularly problematic in capitalist businesses. Workmanship is the productive aspect, involving the use of resources like land, labour, and capital to make useful goods and services. Predatory behaviour, on the other hand, includes activities that enhance profit without adding to the productive capacity of the economy. The former is socially beneficial (setting aside the issue of environmental exploitation and decay); the latter is ultimately counter-productive—although it may be an attractive strategic option in the short term. Both aspects coexist in the real economy.

Somewhat schematically, this dualism can be described as a tension between *industry* and *business*. Those terms are often used interchangeably in popular discourse (and elsewhere in this book), but the suggestion here is that they represent contrary tendencies. Industry is productive activity focused on the use of the physical means of production and taking advantage of technological possibilities in the development of new products or better ways of making existing products. This is the realm of the engineers. Business, on the other hand, focuses on pecuniary matters. It is concerned with monetary values and financial flows—with the so-called 'bottom line'. This, and this alone, is the interest of the owners of the businesses, particularly where they are 'absentee owners', shareholders having no direct involvement in the management of the enterprises. This is the world of the financiers.

The tension between the engineers and the financiers is manifest at a number of points. The *management of technological change* is one point. Engineers are concerned with the development of new technologies, but this may undermine the value of existing capital equipment, even make it obsolete. Technological change may therefore be perceived as working against the interests of the absentee owners of businesses. One way of handling this dilemma, Veblen noted, is for business managers to try to eliminate inter-firm competition, or at least to reduce it to a level that enables them to exercise some control over the rate and form of technological process. Innovations may be suppressed, contrary to the interests of both the engineers and consumers. This incompatibility of modern technology with competition was Veblen's explanation for the great wave of mergers and cartel formation taking place in his time. In the present age, the desire to control technology continues to be a major factor influencing business strategy and industrial concentration. It is a two-way process, though; being in the forefront of new technological developments can be a key factor in the growth of businesses, while big businesses are better able to control the form that technological change takes.

Veblen also sought to explain the *tendency to economic depression*. He considered that, even if mergers and the formation of cartels produced coordination on the supply side of the economy, the problem of ensuring sufficient demand for the growing volume of goods and services would likely remain. Prodigious productive capacity was being developed, but the distribution of income set a limit to what could be sold at the prices required by monopolists in order to give them an acceptable rate of return on capital. Echoes of the overproduction and underconsumption problems discussed by Marx are clearly audible here. Veblen's analysis of the wasteful expenditures of the 'leisure class' drew attention, in effect, to a partial solution. Wasteful public expenditures—on grandiose public edifices, diplomatic and ecclesiastical establishments, military service, and armaments—could also play a part. However, Veblen doubted that these wasteful expenditures would be capable of growing indefinitely at the same rate as the productive power of industry. Hence, he forecast a great depression. His analysis of it was loose and imprecise, but the conclusion that tendencies towards depression were endemic in the economic system preceded Keynes's analysis by almost three decades.

Veblen further noted that the most 'successful' form of wasteful expenditure is *war*. War is hell, but it gives a great stimulus to an economy with an inbuilt tendency to depression. His analysis proved prescient, for World War I broke out in 1914. Veblen also predicted the rise of *fascism* and the emergence of the *corporate state*, a scenario in which military authoritarianism and the interests of capitalist big business would prevail over nominally democratic institutions. By raising these concerns, he foreshadowed one of the major themes raised by institutional economists today: the awkward, even incompatible, relationship between capitalism and democracy.[8]

CONCLUSION

Thorstein Veblen's work provided a substantial foundation for the development of institutional economics. It may be regarded as everything that the neoclassical economists' work was not—and still is not. It was interdisciplinary in character, with strong historical and anthropological emphases. It examined the evolution of the economy rather than the properties of posited equilibrium tendencies. It explored the origins of the very things that orthodox theorists normally took (and continue to take) as given: tastes, technology, social structure, and economic inequality. The focus on these matters, particularly on the effect of tastes and technology, enabled Veblen to illuminate the discordant aspects of the economy. He showed an economy rife with waste and internal contradictions, not an economy producing harmonious outcomes. This is the reasoning of an uninhibited social scientist developing a trenchant critique of the economic basis of the society of his day.

Was Veblen the American equivalent to Karl Marx? In a society with strongly conservative characteristics based on a deep attachment to capitalism as the expression of economic individualism, Veblen was about as radical as someone seeking a significant audience for their views can be. His analysis was penetrating and challenging. However, a balanced assessment of his contribution must also acknowledge two contrary features. First, there is not the same analytical rigour in his work as is found in Marx's political economy. Veblen's rejection of neoclassical theory led him to a looser style of reasoning, characterised by social observation and witty criticism. Second, Veblen had no political program comparable to that proposed by Marx. His analysis of the contradictions and wastes of the American economy and society did not lead to substantial proposals for different economic and social arrangements that would offer more favourable prospects for progress. There is the hope, even the expectation, that the engineers may take over from the financiers as the economic managers of society, but no analysis of any such transition and no manifesto for an alternative political economic order. This is not to belittle the importance of his work. Veblen paved the way for a significant dissident tradition in economic thought: the tradition of institutional economics.

CHAPTER 25

A Dissident Tradition in Economics

What are the characteristics of institutional economics?
What significant contributions has this tradition made to economic thought?
What impact have institutionalists had on economic policy in practice?

Many dissident economists, following in the footsteps of Veblen, have been concerned to understand economic issues in their social context. They do not form so clearly a defined school of thought as Marxist and neoclassical economists. They have no clear analytic framework equivalent to Marxist value theory or neoclassical marginal analysis. Indeed, institutionalists normally reject *both* value theory and utility theory as abstractions that are not empirically operational. Their preference is for open-ended, less explicitly theoretical lines of enquiry. This attracts less academic prestige. Nevertheless, institutional economists can claim to have had a major influence in shaping various aspects of economic policy, not least the development of the welfare state as a means of tempering the instability and inequality generated in a capitalist economy.

The loosely bounded character of the institutional economics tradition is both its strength and weakness. It opens up possibilities for illuminating analyses of the connections between economic, social, and political issues. It has also opened up new lines of enquiry, helping to spawn academic disciplines like economic statistics and industrial relations. On the other hand, critics of institutionalism claim that its loosely bounded character is symptomatic of lack of analytical rigour.

Some stocktaking of the contributions of, and the competing claims about, institutional economies is warranted. One way of doing this is to look at the work of the major figures in this institutional economics tradition. This will illustrate the general characteristics of institutional economics (which are described in box 25.1). These characteristics, while not applying equally to all practitioners of institutional economics, indicate the broader orientation of this tradition in political economy.

AMERICAN INSTITUTIONALISM

Veblen's pioneering work opened the way for significant numbers of other economists seeking an alternative to orthodox neoclassical economics. Their alternative has developed many branches. Politically, institutionalism has tended to become more conservative as Veblen's breadth of vision has given way to more detailed contributions to empirical research. However, as the work of institutional economists in the twentieth century came to be more acceptable to the political establishment,

Box 25.1

Principal characteristics of institutional economics

Institutionalists have generally been critical, indeed often downright dis-respectful, of economic orthodoxy. This *iconoclasm* has exposed the shallowness of the 'conventional wisdom' in economics, thereby clearing the decks for more down-to-earth institutional investigations.

Institutionalists have been concerned, first and foremost, with the study of the real world, emphasising its complexity, but also trying to discern recurrent patterns. This *empirical* approach is the antithesis of the 'armchair theorising' that has tended to dominate mainstream economics.

Institutionalists have generally been concerned with reintegrating econom-ics with sociology, politics, and the other social sciences. The world does not come in neat analytical compartments, they argue, so the analysis of it must have a correspondingly *interdisciplinary* character.

Institutionalists also emphasise the pervasive role of ideology in shaping economic behaviour, and the inevitability of *normative* judgments shaping eco-nomic analysis. From this perspective, the notion of 'positive' economics is a fiction. Values influence all aspects of economic and social enquiry.

Economic systems are constantly changing. Institutionalists argue that the methodology of economic enquiry must therefore be *evolutionary*, emphasis-ing the forces that shape the development of the institutions of capital, labour, and the state, and the corresponding processes of social change.

A common theme in institutional economics is that the development of the economic system can be, indeed invariably is, steered by the state. Economic knowledge thereby becomes a key element in the process of taking control of our own destinies. This *reformist* view of the state tends to situate institutional economists, politically, in a broad middle ground between conservative neo-classicals and revolutionary Marxists.

some of the reformist prescriptions had a significant influence on public policy. In the United States especially, institutional economics was a serious rival to ortho-dox economics during the first half of the century. It continues to be a source of constructive dissent.

In listing the major contributors to this political economic tradition, it is appro-priate to begin with John Commons (1862–1945). His publications included a ten-volume *Documentary History of American Industrial Society* (1910–11). He also wrote *The Legal Foundations of Capitalism* (1924), which examined the relationship between the economic and legal systems—an important connection because, to this day, these continue to be the twin foundations of social order. Commons empha-sised the need to study *the economy as a going concern*, evolving in response to real pressures, rather than abstract principles. His writings were packed with the results of his painstakingly detailed and descriptive institutional enquiry—the sort of work that everyone says is useful but few ever read. However, he had a strong, practical influence in his own day, particularly in the development of the policies of the 'New Deal' introduced by President Franklin D. Roosevelt to combat the chronic economic and social problems of the Great Depression.[1]

Wesley Mitchell (1874–1948) was another prominent American institutional economist. A friend and former student of Veblen, he is renowned for his large-scale investigations of trends in capitalist development, especially the cyclical character of economic growth. He compiled enormous volumes of statistical data to describe and analyse these trends. 'Measurement without theory' his critics called it. Arguably, one can discern in this work the origins of the discipline of economic statistics, later to become econometrics. It is an interesting connection, at first sight not fitting comfortably with the general character of institutional economics as a dissident current in the economics discipline.[2] However, there is actually a common theme here: the emphasis in institutional economics on *empirical observations* of the real world rather than abstract theorising. Mitchell emphasised the quantitative aspects of this empirical enquiry. Computers, of course, have made the analysis of large-scale data sets of economic variables much easier today than it was in Mitchell's time.

Gardiner Means (1896–1988) made equally important contributions to understanding the *qualitative* changes in twentieth-century capitalist development. Together with Adolph Berle (1895–1971), he is best known for the book *The Modern Corporation and Private Property* (1932),which explored the significance of the separation of ownership from control in the modern corporation. Treating the 'firm' as a single decision-making 'entrepreneur', still a pervasive tendency in mainstream economic reasoning, was shown to be out of kilter with what was happening to real firms. The growth of *absentee ownership* (shareholders who have no direct managerial role) opened up major potential conflicts of interest in the running of the corporations. The detailed study of these changes and tensions by Berle and Means was a significant contribution to understanding the consequences of the 'managerial revolution'. Their work continues to resonate today, as corporate power becomes both more concentrated and globalised.[3]

One final example of the major figures in the tradition of American institutionalism is Robert Heilbroner. He comes close to rivalling John Kenneth Galbraith as its outstanding representative since World War II. A big thinker and prolific writer, Heilbroner, perhaps more than any other modern political economist, has been willing to speculate on the future prospects for capitalism—not the short-term trends in economic indicators beloved of the financial market pundits, but the broad trajectory of economy and society over the decades ahead. His *An Inquiry into the Human Prospect* (1975), for example, reflects on the pressures resulting from population growth, environmental stress, and military conflict. It looks at the capacity of our political institutions to effect the necessary adaptations and at the limits of 'human nature', thereby boldly stepping beyond the usual limits of political economy into the realm of social psychology. The evolutionary perspective is blended here with an emphasis on the limits of industrial society, or what he elsewhere calls 'business civilisation'. Heilbroner anticipates *convulsive change*, that is 'change forced on us by external events rather than by conscious choice, by catastrophe rather than by calculation'.[4]

Box 25.2

Gunnar Myrdal (1898–1987)

The Swedish political economist Gunnar Myrdal is the most distinguished non-American in the institutional economics tradition. As well as being an academic economist, he was a member of the Social Democratic Party in the Swedish parliament, serving for a couple of years as Minister for Trade and Commerce and contributing significantly to developing the institutions that have made Sweden one of the most economically secure and egalitarian nations of the world.

His numerous books include *An American Dilemma* (1944), which examines the problem of racial discrimination; *Economic Theory and Underdeveloped Regions* (1957), which analyses how processes of circular and cumulative causation accentuate regional economic inequality; *The Political Element in the Development of Economic Thought* (1954), which shows that economic analysis has never been value free; and *Asian Drama* (1968), a three-volume work on the problems of economic underdevelopment.

He was awarded the Nobel Prize in Economic Sciences in 1974, although he reportedly said afterwards that he regretted accepting it because his whole professional career had been spent arguing that economics cannot be a science! In *The Political Element in the Development of Economic Thought*, he wrote: 'Every economist is painfully aware that there exists widespread doubt about the supposed "scientific" character of economics. The distrust is, indeed, well founded'.[12] He further argued that there were three main focal points for the 'political speculation which has permeated economics from the very beginning': the idea of 'value', the idea of 'freedom', and the idea of 'social economy or collective housekeeping'. The last of these is particularly interesting, touching as it does on different views about the link between the household and the national economy, and the role of the state in national economic management.

The Swedish economy is perhaps the most striking example of the concept of 'social economy' being given its broadest interpretation in practice. In effect, it constitutes a major experiment in seeking to blend capitalism and socialism. Instead of 'social liberalism', whereby problems like poverty and unemployment are seen as frictions in an otherwise harmonious system, the Social Democrats, in conjunction with the Labor Organisation, developed policies to challenge capitalist principles on a programmatic basis. These policies have included reduced wage differentials, a high progressive income tax, the pursuit of full employment through a permanent labour-market policy, industrial democracy, and the use of superannuation funds to finance nationally targeted investment priorities. Sweden's welfare state, although recently under challenge, has been the envy of the world.[13] Even the self-proclaimed right-wing 'Republican Party reptile' P.J. O'Rourke has conceded that it constitutes 'good socialism'.[14]

CIRCULAR AND CUMULATIVE CAUSATION

How economic and social change occurs is a central theme in institutional econom-ics. Perhaps the most significant interpretation, with important implications for understanding modern capitalism and the formulation of public policies, is the prin-ciple of circular and cumulative causation. The notion has its roots in Veblen's writing and has since been developed by other institutional economists, most notably Gunnar Myrdal.[5] Its key postulate is that *economic inequalities, once established, tend to self-perpetuate and grow*. In one respect, this theory is an uncomfortable product of institutionalism because its practitioners are usually suspicious about claims regarding universal economic principles. Circular and cumulative causation looks like a general theory proposed by critics of general theory! Perhaps the best way of interpreting it is as a notion that can be applied in numerous specific contexts, ranging from the analysis of sexual and racial discrimination, to regional and national underdevelop-ment, and the formulation of industry policies. It is not so much a general theory as a 'way of seeing' that opens up new directions in analysis and policy.

The contrast with the equilibrium tendencies posited in neoclassical theory is cer-tainly striking. Recall the analogy of the ball on a saucer, invariably tending to a middle position in spite of 'external' disturbances—this is the essence of the neoclassical view of the economy in equilibrium. In circular and cumulative causation theory, if there is any equilibrium at all, it is the equilibrium of a pencil standing on its end. Once dis-turbed, the pencil will fall further and further away from its initial vertical position. This analogy illustrates the contrast with neoclassical theory, or 'equilibrium economics' as Nicholas Kaldor, another of the proponents of the principle of circular and cumulative causation, labels it.[6] However, it does not adequately convey the key feature of the institutional economic reasoning, which is more about *processes* than end states. Circular and cumulative causation processes arise because relationships in the real world between economic and social variables are seldom linear. Economic changes interact with social changes in ways that open up opportunities for economic growth and social progress. Meanwhile, problems beget problems.

Consider some examples. One obvious case in point is *racial discrimination*, the focus of one of Myrdal's early books.[7] If ethnic 'minority groups'—such as people of African descent in the United States or the Aboriginal peoples of Australia—are subject to discrimination, they are consigned to systematically inferior economic and social circumstances, usually manifest in lower incomes and higher unemploy-ment. These circumstances cause the victims of discrimination to cluster in areas where housing is cheaper, to wear clothing of inferior quality, and perhaps also to adopt self-destructive or anti-social patterns of personal behaviour. That provides a basis and apparent justification for further discrimination against them. A *vicious cycle* of disadvantage and prejudice develops.

A similar story can be told about *unemployment*. People who lose their jobs (or have difficulty finding a first job) usually experience a predictable sequence of responses, their optimism about their personal employment prospects turning to pessimism the longer they remain out of work. The personal characteristics, such as regular timekeeping, that employers usually look for in job applicants may atrophy.

Potential employers are also often suspicious of people who have significant gaps in their employment record. Eventually the unemployed people may rationalise their own situation by saying they do not want to work, anyway—then, it seems, they are not failures in their own eyes. The 'dole bludger' or 'work-shy' welfare recipient is thereby created. Conservative political campaigns then turn these 'undeserving' individuals into scapegoats for the unemployment problem, a process generally supported by the tabloid press and other capitalist-owned media. The victims become the problem.

This sort of sequence, writ large, is central to the problem of economic *under-development*. To quote the economic historian, Ragnar Nurske:

> a poor man may not have enough to eat; being undernourished his health may be weak; being physically weak, his working capacity may be low, which means that he is poor, which in turn means that he will not have enough to eat; and so on. A situation of this sort, applying to a country as a whole, can be summed up in the trite proposition 'a country is poor because it is poor'.[8]

This is a simple but powerful insight into the general nature of international economic inequalities, although it does not address the origin of the inequalities. It stands as a powerful antidote to the conventional economic claim, from Ricardo onwards, that more 'openness' in economic intercourse is necessarily to mutual advantage. The creation of a 'level playing field' may tend to give the already big players even more competitive advantage, accentuating the international economic inequalities.

Within nations there are also observable tendencies towards cumulative *regional inequality*. Particular cities and regions lead the way in economic growth, usually because of the inherent advantages of being first. Those with the 'head start', for whatever historical or geographical reasons, forge further ahead. Their better developed infrastructure makes them attractive to both capital and labour, with the result that migratory flows accentuate the core regions' growth. Meanwhile, emigration from the peripheral regions causes them to lose their younger and more entrepreneurial people. These are what Myrdal calls some of the 'backwash effects' in regional economies.[9] At the same time, firms in the core regions, having the best access to both consumer markets and factors of production, develop economies of scale, and external economies arise as firms cluster in those localities. There may then be some 'spread effects' from this growth, benefiting firms in neighbouring regions who serve the core regions with foodstuffs or ancillary services. However, the 'backwash effects' normally dominate, increasing regional economic inequalities. The 'urban bias' in poorer nations tends to have a similarly circular and cumulative character.[10]

These illustrations of the processes of circular and cumulative causation present a rather depressing picture. The possibilities for more balanced economic and social progress seem to be receding. Greater inequalities—racial, international, and regional—seem inevitable as a result of the operation of 'normal' socioeconomic processes. However, once understood, circular and cumulative causation analysis opens up more positive possibilities of change. It enables us to envisage what is needed to generate radically different outcomes. With strong policy commitments (and a little bit of luck), vicious cycles can be turned into virtuous cycles. Affirmative action policies can help to reverse the disadvantages suffered by 'minorities'. More balanced regional development can be fostered by policies that locate *growth centres* in underdeveloped regions, giving them the opportunity to become counter-magnets to the otherwise cumulatively dominant metropolitan centres. More effective *industry policies* can also be constructed, recognising the technical interdependencies of industries and developing institutions to foster the cooperation of firms within those industries.[11]

No general panacea is implied. Regional and industrial inequalities are difficult to redress and always entail 'opportunity costs' if the policy measures divert public expenditures from elsewhere. The problems of international economic inequality are particularly hard to resolve because of the need for international cooperation in the pursuit of solutions. Problems of social exclusion, stigmatisation, and racial discrimination are also never easy to turn around because of their socially embedded character. Long-term commitments, emphasising a necessary role for the state as a manager of the process of reform, are required. This means more than the augmentation of the 'market economy' with selective government 'intervention': it entails a holistic approach to economic and social policy within the context of the welfare state.

THE WELFARE STATE

The state features more prominently in institutional economics than in the other traditions of economics already considered in this book. This is linked to the generally *reformist* inclination of institutional economists, who are always looking for ways in which institutions can be developed and adapted to resolve socioeconomic problems and for ways to manage the evolution of economic society. Probably the most important expression of this reformist inclination, linking the concerns of institutional economics with the practical politics of social democracy, is the *development of the welfare state*. This was indeed one of the great practical political economic achievements of the twentieth century, tempering the capitalist economy with institutional means of enhancing economic security and redressing economic inequality. Since it is a development in danger of being rolled back in many countries in the early twenty-first century, the target of neo-liberal austerity measures, it is important to consider this legacy of economic and social reform.

It is usual to think of the welfare state as having experienced its most spectacular development in the years after World War II. Yet its foundations were laid earlier—during the late nineteenth century in Germany and the United Kingdom. Many intellectuals, as well as practical politicians, contributed to its development, supporting social reform based on legislative change and the extension of government's role to foster social institutions with humanistic goals.

One such important intellectual was John Hobson (1858–1940), a British economist who wrote prolifically on economic and social issues in the early twentieth century. He has been described as 'the Godfather of the newly formed British Labour Party'.[15] His wide-ranging concerns included the analysis of the causes of economic depression, imperialism, monopolies, and economic inequality. Denied a university post because of his unorthodox views, he may be seen in retrospect as a visionary of the welfare state. As Daniel Fusfeld puts it: 'Hobson believed that government action could end poverty, unemployment, and insecurity, and could establish a society in which human happiness prevailed. Utopian, yes—but this was the vision that lay behind English social legislation. Hobson did not originate it, but he was one of its best spokesmen'.[16] Here indeed was a foundation on which practical reformers like Britain's Lord Beveridge would later build, establishing the welfare state in practice by extending the provision of social security, pensions, unemployment insurance, public education, and public health facilities.

The welfare state has found its most fully developed form in the Scandinavian nations—Denmark, Norway, Sweden and Finland. The Swedish political economist Gunnar Myrdal was a significant contributor to this process (see box 25.2). The Scandinavian experience suggests that having social democratic parties in government is crucial for the full realisation of welfare state ambitions. However, even some conservative political parties have, in the past, accepted its logic. Both in the United Kingdom and Australia, for example, conservative governments during the 1950s and 1960s consolidated and, in some respects, extended welfare state provisions. Political economists were wont to say that this indicated that the welfare state served capitalist interests in the long term—ensuring a healthy workforce with the requisite skills; ensuring the high levels of consumer spending on which the economy depends; and contributing to the 'legitimation' process, which prevents any fundamental challenge to the prevailing socioeconomic system.[17]

So, was the welfare state *given or won*? Its realisation was the product of social and political struggle. Its development was also increasingly accepted by capitalist interests, who could see the economic benefits it generated. The Achilles heel, it seems, is the issue of how to finance it. There is no problem in principle. Taxes are the means by which revenue can be raised to finance welfare state expenditures. It is just a matter of allocating some of our national income, via taxes, to finance our collective social needs. In practice, though, this process is beset with tensions. In the early 1970s, the economist James O'Connor, drawing on Marxist as well as institutionalist reasoning, argued that a *fiscal crisis of the state* would frustrate further development of the welfare state.[18] The reluctance of upper income groups and businesses to contribute the tax revenues necessary to finance a comprehensive welfare state has since been the major source of tension in practice. The ascendancy of neo-liberal ideologies has concurrently undermined the perceived legitimacy of this substantial role for the state. This continues to be a focal point for contemporary political economic debate and struggle—a powerful reminder that the evolution of economic institutions is not free of contradictions.

A NEW INSTITUTIONALISM?

This brief survey of the major institutional economists and their practical contributions would be incomplete without considering the significance of what in recent years has been described as 'new institutionalism'. Its leading practitioners include the American economists Oliver Williamson and Richard Langlois. 'New institutionalists' are concerned with analysis of the relationship between individual and institutional behaviour.[19] Corporate hierarchies and non-market institutions are studied in relation to the rational choices of self-interested individuals within them. The underlying view is of society as a market in which individuals have continual opportunities to make mutually beneficial exchanges. Contracts may be made (explicitly or implicitly) between the parties in order to specify future rights and obligations. What bedevils the process is the pervasive problem of *transactions costs*. The costs of gathering information and specifying and enforcing contracts, for example, must be taken into account. The resulting institutional arrangements are therefore an outcome of more complex negotiations than normally assumed in mainstream economic theory.

This way of interpreting business behaviour, and social behaviour generally, is helpful in drawing attention to the effect of transactions costs on economic choices. However, putting the individual at the centre of attention gives a distinctly neoclassical orientation to this 'new' institutional economics. Much of the transactions-cost theory makes assumptions about individuals with given preferences. This tends to give primacy to the market, as in neoclassical theory. 'In the beginning there were markets', says Williamson in one of his books.[20] From that beginning some individuals go on to create firms and hierarchies, which endure if they can keep transactions costs down. Williamson claims a close connection between this focus on transactions costs and John Commons's idea of a transaction, but there is a fundamental difference of emphasis. As Geoff Hodgson puts it, 'for Williamson the unit of *analysis* is the given, abstract, atomistic and "opportunistic" individual, whereas Commons presupposes and stresses the organic and collective quality of institutions'.[21] What fades from view in the 'new' institutionalism are the characteristic concerns of 'old' institutionalism, such as how preferences, aspirations, and behaviour are moulded by circumstances and become embedded in the habits and customs of the people. Here, it seems, is a case where the 'new' is not an advance on the 'old'.

In a similar vein, it is pertinent to note the awkward relationship between 'new growth theories' and the 'old' institutionalist principle of circular and cumulative causation. There has been a recent flurry of concern with studying the *path-dependent character of economic growth*. This is the essence of the so-called 'new growth theories'.[22] The central proposition is that what happens tomorrow depends crucially on what happened yesterday and on what exists today. That may sound banal, but it is of some considerable economic significance. It means that the economic growth that a region or nation can achieve is constrained by its past experience. To give an example: implementing a particular government economic policy (such as tighter monetary policy) tends to change the overall level of national economic activity, which in turn affects future growth prospects and limits future policy options. This 'path dependency' has long been recognised by the proponents of circular and cumulative causation. However, the formal models of the new growth theorists purge the circular and cumulative causation theory of its qualitative insights into economic and social *processes*. As with the tension between the 'new institutional' theories of the firm and the older institutionalist tradition, the key difference is one of economic methodology—whether to make the simplifying assumption necessary for the construction of formal models or to emphasise the complex, qualitative changes associated with evolutionary processes.

Box 25.3

Joseph Schumpeter (1883–1950)

Joseph Schumpeter is not usually considered an institutional economist, but his work has many of the characteristics of institutionalism. He was certainly a 'big thinker', seeking to understand the trajectory of the economic system as a whole.

He grew up in an aristocratic household in Vienna before World War I. At that time, Vienna was a thriving centre of learning in the social sciences, and Schumpeter became interested in both neoclassical and Marxist economics, although his own work did not fall clearly into either category. He fled Europe as fascism spread and spent most of his professional career in the United States. While a professor at the Massachusetts Institute of Technology (where his penchant for wearing riding boots, even to faculty meetings, was notorious), he wrote the most comprehensive survey of the history of economic thought published to that date.

His best known political economic contribution is the book *Capitalism, Socialism and Democracy* (1943). In it he poses the question, 'can capitalism survive?' and answers, 'No, I do not think it can'. He saw the most attractive feature of capitalism as the dynamism generated by entrepreneurship and innovation, which created a 'perennial gale of creative destruction'. This feature would be eroded, he anticipated, by the development of large corporations. A managerial class would emerge, more concerned with sheltering from the perennial gale of creative destruction than in fostering it. The dynamism of the system would be throttled. This, he predicted, would pave the way for the change to socialism. It was a change that he saw as both regrettable and inevitable. Politically, this was indeed 'Marx upside down'.

Schumpeter viewed competition as crucial to the dynamism of capitalism, but it was competition among entrepreneurs seeking monopoly profits, not competition in perfectly competitive markets *à la* neoclassical theory. From this perspective, oligopoly is actually preferable to perfect competition because it enables firms to make sufficient profits to invest in research and development. However, the inherent danger is that 'rationalising' innovation eventually leads to it being prone to stagnation.

There has been a recent revival of interest in Schumpeter's economic analysis, sometimes labelled 'neo-Schumpeterian'. The modern variant is less concerned with the broad political economic trajectory of capitalism than with pragmatic aspects of industry policy. It sets aside Schumpeter's personal conservatism in favour of a more 'interventionist' approach to fostering innovation in industry. This focus on innovation as the key to economic dynamism underlies public policies of expenditure on education and training, and research and development. It is hoped that these will promote a 'high road' for economic development, providing interesting and secure careers. If so, it is a more attractive alternative than the 'low road' that emphasises cost reduction, particularly wage-cutting, as the means of securing national competitive advantage.[23]

CONCLUSION

Institutional economists have had diverse concerns. They form a motley crew, some would say. However, their contributions to political economy are important in at least three respects. They have been a consistent source of *critique* within the economics profession, challenging the dominance of neoclassical theorising and the 'unrealism' of its principal underlying assumptions. They have contributed useful *concepts*, such as the principle of circular and cumulative causation, for understanding and seeking to shape the evolution of economic society. They have had a significant practical *influence* on policies to ameliorate the extremes of a capitalist market economy, particularly through the development of the institutions of the welfare state.

A common element in all those contributions is the concern of institutional economics with economic power—its abuses and uses. This theme is further developed in the next chapter, looking in particular at the work of one of the great figures of the economics discipline during the last half century, the American political economist John Kenneth Galbraith.

CHAPTER 26

Economic Power

An institutionalist perspective

What are the principal sources of economic power?
How does John Kenneth Galbraith analyse the power structures in contemporary capitalism?
Can the power of capital be matched by the power of a reforming state?

The analysis of economic power is central to political economy. Indeed, this is its most obvious point of departure from the neoclassical orthodoxy. Power in neoclassical economics is limited to the study of power in the market place—the power exercised by consumers over firms as they make their purchasing decisions, or the power of monopolists to raise their prices above the level that would prevail under mere competitive conditions. It is a myopic view, focusing on only part of a bigger picture. As Marx emphasised, there are more *systemic* dimensions of power, such as the power that capital as a class exercises over labour.

Institutional economists have emphasised other types of power—the power that business corporations may exercise over governments, for example, and the power that they can exercise over consumers through processes of commercial advertising. Collective organisations, such as workers in trade unions or environmentalists in active pressure groups like Greenpeace, may enable other groups to exercise power to offset the power of corporate capital. The relative strength of these different kinds of power, and their sources and uses, warrants attention.

Particular focus here is given to the contributions of the distinguished political economist John Kenneth Galbraith. His numerous books have ranged over almost every conceivable aspect of political economy, but the study of power has been a consistently central theme.

THE ANATOMY OF POWER

Galbraith analyses power in a book devoted to this topic, appropriately called *The Anatomy of Power*.[1] He distinguishes three forms of power: condign, compensatory, and conditioned. *Condign power* is associated with coercion and punishment. It is the type of power exercised by a slave-owner over his slaves. More mildly, it is evident in all social behaviour constrained by the fear of rebuke. The common element in condign power is that submission occurs as the result of threatened or actual adverse consequences. *Compensatory power*, by contrast, works by offering rewards. If the fear of rebuke is a mild form of condign power, the pursuit of praise is its equivalent in terms

Box 26.1

John Kenneth Galbraith (1908–)

Galbraith has been a towering figure in modern institutional economics, both literally (being more than six and a half feet tall) and figuratively. He has made an enormous contribution to enhancing popular understanding of the modern economy. His numerous books on political economy have almost certainly been more widely read than those of any other twentieth-century economist.

Galbraith was born in 1908 into a Canadian farming family of Scottish descent. He studied agriculture at the University of Toronto and completed his PhD at the University of California, Berkeley. During World War II he was appointed Deputy Director for Price Administration for the US government, a post that gave him practical experience in the exercise of regulatory processes to control inflationary pressures, which invariably occur in wartime.

He became Professor of Economics at Harvard University, lectured at many other universities, and was elected President of the American Economics Association in 1972. He had a long-standing association with the Democratic Party, giving advice to presidents, including John F. Kennedy, who appointed him US Ambassador to India in the period 1961–63. He also wrote a novel and a book on Indian painting.

However, it is for his writing and public speaking on political economic issues that he is best known. Books such as *American Capitalism* (1952), *The Affluent Society* (1958), *The New Industrial State* (1967), *Economics and the Public Purpose* (1974), *Money* (1975), and *The Culture of Contentment* (1992) have been best-sellers. He also made a widely acclaimed television series called 'The Age of Uncertainty', which critically and wittily assessed the relationship between economic history and the development of economic ideas. For over half a century his has been an outstanding voice against the 'conventional wisdom' of conservative economists. Strong echoes of Thorstein Veblen's concerns are to be found in his writing—the shallowness and waste of consumer society, the shifts in power over key economic decisions, and the evolutionary character of the economy. Like Veblen, Galbraith has also enjoyed ambiguous status in the economics profession: he has been widely praised for his elegant writing and engagement with the major practical concerns of the day, but he has also been derided for his dissident views and preference for verbal argument rather than formal economic modelling.

His son, James K. Galbraith, has followed in his footsteps as a prominent critic of mainstream economic theory and of what passes for orthodoxy in the realm of economic policy.

of compensatory power. More specifically in the modern economy, compensatory power usually takes the form of pecuniary reward. Submission to the economic purposes of others finds its compensation in a monetary payment. This is central to the functioning of capitalism. So, too, is the third type of power, *conditioned power*, which is exercised by changing people's beliefs. As Galbraith puts it, 'persuasion, education, or the social commitment to what seems natural, proper or right causes the individual to submit to the will of another or of others'.[2] Submission may not be, indeed normally is not, conscious. The essence of conditioned power is willing, even enthusiastic, compliance. Social conformity is its hallmark.

So, what differentiates those who wield power from those who submit to it? Galbraith continues his analysis of power by identifying its three sources: personality, property, and organisation. *Personality* in this context is broadly interpreted as the qualities of leadership, ranging from physique to personal persuasiveness. 'Charisma' is one commonly cited manifestation—albeit one that is notoriously difficult to define. *Property* is the more obviously economic source of power. This is the power that derives from wealth, including command over resources, and the capacity to hire and dismiss employees. However, according to Galbraith, it is *organisation* that is the most important source of power in modern societies. The power of corporate executives or of senior state bureaucrats derives from their organisational positions, not primarily from their personalities or personal property. On their retirement, the organisational basis of their power disappears overnight. Power attaches to their office, not their person. Similarly, in the political arena, the power of a politician derives from having a senior position in government or having the capacity to influence colleagues in such positions. Again, on losing office, the power usually disappears; the retired politician may command an interested audience but usually wields little or no power.

Rather more contentiously, Galbraith asserts a general correlation between the three types of power and the three sources of power. According to this reasoning, the exercise of condign power is most directly associated with power structures based on personality or leadership; compensatory power has its strongest linkage with power structures deriving from property; while conditioned power is characteristic of organisational sources of power. These he calls 'primary but not exclusive associations', conceding that there are also 'numerous combinations of the sources of power and the related instruments'.[3] The taxonomy starts to look less tidy.

Galbraith's *Anatomy of Power* is a useful starting point for thinking about the avenues through which power is exercised, but deeper insights come from other works, particularly those he has himself identified as his principal political economic quartet: *American Capitalism*, subtitled *The Theory of Countervailing Power*; *The Affluent Society*; *The New Industrial State*; and *Economics and the Public Purpose*. Figure 26.1 shows the major themes developed in them and is a succinct summary of his important contributions to the understanding of power in modern capitalism.

TECHNOLOGY, PLANNING, THE CORPORATION

Technology has a leading role in Galbraith's conception of the economy. He regards capitalism as being, in substantial measure, the offspring of technology.[4] He emphasises the incessant pressures for economic change due to 'the systematic application of scientific or other organised knowledge to practical tasks'.[5] These tasks involve the provision of services as well as the production of goods, particularly at the present time, when the spread of information technologies has been so rapid. Relentless technological change has always been a prominent feature of capitalist development. The building-up of vast productive capacity based on increasingly sophisticated production and transportation technologies is perhaps the source of its greatest achievement. What Marx called the 'forces of production' have indeed been revolutionised.

Does this constitute a technological imperative? Galbraith's critics accuse him of *technological determinism*, of implying that technological change has a life of its own rather than being a product of capitalist interests.[6] Indeed, technology may have its own partially independent momentum, driven by the findings of scientists researching new materials, processes, and applications, for example. This independence is lessened, of course, as research becomes more dependent on corporate funding. Much of the research leading to innovation is now done by the companies themselves, particularly when associated with new product development. So, the form and direction of technological change is directly linked to capitalist interests. This has major implications for the organisation of the companies, their relationship with one another, and the broader society.

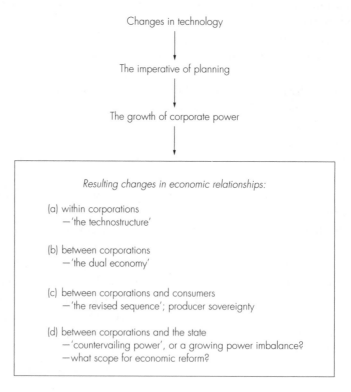

Figure 26.1 Elements in Galbraith's analysis of economic power.

Galbraith's analysis emphasises that an economy based on increasingly sophisticated technology must necessarily be a *planned* economy. In a capitalist system, it is the big firms who are the planners. They need to make long-term, large-scale commitments of capital because the capital goods embodying the complex technologies are so expensive; and the commitment of funds to research and development adds further to the cost. Therein lies a paradox: the capitalist system, whose supporting ideology emphasises free markets, has become characterised, in practice, by institutions engaged in planning as a means of limiting market uncertainties. A world of rapidly changing technologies is always one of uncertainty. Committing capital to the purchase of equipment based on a particular technology is a risky business, for those capital goods can be quickly superseded by further innovations. It is for this reason that planning is inescapable. The competitive market place is too unstable, too focused on the short term, for a technologically sophisticated economic system requiring long-term, large-scale commitment of capital.

Does this comprise a 'new socialism'?[7] As the corporate sector of capitalism becomes a planned economy, does the system take on a characteristic more commonly associated with the socialist alternative? This possibility, sometimes labelled the *convergence* thesis, is a controversial interpretation of the long-term trajectories of capitalism and socialism. In essence, it is the claim that the rival systems, notwithstanding their competing ideologies, must necessarily come to look alike because all economic activity is shaped by common technological and organisational imperatives. But the term 'new socialism' does not necessarily connote a complete convergence; it certainly does not mean that capitalism fades away. What Galbraith is talking about is a system run by corporations for corporations. The planning is for *private* interests rather than the pursuit of broader social goals. It only takes on a more broadly socialist character if the corporations are forced—by the 'countervailing power' of governments or trade unions, for example—to assume wider social responsibilities. In Galbraith's analysis, 'new socialism' implies a substantial role for the state in managing and steering the capitalist economy, notwithstanding the rhetoric equating capitalism with 'free markets'.

Overall, the picture presented by Galbraith is one in which several hundred giant corporations, able to control technology and plan for their own corporate interests rather than simply responding to market forces, dominate the economy. This corporate sector of the modern economy controls an essential part of contemporary industry. Its enormous economic power reshapes economic relationships—within the corporations; between firms; and with consumers, workers, and governments.

POWER WITHIN CORPORATIONS

Those who control the information necessary for the day-to-day running of the corporate economy are, according to Galbraith, the focal point in the exercise of corporate power. These people he labels collectively the '*technostructure*', comprising 'all who bring specialised knowledge, talent or experience to group decision-making'.[8] Technicians, scientists, engineers, financial controllers, market researchers, and human resource managers are among its members. University qualifications are the norm—so, economics undergraduates, in particular, may be reassured to know that they are on the road to joining the most powerful group in modern capitalism.

It is important to distinguish the technostructure from the owners of the big corporations. The crucial feature of the former is not ownership, nor even an elevated position in the organisational hierarchy: it is *control of information*. The technostructure has the detailed knowledge about running the business, whereas the owners have only a pecuniary interest in the outcomes. This aspect of Galbraith's analysis builds on the earlier work of institutional economists Berle and Means (discussed in the preceding chapter), which explored the significance of the separation of ownership from control in the modern corporation. Galbraith goes one step further, however, distinguishing between the formal power of the capitalist owners and the practical power of the technostructure, which derives from its control over the sources and uses of information. The latter has more day-to-day opportunity to shape how capitalist businesses operate in practice.

Galbraith justifies his emphasis on the power of the technostructure with a characteristically neat argument. Under feudalism, he notes, land was the key factor of production, so the owners of land were the dominant class. With the development of industrial capitalism, capital became the key factor of production, and power switched to its owners and controllers. With the advent of the 'information age', those who generate and control information become the key group. Here is a strong contrast, both with the neoclassical assumption of the firm as a single decision-maker and with the Marxian view of the continuing dominance of the capitalist class. Galbraith emphasises the latter contrast as follows:

> Once all economic and social thought turned on a bilateral economic and social structure. There were capital and labour, the capitalist and the worker. There were also, to be sure, farmers. And intellectuals and others. But capital and labour, capital versus labour, that was the basic dialectic. Marx had an authority here that would have surprised even him. This is no longer the case in the advanced industrial countries. The great political dichotomy—the capitalist and the working masses—have retreated into the shadows. It survives not as a reality but as mental commitment. In place of the capitalist there is now the modern great corporate bureaucracy. Not capitalists but managers.[9]

Whether or not the managers serve the capitalists is, of course, the crucial question. In general, one may expect them to do so.[10] However, according to Galbraith, there is some evidence of a self-serving tendency. Managers, he notes, are commonly concerned with corporate *growth*, even at the expense of profit maximisation, since therein lies the strongest correlation with their own employment security, income, and prestige. This reinforces the growth-orientation of the modern capitalist system as a whole, what Galbraith had earlier called 'the paramount position of production'.[11] Evidence of yet more directly self-serving tendencies today are the increasingly generous managerial remuneration packages and the perquisites of office. But these prodigious incomes are mainly enjoyed by chief executive officers (CEOs) and other top managers; the members of the technostructure generally receive rather more modest rewards, notwithstanding their key role in actually running the corporations.

POWER BETWEEN CORPORATIONS

The scope for the discretionary exercise of managerial power depends crucially on the relationships between the corporations themselves. These relationships are both cooperative and competitive. Large firms in the corporate sector must continually make strategic decisions about the use of power. Theirs is a world that neoclassical economists describe as *oligopolistic* (see chapter 21), using this term to describe the structural relationship between firms in a particular *industry*. In modern capitalism, by contrast, large corporations often straddle different industries, making a range of products that defy categorisation in a single industry sector. This is the essence of the corporate economy—what Galbraith calls the *planning system*.[12] It comprises large corporations that are individually powerful in shaping their own market shares, their corporate culture, and their organisational practices, and that are collectively powerful in reshaping the world in their own image and interests.

Alongside this planning system is a *market system* comprising smaller businesses where more traditionally competitive practices operate. Galbraith concedes that the sort of market principles discussed by neoclassical theorists under the rubric of 'imperfect competition' may have some role to play here. He thereby reinterprets the neoclassical theory of oligopoly as relevant to the realm of relatively small rather than big business. But the situation is complicated by the *dependence* of these firms in the market system on the giants in the planning system. The former usually supply the latter with intermediate products, with services, and with subcontracted elements in the production process. This dependent, or subordinate, character of the market system is its most general characteristic. The dualism of the planning and market systems involves a dramatic asymmetry in the distribution of economic power.

CORPORATIONS AND CONSUMERS

What about the consumers? Their purchases are essential for the corporations to achieve their goals and, generally, for the relentlessly growth-oriented capitalist system to continue functioning. According to the neoclassical theory of consumer sovereignty, it is the consumers' preferences that call forth the products: the pattern of consumption thereby determines the pattern of production (or at least *what* is produced). Galbraith posits that the reverse situation is more typical. This is what he calls 'the revised sequence', perhaps the most controversial of Galbraith's claims about the use of corporate power in modern capitalism.[13] According to his reasoning, it is imperative that large firms seek to control the demand for their products as far as possible. This is integral to long-term corporate strategy and made necessary by the major commitments of capital necessary for the large-scale production of their goods. Hence the channelling of prodigious resources into commercial advertising and other sales promotion activities, designed to create product acceptance and ensure consumer 'brand loyalty'. The preferred pattern of production thereby shapes the pattern of consumption. *Producer sovereignty* replaces consumer sovereignty.

Stated so baldly, the argument is not wholly compelling. It is not as if firms can simply mould and exploit gullible consumers—at least not all the time. Galbraith himself acknowledges important exceptions to producer sovereignty and the importance of the context within which product choices are made.[14] New products, even extensively advertised ones, sometimes fail. And 'brand loyalty' can wane when rival firms are simultaneously pursuing extensive sales promotion activities for their own products. Market research also provides something of a feedback loop, ensuring that the 'want-creation' process has some basis in consumers' potential preferences, founded on aspirations or psychological fears that can be exploited for commercial advantage. Most significantly, it all takes place in a broader social context that glamorises consumption. A widespread acceptance of the consumerist ethos—'I consume, therefore I am'—is the necessary condition for the effectiveness of producer sovereignty.

The inclusion of these contextual considerations gives Galbraith's argument greater force and generality. It also raises some profound questions about the purposes of economic activity in an affluent society. Is there a reliable connection between consumption and happiness? Does the production of ever more goods and services contribute to a good society?

Galbraith's analysis has an explicitly normative dimension. It is not simply a matter of countering the neoclassical theory of the consumer with a more 'realistic' view of the power relationships involved in consumption processes in practice. It is also a matter of drawing attention to the roots of pervasive social problems. Perhaps most fundamental is the tendency towards ever higher levels of goods and services being consumed. Consumption has its purposes, but they are increasingly *social* in character, once basic needs for food, clothing, and shelter have been met. Even those basic goods come to be consumed increasingly as means of social display. On the subject of clothing, for example, Galbraith says 'to a marked extent, attire remains to this day ... a prime badge of social position and distinction'.[15] An echo of Thorstein Veblen is clearly audible. If we can distinguish between needs and wants—and Galbraith differs from the neoclassicals in arguing that we can and should—and if the wants are becoming increasingly frivolous, then there is no necessary connection between increased consumption and social well-being.

The tendency towards the dichotomy of *private wealth and public squalor* makes the situation yet worse.[16] According to Galbraith, private sector consumption tends to expand at the expense of the quality of the public sector. So, we have fabulously expensive private cars, but inadequately maintained public roads on which to drive them. Our poorly funded public education and public health systems struggle to maintain quality alongside vastly more affluent private schools and elaborate private medical services. These are striking examples of 'social imbalance' in modern capitalism.

CORPORATIONS AND THE STATE

Can we look to the state to rectify problems of 'social imbalance' and, generally, to manage capitalism in the public interest? Indeed we must, says Galbraith. However, we also need to recognise the major tensions arising from the power relationships between corporations and the state. The focus on the balance of power between the corporations and the state is the crux of Galbraith's political analysis and, as we shall see in chapter 37, is crucial in the construction of modern political economy.

In his early writing, Galbraith was relatively optimistic that the growing power of corporations would be checked by other sources of *countervailing power*, particularly the power of government and unions.[17] His later work emphasises the problems of growing *power imbalance* as the corporate sector has become ever more dominant. But this imbalance can be corrected by strengthening the capacity of the state. Hence, the need for a theory, and program, of economic reform to curtail corporate power and pursue 'the public purpose'.[18]

At one level, this reformist position echoes the 'liberal interventionism' of some orthodox economists, giving primacy to the market but acknowledging a supplementary role for the state. The 'market failure' perspective is evident in Galbraith's proposition that 'there are some things the market system does not do well or sometimes even badly. These must be the responsibility of the state'.[19] However, for Galbraith, the range of such intervention is atypically broad. Ensuring that all citizens have access to a basic source of income, to a decent educational system that may facilitate upward social mobility, to low-cost housing, and to good health services, and ensuring that there is funding for the sciences and the arts, that peace is maintained, and that recession is avoided—these are the characteristic policies that he regards as necessary, if we are to live in a good society. 'This requires positive government intervention', says Galbraith, adding, with his characteristic humour, that 'prediction and prayer, the instruments of policy in past years, will not serve'.[20]

Support for systematically reformist policy measures, he had earlier argued, might be expected to be forthcoming from *the educational and scientific estate*, comprising the better educated and more economically advantaged social strata.[21] However, in recent years, Galbraith's writing has become more pessimistic about this potential source of support for economic and social reform. The political will to effect the reforms is evidently lacking (at least in the United States, which is his principal focus), particularly among the members of the middle class who might be expected to have the most enlightened reformist views.

What Galbraith wryly calls the *culture of contentment* has now become dominant.[22] An affluent electoral majority, enjoying the fruits of a consumer society, has become defensive, conservative, and fearful of change. Its members no longer look to government as an instrument for social betterment. Instead, their concerns have turned inwards, away from political processes and the collective provision for social needs, to market processes and individual provision. They inhabit a demi-world of private schooling, private health insurance plans, and private houses, often in private security-patrolled 'gated communities', insulated from the social underclass. They are extremely reluctant to pay the taxes that would be necessary to fund higher levels of government expenditure on the provision of public goods. It is a deeply disturbing situation, one which has also been emphasised by prominent American political scientist Christopher Lasch in his book *The Revolt of the Elites*.[23] Both Galbraith and Lasch are talking about an economic system effectively out of the control of the political process.

TOWARDS THE 'GOOD SOCIETY'?

Galbraith's political economy exhibits both the pessimism of the intellect and the optimism of the will. The latter aspect continually prevails. The last section of *Economics and the Public Purpose* explores the possibilities of significant political economic reform—notwithstanding the powerful reasoning in the preceding chapters about the concentration of economic power that might be expected to stand in its way. His more recent book, *The Good Society*, presents a significant reformist agenda for capitalism in the years ahead.

First and foremost, Galbraith argues, public policy must address the fate of the 'underclass'—the social stratum comprising people excluded from the 'culture of contentment'. Some are unemployed or have only marginal attachment to the workforce, effectively forming a modern industrial reserve army. Some do heavy repetitive industrial work. Others are engaged in doing the jobs that make life pleasant for the corporate bureaucrats, the diverse smaller entrepreneurs, the lawyers, doctors, teachers, and other professionals—'the cultural elite, as it has been called, and the large pensioned and rentier community'.[24] Members of the underclass harvest their fruit and vegetables, clean their streets, and collect their garbage. A very broad interpretation of 'underclass' is evident here, straddling traditional views of the working class, economically marginalised segments of society, and minorities subject to discrimination. It serves Galbraith's purpose in drawing attention to the continuing need for public policy to be concerned with economic inequality. At bottom, it is a concern for social order, a concern that 'those who have no other outlet for political expression may well take to the streets in protest or … escape civilised reality into drugs and crime'.[25]

Generally, the case for public policy to assist the 'underclass' reflects an egalitarian political sentiment, or as much of one as can, seemingly, be tolerated in modern American society. Hence, the case for policies to expand employment opportunities, improve opportunities for upward social mobility, and, as a last resort, for the state to provide basic income. As Galbraith says, 'there can be no claim to civilised existence when such a safety net is not available'.[26] It is symptomatic of the welfare state being in retreat that such a case even needs to be restated.

The rationale for direct government provision of public goods also has an egalitarian dimension to the extent 'that many of these services—public works, parks, and recreational facilities, police, libraries, and many others—are more important for, more needed by, the poor than the affluent'.[27] On the other hand, the case for extending public provision in the arts and the sciences, including medical research, reflects their general neglect in a market economy with a short-term orientation. Galbraith notes that 'some of our most important American achievements of recent generations—the great improvements in agricultural productivity, modern air transport, advanced electronics—have depended heavily on public investment'.[28]

Public investment is also necessary because, according to Galbraith, 'the tendency of the market system to periods of despondency and depression', is a basic feature of the capitalist market economy.[29] The echoes of Marx in this view of capitalism are drowned out by the Keynesian commitment to, and confidence in, the possibilities of remedial policies being implemented by governments. Indeed, this is the characteristic political stance throughout the Galbraithian analysis: the continued reassertion of the need for our political institutions to effect the necessary remedies for pervasive socioeconomic problems. It is an exemplary social democratic stance.

Galbraith is not blind to the obstacles to reform. His earlier calls for the *emancipation of the state*, freeing government from domination by corporate interests, and for the *emancipation of belief*, challenging the dominance of orthodox economic beliefs in particular, illustrate the immensity of the task.[30] Indeed, therein lies a tension between Galbraith's analysis and his prescriptions. The penetrating analysis of the power structures shows the obstacles to the reforms that are advocated. It is a tension that cannot be resolved purely in the realm of political economic analysis. As Galbraith has repeatedly emphasised, it is the 'march of circumstances', not the theories and wishful thinking of economists, that is ultimately decisive.[31]

CONCLUSION

Taking Galbraith's political economy as a case study provides useful insights into the analysis of modern economic institutions and their power. It also draws attention to the forces driving political economic change and the possibilities for steering change by the exercise of political power. It regards orthodox economics as being fundamentally misleading because of it emphasises equilibrium conditions, implicitly treating the economy as a stable, immutable structure. Galbraith's alternative analysis is evolutionary economics *par excellence*. The capitalist economy is understood in terms of technology-driven changes, moulded by powerful institutions, and reshaping economic structures, social behaviour, and political possibilities.

Galbraith's analysis of this world of powerful economic institutions is correspondingly wide-ranging. It lacks the precision—certainly the formal model construction—of neoclassical theory (and, to some extent, of Marxist economics, too). It is on these grounds that Galbraith has often been a target for criticism among more conservative economists, and even some on the political Left. This reflects a general tension in political economic analysis—between elegance and relevance. In Galbraith's work, elegance comes through the careful crafting of arguments and through his mastery of the English language, not through the use of formal theory, diagrams, and mathematics. Indeed, the study of economic power—its sources, uses and abuses—brooks no facile formalisation. Galbraith's analysis is more directly relevant to contemporary economic, social, and public trends. He writes primarily about the United States, but his vision also embraces developments on the world stage. It thereby links with analyses of recent institutional changes in the process of corporate 'globalisation'.

CHAPTER 27

Corporate Globalisation
Transnational institutions

What are the main dimensions of the process of globalisation?
What are the implications for political economic analysis and policy?
How does globalisation change the balance of economic power?

'Globalisation' is one of the most frequently noted trends of the present time. It is also one of the most hotly debated concepts in political economy. At one extreme are those who consider globalisation to be a relentless process, driven by technological and commercial imperatives and rapidly undermining the sovereignty of nation states, perhaps even destroying the political economic significance of national boundaries.[1] At the other extreme are the 'globalisation sceptics' who argue that there is nothing new about international commerce and that the task for nation states, as ever, is to determine how to reconcile it with the pursuit of national economic interests.[2] Analytically, many questions arise in such debates. How is globalisation to be defined? How does the globalisation of capital relate to the globalisation of labour, of the state, and of non-governmental organisations? Is globalisation orchestrated by a trans-national capitalist class? Are nation states independent of such interests? What are the implications for democratic processes? Who wins from globalisation? Who loses?

Institutional economists have a head start in contributing answers to these questions because of their long-standing concern to understand the evolving characteristics of economic society. Their focus, as set out in the three preceding chapters, is on what is distinctive about the *institutions* of capital, labour, and the state; how they are changing over time; and how the economic, social, and political aspects of that institutional behaviour interact. The work of Australian political economist Ted Wheelwright exemplifies these concerns. The subsequent analysis draws on his pioneering contributions to the analysis of globalisation.[3]

TRANSNATIONAL CORPORATIONS

It makes sense to begin by looking at the major institutional actors. In the drama of globalisation these are, first and foremost, the transnational corporations (TNCs). These are companies that have subsidiaries or associate companies in more than one country—often in many countries. Their distinctive feature is not that they engage in international trade, but that they have financial sources, manufacturing operations, administrative offices, and marketing operations in different countries.

Box 27.1

Ted Wheelwright (1921–)

Ted Wheelwright has been an inspiring figure in the development of Australian political economy. He taught at the University of Sydney for more than three decades, retiring in 1986. As a teacher, he was much respected by his students for his emphasis on up-to-date developments in the real world rather than the repetition of outdated theories. Like Galbraith, he was always inclined to poke fun at the 'conventional wisdom' in economics—but with serious intent.

His research and writing focused on the analysis of 'globalisation' long before that term became popular. He pointed to the dangers of overreliance on foreign investment. He emphasised that transnational corporations have created a 'new corporate world economic order'. He predicted that governments seeking to attract investment by transnational corporations would tend to become 'client states'—effectively at the service of the corporations.

These developments, Wheelwright argued, would accentuate the tendency for the economic interests of capital, supported by the exercise of state power, to work against the interests of ordinary working people. A two-volume history of Australia, written in conjunction with economic historian Ken Buckley, extended this working class perspective to a broader description and critique of capitalist development 'down under'. Other themes in Wheelwright's political economy include the ascendancy of Asian capitalism and the influence of Japanese investment on other nations, particularly Australia. His writing has also been consistently critical of the concentration of corporate power and of the complicity of orthodox economics in this process. He established the Transnational Corporations Research Project as a means of encouraging research on global big business.

Together with other dissident political economists, Wheelwright also participated in the long struggle to establish political economy courses at University of Sydney—a focal point in Australia for the challenge to conservative economic orthodoxy. The struggle bore fruit in 1975 with the introduction of the first of a sequence of undergraduate units of study in political economy. Other course developments, both undergraduate and postgraduate, followed. The *Journal of Australian Political Economy* was introduced as a means of disseminating political economic analyses and ideas, both within academe and in the community at large. More than a quarter of a century later, these initiatives are flourishing. They make the University of Sydney one of the key centres, internationally as well as nationally, of teaching and research in political economy.

There are many such companies. United Nations sources refer to some 600 000 TNCs. About 1 per cent of these own half the total assets.[4] They control about half the world trade in non-agricultural products. They have twice the amount of reserves of national currencies as the official government institutions (treasuries and reserve banks) of the countries of the world. Their prodigious growth continues.

Many are now bigger than nations. Of the world's 100 largest economic entities, ranked according to market capitalisation, only 29 are nations, while 71 are TNCs.[5]

These TNCs have their headquarters in various countries. Among the best known TNCs with headquarters in the United States are General Electric, Ford, General Motors, Microsoft, Exxon Mobil, IBM, and Coca-Cola Amatil. TNCs based in Europe include Vodafone, Nestlé, Glaxo Smith Kline, and Royal Dutch Shell. The biggest TNCs based in Japan are Sony, Toyota, Nippon T&T, and Mitsui. North America, the European nations, and Japan together account for the overwhelming bulk of TNC headquarters. The products of these corporations cover the gamut of consumer goods, from processed foods and cigarettes, to pharmaceuticals, cars, televisions, and other electronic consumer durables; and also the full range of producer goods, such as steel, aluminium, chemicals, and plastics.

Alongside the giant firms producing those tangible products are other institutions carrying out purely *financial* functions. Most prominent among these are the banks, many of which have themselves become TNCs. Until the 1980s, most banking institutions were national, having 'overseas' operations as an adjunct to their major domestic activities. Since the 1980s, however, there has been a dramatic, although less than complete, globalisation of financial services. The major banks, whether originally based in New York, Tokyo, London, Paris, or any other city, now carry out their banking operations in numerous countries worldwide. This growth of the transnational banks—and of global finance generally—is in the interests of TNCs producing goods and services. The transnational banks help them arrange their global financial requirements, and thereby play a key role in the globalisation of productive capital. The banks themselves are also in a position to be global profit maximisers, arranging their activities on a world scale in order to minimise the constraints imposed by nationally based regulatory agencies. This gives them tremendous economic power.

INDUSTRIAL CONCENTRATION, WORLD INDUSTRIES, CONGLOMERATES

The growth of TNCs has generated significantly different patterns of industrial concentration. One conventional national measure of concentration is the proportion of the total output in a particular industry that is produced by the largest, say, six firms in that industry. Where TNCs dominate, such measures of concentration are typically increased. The process has now broken the bounds of national economies. It has led to the development of 'world industries' in which a handful of TNCs are the dominant players.

Already by the 1980s, according to Ted Wheelwright and researcher Greg Crough, six firms controlled two-thirds of the output of aluminium in the capitalist world economy, seven firms controlled half of oil refining for the manufacture of petrol, seven firms controlled 80 per cent of the production of tobacco products (other than that in the hands of state tobacco monopolies), eight firms controlled two-thirds of the output of computers, and ten firms produced more than 80 per cent of the cars.[6] Industrial concentration on a global scale has proceeded apace. It has also affected *service* industries, although these have traditionally been much

Rank	Entity	Total market capitalisation (US$ billion)	Rank	Entity	Total market capitalisation (US$ billion)	Rank	Entity	Total market capitalisation (US$ billion)	Rank	Entity	Total market capitalisation (US$ billion)
1	USA	14 016	26	Vodafone (eur)	184	51	Greece	101	76	Deutsche Tel (eur)	71
2	Japan	2 955	27	Intel (us)	182	52	Home Depot (us)	99	77	Abbott Labs (us)	69
3	UK	2 423	28	Finland	182	53	Nippon T&T (jap)	97	78	Pharmacia/Monsanto (us)	69
4	France	1 380	29	South Korea	180	54	Roche/Genen (eur)	97	79	Morgan Stanley (us)	67
5	Germany	1 241	30	AIG (us)	178	55	Total/Fina/Elf (eur)	96	80	Telefonica (eur)	67
6	Switzerland	738	31	IBM (us)	173	56	Chevron/Texaco (us)	93	81	Amgen (us)	67
7	Canada	700	32	Merck (us)	166	57	Morgan Chase (us)	90	82	Norway	65
8	Italy	705	33	AOL/TimeWarner (us)	159	58	AT&T (us)	88	83	UBS (eur)	64
9	Hong Kong	627	34	GlaxoSmithKline (eur)	155	59	Berkshire Hathaway (us)	87	84	Dell Computer (us)	64
10	Holland	600	35	Singapore	151	60	Oracle (us)	86	85	Israel	63
11	Spain	521	36	SBC Comm (us)	145	61	BankAmerica (us)	86	86	Sun Microsystems (us)	62
12	General Electric (us)	436	37	Belgium	137	62	Eli Lilly (us)	86	87	PepsiCo (us)	62
13	Australia	373	38	Cisco (us)	136	63	ProctorGamble (us)	86	88	Sony (jap)	61
14	Sweden	306	39	Verizon (us)	132	64	Tyco/Mattel (us)	85	89	Portugal	61
15	Taiwan	302	40	Toyota (jap)	132	65	Ireland	84	90	Vivendi/Univ (eur)	61
16	Microsoft (us)	290	41	Mexico	130	66	AstraZeneca (eur)	83	91	Texas Instruments (us)	59
17	Exxon Mobil (us)	282	42	Johnson & Johnson (us)	129	67	Wells Fargo (us)	82	92	Chile	59
18	Pfizer (us)	237	43	Nokia (eur)	125	68	China Mobile (hk)	80	93	ING (eur)	59
19	Citigroup (us)	233	44	Coca-Cola (us)	120	69	EMC (us)	76	94	Nortel (can)	58
20	South Africa	218	45	Malaysia	117	70	Fannie Mae (us)	76	95	Amgen (us)	57
21	Wal-Mart (us)	212	46	Bristol-Myers (us)	114	71	Nestlé (eur)	76	96	France Telecom (eur)	57
22	Royal Dutch (eur)	201	47	Denmark	111	72	BellSouth (us)	76	97	Viacom/CBS (us)	57
23	WorldCom (us)	192	48	Philip Morris (us)	105	73	American Home (us)	74	98	Qwest Comm (us)	57
24	Brazil	192	49	Novartis (eur)	104	74	AT&T Wireless (us)	74	99	Aventis (eur)	56
25	BP Amoco (eur)	185	50	HSBC (eur)	103	75	Allianz (eur)	71	100	Hewlett-Packard (us)	56

Total market capitalisation of stock markets (domestic equities only) and market capitalisation of the world's biggest companies as as at 28 February 2001.

Sources: *International Federation of Stock Markets and Hoover's Stockscreener Search Engine.*

Table 27.1 Countries and companies: the world's 100 largest capitalist economic entities

more localised in their focus than manufacturing industries. Twenty years ago, for example, people referred to the 'big eight' accounting firms who provided financial services internationally, mainly to other businesses; now, as a result of mergers in the industry, it is the 'big five'.

Having only a relatively small number of players does not mean that competition disappears. On the contrary, competition among TNCs for market share is often vigorous. However, it is usually *non-price competition*, focusing on product differentiation and corporate image, for example. It is not the competition of the perfectly competitive markets analysed by neoclassical economists. Even the stylised neoclassical theories of 'imperfect' market structures, such as monopolistic competition and oligopoly, have dubious relevance in relation to industries characterised by such striking concentrations of economic power.

The situation is further complicated because many of the TNCs are *conglomerates*. They are giant organisations with diverse productive activities straddling different industries.[7] Because they are engaged in many industries, it is hard to analyse them using the conventional economic notions of industries and firms. The image of an industry as comprising firms that make broadly similar products does not apply where conglomerates exist. The proliferation of conglomerates in recent decades therefore challenges the basic categories of orthodox economics. It also challenges political economists considering the significance of this further concentration of economic power.

THE NEGATION OF THE MARKET?

A market system imposes some discipline on economic life. According to neoclassical economists, it ensures that the pattern of goods and services produced will correspond to the pattern of consumers' preferences. To the extent that the economic prosperity of TNCs, including conglomerates, depends ultimately on them selling their products, the market continues to exert that ultimate discipline. However, many of the activities of TNCs are concerned with bypassing, even undermining, the market system. Many of their transactions do not occur through markets. Over a third of global merchandise trade is between TNCs and their subsidiaries: in other words, it is *intra-corporate* trade.[8] It opens up possibilities for 'business reciprocity'—the practice of making sales to, and purchases from, corporations that are customers of conglomerates. As Crough and Wheelwright note: 'this new kind of "market" responds much more to the procedures developed to maximise global profits by head office than to traditional market signals or the administrative fiats of national governments. Hence a new form of "international" capitalism is born, very much less susceptible to traditional market forces, beyond the control of any national government; and no international government exists'.[9]

There are some apparent advantages for consumers arising from this increasingly global character of production and distribution. The companies may reduce costs by taking advantage of economies of scale and of global sourcing of their production and financial requirements; and consumers may benefit in so far as inter-firm competition leads to part of those savings being passed to consumers in the form of lower product prices. Consumers gain easier access to products from distant lands—

they can, effectively, shop in a global bazaar. For those consumers who are themselves internationally mobile, there may be some advantages in the standardisation
of product quality: a can of Coke, a packet of Dunhill cigarettes, or a night in a
Holiday Inn hotel each has a predictable standard, almost irrespective of the place
where it is purchased. Other, less mobile, consumers may derive psychological pleasure from buying products commonly identified through commercial advertising
with international celebrities or global brand imagery.

Meanwhile, some profound concerns arise from the concentration of economic
power in the TNCs. The promotion of *consumerism*, accentuated by the quest for
maximum penetration of global markets, is the most obvious. Whether it is sustainable in the longer term is a moot point. Whether it even leads to greater consumer
satisfaction is also dubious, since the process of sales promotion increases aspirations
at the same time as promising to satisfy those aspirations. The greater uniformity of
products is also a mixed blessing, as some say it tends to undermine cultural diversity.
This process is particularly evident in the media and entertainment 'industries'. Any
benefits consumers derive from having access to a range of global products have to
be set against the impact on local economies. Local industries may be destroyed or
taken over by TNCs, and regional economies may become increasingly dependent
on decisions taken by businesses with no roots in the locality. It has been said that the
ideal factory would be one that is built on a floating platform that could be towed
around the world to where wages and other cost considerations would make it most
advantageous to produce at the time.[10] It is a fantasy, but one that accords with the
processes actually shaping the global distribution of production and jobs.

A CHANGING INTERNATIONAL DIVISION OF LABOUR

Whether globalisation gives rise to a 'new international division of labour', and
what form it takes, has been one of the more controversial issues in modern political economic analysis.[11] Division of labour, as emphasised by Adam Smith, involves
different people working on different stages in a production process. It has long
been a feature of international economic specialisation. However, there has been a
significant reorientation of its geographical form in recent years. It has become
increasingly differentiated on a world scale because TNCs can divide their activities
between operations in different regions and nations.

Some manufacturing jobs have been relocated to countries of the developing
Third World. Free-trade zones and export-processing zones are particular focal
points for industrialisation in the former colonial nations. The host governments
usually offer cheap premises, 'tax holidays', low-wage and sometimes union-free
labour to attract TNCs to operate there. Rapid, but unbalanced and dependent, patterns of economic growth are the usual outcome. Industrial output surges, but often
with little linkage to the rest of the national economy. There is always the fear that
the TNCs may pull out if they are not given yet more generous incentives to stay.

The other side of the coin is the partial deindustrialisation of the formerly more
economically developed nations. Jobs losses in particular manufacturing industries
have been significant. The loss of jobs in clothing manufacture in Australia following
the reorientation of the industry towards 'offshore' production and sources of gar-

ments (e.g. in Fiji) is one case in point. However, it is important to put this trend in perspective. The changing international division of labour cannot wholly account for the relative decline in manufacturing employment in the advanced industrial nations. As a number of economic commentators have pointed out, the total figures do not tally.[12] Shifts of manufacturing plants to lower-wage nations account for only a small part of the total manufacturing job loss, much of which has more to do with the effects of technological change and higher output–labour ratios.

The international division of labour is itself rapidly evolving; so, it is not as if there is a clear divide between the 'old' and 'new' arrangements. Indeed, there are interesting contemporary trends towards greater global mobility of the workers themselves—certainly among the professional and managerial elite at the top of the hierarchy and also, to some extent, among unskilled and semi-skilled workers at the bottom of the workforce hierarchy. Networks of international contracting and subcontracting are also developing as a major feature of contemporary transnational business activity.

SYNCHRONISATION AND DISARTICULATION

These circumstances accentuate *international interdependence*. The buoyancy—or otherwise—of economic conditions comes to be ever more rapidly transmitted between nations. It is summed up in the phrase 'when the United States sneezes, the rest of the world catches a cold'. The recession which developed in 2001 is a case in point. But even changes in the economic conditions of smaller nations can have major international repercussions. In 1997, the sudden deterioration of the Thai economy triggered an economic crisis throughout the countries of South-East Asia. Global interdependence makes it increasingly difficult for any one nation to insulate itself against such 'external' shocks.

The transmission mechanisms are many and varied—direct flows of investment, the demand for goods and services produced for international markets, interest rates for borrowed funds, and the credit ratings applying to those international borrowings, for example. Even the general state of business optimism or pessimism may have a significant bearing on the decisions of TNCs about whether to expand or contract their activities. These factors tend to synchronise economic conditions across nations, for better or worse.

This transnational interdependence also goes hand-in-hand with *disarticulation* within national economies. Where strong linkages exist between industries in a nation, expansion in one industry tends to pull others along behind, leading to generalised economic growth. Disarticulation occurs when these links are weak or broken. Open-cut mining in Queensland, Australia, for example, produces coal that is taken directly to the coast for export to Japan. There is a strong link between coal mining in Queensland and Japanese manufacturing industry, but only a weak link with the rest of the Australian economy. Such regional disarticulation is common in an increasingly globalised economy.

Two obvious consequences are increasingly uneven patterns of regional development and greater regional economic vulnerability. Articulated regions, sometimes transcending national boundaries, as in the case of the Singapore–Johor Bahru (Malaysia)–Bintan Island (Indonesia) triangle, may experience rapid surges of economic growth. Meanwhile, other regions become marginalised, effectively bypassed by the dynamic processes of technological and structural economic change. 'Billa-bong regional economies' is a possible characterisation, drawing on the Australian word for an area of water partly cut off from the main stream. The spectacular economic growth of some areas and the stagnation of others are related phenomena. But even those regions experiencing rapid growth generally become dependent on economic conditions elsewhere, over which the local businesses and governments can exert no significant economic control.

A CHANGING BALANCE OF ECONOMIC POWER

The institutions that have become the most spatially mobile have gained power relative to those that remain localised. The former are most obviously the institutions of capital—the TNCs producing goods and services and the transnational financial institutions who serve their needs while pursuing their own profitability. They can rearrange their activities strategically in the pursuit of their corporate goals. They can minimise their taxation, for example, by the use of *tax havens* or *transfer pricing*.[13] They can reduce costs by relocating their activities to where wages are lowest or environmental standards most lax.

By contrast, the institutions representing workers, consumers, and environmentalists and the institutions of government are generally less mobile and are correspondingly limited in their strategic options. Labour is organised mainly on local and national scales through trade unions, and the proportion of workers in unions has been declining in most of the advanced nations over the last couple of decades.[14] Consumers, to the extent that they have any collective voice at all, have organisations that are mostly national. Environmental organisations have a characteristically local focus. Governments relate to nation states, or components thereof (local governments and state/provincial governments where there are federal systems, as in the United States, Germany, Canada, and Australia). So, by definition, these institutions are more spatially bounded than TNCs. Each has elements of international coordination—the International Labour Organisation, the International Consumers' Association, Greenpeace, and the United Nations, for example—but these do not command direct *economic* power comparable to the transnational institutions of capital.

Some social scientists are now arguing that a *transnational capitalist class* has developed, effectively coordinating the collective interests of capital on a global scale.[15] The class, broadly defined, comprises not simply the senior corporate executives, but also bureaucrats, politicians, and some academics whose activities are increasingly connected with global corporate interests.

The power shift is towards essentially undemocratic institutions. The corporations are ultimately accountable to their own shareholders (an accountability based on the principle of 'one share, one vote'), although, in reality, the fragmented nature of shareholdings leaves effective power in the hands of the major institutional investors and the managers of the corporations. Governments, on the other hand, are the formally democratic institutions, normally elected on the principle of 'one person, one vote'. But their policies are increasingly tailored to suit the interests of the TNCs on whose decisions the prosperity, or otherwise, of national economies depends. Crough and Wheelwright call this tendency the development of a 'client state'.[16] Beggar-thy-neighbour competition between such states in pursuit of investment by TNCs is commonplace. So, the seat of effective power shifts from democratic to essentially undemocratic institutions.

Governments are tending to become 'puppets' of international business, according to this view. They give priority to corporate interests, defining success largely in terms of economic goals, determining foreign policy mainly according to commercial criteria. As Noreena Herz puts it, 'instead of creating a better world for people, governments work to create a better environment for business'.[17]

The much celebrated connection between capitalism and democracy is increasingly questionable in these circumstances. There has been a broad historical correlation between the development of market freedoms and political freedoms. However, this connection now looks more and more tenuous. The growth of power of the TNCs makes private economic interest increasingly dominant relative to the formally democratic institutions to whom we have entrusted the protection and advancement of a broader public interest. As Marxists have long emphasised, one should not idealise national governments, for their activities have always been intertwined with the interests of the capitalist class. The point is rather that, in current circumstances, the scope for independent governmental action is further reduced by the globalisation of capital. In the extreme, political authoritarianism becomes the precondition for maintaining an essentially undemocratic economic system.

CHANGE AND CHALLENGE

These observations about institutional change on a global scale pose big challenges. Analytically, they pose a fundamental challenge to conventional economic theory: to come to terms with a very different world from that depicted in the conventional textbooks. Politically, they pose a major challenge to workers, consumers, environmentalists, and indeed to all who are uncomfortable about simply sitting back and allowing corporations to restructure the world economy in their own interests and after their own image.

Economic discourse has conventionally rested on two major assumptions: the existence of *national economies* and the operation of a *market system*. These underpin the standard division in the discipline between macroeconomics and microeconomics. Macroeconomics is about national economies; microeconomics is about how markets function (or, in neoclassical theory, about how stylised *models* of markets function). The institutional economic analysis of globalisation casts significant doubts on the value of this disciplinary structure.

National economies are not simply 'open economies' in the sense that they engage in international trade: many of the institutions that shape their fortunes have effectively abandoned their national identities. Indeed, domestically based transnationals may operate little differently from TNCs with their headquarters in other countries. So, instead of a world economy comprising an aggregation of national economies, we now have a world economy in which the main components are corporate institutions. That being the case, the conventional construction of macroeconomics, even so-called 'open-economy macroeconomics', looks inappropriate. Similarly, the micro-economic assumption that markets shape economic outcomes looks increasingly untenable in a world shaped by the exercise of corporate power. So, the twin pillars of conventional economics—the assumption of national economies and free markets—seem to stand on ever more shaky ground.

Some institutional economists contend that we now need a *mesoeconomics* to supplement micro- and macroeconomic analysis, if not to replace them altogether. Mesoeconomics—the intermediate between micro and macro—focuses primarily on the institutions wielding the corporate power. As the leading proponent of this view has argued, 'modifying conventional models of international trade and payments to account for the rise of multinational capital is imperative if we are to understand how the world has changed both since Keynes and since Ricardo … Analysis of the modern meso economy and the role of multinational capital is integral to such qualifications of conventional macroeconomic theory'.[18]

Not all political economists agree with this argument for a new institutional 'mesoeconomics'. Some say that the application of the theory of capital accumulation to the study of globalisation is all that is needed. Marxist economists point out, quite rightly, that Marx anticipated the tendency for the relentless capital accumulation process to transcend national boundaries. They emphasise that globalisation is an extension of long-standing processes of imperialism. They sometimes also argue that, far from eradicating competitive processes, the contemporary globalisation of capital extends them on a world scale. From this perspective, it is the inter-corporate competition that drives the TNCs to behave in ways that systematically violate the interests of labour.[19] Whether the processes are predominantly competitive or collusive remains a matter for rival political economic interpretations. What is less in dispute is that the outcome is a world order in which the collective interests of capital dominate.

Marx and Engels ended their *Manifesto* with the famous rallying cry 'Workers of the world unite: you have nothing to lose but your chains'. As Ted Wheelwright has wryly noted, it is the capitalists, not the workers, who seem to have taken that advice, integrating their activities on a global scale, while workers remain organised mainly at the local or national scale.[20] But the situation is not altogether clear-cut, and certainly not static. Campaigns involving international solidarity between nationally based trade unions frequently occur. Other groups concerned with consumers' interests and environmental protection, for example, have developed international linkages, although most activity remains characteristically local. The activist organisational principle 'think global, act local' has obvious resonance in these circumstances. It is not all over …

CONCLUSION

Institutional economics emphasises that there is a material basis to corporate globalisation. It is a process made possible by technological advances, encouraged by neo-liberal policies and compounded by consumerism. The growth of international trade, investment, and financial flows accentuates the economic interdependence and disarticulation of national economies. However, it is the *interpretation* of these trends that is crucial in shaping social and political responses. An interpretation of globalisation as unavoidable, necessary and desirable generates a quite different politics from one that sees it as contingent and malleable.[21] Seeing 'globalisation' as a contested process and a contestable discourse directs attention to political processes and choices.

What political responses to corporate globalisation are appropriate? Some make the case for a defensive nationalism. Others argue for a progressive internationalism which emphasises the globalisation of human rights, environmental consciousness and the interests of labour as a counter to corporate globalisation. Localist responses at the urban or regional level also have the potential to build alternative community structures and spawn grass-roots movements to challenge the hegemony of multinational capital.[22] All three levels—local, national, and international—are important. The main issue for those concerned about the corporate globalisation process is how to articulate the various progressive policies and struggles. Of course, there are strategic choices to be made, given limited political energies. However, it is inevitable that political groups responding to globalisation will continue to operate at all three levels. So, the key practical challenge is to enhance their effectiveness by sharing information and forging cooperative relationships.[23] By addressing these issues, modern institutional economics links up with contemporary political challenges.

PART VII

Stabilising the Economy

Keynesian economics

CHAPTER 28

The Disillusioned Defence of Capitalism

Why worry about unemployment?
What was distinctive about the economics of John Maynard Keynes?
What are the principal implications of Keynesian economics?

John Maynard Keynes (1883–1946) once said that it would be good for economists to be like dentists. Most of us require the services of a dentist from time to time, but we do not let dentists dominate our lives; and the less we need their services, the better. Is it possible that the economic system could operate in such a way that only occasional minor 'dental' repairs would be needed?

To try to perfect the economic system is a worthy goal. Marxist political economists, you will recall, have always claimed that it requires radical change. They contend that capitalism is inherently conflict-ridden and crisis-prone, and so the quest to perfect it is ill-conceived. The solution must lie in its replacement by socialism (although that still leaves some big questions unanswered about what form socialism should take in practice and how to bring the change about). On the other hand, the neoclassical economists see a competitive market system as basically self-regulating, producing optimal (or, at least, efficient) outcomes. According to the more extreme variations on this neoclassical theme, since most economic problems are caused by governments interfering with the 'natural' operations of the market mechanism, achieving perfection requires reduced government intervention. Whether this idealised market model has anything to do with capitalism in practice is a moot point.

An intermediate, *reformist* inclination is evident in the tradition of institutional economics, as noted in the preceding four chapters. It is also the characteristic policy stance of Keynesian economists, who emphasise the positive role governments can play in stabilising an otherwise unstable capitalist system. The eradication of involuntary unemployment is perhaps its most distinctive target.

UNEMPLOYMENT, DEPRESSION, SOCIAL TURMOIL

The need for economic analysis and policy to focus on the causes of, and cures for, unemployment is obvious. Unemployment is economically irrational. It involves simultaneous underutilisation of economic resources and failure to satisfy social needs. For the involuntarily unemployed people themselves—whether they are unable to find a first job or have been made redundant by their last employer—

there are considerable *personal costs*. These include not only the absence of a regular wage income, but also the severance from the social contacts usually associated with the workplace. Moreover, in a society where people's status is defined primarily by their work, unemployment frequently leads to social marginalisation and social stigmatisation. Employment may be alienating, but unemployment is usually more so. Being out of work for a significant period of time also usually causes skills to atrophy and may lead to attitudinal changes that make it harder to enter or re-enter the workforce.[1]

There are other *social costs* which have to be borne by society at large. In a welfare state, which provides financial assistance to the unemployed, unemployment causes higher government expenditure. Simultaneously, government income is reduced because unemployed people generally pay no taxes. So, there is a strong tendency towards government budget deficits—not altogether a bad thing according to Keynesians, but something that creates pressures to prune other areas of government expenditure, such as health, education, public transport, and infrastructure. Therein lie further contradictions because, in so far as unemployment is linked to ill-health (and there is considerable evidence of such statistical and causal connections), the need for medical services tends to rise. Similarly, to the extent that unemployment is associated with a higher incidence of crime, the costs of policing, incarceration, and other forms of social control also tend to increase.[2]

Fundamentally, though, the problem of unemployment is one of *opportunity cost*. The society has to forgo the goods and services that the unemployed people would have produced were they in useful employment. That is the opportunity cost of unemployment—its cost in terms of opportunities (for production and consumption) forgone. It shows the irrationality of an economic system simultaneously having unused resources and unfulfilled social needs.

Reducing unemployment therefore raises the tantalising possibility of a *win–win* situation, whereby the unemployed people benefit by acquiring jobs while society benefits by acquiring the extra goods and services they produce and the extra tax revenues they pay. Whether or not a reduction in unemployment actually increases social well-being also depends on the nature of the jobs created (alienating or fulfilling?) and the nature of the goods produced (better hospitals, schools, and transport systems, or more environmentally degrading junk?). Such broader considerations apply equally to those currently in employment, of course. Just focusing on the personal, social, and opportunity costs of unemployment provides a strong argument that policies to reduce unemployment make a valuable social contribution.

Keynes certainly thought so. He was analysing the situation prior to and during the Great Depression. It was a time of terrible economic difficulties, causing major social stresses and threatening political turmoil. Here were circumstances crying out for careful analysis and remedial policies.

It is conventional to associate the start of the Great Depression with a single day: 'black Thursday', 24 October 1929, when there was a major financial crash on the Wall Street Stock Exchange in New York. The sharp fall in share values triggered a stampede of panic selling that led to further falls in the following days and weeks. Fortunes were lost. It is said that people checking into high-rise New York hotels at the time were being asked if they wanted a room to sleep in or a room from which they could jump out of a window.

Along with the financial crisis came a crisis in the *real economy*: falls in productive investment, and rapid decline in the levels of output, income, and employment. With the benefit of hindsight, these real economic problems can be seen to have been developing even before the stock market crash. They set in with a vengeance thereafter. The volume of farm produce fell by more than half over the next two years and industrial production fell by almost a half. Nearly a third of all workers suffered unemployment. The adverse economic conditions spread quickly to other capitalist national economies, including Canada (always immediately vulnerable to changes in US economic conditions), the United Kingdom and continental Europe, Australia, and New Zealand. Charitable soup-kitchens provided some assistance to the unemployed, but there was little institutionalised state support for them in those days. People who had no jobs commonly suffered eviction from their homes, destitution, and even starvation.[3]

What had gone wrong? The farms and factories were still there. There was no shortage of people willing to work in them. The problem was that the capitalist economy could not be relied upon to mobilise the unemployed people for socially useful production.

Of course, the problem of economic depression was not new; a deep and prolonged depression had occurred in the 1880s, for example. Earlier still, Marx had pointed out this potentially fatal flaw in the capitalist system, emphasising its innate tendency to generate a 'reserve army of labour' and periodic economic crises. Marx's reasoning, developed many decades before the Great Depression, evidently tallied with the observable conditions of the time, and an increasing number of people came to believe that only *socialism* could provide a solution. Indeed, while the capitalist countries were suffering the Great Depression in the 1930s, the Soviet Union, then the major experiment in constructing a socialist alternative, was experiencing full employment and continuing economic growth. In Germany and Italy, *fascist* governments were offering another solution, mobilising unemployed people to build highways and public housing, and manufacture tanks and bombs. Notwithstanding its authoritarian and racist aspects, the fascist alternative attracted growing numbers of followers. The future of liberal capitalism, flanked on the left by socialism and on the right by fascism, was starting to look very insecure. Both alternatives seemed to be doing so much better economically, and support for revolutionary change was widespread. Marx's famous prediction of 'socialism or barbarism' seemed to be materialising.

This was the economic, social, and political context within which Keynes made his analytical and practical contributions. Although he described capitalism as 'morally objectionable', he judged its reform and survival necessary. Solving the unemployment crisis was the top priority. Keynes did marvellously well in this respect. Not only did he find an explanation for unemployment, but he also showed how appropriate government policies could substantially reduce, if not eliminate, it. The market did not have to be left to find its own equilibrium, Keynes argued; rather, a managed equilibrium of full employment could be engineered. While that would not resolve all economic difficulties, it would create the more stable macro-economic environment within which other economic and social problems could be more readily addressed. This, in the words of his student Joan Robinson, was Keynes's 'disillusioned defence of capitalism'.[4]

Box 28.1

John Maynard Keynes (1883–1946)

Often described as the greatest economist of the twentieth century, Keynes continues to occupy a central place in modern debates about economic analysis and policy.

The son of a Cambridge University academic, Keynes was educated at Eton, England's most elite boys' school, where he excelled at everything: the classics, mathematics, history, debating, rowing. At university, he studied mathematics and became president of the Union and the Liberal Club. He became interested in economics, too, and attended Alfred Marshall's lectures. When he fared rather poorly in an economics test, he reputedly said that this indicated he knew more about economics than his examiners! It was probably true.

After leaving university, Keynes worked in the Civil Service. As a Treasury official he attended the peace conference at Versailles at the end of World War I. Incensed by the Allies' policy of seeking punitive reparations from a vanquished Germany, he wrote a controversial book called *Economic Consequences of the Peace* (1920). He returned to Cambridge as an academic economist and established an enviable reputation for combining economic theory with an understanding of how the world actually works—a rare combination indeed! His most important books were *A Treatise on Money* (1930) and *The General Theory of Employment, Interest and Money* (1936). His influence on the economics profession was through his writing, but he also had direct influence on the formulation of public policy in his role as economic adviser to successive British governments.

On a personal level, Keynes is renowned for his connection with the 'Bloomsbury set'. This was an avant-garde artistic and literary circle whose members also included Lytton Strachey and Virginia Woolf. In 1925, Keynes married Lydia Lopokova, a Russian ballerina—although his sexual preference was widely known to lie in a rather different direction. These aspects of his life, although not directly relevant to his economics, are relevant to an understanding of his distinctive status—as simultaneously an influential figure within the British Establishment and an intellectual and social non-conformist.

Keynes worked hard to inject sense, as he would have seen it, into practical economic policy during the turbulent years of the Great Depression and World War II. He represented the British government at the Bretton Woods conference in 1944, concerned with setting up institutions to provide for a more prosperous post-war period, but was not wholly successful in winning acceptance for his proposals. Worn out by relentless overwork, he died in 1946.

CHALLENGING 'CLASSICAL' PRESCRIPTIONS

Keynes faced a major task in turning round the dominant explanations of unemployment and the preferred policy prescriptions. They were deeply entrenched in the prevailing economic orthodoxy. This was what Keynes called the 'classical' explanation of how the economy functions. The word 'classical' here refers to the ideas of classical political economists like Jean-Baptiste Say and the ideas of neo-classical economists. From Keynes's vantage point, these were all 'classical' ideas because they predated his reconstruction of economic analysis.[5] His first task was to refute these pre-Keynesian orthodoxies.

Say's Law is at the root of the problem. It has numerous variations, but, as summarised in chapter 8, its key proposition is that 'supply creates its own demand'. This implies that prolonged economic depressions cannot be the result of insufficient demand for goods and services. The possibility of unemployment arising for other reasons is not denied: it could be *structural* (unemployed workers having the wrong skills relative to the available jobs) or it could be *frictional* (unemployed workers having difficulty making quick transitions to new jobs), but *demand-deficient* unemployment should not arise. The process of producing goods and services generates the income that is necessary in order for those goods to be purchased and consumed. As Cambridge professor A.C. Pigou put it during the depths of the Great Depression, 'with perfectly free competition … there will always be at work a strong tendency for wage rates to be so related to demand that everyone is employed'.[6] How, then, to account for the observable unemployment in practice? Why had it quite suddenly assumed such massive proportions?

The real world was obviously not behaving like the textbooks said it should. One explanation for the unemployment problem was couched in terms of 'external shocks' to which the economic system was vulnerable. It is a view that remains common to this day. It had originally been a feature of the 'sunspots' theory developed by William Stanley Jevons in the late nineteenth century to explain fluctuations in the level of economic activity. Indeed, if periodic sunspots do change weather patterns, they can impact on agricultural harvests, which may then affect the economy as a whole. However, to base a general explanation of the cyclical behaviour of the capitalist economy on 'external' forces of this kind is quite bizarre. It diverts attention from capitalism's own internally generated contradictions.

The root problem, analytically, in the pre-Keynesian orthodoxy is the denial that there are systemic problems in the capitalist economy. Neoclassical theory is an obvious case in point. The labour market is regarded as operating pretty much like any other market. The changing conditions of demand and supply are held to be mediated by adjustments to market prices. The wage rate, being the price of labour, is the adjustment mechanism. If supply exceeds demand, rather than there being prolonged unemployment, the wage rate falls. That increases the demand for labour, as employers become willing to employ more of the now cheaper workers. The market clears. Unemployment is eradicated. If, in the real world, unemployment persists, it therefore must be because of some impediment preventing the price mechanism from working properly. The solution is obvious: governments must seek to remove these impediments. If trade unions, for example, are preventing wages from falling, their power to do so must be broken (for the workers' own collective good, of course).

THE KEYNESIAN VIEWPOINT

Keynes provided a critique of the prevailing orthodoxy and a fundamentally different interpretation of unemployment. Demand and supply still figure in his story, but the labour market is not treated as if it operates like other markets. A distinctive analysis of money markets is also introduced. The analysis is reoriented to the determinants of the aggregate demand and supply for goods and services, for labour, and for money. This emphasis on the analysis of the economy *as a whole* is the essence of a distinctively *macroeconomic* approach.[7] The macroeconomy is seen to be functioning according to principles that cannot be derived simply by adding up all its microeconomic elements.

Individual markets for goods and services, for example, may clear if prices are flexible, but that does not mean that full employment is guaranteed. The most obvious illustration of this is the wage-cutting favoured by neoclassical economists in Keynes's day (and still frequently advocated today). Wage-cutting has a seemingly obvious rationale: individual employers might indeed be willing to hire more workers if they are cheaper to employ—but only if they are confident of selling the extra products. According to Keynes, wage reductions in practice generally make the unemployment problem worse. If workers have lower incomes, they have less to spend on goods and services, so firms will sell fewer products and consequently reduce their demand for labour, and unemployment will rise. Wage-cutting has perverse effects because it decreases the aggregate demand for goods and services. Indeed, the problem of depressed demand tends to become even more entrenched because businesses usually respond to reduced sales of their products by cutting their investment spending, which then reduces the productive capacity of the economy in the longer term. A *vicious cycle* of economic contraction occurs.

A better strategy, Keynes argued, would be to implement policies to expand the aggregate demand for goods and services, thereby leading to increased levels of employment. How best to do this? Governments do not usually have direct control over the wage rates that employers pay to their employees (although they do have direct control over the wages they pay to their own public-sector employees, and they may also be able to exert some indirect influence on wages in the private sector, especially in countries like Australia where arbitration institutions oversee wage outcomes). However, a government *can* always adjust the level and pattern of its own expenditure in order to pursue the goal of full employment. If it spends more on building schools, hospitals, bridges, or railways, for example, that creates jobs for construction workers. Those workers are then able to spend more on food, cars, and clothing, which creates jobs for farmers and car and clothing manufacturers. The extra incomes lead to extra spending, which then stimulates higher outputs and creates more jobs. A *virtuous cycle* of economic expansion occurs.

Whether this process is virtuous in all respects is a matter of judgment. Producing more goods and services to create more jobs may concurrently entail environmental damage or foster an ultimately unfulfilling consumerism. However, for directly tackling the social evil of widespread unemployment, such as existed when Keynes was writing, the justification for the policy is abundantly clear. Keynes himself felt so strongly about this that he made the memorably puckish statement that:

> If the Treasury were to fill old bottles with banknotes, bury them at suitable depths in disused coal-mines which are than filled up to the surface with town rubbish, and leave it to private enterprise on well-tried principles of *laissez-faire* to dig the notes up again … there need be no more unemployment and, with the help of its repercussions, the real income of the community, and its capital wealth would probably become a good deal greater than it actually is. It would, indeed, be more sensible to build houses and the like; but if there are political and practical difficulties in the way of this, the above would be better than nothing![8]

Students tend to remember this as Keynes's advocating filling mine shafts with banknotes, or digging holes and filling them in again. He meant nothing of the sort. He favoured mobilising the unemployed for *socially useful* production—for 'building houses and the like'. His point is that, from a purely job-creating viewpoint, these other bizarre forms of activity would serve the purpose equally. They would certainly be better than policies of wage-reduction and fiscal austerity.

Increasing government expenditure as a means of resolving economic difficulties was heresy in Keynes's day, and has become so again in our own. For Keynes it was not simply a matter of economic logic; it was also a *moral* imperative. Unemployment was a social scourge. The policies that he advocated for its eradication were based on the presumption that government could, and should, serve broad social purposes. This entails the pragmatic application of economic knowledge to the improvement of existing social conditions.

Job creation had top priority in Keynes's own time because unemployment was so obviously the main economic problem requiring resolution. Some contend that this is still the case. However, Keynesian analysis is equally applicable to the analysis and control of *inflation*. Broadly speaking, the reverse policy measures apply. If inflation is the product of an excess of aggregate demand for goods and services, its reduction requires curtailment of that demand. The reduction of government spending is the most obvious prescription. These are circumstances in which Keynesians might well regard fiscal restraint as appropriate. Cuts in government spending may be supplemented by policies restricting the supply of money and/or raising the rate of interest, if there is a need to further discourage spending in the private sector. Such policies of macroeconomic 'fine-tuning' can steer the economy along the sensible path between unemployment on one side and inflation on the other.

Keynes's own analysis of the economy and economic policy was much more sophisticated than this summary implies. His best known book, *The General Theory of Employment, Interest and Money*, is a particularly complex work, and most students prefer their Keynes in a more clearly organised and digestible form. Nevertheless, his *General Theory* (as it is almost universally abbreviated) can rightly be said to 'stand as one of the three key books in the development of economics … together with Adam Smith's *Wealth of Nations* and Marx's *Capital*'.[9] The parallels are significant. All three works can be criticised for their lack of organisational clarity and their sometimes convoluted reasoning, but all three created significant 'paradigm shifts' in the understanding of political economic matters. They contributed to radical changes in economic thought and political practice.

CONCLUSION

Keynes's ideas have left an enduring legacy. First, and most fundamental, is the inference that understanding the nature of economic problems requires *rigorous analysis*. This is the rationale behind the model-building described in the next two chapters. Intellectual effort is needed to understand and shape the world in which we live. Prejudice will not do. Blaming unemployment on 'too many immigrants', on 'women taking men's jobs', or on 'work-shy welfare recipients' may be effective populist rhetoric for conservative politicians, but it is counter-productive for those who really want to understand and resolve the systemic problems of the modern economy.

Second, there is the *imperative to act*. Explaining the roots of unemployment in terms of a deficiency of aggregate demand, or explaining inflation in terms of excess demand, is not an end in itself. It is a means towards the formulation of effective practical policies—policies of demand management most obviously in these instances. Keynes took the view that 'the ultimate end of rational human action was the generation of as much intrinsic goodness as possible, and in which the means embraced all the sciences, politics and economics included'.[10] Economics, from this perspective, has an ethical purpose. It is the means by which we come to understand the world in order to manage it better in the service of broader social goals.

Third, there is an optimistic view of the capacity of government to pursue those social goals. In particular, government is assumed to be an *effective vehicle for improved economic management*. Here is a point of contrast with the revolutionary Marxist and 'free-market' neoclassical stances. The characteristically Keynesian belief is that government can, and should, contribute to social progress, working within the general context of a capitalist economy to eradicate its most anti-social features. It is not that governments always 'get it right'; governments may indeed exacerbate economic problems—but Keynes would have thought this most likely to be the result of 'muddled thinking'. Soundly advised (by the likes of Keynes!), governments should have a significant role in securing 'the possibility of civilisation'.

CHAPTER 29

Constructing a Keynesian Model

What determines the overall level of economic activity?
How can we understand the various elements shaping the aggregate demand for goods and services?
What are the causes of periodic recessions?

Keynesian analysis focuses on understanding the functioning of a whole economy and the appropriate means of managing it. In principle, that whole economy could be a particular locality or region, a nation, or even the world. Normally it is taken to be the *national* economy, since the nation is the most unambiguously bounded space and national governments the most obvious institutions for the implementation of economic policy. This primary focus on the nation contrasts with the Marxist emphasis on *class* and the neoclassical emphasis on the *individual*, although all would ultimately claim a common concern to understand the economy in its entirety. What Keynesian economics does is provide a basis for a coherent *macroeconomics*. It emphasises a cluster of key variables, the interaction of which determines the overall levels of income, output, and employment.

THE CIRCULAR FLOW OF INCOME

The commonest way of illustrating the Keynesian macroeconomic viewpoint is through models of the circular flow of income. Figure 29.1 shows two variations on this theme.[1] The top diagram shows the simpler case. Here there are just two sets of participants in the economy: households and firms. Households supply the factors of production, and are rewarded with corresponding income flows: wages (paid to workers), rent (paid to landowners), and distributed profits (such as dividends paid to shareholders). Firms supply the goods and services that households purchase out of their incomes. The higher the incomes, the higher the outputs, and, presumably therefore, the greater the number of jobs. In other words, both firms and households benefit from a larger circular flow.

The bottom diagram shows a rather more complex, and more realistic, situation. Here, it is recognised that the circular flow may be reduced by three 'leakages':

- households may put part of their incomes aside as *saving*, which detracts from the demand for goods and services
- households may spend part of their incomes on *imports*, which does not form part of the aggregate demand for locally produced goods and services
- households may have to pay part of their incomes to governments in the form of *taxes*, so that portion of their income does not add directly to the aggregate demand for goods and services, either.

(a) Simplest model

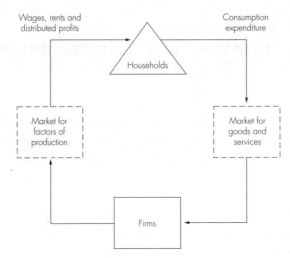

(b) More complex model

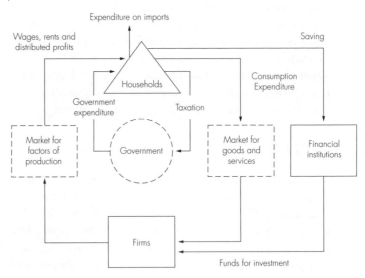

Figure 29.1 The circular flow of income.

The larger these 'leakages' are from the circular flow, the greater is the tendency towards economic contraction.

On the other hand, there are three 'injections' into the circular flow that have the reverse effect, of stimulating the overall level of economic activity:

- firms may invest, spending on plant and equipment to modernise or expand their businesses, which adds to the circular flow of income
- firms may export some of their products, the payments for which also add to the flow of income in the national economy
- government expenditure on social service payments, armaments, public education, infrastructure provision, and so on further adds to the circulating incomes.

There is no reason why the three 'injections' should balance the three 'leakages'. This may not be obvious from the bottom diagram in figure 29.1. It may seem that, if household savings are deposited in financial institutions, and firms borrow funds from those institutions to finance their investment, this pair of leakages and flows is likely to balance. It is not necessarily so. Savings and investment are undertaken by different people—by households and firms, respectively—and so it is quite possible for one to exceed the other. Similarly, there is no reason why the payments received for exports should balance the expenditure on imported goods. Indeed, international trade imbalances of that kind are common. Finally, there is no necessary equality between taxation and government expenditure, unless the government has a commitment to balanced budgets and is capable of actually realising that goal in practice. Keynes himself thought such a commitment unwise since budgetary deficits and surpluses could be used as policy instruments to adjust the level of economic activity.

An understanding of these various 'injections' and 'leakages' in the circular flow of income can help to explain the ups and downs of a national economy. If savings exceed investment, for example, national income tends to decline. At first sight, this seems strange. A high rate of household saving is generally thought to be desirable, surely? Indeed, it is usually good for individual households—thrift, if not inherently virtuous, is a means of personal insurance against future poverty. However, thrift can do more harm than good for the economy as a whole. When people save, they buy fewer goods and services, so the aggregate demand falls, causing the output of goods and services and the national income to decline. People's plans to save may not then be realised because, having reduced incomes, they cannot readily achieve their original savings intentions.

It is *investment*, not saving, that drives economic expansion. Saving is only economically beneficial, from a national economic viewpoint, if it is matched by investment. But businesses will only engage in investment spending when they anticipate a growing demand for their products. That, in turn, is likely to depend on whether national income is growing or contracting. Evidently, striking the 'right' balance between saving and investment is hazardous. Striking the 'right' balance between all the 'leakages' and 'injections' is yet more so.

The model of the circular flow of income is only a starting point for interpreting a complex set of behavioural relationships and economic interdependencies. It can be developed in various ways. Some economists at the London School of Economics and Political Science once built a hydraulic contraption made of pipes and valves, physically simulating the structure of an economy, seen from a Keynesian perspective. Extra water poured into the export revenue tube, for example, would flow through the apparatus, leading to higher levels of consumption and saving (depending on the relative diameters of those tubes) and higher levels of national income and tax revenues (depending on the amount of water diverted from the main flow into the government 'tank'). The consequences of a surge in exports could thereby be predicted. Similarly, one could monitor the 'flow-through' effects of injections of higher government expenditure or business investment, for example, on the overall level of incomes and expenditures. The model was an interesting marriage of Keynesian economics and some simple hydraulic engineering. Gumboots, to be worn at times of excessive 'leakages', were presumably an advisable economic accessory!

Macroeconomic models are now usually constructed in *statistical* form, using computer technology. Such econometric analysis is more sophisticated than the hydraulic contraption, but not fundamentally different in character. Its results depend, like the hydraulic model's, on the assumptions made about each of the variables in the model and their interrelationships. What determines the value of each of the variables? How do they interconnect? A macroeconomic view focuses on the factors shaping the overall supply and demand for goods and services.

AGGREGATE SUPPLY AND DEMAND

It is often said that the Keynesian emphasis on the importance of aggregate demand results in the relative neglect of aggregate supply. This is misleading. Keynes was well aware that the relationship between aggregate demand and supply determines the prosperity of the economy in the long term. In other words, *the crucial relationship is that between the overall demand for goods and services and the productive capacity to supply them*. Building up productive capacity is necessary for economic expansion, increasing national income and employment in the long term. Investment has a crucial role in this process since it is both a source of demand for goods and services and the means by which the extra capacity to supply them is created.

However, at any particular point of time, the productive capacity of the economy can be taken as given. It depends on the number and size of factories, offices, trucks, tools, and so on. The question is how fully they will be utilised. It is understandable that Keynes focused on this more *short-term* question in the 1930s, for the under-utilisation of existing productive capacity caused the chronic unemployment of the Great Depression. In our time, too, understanding the causes of periodic economic downturns can be usefully based on the analysis of capacity utilisation. We need to know under what conditions aggregate demand will be insufficient to ensure that the existing productive capacity is fully utilised? Raising this issue puts the spotlight directly on the determinants of *aggregate demand and its principal components*.

The standard exposition of the Keynesian analysis of aggregate demand identifies five components that together determine the level of national income (Y). These are consumption (C), investment (I), government expenditure (G), exports (X), and imports (M). Thus:

$$Y = C + I + G + X - M$$

If these components are growing (or shrinking in the case of M), then national income will tend to grow. Any spare productive capacity in the economy will be fully utilised. If they are declining (or increasing in the case of M), then national income will fall, and the economy will tend to slide into recession. In the latter case, surplus capacity will become an economic problem. It is therefore important to understand what determines the size of each of the components of aggregate demand.

Consumption

Consumer spending (C) is invariably the biggest item in the national income (Y). It also tends to be fairly stable over time (other than seasonal fluctuation, such as the annual surge in consumer spending at Christmas).

Box 29.1

What shapes consumer spending?

The amount of money consumers spend depends primarily on their income. The typical relationship between the two variables, known as the *consumption function*, is depicted here:

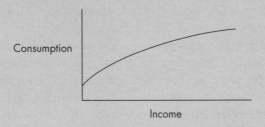

The slope of this line is determined by the *marginal propensity to consume*. This indicates what proportion of each extra dollar received is spent rather than saved. Increases in income are normally associated with increases in consumption, so the marginal propensity to consume will be somewhere between zero and unity. At a hypothetical level of zero income, some consumption would have to occur if the individual (or society) were to subsist; this would presumably require dis-saving from funds accumulated in a previous period or increasing debts to be repaid in a future period. As income rises, consumption rises—but usually at a decreasing rate. Rich individuals can usually afford to save a higher proportion of their income than poor individuals; whole societies can be expected to exhibit a similar tendency.

The marginal propensity to consume for a whole society normally also depends on the *distribution of income*. Because poor people tend to spend all their income, whereas rich people tend to save more, the distribution of income between them affects the overall consumption–saving ratio. The propensity to consume also depends on the *availability of credit facilities*. Some societies have institutional arrangements imposing forced savings requirements, such as the compulsory occupational superannuation schemes in Australia. Beyond these factors, numerous *social and cultural considerations* affect the propensity to consume: the influence of consumerism and commercial advertising; the prevalence of social emulation; and the extent to which consumers feel confident about their future incomes, their personal job prospects, and the state of the economy as a whole.

What determines the total volume of consumer expenditure on goods and services? It depends on *income*, obviously. This is true for individual consumers, and for the economy as a whole. Therein lies a significant analytical problem, though. In trying to explain the level of national income, consumption is identified as its largest component; but we then say that consumption spending depends on national income. It seems to be circular reasoning. The 'get-out' is that not all income is usually spent on consumption: some is *saved*. If we can explain what proportion is saved, a coherent theory of consumption is possible.

So, what determines the level of saving? As noted in box 29.1, numerous social and institutional factors can be expected to have a bearing on the nature of the relationship between income, consumption, and saving. According to Keynesian economics, the rate of interest is *not* particularly important in this respect. In this, Keynes differed significantly from pre-Keynesian economists, who thought that the level of savings would respond positively to a higher interest rate. The pre-Keynesian view sounds logical enough: higher interest rates would mean a higher financial reward for saving, so people would be inclined to save more, would they not? Indeed, people certainly might *want* to save more if the rate of interest were higher. However, because high interest rates deter investment, they also tend to reduce national income, which then reduces people's capacity to save. On the whole, therefore, Keynesians doubt the capacity of changes in interest rates to produce equilibrium between the levels of investment and savings in the economy. Keynesians typically take the view that interest rates shape *how* people save—whether they stuff their savings under the mattress, or put them in bank savings accounts or fixed term deposits, for example—rather than *how much* they save.

Investment

Investment (I) is the second component in aggregate demand. While not usually as large as consumption, it is usually more *volatile*. That is why it is so important as a determinant of the overall state of the economy in the short term. The volatility of investment can cause major fluctuations in the level of national income, output, and employment. It warrants careful analysis.

Investment is undertaken primarily by capitalist businesses. They invest in new plant, equipment, premises, and capital goods in general. Since the profit motive is the driving force (presumed to be axiomatic in a capitalist economy), investment will be undertaken when it is expected to be profitable. This, according to Keynesian economics, will be when the expected rate of return on investment exceeds the rate of interest on funds borrowed to undertake the investment. Box 29.2 explains the reasoning.

It does not matter in principle whether firms are borrowing money to undertake investment or financing it out of past profits. In the former case, the rate of interest is the *actual cost* of obtaining capital; in the latter, it is the *opportunity cost*, since it indicates the rate of return a firm could have earned by lending its money rather than using it for its own investment. (For simplicity here, we assume that borrowing and lending rates, if not identical, move in tandem.) Either way, the rate of interest is a negative influence on investment.

Box 29.2

What shapes business investment?

Investment is expenditure by firms on capital goods. Its aim is to expand firms' productive capacity. The overall amount of investment undertaken by firms depends on the relationship between the marginal efficiency of capital and the prevailing rate of interest, as shown in the following diagram:

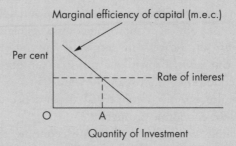

The marginal efficiency of capital indicates the expected rate of return on an additional unit of investment expenditure. Imagine a business person considering the various possible investments that could be made: he or she ranks them in order of expected rates of return, with the most profitable being undertaken first, the second most profitable being undertaken next, and so on. In other words, the marginal efficiency of capital declines as the amount of investment increases. Similar reasoning applies to the economy as a whole. Hence, the downward sloping m.e.c. schedule in the above diagram.

The rate of interest, on the other hand, must usually be taken by firms as given. It is the rate that banks or other financial institutions charge for money borrowed from them. A profit-seeking business person will normally weigh up that cost of borrowing against the income expected to be generated by using the borrowed funds for investment (that is, the marginal efficiency of capital). All projects where the expected rate of return is greater than the rate of interest are profitable to undertake; they would be given the go-ahead. Projects where the expected rate of return is less than the prevailing rate of interest would be unprofitable to undertake. Thus, investment ceases at the point where the marginal efficiency of capital equals the rate of interest (that is, at OA in the above diagram). The higher the rate of interest, the less the amount of investment undertaken.

The positive influence is the expected rate of return. 'Expected' is the key word here. Keynesians stress the importance of *business expectations* in determining the level of investment undertaken.[2] The marginal efficiency of capital is the *anticipated* return on the last unit of investment spending undertaken. If business decision-makers are optimistic about the future, this marginal efficiency of capital will be high; if pessimistic, it will be low. The level of optimism is not simply a matter of whether they get out of bed in the morning feeling cheerful or not; it depends on their judgments about the prospects for profitability of their business, based on assessments of market demand, and on broader perceptions of the state of the national and international economies, as shaped by media interpretations, political pronouncements, and so on. For this reason, governments regularly try to 'talk up' business confidence by presenting rosy assessments of the economy.

Herd behaviour by business investors is common, as is usually the case where there is interdependence of information and strategic decisions. Keynes said that investment, that most crucial influence on a nation's income, output, and employment, is dependent on the 'animal spirits' of business people. Some might think incomplete an analysis that has such a crucial variable depending on 'psychological' factors. Marxist political economy, in contrast, explains the interruptions to the capital accumulation process in terms of the internal *systemic* contradictions of capitalism. But 'animal spirits' are not like 'sunspots': they are shaped by material economic conditions. Marxist and Keynesian economists would surely agree that, as far as the real economy is concerned, dependence on 'animal spirits' is a less than robust basis for economic prosperity.

When things are going well in the economy, they tend to go very well. An increase in investment creates extra jobs and extra incomes; those incomes are then spent on other goods and services, which creates more demand, more output, more incomes, more jobs, and so on. The total impact on national income can be many times greater than the initial investment that began the process. This is *the multiplier effect*, a key element of Keynesian economic analysis. The size of the multiplier depends on the size of the 'leakages' from the circular flow of income. It is highest when these leakages are smallest, that is, when there is a low marginal propensity to save, a low marginal tax rate, and a low propensity to import. Then, the bulk of any extra incomes flow through the economy in a cumulative process of expansion. If, on the other hand, consumers save a high proportion of their extra incomes, spend a great deal on imported goods, or pay high marginal rates of tax (without corresponding increases in government expenditure), the multiplier effects are bound to be more modest. Economic expansion peters out more quickly.

The multiplier effect also operates in reverse. Falls in investment, occuring when those 'animal spirits' take a pessimistic turn, are multiplied in their impact on the decline of national income. Therein lies the principal source of recession. Therein also lies the key reason to emphasise government expenditure as a potential antidote to socially damaging outcomes.

Government expenditure

This third component in the aggregate demand for goods and services may take the form of consumption spending (for example the direct provision by government of services, such as public housing, education and health, or social security transfers that allow poorer people to consume more goods and services than they otherwise could). Alternatively, it may be in the form of public investment (such as building bridges, electricity supply systems, railways, roads, hospitals, schools, libraries, or art galleries). Its macroeconomic effects, including its multiplier effects, can be expected, as a first approximation, to be similar to private-sector consumption and investment.

The principal difference is that government expenditure (G) is a *policy* variable. In other words, it can be determined consciously by the government in order to achieve specific economic and social goals. It can be adjusted, for example, to compensate for variations over time in the volume of private-sector consumption and investment. It can be used as an instrument for economic stabilisation and the pursuit of full employment. That is why it is of such significance from a Keynesian perspective.

Exports and imports

These final two components of aggregate demand are much harder to control. They depend significantly on what is happening in the rest of the world—something over which local economic institutions, whether public or private, usually have no substantial influence. The volume of export sales (X) from any nation may be enhanced by the strategic efforts of local producers, and may be encouraged in various ways by the government, but it depends ultimately on the incomes and consumption preferences of the citizens of other nations. An international economic recession or switch in consumers' tastes can make sudden and substantial dents in a nation's export earnings.

Meanwhile, the volume of expenditure on imports (M) depends on the preferences of local consumers for those imported goods relative to local products. It also depends on the strategic behaviour of firms both inside and outside the country (such as when TNCs have a policy of importing from their subsidiaries or affiliate companies rather than buying from local producers). Governments commonly seek to exert some control over imports, directly through the imposition of *tariffs* and *quotas* on imported goods, and indirectly through campaigns to encourage the purchase of local products. *Exchange rate policy* may also be adjusted as a means of trying to improve the trade balance (X − M), although its effectiveness depends on the elasticity of demand for the exported and imported products. Overall, balancing imports and exports does not happen 'naturally' and constitutes a major challenge for public policy.

These considerations about the various components of aggregate demand draw attention to numerous interdependent relationships, some of which may be responsive to government policy, while others seem to have their own momentum. The savings habits of consumers, the 'animal spirits' of business investors, and the external conditions affecting imports and exports are the elements most difficult to control.

A DIABOLICAL ADJUSTMENT MECHANISM

The next step in developing a Keynesian interpretation of the economy is to ask how the economy adjusts to changes in these components of aggregate demand. For example, what happens when the level of aggregate demand is rising? In the short term (when aggregate supply or productive capacity is fixed), it depends on whether the economy is operating at full capacity or has surplus capacity. If there is surplus capacity, the previously underutilised resources will be put to productive use and unemployment can be expected to fall. On the other hand, if the economy is already operating at full capacity, the expansionary pressures are likely to cause the prices of goods and services to rise. *Inflation* is a probable outcome in the latter circumstances.

The reverse chain of reasoning applies to a reduction in aggregate demand. Inflationary pressures may be eased if the economy was previously operating at full capacity. Increased unemployment of resources (labour, capital, and land) is the more likely outcome, as capacity utilisation falls. This is the *recession* scenario.

These considerations illustrate a Keynesian insight of great social significance: the mechanism that balances aggregate demand and supply is change in the levels of national income, output, and employment. This is usually a painful adjustment process. It entails major social damage when aggregate demand declines—people lose their jobs and face falling incomes. Equilibrium in the economy may be re-established, but it is not necessarily, indeed not typically, an equilibrium of full employment.

Pre-Keynesian economists had generally been more complacent. If, as they argued, the rate of interest serves as the adjustment mechanism between savings and investment, there need be no major volatility in the economic system. Equilibrium in the economy is continually restored without any major social costs (other than fluctuating incomes from interest payments for those with surplus funds to lend). Similarly, if exchange rate adjustments automatically restore balance between national exports and imports, then temporary trade imbalances need cause no concern. It is for those reasons that the pre-Keynesian view (which still has numerous adherents) produces a more *laissez-faire* inclination. It is this political complacency that Keynes and Keynesians have continually challenged.

The Keynesian view does not deny the existence of adjustment mechanisms. In that sense, Keynesian economics still has some of the features of an equilibrium theory. However, the Keynesian emphasis on changes in income, output, and employment as the principal adjustment mechanism leads to a quite distinctive interpretation of the problems of a capitalist economy. If the amount consumers plan to save exceeds the amount firms plan to invest, for example, the national income falls, and the consumers are not able in practice to save as much as they originally intended. A *recession* restores the equilibrium of savings and investment. Similarly, if imports exceed exports, there will be a downward pressure on the national income, tending to reduce people's capacity to spend on imports, or on locally produced goods for that matter. Reduced material living standards occur. The adjustment mechanism in both cases is *the overall level of economic activity*. Therein lies the source of systemic instability, the cause of alternating booms and slumps. Therein lies the Keynesian rationale for significant government intervention in order to stabilise an otherwise unstable capitalist economic system.

CONCLUSION

The Keynesian analysis, focusing on the factors affecting the aggregate demand and supply for goods and services, provides a coherent explanation for some of the recurrent problems of capitalism. The explanation of the problems of unemployment and inflation is particularly powerful. The confidence in the capacity of economic policy to correct these flaws is an equally distinctive feature of Keynesian reasoning, contrasting with both Marxian and neoclassical perspectives. In this last respect, Keynesian economics has more in common with some of the more politically optimistic currents within institutional economics. However, the story becomes rather more complicated when the role of money in the economy is considered. Therein lie further sources of economic instability, but also further opportunities for management of the economy as a whole.

CHAPTER 30

Instability in a Monetary Economy

Does money matter?
How do money markets, goods markets, and labour markets interact?
Is the economy naturally stable? Can it be more effectively stabilised?

Keynesian analysis interprets capitalism as a monetary economy. To understand it requires study of the aggregate demand for, and supply of, goods and services, as considered in the preceding chapter. More than that, it requires study of the significance of money itself in the economy.

An immediate difficulty must be confronted. People usually talk about money and income as if they were the same thing. This is understandable because we usually receive our income in the form of money. However, an important analytical distinction between money and income must be made. Money comprises cash, most obviously, the notes and coins that can be used to facilitate exchange. As normally defined by economists, it also includes other liquid assets, such as bank deposits which can be readily converted into cash (by withdrawing funds from the bank or from an ATM).[1] Income, on the other hand, comprises payments that people receive during particular time periods, as rewards for their work, as interest on their savings, as profits on their investments, or perhaps because of an inheritance or a lucky win while gambling. Income may be received in the form of money or in the form of goods and services.

Distinguishing between money and income is easy, but discerning their relationship is harder. Does the role of money in the economy facilitate or hinder the achievement of higher levels of national income? And does the use of money and the behaviour of financial institutions affect how the economy works, for better or worse? Does including such monetary considerations lead to a different view about the stability or instability of the economy? Does it lead to different prescriptions for economic management? Exploring these questions takes us into some of the more complex dimensions of Keynesian economics. We can start simply, by asking what is the significance of money in the general functioning of the economy. This draws attention to the role of money as a *store of wealth* as well as a *means of exchange*.

DOES MONEY MATTER?

It is sometimes said that 'money is a veil', a shroud that conceals the underlying economic fundamentals. It is certainly prominent on the surface of economic life:

wages are usually paid in the form of cash, cheques, or deposits into a bank account; prices of commodities are set in terms of the amount of money that must be paid in order to buy them; and payments of dividends to shareholders are usually in the form of cheques. However, behind the appearances are *real* economic variables: the quantity of goods and services that a money wage can buy, the quantity of one commodity that will exchange in the market for another, and the claim on real economic resources that a dividend payment represents. The use of money should not obscure these fundamental features.

This view of 'money as a veil' applies to each of the principal currents of economic thought preceding Keynes's restructuring of economic thought, subject to relatively minor qualifications. Each sought to lay bare the underlying economic foundations. Recall classical political economist Adam Smith's famous statement about the relative value of deer and beavers being determined by how much time must be spent catching them: the price of beavers can be specified in terms of deer without any mention of money. In Marxist economics, the ability of employers to appropriate some part of the value produced by labour shapes the relative income shares of capitalists and workers—money enters the story only as a means of facilitating the (unequal) exchanges. In neoclassical theory, the *relative* prices of different goods and services, and of factors of production, are determined by the forces of demand and supply—only when the focus shifts to the *absolute* level of prices does money enter the story.

In the real world, too, economic activities could continue without the use of money. We could rely instead on *barter*, the process of direct commodity exchanges. Life would not be easy, though. If you were paid your weekly wages in commodities—say, ten loaves of bread, six litres of milk, one bicycle, one pair of shoes, and one Spice Girls CD—it would be most inconvenient. You might already have enough shoes, but might need a new pair of jeans, in which case you would need to find someone willing to exchange a pair of jeans that are surplus to his or her requirements for a pair of shoes, which he or she wants. And, you might prefer Limp Bizkit to the Spice Girls, so you would need to hunt for someone with the opposite preference who would be willing to swap CDs. Life in a pure barter economy is complex.[2] It is easier if there is some common medium of exchange. Money usefully serves that function.

If that is all that money did, it would not be of fundamental economic importance. It would not significantly affect the overall level of economic activity, the sectoral composition of the economy, or the distribution of income and wealth. It could rightly be regarded as a veil shrouding the real economy. In building economic analysis, we might properly seek to strip it away in order to reveal the underlying forces at work. Keynes disagreed. He took the view that money *does* affect the functioning of the real economy, particularly the overall level of economic activity. This is because money is more than a means of exchange—it is also a store of value. It may be held not only for financial transactions, but also for *speculative* reasons. Such speculation imparts a greater degree of uncertainty and instability to the economic system. The functioning of *financial institutions* also becomes important in determining the likelihood of prosperity or recession. Money matters, and an understanding of its influence is essential for managing the economy.

THE DEMAND AND SUPPLY OF MONEY

Why hold money? At first sight, doing so seems illogical. Holding substantial amounts of cash, for example, incurs an obvious opportunity cost—the income forgone by not putting that cash into some interest-earning form. If, instead of holding cash, you put your money into an interest-earning deposit account at a bank, you would be making your money 'work' for you. As George Argyrous puts it: 'surely a rational person would either consume their income, and thereby gain immediate satisfaction, or else lend their income to a capitalist and thereby receive an interest payment which will increase their ability to consume in the future. Why give up present gratification for no reward when a reward is available? Money is barren—only a miser can get satisfaction from the holding of cash as such'.[3]

Keynes identified three reasons why rational people—not just misers—might indeed want to hold their income in a liquid form, as cash. These constitute the *three types of demand for money*.

- *Transactions demand*: We usually need to keep some cash handy for our normal day-to-day shopping and other expenditures. If workers are paid weekly, for example, they need this 'pocketful' of money to see them through to the next pay day. Less frequent, say monthly, payments could be expected to result in higher average amounts of money being held.
- *Precautionary demand*: Some additional money may be kept handy as a safeguard against unforeseeable personal problems, such as ill-health or personal accidents, or to take advantage of unforeseen opportunities.
- *Speculative demand*: Financial speculators may choose to hold money rather than interest-bearing assets so that they can buy financial assets at a later date when the prospect of making capital gains is greater.

The first two sources of demand can be expected to be pretty stable and predictable, rising and falling broadly in proportion to national income. The third is potentially much more volatile. Keynes, a successful financial speculator himself, thought that the speculative demand of money was particularly significant in determining how the economy functions—for better or worse.

Consider, for example, a speculator choosing between holding two types of asset: cash and government securities. These securities, sometimes called bonds, command a fixed rate of interest. If the current interest rate is 5 per cent, a bond costing $100 will yield a guaranteed $5 annual income to its holder. That sounds more attractive than simply holding cash, does it not? There is no risk associated with government bonds, unlike shares in corporations and other financial assets whose market prices are volatile. But, what if the rate of interest applying to bonds were to rise to 8 per cent in the next year? The holder of this year's bond, earning only $5 per annum, would want out. The holder would want to sell the old bond in order to buy a new one that would give a higher yield. However, no one would buy that old bond at its face value of $100 because a new bond yielding 8 per cent interest would be a better deal. The old bond will sell in the market for only $100 x 5/8. So, selling it would entail a substantial capital loss. With the benefit of hindsight, it was a mistake to buy the bond in the first place. The speculator would have done better to hold cash and wait for the interest rate to rise before buying a bond. Of course, the problem is that one can never know for sure how interest rates will move in the future. So, whether speculators hold cash or interest-bearing assets depends crucially on their *expectations* about interest rate changes.

Why does any of this matter? If speculation were simply part of an economic 'sideshow' in which people gambled against future price movements, sometimes making capital gains and sometimes making losses, it would be of no great significance (other than the diversion of human energies into what is essentially a *zero-sum game* of no public benefit). Keynes recognised that it is more than this. The activities of the speculators have real economic impacts, affecting society as a whole.[4] This is partly because their speculative activities tend to have self-fulfilling effects.

Consider, for example, a situation where speculators *en masse* are anticipating a rise in interest rates. A surge in inflation or the trade deficit often leads the financial media pundits to make such a prediction. Speculators will then want to hold cash rather than interest-bearing assets. They exhibit what Keynes called a strong *liquidity preference*. However, if the supply of money is fixed, the speculators can only hold more cash if ordinary household savers hold less cash. That means a higher market rate of interest is necessary in order to induce household savers to put the cash that they would have otherwise held into buying interest-bearing financial assets. The effect of the speculators' actions has been to push the interest rate up. Their expectations have become self-fulfilling.

It sounds like a complicated process, producing a strange outcome. The role of the rate of interest is at the heart of the matter. Herein is a striking contrast between the neoclassical and Keynesian views about how the economy works. The neoclassicals expect interest rate changes to continually restore a balance between savings and investment, the market interest rate rising when investment exceeds saving (thus discouraging investment and encouraging saving) and falling when savings exceed investment (thus discouraging saving and encouraging investment). By contrast, Keynesians emphasise that market interest rates do not depend on the overall level of savings, but on whether people want to hold their savings as cash or as interest-bearing assets. But their liquidity preference itself depends on the prevailing rate of interest and predictions about its likely future movements. The overall effect is a tendency to economic instability, accentuated by self-fulfilling expectations.

Whether the monetary authorities can, or should, do anything to stabilise this otherwise unstable economy is an interesting question. The analysis so far has assumed that the *supply of money* is fixed. However, the supply of money in practice is variable. The key question is: who or what determines it? The standard Keynesian view is that it is a policy variable (similar, in this respect, to government expenditure, as analysed in the preceding chapter).[5] The supply of money may be varied by the central monetary authority (for example the Reserve Bank), usually working in tandem with government for social goals, such as full employment and/or the elimination of inflation. So, if speculative activities are causing interest rates to rise, and thereby threatening to cause a recession, it is possible for the monetary authority to intervene in order to offset that tendency. It can, for instance, increase the money supply, which will normally cause interest rates to fall and thus encourage investment and economic growth.[6] From a Keynesian perspective, control of the money supply is, in principle at least, integral to stabilising an economy otherwise afflicted by undesirable fluctuations in the levels of income, output, and employment. It has to be done judiciously in order to avoid creating inflation, but it is an important policy instrument.

A rather different view emphasises the supply of money being determined directly by the banks in the private sector. The banks can lend money to borrowers, including business investors, over and above what they have in deposits. Thus they create *credit money* directly in the act of bank-lending. In effect, the supply of money adjusts continually to demand. The central bank can try to influence this process, but its influence is quite secondary to the pressure of demand for loans from the banks. As James K. Galbraith argues: 'The central bank ... does not control the money supply, only the excess reserves in the system. Banks may or may not lend all the excess reserves and the public may or may not demand loans sufficient to absorb them ... Money is therefore always and everywhere non-neutral. The dynamic consequence is business cycle instability'.[7]

AN INTEGRATED KEYNESIAN MODEL

The analysis of money markets needs to be integrated with the macroeconomic analysis of the markets for goods and services in order to arrive at a total picture of how the economy works. Box 30.1 presents one analytical device conventionally used for this purpose. It is introduced here—cautiously—only because it has been so influential in the teaching of a rather mechanistic, 'textbook' interpretation of Keynesian economics. One recent economic reviewer has argued that it was the embrace of this model by younger economists, rather than Keynes's own ideas as set out in *The General Theory*, that marked the start of what came to be known as the Keynesian revolution.[8] Perhaps its most useful feature is that it draws attention to the role of *the rate of interest as a mechanism linking the goods and money markets*. For example, if a high liquidity preference prevails among those with loanable funds, a high rate of interest is necessary in order to induce them to buy interest-bearing assets and thereby produce money market equilibrium. That high rate of interest will then affect the level of productive output and incomes via its negative impact on investment.

This particular analysis also draws attention to how the money markets and markets for goods and services are linked through *the level of national income*—what was termed 'the diabolical adjustment mechanism' in the preceding chapter. It is a reminder that such equilibrium processes that do exist in the economic system take effect through impacting on people's livelihoods.

However, the IS/LM analysis shown in box 30.1 has limited application (and is somewhat 'out of tune' with the general tenor of Keynes's own views) because it abstracts from the important role of *expectations* in the capitalist economy. Each IS/LM diagram is drawn for a given state of expectations that determine the marginal efficiency of capital and the liquidity preference, and therefore the IS and LM curves respectively. A different set of expectations among investors and speculators would mean different positions for the IS and/or LM curves. Moreover, any change in expectations that causes a shift in one curve would tend to cause a shift in the other. So, there may be no unique equilibrium at all.[9]

Box 30.1

A mechanistic interpretation of Keynesian economics

One neat—perhaps too neat—representation of an integrated Keynesian model is the IS/LM diagram. It shows how the market for total goods and services interacts with the market for money. 'IS' stands for investment and savings, 'LM' for liquidity and money.

The IS curve indicates the various combinations of the rate of interest and national income that bring savings and investment into equality, thereby producing overall equilibrium in the *market for goods and services*. It is downward sloping to the right because the higher the rate of interest, the less the investment and, hence, the lower the national income.

The LM curve indicates the combinations of the rate of interest and national income that produce equilibrium in the *money market*. The higher the national income, the greater the transactions and precautionary demands for money, and the less money available for speculation (given a fixed supply of money at any time). Higher rates of interest are then needed to induce savers to purchase interest-bearing financial assets. So, higher national income is associated with higher interest rates. The curve slopes up to the right, indicating this generally positive relationship.

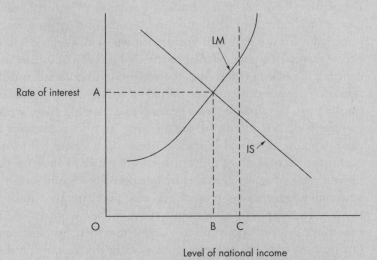

Level of national income

In the situation shown here, the goods and money markets are in simultaneous equilibrium when the rate of interest is at level OA and the level of national income is at OB. Keynesian economists using this model emphasise that there is no necessary connection between this equilibrium and the condition of full employment. The level of national income necessary to bring about full employment might be OC, for example. It would be pure chance if OB and OC were to coincide. In other words, there is no market mechanism ensuring full employment.

The IS/LM analysis is also limited in that it does not—indeed cannot in this two-dimensional diagrammatic form—show how these variables are linked to *labour-market* conditions. All one can say is that there is no necessary convergence between the equilibrium level of national income and the level that would be necessary to establish full employment. It would be quite accidental if the equilibrium level were also the full employment level. Further consideration of the labour market, including analysis of how technological change may affect the ratio of output to employment, is needed in order to assess the prospects for full employment in practice.

THE LABOUR MARKET

Do income, output, and employment move together? So far, this has been assumed. When the output of goods and services is rising, more incomes are generated, and more employees will presumably be hired to produce the growing volume of products. Conversely, if output is shrinking, total income falls and unemployment can be expected to rise. It seems a reasonable assumption to make about the behaviour of the economy in the short term, when its productive capacity is relatively fixed. It is integral to the Keynesian reasoning as it explains changes in the number of people employed by reference to changes in the level of output and national income.

What view about the labour market is implied? Keynesians do not regard it as a market in which changes in wage rates ensure equilibrium. In this respect, Keynesian economics differs both in analytical construction and political implications from neoclassical economics. Neoclassical economists tend to advocate wage reductions to deal with unemployment, since they see it as resulting from the excess supply of labour relative to the demand for labour. Where supply exceeds demand, the price (in this case, the wage rate) should fall. Any 'market imperfections' that impede that outcome should be removed. Keynesians, on the other hand, usually point out that wages are generally not flexible downwards. Of course, wage cuts for particular groups of workers may, and do, occur; but workers, certainly those who are organised in trade unions, can be expected to use their collective organisational strength to resist such cuts. What does often happen, though, is that the *real* value of wages is eroded by inflation. That is one reason why trade unions advocate wage rises to protect the real purchasing power of their members. However, the apparent gains from a rising money wage may be eroded by further rises in the price of goods and services, so that there is no increase in the real wage (the quantity of goods and services that can be purchased with the wage).

In any case, from a Keynesian perspective, a general policy of wage reduction is not a sensible economic strategy for dealing with unemployment because of its negative effects on the demand for goods and services and, therefore, on the demand for labour. Keynesians, while not necessarily supportive of working class interests *per se*, at least recognise the importance of wages as a source of aggregate demand. They emphasise the positive role of wage incomes in the realisation of surplus value (to use the Marxian terminology), rather than the more negative role (from a capitalistic viewpoint) of wage costs in the production of surplus value.

Over a longer period of time, another type of threat to full employment has to be considered. When the nature of *technology* is variable, labour displacement may occur, even though output is increasing. Most goods and services can be produced in various ways, and the type of technology a business chooses to use can be expected to be influenced by the prevailing level of wages relative to the cost of capital goods. So, if wage rates are rising relative to the cost of capital goods, labour displacement is likely. Generally, the effect of technological change is to open up possibilities for increasingly sophisticated methods of production, including automation. Under these circumstances, the conventional Keynesian assumption that income, output, and employment move together is less reasonable.

In the extreme case, increases in output may occur without any corresponding increases in employment. This is the controversial phenomenon of 'jobless growth'. In Keynes's time it could safely be ignored: the immediate task was to get the masses of unemployed people back to work by creating conditions conducive to economic expansion. Nowadays, it seems that policies concerned with the *redistribution of work*—its more equitable sharing throughout the society—are of comparable importance in resolving the persistence of the unemployment problem. This is not to gainsay the enduring value of the Keynesian perspective, only to emphasise the need to subject its underlying assumptions to critical scrutiny in contemporary conditions.[10]

CONCLUSION

The analysis of capitalism as a monetary economy is a distinctive feature of Keynesian economics. 'Money', according to the old adage, 'makes the world go round'. Keynes showed that it also makes it go up and down. Monetary factors, especially those associated with speculation, impart additional sources of instability to the economy. Where speculators have a high liquidity preference, for example, the savings that would otherwise be available for productive investment, may be diverted instead into speculative activities. Upward pressure is exerted on the market rate of interest, with potentially damaging consequences for investment, employment stability, and economic growth.

Keynes said that 'if the capital requirements of the economy are determined as a side-effect of a casino then the job is likely to be ill-done'.[11] He also expressed a broader concern about the adverse economic consequences of the persistence of the 'rentier' class—those who derive incomes from the ownership of assets without contributing directly to productive activity. Keynes welcomed the prospect of the 'euthanasia of the rentier'.[12] In this respect, the Keynesian view is akin to Veblen's, at least in distinguishing between the contribution of those who use capital productively and those who pursue more 'predatory' purposes. It contrasts with the Marxian view about the need to challenge the dominance of the capitalist class as a whole. What all these viewpoints—deriving from Marx, Veblen, and Keynes—have in common is the recognition of systemic structural flaws in the capitalist system. Politically, what distinguishes the Keynesian view is its emphasis on the role that governments can play in redressing these adverse aspects of the capitalist economy by seeking goals such as full employment without inflation.

CHAPTER 31

Macroeconomic Policy

The visible hand

Why do governments face an economic policy imperative?
What are the principal policy instruments advocated by Keynesian economists?
Do they work?

It is one thing to analyse capitalism; it is another to manage it. Most of the key deci-sions affecting the overall level of economic activity are taken by self-interested actors in the economic drama—employers, consumers, investors, and speculators. Yet we generally hold the elected governments of nation states responsible for the prevailing economic conditions. In certain respects this is a distinctively Keynesian legacy—holding governments, rather than capitalist businesses or the capitalist sys-tem in general, accountable for problems like unemployment or inflation. It is based on a view of the state as the guardian of national economic performance.[1]

What should governments do? What follows from Keynesian economic analysis about the appropriate form of economic policy? How effective are such policies, and why have they not been more systematically implemented?

THE ECONOMIC POLICY IMPERATIVE

The argument that governments are responsible for national economic perfor-mance rests on essentially three pillars. First is the observation, stressed in the preceding three chapters, that the capitalist market economy is not adequately self-regulating. Keynes swept complacent *laissez-faire* views aside. In Galbraith's words:

> It was the historic achievement of John Maynard (later Lord) Keynes in the mid thirties, in the wake of numerous less reputable voices (who lacked Keynes' prestige and the sav-age reinforcement of the circumstances of the Great Depression), to destroy Say's Law virtually without trace and therewith the illusion of a self-righting economy. After Keynes it was accepted that there could be a shortage (or surplus) of purchasing power in the economy and that neither wages nor interest rates reacted usefully to correct it. A reduction in wages might merely reduce purchasing power—aggregate demand, as it came to be called—yet more and make things worse. In the absence of sufficient demand even the lowest interest rates, as the Depression experience showed, would not encour-age the needed investment and thus enhance demand. Stagnation would continue. The only answer was for the state to intervene.[2]

The second pillar in the case for government economic policy has more to do with political philosophy than economic analysis. It is the view of the state as an instrument for the pursuit of social goals and, generally, as the embodiment of the public interest. Individuals may act on the basis of self-interest and greed, but the state can pursue nobler goals. This is an essentially liberal democratic stance, but not incompatible with an evolutionary socialist perspective. As Rod O'Donnell puts it, 'while rejecting *laissez-faire* capitalism and state socialism as global frameworks, Keynes sought a fusion or "amalgam" in which the best features of each could be retained and the worst discarded'.[3]

The third pillar is confidence in the *capacity* of the state to act systematically in the pursuit of the goal of social betterment. This does not deny the possibility of making mistakes. However, it does assume some degree of coherence in the organisation of the state, and its ability to apply economic policy in a rational and deliberate manner. It requires, as a bare minimum, that the government should have good information about the national economy and an effective array of policy instruments with which to manage it.

THE INFORMATION BASE

Any management system depends on the existence of a good information base. For national economic management that means a comprehensive system of *national economic accounting*. Governments need to know the trends in national income, expenditure, output, and employment in order to judge whether particular forms of economic steering are appropriate. Historically, the development of Keynesian economics, together with the work of economists such as Colin Clark and the institutionalist Wesley Mitchell, helped to establish consistent annual national economic accounts. Those national accounts do not use neoclassical concepts like marginal product and marginal cost, nor Marxist value categories like the rate of surplus value or the organic composition of capital; they use Keynesian economic concepts like aggregate consumption and investment expenditures, as discussed in the preceding three chapters.

Ensuring the accuracy of these accounts is a problem. In practice, the estimation of the annual aggregates is rather rough-and-ready. Sometimes quite major revisions to each year's data occur, often over many subsequent years, as errors are located and new information comes to light. Quarterly national income accounts are worse still—perhaps not worth the paper they are written on—because the trends they show are commonly revealed by subsequent revisions to have actually been moving in the opposite direction. Such elements of unreliability in the data base make the process of 'fine-tuning' the economy more difficult. However, they are not an absolute impediment. Interpreted cautiously, and supplemented by other data sources like surveys of consumer confidence and business investment intentions, national income accounts provide a useful foundation for policy formulation.

POLICY INSTRUMENTS

In addition to a good information base, economic management requires a range of effective policy instruments. It is useful in this regard to distinguish between policies for short-term macroeconomic *stabilisation* and grander measures to steer economic *growth and development* in the longer term. These may be seen as the two faces of Keynesian economic policy, reflecting liberal and radical interpretations of the contribution by Keynes. Fiscal and monetary policies are the basic stock-in-trade of the liberal interpretation, while the more radical view also embraces policies to shape the distribution of incomes, and the patterns of investment, industry development, and trade. Each of these forms of policy requires careful consideration of their potential and their pitfalls.

Fiscal policy

Fiscal policy is the most direct means of managing the overall level of income, output, and employment in a national economy. It entails adjustments to government expenditure and taxation. Of course, governments usually do an annual stocktaking of their spending and income anyway, and vary expenditure patterns and tax rates to accord with their political priorities. From a liberal Keynesian perspective, the key issue is the overall *fiscal stance*—whether expansionary or contractionary. The standard prescription is for a budgetary *deficit* (an excess of expenditure over taxation) to deal with recession and unemployment, and for a budgetary *surplus* (an excess of taxation over expenditure) to deal with excess demand and inflation.

This emphasis on judgments about deficits and surpluses stands in striking contrast to the pre-Keynesian view (revived in recent years as a new orthodoxy) that governments should seek a *balanced budget*. A balanced budget—not spending more than you earn—sounds like a prudent basis for household management, but, as Keynes emphasised, it is usually not good macroeconomics. Keynes thought that, over the whole of an economic cycle, perhaps spanning a decade or more, it would be sensible to roughly balance expenditures and taxation levels; but that, in any one year, it would be better to use fiscal policy in a *counter-cyclical* manner.

Deficits and surpluses tend to happen anyway, as the economy moves between periods of recession and growth. During a recession, social security expenditures rise because there are more claimants for unemployment benefits, for example. Meanwhile, tax revenues tend to fall because average incomes are lower. Both income taxes and consumption taxes generate less revenue in those circumstances. So, a natural tendency towards budgetary deficit exists during a recession. This is good, Keynesians argue, because that injection of government expenditure into the circular flow of income helps to raise the overall level of economic activity and bring the recession to an end. The reverse reasoning applies in a boom: government social security expenditures tend to fall and tax revenues tend to rise, causing a budget surplus that damps down the rate of economic growth, and reduces potential inflationary pressures.

There is a strong case for supplementing these *automatic* stabilisers with *discretionary* fiscal policy to smooth out the ups and downs in the level of economic activity even more. On this reasoning, governments should run even larger deficits in times of recession in order to 'kick start' economic recovery, either by cutting tax rates or increasing expenditures. That is the best time to spend on infrastructure construction projects that will create jobs. In boom times, on the other hand, bigger surpluses can be engineered by increasing tax rates or cutting back on government spending.

There are significant pitfalls in the application of these discretionary fiscal policies. The timing has to be good, otherwise there is the danger that the policies may accentuate rather than dampen the amplitude of the economic cycle. The effect of fluctuations in government expenditure on investment expenditure in the private sector also needs to be considered. How changes in a government's fiscal stance impact on volatile business expectations will have a major bearing on the macroeconomic outcomes. The distributional consequences of changing patterns of taxes and expenditures also warrants further attention—there are always winners and losers in such policy changes. And, as a matter of political expediency, the relationship between the economic cycle and the political electoral cycle can be expected to have an influence on a government's fiscal policy stance. Increasing spending before elections in order to woo voters and increasing taxes after being elected may be effective, albeit cynical, politics.[4] However, it makes no positive contribution to, and may significantly undermine, macroeconomic stability.

These features notwithstanding, discretionary fiscal policy has the obvious appeal of providing a direct means of levelling out the ups and downs to which the capitalist economy is otherwise prone. It simultaneously extends political decision-making over the allocation of economic resources in order to achieve broader social goals.

Monetary policy

Governments may also influence the general state of the economy through their influence over the supply of money and the cost of borrowing it. The instruments of monetary policy can be used either as supplements or as alternatives to fiscal policy for the purposes of demand management in a counter-cyclical economic strategy. Few would claim that monetary policy can contribute, like fiscal policy, to broader social goals in the long term, but it can have a significant effect on economic conditions in the short term.[5]

The relevant policy instruments, in principle, are clear. Governments directly control the issue of notes and coin; they may indirectly influence the extent to which banks and other financial institutions extend credit facilities; and they may determine the general direction of change in interest rates. Through these measures they can influence the levels of consumption and investment in the private sector of the economy and thereby seek to steer the economy towards a more stable growth path consistent with full employment without inflation.

In practice, things are much more complicated. Indeed, developments since Keynes's time bear heavily on how monetary policy can actually be applied. First, governments often do not have the policy instruments *directly* at their disposal. Monetary policy is commonly in the hands of central banks that have a considerable degree of independence from governments. The extent of such independence in policy varies: the German *Bundesbank* has had more than the Bank of England, and the Reserve Bank of New Zealand has more than the Reserve Bank of Australia, for example. The goals that the central banks should pursue (whether full employment or the control of inflation, for example) are also matters of intense political controversy in many countries. The dominant tendency seems to be towards the central banks being given more independence and asserting the control of inflation as their main, if not sole, concern. This makes monetary policy less directly amenable to a Keynesian policy agenda, and puts the coherence of monetary policy in relation to other aspects of government policy in question. So, when economic commentators talk about the 'policy mix' between fiscal and monetary policies, it is important to remember that the responsible authorities are not necessarily the same, and sometimes not working comfortably in tandem, the frequent exchange of information between them notwithstanding.

A second consideration is how monetary policy has been constrained by the process of *financial deregulation* that has taken place in many nations in the last two decades. Deregulation has meant that some of the direct controls over financial institutions that were previously exercised by governments and/or central banks have been relinquished. Its vigour has varied from country to country. Direct controls over how banks hold their assets (how much should be held as government securities, for example) and of how they allocate their lending (what proportion should go to house-purchasers rather than business, for example) have been common casualties. The proponents of financial deregulation have consistently claimed that the result would be a more competitive and efficient banking sector; the outcomes have often been rather different in practice.[6]

The main effect of deregulation, as far as monetary policy is concerned, has been to leave the central monetary authority with *indirect control over the general level of interest rates* as its main, if not sole, remaining policy instrument. It can be a potent policy. Changes in the interest rate at which a country's central bank lends to other banks usually flow through into corresponding changes in the rates that banks charge, and pay, their customers. It tends to be a process of follow-the-leader, although individual financial institutions make their own judgments about how quickly and how closely to follow. The changes in prevailing interest rates then affect consumption and investment behaviour. Higher rates (a 'tight' monetary policy) make indebtedness more expensive and therefore tend to discourage both consumer spending and business investment, while low rates ('cheap money') can be expected to have a stimulatory effect. So, interest rate policy can be a powerful means of influencing the overall level of economic activity—for better or worse.

As with fiscal policy, there are potential pitfalls. Indeed, the problem of *timing* is more severe in the case of monetary policy. There are usually long and uncertain time lags between the policy process and its economic effects. It may be some time before the monetary authority sees the need for a policy adjustment (the 'recognition lag'), and more time may elapse before it decides which particular adjustment to monetary policy is appropriate (the 'implementation lag'). There may then be a significant period during which consumers and business people decide how to modify their plans for consumption and investment spending (the 'decision lag') and yet more time before those decisions affect the output of goods and services produced (the 'impact lag'). By that time, the prevailing national economic conditions may be markedly different. In the worst-case scenario, a supposedly counter-cyclical policy can turn out to accentuate the amplitude of the cycle.

Monetary policy also tends to have a *non-symmetrical* impact. It is most powerful as a contractionary measure. Higher interest rates can be relied on to depress the level of economic activity. Raising the cost of borrowing money has a particularly strong impact on investment by small businesses and on home loans (and therefore on the construction industry). However, monetary policy sometimes works less well in the opposite direction. Interest rate cuts will not necessarily stimulate business investment, for example, because business people also have an eye on the market for their products. If they are experiencing stagnant demand and are pessimistic about future prospects, investment will stay low despite falling interest rates.

Finally, the impact of monetary policy tends to be *non-selective*. An increase in interest rates usually has depressing effects on investment levels throughout the economy. This can be problematic because different regions or industries in a nation may be experiencing quite different economic conditions—some may be buoyant, while others are economically stagnant. An interest rate rise designed to choke off inflationary pressures in booming regions may send other regions into recession. The same may occur with fiscal policy, but in that case there is the possibility of targeting public expenditures at particular regions or industry sectors according to the prevailing economic conditions in those regions or sectors. In the case of monetary policy, no such possibility exists.

None of this means that monetary policy is redundant or unimportant. On the contrary, the monetary policy stance adopted by a government and/or the central bank normally has a significant bearing on the state of the economy. Its relationship to the government's fiscal policy stance—whether expansionary or contractionary—determines the 'policy mix' (about which conventional economic policy commentators argue incessantly). However, if that were the be-all-and-end-all of government economic policy, it would be a very limited agenda. In practice, other policies may be more important in fostering the conditions for economic prosperity in the longer term. Such measures include incomes policies, investment and industry policies, and international economic policies.

Incomes policy

Incomes policies require a more extensive role for government in economic affairs. Managing the relative shares of wages, profits, rent, interest, and other incomes is no easy matter, but a number of policy instruments are available if governments choose to use them. The share of labour in the national income can be influenced by setting minimum wage standards or, where centralised arbitration systems exist, intervening generally in the processes of wage-fixation. Direct controls over professional fees and rents may also be implemented in seeking to control non-wage incomes. Direct control over profits is harder in a capitalist economy, but, in so far as profit is a surplus payment, policies to control the other income sources that are costs to business can have some indirect effect.

Why would a government make these more extensive policy interventions? It may do so because of a concern with *social equity*, although that need not involve policies to influence income shares at source—it could equally be the focus of redistributive policies through taxation. A more fundamentally *economic* rationale for incomes policy is that income shares have a bearing on the overall level of economic activity. Consider, for example, a situation in which workers spend all their income, but capitalists save a significant proportion of theirs. Under these conditions, a redistribution of income from capital to labour would increase the total level of consumption, fuelling aggregate demand and thus, ironically, adding to the income stream of capitalists, too, in the longer term. Capitalists, acting individually, would never seek to initiate such redistributions, although they would ultimately benefit from the resulting boost to the level of economic activity. Incomes policy becomes a role for government because, while it improves conditions in the economy as a whole, none of the other players has the collective capacity to implement it.

Of course, all government economic activity has distributional consequences. In practice, the issue is only whether incomes policy should be implicit and passive, or explicit and purposeful. If the latter, then it can be linked more directly to goals, such as the pursuit of a more equitable society. Keynes himself thought that a less unequal distribution would be both economically and socially desirable. In his own words: 'I believe that there is social and psychological justification for significant inequalities of income and wealth, but not for such large disparities as exist today … Much lower stakes will serve the purpose equally well, as soon as the players are accustomed to them.'[7]

Incomes policies in practice do not necessarily produce egalitarian outcomes. The Labour government in the United Kingdom in the 1970s, for example, adopted a 'social contract' with the trade union movement that emphasised control over wage increases to combat inflationary pressures, but the absence of any corresponding regulation of the incomes of capital led to the policy becoming widely regarded as a 'social con-trick'. The Labor government in Australia between 1983 and 1996 also used an incomes policy, rather more successfully, as part of its Accord with the trade union movement; but it also eventually suffered loss of support because, among other things, the wage restraint was unmatched by any control over the sources and disposition of non-wage incomes.[8]

Investment and industry policy

From a Keynesian perspective, the level of expenditure on investment in the economy is crucial for two reasons. In the short run, it boosts the level of effective demand, raising incomes, output, and employment. In the long run, it adds to productive capacity. Because it impacts on both aggregate demand and aggregate supply, it is a key determinant of economic prosperity. Yet, as previously noted, when left purely in private hands, investment tends to be volatile, fluctuating according to changes in the 'animal spirits' of business people. Is there a role for government here, too, in the regulation, stabilisation, or direct control of investment expenditures?

Keynes used the memorably enigmatic phrase 'a somewhat comprehensive socialisation of investment' to indicate what he thought might be needed. To quote him in full:

> It seems unlikely that the influence of banking policy on the rate of interest will be sufficient by itself to determine an optimum rate of investment. I conceive therefore that a somewhat comprehensive socialisation of investment will prove to be the only means of securing an approximation to full employment; though this need not exclude all manner of compromises and of devices by which public authority will cooperate with private initiative.[9]

Not surprisingly, debate continues about what is implied by such an open-ended policy prescription. Possibilities include joint ventures between government and private-sector enterprises, and interventionist industry policies designed to create the conditions for more stable and/or buoyant patterns of private-sector investment. Although Keynes did not personally favour the extension of government ownership of key industry sectors ('nationalisation'), a similar logic applies. Because investment is so important to the state of the economy, it cannot sensibly be left to business people alone.

One particularly interesting possibility arises from the expansion of superannuation schemes in recent years. The workers' savings in those superannuation funds could be systematically steered into investment projects of national economic benefit. This would build a direct bridge between savings and investment. The savings in the superannuation funds—'pension funds' as they are sometimes called—are normally invested in shares, government bonds, real estate, and other financial assets in order to maximise private rates of return. Capitalist investment criteria currently prevail. If, instead, the process were coordinated through a *national investment fund*, the savings could be channelled into the development of particular industries that the government wishes to promote—technologically advanced sectors requiring substantial research and development expenditures, for example, or industries conducive to more ecologically sustainable development. 'Picking winners' this is sometimes called, especially by critics who are worried by the possibility of governments picking losers. Some nations, such as Sweden, have used national investment schemes as instruments for successful industry development.[10] Some level of public-sector investment is integral to the financing of infrastructure and public goods, anyway—a fact acknowledged as necessary by economists across the political spectrum ever since Adam Smith. The issue in practice is deciding on the most appropriate public–private balance and how best to achieve it. These are political economic decisions *par excellence*.

THE INTERNATIONAL CONTEXT

The assumption of a *national* economy, and of the possibility of managing it systematically, pervades most discussion of Keynesian economics. However, policies that treat the national economy as if it were a closed economy are always going to be of limited effectiveness. This was so in Keynes's time; it is even more so in the current age of 'globalisation'. The most modest response to the challenge involves using policy instruments that impinge on the relationship between the national economy and the rest of the world—exchange rate policy, and tariff policies, for example. The more ambitious response is to seek to influence the broader international economic conditions themselves—through international agreements on trade, debt, and taxation, for example.

It is axiomatic that a nation's 'external sector' has a significant bearing on its overall level of income, output, and employment. The standard Keynesian macroeconomic analysis shows that a trade deficit ($M > X$) will have a depressing effect, unless offset by a government budgetary deficit (and the latter may not be a sustainable option if the trade deficit persists across all stages of the economic cycle).

Putting *tariffs* on imported goods is a direct means of addressing the problem, for a tariff operates as a tax, the effect of which is to make imports relatively more expensive for domestic consumers. Whether the effect is to reduce expenditure on imports depends on their elasticity of demand, which in turn depends on the availability, price, and quality of locally produced substitutes. There are also some strategic considerations, such as whether the imposition of tariff protection is likely to cause other national governments to retaliate by increasing tariffs to give more protection to their own industries. They do not necessarily do so, but, if they do, export sales may decline along with import expenditures.

Some similar considerations apply in respect of *exchange rate* policy. If the relativities between currencies are not fixed, governments may seek to manipulate the exchange rates in order to achieve better trade outcomes. Central banks regularly 'intervene' as buyers and sellers in foreign exchange markets, usually in the attempt to stabilise otherwise volatile currency prices. They may even make a 'profit' if they buy their own country's currency when its price is falling and if that purchase turns out to be effective in reversing the trend. In the longer term, the key question is: what exchange rate will have the most beneficial effect on the trade balance? It is often said that a lowered value of the local currency helps in this regard, since it makes locally produced goods cheaper, and therefore more 'competitive', in international markets, while making imports dearer in the local currency. Whether this does actually improve the trade balance depends, again, on the elasticity of demand for those exports and imports. It seems that there are few certainties in this approach to managing the 'external sector'.

Keynes thought that these nationally based policy instruments should be used selectively in national economic management. He also thought that they needed to be complemented by more proactive interventions in the international arena. The key question in Keynes's day was what international monetary arrangements would be conducive to prosperity in the world economy following the devastating effects of the Great Depression and World War II. At the Bretton Woods conference in 1944, at which Keynes represented the British government, Keynes was opposed to the adoption of floating exchange rates and wanted a scheme for expanding international finance, including an expanded international currency unit ('Bancor') that would not need to be fully backed by gold or international currencies. The actual outcome of the Bretton Woods negotiations was closer to the proposal advocated by Harry White, the American representative, which gave a more central role to the US dollar as an international reserve currency. But Keynes's energetic participation was not in vain; it contributed to an agreement that did create more stable conditions for the settlement of international debts and which helped foster growth—in the more advanced economies at least. The subsequent quarter-century 'long boom' rested, in part, on these international political economic arrangements.

In our own time, there is a quite different proposal for international economic cooperation. This is the *Tobin tax*, first proposed by the US Keynesian economist James Tobin, winner of the 1981 Nobel Prize in Economic Sciences. It is frequently advocated as a means of discouraging international currency speculation. It would be a tax on all international transactions, probably set somewhere in the range of 10 to 25 cents per $100 value of currency transacted. Its effect would hit hardest at currency transactions of a short-term, speculative nature, rather than those directly concerned with the financing of international trade and investment. Whether it would indeed discourage speculation would depend on the rate at which the tax was set, but if it did *not* do so it would generate considerable revenues that might be used to help the development of poorer nations in the world economy. That would depend, of course, on there being effective monitoring and compliance, based on intergovernment agreements to enforce a uniform system. At present, it remains a 'pipe dream', but today's pipe dream can be tomorrow's policy.[11]

CONCLUSION

Managing a capitalist economy is never easy. Many of the key decisions are in private rather than public hands. Governments can seek, at a minimum, to play a steering role. Keynesian political economy indicates how to do so, showing the data requirements, the necessary policy instruments, and the principles and pitfalls that determine their use. A key ingredient in this policy process is *political will*. Keynes argued that governments could and should strive towards important social goals through the pursuit of policies to expand job opportunities and create the conditions for long-term prosperity.

Given that political will, there are numerous weapons in the armoury of government economic policy. Fiscal and monetary policy instruments are those most commonly associated with a Keynesian policy approach to macroeconomic 'fine-tuning'. However, a broader interpretation of Keynesian economics also includes incomes policy, investment policies, industry policies, exchange rate and trade policies as means of producing a more buoyant economy in the long term. The development of international agreements designed to create more stable conditions in the world economy, bridging national and global concerns, is a further concern. So, there is potentially much more to a comprehensive Keynesian policy approach than merely 'fine-tuning' the level of aggregate demand in a national economy.

Assumptions about the adequacy of economic analysis and of economic information, such as national income accounting, underpin these policy prescriptions. So do political economic judgments about the nature of the state, its capacity to use the policy instruments effectively, and the ethical basis of public policy. Not surprisingly, these are matters of disagreement. They were in Keynes's time, and they are today. This helps to explain why the political economy of Keynes is such a contested legacy.

CHAPTER 32

The Keynesian Legacy

Revolution, counter-revolution, renaissance?

Was there a 'Keynesian revolution'?
Why did Keynesian policy prescriptions fall from favour?
What does post-Keynesianism offer? Are Keynesian ideas still relevant?

'In the long run we are all dead' is the one quotation from Keynes that students invariably get right (while usually missing his point). 'Yes, but not all at once,' added Joan Robinson later. A focus on short-run economic problems and their immediate resolution is necessary, socially and politically, but it is not enough. Dealing with widespread unemployment was the obvious short-run priority in Keynes's time, although that problem has in recent decades re-established itself as a seemingly long-run, if not permanent, feature of modern capitalist economies. Keynes was also concerned, generally, with the conditions conducive to economic and social progress. Joan Robinson's quip is a reminder that society, as an ongoing entity, has to be equally concerned with those long-term goals.

How have Keynes's ideas fared in this longer-term context? We conclude our consideration of Keynesian economics by looking at its influence and the subsequent backlash against it. How could it have once commanded widespread respect but become vulnerable to the resurgence of pre-Keynesian views? Whither Keynesianism now?

FOUNDATIONS FOR A PARTIAL REVOLUTION

Keynes expected his *General Theory* to 'largely revolutionise … the way the world thinks about economic problems'.[1] Indeed, his ideas had a dramatic impact on economic analysis and policy between the 1930s, when his *General Theory* was published, and the 1970s, when his ideas fell foul of the monetarist economists. They constituted the basis for a new orthodoxy in economics for approximately three decades. The initial resistance was strong, both among academic economists and among business people and politicians uncomfortable with the 'interventionist' approach to the management of capitalism that his ideas implied.[2] The force of actual political economic circumstances proved stronger. The termination of the Great Depression by the onset of World War II was the most obvious factor. Economic conditions had been improving slowly during the middle to late 1930s, but sharply deteriorated again in 1937–38. The war restored full employment to the capitalist nations. War preparations had already reduced unemployment in Nazi Germany, prompting Galbraith's subsequent ironical remark that Adolf Hitler was 'the true protagonist of the Keynesian ideas'.[3] Keynes would not have approved, of course, favouring employment for socially useful, peacetime production. However, in purely macroeconomic terms, the effect was similar. Many people who might otherwise have been unemployed in countries were enlisted in the armed forces; others were employed in industries producing munitions, uniforms, and so on. In nations partly cut off from international trade by naval blockades, more land was brought under cultivation to feed the citizenry. The whole process—the 'war effort'—was coordinated by the respective national governments.

The war itself inflicted widespread economic devastation on the countries at the centre of the action. Both in the victorious and defeated nations, the bombing had destroyed houses, factories, bridges, roads, railways, ports, and electricity supply systems. After the war, this infrastructure had to be rebuilt. Even in nations geographically distant from the principal theatres of war (such as Australia and 'mainland' United States), a major backlog in the building of houses and social infrastructure had developed because resources had been diverted to the war effort. There was much work to be done when the war ended. That ensured the continuation of full employment, although the transition from military to peacetime production was not always smooth.

Politically, too, this economic reconstruction and expansion was imperative. People make enormous personal sacrifices during times of war, foregoing much of the consumption they normally enjoy. Their homes may be bombed, and sometimes family members killed or maimed. Such sacrifices need to be justified as the price to be paid in the struggle for a better society, or at least compensated by a significant *social dividend*. After World War II, it was inconceivable that the people who had made such sacrifices would tolerate a return to the conditions of the Great Depression. A more prosperous and secure society had to be engineered in the victorious nations. Having won the war, it was now necessary to 'win the peace'.

Meanwhile, the countries that lost the war would have to be reconstructed under international supervision—a process dominated in practice by the United States. The short-sightedness of impoverishing the defeated nations through punitive war reparations had been realised in the years following the end of World War I. Keynes had warned at the time about the likely adverse consequences of pursuing that strategy and, in practice, the rise of fascism had proved his point. For all the capitalist nations, victors and vanquished alike, policies to promote economic prosperity were the priority after World War II.

These political economic conditions were fertile ground for the acceptance and implementation of Keynesian economics. Governments in the major capitalist nations committed themselves to the pursuit of full employment as the primary economic objective. The British government, for example, formally committed itself to full employment in 1945, and the Australian government issued a White Paper on full employment in the same year. In the United States, the Employment Act of 1946 proclaimed 'the continuing policy and responsibility of the Federal government to use all practical means … to promote maximum employment, production and purchasing power'.

Concurrently, the foundations for a more extensive *welfare state* were being laid, with governments in the leading capitalist nations introducing legislation to extend social security provisions, provide more public housing, provide better public education, and (with the notable exceptions of the United States and Australia) establish publicly funded national health services.[4] Public-sector employment expanded. Firms in the private sector also received a boost from the stimulus to the demand for their products, and they took on more employees in order to expand output and make more profit. The marriage of Keynesian economics and welfare state commitments proved remarkably fruitful. Some say it was the saviour of capitalism in those turbulent times.

Whether, and to what extent, the subsequent 'long boom' in the major capitalist economies was a product of Keynesian economic policies continues to be a matter of controversy. Sometimes the causal connection is simply assumed. The period from the late 1940s to the early 1970s was one of sustained economic growth in the major capitalist nations, with full or near-full employment and generally low rates of inflation (with the significant exception of the Korean War period in the early 1950s when inflation surged). Keynesianism was the official basis of policy, right up to the early 1970s when US president Richard Nixon made the famous statement 'we are all Keynesians now' (just when it was ceasing to be true). *Ergo*, Keynesianism caused the long boom. One may equally posit the *reverse* causation: the prosperity of capitalism made some degree of Keynesian policy interventionism tolerable to the corporate interests, who would otherwise have vigorously opposed it. One thoughtful analyst of the period suggests that, to the extent that government policies underpinned the long boom, they were more to do with policies for industry development and the building of appropriate regulatory institutions than Keynesian macroeconomic demand management.[5]

One of the problems of making grand claims about Keynesian policies underpinning the long boom is that Keynesianism then takes the blame for its eventual collapse. And collapse it did. In the 1970s, economic growth stalled in most of the advanced capitalist nations, unemployment rose, and inflation surged. Was this indicative of a failure of Keynesianism? *Left-wing* critics, drawing on Marxist analysis, say that it showed Keynesianism to be incapable of resolving the inherent structural contradictions of capitalism.[6] The contradiction between the necessary conditions for the production and realisation of surplus value remains. Keynesian policies, boosting aggregate demand, facilitate the realisation of surplus value. However, in so far as those same policies cause wage levels to rise (and if labour gains more bargaining power when full employment prevails), the conditions for the production of surplus value are eventually undermined. So, the tendency towards economic crisis reasserts itself.

Echoing some of these concerns, but couching them in more acceptably conservative language, is the *right-wing* critique of Keynesianism. Milton Friedman (1912–) has been its best known exponent, arguing that Keynesianism in practice caused more problems than it solved. As he saw it, the extension of state 'intervention' during the years of the long boom directly caused inflation and, more generally, throttled the dynamism of the free-enterprise system. Friedman's view is that Keynesian attempts to 'fine-tune' the economy should be abandoned.

Box 32.1

Milton Friedman (1912–)

Milton Friedman is the best known of the right-wing economists responsible for the ascendancy of neo-liberalism in economic analysis and policy. In the 1950s and 1960s, teaching at the University of Chicago, he was a persistent exponent of free-market economics. His stridently free-enterprise views and antipathy to Keynesianism made him a somewhat marginal figure. He was at odds with the economics profession's general acceptance of the pragmatic marriage of Keynesian macroeconomics and microeconomics (what the more liberal-interventionist economist Paul Samuelson proudly proclaimed as the 'neoclassical synthesis'). Friedman's methodological view, that the test of an economic theory is not the reasonableness of its assumptions but only the accuracy of its predictions, was also widely regarded as extremist.

From early in his career, he showed a willingness to combine economics with politics. His book *Capitalism and Freedom*, published in 1962, made an explicitly political case against any semblance of economic collectivism. It was in tune with Cold War ideology, emphasising the virtues—political and economic—of the 'free-enterprise' system.

When there was a sudden intensification of economic problems in the capitalist nations in the 1970s, it seemed as if Friedman's time had come. He had a political platform for his critique of Keynesianism and his advocacy of a neo-liberal alternative. His monetarist views, based on the pre-Keynesian 'quantity theory of money', were supported by empirical economic analysis founded on the extreme methodological proposition that he had earlier enunciated. Inflation, he sought to demonstrate, was the product of too much expansion of the money supply, fuelled by excessive government intervention in the economy. Politicians such as former British prime minister Margaret Thatcher seized on his *laissez-faire* prescriptions. Milton Friedman became a household name, synonymous with monetarism and the broader political program of 'slimming the state'. In Chile, after the US-backed overthrow of the government of Salvadore Allende in 1973, US economic advisers (known as 'the Chicago boys') recommended a yet more audacious experiment in free-market economics involving privatising public enterprises, removing government regulation of business, and creating glaring disparities in the distribution of income and wealth.[8]

Friedman can claim to have rivalled J.K. Galbraith as the most popular interpreter of contemporary economic affairs in the late twentieth century—although consistently arguing from the opposite political position. He made a television series of his best-selling book *Free to Choose*. His combination of neoclassical economics and right-wing libertarian politics has been distinctive and highly influential.

According to Friedman, economic policy should simply ensure the steady expansion of the money supply at a rate matching the long-term growth of economic output. This is the essence of the *monetarist* position that was embraced—but not consistently implemented—by right-wing politicians in the 1970s and 1980s.[7]

MONETARISM AND THE 'NEW CLASSICAL' REVIVAL

Monetarism has its roots in pre-Keynesian economics, specifically in the quantity theory of money. This is most simply expressed as the 'equation of exchange':

$$MV \equiv PQ$$

In this formulation, M is the money supply; V is the velocity of circulation (the rate at which money moves around the economy); P is the general price level for goods and services (a measure of inflation); and Q is the output of goods and services produced in the economy. This equation of exchange is written as an *identity* ($\equiv$) because its proponents say it is true by definition; thus, for any given level of output (Q), changes in the money supply (M) and the price level (P) will always move together, assuming the velocity of circulation (V) is fixed. In other words, the effect of increases in the money supply, over and above increases in the volume of goods and services produced, is always to raise the general price level. Expansionary monetary policy causes inflation. So, too, will expansionary fiscal policy, if budgetary deficits are financed by money supply increases.

According to monetarists, inflation is a scourge: it erodes the value of savings, creates greater economic uncertainty among consumers and investors, and becomes self-perpetuating because it comes to be 'built into' consumers' and investors' expectations and the behaviour resulting from those expectations. However, since its cause is clear—excessive growth in the money supply—its remedy is equally obvious. Governments must restrict their policies to the management of a slower and steadier expansion in the supply of money that is just sufficient to match the growth in the output of goods and services.

Monetarists acknowledge some safety valves. If workers are willing to work harder at the current wage rate, for example, total output can be raised and the inflationary pressures thereby alleviated. Alternatively, inflationary pressures are reduced if households are willing to save more of their income at the current rate of interest; the problem of 'too much money chasing too few goods' then becomes less severe. In both cases, sacrifices must be made—harder work and deferral of the gratification from consumption. Austerity or 'belt-tightening', targeted particularly at the working class and those benefiting from an expansion of state support, is the implied antidote to the forces that otherwise fuel inflation. As former Australian prime minister Malcolm Fraser (himself only a half-hearted convert to monetarism) said at the time when monetarism was coming into vogue, 'Life isn't meant to be easy'. It certainly is not easy when monetarists are in charge.

On closer examination, the monetarist interpretation of the 'equation of exchange' can be seen to rest on some dubious assumptions. The economy is taken to be operating at full capacity, for example. If it were not, it is possible that an increase in the money supply *could* flow through into increased output. The monetarist

Box 32.2

A trade-off between unemployment and inflation?

The *Phillips curve* is a popular means of interpreting the relationship between unemployment and inflation. It takes its name from a diagram constructed by A.W. Phillips, a New Zealand economist working in London during the 1950s (also the inventor of the hydraulic model mentioned in chapter 29). He plotted the levels of unemployment and inflation in the British economy over a number of years and found a generally inverse relationship. The years when unemployment was high generally had low inflation, while the years when unemployment was low typically featured a higher rate of inflation.

The nature of this unemployment–inflation relationship evidently changed throughout the major capitalist nations in the 1970s. The diagram below plots conditions in the United States. The scatter of observations for the 1960s suggests a pretty standard Phillips curve relationship: the curve slopes downwards to the right (as represented by the line drawn through the lower part of the scatter). Then, starting in 1970, things seem to go haywire. Some years (1970–71, 1972–73, 1974–75, 1977–78) exhibit the normal inverse relationship, but some (1969–70, 1973–74, 1979–80) show both unemployment and inflation rising together, and others (1971–72, 1975–76, 1976–77) show unemployment and inflation falling together. It seems pretty chaotic.

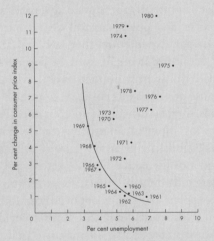

What had gone wrong? An empirical description cannot indicate the *causal* factors underlying this change in the patterns of unemployment and inflation. Posited explanations were plentiful at the time; some blamed trade unions (for seeking wage increases in excess of labour productivity growth). Others blamed governments (for the failures of macroeconomic 'fine-tuning'). Reviewing the current state of opinion, one orthodox economist concludes that the 'inflation–unemployment trade-off has a secure place in economics … [but] the bad news is that the dynamic relationship between inflation and unemployment remains a mystery'.[9]

assumption of a fixed velocity of circulation (V) is also questionable. In practice, the speed with which money circulates may vary according to institutional factors, such as how frequently people are paid and how much cash they choose to hold for transactionary and precautionary purposes. If changes in the money supply *interact* with changes in the velocity of circulation, the direct relationship between M and P (the posited inflationary effect of expanding the money supply) ceases to be inexorable. But questioning assumptions like this is not a characteristically Friedmanite methodology. Look at the evidence, Friedman says, not at the reasonableness of the underlying assumptions.[10] And the evidence, during the 1970s in particular, revealed the emergence of a dual problem of unemployment and inflation, or 'stagflation' as it came to be known. This heralded a new era of troubled economic times. Its interpretation in terms of the 'Phillips curve' is set out in Box 32.2 on the preceding page.

Keynesian economics, at least in its mechanistic interpretations, had difficulty in coming to terms with *stagflation*. In the simple Keynesian model, there is either unemployment (in which case an expansionary approach to demand management is warranted) or inflation (requiring a contractionary demand management policy stance). Coping with the two problems simultaneously is problematic, both analytically and in terms of appropriate policy response. No doubt Keynes himself—ever flexible and shrewd—would have proffered a solution. However, the more pedestrian policy analysts—schooled in the mechanistic interpretation of his ideas associated with the 'neoclassical synthesis'—were thrown into disarray when stagflation hit in the 1970s. This created the political vacuum that the monetarists were able to fill.

The monetarists at the time argued against expansionary fiscal policies (as right-wing economists and politicians still do). If extra government spending 'crowds out' private-sector expenditure, they say, it is impotent as a means of boosting the national economy. It might even be counter-productive, causing the national income to fall. So, it is important to ask why such '*crowding-out*' might occur. Perhaps because governments compete with business investment in the market for loanable funds, thereby driving up interest rates. Perhaps because of a general political antipathy by capitalist enterprises to any increase in government spending, bringing on a 'capital strike' in response to what they perceive as 'creeping socialism'. The evidence for such effects is sketchy, at best.[11] If anything, there seems to be a stronger 'crowding-in' effect, as government spending—on infrastructure, for example—opens up further opportunities for private-sector profits and capital accumulation. Notwithstanding this contrary evidence, the assumption of 'crowding-out' continues to pervade conservative political economic discourse. It is an influential legacy of monetarism.

The monetarists' critique of fiscal policy did not lead, contrary to widespread popular belief, to an advocacy of stronger reliance on monetary policy *per se*. Monetarists emphasise the pitfalls in using *both* monetary and fiscal policies as instruments of 'fine-tuning' (as discussed in the preceding chapter). Instead, they argue for a slower and steadier expansion of the money supply that is just sufficient to match the growth of output. They reject the use of discretionary monetary policy aimed at smoothing the economic cycle. This is the essence of the pursuit of a *simple monetary rule* as the principal instrument of economic policy. Some of the more extreme monetarists—to the political right of Milton Friedman, if that is possible—have argued even against that, saying that government should have no role at all, and should leave the creation and control of money to the private sector!

Perhaps the most distinctive feature of monetarism, as it came to be adopted in practice, was the emphasis on the need to 'fight inflation first'. The case for so doing is usually argued in terms of the need to restore the economic system to its natural equilibrium state, before 'excessive' government intervention and 'excessive' wage demands had triggered the inflationary process. The effect of so doing is to jettison the commitment to full employment. Instead, monetarists argue that a *natural rate of unemployment* should be allowed to prevail. This is commonly defined as a 'non-accelerating inflation rate of unemployment' (NAIRU). Formally, this is the rate of unemployment below which the tendency towards inflation in the economy becomes pronounced. In practice, supporters of this concept use it to justify, more or less, whatever rate of unemployment currently prevails.[12]

Why bother with monetarism? Monetarism *per se* was a fad that petered out in the 1980s, as successive governments abandoned their official commitment to the sort of monetary targeting that Friedman advocated. Few economists would call themselves monetarists now, preferring the labels 'new classical' and 'new Keynesian'. However, there is a remarkable continuity in practice with monetarist reasoning. The NAIRU has continued to feature prominently in policy documents.[13] The preference for monetary policy over fiscal policy seems to have become institutionalised. One reviewer of the current state of play in macroeconomic theory and policy concludes that 'the influence of monetarism on how we all think about macroeconomics today has been deep, pervasive and subtle', indeed so pervasive as to constitute 'intellectual hegemony'.[14] Governments and central bankers continue to prioritise the control of inflation over policies for full employment, even though the inflationary tendencies of the 1970s have not recurred. At the start of the twenty-first century, most of the capitalist countries were back at the low inflation–high unemployment end of the Phillips curve (see box 32.2).

The case against running budget deficits as a conscious policy measure has also been buttressed by the so-called 'twin deficits' thesis, which posits a link between government budgetary deficits and external current account deficits. Like the evidence for 'crowding-out', the evidence supporting a 'twin deficits' connection is flimsy, at best. Some government spending may directly increase imports (such as the purchase of foreign-made fighter aircraft), but other government spending may help to increase exports (such as research and development subsidies or industry-development policies to assist local firms). There is no reliable general connection between the size of budgetary deficits and current account deficits in practice.[15]

Notwithstanding these conceptual and empirical difficulties, governments of a neo-liberal bent now tend to eschew the use of discretionary policies for counter-cyclical purposes. Fiscal policy is the most obvious casualty. The Keynesian view about using deficits and surpluses in a discretionary manner according to the state of the economy has given way to a general commitment to *balanced budgets* (or, better still, surplus budgets, which supposedly show the government's fiscal rectitude). Actually, this commitment is seldom realised in practice, since the automatic stabilisers (described in chapter 31) continue to cause budgets to move into deficit during recessions and into surplus during booms, whatever the declared intentions of the government. Meanwhile, discretionary monetary policy seems to have become re-established as the principal policy tool to control the economic cycle. This is ironic in that the pervasive problems associated with monetary policies (also described in chapter 31) featured prominently among the reasons put forward by monetarists for the adoption of a simpler, long-term monetary rule. It is doubly ironic that, in the meantime, financial deregulation has effectively left pressure on interest rates as the only available policy instrument—and that is usually in the hands of appointed central bankers than elected governments.

Perhaps the most extreme variation on this theme of anti-Keynesian economics comes in the form of the 'policy ineffectiveness proposition'. Here is the claim that, because people have *rational expectations* about the future, economic policy is generally impotent. People anticipate the consequences of any change in policy and, by modifying their behaviour appropriately, negate its effects. According to this reasoning, as people come to know more about the economy and anticipate government policy changes, the policies become ineffective. If 'rational' people know that economic policies are ineffective, the policies in practice work only if people make systematic errors. This sort of reasoning is typical of what has come to be known as 'new classical' economics.[16] Its emphasis on individual choice and general equilibrium outcomes means it has more in common, both analytically and politically, with neoclassical economics than with classical political economy. Like the posited 'natural rate of unemployment', the effect of the 'policy ineffectiveness proposition' is to buttress free-market ideology. Notwithstanding some analytical novelty, the practical upshot looks more like a revival of an old-time religion.

POST-KEYNESIAN ECONOMICS

Where does all this leave Keynesian economics today? Rather schematically, two types of Keynesian economics can be identified. One is what has earlier been called the mechanistic interpretation of Keynes, illustrated by the analysis summarised in box 30.1. Analytically, it stresses the equilibrium tendencies in the macroeconomic system—albeit not guaranteeing full employment. Politically, it accepts the case for a limited set of discretionary fiscal and monetary policies to 'fine-tune' the economy, reconciling equilibrium with full employment, but otherwise leaving the economy to function largely according to the principles of private enterprise. In the economics textbooks, this is the interpretation of Keynes that Paul Samuelson proudly proclaimed as the 'neoclassical synthesis', combining neoclassical microeconomics with a mechanic interpretation of Keynesian macroeconomics. It is what Joan Robinson later called, rather less flatteringly, 'bastard Keynesianism'—the illegitimate product of marrying Keynes to neoclassical theory. 'Neo-Keynesianism' is a less pejorative term. Its practical influence shaped government policies. However, it was always incoherent, politically if not analytically, because it spliced together a microeconomics emphasising the general desirability of free markets and a macroeconomics stressing the need for recurrent government 'intervention'.

This mainstream interpretation of Keynesian economics was the obvious casualty of the stagflation era and the monetarist assault. Many of the orthodox economics textbooks have since been purged of their residual Keynesianism, a process that their authors have sometimes sought to justify by claiming the need for better developed 'micro foundations of macroeconomics'.[17] Such a quest for greater analytical coherence is eminently reasonable. The problem is that coherence is (re-)established on the neoclassical terrain. In effect, it constitutes a return to pre-Keynesian economic theory, but under the name of 'new classical' economics. Concurrently, in the policy arena, the primary emphasis of government policies has switched from macroeconomic management to 'microeconomic reform'.[18] This is no coincidence. This policy push, which focuses on labour-market deregulation, privatisation, and trade liberalisation, is based on the reassertion of free-market economics. It constitutes a return to pre-Keynesian economics in the realm of public policy.

A second, quite different, interpretation of Keynes is possible, providing the basis for *post-Keynesian* economics. It places more emphasis on Keynes's view of the economy as an inherently unstable system—indeed, one might argue, not really a 'system' at all. The crucial, but volatile, character of investment—responding to the 'animal spirits' of business people and needing 'somewhat comprehensive socialisation'—is a focal point. So, too, is income distribution, since it has a major influence on the size of the multiplier and the determination of the overall state of the economy, as well as being a crucial social concern in its own right. These original concerns of Keynes were marginalised, if not lost altogether, in the dominant neo-Keynesianism. From a policy perspective, they are incompatible with a *laissez-faire* stance, perhaps even a 'liberal-interventionist' stance. Their re-emphasis by post-Keynesians puts more extensive policy reforms on the agenda. Incomes policies and industry policies are particular focal points. There has also recently been a strong advocacy of policies to combat unemployment, by extending the role of the government as 'employer of the last resort'.[19]

Post-Keynesian economic theory, drawing on more radical interpretation of Keynes, has been influenced by the work of Keynes's colleague at Cambridge, Piero Sraffa. Sraffa's contribution is based primarily on a mathematical model of 'the production of commodities by means of commodities' that shows the structure of the economy as a whole can be analysed without recourse to the market theories of the neoclassical school.[20] The technical interdependencies of the different sectors of the economy are the key. (In this respect, the theory parallels the empirically based input–output analysis pioneered by Wassily Liontieff and used as a tool for economic planning under both capitalism and socialism.) The impersonal economic forces determine the conditions for efficient production, leaving questions of income distribution to other processes of a social and political character. Echoes of both David Ricardo and John Stuart Mill can be heard in the (implicit) politics of this analysis. On a more technical level, Sraffa's work enables post-Keynesian economists to match the orthodox economists 'equation for equation'—should they be so inclined.[21]

The contribution of Michal Kalecki (1899–1970) to post-Keynesian economics is of more direct political significance. Kalecki was a Polish economist working within the Marxist tradition who developed a penetrating analysis of capitalism at about the same times as Keynes was working on his *General Theory*. Like Keynes, Kalecki emphasised the inherent tendencies of capitalism to recession and unemployment, but he went further by emphasising the significance of income distribution and the 'degree of monopoly' enjoyed by capitalist firms. Moreover, he showed the *political* obstacles facing the implementation of remedial Keynesian-type policies. Measures to produce full employment, he argued, would have the effect of increasing the power of labour relative to capital, and would be resisted by employers for that reason.[22] How right he eventually proved to be! This view of the causes of the 'political business cycle' can also help to explain the vulnerability of neo-Keynesian analysis and policy to the assault by the monetarists and 'new classical' economists. The class interests represented by these anti-Keynesians come more clearly into view.

Other contributions to the development of post-Keynesian economics are many and varied. The work of Hyman Minsky (1919–97), for example, has added to the understanding of how financial institutions affect the vulnerability of the economy to economic crises. The complexity of the financial arrangements underpinning modern capitalism produces a 'layering' of debts and financial assets that has the potential to collapse like a house of cards.[23] Alfred Eichner (1937–88) put the pricing and investment behaviour of big businesses ('megacorps') in the spotlight, showing how prices are set in order to generate required rates of return rather than according to market principles of demand and supply.[24] This links up with the more general post-Keynesian concern with the process of 'mark-up pricing', whereby firms with market power administer the prices of their products to reduce risk and increase corporate growth.[25] A common element in these analyses is a rejection of the neoclassical conception of the market as a self-regulating system that ensures economic stability and efficient resource allocation.

These are just a few illustrations of the various currents in post-Keynesian economics.[26] Whether they, and other post-Keynesian contributions, constitute a coherent school of thought, comparable to Marxist or neoclassical economics, is debatable. Perhaps a better parallel is with institutional economics. In both cases there is a group of economists opposed to the prevailing economic orthodoxy, but who have diverse views about what alternative analysis would facilitate understanding, and then changing, modern capitalism. Some concepts, such as the theory of circular and cumulative causation (discussed in chapter 25), are applied by scholars from both institutional and post-Keynesian schools of thought. Some policy reforms, such as incomes policies, industry policies, and extensions of public-sector employment, also command widespread support from both camps. The concerns of these moderate dissidents flow through into the broader issues explored in part VIII of this book, dealing with the main themes in modern political economy.

CONCLUSION

Like Marx, Keynes just will not lie down. He is sometimes said to have created a revolution, both in economic theory and in economic policy. However, it was an incomplete revolution. In the realm of theory, Keynes's ideas were steered into an uncomfortable marriage with neoclassical economics. In the realm of policy, they were interpreted as requiring governments to undertake selective demand management only as an adjunct to the functioning of an otherwise fundamentally sound capitalist market economy. For about a quarter of a century, this neo-Keynesianism seemed to work quite well, both in the realm of theory and policy. However, it proved vulnerable to the monetarist assault when economic conditions changed at the end of the long boom. Now the monetarist alternative, and its 'new classical' variations, seems to have run its course.

Unemployment is still with us. The periodic recurrence of recession continues to bedevil the capitalist economy. Globalisation, by increasing the economic interdependence of nations, makes them ever more vulnerable to the forces generating volatile investment patterns. Confidence in the ability of governments to engineer solutions that provide greater economic security is at a low ebb. The capacity of the state to act as 'demand manager, spender, social guardian and umpire of the competitive process'[27] is profoundly in question. These are conditions crying out for solutions. Drawing on the more radical, albeit less than wholly coherent, legacy represented by post-Keynesian economics makes sense in these circumstances. So too does further exploration of the Marxian and institutional economics traditions. The further development and fusion of these schools of thought can provide a basis for the construction of a modern political economy.

PART VIII

Contemporary Concerns

Modern political economy

CHAPTER 33

A Radical Reformulation

Contributory currents

On what currents of economic thought does modern political economy draw?
What contemporary political economic problems does it address?
What analytic framework can facilitate future progress in political economy?

The challenge for modern political economy is threefold: to further develop the critique of orthodox economics, to combine the currents flowing against the mainstream into a more coherent alternative, and to use that analysis to contribute to progressive social change. These three elements are *interdependent*. Critique is a springboard for the development of alternatives rooted in the real world, explaining the real world and contributing to effective political strategies for dealing with current economic problems. The elements have an *iterative* character, too. The changing character of the real world, itself partly shaped by the application of particular economic ideas, necessitates alternative political economic ideas that can take us in a different direction. This is the essence of *praxis*—the integration of theory and practice—in the development of modern political economy.

The preceding chapters in this book have surveyed the evolving nature of economic enquiry, emphasising not only the principal analytical tools of each of the main schools of thought, but also their distinctive political economic 'world-views'. Each school emphasises different aspects of the same economic system. In that sense, they are complementary, but rival, discourses. Each embodies different assumptions and beliefs about the relationship of the economy to society. It is now time to explore how a more coherent modern political economy can be developed by drawing on these schools of thought to provide a means of understanding—and changing—contemporary capitalism.[1]

MULTIPLE CURRENTS AGAINST THE MAINSTREAM

Look back at figure 7.1 (p. 54) to remind yourself of the principal currents of economic analysis. Historically, classical political economy provides a common basis. The mainstream flows through neoclassical economics, merging (temporarily) with Keynesianism in the 'neoclassical synthesis', and re-emerging in a more purist form in monetarism and modern 'economic rationalism'. The dissident currents challenging this mainstream are Marxist economics, institutional economics, and the more radical interpretation of Keynes represented by post-Keynesian economics.

A first approximation of a definition of modern political economy is that it is a fusion of the last three bodies of analysis. This suggests some *common features of modern political economy*:

- analysis of how an *economic surplus* is generated, who gets the surplus, and for what purposes it is used
- emphasis on *capital, labour, and the state*—their relationships, relative power, and institutional forms
- study of the *evolving* character of the economy, looking at change in actual historical time rather than studying static equilibrium
- identification of processes of *circular and cumulative causation* that shape economic and social developments
- analysis of how resources are *created and destroyed*—not simply how they are allocated—focusing on the role of politics as well as markets in those processes.

The first of these concerns has its source in classical political economy, and then flows through into Marxist and neo-Marxist economics.[2] Arguably, it is the most fundamental and long-standing analytical feature of the political economy tradition, contrasting sharply with the turn taken by neoclassical economics to an equilibrium analysis, in which the notion of economic surplus has no place. But the other four features also sharply distinguish the dissident traditions of political economy from the economic mainstream. Studying the interaction of capital, labour, and the state in real historical time, and focusing on processes that create cumulative changes and shape the creation and destruction of economic resources—these are the hallmarks of political economy.

To define modern political economy in terms of this fusion of the concerns of Marxism, institutionalism and Keynes/post-Keynesianism is both too grand and too modest. It is too *grand* in that it implies synthesis is simple—when it is not. The characteristic concerns of the three schools of thought are quite different. Marxist value theory, for example, sits uncomfortably with Keynesian concepts and with the more descriptive institutional approach to understanding the evolution of economic society. Important differences of emphasis and interpretation, including intra-paradigm as well as trans-paradigm differences, allow no easy reconciliation.

The claim that modern political economy synthesises the three main dissident currents of economic thought is simultaneously too *modest* in that it neglects other potential contributory elements. *Environmentalism* and *feminism* are obvious cases in point. Both have developed as important channels of enquiry and as significant social movements. Environmental analysis and politics focuses on perhaps the most fundamental tension in the modern economy: capitalism's rapacious relationship with nature and its consequent unsustainability. Feminist analysis and politics emphasises gender as a significant source of contemporary social inequality and tension, as important as (some would say more important than) class differences. Both environmentalism and feminism warrant serious attention in the construction of modern political economy. This is not simply a matter of broadening the range of topics discussed. As one feminist writer emphasises, feminists and environmentalists also have in common a belief in the importance of ethical questions in economic reasoning. So, incorporating these concerns imparts a distinctively normative element to modern political economy.

There are other contemporary economic and social analysts whose work is important but who are not easily classified in terms of the major schools of economic thought. French social scientist André Gorz, who has written challengingly about the significance of technological change and the future of work, springs to mind. So do various contributors to the debates about 'post-Fordism', who have raised fundamentally important questions about the direction of recent political economic changes.[3] Contemporary analyses of how ethnicity relates to class and gender also have the potential to enrich our understanding of economy and society.[4] The land question, raised earlier by Henry George, is worth revisiting in the light of contemporary social and environmental concerns, too. There is no shortage of interesting themes. The question is how to structure and integrate their exploration in the most useful way.

RETHINKING POLITICAL ECONOMY

Table 33.1 suggests one framework for organising the various concerns of modern political economy. It focuses on four themes around which political economic analysis can be structured. As with any simple taxonomy, it does not purport to demonstrate how its components should be analysed, nor what concepts are likely to be most useful for that purpose. It merely lists the four themes, indicates some aspects of economic and social thought on which we can draw in each case, and hints at some potential interdisciplinary links.

Table 33.1   Four themes in modern political economy

Themes	Analytical influences	Interdisciplinary links
Economy–nature	Henry George; modern environmentalism	Biological sciences; geography
Economy–technology	Thorstein Veblen; André Gorz; post-Fordism	Industrial relations; engineering
Economy–society	Karl Marx; class analysis; feminism	Sociology; history
Economy–state	J.M. Keynes; 'radical reformism'	Political science

The most fundamental of these four themes is the *relationship of the economy to nature*. Starting here is an acknowledgment that an economy must necessarily be embedded in the physical world. The spotlight immediately turns to the problems associated with existing forms of economic growth that deplete natural resources and pollute the environment. From a strategic policy perspective, the central issue is whether the economy can be restructured so that it is ecologically sustainable. Some economists contend that policy 'fine-tuning', such as better pricing of scarce environmental resources, can make a major contribution to this reform process. But capitalism has a particularly problematic relationship with the environment because of its *systemic* association with exploitation, individualism, and consumerism.

Whether it can be made to meet the prerequisites for ecological sustainability, or, if it cannot, finding out the sort of economic system that could, are matters deserving careful consideration. In such investigations it is useful to place particular emphasis on the role of land and other natural resources in the production and disposition of the economic surplus.

The second theme turns the spotlight on to the *relationship of technology to the economy*. It requires analysis of how the process of economic production shapes, and is shaped by, scientific knowledge and its embodiment in capital goods. More than that, it requires study of the institutions shaping how technology is harnessed for the purpose of enhancing the economic surplus. Veblen's distinction between 'industry' and 'business' is relevant here—manifest today in the tension between productive and speculative uses of the surplus. We are living in an era of rapid technological change, sometimes said to be creating a 'new economy' based in information technologies and more knowledge-intensive production. If so, what are the implications for education and training, for the nature of work, and for social structure? Who acquires the fruits of higher productivity? Why is there a growing gulf between winners and losers—between the workers in primary and secondary labour markets, and between the overworked and the unemployed? Is there a means of reconciling technological and structural economic change with broader social goals? This broad sweep of concerns with how production is organised and how an economic surplus is generated is central to modern political economic analysis.

The third theme concerns the *relationship of the economy to society*. Class, gender and ethnicity are key considerations here. As Marxists have always emphasised, the *capital–labour relationship* is the key to understanding the functioning of the economy—its contradictions, conflicts, and distributional outcomes. From this economic fountainhead of *class* differences, many other dimensions of social inequality can then be seen to flow. Embracing other currents of contemporary social science, such as feminism and studies of racial inequality, necessarily broadens the focus to include gender and ethnicity. This is not simply a matter of describing how economic inequalities are structured according to sex and race, but also of understanding their articulation with class and the changing characteristics of capitalism. Political economic and sociological enquiries merge in the analysis of these contemporary phenomena. The issue of how the disposition of the economic surplus effects the distribution of income, wealth and life chances is a central concern.

The fourth theme is *the relationship of the state to the economy*, including the capacity of governments to deal with the concerns raised by the first three themes—managing the relationship of the economy with the natural world; shaping technology and productivity; and managing the economic outcomes associated with class, gender, and ethnicity. Analysis of the state has always been a major theme in political economy. It has been, implicitly or explicitly, an issue on which the major dissident traditions have taken quite different positions. Whereas Keynesians have had a basically optimistic view of the capacity of the state to redress specific problems like inflation and unemployment, institutional economists have advocated broader economic and social reforms, while Marxist political economists have generally been, at the very least, sceptical of these reformist perspectives. Seeking some common ground among these competing currents of analysis is bound to be problematic. It is more so in the circumstances of modern capitalism, where concerns about ecological sustainability and social justice exist alongside the continuing concerns about economic prosperity. Is using the state as a vehicle for 'radical reformism'—emphasising immediate benefits but prefiguring more radical, long-term transformations—a viable strategy? If not, then what other vehicle can facilitate social progress? Such issues necessarily feature prominently on any modern political economic agenda.

Is this cluster of themes for the organisation and development of modern political economy logical and coherent? It may be regarded as little more than four convenient headings under which we can explore contemporary problems and policy issues. More ambitiously, it may be taken as a first step towards the integration of different 'streams' of political economic analysis. Thus, it successively explores the relationship of capital to nature, technology, socioeconomic structure, and politics. The shift, schematically, is from the fundamental concern with the *nature–economy* relationship, to the *economy–technology* relationship, then the *economy–society* relationship (with particular reference to the associated issues of class, gender, and ethnicity), and, last, to the relationship of the economy and society to *the state* (including its role in managing the tensions arising from the three preceding relationships). Here is a 'nested' and logically sequential set of analytical concerns.

CONCLUSION

In studying political economy today, we are confronted with a formidable legacy comprising various currents of analysis. First and foremost, we need to understand that legacy. However, we also need to *transcend* it; the evolving form of the political economic system in the real world demands nothing less. How best to do this is inevitably a matter about which reasonable people can reasonably disagree.

What is presented here is a suggested way forward. It draws on ideas from classical political economy and Marxist economics, from the tradition of institutional economics, and from Keynes and the post-Keynesians. It incorporates concerns raised by environmentalists, feminists, and other contemporary social scientists. It purports to give some coherence to modern political economy by emphasising four themes concerned with the interrelationships between the economy and nature, technology, society, and politics. Whether it constitutes a useful way forward can only be demonstrated by putting the plan into action—by bringing political economic analysis to bear on the questions of crucial importance in the twenty-first century.

CHAPTER 34

Economy and Environment

How does the economy interact with the physical environment?
Can capitalism be made compatible with ecologically sustainable development?
How does a political economy of the environment differ from 'free-market' environmentalism?

Analysis of the relationship between the natural world and the economic system is of central importance in modern political economy. Indeed, it is of central importance to the future of humankind, not to mention the future of other species threatened by the effects of further environmental degradation. Political economists have to take seriously the growing concerns about the impact of economic activity on environmental quality and the prospects for ecological sustainability. They have a responsibility to contribute to an understanding of the economic causes of environmental decay and of what changes in political economic structures and policies might contribute to effective solutions.

Political economic analysis is enriched by recognising the 'embeddedness' of the economy in nature. All economic activity occurs in a biophysical context, using land and other natural resources, and generating products, including waste products, impacting on the environment. To neglect such connections is not only to limit the potential contribution of political economic analysis to environmental concerns, but also to impoverish the study of the economy.

This chapter considers how to cope with these challenges. Attention is given to proposals for extending orthodox economic reasoning to the study of environmental issues, since this has been a major element in the drive towards 'free-market' environmentalism. This is contrasted with the view that the embrace of market principles is part of the problem, rather than part of the solution. Henry George's ideas about land are revived and integrated with broader environmental concerns. All this is intended to contribute to a better understanding of economy–environment interactions and the requirements for ecological sustainability.

THE NATURE OF ENVIRONMENTAL PROBLEMS

Environmental stresses takes various forms and are manifest on various spatial scales. Some affect the planet in its entirety—the problems of global warming and the damage to the ozone layer are the most obvious examples. Concurrent concerns with more localised problems include the environmental effects of particular urban and industrial developments; of inappropriate farming, fishing or forestry practices; and of the disposal of effluents caused by waste-generating economic and social activities.

How best to classify these diverse concerns? One useful basis has been suggested by David Attenborough, whose television documentaries have consistently emphasised the need to more effectively care for the natural environment. Attenborough distinguishes between the effects of:

- *overharvesting:* taking resources from forests, seas, and nature in general at a rate faster than that at which they are replenished
- *introduction of alien species:* relocating plants and animals, deliberately or accidentally, thereby upsetting the local ecological balance and causing the loss of other species of flora and/or fauna
- *destruction of habitat:* converting wilderness into agricultural or urban land, thereby reducing biodiversity and also often causing species loss
- *'islandisation':* the process whereby patches of natural habitat become cut off from one another by degraded environments, such as those converted from natural to agricultural or urban land uses
- *pollution:* using the physical environment as a receptacle for waste products, with damaging consequences for the quality of the environment and its capacity for renewal.[1]

In Attenborough's judgment, all five processes are currently happening at an unprecedented rate. They are not all of recent origin, but there is a strong general correlation, in the last half century in particular, between their intensification and the relentless growth of population and economic activity.

There are echoes here of the warning about the unsustainability of demographic and economic trends issued three decades ago by the team of scientists sponsored by the Club of Rome.[2] There has been incessant debate about the nature of the causal connections in the intervening years.[3] The role of *population growth* has been the subject of particularly intense controversy.[4] It has a direct connection with the severity of the pressures on finite environmental resources. However, distributional elements have to be considered. An extra body in one of the affluent nations, for instance, adds many times more to demands on natural resources than an extra body in one of the poorer nations—although there, too, the increased pressure on the physical environment may be intense. *Economic* growth has yet more fundamental consequences for environmental quality. It is directly implicated in at least the first and last of Attenborough's five factors. However, it is important to recognise that the extent of environmental damage depends on the form the economic growth takes. The technology on which it is based, the spatial distribution of the growth, whether it uses renewable or non-renewable resources, the extent to which materials are recycled—all these factors have a major bearing on the relationship between economic growth and environmental quality. A principal task for modern political economy is to contribute to analysing these connections.

ECOLOGICALLY SUSTAINABLE DEVELOPMENT

Figure 34.1 presents a simple schematic representation of the principal economy–environment interactions. It contrasts a 'throughput' economy with a 'spaceship' economy. In the former, the economy has a rapacious relationship with the environment, treating natural resources as inputs, and using the physical environment

as a receptacle for outputs, including waste products. In the latter, the nature of economic activity, the type of resources used, and the emphasis on their re-use reduces,
if not eliminates, the damaging consequences for the physical environment. The
inference is that the latter economic arrangement would be more conducive to
ecologically sustainable development.[5]

(a) A 'throughput' economy

(b) Dual impact of a 'throughput' economy on the environment

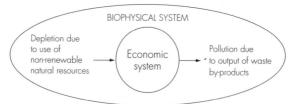

(c) A 'spaceship' economy more in harmony with the environment

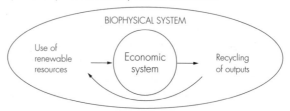

Figure 34.1   Economy–environment interactions.

Ecologically sustainable development—ESD for short—has been one of the
'buzz words' of the last decade (perhaps surpassed in popular political economic discourse only by 'globalisation'). Its meaning is not always clear. One way of defining
it is in terms of its *four essential principles*, two of which are fundamentally biophysical and two of which are more socioeconomic in character:[6]

Biodiversity

ESD requires, first and foremost, that destruction of species be avoided and biodiversity thereby maintained. This requirement has a moral dimension, emphasising the
responsibility of humans to ensure that their domination over nature is not at the
expense of the survival of other species—both fauna and flora. A supplementary economic rationale exists, too, for any reduction in the gene pool associated with loss
of species thereby destroys an asset with significant economic value—in medical
applications, for example.

Ecological integrity

ESD requires that the health and resilience of natural life-support systems be maintained. This does not rule out all temporary environmental damage, for ecological systems have natural mechanisms for self-repair. Winds, waves, and water currents are effective dispersal mechanisms; and waste materials that are organic eventually biodegrade. However, beyond 'threshold' levels of pollution or resource depletion, irreversible environmental changes may be precipitated. Ecological integrity requires that these threshold levels not be surpassed.

Intergenerational equity

ESD also requires that each generation bequeaths to the next a physical environment in no worse state than when it was inherited. In other words, we should not live at the expense of future generations. This is a key socioeconomic principle, although its interpretation is somewhat ambiguous. Whether improvements in the quantity or quality of some resources constitute adequate compensation for the damage to others is a debatable point, for example. How we deal with this sort of issue is linked to the fourth ESD principle, which emphasises how we value nature.

Constant natural capital

ESD requires that there be no depletion of the total stock of productive soils, fresh water, and other available natural resources. It is a tall order, since current patterns of economic growth commonly use non-renewable resources, or use renewable resources more rapidly than nature can replenish them. A commitment to maintaining constant natural capital requires a means of regulating the use of resources (whether through the price mechanism or through more direct control over the exploitation of resources) and a mechanism for natural resource accounting (a 'stocktaking of assets').

The latter requirement, for a means of *natural resource accounting*, has immediate political economic implications. Our current framework for national economic accounting—based on Keynesian concepts—has no place for such measurement. This contrasts with normal business accounting practices. Businesses calculate (normally as a legal requirement) both *profit and loss statements* and *balance sheets* annually.[7] The former shows incomes and expenditures over the year; the latter shows assets and liabilities at the end of each year. No business would consider a profit (shown in the profit and loss account) that has been generated solely by running down its assets (shown in the balance sheet) to be sustainable in the longer term. However, because there is currently no equivalent to the balance sheet in our national income accounting, we cannot tell whether our income, as a nation, has a sustainable character. Some economic activities may generate income without depleting the stock of natural capital, but others clearly do not; for example, the proceeds from the export of minerals are matched by the reduction in the value of the nation's natural capital.

Here is an obvious lacuna in current national accounting practices. To fill it, a system of 'stock' accounting (including natural resource stocks) needs to be developed to supplement the existing 'flow' measures of national income. Then, we would be in a position to see whether we are indeed living at the expense of nature and of future generations.

Seeing is one thing; acting is another. The key issue is to consider what policy measures would facilitate a transition to ESD.

FREE-MARKET ENVIRONMENTALISM

The usual response of orthodox economists to the problem of environmental decay is to interpret it in terms of markets and to propose 'environmental pricing' solutions.[8] The key concepts underlying this reasoning are 'market failure' and 'externalities'. They derive from the neoclassical theory discussed in chapter 23. Market failure is said to exist because no price normally applies to the use of 'environmental goods' like clean air and water, so consequently they are overused—for example as receptacles for the waste products of economic activity. Even where prices do apply, as in the case of fossil fuels used for energy, the prices do not reflect the full social costs, for the consumption of these items has negative spillover effects, such as atmospheric pollution. These negative spillovers are said to be the 'externalities' of an imperfect market economy.

The policy implication is to make adjustments to the price system so that these environmentally damaging effects do not occur. In effect, the environmental improvement comes through changing the economic *incentives*. Putting prices on environmental goods—by imposing taxes on their use, for example—provides an incentive to limit the demand for them. It also creates an incentive to develop alternative technologies that do not require the (now more expensive) resources. 'Internalising the externalities' thereby brings the prices to the consumers of environmental goods into line with the social costs arising from their use. The consumers can still exercise their freedom of choice, but the changed price structure applying to environmental goods aligns the 'equilibrium' market outcome more closely with the 'optimum' social and environmental outcome.

This is impeccable neoclassical economic reasoning. It can be extended with greater theoretical sophistication and more practical examples, enabling neoclassical economists to claim that they have a clear answer to the environmental challenge. The basic message is that the resolution of environmental problems requires more, and more effective, markets. It is a message with obvious appeal to those who are attracted by the prospect of having both individual market freedoms and responsible environmental outcomes. Politically, it has become increasingly influential, both within individual nation states and in international forums where responses to the global environmental challenge are discussed.

The necessary policy instruments are readily at hand. *Tradeable pollution permits*, for instance, may be issued by governments, constituting the sale of the right to pollute up to a specified level.[9] Bought and sold in the market, these permits go to the highest bidders. Those who cannot afford to buy them have to cease their polluting activities. *Carbon taxes* could also be introduced. Levied on commodities according to the quantity of fossil fuels that go, directly and indirectly, into their making, a carbon tax could be expected to discourage the consumption of those commodities.[10] Aluminium products, notoriously energy-intensive to make, would become much more expensive, for example, thereby providing an economic incentive to switch to the production and consumption of substitutes that are less environmentally damaging. Raising existing petrol taxes should, in principle, also provide an incentive to switch from cars to other modes of transport that make fewer demands on the depleting stock of fossil fuels. In practice, switching of this sort is impeded by the lack of good quality public transport in many suburban and rural areas, which causes demand for car travel to be quite price inelastic. However, the incentive to switch to more fuel-efficient vehicles is potentially a significant contributor to reducing environmental stress.

Pragmatically, such 'ecological taxes' appeal to governments because they also generate revenues. Therein lies a conundrum: the more inelastic the demand for the product causing the environmental damage, the greater the revenues from environmental taxes, but the smaller the reduction in environmentally damaging activities. Of course, even where demand is inelastic there may be indirect environmental benefits, if the extra revenues generated by the taxes are spent by the governments on repair of environmental damage. There are political constraints on this, though. Governments usually feel it necessary to compensate motorists for having to pay higher petrol prices, for example, by promising to allocate the additional tax revenues to expenditure on roads. A process of circular and cumulative causation results.

Perverse effects can also result from raising the prices of scarce environmental goods. As the populations of large cats and rhinos dwindle in Africa, the market prices for skins and rhino horns rises. That provides an extra incentive for hunters, acting illegally, to capture and slaughter more animals. Without extreme vigilance by regulatory authorities, the rate of depletion increases. In such a case, the process of circular and cumulative causation, working through the price mechanism, produces an 'equilibrium' of ecological catastrophe.

The distributional *consequences* of environmental policies also warrant consideration. Here lies a fundamental problem with all 'market-based' approaches to environmental concerns—their adverse impacts on *equity*. To the extent that environmental taxes add to the prices of scarce environmental goods, they push them increasingly beyond the reach of the poor. Access to the environmental requirements for a healthy life—in the extreme, for life itself—becomes increasingly restricted to the wealthy.

Structural constraints are also problematic. Like neoclassical theory in general, the case for 'environmental fine-tuning' through adjustments to the market mechanism assumes ease of substitution in the patterns of production and consumption. In practice, this is not necessarily the case. Inertia commonly arises from the existence of structural constraints, such as the spatial forms of urban and regional development, the distribution of employment opportunities, and the existing state of technology. These limit the capacity of production and consumption patterns to adjust in response to price changes. In the longer term, all these factors become variable, one might reasonably argue, but resistance from existing political economic interests still has to be countered. Opposition from the powerful institutions of corporate capital to policies that are seen to undermine the perpetuation of consumerism may be anticipated, for example. Such considerations suggest the need for an analysis of the causes of environmental decay that has a more political economic character.

Box 34.1

Reallocating environmental problems to poorer nations?

On 12 December 1991, the chief economist of the World Bank, Lawrence Summers, wrote an internal memo, which was leaked to the environmental community. It read as follows:

'Dirty' Industries: Just between you and me, shouldn't the World Bank be encouraging MORE migration of the dirty industries to the LDCs [Less Developed Countries]? I can think of three reasons:

1　The measurement of the costs of health impairing pollution depends on the forgone earnings from increased morbidity and mortality. From this point of view a given amount of health impairing pollution should be done in the country with the lowest cost, which will be the country with the lowest wages. I think the economic logic behind dumping a load of toxic waste in the lowest wage country is impeccable and we should face up to that.

2　The costs of pollution are likely to be non-linear as the initial increments of pollution probably have very low cost. I've always thought that underpopulated countries in Africa are vastly UNDERpolluted, their air quality is probably vastly inefficiently low compared to Los Angeles or Mexico City. Only the lamentable facts that so much pollution is generated by non-tradeable industries (transport, electrical generation) and that the unit transport costs of solid waste are so high prevent world welfare enhancing trade in air pollution and waste.

3　The demand for a clean environment for aesthetic and health reasons is likely to have very high income elasticity. The concern over an agent that causes a one in a million change in the odds of prostate cancer is obviously going to be much higher in a country where people survive to get prostate cancer than in a country where under 5 mortality is 200 per thousand. Also, much of the concern over industrial atmosphere discharge is about visibility impairing particulates. These discharges may have very little direct health impact. Clearly trade in goods that embody aesthetic pollution concerns could be welfare enhancing. While production is mobile the consumption of pretty air is a non-tradeable.

The problem with the arguments against all of these proposals for more pollution in LDCs (intrinsic rights to certain goods, moral reasons, social concerns, lack of adequate markets, etc.) could be turned around and used more or less effectively against every Bank proposal for liberalisation.

This is a rather startling example of neoclassical economic reasoning applied to environmental policy. It is the more startling because it comes from the chief economist of an institution ostensibly concerned with the welfare of the poorer nations. A similar argument could be made for the further concentration of environmentally degrading activities in poorer neighbourhoods in the more affluent nations. Considerations of equity and social justice evidently have no place in such reasoning. Nor is there recognition of the greater incentive to reduce pollution if you have to live in your own mess.

THE POLITICAL ECONOMY OF ENVIRONMENTAL DECAY

Consider the influence of *corporate power*. This may systematically limit the range of technologies and consumer choices, effectively ruling out more ecologically sustainable options. An obvious example is transport, which is central to the problem of environmental damage, both as an energy-user and as a pollution-generator. The major automobile manufacturers, oil companies, highway construction companies, and suppliers of motor vehicle components and accessories collectively comprise a 'roads lobby', which has a well-documented track record of suppressing innovations that might threaten their economic interests and of pressuring governments to pursue policies consistent with those interests.[11]

The wielding of this corporate power was significant in the effective destruction of the public transport system in many US cities, for example. The classic case is Los Angeles. In the late 1930s, National City Lines, a holding company formed by General Motors, in conjunction with the Firestone Tyre and Rubber company and Standard Oil of California, bought the light rail systems that served the scattered communities of the southern California region. It ripped up the tracks and replaced the rail service with buses (built by General Motors, running on Firestone tyres, and fuelled by Standard Oil). The deteriorating quality of service effectively forced most citizens to turn to private cars in order to move around the area. This, of course, was a transport option immensely more lucrative for General Motors, Firestone, and Standard Oil. The state responded by building more and more freeways to accommodate the cumulative growth in vehicle use. A region of fragrant orange groves and clean air was thereby converted into a sprawling metropolis with chronic problems of traffic congestion and atmospheric pollution levels regularly exceeding recommended health limits. No doubt, rising incomes would have led to growth in private car ownership, anyway; however, the process was accelerated by the corporations restructuring the transport options to serve their own purposes, irrespective of the environmental damage this caused. National City Lines was responsible for the removal of light-rail operations in more than a hundred other cities around the USA. A conspiracy against the public interest? A federal grand jury ruled it to be so, under anti-trust legislation. The corporations were fined $5000.[12]

A sad footnote to the story is that the city of Los Angeles, recognising the need to restore better public transport, has since rebuilt some of the light rail system at enormous public expense. However, it is having difficulty making it economically viable because, as residential and commercial activities have developed the sprawling, low-density suburban patterns characteristic of car-oriented cities, fixed-route public transport systems have become a less effective means of serving people's transport needs.[13]

This example is by no means exceptional. Expanding corporate power and profits through consciously violating ecological sustainability is common. Producing goods with *built-in obsolescence* is a case in point. This involves making products with working lives that are shorter than necessary, or making frequent style changes to products to render earlier lines unfashionable or redundant. It enhances producers' profitability, but at the expense of two forms of environmental damage: the greater use of resources to make the larger outputs of products, and the disposal of the discarded products. These are the familiar features of a junk economy based on the production of 'disposable' products. The profligate use of packaging, an integral part of many firms' marketing strategies today, accentuates the problem.

Consumers come to be complicit—sometimes reluctantly, sometimes enthusiastically—in these processes. Indeed, this is the essence of *consumerism*. Fostered by relentless sales promotion, the high levels of consumption, on which the modern capitalist economy depends, come to be regarded as normal, desirable, even laudable. Consumerist ideology thereby becomes central to the process of environmental decay, while the related ideology of *individualism* has the concurrent effect of eschewing concern with collective responsibility for finding solutions. As the economist Ken Boulding once put it, 'the presence of pollution is a symptom of the absence of community'.[14] *Homo economicus*, it seems, is not the ideal candidate for the job of securing ecological sustainability.

These various considerations lead to the conclusion, contrary to the claims of free-market environmentalism, that the market economy is the problem, not the solution. In its modern form, shaped by corporate power, consumerist practices, and the prevailing ethos of individualism, it stands as the antithesis of ESD.

What is to be done? Institute changes to the ownership and/or control of economic activities in order to sever the nexus between corporate interests and environmental damage? Instigate a 'values revolution' to shift consumer behaviour to more environmentally conscious practices? Lower consumption levels, at least in the more affluent nations, in order to allow the less developed nations some prospect of parity in their living standards within the ecological limits set by 'spaceship earth'?[15] Even such radical changes may not be sufficient to achieve ESD on a global scale, unless they embrace the spiritual and moral issues at the heart of the environmental crisis.

LAND, NATURAL CAPITAL, ECOLOGICAL BALANCE

Our relationship with land, to nature generally, has an inherently spiritual dimension. Consider the Aboriginal peoples of Australia, who lived in harmony with nature for more than 40,000 years before the European invasion of the continent. Their relationship with the land was integral to their culture, to their very being. Of course, it is difficult to reconcile that sort of relationship with nature with the structures of an affluent, urbanised, industrial society. However, policy changes can render nature less vulnerable to exploitation for personal economic gain.

Henry George's ideas warrant revisiting in this context. George was concerned (as we saw in chapter 11) with the effects of private land ownership and the potential for land taxation to redress economic inefficiencies and socioeconomic inequities. The type of analysis he developed can be extended from land to nature in general. Such an analysis recognises that the privatisation of natural assets allows a *rent* to be appropriated, and that therein lies the root of a range of economic, social, and environmental problems.

Incomes from rent derive from the economic surplus generated by the application of capital and labour to nature. The owners of privatised environmental assets derive that income solely as a result of their ownership of the resources. As economic growth proceeds, they usually capture increasingly large *unearned increments* from the fruits of growth. If urban development, for example, raises the price of urban land—as it usually does—that increases the rental income of existing landowners. They also stand to make unearned income from capital gains on the sale of their property. Not surprisingly in these circumstances, land is commonly held for speculative purposes. Henry George argued that the site rents (based on the unimproved capital value of the land) should be taken as tax, and the revenue thus collected be used to finance social expenditures. *Resource rent taxation* constitutes a broader application of the same principle—capturing for public purposes the economic surplus that would otherwise go to the owners of scarce environmental resources.

A case can be made for extending some such means of surplus-capture to all environmental assets. These include land, other natural resources, and 'common heritage capital'.[16] The latter includes human-made as well as natural assets whose value derives from their uniqueness or social significance. The use of bandwidth for radio, television, mobile phone, and other communications purposes is also relevant in this connection. Media and telecommunications companies currently derive enormous rents from their use. More extensive application of resource rental taxation can be of great value as a means of constraining the use of, and generating public revenues from, all these resources. No problem of trade-off between revenue-raising and environmental effectiveness need arise, as it does with taxes on the consumption of goods with environmentally damaging consequences, because the tax is on rent. Therein lies the advantage of a policy designed to capture an economic surplus.

There is a moral, as well as an economic, element in this analysis and policy—the principle that nature is not to be exploited for financial gain. More extensive land and resource rent taxation stops short of the comprehensive socialisation of natural assets, and it is no panacea for environmental problems that are deeply embedded in existing institutional practices, power structures, and prevailing ideologies. However, it could effectively capture for public purposes the economic surplus arising from the use of environmental assets. Whether, in the longer term, any such radical reformist measures can trigger the broader 'values revolution' required for the achievement of ecological sustainability remains an open question.

CONCLUSION

Consideration of environmental problems and policies paves the way for the construction of an alternative ecological economics.[17] It indicates, albeit tentatively, how the general principles of modern political economy outlined in the preceding chapter can be applied to environmental analysis and policies. The focus on an *economic surplus* draws attention to land, and nature generally, as a source of unearned income, and to a potentially effective means of limiting environmental damage from the exploitation of the environment. A focus on *capital, labour, and the state* puts the significance of corporate power into the spotlight, including its impact on transport options and the production of goods with built-in obsolescence. The concern with *evolution* is manifest in the analysis of how the economic system can be restructured to satisfy the requirements for ecologically sustainable development. The process of *circular and cumulative causation* is illustrated by the 'vicious cycle' of environmental decay that occurs in the absence of such remedial measures. Finally, the political economic emphasis on long-term processes of *resource creation* and destruction contrasts with the typical neoclassical economic focus on how markets allocate a given set of 'environmental goods'.

This alternative political economic perspective shows the need for a holistic view of the quality of the environment, the sustainability of the economy, and the prevailing ideologies and power structures. It also links with contemporary political economic concerns about technology, industry, and work.

CHAPTER 35

Technology, Industry, Work

Is capitalism changing to a 'new economy'?
Is it useful to interpret recent political economic changes as a shift towards post-Fordism?
Does speculation impede the quest for a more productive economy?

Any analysis of the modern economy must pay due regard to questions about how the technical and social organisation of production affects the prospects for material progress. Do new technologies necessarily contribute to higher productivity and/or open up possibilities of liberation from toil? Or is the potential for progress being sidetracked because our economic institutions are unsuited to realise that potential? These big issues have always been central to political economic enquiry. Recall Adam Smith's focus on the division of labour as the driving force of economic progress (but causing the workers to become 'stupid and ignorant'). Recall Karl Marx's analysis of the connection between the development of the forces and relations of production, showing therein the sources of workers' alienation and exploitation. Recall Veblen's worry that the 'instinct of workmanship' in industry would be negated by the 'predatory instinct' of business people. Recall Schumpeter's pessimistic prediction that the progressive role of innovation in industry would be throttled by the development of large corporations.

Similar concerns come in many guises in our own time. Some argue that we are now experiencing a transition from a Fordist to a post-Fordist organisation of production, with major implications for the nature of work and the distribution of political economic power. Some point to the technological changes, particularly information technologies, that are ushering in a 'new economy'—although what is new about it and who benefits from the novelty remain matters of controversy. 'The end of work' is posited as one possible outcome, as the technological changes displacing workers from their previous occupations fail to create a comparable number of new employment opportunities. For social scientists emphasising the liberating effects of technology, this is not necessarily an unwelcome scenario; it shifts attention from the Keynesian concern with job creation to the design of institutional arrangements for a more equitable distribution of working time and incomes.

It would be an exaggeration to say that there is a comprehensive and analysis of these issues in modern political economy. Rather, what exists is a rapidly expanding literature that is exploratory in method and diverse in political perspectives. This chapter seeks to identify some of the most significant themes.

TOWARDS A 'NEW ECONOMY'?

How is capitalism changing? Sectoral shifts, affecting the balance of output and employment between agricultural, manufacturing, and service industries, are on-going. Concurrently, firms and markets are undergoing transformations, as they channel investments into new and diffusing technologies. This is the essence of what Ed Nell calls 'transformational growth', involving qualitative as well as quantitative change.[1] How to understand it and judge the significance of the effects of the technological changes are the key issues.

Popular interpretations centre on the role of technology in the development of a 'new economy'. Indeed, few doubt that new technologies are affecting many, if not most, aspects of economic and social life. The 'microelectronic revolution' has led to computer technologies affecting an ever wider range of industries and economic activities. Developments in biotechnology are having dramatic economic and social effects. The development of robotics is also starting to have significant consequences for production processes. Some contend that the magnitude of the economic changes wrought by these innovations is comparable to the effects of earlier technological transformations, such as the development of railways in the mid nineteenth century and motor cars in the early twentieth century.

Does the ever wider application of technological change constitute a basis for the development of a 'new economy', augmenting—and displacing—the 'old economy' based on mining, heavy engineering, and other traditional manufacturing and transport industries? What is implied is not simply a change of production technologies, but also fundamental changes in economic and social structures. Social theorists such as Manuel Castells have heralded the arrival of an 'informational economy', while terms like 'network society' and 'knowledge economy' have gained currency.[2] Economist Lester Thurow contends that a third industrial revolution is occurring, at least in the United States, with impacts similar to that of the steam engine and the development of electricity.[3] Discussion of this posited revolution is often couched in exhortatory terms, advocating greater priority in public policy to developing the knowledge base and skills to ensure that companies—and whole nations—are at the forefront of the processes of change.

On closer inspection, the evidence of the impact of new technologies on productive activity remains ambiguous. It is not self-evident that the overall effect is to expand the array of opportunities for capital accumulation. The development of e-commerce, for example, may be threatening to profitability, and thus to the economic surplus available for investment in innovation, because it enables customers to more readily 'shop around' for the cheapest priced products by browsing the Web.[4]

Even the basic issue of what constitutes the 'knowledge economy' is ambiguous. According to one writer, it is much broader than information technology, and may also include 'the development of aerospace, artificial intelligence, bio-technology, eco-tourism, gene technology (including genetically modified food, gene shears and cloning), medical technology, miniaturisation, multimedia, nano-technology, new materials, pharmaceuticals, solar and other renewable energies, telecommunications, waste use and re-use'.[5] This broader view suggests that the development of the knowledge economy depends essentially on fostering the necessary human capital. The political economic focus shifts from technology *per se* to the role of labour, albeit primarily intellectual rather than manual labour. Therein, however, lie big difficulties, such as the tension between privatisation of knowledge as a means of generating greater profits and the assertion of a public interest in how the knowledge is used (for instance, the potentially hazardous consequences of genetically modifying food).

Overall, it is not clear that the posited 'new economy' changes anything fundamental about capitalism—the relationship between capital and labour, the process of surplus-generation, or the tensions over the use and distribution of the economic surplus yet *something* new seems to be afoot.

FROM FORDISM TO POST-FORDISM?

One group of social scientists claiming that a fundamental political economic transformation is currently occurring comprises the theorists of 'post-Fordism'. The shift from 'Fordist' to 'post-Fordist' economic arrangements is said to constitute a significantly different form of capitalism.

'Fordism' is the label applied to the phase of capitalist economic development based on mass production for mass markets. Henry Ford, the American car maker, is generally regarded as its pioneer. He introduced the use of the endless-chain conveyor-belt into car production, facilitating a detailed division of labour and an enormous increase in labour productivity. He paid his workers $5 per day to accept the new working arrangements, a wage rate much higher than that then prevailing in US industry (a decision he later described as 'the best cost-cutting move I ever made'). Nearly 17 million of Ford's standard black Model T cars rolled off the production line between 1908 and 1927, revolutionising the vehicle industry and the transportation system. Other car makers followed suit. The basic principle of standardised mass production spread to an ever wider range of industries. By the 1950s and 1960s, 'Fordism' had become the norm for industrial production, not only in the United States, but also in other industrialised countries. The theorists of post-Fordism generally see this period of the 'long boom' as the zenith of the Fordist system, the years when it reached its most well-developed form.

What are the essential features of Fordism as a *regime of accumulation*? As shown in table 35.1, the characteristic Fordist production units are large factories. Inter-firm relationships are competitive, at least as far as market shares are concerned, with oligopoly—'competition among the few'—being the usual market structure. The products are standardised, made by methods of mass production, for sale in mass consumer markets. Work is organised in terms of a detailed division of labour and is typically monitored and regulated by hierarchical modes of control. 'Scientific management', pioneered by F. W. Taylor as a means of asserting that control, is applied more or less explicitly, along with techniques, such as 'time-and-motion study', which seek to minimise the discretion exercised by workers in deciding how the work is done.[6]

What about the features of Fordism as a *mode of social regulation*? Rather more contentiously, table 35.1 suggests that the application of Fordism in industry tended to go hand-in-hand with a broader set of 'macro' economic and social arrangements: the regulation of the capital–labour relationship (through the use of arbitration and

Table 35.1 Contrasts between Fordism and post-Fordism

	Fordism	Post-Fordism
Regime of accumulation:		
Structure of industry	Large factories	Networks of small production units
Inter-firm relationships	Competitive	Competitive and cooperative
Outputs	Standardised products for mass markets	Diverse products for niche markets
Capital	Machinery for mass production	Reprogrammable machinery, e.g. CAD/CAM
Labour	Detailed division of labour	Multiskilled workers
Workplace relations	Hierarchical; 'scientific management'	Partial autonomy; 'flexibility'
Mode of social regulation:		
Broader socioeconomic system	Macro-regulation; Keynesian policies; welfare state	Deregulation; privatisation; 'neo-liberalism'
Political disposition	Centralised	Decentralised
Cultural character	Modernist	Post-modernist

other regulatory institutions, for instance), the implementation of Keynesian policies, and the development of the welfare state.[7] Looking at the extension of Fordist arrangements during the 'long boom' years in particular, the inference is that these 'macro' arrangements were part of a political 'deal'. An implicit social contract compensated workers for their acceptance of alienating Fordist workplaces by giving them greater economic security and the social benefits arising from the welfare state. This can be regarded as part of a broader 'capital–labour settlement'.

This is a neat characterisation of Fordism, as both a set of business practices and a socioeconomic system. It may be deceptively neat. Many of the features of Fordism were evident during the 'long boom' era. However, the *causal* connections between the 'micro' aspects and the 'macro' characteristics of the period are unclear. A rather more modest inference posits correlation rather than causation. Either way, the combination of these 'macro' economic, social, and political conditions with Fordist workplace practices looked like a winning formula. The economic crisis caused by the collapse of the 'long boom' in the 1970s changed all that. This is what is said to have ushered in the 'post-Fordist' alternative, which was driven by the quest to restructure industries in order to establish renewed conditions for capital accumulation.[8]

What is different about post-Fordism? As shown in table 35.1, business production units are typically smaller, and networks of cooperative inter-firm relationships develop. Competition for market share continues, but the competing firms may simultaneously cooperate by pooling information about technologies and market trends, perhaps setting up industry service organisations for this purpose. As for the types of products being made, these are diverse and may be individually 'customised' for small niche markets. Modern technologies are used, often involving computer-assisted design (CAD) and computer-assisted manufacturing (CAM). The reprogrammable nature of the machinery imparts more flexibility to production. So does the use of multiskilled labour, often organised in workteams with partial autonomy in determining how the tasks are organised and executed. 'Just-in-time' (JIT) systems of managing the production flows may also obviate the need for substantial stocks of raw materials and spare parts to be kept 'just-in-case' they are needed.[9]

It is not claimed that all firms and industries have made this transition. Indeed, post-Fordist theorists often contrast Fordism and post-Fordism in a rhetorical manner, as a challenge. The challenge is for firms to adopt the new practices. The alternative is to stick with the old ways, incorporating new technologies and management practices only in so far as they preserve the organisational patterns and social relations of Fordism (a conservative response said to result in 'neo-Fordism'). It sounds rather like 'an offer you can't refuse': embrace the new system or go under. In practice, both systems coexist in different industries and sometimes side-by-side in the same sector.

The association between 'post-Fordism' in industry and the changes in the broader socioeconomic system—between the regime of accumulation and the mode of social regulation—is also less clear-cut than table 35.1 might seem to suggest. As noted in earlier chapters of this book, the neo-liberal political program—scaling back Keynesian policy measures, deregulating capital and labour markets, privatising public enterprises, and squeezing the welfare state—has been in the ascendancy in the last quarter of a century. This is the period during which post-Fordism is said to have been challenging Fordism as the dominant model of capitalist production. As with the correlation between Fordism and the 'capital–labour settlement' of the 'long boom' years, the causal connection is contentious. The *rhetoric of 'flexibility'* has certainly been characteristic of both the 'micro' (industry) and 'macro' (state) spheres in this more recent era, but that does not 'prove' that neo-liberalism necessarily accompanies post-Fordist production arrangements. Indeed, many proponents of post-Fordism see any association with neo-liberalism as negating its potentially progressive political possibilities.

Table 35.1 also posits a link between the economic shift to post-Fordism and a broader social and cultural shift to 'postmodernity'. This may be regarded as a flight of fancy. It is mentioned mainly to indicate an aspect of modern political economy that has some connections with contemporary 'cultural studies'. *Postmodernity* as a social phenomenon is associated with a shift from the primacy of class relationships to more complex dimensions of social identity that emphasise diversity and difference. *Postmodernism* as a form of social enquiry emphasises competing discourses and the impact of language and media on how we see and relate to the world around us (if, indeed, any such world exists independently of how we see it). Post-Fordism, like any '-ism' or 'totalising discourse', does not sit altogether comfortably among such concerns. However, there have been some interesting explorations of how economic arrangements emphasising 'flexible specialisation' relate to the cultural context of postmodernity.[10]

How significant is post-Fordism in practice? Its proponents point to particular regions that have achieved economic prosperity through the adoption of at least some of its characteristics. These *new industrial spaces* include Silicon Valley in California, the central-northeast region of Italy (the city of Bologna in particular), Baden-Württemberg in Germany, and the M4 motorway corridor in England. These regions are geographically distinct from the former heartlands of Fordist production like the Midwest and northeast region of the United States, the Milan–Turin–Genoa triangle in northwestern Italy, the Ruhr in Germany, and the Midlands in England. They differ in many respects. Some see them as modern expressions of the 'industrial districts' discussed a century ago by Alfred Marshall. Others posit a connection with a neo-Schumpeterian view of innovation and technological change as the key ingredients in industrial success.[11]

From a modern political economic perspective, perhaps the most interesting question is whether these regional enclaves of so-called 'hi-tech cottage industries' are forerunners of a system that can be expected to spread *or* whether their existence is made possible by the continued prevalence of Fordist arrangements elsewhere.[12] The issue is of considerable policy significance. Proponents of post-Fordism commonly posit the model as desirable, if not inevitable. The policy implication is that communities and governments should be trying to foster the development of *industry clusters* with these characteristics. From this perspective, post-Fordism is a formula for being a winner, regionally or nationally, in circumstances of increasingly vigorous global competition. Post-Fordism is also held to open up possibilities for more interesting work, the extension of industrial democracy, and the decentralisation of political economic power.[13]

Critics, on the other hand, argue that the 'flexibility' post-Fordism offers is generally used as a means to divide the workforce and extend the power of capital over labour. They also point to the implicit technological determinism, arguing that the assumption that new production technologies lead to new work opportunities and more progressive social outcomes neglects the capitalist power relations that shape how the technologies are used in practice.[14]

REDISTRIBUTING WORK IN A TECHNOLOGICALLY ADVANCED SOCIETY?

Recent structural economic changes—whether usefully characterised as the development of a 'new economy' or as a transition to 'post-Fordism'—certainly pose major challenges for the future of work. Some fundamental questions about the *distribution of jobs* arise. For example, how will work be shared between those with educational attributes and skills in high demand and those who are less able to command roles as 'symbolic analysts', to use Robert Reich's term?[15] A striking 20:80 ratio is posited by H-P. Martin and H. Schumann as the most likely outcome, a situation in which only a minority of the population (perhaps 20 per cent) will benefit from the hi-tech/advanced-human-capital growth path, while the majority (perhaps 80 per cent) will be marginalised, consigned to a diet of 'tittytainment' (the modern equivalent of 'bread and circuses').[16] A shorter standard working week for all is one possible policy response to this otherwise strongly polarising tendency. European nations, France in particular, are taking the lead in reducing working hours in order to spread the work (and leisure) more broadly across the population. Companies like Volkswagen, Hewlett-Packard, and Digital Equipment have successfully implemented shorter-working-hours policies to prevent dramatic numbers of job losses.[17]

Of course, there is a problem with shorter hours if the corollary is lower wages. Whether this is a necessary part of the deal depends, *inter alia*, on how productivity per hour is affected by the changes in hours worked. In any case, workers' willingness to accept wage–leisure trade-offs may be greater than generally believed; surveys indicate that as many as 50–60 per cent of workers would prefer shorter hours to higher wages.[18] Some employers and workers will inevitably resist change, but there are relatively modest measures that could be widely implemented in order to facilitate shorter hours for those who are enthusiastic. Possibilities include (1) taking the benefits of productivity improvements as shorter hours rather than higher wages; (2) changing working-time arrangements—to a four-day week, for example; and (3) allowing workers to take long periods of leave without pay, with income spread over working and non-working periods.[19] Governments can provide taxation incentives to encourage such redistribution of working time.

The French social scientist André Gorz posits a more radical response to the challenge of combining new technologies with an equitable sharing of work, also emphasising how we can enjoy more leisure time.[20] Gorz suggests that a lifetime commitment of, say, twenty thousand hours from each person would be sufficient, given modern technology, to generate the goods and services needed for a reasonably affluent society. Ideally, individuals should have choice about how they organise this—whether in full-time work leading to early retirement, in more continuous part-time work, or in blocks of work interspersed with periods of education or recreation. Ideally, too, the income stream should be reasonably consistent over time, irrespective of the pattern of work. This throws up a major challenge for capitalist institutions, for which the direct nexus between work and wages has always been a central feature.

Gorz's analysis presents us with a vision of a post-capitalist society—even a 'post-industrial' society—in which the relationship between work and nature, economy and social structure is transformed. Yet its achievement is inconceivable without a fundamental shift in prevailing economic structures and ideologies. There would also need to be a major cultural shift, involving significant changes in the role of men and women in families, in communities, and in social arrangements generally. The conventional notion of 'breadwinner' is already breaking down as both men and women juggle increasingly complex patterns of paid and non-paid work. Whether reducing the dominance of work—both for those who have too much of it and those who have too little of it—would reduce the stress associated with these imbalances and social shifts depends on the social valuation of leisure, of people's contributions to community organisations, and of citizenship in general. Taking advantage of technological change to liberate *Homo economicus* is an enormous political economic challenge.

PRODUCTIVITY OR SPECULATION?

A growing economic surplus is made possible by technological changes and increases in labour productivity. What determines its disposition? Is the surplus used for wealth-enhancing or wealth-redistributing purposes? *Productive investment* generally has the former characteristic; *speculation* the latter. Productive investment, as Keynes emphasised, adds to the aggregate demand for goods and services in the short run and to the capacity of the economy to supply more in the long run. Speculation, on the other hand, adds nothing to the wealth of society: it is a 'zero-sum game' in which the winners make gains at the expense of the losers. Worse, to the extent that speculation diverts resources from more directly productive purposes, it is a 'negative-sum game' for society as a whole.

The distinction between productive investment and speculation is not always clear in practice.[21] Some markets characterised by speculative activities seem to be necessary adjuncts to productive economic activity in a capitalist economy. If people are to be willing to advance their savings to businesses by buying shares, for example, there must be 'secondhand' markets where they can re-sell those shares if they need cash or if they judge their original purchases to have been unwise. As soon as those markets are established, though, they become arenas for speculative buying and selling. Similarly, foreign exchange markets are needed to facilitate foreign trade and foreign travel, but the overwhelming bulk of transactions in those markets have nothing to do with those 'real' activities; currencies are bought and sold according to their expected future price movements in the hope of securing capital gains.[22]

'Futures' markets are a yet more striking example. Farmers may need to insure against big fluctuations in their incomes by entering into 'futures' contracts that effectively give them a guaranteed price for their produce. But those 'futures' markets, whatever their original economic rationale, then become magnets for speculative funds. In practice, this has been one of the most striking contemporary trends. It has been estimated that the growth of volume of transactions in markets for futures and other derivatives grew sixfold in only six years in the 1990s—a decade of phenomenal proliferation of financial instruments in the global economy.[23]

The term 'casino capitalism' (introduced in chapter 4) draws attention to these speculative tendencies in the current economy. Seymour Melman refers to the quest for 'profits without production', attributing the low productivity growth in the United States to 'the looting of the productive capital of the system on behalf of short-term money making (and military-political power)'.[24] There is an obvious parallel with Thorstein Veblen's earlier criticisms of the ascendancy of the financial managers over the production engineers. According to Melman, the influence of the financiers has increased dramatically. The production managers—the 'organisers of industrial work'—were once the key personnel, then the marketing executives, but now the 'financier–strategists' are in control, focusing on 'combining disparate firms into conglomerates … [and] maximising the short-term profit-making opportunities afforded by tax laws, securities transfers, the milking of production assets and other financial legerdemain'.[25]

In the language of Marxist political economy, this would imply a systemic shift from (1) the production of surplus value to (2) the realisation of surplus value, and thence to (3) the circulation of capital and the subdivision of surplus value. Of course, all three aspects are continually relevant to capital accumulation. Indeed, for capital as a whole, the notion of 'profits without production' is nonsensical. Melman's point can be reinterpreted as a claim that (3) has come to be a disproportionate concern in modern capitalism, involving financial pursuits that redistribute income without contributing directly to the generation of value.

To develop this analysis rather more fully, it is useful to distinguish between the *sphere of production* and the *sphere of circulation*. In the former, money capital is used for the purchase of labour power and the means of production, and the power of the owners of capital is used to appropriate surplus value from the value of commodities produced by labour. In the sphere of circulation, the money capital obtained through the sale of the commodities is channelled into the financing of further economic activities in order to facilitate the accumulation of capital as a whole. These activities include further rounds of commodity production, of course, but may also involve indirect but necessary adjuncts to the production process, such as those activities performed by capital and the state to ensure economic and social reproduction. Exchange of financial assets (whether shares, titles to real estate, futures, insurance policies, or whatever) have their place here in the sphere of circulation.

Because surplus value is generated only in the sphere of production, the profits of enterprises engaged in the sphere of circulation—including banks and other financial institutions—must derive ultimately from that source. In effect, the financial institutions rely on 'capturing' a subdivision of the surplus value generated elsewhere in the economy.

The relative sizes of the sphere of production and the sphere of circulation are not fixed. A tendency towards speculation tilts the balance towards the latter. A larger share of the economic surplus is then captured by enterprises operating in the sphere of circulation—as the result of high interest rates charged on loans to productive enterprises, for example. Similarly, the share of wage incomes captured by enterprises in the sphere of circulation depends on the level of mortgage rates, consumer credit charges, and insurance premiums.

Speculation also tends to expand the sphere of circulation (and hence its relative share in total income) by increasing the range of financial transactions. The development and rapid growth of 'futures' is a case in point. The proliferation of financial intermediaries also creates a situation where each slice off their own margins from the remaining economic surplus. The corollary of this is that the share of the total surplus retained by the sphere of production is reduced. Hence, the problems of low productive investment.

There is an important caveat. In so far as the increased income share being absorbed in the sphere of circulation comes partly from wage earners, the problems of inadequate investment cannot be attributed to the effect of speculation. So if, for example, speculation compounds the tendency to inflation of house prices, it raises the cost—particularly for first-home buyers—of obtaining housing. The principal diversion of incomes is then from wages to the profits of financial institutions. There also may be a secondary diversion from the profits of industrial enterprises to landowners, to the extent that commercial property rents are also affected by land speculation; this, too, as the followers of Henry George remind us, is an impediment to the productive use of the economic surplus.

CONCLUSION

Technology does not directly 'determine' the way in which economic production is organised, still less how its fruits are distributed. Its effects are mediated by the exercise of economic power. The interaction of these technological and political economic forces can be regarded as shaping the *social structure of accumulation*. This is 'the specific institutional environment within which the capitalist accumulation process is organised'.[26] It reflects the nature of business organisations, the financial institutions and credit system, the character of class relationships, and the pattern of state involvement in the economy. Looking back at the last two centuries of capitalist development, the US political economists advocating the use of this concept identify three periods characterised by different social structures of accumulation: (1) the creation of a working class ('proletarianisation'), (2) its subjugation to increasingly uniform productive requirements ('homogenisation'), and (3) its division by industry and occupation according to gender and ethnicity ('segmentation').[27]

The concerns of this chapter can be interpreted as exploring whether a different social structure of accumulation is now emerging. Arguments about the 'new economy', 'post Fordism', and the speculative uses of capital are aspects of this political economic exploration. At this stage, it seems premature to assert that a new social structure of accumulation has arrived. However, in so far as there is a central theme in political economic changes in the current period, it seems to be 'flexibility' in serving the interests of capital: flexibility in the flow of funds between alternative uses (including speculation), flexibility in labour markets (resulting in less economic security for labour), and flexibility in the organisational forms of capital.[28]

Political choices are not thereby eradicated. Workers—and citizens in general—can be more or less compliant when faced with the possibility of a transition to a new social structure of accumulation. The form of flexibility posited by André Gorz, for example, would take us in a markedly different direction. It would require concerted political action to achieve. The state is obviously crucial in this respect. It necessarily has a major influence, whether as facilitator of the transition to a social structure of accumulation offering capitalist employers the sort of flexibility they seek, or as an instrument for the pursuit of an alternative future *à la* Gorz. Equally important is whether there is sufficient unity of interests in contemporary capitalist society to pursue progressive alternatives, or whether this possibility is impeded by social divisions. It is with these questions about the political economy of state, class, gender, and race that the next two chapters are concerned.

CHAPTER 36

Class, Gender, Ethnicity

Is class relevant in modern capitalism?
What shapes the gender dimension of economic inequalities?
Does capitalism eradicate or foster racism?

Analysis of socioeconomic inequalities has always been a central concern of political economy. Recall David Ricardo's description of the study of distribution between classes as 'the principal problem of political economy'.[1] For Marx, the study of the capital–labour relationship was the key to understanding the capitalist system, linking distribution with production, growth, and economic crises. Keynes, whose primary concern was with macroeconomic aggregates, recognised the importance of income distribution as an influence on the state of the economy and a legitimate focus for public policy. Prominent figures in the institutional and post-Keynesian traditions, including Galbraith, Myrdal, Kalecki, and Robinson, have also made the study of economic inequality part of their political economic analyses. Other modern scholars concerned with the problems of economic development and underdevelopment, such as Amartya Sen, winner of the 1998 Nobel Prize in Economic Sciences, place the issue of inequality at the forefront of their studies.[2]

Neoclassical economics is the obvious exception. As noted in chapter 22, some of the pioneers in this tradition sought to use marginal productivity theory as an explicit justification of the economic inequalities generated in 'free-market' economies. In the past century, any systematic concern with economic inequality has usually dropped out of the picture, the existing distribution of income and wealth being taken as 'given' for the purposes of constructing models of resource allocation. Thus, the neoclassical concern with efficiency has virtually eclipsed concerns with equity, which is labelled 'political' and hence not properly the concern of 'scientific' economic enquiry. To the extent that equity issues enter the analysis at all, it is usually with reference to the 'efficiency–equity trade-off', thus implying that the pursuit of distributive justice comes at a significant price in terms of its negative economic consequences.[3]

The marginalisation of concern about economic inequality in orthodox economics is an imbalance that warrants redress. Economic inequalities, their causes, consequences, and possible reduction, are among the key issues of the present time. As noted in chapter 4, there is considerable evidence that inequalities have recently been increasing, both within and between nations. Understanding the causes and formulating possible remedies is a major challenge. It is no less a challenge for political economy than for orthodox economics and requires reconsideration of some key concepts in political economic analysis. Whether the long-standing concern with 'class' is still relevant, and how class relates to inequalities associated with gender and ethnicity, are issues requiring particular attention.

RECONSIDERING CLASS

The obvious starting point for a reconsideration of 'class' in political economy—its definition, its interpretation, and its usefulness—is Marx. It was with Marx's analysis that the concept of class took on its radical character. Marx and Engels used the term in their polemical writing, beginning the *Manifesto of the Communist Party* with the words: 'The history of all hitherto existing societies is the history of class struggles'. Class was also an important concept in Marx's theoretical works, such as *Capital*, and historical works, where it is employed as a means of explaining economic, social, and political change. Of course, class has always been central to the characteristically Marxist political prescription that urges workers to recognise their collective interest in transforming capitalism into socialism.

How relevant are these ideas today? At first, they sound archaic. Many people are uncomfortable about even using the word 'class', perhaps because of its association with the political program of Marxism and its exhortation to class struggle. For those who prefer to see no discontinuities in the social appearances, values, and aspirations of the citizenry of modern capitalist society, even *talking about class* is regarded as a source of unnecessary social division. It is a perspective that reflects the absence of a prevailing class-consciousness. It does not necessarily refute the relevance of class as an *analytical tool*.

How is the concept of class actually used in Marxist political economy? It is not a matter of 'social pigeon-holing', of putting people into categories according to their personal characteristics, or their perceptions of their own social status. The characteristic Marxist concern is with class *relationships* rather than class positions. It is the posited asymmetry of class relationships that is distinctive. Not that there is anything particularly novel about that. As Marx and Engels emphasised, in every form of society a dominant class has been able to systematically organise the extraction of surplus labour from another class. This was quite blatant under slavery and feudalism. Under capitalism, it continues—albeit in a less immediately visible form—in the relationship between capital and wage-labour. As argued in chapter 14, because workers in general are not paid wages equivalent to the full value of the commodities that their labour creates, there is an economic surplus that takes its most immediately obvious form in the profits of business enterprises. Despite all the changes to capitalism that have occurred since Marx's time, as long as profits continue to be generated in this way, the *economic* basis for class division remains.

From this perspective, it is immaterial whether capitalist employers are nice or nasty people, whether they have extravagant or frugal lifestyles, or whether they exhibit 'ruling class' or more 'matey' personal manners. Class derives from the *structural* relationship of capital to labour as the basis on which a capitalist economy functions.

According to Marxist political economy, this capital–labour relationship is essentially *contradictory*: it requires cooperation between parties who have fundamental conflicts of interest. *Cooperation* is necessary to 'keep the wheels of industry turning', whether in transnational corporations or small businesses, whether in extractive, manufacturing, or service industries, and whether unionised or not. Without this cooperation, both the owners of capital and the workers lose income. However, there is a simultaneous *conflict* of interest under capitalism, manifest in the continual contest over the distribution of the total income generated—the wages and profit shares—and in friction over managerial prerogatives, the rights of labour to organise collectively, and so on. This uncomfortable nexus between cooperation and conflict is the essence of the capital–labour class relationship.

Certain things follow from this way of conceptualising class. The focus on relationships to the means of production gives the definition of class a distinct *economic* character. This contrasts with sociological views of class. The Marxian approach does not define class according to *income*: capitalists can be rich or poor. It is the *source* of their income that differentiates them from workers. By the same reasoning, people's different *consumption* patterns do not define their class position: capitalists may ride bicycles while workers travel in expensive cars; and workers may go to work in overalls or suits. Of course, people's income levels and patterns of consumption, in so far as they correlate to ownership of the means of production, may be useful secondary indicators of class position, but they are not of themselves defining features.

Nor need *class-consciousness* be a defining feature. Individual workers sometimes perceive themselves to have common interests with other workers in the same firm, in other firms, or in distant lands. They often do not. Indeed, they may perceive themselves to have more interests in common with their employers. That will have a significant bearing on their behaviour, including their political inclinations, but it does not refute their class position as workers. The definition of class is based on *objective* rather than subjective characteristics.

These are bold assertions. For those who feel uncomfortable about using the term 'class' at all, such reasoning may reinforce the discomfort. The point is an analytical one—to establish a clear starting point for class analysis, quite different from popular perceptions of what class might mean. This provides a basis for considering how class analysis may be adapted to deal with an array of contemporary concerns: the significance of the 'middle class', the effect of spreading share-ownership, the general lack of class-consciousness, the effect of intra-class inequalities, and the interaction of class with other dimensions of economic and social inequality. These concerns impart more subtlety to the consideration of class and reflect the complexities of class in the real world.

The question of the 'middle class' is particularly important in considering the contemporary relevance and meaning of class. The Marxist analysis begins with what is essentially a *two-class model*: *bourgeoisie* and *proletariat*, or capitalist class and working class. Marx conceded that reality was more complex—that self-employed artisans and a *petit bourgeoisie* existed alongside these two major classes, for example—but the expectation, forcefully argued in the *Communist Manifesto*, was that capitalist development would tend increasingly to polarise society.[4] Has it done so? The prominence of a 'middle class' in modern capitalist societies would suggest not. People commonly talk nowadays about this 'middle class' as the largest social group, and the majority of people almost invariably describe themselves as 'middle class' in surveys of personal class identification. The traditional Marxist response is to describe this as evidence of their 'false consciousness', of a subjective misreading of the objective reality of class. According to this reasoning, while self-identification as 'middle-class' may serve people's personal social and psychological needs, the majority of them derive their income principally from the sale of their labour power and, as such, they are working class.

On this reasoning, class is not determined by whether you work in 'white-collar' or 'blue-collar' jobs, whether you are employed in mental or manual labour, in 'hi-tech' or 'smokestack' industries, or whether your remuneration is called a 'wage' or 'salary'. It is matter of whether you own the means of production or not. This is not to say that the 'false consciousness' of people describing themselves as 'middle class' is irrelevant. On the contrary, it is a powerful explanation for their failure to act in the unified manner that Marx advocated and predicted—to form a 'class for itself' rather than be merely a 'class in itself'. The political inference is clear: these workers need to be persuaded to abandon their 'false consciousness'. Much of the political activity of far-left political groups continues to be based, explicitly or implicitly, on this presumption.

A rather more sophisticated response to the question of the 'middle class' recognises that changing economic conditions have indeed changed the class structure. One aspect is the *spread of share-ownership*. In countries where there has been substantial privatisation of public enterprises and where there has been a vigorous political promotion of 'people's capitalism', many workers have bought shares in private-sector businesses. The overall distribution of share-ownership usually remains sharply concentrated, and the dividend payments for 'mum-and-dad' shareholders are usually small relative to their wage incomes.[5] However, the recipients feel themselves to have some stake in both capital and labour—as indeed they have. Many other workers with savings in superannuation funds, which are partly invested in capitalist businesses, may also feel themselves to have a similar dual interest. Ascription to the 'middle class' looks a more reasonable response in these conditions.

The effect of *intra-class* economic inequalities also needs to be considered. Among those who derive their income principally from the sale of their labour power there are striking income differentials, which have been accentuated by recent technological and structural economic changes. Workers with key specialist 'know-how' often command quite impressive wage incomes. Others in more traditional working-class occupations have been fighting a rearguard action, many being forced into casual and part-time work in the secondary labour market or into the 'reserve army of labour'. Some have been permanently excluded from the waged workforce. This range of economic circumstances sits uncomfortably with a notion of common working-class interests.

Meanwhile, there is blurring of the boundaries of the capitalist class. Senior executives in large corporations often receive massive remuneration packages, sometimes—but not always—including shares in the companies that employ them. They are employees, but their incomes are many times bigger than those who own and control their own small- or medium-sized business, even though the class position of the latter, formally, is more unambiguously capitalistic.[6] The tension between ownership and control in the modern corporation, a central concern of institutional economists, underpins this difficulty of imposing a clear definition on the capitalist class. The resulting fuzziness in class delineation is problematic.

Three principal types of response are possible. One is to take the traditional position that the capital–labour relationship is a *functional* relationship independent of the identity of the capitalists and the workers, of the degree of inequality in the distribution of income, and of people's perceptions of how they relate to the socioeconomic system. It is a position that separates economic analysis (of the distributional shares of capital and labour, for instance) from social analysis (of the extent of personal inequalities, for example) and from political analysis (of how people respond to economic and social inequalities, for instance). This disciplinary fragmentation of class analysis sits awkwardly with a political economy perspective.

A second response is to recognise that contemporary capitalist economic and social developments necessitate a more flexible approach to the definition and interpretation of class. This means modifying, if not scrapping altogether, the traditional Marxist dual-class thesis and the concept of 'false consciousness'. The model from some of the early work by sociologist Erik Olin Wright, reproduced on the next page in box 36.1, illustrates one step in this direction. Six categories, rather than two, are identified. This recognises that supervisors, managers, semi-autonomous wage earners, and self-employed business people may indeed have distinct class characteristics that are not reducible to the working class–capitalist class dichotomy.

How the members of these *intermediate socioeconomic categories* (or 'contradictory class locations') align politically is crucial to the functioning and stability of capitalism. If they see themselves as having common cause with the working class, their combination produces a powerful force that is potentially challenging to the prevailing political economic order. The late twentieth-century experience of 'people's power' toppling tyrannical and corrupt governments in the Philippines and Indonesia, for example, comes to mind in this context; here were broad, cross-class coalitions that successfully challenged the political, if not economic, order. If, as is usually the case, those in 'contradictory class locations' see their interests aligned with the capitalist class in maintaining the present political economic system, a more conservative scenario prevails. If some of the working class share that perception too, as is also often the case, the conservatism is yet more pervasive.

Antonio Gramsci's notion of *hegemony* also warrants consideration in this context. Hegemony entails the widespread acceptance of beliefs supportive of a particular political economic arrangement.[8] The hegemony of 'bourgeois' values is partly a product of people's conditioning (through institutions such as the media, the churches, and the education system) and partly a product of their practical need to 'fit in' with the existing socioeconomic arrangements.[9] The dominant ideologies are commonly accepted by those whose objective class position might otherwise lead to a more radical political stance. Therein lies an important explanation for the coexistence of class inequality and widespread political conservatism. Its political implications are far-reaching. Instead of trying to exhort workers to see the error of their ways by exposing the 'true' nature of capitalist class relations, the emphasis switches to challenging the institutional arrangements whereby capitalist ideology is perpetuated. It is a theme to which we return in the penultimate chapter.

A third approach imparts yet more fluidity to the interpretation of class by emphasising *distributional struggles* rather than structural class relationships. This is what its proponents call 'postmodern Marxism'.[10] The emphasis is on replacing an

Box 36.1

Class in contemporary capitalism

The following model, developed by Erik Olin Wright, shows a simple way of reconciling class analysis in the Marxist tradition with a recognition that the economic conditions of modern capitalism do not produce a simple dichotomy of capital versus labour.

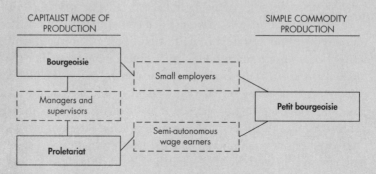

The capitalist class and the working class are represented as the key groups within the capitalist mode of production. Between these classes are managers and supervisors in 'contradictory class locations'. Meanwhile, a sector of simple commodity production, not eradicated by the forward march of capitalism, ensures the continued significance of a self-employed class or *petit bourgeoisie*. Small employers and semi-autonomous wage earners are represented as intermediate groups between the main categories, having hybrid characteristics in terms of (1) their ownership and control of property and investment, (2) their control over the physical means of production, and (3) their control over the labour power of others and over the sale of their own labour.

The model illustrates how class analysis can be developed. It provides a basis for both empirical measurement (such as the relative size of each of the groups in different nations) and political analysis (of class-consciousness or electoral behaviour, for instance). E.O. Wright's recent work provides more complex illustrations of how sociological analysis can be blended with the concerns of political economy.[7]

essentially dualistic conception of class with a more complex and nuanced analysis of class relationships that emphasises the processes of class formation operating at specific times in particular places. The analysis retains a Marxist character in stressing the existence of an economic surplus; however, there is no presumption that the surplus goes directly as income to the capitalist class. Rather, the surplus is the focus of numerous distributional struggles. Environmental movements, for example, can be effective in acquiring some of the surplus for cleaning up hazardous wastes or restoring environments degraded by capitalist enterprises. These struggles over the surplus are regarded as being as significant as struggles between capital and labour within the capitalist mode of production—the traditional Marxian focus. This reorientation of the analysis also draws attention to the articulation of class with gender and ethnicity.

RECOGNISING GENDER

Gender divisions in society are more visible than class divisions because there is no ambiguity about the basis of classification—people are either male or female. The term 'gender', however, refers specifically to the *socially constructed* roles for men and women. Gender inequalities are not necessarily based on biological differences. Often, the fact that men and women do different jobs is not attributable to their different physical capabilities. Men and women may face a different array of economic opportunities, and their average income levels are characteristically uneven. Any analysis of the political economy of inequality needs to take account of this gender dimension of the way in which the economy functions, as well as the class dimension. Then we are in a better position to consider strategies for change.[11]

Gender and class dimensions of inequality are not synonymous, of course. One way of conceptualising their relationship is in terms of the relationship between *patriarchy* and *capitalism*.[12] Put most simply, patriarchy is the power structure in which men dominate women, and capitalism as the power structure in which capital dominates labour. Analytically, the task is to examine the relationship between these two structures that are so closely linked in the real world. One way of doing this is in terms of the Marxist model of the circuit of capital, introduced in chapter 16. This situates gender within the sequential conditions for accumulation. The three conditions that are directly relevant in this context are the reproduction of labour power, the production of surplus value, and the realisation of surplus value. In each case, gender inequalities can be seen as functional for capital in the sense of helping to ensure that the requirements necessary for its expansion are met.

The *reproduction of labour power* is the fundamental precondition for the continued functioning of the economic system. First and foremost, it means producing and raising children. This is characteristically 'women's work'. Men play only a small part in biological reproduction—often a very small part indeed! Notwithstanding the fact that more men are involved in childrearing today than in the past, women remain the principal carers and rearers of children. In the advanced capitalist nations at least, it is also common for mothers to have to combine their role as childrearers with participation in waged work.[13] Other domestic labour also generally falls to women. Sustaining the existing workforce—maintaining health, providing adequate nutrition, and creating leisure activities conducive to physical and emotional well-being—is an important aspect of economic and social reproduction that is based in the household.

Not surprisingly, the study of domestic labour and the associated gender inequalities is a primary focus of feminist political economic analyses. The household is commonly said to constitute a *private sphere*, subordinate to the *public sphere* of paid employment and the political and economic institutions usually dominated by men.[14] It is typically excluded from the gaze of orthodox economics because the economy, from a neoclassical perspective, is defined in terms of production for market exchange. Yet, according to various estimates, the value of domestic economic production carried out in the household—disproportionately, but not exclusively, by women—amounts to about half of the gross national product.[15] The neglect of this crucial economic contribution of domestic production constitutes a significant gender bias in orthodox economics.[16]

How to situate the household sector in a reconstructed modern political economy is a contentious matter. At first sight, much, if not all, household production seems to have a non-capitalist character. Useful goods and services are produced, but usually for direct consumption rather than for market exchange; and, rather than direct wage-labour, intra-household income transfers are typical. Some families in which both men and women have paid jobs purchase domestic services (such as cleaning, ironing, cooking, even dog-walking) rather than do all their own domestic labour, but most is still done by members of the household. The provision of these services in the household is crucial to the functioning of capitalism. Capitalist employers need new generations of workers who are fed and reasonably well educated—'job-ready', so to speak. Schools and hospitals also have a role to play in the functions of social reproduction, but the nurturing capacity of the household is fundamental to the requirements of the economy as a whole.

The labour expended within the household is also provided typically at no direct cost to capital. There may be an indirect contribution, to the extent that firms pay taxes, and to the extent that those taxes go partly to family support payments, child allowances, and other transfer payments to households. However, unpaid domestic labour is an effective means whereby the cost of reproduction of labour power is shifted from firms on to the state and households themselves. Looked at from this viewpoint, it suits the class interests of capital to retain the household—and its typically gendered division of labour—as a subordinate, 'non-capitalist' sector of the economy and society. One might draw a parallel with the advantages the advanced capitalist nations derive from their coexistence with a poorer Third World that serves as a source of cheap resources, and mobile and disposable labour.

The *production of surplus value* is the second requirement for capital accumulation. The gendered character of *waged work* is the central feature here. Marxists have sought to apply the concept of the 'reserve army of labour' in this context because many women have had a more marginal attachment than men to the waged workforce. A striking historical example of this 'reserve army' characteristic was the sudden entry of women into paid jobs during World War II (to 'support the war effort') and their subsequent return to unpaid domestic duties after the war (resuming 'their proper place in the home').[17] However, the growing proportion of women who have become permanent members of the waged workforce in recent decades sits uncomfortably with the view of women as a 'reserve army'. Far from being marginal to wage-labour, more and more women have become direct and regular contributors to the production of surplus value.

The more persistent problem is the gendered division of labour in waged work. *Labour-market segmentation* entails distinctive concentrations of men and women in different industries and occupations, that is, in different labour-market 'segments'. Women have been disproportionately represented in occupations that are perceived to be extensions of their traditional household work—nursing, cleaning, primary education, the preparation of food, clothing manufacture, and clerical work, for example.[18] The patterns are not static; in the nineteenth century, for example, secretaries were usually male—the occupation becoming characteristically female only in the twentieth century. The gender composition of bank tellers has seen a similar shift more recently. In other fields, such as nursing and clothing manufacture, the gendered character of work remains striking. In the modern economy, the services sector has a range of occupations where face-to-face interactions are the key and client emotions have to be managed; not surprisingly, these are occupations where women are concentrated, too.[19]

Labour-market segmentation has a strong association with *gender-biased wage inequalities*. In so far as average wages tend to be lower for characteristically 'female' jobs, it is not surprising that a gendered inequality in the overall distribution of wage incomes persists. The higher incidence of part-time work among women also biases the distributional outcomes. Even after accounting for that factor, a ratio of about 4:5 for women's average full-time wage incomes relative to men's is typical.[20] Recognising the importance of redressing such systemic economic discrimination according to gender, governments have sought to prevent employers making differential wage payments to men and women doing similar jobs. However, where men and women are doing different jobs, a requirement of 'equal pay for equal work' does not eliminate gendered wage inequalities. The more complex principle of 'comparable worth' needs to be applied to wage-setting in those circumstances.[21]

The problem of *differential promotion prospects* is a further source of gender bias. Ensuring wage parity for people in different occupations, even breaking down the labour-market segmentation process, does not ensure equality of gender outcomes if there is gender bias in promotion processes. The problem of women 'interrupting' their career for childbirth is commonly cited as a justification for the observable inequalities that exist in this respect. Claims about a *glass ceiling* inhibiting women's career progress, including the progress of women who do *not* have children, suggest a more profoundly discriminatory process associated with perpetuating the 'boys' club' character of many business enterprises. The 'glass ceiling' may work against the interests of capital in the long term, for failure to take full advantage of the potential leadership roles of women constitutes a waste of human capital. Its persistence implies that, in this respect, patriarchal influences dominate.

In general, the gendered division of labour in waged work serves capitalist interests to the extent that it facilitates the production of surplus value by keeping down wage costs. This is the result, directly, of women's wages being lower than men's, on average. It is the result, indirectly, of gendered divisions among workers undermining the collective bargaining power of labour—the 'divide-and-rule' process at work.

What about the *realisation of surplus value*? This third requirement for capital accumulation has a less obvious link with gender divisions in the economy and society. For the capitalist system as a whole, the realisation of surplus value in a monetary form as profit depends primarily on the maintenance of a high level of demand for goods and services. Both men and women are consumers and, as such, both contribute to meeting this particular systemic requirement. However, women have usually managed a larger share of the consumption process—especially in the purchasing of clothing and day-to-day food and household items, rather than 'big-ticket' items like cars and electrical goods. The advertisers certainly seem to think women are the key consumer group, judging from the way they target commercials at them. These commercials commonly play on the presumed fears and aspirations of women—to be the 'perfect mother' who feeds her children the right breakfast cereal and washes their clothes in the most effective laundry detergent, for example. The role of women in the management of consumption is thereby linked with the perpetuation of sexist stereotypes. This reasoning suggests that women as 'shoppers', as well as 'housewives' and 'workers', are crucial to the functioning of the capitalist economy. This is the sense in which Galbraith describes women as comprising 'a crypto-servant class'.[22]

The distinctive economic positions of women and men can be analysed in various ways.[23] The political economic perspective presented here has a distinctly Marxist feminist angle, emphasising how the gender division of labour helps capitalism meet its own systemic requirements for reproduction and growth. This is not to deny some fluidity in patterns of gender inequality, or that government policies of anti-discrimination and affirmative action can make a difference. Certainly, it does not imply passivity in response to a situation of structural disadvantage. Indeed, it is a chain of reasoning with a politically powerful punchline—that the movement for gender equality, if it is to be fully successful, also involves a struggle against the prevailing structures and interests of capital.

EMPHASISING ETHNICITY

Economic inequalities according to ethnicity parallel gender inequalities in some respects. People of different ethnic origin are usually clustered in different types of occupations. They may face an unequal array of economic opportunities. Their average income levels are sometimes markedly uneven.

The nature and extent of those inequalities varies from country to country. In the United States, for example, the relative economic disadvantage of African Americans is notorious; even after nearly a century and a half of freedom from slavery, and despite government programs to promote 'black capitalism', economic disadvantage remains entrenched. The relative economic disadvantage of others, particularly people from Central and South America and the Caribbean islands, is equally striking. In England, immigrants from India, Pakistan and, again, the Caribbean have been the major groups to experience economic and social disadvantage. In Australia, the most disadvantaged ethnic groups are the Aboriginal peoples, but recently arrived immigrants, especially those from non-English-speaking-backgrounds, face particular problems in establishing socioeconomic equality. Immigrants to any nation usually 'do it tough' before they establish themselves; and in societies where racism is pervasive, a further impediment exists to achieving parity in economic opportunities.[24]

Is there a connection between racially discriminatory practices and the operations of capitalism? Since racism predated capitalism, it would be facile to suggest a simple or direct causal connection. One view is that it is quite *independent* of the economic system. From this perspective, racism, and the associated processes of discrimination and socioeconomic disadvantage, are not attributable to capitalism, and are equally likely to characterise any other socioeconomic system that might succeed it. Its roots are not economic—or, at least, not systemically so. The solution, accordingly, is independent of the economic arrangements of society—it is a matter of changing personal attitudes through public education or of developing institutions that foster greater mutual understanding among different ethnic groups.

Among social scientists who recognise an *economic* dimension to racism there are sharply divided views about whether capitalism ameliorates or accentuates the problem. In the former camp are neoclassical theorists, such as Gary Becker, who won the 1992 Nobel Prize in Economic Sciences for his application of orthodox economic reasoning to social phenomena. The neoclassical construction of his analysis emphasises the exercise of *individual choice* in competitive markets. It generally takes the tastes informing those choices as given. So, in respect of racial discrimination, we assume that some employers have a preference for white employees over black employers, that is, that they have some sort of 'racist inclination'. That being so, white workers will be in greater demand. In a market economy, that will cause the prevailing wage rates for white workers to be above those of black workers. So, racially discriminating employers must pay bigger wage bills than non-discriminating employers for the same number of workers. The former will have higher costs of production and therefore lower profits. In a competitive market economy, they will eventually be driven out of business. Only the non-discriminating employers will remain.[25]

Milton Friedman, taking a similar view, has argued that 'a businessman or entrepreneur who expresses preferences in his business activities that are not related to productive efficiency is in effect imposing higher costs on himself than are other individuals who do not have such preferences. Hence, in a free market they will tend to drive him out'.[26] Thus, capitalism eliminates racism.

Like neoclassical economics in general, the preceding argument rests on some distinctive assumptions. The origin of the original 'preference' for white over black (or whatever is the relevant racist inclination) is unquestioned. Both labour and commodity markets are assumed to operate in a competitive manner. There is no requirement that workers doing the same job be paid the same wage, irrespective of their race. This last assumption sits awkwardly with the fact that anti-discrimination regulations have now become common in practice. The neoclassical analysis would predict that such regulations would likely cause higher rates of unemployment among the less-favoured ethnic groups: in other words, enforced wage parity benefits those fortunate to be employed, but at the expense of those who now find it harder to get work at all.

From a political economic perspective, the problem of racial discrimination looks quite different. Racism is seen not so much as a matter of individual preference but as a feature of the normal functioning of institutions—*a systemic rather than personal phenomenon*. The origins of the discriminatory preferences and the institutional mechanisms by which they are reproduced come under more critical scrutiny. So do the economic interests with a stake in their perpetuation. This imparts an essential historical dimension to the analysis. It also puts capitalism back in the dock. If, for example, the perpetuation of racism results in divisions among workers that undermine their propensity to achieve higher wages through collective action, then one may judge that to be in the general interests of capital, irrespective of individual employers' racist or non-racist preferences. The 'divide-and-rule' strategy, while not necessarily *causing* the racism, may thereby *perpetuate* it to the advantage of capitalist employers.[27] The political implications of this view are strikingly different from those of the neoclassical analysis. The inference is that, like the movement for gender inequality, the movement against racism must challenge the prevailing power structures of capitalism as a necessary, but not sufficient, precondition for eradicating economic disadvantage.

The *principle of circular and cumulative causation*—introduced in chapter 25 in the context of the study of institutional economics—has particular relevance to the explanation of racism and its perpetuation. It helps to explain why a disadvantaged minority group, identifiable by its skin colour, for example, may face a vicious cycle of discrimination and material disadvantage. Being relatively poor, its members are likely to be poorly dressed, poorly educated, and more inclined to anti-social behaviour, such as crimes against property. That fuels the belief that the minority group is inherently different, unworthy of a helping hand, and probably best avoided, if not actively suppressed. In effect, the legacy of past discrimination becomes a justification for further discrimination.

Add the *spatial* dimension and the problem is compounded. This is most obviously the case in 'ghettoes', where minority groups are geographically concentrated. The possibility of an individual achieving upward economic and social mobility is thereby made more remote. However, spatially targeted policies can play a significant role in the redress of economic inequalities in these circumstances. The same applies to inequality between classes; spatial segregation accentuates the differences of access to economic opportunities, but also provides a basis for policies to ameliorate, if not eradicate, the inequalities. In both cases, however, the precondition for the redress of inequalities is a government with a strong commitment to using vigorous income redistribution and anti-discrimination policies.

If the market will not eradicate discrimination—if, indeed, the most powerful participants in the market profit from it—then it necessarily becomes a concern for the state. Proponents of purposive intervention, sometimes drawing on the principle of circular and cumulative causation, contend that policies of *affirmative action* are needed. The victims of discrimination must be given explicit preference (in education and employment, for example) for a period of time before equality of opportunity can eventually be established. Not surprisingly, opponents of such a policy call it 'reverse discrimination' and emphasise its apparent incompatibility with efficiency in the use of human resources during the period of transition.[28] A 'level playing field' is evidently an admirable goal, but the path towards it is fraught with conflicting economic interests and political judgments.

CONCLUSION

The analysis of economic inequalities according to class, gender, and ethnicity is central to modern political economy. This chapter has merely touched on some of the major concerns, and indicated some lines of fruitful enquiry. A further analysis would emphasise the *interconnections* between these three dimensions of socioeconomic inequality, recognising that the socioeconomic conditions of disadvantaged groups are multidimensional. The different economic positions of black, female employees and white, male employers, for example, are attributable to differences of race, gender, and class that are multiplicative rather than additive.

Integrating considerations of class, gender, and ethnicity illuminates the complex patterns of social stratification. These issues of social structure are also integral to the dynamics of capitalist development, affecting the process of capital accumulation as well as the distribution of income, wealth, and economic opportunities. In other words, they are of fundamental economic, as well as social, significance.

Equally important are the politics. The complexity of class, gender, and ethnicity as dimensions of 'who gets what' in the modern economy is matched by the complexity of social struggles to make a difference. The drive to eradicate exploitation, discrimination, and oppression takes many forms, generating more diverse social movements than a more traditional focus on the binary opposition of capital and labour would suggest. Focusing on the study of these inequalities and the social movements to which they give rise is the source of much of the politics in modern political economy.

Deciding on the appropriate policy responses to inequalities associated with class, gender, and ethnicity is a contentious matter. The traditional focus of those committed to the eradication of unjustifiable inequalities has been the 'politics of redistribution'. This seeks to create greater equality of opportunities, even equality of outcomes, through the redistribution of income and social expenditures. A quite different approach emphasises the 'politics of recognition', emphasising the distinctiveness of minority groups and the desirability of maintaining the cultural differences, while at the same time reducing economic inequalities.[29] This entails an official commitment to 'multiculturalism' and the recognition of the special rights of indigenous peoples in respect of land, for example. The two approaches do not sit comfortably together. Can public policy move on both fronts simultaneously? It is a big challenge for the institutions of the state.

Thus, concerns about economic inequality, like other contemporary concerns about environmental decay, technology, industry and work, lead us to reflect on the potential for political control over market processes in the pursuit of broader social goals. It seems that all roads lead to the state ...

CHAPTER 37

The Political Economy of the State

What is the state?
Whose interests does it serve?
Can the state be used as an instrument for economic and social progress?

Analysis of the state is central to political economy. It makes no sense to treat it as external to the economy, as a *deus ex machina* that 'intervenes' intermittently in an otherwise self-regulating economic system. The state has been integral to the history of capitalist development. It has been involved in providing infrastructure and services, regulating business behaviour and markets, establishing and enforcing property rights, managing trade relationships, imposing taxation, and spending public revenues (making governments, without exception, the largest consumers of economic resources within individual nations). The precise form of these activities has varied from country to country, according to particular historical conditions. A comprehensive political economic analysis needs to identify both the general patterns and the more nation-specific aspects. Understanding how the state is shaped by competing political economic interests and ideas is the core *analytical* concern.

For those who would wish to engineer new directions of economic development, whether capitalist or otherwise, the question of the state also raises the explicitly normative *political* concerns. Judging what role the state can play is the key issue in formulating political strategy, whether the intent is to expand or contract the range of 'hands-on' functions the state performs. Social democrats contend that the long-term trend is, and should be, towards expanding the sphere of politics—making more of our economic and social choices inherently political.[1] How best to steer the state and use public policy to mediate between the interests of capital and labour—between differences of class, gender, and ethnicity generally—then becomes the focus. For those of a more libertarian disposition, the question is how best to roll back the state and thereby extend the realm of individual (market) freedoms.[2] Either way, a *prescriptive* view of the state is implied.

Perhaps it is because these analytical and prescriptive elements inexorably intertwine in discussions of the state that the topic is notoriously complex, if not confusing. Analysis of what the state *does* tends to be mixed up with prescriptions about why it *should* do those things or do different things. This chapter seeks to impose some order by setting up a general framework for analysis of the state, before examining each of the three principal prescriptive positions: radical, reformist, and conservative.

AT THE INTERSECTION OF DEMOCRACY, CAPITALISM, AND BUREAUCRACY

The state comprises a set of interrelated institutions. At its core is the government. Indeed, the government is so obviously central to the state that one may be forgiven for using the two terms interchangeably. However, therein lies the source of some confusion because the state includes other institutions, too. Alongside governments—and acting as a partial check to their activities in formally democratic states—are parliamentary assemblies. Political parties not in government oppose, and may use whatever channels are formally open to them to impede particular government policies. Where there are bicameral parliamentary arrangements, for example, and an opposition 'has the numbers' in the upper house, that may constitute a major constraint on a government's power. So, too, may tensions with subnational governments, where federal arrangements exist within a nation's polity—as in Australia, Canada, Germany, and the United States, for example. Other checks and balances arise from the relationship between governments and other institutions within the state apparatus, such as the public service, the judiciary, and the armed forces.

Generalising about the state as if it were a unified entity is fraught with difficulty. Yet, the other extreme, of restricting analysis of the state to the individual institutions within it, is problematic for different reasons. Rich descriptive detail is generated— the very stuff of 'political science'—but there is a loss of perspective on broader political economic aspects. This is indicative of a universal tension in social enquiry, of course, between the focus on the specific and the general. An intermediate construction recognises the need to keep the focus on the whole, but to emphasise tensions between the parts. In the case of the state, this requires differentiation between its democratic, capitalistic, and bureaucratic aspects.[3]

The state is *democratic* in so far as it is accountable to the public at large and subject to control through electoral processes. In the advanced industrial nations with long democratic traditions, we tend to take that for granted, while grumbling about imperfections of the democratic arrangements in practice. However, not all parts of the state are democratic, even in principle. Public servants, judges, and military personnel are typically recruited, promoted, and dismissed according to institutional procedures in which the public has no direct voice.[4] Direct elections are focused primarily on the periodic contest for seats in parliamentary assemblies. Under the Westminster system, government is then formed by the party with the majority of seats, or whatever workable coalition of minorities can achieve an effective majority. To the extent that the elected government then has power over other elements within the state—through appointing senior public servants and policy advisers, for example—it may be said that the democratic impulse radiates outwards to other parts of the state (although, in practice, the processes are often soured by the influence of political patronage).

Not all countries have even this imperfect democratic element at the core of their states. Dictatorships have been common, particularly in many of the former colonial nations of Africa and South and Central America. In those cases, it is the political inclinations of the senior military personnel and control over the armed forces that is decisive. Such interludes of democratic government as may occur depend heavily for their stability on the elected political leaders commanding the loyalty of the military. In countries that pride themselves on democratic traditions that have had no recourse to military intervention, there is often evidence of *economic* forces producing rather different forms of political closure. In the United States, for example, it is inconceivable that any presidential contender who did not have, or could not raise, millions of dollars to finance their electoral campaign would be successful. Generally, economic inequality can effectively subvert the egalitarian principles formally underpinning democracy. As Galbraith reminds us, 'forthright purchase of votes was commonplace in various parts of the United States until comparatively recent times'.[5] Rather more circumspectly, Arthur Okun notes that 'money is used by some big winners of market rewards in an effort to acquire extra helpings of those rights that are supposed to be equally distributed'.[6]

The influence of these economic factors brings us to a second theme: the extent to which the state is a *capitalist* state. The relationship of capitalism to the state is a characteristically political economic concern that may be seen as a specific example of the base–superstructure perspective discussed in chapter 13. The focus is on how the functioning of political institutions is constrained and shaped by the structure of the economic system, and the interests of capital in particular. Phrases in the political economic literature such as 'the capitalist state' and 'the state in capitalist society' directly draw attention this connection.[7] It is not simply a matter of economic wealth buying political influence. What is at issue here is a more systemic relationship. At root, it is structural. If the state is concerned with managing or steering the economy, it must have due regard to the dominant interests within it whose co-operation is essential for the achievement of successful outcomes. To put the point negatively, if the state fails to ensure the conditions for capital accumulation and an economic crisis occurs, this is likely to precipitate political crisis and change of government. Not surprisingly, it is a scenario that senior decision-makers within the state would normally wish to avoid. Working in tandem with the interests of capital has a self-evident logic in these circumstances.

The third aspect of the state is its *bureaucratic* character. Recognising this aspect shifts our gaze to the *internal* structures within the state and how they shape its functioning. Instead of looking at how the state responds to external pressures—whether from the citizenry via democratic processes or from capitalist economic interests— the bureaucracy itself now comes under scrutiny. The term 'bureaucracy' is not used here in a derogatory sense. Indeed, as the sociologist Max Weber emphasised, bureaucratic procedures are generally necessary in large organisations to ensure that there is consistency in the processes of public administration. However, once a large state apparatus is created, its members do tend to develop their own interests, which may be different from, even contrary to, those of their 'political masters' in government. Viewers of the famous BBC television series 'Yes, Minister' and 'Yes, Prime Minister' will be familiar with this theme. Those with experience of working in large institutions, whether in the public or private sectors, will probably have firsthand experience of it. Its normal manifestations are an emphasis on the desirability of continuity in public administration and security for public administrators. Policy paralysis is a predictable outcome when these concerns are at odds with the reforms sought by governments. In the extreme, but only in the extreme, explicit corruption of state officials is implied, in which case the bureaucratic character of the state tends to be more closely aligned to its capitalistic character.

A schematic representation of these three influences on the state, together with quotations emphasising each aspect, appears in figure 37.1. How the three dimensions *interact* is the key analytical question, of course, because it is evident that they are not wholly compatible. Further exploration of this can usefully be couched in terms of competing viewpoints about the politics of using the state apparatus to achieve socio-economic change. Not surprisingly, there are three broad positions, corresponding to their respective emphases on democracy, capitalism, and bureaucracy.

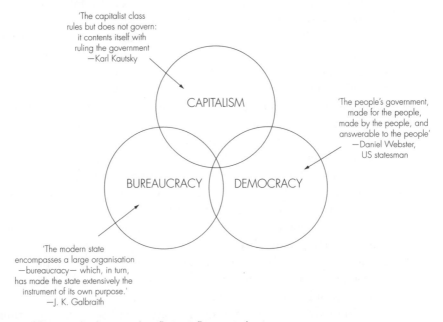

Figure 37.1   The state of the state: the diverse and conflicting influences in the state.

THE STATE AS AN INSTRUMENT FOR SOCIAL PROGRESS

One does not necessarily have to be of a democratic temper to see the state as an instrument for social progress. As noted in chapter 9, the tradition of mercantilist thought and practice, prevalent in the seventeenth and eighteenth centuries, saw a strong state and a strong economy as the twin necessities for national power. This was in an age before democratic rights were extended to the people as a whole. Emphasising the need for state-directed policies to ensure strength and stability was a pragmatic response to conditions of growing international economic rivalry. It was this mercantilist emphasis on the necessary regulatory role of the state that Adam Smith reacted against, arguing that it tended to stifle enterprise. But even Adam Smith was cautious about the consequences of market freedoms. He supported British colonialism and the naval power that the state provided to support it, seeing this as securing the big market necessary for the detailed division of labour and for greater economic liberties in Great Britain. Smith also thought that a significant role for government, supplemented by the moral influence of the Church, would continue to be necessary to ensure the 'social bond' that the pursuit of commercial gain might otherwise threaten. Thus, a conservative concern for social stability continued to put the state in the spotlight, despite the growing influence of 'economic liberalism'. The awkward blend of these two currents, observable in Smith, continues today in the positions to the right of centre in economic policy debates.

The 'statist' inclination had yet stronger roots in Germany. Friedrich List, author of *The National System of Political Economy* published in 1841, is particularly notable for his view about the importance of national strength for economic survival.[8] The liberal case for freedom of trade might suit British interests, he argued, but would likely result in greater British domination over less economically developed nations. German national interest required a different, state-centred, approach. German intellectual culture was also of less liberal inclination than its British counterpart, emphasising a more corporative sense of community. The German 'historical school' of economic enquiry reflected this—stressing the social and historical context of economic activity, rather than the abstract theorising based on 'rational economic man', which became the hallmark of the British approach to economic analysis. As noted in chapter 24, this historical school was to have a major influence on the development of institutional economics.[9]

These differences of analytic orientation are not of purely historical and academic interest. They were—and continue to be—manifest in different views about the appropriate role of the state in economic management. The modern *neo-liberal* view, emphasising the virtues of free trade and individual enterprise, contrasts with the *corporatist* view of the state, which emphasises the need to consciously engineer and secure cooperation between the major interest groups in the economy. The latter inclination is reflected in various ways in the works of Veblen, Galbraith, and contemporary post-Keynesian advocates of incomes policies (as discussed in chapters 24, 26 and 31, for example).

An 'interventionist' position on the state is even to be found within the neoclassical economic tradition. As noted in chapter 23, the economic problems arising from the niggardly supply of public goods in free-market economies, and the problems of imperfect competition and of 'externalities', may be held to justify a substantial ameliorative role for the state. This strand of neoclassical economics thereby concedes there is a significant case for government in correcting the anomalous tendencies in 'free-market' economies. The assumed primacy of the market remains distinctive, though. The state intervenes only to apply 'band-aids' to an otherwise healthy economic body. The implicit presumption is that enlightened state policies can help to reconcile capitalism with broader social concerns about efficiency, equity, and environment. Only the lightest touch is needed, however. Here, in effect, is a view of the state as an instrument of reform by *default*, stepping in only when the market fails to ensure an optimal allocation of resources.

The view of the state in Keynesian economics, at least in its mainstream 'bastard Keynesian' interpretation, has a similar character—although it recognises the need for a more substantial range of policy measures. Government intervention is warranted, according to this perspective, because of the basic flaws of a free-market economy. In this case, the principal difficulty is that of ensuring continuous full employment and, as a secondary concern, controlling inflationary tendencies. That provides a rationale for government policies to manage and stabilise an otherwise unstable economy. It may even extend to 'a somewhat comprehensive socialisation of investment'. Again, there is no significant political economic *analysis* of the state; instead, the implicit assumption is that it can be an instrument for effective reform, just so long as it is informed and guided by people of intelligence and sound values (like Keynes!).

Fabianism shares this latter presumption, but marries prescriptions about reform to goals of an explicitly socialist character. The early Fabians, like Sidney (1859–1947) and Beatrice Webb (1858–1943) and George Bernard Shaw (1856–1950), considered that greater knowledge about economic and social conditions would be the key to forging incremental improvements in public policies. Finding out about the conditions in which people work, their occupational health hazards, patterns of remuneration, and attendant social problems, for example, would lead to legislative and regulatory changes producing more socially beneficial economic outcomes. The state would be the vehicle for that process of reform.[10] The enfranchisement of all citizens would ensure that the state—or at least the government—would no longer represent the interests of only the dominant class. Not surprisingly, when these sentiments were becoming widespread in the early twentieth century, Fabians saw the then newly established Labour parties as instruments of reform. Subsequent disillusionment with the ability, or even the inclination, of Labour parties to engineer evolutionary socialism in practice has weakened the Fabian tradition over the last half century. Yet it remains a significant intellectual current in the analysis, and advocacy, of progressive economic reforms.

The underlying tension in any reformist political economic agenda is between *strong reformism* and *weak reformism*. The former runs the risk of provoking a destabilising backlash from those who own and control the bulk of the capital, if the policies go against their interests. The latter runs the risk of loss of support among the citizenry if the slow pace of reform leaves expectations and aspirations for change frustrated. There is no easy solution to this dilemma. As the British socialist intellectual R.H. Tawney said, you can peel an onion layer by layer but you can't skin a tiger paw by paw (and capitalism, by this reasoning, is surely one big pussy cat).[11]

The notion of 'radical reform' may be considered a practical response to this dilemma. The British political economist Stuart Holland talks about this as a means of bridging the long-standing divide between reformist and revolutionary currents in leftist politics; in effect, it is the assertion of the strong reformist case.[12] André Gorz, the French social scientist whose prescriptions for radical change in the distribution of work and incomes were considered in chapter 35, has reasserted this view more recently. In his words, 'the task of politics here is to define intermediate strategic objectives, the pursuit of which meets the urgent needs of the present while prefiguring the alternative society that is asking to be born'.[13] This sounds like a remarkable blend of pragmatism and idealism. However, it is not difficult to cite positive examples. One is the redistribution of working time, dealing with the immediate problems of unemployment and overwork, while simultaneously 'prefiguring' more fundamental

challenges to the capitalist wages–work nexus in the longer term. Another is the introduction of a carbon tax as a practical policy measure to deal with environmental decay,
and as a step towards producing the attitudinal and structural economic changes necessary for the transition to ecological sustainability. As with Fabian socialism, the
advocacy of such reforms is based on the underlying presumption that the state can be
a vehicle for economic changes that address fundamental social needs violated by the
immediate interests of capital.

SERVING THE INTERESTS OF CAPITAL

Other currents in political economy—Marxism, most obviously—are less sanguine
about the possibilities of progressive reform. Indeed, scepticism towards claims about
the state serving the 'national interest' is well-nigh axiomatic, Marxists seeing such
claims as typically masking a class interest. The key question is: how does the state
actually relate to the conflicting class interests in a capitalist society? The characteristic answer emphasises the dominant tendency to serve the interests of capital. The
simplest and most often cited expression of this view is the statement in the *Manifesto
of the Communist Party* by Marx and Engels: 'the executive of the modern state is a
committee for managing the common affairs of the capitalist class.'[14]

The supplementary questions are *why* and *how* this role is played by the state. It is
in answering these questions that a distinction between structuralist and instrumentalist theories of the capitalist state is usually drawn.[15] The *structuralist* approach
emphasises the pressure on the state to act in this way because of the necessity to
secure the conditions for *capital accumulation*—it must prioritise the pursuit of economic growth. The state is also necessarily concerned with *legitimisation*—it must
ensure that the existing socioeconomic structure is regarded as legitimate in the
eyes of the citizens. The former requires that the government, and the state in general, be continually mindful of the need to ensure profitability, not necessarily for all
firms, but for capital in general. The latter may require some ameliorative policy
measures, such as income redistribution or welfare state provisions to help the poor.
The task is to find an effective combination of policies for capital accumulation and
legitimisation—for example by devising a tax system that is effective in producing
the necessary revenues, without violating capitalist class interests.[16] Maintaining the
structure of the capitalist economy and society requires nothing less.

The *instrumentalist* variant on the Marxist theory of the state puts more emphasis on
the *personnel* within the state apparatus. In so far as politicians, judges, and senior members of the armed forces and public service have backgrounds and values in common
with members of the capitalist class, they can be expected to have common interests,
too. The 'old school tie' and club memberships play a part in this story. So, too, does
freemasonry—at least in certain sections of the public service and the police force.[17] This
starts to make the process linking economic and political interests and ensuring coherence within the state apparatus sound conspiratorial. Perhaps, but it is not necessarily
so. All one need posit is that the confluence of interests and values between the dominant economic class and the political elite leads to a generally harmonious relationship.
The use of the state as an instrument by the capitalist class then becomes relatively

uncontroversial, notwithstanding the veneer of accountability to a broader citizenry.

The globalisation of capital is often said to compound this tendency for the state to serve the general interests of capital. As argued in chapter 27, globalisation tends to further constrain the policies of states, to the extent that there is a fear of capital flight in response to 'unsympathetic' government policies. Trying to create the conditions conducive to investment by multinational businesses tends to force states into *beggar-thy-neighbour* competition. Reducing wages, trade union rights, business tax rates, and environmental protection are the characteristic policy responses. Faced with these dominant pressures, Marxist political economists argue that the prospects of progressive reform have become yet more remote.[18]

However, this implies a greater degree of unanimity than is actually the case. Marx himself did not develop a comprehensive analysis of the state, and there are numerous places in his writing where one may discern support for particular measures of reform. Notwithstanding the polemical, revolutionary tone of the *Manifesto*, one can find in it a 'shopping list' of reformist demands, on which he and Engels thought the movement for socialism could focus. The socialist tradition has been replete with controversy about the possibility of progress through the state ever since the 'revisionism' debates between Marx and Eduard Bernstein in the late nineteenth century. Bernstein argued that an evolutionary transition from capitalism to socialism was possible, a view that Marx denounced as incompatible with a revolutionary perspective. The controversy continues in today's debates over the scope for 'radical reform'.

Almost without exception, states have played a greater role in capitalist economies over the last century. While many of these state functions have directly served the interests of capital, this has not been the case all the time. The extensions of protection against racial and sexual discrimination in the workplace, occupational health and safety provisions, environmental protection, and urban 'zoning' to prevent incompatible land uses are just a few examples. Of course, one may take the view that any policies serving to defuse potential social discontent are, by definition, in the interests of capital, but this is a very uncompromising stance. On that reading, just about anything the state does fulfils its pro-capitalist functions of facilitating accumulation and/or ensuring legitimisation. The role of the state in serving the interests of capital becomes a tautology so long as capitalism remains the dominant economic system.

THE STATE AS AN IMPEDIMENT TO SOCIAL PROGRESS

A quite different critique of the state comes from an *anarchist* position. Anarchists have had a bad press, but they have a coherent political philosophy. One recurrent theme is the preference for voluntary cooperation rather than the exercise of state power. The state is generally seen as an instrument of oppression—in this sense an even more fundamental obstacle to social progress than the class exploitation on which Marxist political economy focuses. It is a chain of reasoning that derives, in part, from the *aversion to coercion*. As Giovanni Baldelli puts it, 'coercion, whether by society or individuals, runs counter to the needs and purposes of the individual and is therefore evil. It forces a human being to behave according to the needs, feelings, thoughts and will of another, as if he had none himself'.[19] The state, as the source of officially sanctioned coercive power, is necessarily a principal target of this ethically based anarchist critique. In a capitalist society, this position converges with the Marxian view of the state; but anarchists go further in arguing that the problems with the state apply to other social formations, not only the capitalist state. The state, from this perspective, is fundamentally problematic.

Coming from a different political perspective, but arriving at essentially the same conclusion, are the proponents of *public-choice theory* within orthodox economics. Strange bedfellows indeed! In principle, public-choice theory is not aligned to any particular political belief, but in practice it shares the same assumptions about individualism and the rationality of market exchange that pervade neoclassical economic theory. As D.C. Mueller puts it, 'the assumption that the electorate is ignorant and greedy underlies much of the public choice literature'.[20] According to the public-choice theorists, such an electorate gets the politicians it deserves! Favours are bestowed on interest groups in order to gain their political support, thereby creating 'inefficiencies', 'distortions', and 'overload' in the aggregate, as the number of government promises and policies extends beyond the capacity to deliver. The public service bureaucracy, not being subject to the 'market for votes', has a yet stronger propensity to inefficiency, according to this reasoning. The resulting problems of 'government failure' far outweigh the problems of 'market failure'. 'Slimming the state' by reducing the range of functions that government performs is the characteristic prescription.

Public-choice theory has been subjected to trenchant critique.[21] Essentially, the theory extends neoclassical reasoning from the economic into the political arena. As such, it carries all the general limitations of that theory, as discussed in chapters 18–23, while also having the disadvantage of being applied in an arena where 'market logic' is of more dubious status. The presumption that political actors behave like *Homo economicus* is particularly contentious. There is an essentially collective element in political choice that requires explicit consideration of the processes by which collective goals are formulated and implemented. The assumed 'purity' of the market system with which the 'corrupted' political process is contrasted is deeply problematic. In the words of Peter Self:

> Those thinkers such as Friedman and Hayek who laud the market system, and want it to operate largely free from control, seem to be living in a vanished world. Theirs is a world of individuals bettering themselves and their society through hard work, enterprise and saving in some useful trade or occupation. Such individual efforts are still highly valuable to society and still continue to be made, yet they seem rather far removed from modern economic realities. The virtues of hard work and saving lose much of their moral appeal in a society where economic growth is directed more towards titillating individuals into consuming luxuries than meeting more basic needs; and the virtues of private enterprise seem less obvious when it takes the form of financial speculation, monopolistic profits or tendentious advertising.[22]

The 'free-market' alternative has a less clear rationale in these circumstances. So, notwithstanding the scepticism about the state expressed by libertarians on both the political Left and Right, we come back to where we started—wondering about the way in which collective control over our economic destinies may be implemented.

THE STATE AS AN ARENA OF STRUGGLE

What are we to make of these competing views of the state? The most even-handed approach is to acknowledge at least a partial truth in each of the three principal viewpoints.

From the proponents of the state as an instrument for social progress comes the simple, but fundamentally important, observation that *the presence of the state is not at issue*. As Evan Jones puts it, 'reformers see policies for stabilisation and regulation not merely as desirable but as inevitable. Societies (including the business community itself) will not tolerate the anarchy of unregulated commercial activity. When one set of stabilisation measures breaks down, a new set will ultimately have to be formulated and constructed. Measures of economic and social stabilisation have to be on the policy agenda, whether one likes it or not'.[23] So, the key issue from a political economic perspective is not *whether* to have public policies but *what type* of public policies to have. Will they be consciously developed and systematically co-ordinated or *ad hoc*? Will they be coherent or incoherent?

From the Marxist political economists comes a similarly basic, but also fundamentally important, observation: *the importance of power inequalities in shaping public policy*. The power of capital in general is a central consideration, but it continually vies with the power of labour. The latter depends on the effectiveness of its industrial and political organisation and its links to other social movements, such as those concerned with issues of social justice, human rights, and environmental quality. Political coalitions that bring together the interests of labour with social movements can potentially be a significant challenge to the interests of capital and a powerful force for political economic change.[24] Moreover, the interests of capital are not always unified; different 'fractions' are commonly divided. Multinational capital versus local small business, manufacturing against mining, rural interests versus urban capitalist interests—the types of intra-class conflict are many and varied. Proponents of progressive reforms can take advantage of that by making alliances with supportive fractions of capital in the process of lobbying state personnel.

From the more libertarian perspective comes the reminder that *the possibility of abuse of state power* is ever present. Analytically, this suggests the need for investigation of governmental and administrative processes to be part of political economic enquiry—not leaving this matter exclusively to the separate discipline of 'political science'. Politically, it suggests the need for emphasis in policy processes to be placed on measures of public accountability, challenging the self-serving practices of corrupted political elites, and fostering a genuine commitment to 'public service'.

Putting these three themes together produces a view of the state as an arena of struggle. The competing views about the state can be interpreted in this context as ideologies marshalled for political economic purposes.

This draws attention to the articulation of its democratic, capitalist and bureaucratic aspects. This chapter has considered the three aspects separately, but in practice thay are interwoven. On any specific policy issue, whether it be tax reform, tariff policy or superannuation policy, the interests of the general public (and segments thereof), the capitalist class (and factions thereof), and the bureaucracy (and different departments therein) vie for influence.

CONCLUSION

The analysis of the state is not a matter of purely academic concern. It is crucial for all who are concerned with contributing to progressive political economic change. Each of us has limited personal time and energy, so the strategic question of how to use that time and energy is crucial. Seeking change by working *within* the apparatus of the nation state, as a public servant, or by becoming a politician, is one option. Working *against* the state, through participation in protest movements of various kinds, is another. Building alternative communities, perhaps in conjunction with strategies focused on *local government*, is a third strategy. On a quite different spatial scale, seeking to influence *supranational institutions* like the United Nations, the International Monetary Fund, the World Bank, and the World Trade Organization, is a fourth possibility. It may be asking too much of political economic analysis to resolve the personal dilemma of how best to channel your energies for socio-economic change—choosing from among these options for working in and/or against the state—but it helps to clarify the broad strategic options.

There is a strong contrast here with conventional economics, most of which has little to say about the nature of the state. Neoclassical economics is essentially a theory of markets. It offers few significant insights into improving the effectiveness of public-sector management. Its major contemporary application, public-choice theory, is largely a supporting ideology for a right-wing libertarianism. It is not so much an analysis of what the state does, as an explanation of why it should stop doing it.

While modern political economy offers no ready-made alternative to fill this vacuum, it does situate the question of the state in a broader analysis of modern capitalism. It identifies the state as an arena of struggle—of conflicts arising from the capital–labour relationship in the sphere of production, of conflicts over distribution, and of a wide range of other tensions in modern capitalist society. It is a reminder that the economic is not separable from the political. This is the crux of political economy.

PART IX

Whither Political Economy?

Conflict and progress

CHAPTER 38

Why Do Economists Disagree?

What different theories of knowledge underpin the competing approaches to economic analysis?
What ideologies underpin the disagreements?
Is reconciliation and/or synthesis possible?

The contest of economic ideas is ongoing. Controversies, discord, even bitter confrontations, pervade economic debate. This makes the subject interesting, albeit difficult, to study. It is frequently perplexing to members of the general public who, not unreasonably, expect economists to 'get their act together' and speak with a more unified voice. The reasons for the lack of harmony warrant further consideration. Is it a matter of personal caprice—the product of the cantankerous disposition of economists? Such a possibility cannot be wholly discounted. However, we have already seen enough of the contest of economic ideas to indicate some more fundamental reasons for the disharmony. Underlying the competing schools of thought are different methodological and philosophical positions. It is time to make them explicit.

Economists disagree about what they consider the appropriate *methods of enquiry*, and this is reflected in their different constructions of economic analysis. Their disagreements also derive from distinctive *value judgments*, based in rival traditions of political philosophy. These differences underpin the endless professional disputes over the relative merits of theoretical modelling, applied research, and historical/institutional investigations, of 'big-picture' assessments versus more detailed case studies, even of what constitutes useful 'facts'. They further underpin the sharply divergent views about what would make the economy serve social needs better, about what those social needs are, and how such changes might best be effected.

HOW DO WE KNOW WHAT (WE THINK) WE KNOW?

Economic disagreements are rooted in different views about the nature of knowledge itself. It is interesting to see how this fundamental issue—formally, *epistemology*—shapes economic enquiry. It is related to the general question of how we understand the world in which we live.

Think back to being a child. It was a very small world, was it not? A baby's personal range of vision is initially very limited. Mobility remains restricted, even as eyesight improves. For the first few months, the relevant world is the cot, the mother (or whoever else does the feeding), and little else. Then, little by little, the world expands as the child grows. *Spatially*, it expands from the bedroom to the whole house, then to the neighbourhood, later a school, and then perhaps to a university and the broader world of work and recreation, maybe eventually involving nation-wide or international (even interplanetary?) travel. *Socially*, a similar cycle is typical—beginning with parents and siblings, and widening to include neighbours, schoolmates, teachers, work colleagues, and others.

What has this to do with the nature of knowledge? The point is that, as the relevant social and spatial scales widen, we are confronted with a correspondingly expanding array of experiences and information. It sometimes threatens bewilderment. Modern information technologies accentuate this. We have to develop some means of sorting out what information is useful and what is not. We have to have some basis for deciding what, among all the information to which we are exposed, we accept.

The initial basis is *authority*. In the early stages of our lives, our parent(s) effectively define for us what is true. We look to them as the source of authority. Eventually, though, the statement 'because mummy says so' starts to have a hollow ring. Then comes the perplexing, but delicious, moment when you discover your parent(s) have got something wrong, or at least seem to be at odds with other authority figures. Who are those rival authorities? Other parents, schoolteachers most obviously, and perhaps priests or other religious figures. As they arrive on the scene, parental fallibility becomes evident. However, the new authorities may eventually prove fallible too, losing our respect as repositories of useful knowledge. At university you may find courses of study purposely constructed to emphasise the disagreements within and between various disciplines. And books like this. If the 'experts' cannot agree, authority based on expertise collapses as an effective basis for sifting information and deciding what is true, rather than what is merely expedient.

What alternatives exist? *Faith* is a possibility. In an uncertain world, faith may serve valuable purposes—as a source of personal love, strength of commitment, and direction in life. However, it cannot reasonably serve as a basis for making judgments about the truth of competing claims about knowledge. It is, in effect, an extreme version of the 'authority' approach. It also entails an element of arbitrariness: in whom does one have faith? In Jesus or Mohammed, in Karl Marx or Milton Friedman? In practice, competing schools of thought in many academic disciplines comprise practitioners sharing more or less unquestioned beliefs. Economists adhering to a particular school of thought usually exhibit faith, perhaps most strikingly in the cases of Marxism and neoclassicism. It is less evident in the case of the politically intermediate and less clearly bounded schools of institutionalism and post-Keynesianism. But, in all cases, as a basis for making judgments that have legitimacy beyond a circle of fellow disciples, faith simply will not do.

A pragmatic alternative focuses on the *organic* character of the acquisition of knowledge. Think again of that expanding universe we confront as we grow up. The bases on which information is accepted or rejected as we start to 'make up our own minds' may be quite varied. Sometimes it is a matter of 'seeing is believing': we observe the characteristics of things and the connections between them. Sometimes it is a matter of logic: we accept propositions because they are based on sensible reasoning. Sometimes it is a mixture: we do not see the light in the refrigerator go out when we close the door (unless we foolishly climb inside), but we accept that it (probably) does because we observe that other switches in the house turn lights on and off, and we accept (usually implicitly) some theory about electricity that enables us to extend that generalisation. Little by little, our prior experiences interact with information generated in new situations, which is accepted or rejected according to its consistency with those prior understandings. In effect, whether or not something is accepted as 'true' depends on whether it fits in with what we already believe.

This organic view of the processes by which we sift and acquire knowledge emphasises that knowledge does not accrue in a random way. Rather, it accrues through the use of an 'image' that helps us to sift through the array of information with which we are presented in our daily lives.[1] An 'image' gives us a relatively coherent framework for interpreting the world in which we live. It is resilient in the face of new information that does not fit—but not indefinitely so. Repeatedly challenged by information that is fundamentally incompatible with it, the 'image' itself may eventually be radically, and perhaps quite suddenly, transformed.

It is tempting to draw a parallel with Kuhn's notion of paradigms in scientific enquiry and how these may periodically be transformed (as discussed in chapter 7). But the issue here is more about how individuals respond to information that conforms to, or challenges, their existing understanding and beliefs. It is an issue that goes to the heart of, not only our personal development and learning experiences, but also the very nature of knowledge itself.

EPISTEMOLOGY AND ECONOMICS

The different theories of knowledge, and how they influence the nature of economic enquiries, can be formally classified in the following manner.[2]

Empiricism

Empiricists regard *experience* as the source of all knowledge. In other words, it comes through direct engagement with the real world—through seeing, touching, hearing, smelling, tasting. In respect of the social sciences, sight is the most important of these sensory bases for knowing. 'Seeing is believing' is the familiar popular expression of this view.

The research method implied is *observation* and *induction*. Question: how to find out? Answer: go and look. A process of sifting through the observations can then be undertaken in order to find patterns that can form the basis for generalisations. This is the essence of the inductive method.

This research method is characteristic of substantial parts of the work of institutional economists. As illustrated in chapters 24–7, institutional economists have eschewed the construction of abstract economic theory in favour of an empirical approach to the study of the economy. This is perhaps most strikingly the case in the 'measurement without theory' undertaken by Wesley Mitchell in his studies of economic growth and fluctuations. It is also characteristic of those institutional economists who have emphasised the close observation of corporate behaviour. Others, like Veblen and Galbraith, more concerned with broad generalisations, claim to derive their insights from observations (of the behaviour of the 'leisure class' or the 'technostructure', for instance) rather than from explicitly theorised positions. Even the notion of the economy as a 'system' sometimes sits uncomfortably with the institutional economists' down-to-earth study of distinct economic events, actual economic institutions and their changing character over time.

Rationalism

Rationalists regard *reason* as the primary means by which we come to understand anything. Knowledge, from this viewpoint, is the set of logical implications of innate ideas. In social enquiry, for example, propositions such as the 'primacy of the individual in society' or the 'self-interested character of individual motivation' are innate ideas on the basis of which more complex theories can be constructed.

The associated methodology is one of *deduction* and model-building. Propositions are deduced logically from the presumed self-evident axioms. No direct observation of the real world is required—hence the common representation of this process as 'armchair theorising'.

It is characteristic of neoclassical economics. One of the founders of the neoclassical tradition, W.S. Jevons, made this position explicit when claiming that 'the science of Economics, however, is in some degree peculiar, owing to the fact that its ultimate laws are *known to us immediately by intuition* or at any rate are furnished to us ready made by other mental or physical sciences' (italics added).[3] As illustrated in chapters 18–23, the deductive method is central to the model-building process in neoclassical theory. Starting with the innate idea (or assumption) that consumers maximise utility, neoclassicists construct a model of their optimising behaviour that requires no observation of actual consumers. Similarly, basing a model of the firm on the assumption of profit maximisation leads to the deduction of the 'marginal cost = marginal revenue' decision rule—it requires no study of real firms.

Critical rationalism/critical realism

Critical rationalists regard experience as the source of knowledge but recognise that experience is usually dependent on theory. It is usually selected, organised, and interpreted according to already held theoretical concepts. However, the soundness of those theoretical concepts needs to be reconsidered in the light of experience. A continuous *iterative process* is implied, combining empiricism and rationalism through the confrontation of experience and reason.

The research method of critical rationalists typically involves the *juxtaposition of model-building and observation*. The models are 'tested' against observations of the real world and rejected if they prove unsatisfactory. Falsifiability is the essential characteristic of competing hypotheses—continually attempting their refutation is the required scientific practice.

Macroeconomics developed from the basis of *Keynesian economics* makes some claim to using this methodology. Macroeconomists in general love model-building, using their models to interpret and predict measurable macroeconomic trends. However, in practice, some of the models seem to have a longevity warranted by neither their explanatory power nor their predictive accuracy.[4] So, while many economists would wish to claim that they adopt a critical-rationalist stance—indeed, this is the most 'respectable' methodological position in the profession—there is a tendency not to practise what is preached. Moreover, there is also ambiguity about what constitutes satisfactory or unsatisfactory performance of these models: should it be their explanatory power or their capability to yield good predictions?

Picking up on this last concern, the proponents of 'critical realism' challenge the emphasis critical rationalists usually place on statistical modelling and predictive capacity. They argue that more attention needs to be focused on the structures, powers, and processes that explain observed economic and social phenomena.[5] This emphasis on *causal* structures is a distinctive feature of the critical realist alternative, and is more characteristic of research in modern political economy, drawing on institutionalist and Marxist traditions.

Praxis

It is also important to consider the *social* construction and use of knowledge. Social scientists emphasising this feature often take the view that passive, detached observation is not fruitful, producing only 'unreal' abstractions. Useful knowledge comes through direct *interaction* between the investigator and the world being investigated.

The associated research method this implies is direct *participation* in the process being studied. Such direct engagement is the antithesis of scholarly detachment. In the case of social enquiry, it means becoming involved in processes of social change. It means coming to know more about the world through participating in changing it.

In political economy, this method is obviously characteristic of *Marxism*, but it is also evident in *feminism* and *environmentalism*. These are simultaneously bodies of analysis and political programs. A view of knowledge as socially constructed has also had widespread influence in other social sciences through the work of Michel Foucault.[6]

Again, significant qualification of these generalisations is warranted. In Marxism, for example, there are both rationalist and empiricist elements. The Marxist theory of value is essentially rationalist in construction. It takes as axiomatic the proposition that labour is the source of value and develops the critique of capitalism (as a system of class exploitation) by logical extension of that reasoning. Meanwhile, an empiricist element comes through the detailed study of industry, of the conditions of the workforce, and of the historical development of capital–labour relations. Modern Marxists differ markedly in the extent to which they adopt these different epistemological stances in their research.

The element that distinguishes Marxists in practice from those who are merely scholars of Marxism is *praxis*. Praxis is not simply a matter of applying economic analysis to the 'real world'; rather, it is a matter of developing the analysis through the process of active political engagement. Feminism and environmentalism also have this essential element of praxis. Understanding patriarchy is inseparable from the political process of trying to eradicate it. Understanding environmental decay is part and parcel of the process of promoting change to ensure a more ecologically sustainable political economic system. Rationalist, empiricist, and critical-realist elements may be identified in various works within these traditions, but this emphasis on praxis is the most distinctive element.

Economic discourse as 'conversation'

These four categories of theories of knowledge and research methodologies are not, in practice, clearly separated. The third obviously overlaps with the first two, while the fourth cuts across the first three. A fifth category can also be added. This is qualitatively different because of its emphasis on the *contingent and subjective* characteristics of knowledge.

Recent contributions by two economic geographers put this alternative view in a positive light. Alan Scott talks of 'a conception of knowledge as an assortment of relatively disconnected (but internally reasoned) fragments, partially formed constellations of ideas and attitudes that are picked up, worked on for a time, then pushed aside again as the tide of social change sweeps along'.[7] Trevor Barnes argues further: 'Knowledge is acquired in many different ways; there is no single epistemology that reveals "the truth". To see how knowledge is acquired, we must examine the local context; that is we must see how knowledge is obtained, used and verified in a particular time and place'.[8] This is a relativist viewpoint, denying the existence of absolutes in knowledge.

Support for this pragmatic stance to the pursuit of knowledge may be derived from Richard Rorty's view that metaphors rather than statements determine most of our philosophical convictions. Rather than seeking 'to hold a mirror up to nature', Rorty prefers the metaphor of 'conversation'. Acquiring knowledge is not a matter of 'getting reality right', but rather a process of open-ended engagement—'a matter of acquiring habits of action for coping with reality'.[9]

This sceptical stance is more in tune with the contributions of those, like Thomas Kuhn and Paul Feyerabend, who stress the *social* characteristics of the research process. It is also consistent with McCloskey's observation that the 'rhetoric' of economists employs a wider array of persuasive techniques than any formal methodology would allow.[10] It is how most economists actually work. What distinguishes the political economists is that they are more frank about this. Whereas the orthodox economists see 'applied' work emanating from their hypothetico-deductive core theory, modern political economists tend to be more eclectic in practice, as illustrated in the preceding four chapters.

Extreme relativism is a feature of *postmodernism*. It not only denies the possibility of objective knowledge, but also the existence of any 'reality' beyond, or independent of, the various discourses of the investigators. Therein lies a methodological vacuum, putting into question the possibility of progress in political economy, or social science generally. The postmodernist stance is capable of yielding valuable insights into how people in different walks of life interpret their own situation and experiences. However, from a political economic perspective, the problem is that such epistemological agnosticism provides no basis for assessing the relative effectiveness of different explanations of economic phenomena: your 'truth' is simply what you see.[11] So, whatever its relevance as a basis for cultural studies (where it has been particularly in vogue), this methodology seems incapable of providing a basis for a coherent analysis of material economic conditions.

The interim conclusion to this chapter is obvious enough. It is that, because different views of knowledge underpin different schools of economic thought, *synthesis* is difficult. One might wish to bring together the useful contributions of each school, but doing so butts up against the existence of irreconcilable methodological differences. The descriptive work typical of institutional economics cannot be simply 'pooled' with the abstract theories of neoclassical economics. Macroeconomic modelling is bedevilled by disagreements over the relevant evidence and testing procedures to apply. The praxis of the Marxists is anathema to the neoclassical theorists, while the 'armchair theorising' of the neoclassicals is equally unacceptable to the Marxists. The institutional economists join the Marxists in rejecting neoclassical methodology as a legitimate basis for trying to understand a complex and changing world, but shy away from the value theory on which much of Marxist analysis has been based.

To make matters yet more complex, these *methodological* obstacles to a synthesis of the competing schools of economics are accentuated by fundamental differences of an *ideological* nature.

IDEOLOGY IN ECONOMICS

Ideologies are systems of belief. They may provide support for an existing social, economic, or political order, or be the basis for a critique of it. Pro-capitalist ideology continually vies with anti-capitalist ideology, for example. There is nothing unusual about that; all societies have dominant ideologies, but critical, even subversive, alternatives are common, too.

Such ideologies pervade society. All of us are influenced by them, knowingly or unknowingly—usually the latter. Indeed, the hallmark of an effective ideology is its broad acceptance, such that the views it embodies come to be regarded as 'natural' or self-evident. Where the dominant ideology legitimises the existing socioeconomic arrangements, the *status quo* is likely to face no major challenge from within; but more volatility can be expected if a critical, or subversive, ideology becomes widespread. In the extreme, those dissident ideologies may fuel revolutionary challenges.

Economics has always had an ideological character. This is hardly surprising, given the central importance of economic interests in shaping social order and political processes. It is not necessarily the case that economists consciously set out to serve this ideological function. They certainly do so sometimes, but, even if they do not, interest groups will filter out and select the particular economic ideas that suit their purpose.

Because economic discourse has this inherently ideological character, it is futile to debate whether the subject is, could be, or should be *value-free*. Economists have wasted much ink on such claims, sometimes even titling their textbooks 'positive economics' in order to advertise their purportedly value-free character.[12] In practice, different currents of economic analysis have always been intertwined with value judgments and have served political functions.[13] That is not to denigrate the subject; rather it is to acknowledge its practical importance in the real world. The presence of ideology only becomes a problem when it takes the form of mystification. If, for example, the centrality of the perfect competition model in neoclassical theory leads to the belief that capitalism is actually like that model, therein lies mystification.

On the other hand, the ideological character of economics can be a positive attribute. *If* perfect competition is indeed an 'ideal' state, one may infer that making real-world market structures perfectly competitive would be a desirable aim of economic policy.

Looked at in this light, the ideological element in economics can be integral to its policy-oriented or strategic purposes. The key question then becomes: which purposes? One has to ask *what vision of society* informs the construction and practical use of economic ideas. This, not surprisingly, is where economists disagree.

POLITICAL PHILOSOPHIES

Some of the differences in political stance adopted by classical political economists, neoclassical economists, Marxists, institutionalists, and Keynesians should be clear from preceding chapters. However, it is useful to step back to see from where they spring. Their common basis in *humanism* is an important starting point. Humanist views about our relationship to the world in which we live became prevalent in the seventeenth and eighteenth centuries. They provided the philosophical foundation for modern approaches to the arts and sciences, to social enquiry in general, and political economy in particular. Three key features of these humanist principles can be identified:

- as the terminology implies, humanism is a *human-centred*, rather than a God-centred, outlook
- humankind is regarded as the *embodiment of reason*—capable of controlling the social environment and thereby influencing its own destiny
- *social progress* is possible.[14]

These propositions, so seemingly 'normal' now, were deeply challenging to beliefs about human destiny and the 'will of God'. The challenge to the expectation that life for one generation would be pretty much as it had been for preceding ones was particularly fundamental from a political economic perspective. Having opened up the possibility of progress, all sorts of technological, social, economic, and political innovations could then operate. The gate was opened for scientists and engineers to reshape nature for that social purpose.

The gate was also opened for political ambitions and political acts seeking to create a better future for the masses of ordinary people previously consigned to lives of drudgery and servitude. Liberation through political economic transformation beckoned. The Declaration of Independence of the United States of America in 1776 (the same year that Adam Smith's *Wealth of Nations* was published), abolitionists' speaking-out against slavery, the French Revolution of 1789, and the French Constituent Assembly's passing of the Declaration of the Rights of Man and the Citizen are all examples of this quest for liberation from servitude and the will to assert the dignity of all people. The French revolutionaries' famous rallying cry of 'liberty, equality, fraternity' is an enduring symbol of belief in the possibility of social progress.

From this common basis in humanism came the two great traditions of political thought of the last two centuries: *liberalism* and *socialism*. These two rival political philosophies may be differentiated according to their key beliefs:

- the liberal focus on *individual* initiative contrasts with the socialist focus on *collective* action
- the liberal emphasis on reward according to *merit* contrasts with the socialist preference for distribution according to *need*
- the liberal inclination towards equality of *opportunity* contrasts with the socialist emphasis on equality of *outcome*
- the liberal ideal of individual *freedom of choice* and free enterprise contrasts with the socialist preference for *community values* and social ownership or control of the means of production.

In terms of their political economic implications, the attitudes to *private property* and *the state* constitute the crucial differences. The liberal philosophy is favourably inclined to the institution of private property, of course. This has its clearest expression in Adam Smith's claim that the 'invisible hand' of the market would, subject to certain qualifications, reconcile self-interest with socially beneficial economic outcomes. This positive attitude to the market has as its corollary a more cautious, often negative, view of the state. Herein lies a significant tension between the general tradition of liberal political philosophy and 'economic liberalism' in particular. The latter's antipathy to the state, flowing through into modern neo-liberalism, is not characteristic of liberalism in general. However, a general wariness of the political economy of the state is understandable in the historical context. In the eighteenth century, when the state was enmeshed in mercantilist practices, it was understandably seen as an obstacle (in Great Britain particularly) to the individualistic, free-enterprise principles that the classical political economists espoused. The direct link between the state and the interests of landowners was further reason to presume that the state would pursue sectional interests ahead of general community interests. To put the economic liberal view in class terms, it extended the freedoms of private property *vis-à-vis* the state, thereby opening up more economic opportunities for the ascendant capitalist class.

Socialism, by contrast, has always been more hostile to private property, at least in regard to ownership of the means of production. Socialists have no antipathy to private property *per se*; they oppose it only when it conveys the power to employ and exploit others. Socialism thereby shares with liberalism an emphasis on the desirability of personal freedom, but 'freedom of the individual' is held to be an illusory notion because people only become free (or unfree) in a social context. The *class* character of capitalism prevents freedom being enjoyed by all. The state provides no solution to this problem because, under capitalism, it operates generally to support the interests of the capitalist class, as discussed in the preceding chapter. Freedom, this chain of reasoning suggests, requires a simultaneous assault on private property in the means of production and on the class-biased character of the state. This is the essence of the revolutionary socialist project.

During the last century, these two great traditions of political philosophy had to come to terms with major changes in the nature of private property and the state. Therein lies the explanation of further significant ideological divisions between competing schools of economic thought.

What were those major changes within the two great traditions of political philosophy influencing economic beliefs? For *liberalism*, the major challenges have arisen from the growth of corporate power and the substantially more extensive functions carried out by the capitalist state. Responses to these trends, which sit so uncomfortably with the basic tenets of classical liberalism, have been basically of two forms. Some have 'maintained the faith', arguing that the trends are fundamentally undesirable, and that the task of liberalism is to stem, if not reverse, the tide. Hence the rhetoric, if not the policies, consistently emphasising the need to split corporate giants into smaller enterprises and to 'slim the state'. This is the position of the right-wing libertarians, or neo-liberals, in so far as they do not ignore corporate power altogether. Other liberals have taken a more pragmatic stance, welcoming (albeit with reservations) the expansion of the state as a balancing force against corporate power and as a vehicle for the extension of market-augmenting policies in pursuit of goals like equality of opportunity. This is the general position of modern liberal democrats.[15]

Somewhat similar tensions have shaped the development of *socialist* ideologies over the last century. The most obvious dilemma has been how to respond to the changes, actual and potential, in the character of the capitalist state. The extension of democracy has made the state less obviously an instrument of class domination. With universal suffrage and with the development of labour and social democratic political parties, there arose in the twentieth century the tantalising prospect of pursuing socialist goals, not through revolution, but through incremental changes to public policies. Chapter 37 considered the different responses to these new political opportunities.

Mirroring the split in the liberal tradition, the split between the evolutionary and revolutionary wings within the socialist tradition is explicable in these terms. The revolutionaries in the Marxist camp have 'kept the faith' in the need for a rupture with the capitalist state as a precondition for the achievement of socialist goals. Their scepticism about the possibility of incremental reform is reinforced by the current processes of corporate globalisation. Radical reformists, on the other hand, advocate seeking whatever progressive reforms are possible, working within the state in the attempt to transform its character in a more socialist direction. From this perspective, the globalisation of corporate capital adds to the difficulties of reformism, but does not fundamentally negate the possibilities of using democratic institutions—local, national and international—in the pursuit of socialist-oriented goals.[16]

Thus, four principal strands of political philosophy and practice can be seen to have evolved from a common basis in humanism. These are libertarianism, liberal democracy, social democracy, and revolutionary socialism. They form a *spectrum* rather than four distinct categories. Figure 38.1 lists selected economists whose political stance illustrates the different positions on this spectrum. Rather more contentiously, the major schools of economic thought are represented in terms of the part of the spectrum occupied by the principal practitioners within each school. In each case there is a range, but it is a sub-set of the full set of political positions.

A more fully comprehensive stocktaking would also need to consider other minority positions. Left libertarianism (anarchism), conservatism, and the Catholic corporatist tradition spring to mind in this context. However, this analysis suffices to

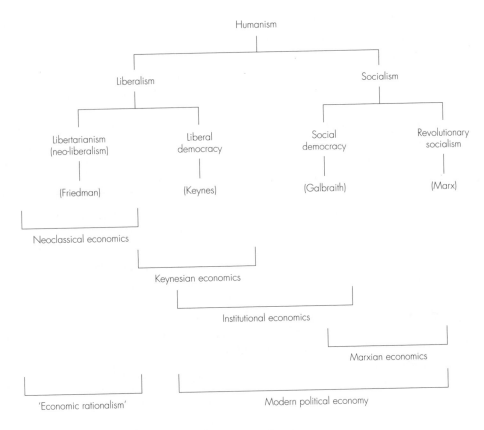

Figure 38.1 Competing political philosophies and currents of economic thought.

illustrate the connections between the major schools of economic thought and the most influential political philosophies.

If nothing else, this analysis brings into sharp relief the political obstacles to the synthesis of economic analyses. Keynesians, Marxists, and neoclassical and institutional economists cannot be expected to easily find points of agreement given the fundamentally different political philosophies that infuse their economic analyses. Just as differences in the underlying theories of knowledge and research methodologies impede an easy synthesis of economic ideas, so too do these fundamental differences of political judgment and political purpose.

CONCLUSION

Because economic prescriptions are rooted in different frameworks of analysis and competing political ideologies, they must be subject to continual scrutiny. As a guiding first principle, it is essential to exercise *constant vigilance* about the nature of economic propositions—their sources, underlying assumptions, and political purposes. A second principle is to *subvert the dominant paradigm*, for progress in understanding and changing the world is more likely to come from the clash of ideas rather than the linear accretion of theory-dependent knowledge. Third, it is good to remember that *diversity is preferable to uniformity*. As the philosopher Paul Feyerabend has argued, the semblance of absolute truth is usually the result of absolute conformism.[17] A range of political economic perspectives, though sometimes perplexing, is the hallmark of an open society.

These principles recognise the impossibility, perhaps even the undesirability, of a complete synthesis of the competing economic analyses. This may seem a rather negative conclusion, pessimistic about the possibility of progress in political economy. That is not the appropriate inference. By recognising the differences between the schools of economic thought, which derive from their views on the nature of economic knowledge and their preferred political philosophies, we can see what each has to offer. We can draw from the various analytical 'tool kits' the tool that is appropriate for the task at hand. We can reconstruct a modern political economy to come to terms with the complex and changing character of the world around us.

The obstacle to progress, looked at from this viewpoint, is not the diversity of the discipline but spurious notions like 'economic science' and 'positive economics'. Their denial of legitimate diversity constitutes dogma. It is better to live with the diversity, sorting out facts, judgments, and ideals as systematically as we can and with as much cool objectivity as possible in practice.

This conclusion is deliberately couched in a pluralist manner to draw attention to the obstacles to its realisation in practice. It is the absence of a 'level playing field' for economic ideas that gives the challenge of political economy its distinctively radical edge.

CHAPTER 39

A Level Playing Field for Economic Ideas?

What are the institutions that shape the influence of economic ideas?
What biases are thereby imparted in economic prescriptions and beliefs?
What can be done to foster the dissemination of progressive political economic ideas?

Economics is not unusual in being a controversial discipline riven by competing currents of analysis. What is distinctive is the direct link between the competing ideas and competing *material interests*. Some economic ideas provide legitimacy for the existing social order and therefore have ready appeal to those with a large stake in its maintenance. Others provide a critique of contemporary capitalism, giving inspiration to those who see themselves likely to benefit from its 'root-and-branch' transformation. Yet other economic ideas, with reformist implications, appeal to specific groups whose economic circumstances could be improved as a result of particular economic policies—consumer groups, small business people, or farmers, for example.

This is not to imply that self-interest alone determines the acceptability of competing economic ideas. The association between economic ideas and broader social values and judgments—different views about what constitutes a 'good society'—is also important, especially for a broad stratum of intellectuals. Nor is it to imply that the relationship between the *contest of ideas* and the *contest of interests* is always simple. Neoclassical economics, for example, does not directly justify the dominant position of those who own and control the means of production. Indeed, it does not mention such 'class' interests at all. Its critics contend, however, that it serves the interests of capital by presenting the market economy in its most favourable light, thereby making capitalism appear a more efficient and equitable arrangement than it actually is. Hence the view of orthodox economics as 'bourgeois ideology'.

How is an economic ideology like this disseminated and perpetuated? How does it retain its dominance in the face of competing views like Marxist and institutional economics, which draw attention to the conflicts, contradictions, and abuses of economic power that capitalism fosters? How, indeed, does it come to be accepted even by many people whose interests it would seem to violate? These questions are explored in this chapter with reference to the key institutions involved in the transmission and propagation of economic ideas. The contest of ideas takes place, not on purely intellectual terrain—a 'level playing field of economic ideas'—but within institutions that systematically favour some viewpoints and marginalise others. Most prominent among these institutions are schools and universities, the public service, the media, 'think-tanks', and, of course, the institutions of corporate capital itself.

SCHOOLS AND UNIVERSITIES

The teaching of economics—to millions of students worldwide annually—is constrained by the prevailing orthodoxy within the curriculum. What is in the textbooks shapes what is taught in the classroom. Some of the 'better' students subsequently become academic economists, going on to produce further rounds of basically similar textbooks. It is not a totally closed loop. Some teachers take advantage of whatever academic freedom they enjoy to explore more dissident ideas, in pursuit of the principles of liberal education that educational institutions usually formally espouse.[1] Books that suggest a less conventional approach to the teaching and study of economics occasionally appear. These are exceptions to the general rule, however. What has to be explained is *why* and *how* the orthodoxy retains its dominance.

The simplest explanation is *inertia*—the tendency of teachers to simply reproduce, with minor embellishments, what they themselves were taught. It is undoubtedly a major factor, strikingly evident in the structure of the leading international best-selling textbooks over the last half century. Ever since Paul Samuelson's introductory *Economics* effectively defined the field over half a century ago, there has been remarkable consistency in the basic structure of the standard textbooks, and even in the details of the models they present. The influence of Keynesian analysis has waned somewhat during that period, as a consequence of the monetarist assault and the neoclassical push to develop the 'micro foundations of macroeconomics'. However, the basic division of the subject into micro- and macroeconomics remains well-nigh universal, while chapters with the headings 'demand and supply', 'perfect competition', 'factor markets', and so on appear with monotonous regularity. Total uniformity is only impeded, it would seem, by such minor product differentiation as is required for textbook marketing in conditions of monopolistic competition. Teachers of orthodox economics—dominated by this neoclassical approach—will often frankly admit they teach it because 'this is what economics is', even though they may have personal doubts about its usefulness in illuminating the real world. This is not mere cynicism (although that is not unknown); fundamentally, it is the effect of systemic disciplinary reinforcement.

How the orthodoxy maintains its dominance reflects the pervasive influence of *authority structures* within educational institutions. Recall the discussion in the preceding chapter of how people are influenced by authority figures, such as parents and teachers, in the process of finding out about the world in which they live. Although 'authority' is a fundamentally flawed basis for the definition of useful knowledge, its use seldom, if ever, disappears. It is certainly pervasive in educational institutions. Think of students writing university essays; they support their arguments with quotations from, or references to, the leading authorities in the field. The students who most effectively craft their essays from those sources are awarded the best marks and go on to honours, and sometimes postgraduate, degrees. If they become academics, they enter at the base of hierarchical employment structures within faculties, where the senior professors are the dominant authority. It is compatibility with the judgments of these senior academics that is commonly crucial in career success. Dissidents have a harder time—if they manage to survive at all. The senior academics also act as editorial 'gatekeepers' for the leading professional journals, deciding what will be published and what will not. Their status gives them the effective authority to decide what will see the light of day.

This is a sequence of *professional socialisation* in which the processes of reproduction have a self-reinforcing character. It is not peculiar to the economics profession, but it is certainly pronounced in this field. Of course, there *is* often lively debate among academic economists, but it is mainly within parameters set by the prevailing orthodoxy. At times, the exclusion of dissident views is conscious, such as when the key decision-makers in the less prestigious educational institutions seek to emulate the more prestigious universities, which are the citadels of orthodoxy. At other times, it is the result of wilful negligence or disinterest—as in the case of the orthodox economics professor who said of a junior lecturer (with a strong post-Keynesian orientation) that he had decided not to renew his contract because he could not see the point of his work.[2] In the more extreme case, dissident views are simply purged from a faculty because they directly challenge the prevailing orthodoxy in the profession.[3]

If these processes of professional reproduction—and occasional blatant discrimination—were purely internal to the educational institutions, one might think them of minor significance. The tendency towards conformity is regrettable, to be sure. Inculcating students in a particular analytic framework rather than exciting them with more profound intellectual challenges is a missed educational opportunity. Discrimination against dissidents also results in a depletion of the 'human capital' that could counter the tendency to disciplinary stagnation. But the bigger problem is that these processes within educational institutions have wider social consequences. The students themselves tend to change as a result of studying economics, becoming less inclined to altruism and cooperation and more imbued with individual materialistic values.[4] This is, in effect, the cloning of *Homo economicus*. The teaching of economics also affects—it is tempting to say infects—the functioning of other institutions in the wider society. The biases flow through into the world of practical economic policy.

THE PUBLIC SERVICE

Many of the best economics graduates—usually those who have most thoroughly absorbed the orthodoxies at the core of the syllabus—are employed in the public service, particularly in key policy departments like Treasury, and in other important institutions such as the Reserve Bank. Although their initial responsibilities may be quite minor, some eventually attain senior positions where they can exert a substantial influence over the administration of economic policy and the advice given to government ministers about desirable policy changes. What sort of influence and advice? There is significant evidence that its tenor derives from their earlier economic studies. It does not necessarily come directly from particular textbook models, rather from the general orientation imparted by their schooling in orthodox economics.

One interesting study by Michael Pusey, for example, shows that the values held by senior Australian public servants have strong connections with whether they specialised in economics during their university studies.[5] Pusey conducted in-depth interviews with these bureaucrats, revealing a pervasive adherence to 'economic rationalist' values. Important differences were revealed between the attitudes of those who had studied economics at university and those with a more liberal education. The former were twice as likely to say that the distribution of income is biased to wage and salary earners, and to say that trade unions have more power than business interests. They were significantly more likely to approve of deregulation of the labour market, and to deny the existence of any exploitative character to capital–labour relationships in a market economy.

Pusey's study provides evidence that the character of a university education does indeed have a lasting effect on attitudes to public policy. He judges this to be 'an even more powerful predictor of orientations to policy and management than such other variables as age, socioeconomic status, school, years of service in the Public Service, seniority in the SES [Senior Executive Service] and perhaps even gender'.[6] He does not claim it to be the sole influence undermining a broader view of the state as an instrument to steer the economy and temper its inequalities with welfare state provisions and income redistribution. The aversion to policies for industry development, for example, is as much the product of the agencies responsible for industry policy being marginalised in the decision-making processes relative to the central agencies, such as Treasury, where the orthodox economists dominate. In all these respects, the hollowing-out of state capacity for effective economic management can be seen as a product of 'economic rationalism' invading the public service. The product is indeed a dramatic set of 'interventions' (using the term in its proper sense, to denote acts that radically change the character of the state). Therein lies a great irony because, to be consistent, one might think that the first act of a free-market economist in the public service should be to resign!

THE MEDIA

There is also a direct link between economics education and the media. Some of the best economics graduates go directly into journalism, including financial journalism as well as more general current affairs reporting. Their usually limited exposure to competing frameworks of economic analysis may constrain how they report and interpret economic developments in the real world. Whether this effect operates as strongly as it does for public policy bureaucrats is doubtful, though. Any such bias is likely to be tempered by the broadening effect of previous studies in other social sciences or in communications. Journalism also seems to attract rather less conformist individuals, and giving a 'new angle' on the developments being reported is a distinctive aspect of the journalistic ethos.

In practice, the constraining influence within the media is the nature of the organisations within which the journalists work. Most are themselves capitalist organisations. In the print media, in radio, and in television, the principal businesses are run for profit and therefore have a collective interest in reproducing the conditions of capital accumulation. Writing of the print media in particular, British media analyst Wayne Parsons sums up the situation as follows:

> Newspapers in many senses could be said to lie at the very core of the capitalist process and the 'free market' idea and consequently have a key role to play in the way in which 'economic culture' is communicated and its myths and discourse sustained and propagated

… They not only sell the information which keeps the wheels of the economy turning but in so doing they also purvey and reinforce the values and ideas, language and culture, which underpin the existence of the market economy … [They] serve as crucial mediators between the price system and the political system, and enable politicians, businessmen and men of ideas to set the parameters of ruling opinion.[7]

How does this 'translate' into particular journalistic limits? Media proprietors, most notoriously Rupert Murdoch, are not averse to direct interference in determining editorial content. Usually, however, they rely on appointing editors whose general 'line' will make such interventions unnecessary. An implicitly accepted set of beliefs about what constitutes acceptable limits on 'sensible' opinion prevails. The American author Daniel Hallin talks about this in terms of three regions: the 'sphere of consensus', the 'sphere of legitimate controversy' and the 'sphere of deviance'.[8] The first constitutes accepted wisdom—evidently requiring no debate, nor even a disinterested journalistic stance—and the journalist's role is as 'advocate or celebrant of accepted values'. The second allows for controversy in political and economic debate, but within the parameters set by the two-party system, the associated electoral contests, and legislative and administrative processes. It is lively, but limited. The third is simply off-limits. It is 'the realm of those political actors and views which journalists and the political mainstream of the society reject as unworthy of being heard'. If journalists do venture into this last territory, it is usually to expose or condemn, thereby reinforcing the consensus.[9]

This analysis has proved to be particularly prescient for the current era during which neo-liberal values have been dominant, if not hegemonic, in discussion of economic policy. Tariffs on imported goods are bad because they create 'economic distortions'—all that need legitimately be discussed is the timing and the rate at which they should be reduced for different industries. Public enterprises, lacking the drive of the profit motive and the disciplining effect of competitive markets, are inherently inefficient—the principal questions are only about the selection of priorities for privatisation and the appropriate extent and prices of asset sales. Dissident voices on these issues do occasionally get a hearing, but the dominant feature is continuous reinforcement of the limits of acceptable political economic discourse.

Individual journalists also rely extensively on information about economic issues that is provided by institutions who are themselves not disinterested. Facing the pressure to produce articles and features on a regular, sometimes daily, basis, journalists have recourse to the most accessible information sources. These include the research departments of major banks who feed regular bulletins on contemporary economic affairs to the journalists. Some of the most assertive of the 'information providers' are corporate-funded 'think-tanks'.

'THINK-TANKS'

It should come as little surprise that the large, powerful institutions of corporate capital fund other organisations to produce information and promote values conducive to their interests. Often nominally established as 'research centres', these 'think-tanks' are usually directly concerned with propaganda. Not much thinking necessarily occurs. Their typical *modus operandum* is the dissemination of more or less subtle pro-business information and more or less blatant 'free-market' ideology through schools and the media, and the direct lobbying of decision-makers in government and other public institutions. They make common cause in this endeavour with right-wing economists, including some of quite senior professional standing.

A particularly illuminating analysis of 'think-tanks' and their international impact is provided in Richard Cockett's book *Thinking the Unthinkable: Think-tanks and the Economic Counter-revolution*.[10] What is the counter-revolution to which Cockett refers? Essentially, it was an organised reaction against the influence of Keynesian economics, which its critics claimed was paving the way for 'collectivism' and 'welfarism' in public policy. Right-wing libertarian intellectuals and capitalist business people, not necessarily having much in common in other respects, found unity in their opposition to what they regarded as a pernicious assault on 'free-market' capitalism. 'Think-tanks' like the Mont Pelerin Society (composed of conservative economists from all over the world), the Institute of Economic Affairs (in the United Kingdom), and the Centre for Policy Studies (also in the UK) provided the vehicle for their cooperation. Financed by individual business people, most notoriously the wealthy chicken farmer Anthony Fisher, these 'think-tanks' provided means by which the views of economists like Milton Friedman and Frederik von Hayek would have a wider influence in society. Their impact on politicians in the 1980s is now legendary, former British prime minister Margaret Thatcher, in particular, being greatly influenced by their work. It is little exaggeration to say that therein lay much of the momentum for the neo-liberal ascendancy in matters of economic and social policy.

The work of these 'think-tanks' is ongoing. In the United States, the best known among literally hundreds of conservative and neo-liberal 'think-tanks' are the Heritage Foundation and the Hoover Institute. In Australia, the list includes the Institute for Public Affairs, the H.R. Nicholls Society, the Centre for Independent Studies, the Tasman Institute, and the Sydney Institute. The occasional critical, even 'left-of-centre' research centre is set up by progressive activists in the attempt to

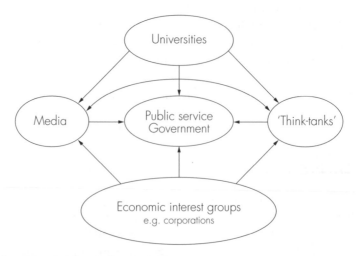

Figure 39.1 Institutions determining the influence of economic ideas.

provide some balance.[11] However, the difficulty of obtaining financial support is a perpetual problem for research centres of genuinely independent inclination. Corporate funding causes a seemingly inevitable right-wing bias in the overall character of 'think-tanks'.

EXTENDING THE INTERESTS OF CORPORATE CAPITAL

Figure 39.1 illustrates some of the important links between these various institutions, which, individually and collectively, 'tilt the playing field' on which economic ideas compete. Underpinning the processes are the interests of corporate capital. The corporations themselves are not always the most visible elements. Senior corporate executives themselves are usually too preoccupied with their own immediate economic and managerial concerns. Working to ensure a healthy 'bottom line' for their businesses (or to maximise their own personal remuneration packages) usually leaves little time for taking an explicitly ideological line. Employer associations exist to give clearer focus to those common or collective interests.[12]

The funding of right-wing 'think-tanks' results in a greater number of ostensibly independent voices representing business interests. The development of global corporate capitalist organisations, like the World Economic Forum, also provides institutional focal points for the reinforcement of common interests and values.[13] These are important adjuncts to the direct influence of corporate interests through the media and their sponsorship of 'think-tanks'. There is also direct corporate lobbying of politicians, ranging from the provision of selective information favouring business interests to the outright corruption of the political process.

Does this all add up to a conspiracy? Opinions differ. At the least, it constitutes a set of interacting influences that operates to support common corporate goals. At the other extreme, it amounts to the 'hijacking' of the educational, informational, and political institutions that should be the guardians of a free and open society. Either way, it strengthens the nexus between economic ideas, economic interests, and their political expression.

CONCLUSION

This book is about political economy as the contest of *economic ideas*. It is simultaneously concerned with the contest of *economic interests*. The history of economic thought is replete with examples of how the ideas and interests intertwine. Not surprisingly, the competing interest groups now actively seek to promote the economic ideas that serve their own interests. Predictably, the most economically advantaged interest groups are best able to fund and directly influence the outcomes of this contest. Therein lies systemic bias. The continued dominance of neoclassical theory as the core of economic orthodoxy may be interpreted in these terms—as expressing the interests of those with the biggest stake in maintaining the existing political economic order.

It is a conclusion that requires qualification. Neoclassical economics seems rather ill-suited to being a legitimising ideology for capitalism in practice. It may be a perfect supporting ideology for a competitive free-market system.[14] However, its focus on an abstract realm of pure competitive markets sits uncomfortably with the real world of corporate power at the start of the twenty-first century. Some might reasonably conclude that a better ideology for capitalism would be an economic analysis that studied capitalism *as it actually is* and provided an explicit justification for the concentration and exercise of corporate power. Attempts to develop a theory of the 'soulful corporation' may be interpreted in this light, but, lacking the conceptual elegance of neoclassical theory, they have never seemed to develop a significant foothold in orthodox economics.[15] The popular saying 'what is good for General Motors is good for the United States' reveals the tension in a folksy way. It is a saying about which neoclassical economists, with their preference for perfectly competitive markets, should presumably feel uncomfortable. Their theory is of an 'ideal' world, and should lead to quite trenchant criticism of the corporate character of 'actually existing capitalism'. Wily exponents like Milton Friedman may argue that competition between giant corporations is an acceptable substitute for perfect competition in practice, but this blending of neoclassical reasoning with political pragmatism lacks coherence. And whenever there is incoherence in the dominant economic ideology, there are opportunities for alternative views to have critical impact.

Whether modern political economy, as articulated in chapters 33–7, has any chance of trouncing, or even severely denting, orthodox economics remains a matter of opinion. Some thirty years ago, when there was a particularly strong movement of young political economists challenging the economic orthodoxy, Galbraith said, 'I would judge as well as hope that the present attack will prove decisive.'[16] He was wrong, or at least substantially premature, in this judgment. However, the challenge continues. It can be expected that modern political economy will exert increasing influence as it is more thoroughly developed and as the disjuncture between orthodox economic theory and observable features of the real world becomes more glaring. Ultimately, its prospects are inexorably linked to the fate of the capitalist economy itself.

CHAPTER 40

W(h)ither Capitalism?

What structural contradictions drive political economic change?
Who are the practical agents of practical political economic change?
What sort of political economic arrangements could replace capitalism?

Has capitalism a future? It certainly has an impressive past, and is proving to be more durable than Karl Marx or Joseph Schumpeter, for example, anticipated. The dynamism of the system is its strength. But can it continue to survive the stresses generated by its own disrespect for existing social structures, technologies, and states of nature? And what could replace it? The demise of the major twentieth-century experiments in building an alternative political economic system on 'communist-state' rather than capitalist principles signals no final victory for capitalism. Rather, the closure of a chapter of Cold War rivalry enables our attention to be turned to questions about the long-term viability of the existing economic arrangements. Our attention can focus on how the capitalist system is evolving and what sort of alternative political economic system might develop in the twenty-first century.

One way of addressing these themes is by drawing on the contributions to the development of political economic analysis reviewed in the preceding chapters of this book. Marx, for example, emphasised features of the capitalist economy that endure—its basis in the pursuit of profits through capital accumulation continues to be a source of phenomenal economic growth and social change. Marx was equally prescient in pointing to the *contradictions* generated by the capital accumulation process—manifest as problems of alienation, exploitation, and recurrent economic crises. Where the Marxist analysis is incomplete, and historically in error, is in positing a direct connection between those structural contradictions and the agents of social transformation. The *Manifesto of the Communist Party* posited: 'What the bourgeoisie produces, above all, is its own gravediggers. Its fall and the victory of the proletariat are equally inevitable'.[1] But the 'gravediggers' have evidently not done the job. The call for the 'victory of the proletariat' now has a decidedly hollow ring. The claim that any particular political economic future is 'inevitable' sounds too deterministic to people living in a more sceptical age, even after making allowances for the rhetorical flourishes of the *Manifesto*.

Revisiting Keynes also provides a springboard for useful reflections about the possibilities for *reforming* capitalism. Keynes thought that a more rigorous under-standing of economic processes, married to an enlightened view of the state as an instrument for progress, could result in the eradication of unemployment, the ame-lioration of the sources of economic insecurity, and perhaps the diminution of rentiers' capacity to reward themselves without making any productive economic contribution. Here, too, things seem to have turned out rather differently in practice; the reformist road has proved to be littered with obstacles, and those socioeconomic problems persist and proliferate. However, the underlying belief that economic knowledge should be used in the formulation of public policies for social betterment remains strong, despite the ascendancy of neo-liberalism.

A reconsideration of the institutional tradition in economics, from Veblen to Galbraith, is also pertinent to reflections on the future for capitalism and the potential for political economic reform. More than the other major economic traditions, institutionalism has stressed the interconnections between technological change, the evolution of the economy, and the social implications of economic change. In his own reflections on the future of industrial society, , the American 'big-picture' institutionalist Robert Heilbroner blamed the sundry disappointments of both capitalism and socialism in the twentieth century on the common reliance on 'the presence of scientific technology and the industrial civilisation that is built on it'.[2] This draws attention to the troubled relationship between advances in technique and productivity, on the one hand, and human 'happiness' on the other. If, as Galbraith has also frequently emphasised, no reliable connection exists, then a sustainable and satisfying common future requires a major reorientation of the economy away from 'money-making' towards broader social and environmental goals.[3] Whether capitalism has the adaptability to meet this challenge then appears as the key question. Can it match its proven effectiveness as a machine for expanding capital, by grinding out more and more commodities and persuading us that we want to consume them, with its effectiveness in serving broader social and environmental goals?

Here are fundamentally important issues to puzzle over. Revisiting the claims of Marx, Keynes, and other great figures in the development of political economic thought is not only a means of understanding what went wrong. It can also be a focal point for considering how best to cope with the contradictions of contemporary capitalism. Both nationally and internationally, the system exhibits profoundly unsettling characteristics—glaring socioeconomic inequality, recurrent instability, and, even for those workers not relegated to the ranks of the unemployed, persistent insecurity. The capital accumulation process seems incapable of delivering indefinitely on the promises of a relentlessly consumerist society. The very possibility of continuing with such a growth-oriented economic system looks increasingly doubtful because of the environmental constraints of a finite planet. Capitalism is both highly successful and in deep trouble.

Exploring this conundrum requires critical examination of some interrelated issues—what drives political economic change, what structural contradictions are embedded in the capitalist economy, whether those contradictions generate agents capable of producing fundamental social change, and what alternative vision might inspire that change.

DRIVERS OF POLITICAL ECONOMIC CHANGE

What might cause the complex structure of modern capitalism to fundamentally change? *Technological progress* is one such possibility. If, in the extreme, it resulted in the eradication of labour from the processes of production, capitalism could not survive. Wage labour and the expenditure of wage incomes on the products of capitalist businesses are essential to capitalism. In a fully automated economy, a distributional mechanism other than a wages system would have to be developed in order to circulate the fruits of productive activity throughout the society. That would indeed be an ironic means of fulfilling the prophecy of Marx and Engels that 'the development of modern industry ... [would] cut from under its feet the very foundations' on which the capitalist economy is based.[4]

Alienation is a second tension with the potential to drive political economic change. The problem, stressed in Marx's early writings, such as the *Economic and Philosophical Manuscripts* of 1844, continues to pervade industrial society. Some say alienation is a general problem of the human condition—the condition of being castaways on this planet, trying to cope with the 'unknowableness' of the reason for our existence. From a more political economic perspective, it is a problem arising from how our particular economic system is organised, with workers divorced from control over their own labour process and from the products of their work. In Marx's time, the transformation of peasant and artisan patterns of working and living brought the origins of this economic alienation into sharp focus. Numerous studies of working conditions over the last century have shown the ongoing links between alienation in the workplace and an array of industrial and health disorders. It is equally evident that alienation has *not* been a stimulus for radical challenge to the existing economic order. For most workers, it seems, growth in material living standards has been adequate compensation for the acceptance of the alienation of labour under capitalism. And many capitalist businesses are now using increasingly sophisticated managerial practices to give at least the veneer of job-satisfaction to workers, individually and in small workteams. Yet it would be facile to dismiss alienation as a driver of political economic change. It now takes more diverse forms, as social, environmental, and political alienation.[5] As market criteria increasingly dominate our lives, their clash with a holistic view of ourselves in relation to nature, society, and polity becomes an ever more profound source of discontent.

What about *exploitation*? Political economists ever since Marx have recognised that the appropriation by capitalist employers of part of the value created in production by workers is at the core of class conflict. This structurally based exploitation is the most striking source of the economic inequality between wage earners and those who derive their income from the ownership and control of the means of production. Profits depend on its continuation. But other incomes, such as those of landowners, also ultimately derive from the exploitation of labour, as does the income of supervisors and other workers who do not directly generate value in the production of goods and services. This is one among many reasons why the continuing process of exploitation has not led to a greater class-consciousness among workers and to the overthrow of the capitalist system, as Marx predicted. The complexity of the channels of exploitation operates against solidarity—some workers in industrialised countries benefit from the higher rate of exploitation of Third World workers, while some administrative, technical, and supervisory workers regard themselves as an 'aristocracy of labour', not having interests in common with other workers. The popular use of the term 'exploitation' to describe only extreme cases of 'speed-up', unusually low wages, or particularly adverse working conditions indicates the general acceptance that some part of the income generated through work is due to the employer. Income shares, not the nature of economic system itself, have become the battleground. On that battleground, those who own and control the bulk of the capital have won most of the battles.

STRUCTURAL CONTRADICTIONS

So, has capitalism triumphed? Political economists have long considered the recurrence of *economic crises* to be capitalism's 'Achilles heel'. Marx thought this tendency to crises would create the material conditions in which radical change of the system would be both possible and necessary. Keynes agreed that, left to its own devices, capitalism could not ensure continuous full employment, although he envisaged the possibility of significant repair. Institutionalists have also emphasised the need for economic regulation to deal with systemic instability. The problem evidently persists. An economic system that cannot consistently reproduce itself and expand—lapsing instead into periodic recessions with large-scale unemployment, and financial turmoil—necessarily has an uncertain future. So it is worth reflecting on the nature of the structural contradictions underpinning this systemic instability.

What about the problem of *disproportionality*? Does the increased complexity of industry make more likely the possibility of structural imbalances, as Marx anticipated? Without central planning, incompatibility between the production decisions of firms in the different sectors of the economy producing capital and consumer goods is always likely. The resulting gluts and shortages have the potential to trigger generalised recessions. As noted in chapter 17, this is a specific manifestation of a general problem arising from the 'anarchy of capitalist production'. One might surmise that the complex planning processes now undertaken by the giant corporations themselves—and the collusion between them—might provide a source of stability, but sectoral coordination remains an ongoing problem of modern capitalism. Indeed, it may be increasing in scale as governments, under the influence of neoliberal economic ideology, withdraw from the regulatory measures and processes of indicative planning that have imparted some degree of stability in the past.

Whether economic crises associated with the *tendency of the rate of profit to fall* are likely to recur is yet more contentious. To the extent that industrial expansion leads to a higher organic composition of capital, as mechanisation continues and the capital–labour ratio rises, then one may infer that there will be a long-term tendency for the rate of profit for capitalist industry as a whole to be squeezed. However, offsetting tendencies, such as increased productivity and increased intensity of labour, pull in the opposite direction. Aggregate profit rates are apt, for this reason, to exhibit cyclical tendencies rather than a downward secular trend. Politically, it is buoyant profits (and their distribution to corporate executives via inflated remuneration packages and share-ownership) that fuel anti-capitalist sentiments—not a tendency to falling profits! But the relentless process of capital accumulation, particularly in a period of labour-displacing technological progress, continues to generate fundamental tensions.

At the present time, unemployment is the most obvious manifestation of the structural contradictions of the capitalist economy. Neither Marxist nor Keynesian economists find anything surprising about that. Marxists have always argued that the existence of a reserve army of labour is integral to the accumulation process. Keynesians have consistently emphasised that there is no inherent tendency towards a full-employment equilibrium; and the rejection of Keynesian policy by neo-liberals more concerned with balanced budgets adds further to the likelihood of recurrent, if not persistent, unemployment. The problem now assumes increasingly troubling forms. The tendency towards 'jobless growth' brings into question the future of wage-labour as the principal means by which income 'trickles down' to the bulk of society and social stability is maintained under capitalism. Can the economic system be adapted in such a way that work is more evenly distributed? The French government has made important attempts to do so, imposing a limit on the permissible length of the working week. The alternative is a society increasingly polarised between those who benefit materially from the capital accumulation process and those who have only a marginal attachment to the mainstream economy.

The problem of *underconsumption* is a related issue. In so far as wage incomes are pushed down and/or made more unequal, then the issue of who will buy the outputs of the production process becomes more problematic. Of course, luxury consumption by capitalists and the minority of the workforce in well-paid positions provides one avenue for the absorption of the economic surplus, as does consumption and investment expenditure by the state. Veblen drew attention to these aspects of consumption spending a century ago, and they have grown spectacularly since then. However, the capacity of the system to continue matching the growth of productive capacity with a corresponding growth of effective demand for goods and services is more troubling at a time when global competition increases the downward pressure on wage rates.

Of course, the counter-tendencies are many. Waves of *new product developments*, based on new technologies, have made electronic equipment, personal computers, mobile phones, and so forth, the focal points for growth of production and consumption. Consumerism, promoted by *commercial advertising*, underpinned by the proliferation of *credit*, and fostering the global expansion of markets for consumer goods, continue to spread. Contemporary political economists, such as Sweezy and Galbraith, have addressed the issues, pointing to the vast resources 'propping up' the economy in this way. Yet therein lie further tensions and sources of potential crises. Catering to the contrived wants of a consumerist society becomes ever more patently unsatisfying. As Esterlin puts it, the 'triumph of economic growth is not a triumph of humanity over material wants: rather, it is the triumph of material wants over humanity'.[6]

Consumerism also generates enormous social waste, partly in the sales promotion process itself and partly in the built-in obsolescence of the products. To the extent that the accumulation of capital depends on the proliferation of credit, it also means that the system becomes ever more vulnerable to crises emerging from financial institutions: 'casino capitalism' is an inherently unstable system.[7] Modern capitalism also makes rapacious use of the physical environment: as such, it is an inherently unsustainable system. Of course, if economic policies could switch the focus from aggregate production and consumption to redistribution and restructuring for sustainability, one could be more optimistic about the prospects for dealing with these tensions. However, as we have seen in previous chapters, the current structures of political economic power are ill-suited to the management of such progressive transformations. An economic system based on production for profit has its own internal dynamic, but it is not one conducive to social equity, economic security, or ecological sustainability.

AGENTS OF CHANGE

If Marx, Keynes, Veblen, and other significant figures in political economy were fundamentally right in their depiction of capitalism as a system based on fundamental contradictions, why has it not been subjected to more radical challenge? And who now could precipitate major systemic change? Such considerations switch attention from structure to *agency*.

Marx thought that an increasingly politicised and cohesive *working class* would be the driving force of social transformation. However, the belief that this class, organised internationally, would have history on its side lacks evident credibility today. Workers, collectively organised through trade unions, engage in intermittent struggles against capitalist employers. The organisation of labour sometimes transcends national boundaries, with unions in different countries working together to inhibit further reductions in working conditions—as in the case of waterside and maritime workers. However, the collective struggles of working people are, for the most part, redistributive rather than transformative in their goals.[8] The waged workforce has been partially incorporated into the existing political economic system.

There are many reasons for this incorporation. As we have seen, the capitalist system generates pressures for both cooperation and conflict. An emphasis on only the conflicting interests—on recurrent or prolonged strikes, for example—impoverishes workers as well as their employers in the short term, while providing no guarantee of material improvement further down the road. It is an option to which workers resort only when they are in desperate circumstances. In any case, potential solidarity is frequently impaired by nationalist, racist, and sexist ideologies and practices that set worker against worker. Other pervasive ideologies—regularly voiced by conservative politicians and in the mainstream media—set workers against 'undeserving' welfare recipients, particularly the unemployed. Add the hegemonic effects of capitalist ideology, educational institutions, and a repressive state apparatus and the reasons for the waged workforce's tendency to work within rather than against the system become increasingly evident.

It follows that whatever can be done within those institutions—the state, the media, and the educational institutions—to develop progressive ideas and practices contributes to building a viable alternative to capitalism. Indeed, that alternative can—and must—be fostered within the institutions of the existing political economic order. The sharp distinction that radical activists have sometimes drawn between reform and revolution is not helpful in this respect. The denigration of the former because it does not directly achieve the latter deflects attention from the important work to be done now. Working *within the state* to develop alternative economic strategies and programs of progressive social reform takes advantage of avenues for change made available by the existence of political institutions capable of controlling the economy. That is why the challenge to the prevailing neo-liberal ideologies and practices—and the underlying economic theories—is so important. Not only politicians, but also reform-minded public servants, teachers encouraging critical inquiry, and investigative journalists have important roles to play in this process.

There are other potential agents of change. The *unemployed* and the otherwise economically dispossessed have the least direct stake in the existing economic structures. They may lack the direct capacity of an organised working class to impair the functioning of the economic system, but they have the indirect capacity to challenge its legitimacy and capacity for reproduction. They have less to lose. Their activism was important during the 1930s when facing the challenges of the Great Depression. With the development of the welfare state, a 'social safety net' has been provided for many of the economically marginalised (although its form is subject to continual contestation). Yet, economic marginalisation continues to be associated with social pathologies and challenges of various forms. The resort to crime on the part of a social 'underclass' is perhaps the least consciously political, but the most widely feared, consequence throughout contemporary capitalist society, particularly in the United States. The wealthy are taking refuge in residential and commercial enclaves patrolled by private security guards. The jails fill. As modern capitalism takes this economically polarising and socially repressive form, Marx's prediction of 'socialism or barbarism' looks increasingly relevant.[9]

Environmentalists and other *social movements activists* are also challenging the existing structures of political economic power. By comparison with the economically dispossessed, they also have more coherent strategies for change. The focus on the tensions between environment and economy is of particular importance. If the crisis of contemporary capitalism is increasingly an environmental crisis—an incapacity to live within the sustainable limits of nature—then it is not surprising that the agents of change reflect this primary contradiction. 'Environmentalists of the world unite' may be the relevant rallying cry today. And we are all environmentalists in so far as our capacity to live in some degree of harmony with nature is essential to our well-being and, ultimately, our continued existence. Traditional Marxism does not sit comfortably in this context to the extent that it shares with orthodox economics—indeed with 'economic liberalism' in general—a presumption of the dominance of humankind over nature.[10] A more reciprocal or symbiotic conception of economy–ecology relationships is needed as a theoretical underpinning for contemporary socialist and environmental politics. As capitalism marches onwards, its contradictions evolve; therefore, corresponding changes are needed to how we understand it and to the practices through which we seek more progressive outcomes.

The role of *the state* in this process is crucial. Therein lie other contradictions. On the one hand, there is a strong tendency for governments to support the interests of capital in general because to do otherwise is to court economic crisis and political instability. On the other hand, the institutions of the state continually offer enticing possibilities of extending democratic political control over the economic system. Analytically, the further exploration of such possibilities can draw on the contributions to political economy of reformers such as Keynes, Myrdal, and Galbraith, as previous chapters have indicated. Politically, the task is to counter the hegemony of neo-liberal ideologies and practices which have given that social democratic commitment such a battering during the last two decades. The challenge is to develop a more progressive alternative economic strategy.

TOWARDS AN ALTERNATIVE SOCIALISM?

Into what the economic system could then be transformed warrants careful consideration. Some form of socialism has usually been seen by political economists as the principal alternative to capitalism. Notwithstanding the disappointing twentieth-century experience of the command-administrative model used in the former Soviet Union, the sources of appeal of some other kind of socialist alternative are enduring. There is the appeal of *rationality*—the replacement of the so-called 'anarchy of capitalist production' with a planned economy geared to the satisfaction of social needs. There is the appeal of *equity*—the replacement of a class society with a society that, if not classless, delivers more equal living standards than capitalism ever could. There is the appeal of *democracy*—the extension of democratic principles to all aspects of our lives, including our working lives. There is the appeal of *liberty*—the freedom from exploitation and oppression, which is a precondition for voluntary cooperation in the construction of social order. There is the appeal of *social solidarity*—the process of working together in pursuit of these interconnected goals.

To this list it is important now to add the appeal of *sustainability*—living in harmony with nature, not simply because it is ultimately necessary for economic reproduction, but also because it is an essential element in a full and balanced life. Capitalism, whatever its capacity to generate material affluence—and to commodify more and more aspects of our lives—cannot readily deliver on this aspiration. Indeed, the more it moulds us in the image of *Homo economicus*, the more unsatisfying and unsustainable it becomes.

How to translate these principles into practice is the big question. It requires the development of an alternative to both capitalism and the command-administrative model. The latter, based on the distinctive trilogy of state ownership of the means of production, central planning and a one-party state, has shown itself to have politically authoritarian, economically inefficient, and environmentally degrading tedencies. But *it is not the only possible form of socialism*. Exploring viable alternatives requires consideration of what 'a good economy and society' for the twenty-first century could look like and of the transitional process for 'getting from here to there'.[11]

First, there is a need to consider *technology and its implications for work*. Modern technology opens up tantalising possibilities of liberation from toil. Work may be part of the human condition, but it need not be alienating labour and it can be more equitably shared. Evidently, modern capitalism has great difficulty adapting to these technological possibilities, although the system has played a major role in precipitating them. The possibility of a socialism that allows greater personal flexibility in working lives (involving continuous part-time work or periods of full-time work interspersed with periods of leisure, education, or other creative pursuits) has considerable appeal. How to balance the progressive 'liberation from work' against the concern to extend 'social employment', to build the infrastructure, and to provide the services to satisfy social needs remain open questions.

Second, there is the question of *how to combine markets and planning*. A capitalist market economy has an inbuilt tendency to produce inequitable outcomes. But, the alternative of economic planning, particularly of a centralised kind, is also problematic. Being sensitive to the complex patterns of consumer preferences, industrial production possibilities, and new technologies is a major, some would say impossibly difficult, task. So, the key question is how planning—shaping the broad directions of economic development to serve social purposes—can be combined with some role for markets in 'fine-tuning' the system. There are some interesting possibilities. With the aid of modern computer technology, regional and sectoral planning can be used to set the broad parameters for economic development without negating the freedom of consumer choice that markets permit.[12] Importantly, that planning framework can—and must—embody goals of ecological sustainability by regulating the use of environmental assets and by responsibly husbanding non-renewable resources.

How to *control investment* is the third issue. The private appropriation of an economic surplus and its disposition to serve particular class interests is the essence of the capitalist system. Under socialism there must still be a surplus. Not all the value created by labour can be returned to the workers as wages, or there would be no funds available to replace worn-out plant and machinery or for investment in collectively needed infrastructure. The essence of a viable socialism is not the eradication of the economic surplus, but the control of that surplus for social purposes. How much surplus and how it is used then become essentially political decisions. Here are some echoes of Keynes's enigmatic reference to a 'somewhat comprehensive socialisation of investment'. The use of superannuation or pension funds for investment projects serving broad social interests is one modern means of pursuing this goal.[13]

The appropriate *form of ownership* in industry is also a contentious matter. It is conventional to associate capitalism with the private ownership of the means of production and socialism with collective ownership. But various forms of collective ownership are possible. Collective ownership by the state of all productive enterprises raises the spectre of an overcentralised economic system. It is neither necessary nor desirable. One can conceive, as a compromise, of a three-tier system in which the 'commanding heights' of industry are either publicly owned or regulated by 'planning agreements' to ensure corporate commitment to community service obligations, while medium-sized firms are organised as worker cooperatives, leaving small businesses to be operated as private enterprises.[14]

Industrial democracy also warrants consideration as a means of diffusing control to the populace. Democracy under capitalism is restricted to the political sphere, focusing mainly on periodic parliamentary elections. Socialism needs to take democracy more seriously, particularly with regard to democracy in the workplace. At a minimum, it is a matter of designing mechanisms so that multiple social interests—'stakeholders', to use the modern jargon—are represented in decision-making processes in all economic institutions, rather than only the interests of a managerial or capitalist class.

Does this mean modern socialism should be a *classless society*? It is easy enough to contrast the capitalist tendency to reproduce poverty amid affluence with a socialist vision of classlessness. But how much inequality could a modern socialist society permit in practice? What, for example, would be the tolerable limit of the ratio of the highest income to the lowest? Would, say, 3:1 be appropriate as a means of allowing for material incentives, while still emphasising social cohesion?[15] The policy instruments by which more egalitarian outcomes are to be achieved also need consideration—policies on inheritance and other sources of cumulative wealth, policies to balance wages against other income sources, and more progressive income taxation, for example.

So what is the basis for economic motivation? Replacing the capitalist dynamic of profit-seeking with the collective pursuit of social needs is easy to posit in the realm of rhetoric. It highlights the need to redress the perpetual imbalance between 'private wealth and public squalor' that Galbraith has stressed. But it seems a tall order to redress that imbalance by the appeal to collective rationality alone. Altruism and social responsibility surely warrant greater encouragement but seem unlikely to provide a sufficiently robust basis for a productive socialist economy in the foreseeable future. However, the situation changes if the emphasis on the relentless pursuit of economic growth should be tempered with greater concern for ecological sustainability. Inculcating the motivation to maximise profits, outputs, and market shares then becomes less important than inculcating the desire to identify and attain more socially and ecologically balanced outcomes.

Underpinning all these concerns are difficult issues about the *functions of the state*. The eventual 'withering away of the state' has long been a cherished ideal of libertarian socialists. It is a useful antidote to the general perception of socialism as requiring an all-powerful regulatory state. However, some coordinating role for government is indispensable if collective social goals are to be achieved. Liberty is not inversely proportional to the size of the state, since states may ensure freedom *from* things (like oppression and exploitation) as well as limit freedom *to* do other things (such as engage in individual pursuits deemed to be against the public interest). There is no simple formula for balancing these competing concerns. The extension of political control over economic issues is the essence of democratic socialism—and the state is necessarily central to this process. The state would still be an arena of struggle under socialism, as it is under capitalism, but its operation would be freed from the constraints imposed by capitalist class interests.

Other *constraints arising from the global economy* would remain. The institutions of multinational capital make it difficult for an individual country, whether it be socialist or not, to take an independent policy direction. Capital strike is an ever-present threat. However, a nation's vulnerability to this problem can be reduced by the development of institutional mechanisms to channel local savings directly into the required investments. Threats of withdrawal by multinational capital would not then be such a damaging prospect. Autarky, or complete self-sufficiency, is not necessarily implied. Indeed, the globalisation of human rights, labour organisations, and environmental consciousness can be progressive antidotes to the globalisation of capital. They have the potential to give strength and support to new forms of socialism.

Is there is a real possibility of any such alternative political economic path coming into being? The prevailing characteristics of global capitalism are not particularly encouraging in this respect. However, the future is inherently uncertain. Flux, contradiction, and dialectical processes of change are constant features on the political economic landscape. Change is inevitable; the key questions are: in which direction? and driven by whom? The preceding list of concerns is an elaboration of those themes. It illustrates Joan Robinson's renowned claim that the answers to most economic problems are political questions.[16]

CONCLUSION

The ultimate purpose of political economy is to contribute to changing our world for the better. Understanding the world better is a good first step. As we have seen, this concern has been common to many currents of analysis within political economy. Those currents of analysis have themselves been closely linked to competing political philosophies, embodying different value judgments about the economy and society and how progress might be achieved.

In these circumstances, it would be facile to expect consensus on what comprises an ideal economic system or on how to attain it. Whether the existing structures of capitalism offer an acceptable means of catering for our individual and collective economic needs is a matter of judgment. So, too, is the compatibility of the existing economic system with our social needs and environmental conditions. Whether the economic system is sufficiently adaptable to resolve its internal contradictions and external stresses also remains an open question. However, one thing is certain—that the economy in fifty, maybe even twenty, years time could not possibly be the same as it is today. 'Imagining' how it might be is not a matter of crystal-gazing or dreaming of Utopia. The future will be shaped by how we address the practical problems that dominate our concerns early in the twenty-first century. From this perspective, the test of our study of political economy is whether it contributes positively to understanding and resolving contemporary economic, social, and environmental problems. If it provides principles for progressive political purposes, that is a bonus.

A changing analysis for a changing world is implied. In developing that analysis, we can usefully draw on the established currents of political economic thought. We do not need to reinvent the wheel, but we do need to set it rolling purposefully in the right direction.

Glossary

aggregate demand: the total expenditures on goods and services within a community (generally a nation). According to Keynesian economics, it is the sum of expenditure on consumption, investment, government spending, and exports less expenditure on imports.

aggregate supply: the capacity (or potential) of the economy to produce goods and services.

barriers to entry: impediments restricting new firms setting up in an industry.

Bretton Woods: the place in the USA where an international conference was held in 1944 to consider arrangements for the management of international payments. The governments represented at the conference agreed to establish a regime of fixed exchange rates, with the US dollar as the major reserve currency, convertible for gold; and new international institutions such as the International Monetary Fund and the International Bank for Reconstruction and Development (part of what is called 'the World Bank').

budget deficit (surplus): where government spending is more than (less than) government revenue. A surplus or deficit may or may not be planned.

capital: a widely used term that normally refers to capital goods, which are manufactured goods used in the production of goods and services (e.g. factories, trucks, machinery, tools). The term may also be used to mean money capital, i.e. stocks of money generated by past savings or borrowing (which can be used, *inter alia*, for the purchase of capital goods). A third use of the term is to refer to capital as a social relation (involving command over resources). In this third sense, reference may be made to a capitalist class, i.e. the group of people who own and control most of the capital.

capital accumulation: the process whereby capital is increased. This is a major impetus for economic growth. A slowing in the rate of capital accumulation is typically followed by an economic crisis.

capitalism: the particular type of economy based on private ownership of the means of production and the pursuit of profit. The term 'monopoly capitalism' may be used where there are large concentrations of ownership and control of capital. 'Competitive' or 'free market capitalism' are terms usually implying a wider spread of wealth and enterprise throughout the economy.

casualisation: the process whereby proportionately more jobs come to be under a contract of 'casual' employment, lacking security of employment.

circular and cumulative causation: the process whereby the political economic conditions at a point of time shape subsequent political economic changes, causing greater divergence from the initial conditions. Small differences thereby become magnified; political economic inequalities relentlessly increase.

class: the division of society according to economic circumstances. Different views of class in political economy associate it with inequalities of property, power, and income.

commodity: any good or service produced for sale rather than for personal consumption by its producer.

comparative advantage: the principle (developed by David Ricardo) whereby countries are said to benefit mutually by specialising in the production of different types of commodities, then trading with each other.

competition: a process of rivalry in economic behaviour, eg. between firms seeking to expand their respective market shares.

concentration and centralisation of capital: a term used in Marxist economics to denote the processes transforming competitive capitalism into monopoly capitalism. Concentration results from the growth of individual business enterprises, whereas centralisation means that the enterprises combine together into fewer units, through mergers and takeovers.

conglomerate: a company that has economic activities in many industries. Note that the development of conglomerates undermines the coherence of the notion of 'industry' as a means of classifying firms.

conspicuous consumption: consuming goods and services in a matter intending to impress, so that the satisfaction derives from the effect on other people, rather than from the subjective utility of the good itself.

consumer sovereignty: the view that consumers are independent and free to choose, exercising economic power because how they spend their incomes determines what products will be produced. This proposition is subject to radical critique, some arguing that *producer sovereignty* (whereby firms mould consumer preferences to suit their own corporate goals) is more characteristic of the modern economy.

consumption: the largest item in national expenditure, comprising the total spending by consumers on goods and services. 'Consumption' may also refer to the actual process of using a good or service, e.g. consuming a chocolate bar, or 'consuming' the service of a house by living in it.

corporate power: the capacity of large corporations to use their economic resources to serve their own corporate goals.

countervailing power: the power of one group (e.g. government, trade unions) to match and to resist the power of other groups (e.g. corporations).

currency: the notes and coin that are the current medium of exchange in a country. The *exchange rate* is the rate at which different national currencies can be exchanged for each other, i.e. the ratio of values or prices of two currencies.

current account deficit (surplus): where payments flowing out of a nation are greater than (less than) payments flowing in. Payments flowing out typically comprise expenditure on imports plus interest and dividends paid to overseas lenders and investors. Payments flowing in typically comprise revenues from exports plus interest and dividends paid by overseas borrowers and recipients of investment. The current account is to be distinguished from the capital account, which accounts for transactions in financial assets.

demand, law of: the generally inverse relationship between the price of a commodity and the quantity of it that consumers purchase.

deregulation: the reduction or removal of state regulations on privately owned businesses. Such regulations may involve, for example, requirements concerning environmental standards, working conditions, occupational health and safety, or the reporting of information about business finances.

disarticulation: the severing of economic linkages between industries or regions.

division of labour: the specialisation of workers in particular parts or operations of a production process. It means that different workers are doing different types of jobs. It may (but does not necessarily) increase economic efficiency and thus enable the production of greater volumes of output. The *international division of labour* extends the process beyond individual nations, leading to a situation in which countries specialise in different types of employment (e.g. farming, mining, manufacturing, provision of services). The character of the international division of labour is changing as a result of the processes of globalisation.

ecological sustainability: the compatibility of the economy with the physical environment. It requires that ecological systems are not irreversibly degraded by economic activities. The extent to which an economic system is ecologically sustainable is a criterion (along with efficiency and equity) by which it can be evaluated.

economic crises: collapses in investment that cause interruptions to economic growth. Depending on their severity (and the preference of the writer) they may alternatively be known as slumps, depressions, and recessions.

economic growth: an increase in the value of goods and services produced. Economic growth is commonly measured in terms of Gross Domestic Product (GDP), but it is increasingly widely recognised that GDP is poorly correlated with national well-being.

economic rationalism: the belief that economic goals should have priority over social goals, and that such goals are better served by markets than by the involvement of the state, because markets ensure the convergence of private goals and the social good.

economies of scale: the cost advantages of large-scale production, arising where expansion of productive capacity causes total production costs to rise less than proportionately.

economy: a system for organising the production of goods and services, the distribution of income and wealth, and the exchange of commodities. *Economics* is the study of the economy. *Political economy* broadens the study of the economy by recognising the interconnections between the economy, the society, and political processes. The term 'political economy' can refer either to the system or to the study of it.

efficiency: the effectiveness with which economic resources (land, labour, capital) are used to achieve given social ends. Note that because efficiency concerns means, not ends, it is always important to ask 'what end?', i.e. efficient in achieving *what?* For example, one may refer to the efficiency of a firm in producing particular outputs.

elasticity: the responsiveness of one economic variable to changes in another, e.g. the price elasticity of demand is the responsiveness of demand for a commodity to a change in its price, whereas the price elasticity of supply is the responsiveness of supply of a commodity to a change in its price. The income elasticity of demand is the responsiveness of change in demand for a commodity to changes in the income of consumers.

equilibrium: a situation in which the forces making for change in opposite directions are in balance, so there is no tendency for change. For example, a market is in equilibrium if the quantity supplied at the prevailing price exactly equals the amount consumers want to buy at that price.

equity: fairness (e.g. in the distribution of income). This definition of 'equity' is different from the meaning of the term in finance, where 'equity' means the shareholders' stake in the ownership of a corporation.

exploitation: according to Marxist economics, exploitation is the process whereby surplus value is generated in a capitalist economy. More generally, it refers to the situation in which one class derives income from the labour undertaken by another class.

factors of production: inputs into the process of producing goods and services: land, labour, and capital. Neoclassical economists commonly model the firm as if it were an 'entrepreneur' combining these factors of production. The concept of factors of production 'de-personifies' land, labour, and capital, and effectively denies their social dimensions.

fiscal policy: the adjustment of government revenues and expenditures in order to affect the level of national income, output, and employment.

gender: the division of society according to the differential circumstances of men and women. Whereas sex is biologically determined, gender is socially constructed, e.g. the gender division of labour in household work and in paid work.

globalisation: the process whereby the significance of national boundaries is eroded as the density of international interconnections intensifies. Globalisation has not only economic dimensions (e.g. trade in commodities, international investment, and finance) but also social and cultural dimensions (e.g. globalisation of environmental consciousness, of consumerism, or of human rights).

ideology: a system of belief. Ideologies, embodying particular value judgments about the economy and society, commonly give legitimacy to a particular socio-economic order, e.g. neoliberal ideology as a justification for 'free market' capitalism.

imperialism: the political economic processes whereby strong classes in some nations dominate over the people of poorer ones. Its hallmarks are empire building, territorial expansion, and domination of the weak by the strong on an international scale. Lenin called it 'the highest stage of capitalism'.

industry: comprises the firms making broadly similar products, e.g. the car industry, the steel industry.

inflation: rising prices. Inflation is normally measured by a consumer price index (CPI), which indicates how the price of a typical 'basket of goods' varies over time.

investment: a significant item in national expenditure, comprising spending on capital goods, usually undertaken by firms and governments. This definition is different from the use of the term 'investment' in everyday language to mean the purchase of any asset, such as a government bond, a share in a company, or a piece of real estate.

labour: normally means work done by human beings, contributing to the production and exchange of goods and services. Wages and salaries are its usual reward. 'Labour' may also refer to the class of people who depend on for their livelihood on income from work, i.e. the working class.

labour power: people's capacity, whether by mental or manual labour, to produce useful goods and services. Converting labour power into labour is a principal concern of capitalist management.

labour theory of value: the view that the value of a commodity depends on the amount of labour that does into making it (given that the latter reflects what is current best practice or 'socially necessary').

laissez faire: a borrowed French phrase indicating that the economy should be left to reflect the decisions of free enterprises in markets, rather than involvement by the state.

land: not simply the part of the earth's surface that is not covered by water. Economically, it also refers to the 'free gifts of nature', such as minerals and soil fertility. Land provides both space and physical resources. Owners of land may receive payments in the form of rent, depending on its economic value.

liquidity preference: the desire to hold one's assets as money rather than in some other (more illiquid) form, such as bonds, shares, or real estate.

marginal cost: according to neoclassical economics, marginal cost is the increase in total costs of production that results from increasing the volume of output by one unit.

marginal efficiency of capital: the expected rate of return on an additional item of investment expenditure, according to Keynesian economics. Firms can be expected to rank investment projects according to their marginal efficiency of capital and undertake those with the highest value first.

marginal product: the increase in output that results from increasing the quantity of a variable factor of production by one unit. According to the principle of diminishing marginal productivity, it declines the greater the amount of the variable factor is put into production.

marginal productivity theory: the view, in neoclassical economics, that factors of production are rewarded in proportion their respective marginal products.

marginal propensity to consume: the proportion of an additional increment of income that is consumed, not saved.

marginal revenue: the increase in the total revenue of a firm that results from its selling one more unit of its output.

marginal utility: according to neoclassical economics, marginal utility is the increase in utility that results from increasing the quantity of the good consumed by one unit. The principle of diminishing marginal utility implies that marginal utility declines the more units of each good are consumed.

market: the place or process whereby exchange occurs between buyers and sellers of a commodity or an asset that can be held as private property.

market failure: the recognition that, in particular circumstances, markets fail to ensure beneficial economic outcomes. Market failures may involve the supply of *public goods* (items that are inherently collective in their consumption) or *externalities* (cost and benefits indirectly affecting people other than those directly engaged in market exchange of the commodity in question, such that there are deficiencies in the formation of prices). Neoclassical economists acknowledge these problems but disagree over their relative importance.

mode of production: how the economy is organised for the purpose of producing goods and services. It involves the use of tangible *forces of production*, comprising the raw materials, capital goods, labour power, and technology. It also involves particular *relations of* production, concerned with how people are organised (e.g. whether by authoritarian/hierachial means or in democratic/participatory ways). This concept is widely used in Marxist economics.

monetarism: the view that government policy should be restricted to a steady increase in the money supply at a rate just sufficient to match the growth in the volume of goods and services produced. This view of monetarism is different from the discretionary use of monetary (or fiscal) policy to even out economic booms and slumps, a policy approach known as *demand management*, or 'macroeconomic fine-tuning'.

monetary policy: the adjustment of the supply of money or the price of money (the rate of interest) in order to affect the level of national income, output, and employment.

money: anything that is generally acceptable as a means of exchange and a means of settling debt. It normally consists of currency on issue (notes and coin) and deposits or credit with financial institutions that is obtainable on demand (through an ATM, for example).

monopolistic competition: a market in which there are very many sellers but where they can influence the price of their own products because of some product differentiation or geographical fragmentation of the market.

monopoly: strictly speaking, 'monopoly' means there is only one firm in an industry. The term is also used more broadly to denote an economy in which the power of big business is dominant, i.e. *monopoly capitalism*.

multiplier: a measure of the effect on national income of a change in one of the components of aggregate demand. For example, if an increase in investment expenditure of $1 leads to an increased national income of $3, the multiplier is 3.

national income: the total value of the flow of goods and services produced in a nation over a specified period, e.g. one year.

neoliberalism: the ideology that seeks to justify the restructuring of the economy to increase opportunities for private profit, often couched in the language of 'market freedoms' and 'individual choice'.

oligopoly: a market in which there are only a few sellers. Strategic interdependence shapes the behaviour of the firms in such market conditions.

opportunity cost: what is foregone by using economic resources in one way rather than another. For example, the opportunity cost of unemployment is the goods and services the unemployed people would have produced if they had jobs. The opportunity cost of attending a university lecture is an hour that you might otherwise spend in the library, in a café, or playing sport.

organic composition of capital: a term used in Marxist economics to refer to the relative values of constant capital and variable capital used in the production of goods and services. A high organic composition of capital in general indicates a production process that is quite mechanised, using a high proportion of capital goods relative to labour.

Pareto criterion: a basis for making judgements about how community well-being is affected by the allocation of economic resources. If a reallocation of resources makes at least one person better off without making anyone worse off it is said to be a Pareto improvement.

perfect competition: the state of affairs in a market in which there are very many sellers providing identical products, so that none can effect the price of its own product, and many buyers so that none can effect the price it pays. All buyers and sellers have perfect information about all relevant products and their prices. This theoretical model has a central place in neoclassical theory.

Phillips curve: the inverse relationshop said to exist between the rate of unemployment and the rate of inflation.

positional goods: goods whose supply is inherently limited, becoming either more expensive or more degraded as rising incomes lead more people to compete to acquire them.

power: in general, the possibility of imposing your will on the behaviour of other people. *Economic power* refers more specifically to the capacity of individuals or, more typically, institutions to exert influence (e.g. over prices, wages, or government policies) because of their command over economic resources.

privatisation: the sale of government-owned enterprises to private owners; the opposite of *nationalisation*. The term 'privatisation' is also loosely applied to any shift of emphasis in the economy from the public sector to the private sector.

profit: the excess of revenue over costs. The nature and origin of profit has been a focal point for debates on political economy.

rate of interest: the price of borrowed money. It may also be regarded as the price of liquidity (i.e. the opportunity cost of holding your assets in a liquid form, as money, rather than in a form that earns interest). In practice there are many different rates of interest. Banks make profits by charging higher interest rates to borrowers than they pay to depositors. When economists talk about *the* rate of interest they normally mean an average of the various rates prevailing in the markets for loans and deposits, or a particular base rate of interest, such as the cash rate set by the central bank.

realisation of surplus value: according to Marxist economics, the conversion of surplus value into profit as a result of capitalist firms selling the commodities that have been produced.

rent: payments to landowners for the use of their land. Rent also has a broader meaning in economics to refer to payments to any factor of production over and above what is necessary in order to maintain it in its current use.

reserve army of labour: a Marxian term used to denote the most marginalised elements of the workforce. It has nothing to do with military conscription! Marx saw the reserve army of labour as having three parts: a 'floating' form comprising workers displaced by technological change or the concentration and centralisation of capital; a 'stagnant' form comprising people in irregular employment; and a 'latent' form comprising workers displaced from agriculture by the encroachment of the capitalist mode of production.

Say's law: the belief that, because producing goods generates the incomes necessary to buy them, there need not be recessions resulting from a glut of unsold products.

saving: income that is not spent on consumption.

socialism: an alternative system of economic organisation, contrasting with capitalism because of its emphasis on collective ownership of the means of production and social control of the economic surplus.

soulful corporation: the view of the corporation as a body serving community interests, or at least tempering its own economic self-interest with responsibilities to the broader community.

speculation: buying and selling with a view to making a profit later when prices have changed (i.e. a 'capital gain'), without making any productive contribution to the economy.

stagflation: simultaneous unemployment and inflation.

state: the institutions of national administration, including the government, the public service, the judiciary, the police, and armed forces. It is in analysing the state that the study of political economy connects with the study of government or political science.

surplus value: that part of the value created by labour that is not returned to workers as wages, but is instead appropriated by capitalist employers. This is a key concept in Marxist economics. *Absolute surplus value* denotes surplus value obtained by lengthening the working day (or week). *Relative surplus value* denotes surplus value obtained by increasing the productivity and/or intensity of labour.

tariff: a tax on imported goods. Tariffs generate revenue for a national government and have the effect of partially protecting firms in that nation from overseas competition.

technology: the technique for producing goods and services, based on the current state of scientific knowledge. *Technological change* results from advances in scientific knowledge and their application to industry: it may involve the production of new goods and services or new methods of producing existing goods and services.

transnational corporation: a company that has affiliate or subsidiary companies in at least one other country. It is commonly used interchangably with 'multinational corporation', although the former term may imply that the company has more completely transcended its national orgins.

unemployment: underutilisation of labour because people who wish to work cannot get jobs. The unemployment rate is normally measured as the percentage of the total workforce who are seeing work but are currently unemployed. There are debates about the proportion of measured unemployment that is involuntary, and about the adequacy of official unemployment statistics as an indication of the full extent of underutilised labour.

utility: the usefulness of a good or service or, in the neoclassical sense, the satisfaction or pleasure derived from consuming it. The estimation of utility is essentially subjective, varying from person to person according to their particular tastes.

value: the worth attributed to a good or service. This may refer objectively to its intrinsic properties, such as the amount of labour, materials, or energy that go into making it. It may be a more subjective notion, referring to the utility the good or service yields to the person who owns or consumes it. Alternatively, it may simply be regarded as its market price. Debates about these competing interpretations of value have been a recurrent feature in political economy. 'Value' may also be defined as the multiple of price and quantity (as in the total value of output, or value added).

World Trade Organisation: an inter-governmental institution established in the 1990s to determine the rules governing international trade: it is committed in practice to trade liberalisation and removing impediments to the global mobility of capital. The WTO administers the General Agreement on Tariffs and Trade (GATT), which originated in the late 1940s.

Notes

1 WHAT IS POLITICAL ECONOMY?

1 P. Baran and P. Sweezy, *Monopoly Capital: An Essay on the American Economic and Social Order*, Monthly Review Press, New York, 1966, pp. 27–8.

2 For further discussion, see F. Stilwell, 'Neoclassical economics: A long cul-de-sac', in *Economics as a Social Science: Readings in Political Economy*, eds G. Argyrous and F. Stilwell, Pluto Press, Sydney, 1997, pp. 94–7.

3 See, for example, R. Bryan and M. Rafferty, *The Global Economy in Australia: Global Integration and National Economic Policy*, Allen & Unwin, Sydney, 1999.

4 See E. Jones, 'The neglected spirit of reform', in Argyrous and Stilwell, *op. cit.*, pp. 102–8.

5 This interpretation of Keynes was pushed strongly by US economist Paul Samuelson, along with his emphasis on a more mathematical emphasis in the construction of economic analysis.

6 See A. Eichner, 'A guide to post-Keynesian economics', in Argyrous and Stilwell, *op. cit.*, pp. 150–3.

7 This issue is the theme of chapter 34. See also M. Diesendorf and C. Hamilton, *Human Ecology, Human Economy: Ideas for an Ecologically Sustainable Future*, Allen & Unwin, Sydney, 1997.

2 THE PERSONAL IS THE POLITICAL ECONOMIC

1 For information on the relative size of companies and nations, ranked according to market capitalisation, see table 27.1, p. 241.

2 This analysis is set out more fully in F. Stilwell, *Changing Track: A New Political Economic Direction for Australia*, Pluto Press, Sydney, 2000, ch. 9.

3 The distinction between markets, state and community as three types of economic organisation has become pretty standard fare in the social science literature. It is traceable *inter alia* to the sociologist Talcott Parsons, who identified the 'two principal competitors' to the market as 'requisitioning through the direct application of political power' and 'non-political solidarities and communities'. See T. Parsons (ed.), *Sociological Theory and Modern Society*, Free Press, New York, 1967.

4 Geoff Hodgson refers to the 'impurity principle' which normally produces a mixture of market and state systems, and by extension community provision too, irrespective of the 'official' economic structure and ideology. See G. Hodgson, *The Democratic Economy: A New Look at Planning, Markets and Power*, Penguin, Harmondsworth, 1984.

5 For further discussion of the spatial dimension, linking up with the concerns of economic geography, see F. Stilwell, *Understanding Cities and Regions*, Pluto Press, Sydney, 1992. On the recent surge of interest by more orthodox economists in spatial issues, see P. Krugman, 'Space: The final frontier', *Journal of Economic Perspectives*, vol. 12, no. 2, Spring 1998, pp. 161–74.

3 STRUCTURAL ECONOMIC CHANGE

1 See, for example, J. Rifkin, *The End of Work: The Decline of the Global Labor Force and the Dawn of the Post-Market Era*, Tarcher/Putnam, New York, 1996. Other aspects of this problem of 'jobless

growth' are explored in chapter 35. On the forces changing employment conditions, see J. Eatwell (ed.), *Global Unemployment: Loss of Jobs in the 1990s*, Sharpe, New York, 1996.

2 See F. Stilwell, *Changing Track: A New Political Economic Direction for Australia*, Pluto Press, Sydney, 2000, ch. 5.

3 For discussion of these social and cultural aspects of globalisation, see R.J. Holton, *Globalisation and the Nation State*, Macmillan, Basingstoke, 1998. For a comprehensive account of the businesses involved in the globalisation process, and their impact on national economies and policies, see J.H. Dunning, *Multinational Enterprises and the Global Economy*, Addison-Wesley, Reading, Mass., first published 1992.

4 See J. Goodman and P. Ranald (eds), *Stopping the Juggernaut*, Pluto Press, Sydney, 1999.

5 Stilwell, *op. cit.*, ch. 6.

6 The analysis of post-Fordism is a concern of chapter 35.

7 'Economic fundamentalism' is the term used in New Zealand, while 'economic rationalism' is the term used in Australia. See also chapter 23, n. 7.

8 '... and their families', she added, thereby opening a Pandora's box of conceptual confusion, for families may be held to constitute something more than the aggregations of individuals.

9 Chapter 39 returns to this issue of the role of 'think-tanks'. See also R. Cockett, *Thinking the Unthinkable: Think-tanks and the Economic Counter-revolution, 1931–1983*, HarperCollins, London, 1985.

10 J. Robinson, *History Versus Equilibrium*, Thames Economic Papers, Middlesex Polytechnic, London, n.d.

4 A NEW POLITICAL ECONOMIC ORDER?

1 See F. Fukuyama, *The End of History and the Last Man*, Hamish Hamilton, London, 1992.

2 The classic study of this problem of international economic inequality, urging remedial action, is the report of the commission headed by former West German chancellor Willi Brandt: *Common Crisis: North–South Cooperation for World Recovery*, Pan Books, New York, 1983. For a more hard-hitting assessment of the political economic forces impeding balanced economic development, see M. Chossudovsky, *The Globalisation of Poverty*, Pluto Press, Sydney, 1997. See also K. Raffer and H.W. Singer, *The Economic North–South Divide: Six Decades of Unequal Development*, Edward Elgar, Cheltenham, 2001.

3 For a careful review of the evidence, concluding that 'poor countries are not catching up with the rich, and to some extent the international income distribution is becoming polarised', see J. Temple, 'The new growth evidence', *Journal of Economic Literature*, vol. 37, no.1, March 1999, pp. 112–56.

4 W. Ellwood, *The No-Nonsense Guide to Globalisation*, New Internationalist Publications, Oxford, 2001, p. 47; see also R. Swift, 'Squeezing the South', in *Economics as a Social Science: Readings in Political Economy*, eds G. Argyrous and F. Stilwell, Pluto Press, Sydney, 1997, pp. 9–13.

5 The former phrase comes from Susan Strange, *Casino Capitalism*, Basil Blackwell, Oxford, 1986, and the latter from S. Melman, *Profits Without Production*, Alfred A. Knopf, New York, 1983. We return to a fuller consideration of these issues in chapter 35.

6 International Labour Office, *The World Employment Situation: Trends and Prospects*, ILO, Geneva, 1994, cited in J. Rifkin, *The End of Work: The Decline of the Global Labor Force and the Dawn of the Post-Market Era*, Tarcher/Putnam, New York, 1996, p. xv.

7 See, for example, J.K. Galbraith, *The Good Society*, extract in Argyrous and Stilwell, *op. cit.*, p. 273.

8 A. Fishlow and K. Parker (eds), *Growing Apart: The Causes and Consequences of Global Wage Inequality*, Council on Foreign Relations Press, New York, 1999, p. 99.

9 W. Hutton, *The State We're In*, Vintage Books, London, 1995, pp. 105–9.

10 B. Fleay, *Decline of the Age of Oil*, Pluto Press, Sydney, 1995.

11 See, for example, C. Hamilton, *Running from the Storm: The Development of Climate Change Policy in Australia*, UNSW Press, Sydney, 2001.

12 The latter view is forcefully argued in J. Kovel, *The Enemy of Nature: The End of Capitalism or the End of the World*, Zed Books, London, 2002. We return to a fuller consideration of these competing views in chapter 34.

13 See T. Trainer, *Abandon Affluence*, Zed Books, London, 1985 for discussion of this imbalance.

5   UNDERSTANDING AND EVALUATING ECONOMIC SYSTEMS

1 On the economics of 'provisioning', see P. Elkins and M. Max-Neef, *Real-life Economics: Understanding Wealth Creation*, Routledge, London, 1992; and J. Nelson, 'The study of choice or the study of provisioning', in *Beyond Economic Man: Feminist Theory and Economics*, eds M.A. Ferber and J. Nelson, University of Chicago Press, Chicago, 1993.

2 See, for example, R. Holton, *Economy and Society*, Routledge, London, 1995.

3 These dimensions are explored in the six articles appearing in *Economics as a Social Science: Readings in Political Economy*, eds G. Argyrous and F. Stilwell, Pluto Press, Sydney, 1997, pp. 23–45.

4 See, for example, R. Eckersley (ed.), *Measuring Progress*, CSIRO, Melbourne, 1999.

5 See R. Lekachman, *Economists at Bay: Why the Experts Will Never Solve Your Problems*, McGraw-Hill, New York, 1976, p. 122.

6 See, for example, C. Hamilton and R. Denniss, *Tracking Well-being in Australia: The Genuine Progress Indicator 2000*, Discussion Paper No. 35, Australia Institute, Canberra, December 2000.

6   CAPITALISM: ITS DISTINCTIVE FEATURES

1 We return to this issue in the last chapter.

2 In the words of Karl Marx and Friedrich Engels: 'The bourgeoisie has left no other nexus between man and man than naked self-interest, than callous "cash payment". It has drowned the most heavenly ecstasies of religious fervour, of chivalrous enthusiasm, of philistine sentimentalism, in the icy water of egotistical calculation. It has resolved personal worth into exchange value.' *Manifesto of the Communist Party*, Foreign Languages Publishing House, Moscow, 1960 (1848), p. 50.

3 On the study of consumerism, see B. Fine and E. Leopold, *The World of Consumption*, Routledge, London, 1993.

4 For a critique of the generalised use of the term 'interventionist', see E. Jones, 'Government intervention', in *Economics as a Social Science: Readings in Political Economy*, eds G. Argyrous and F. Stilwell, Pluto Press, Sydney, 1997, pp. 29–31.

7   ECONOMIC THEORY IN HISTORICAL PERSPECTIVE

1 K. Boulding, *Economics as a Science*, McGraw-Hill, New York, 1970, p. 2.

2 J. Duesenbury, *Business Cycles and Economic Growth*, McGraw-Hill, New York, 1958, pp. 14–15.

3 T. Kuhn, *The Structure of Scientific Revolutions*, Chicago University Press, Chicago, 1970.

4 This is sometimes known as the 'Hawthorne effect', named after the factory where studies of the workforce produced this notorious result.

5 See D. McCloskey, *The Rhetoric of Economics*, University of Wisconsin Press, Madison, 1985.

6 E.J. Hobsbawm, *Industry and Empire*, Pelican Economic History of Britain, vol. 3, Pelican Books, Harmondsworth, 1979, p. 245.

7 J.M. Keynes used this phrase in concluding an address to the Royal Economic Society in the UK in 1945.

8 My teaching philosophy, which informs this approach, includes a belief in the necessity of an iterative method, whereby one begins with first approximations that can be subsequently developed in more sophisticated ways through further study and reading.

8   CAPITALISM EMERGING

1 P. Dasgupta, 'The population problem: Theory and evidence', *Journal of Economic Literature*, vol. 23, no. 4, December 1995, pp. 1879–1902.

2 A.K. Sen, *Development as Freedom*, Knopff, New York, 1999, p. 23.

3 See P. Ehrlich and A. Ehrlich, *The Population Explosion*, Simon & Schuster, New York, 1990.

4 D. Fusfeld, *The Age of the Economist*, 9th edn, Addison-Wesley, Reading, Mass., 2002, p. 23.

5 The phrase comes from the title of the book by Karl Polanyi, *The Great Transformation*, Beacon Press, New York, 1944.

6 See, for example, E. Meiskens Wood, *The Origin of Capitalism*, Monthly Review Press, New York, 1999; M. Dobb, *Studies in the Development of Capitalism*, Routledge & Kegan Paul, London, 1963; and E.P. Thompson, *The Making of the English Working Class*, Vintage Books, New York, 1966.

7 Great Britain was not ahead of the pack before the eighteenth century. Arguably, the Dutch economy exhibited the most modernising, dynamic economic growth in the preceding two centuries. See J. der Vries and A. van der Woude, *The First Modern Economy: Success, Failure and Perseverance of the Dutch Economy, 1500–1815*, Cambridge University Press, Cambridge, 1997.

8 R. Tawney, *Religion and the Rise of Capitalism*, Harcourt, New York, 1947; and M. Weber, *The Protestant Ethic and the Spirit of Capitalism*, Allen & Unwin, London, 1930.

9 These were the Tolpuddle Martyrs; see Trade Union Congress, *The Story of the Tolpuddle Martyrs*, TUC, London, 1991.

9   PRIVATE VICES AND PUBLIC VIRTUES

1 E.K. Hunt, *Property and Prophets: The Evolution of Economic Institutions and Ideologies*, Harper & Row, New York, 1990, p. 25.

2 *Ibid.*, p. 11.

3 *Ibid.*, p. 10.

4 A. Smith, *An Inquiry into the Nature and Causes of the Wealth of Nations*, Modern Library, New York, 1937 (1776), p. 421.

5 *Ibid.*, p. 423.

6 The original work is B. Mandeville, *The Fable of the Bees: Or Private Vices, Publick Benefits*. For a brief discussion of its interpretation, see J. Robinson, *Economic Philosophy*, Penguin Books, Harmondsworth, 1964, pp. 19–24.

7 The quotation comes from C. Hill, *Protestantism and the Rise of Capitalism*, cited in Hunt, *op. cit.*, p. 33.

8 Hunt, *op. cit.*, pp. 44–5. These assumptions of economic liberalism were, in effect, imported into classical political economy from the philosophy developed by Jeremy Bentham and other 'philosophical radicals' of the early nineteenth century.

9 A.O. Hirschman, *The Passions and the Interests: Political Arguments for Capitalism Before its Triumph*, Princeton University Press, Princeton, 1977 cited in K. Tribe, 'Adam Smith: Critical theorist', *Journal of Economic Literature*, vol. 37, no. 2, June 1999, p. 611. Tribe's article provides a useful discussion of the conservative and radical interpretations of Smith. See also J.T. Young, *Economics as a Moral Science: The Political Economy of Adam Smith*, Edward Elgar, Cheltenham, 1997.

10 A. Smith, cited in D. Fusfeld, *The Age of the Economist*, Addison-Wesley, Boston, 2002, p. 30.

11 Fusfeld, *op. cit.*, ch. 3.

12 A. Smith, cited in Fusfeld, *op. cit.*, p. 35. The gender-biased use of 'man' was the norm in those days.

13 R. Heilbroner, *The Nature and Logic of Capitalism*, W.W. Norton, New York, 1985, p. 113.

14 *Ibid.*, p. 114; see also R. Heilbroner, *The Essential Adam Smith*, Oxford University Press, Oxford, 1986.

15 C. Woodham-Smith, *The Great Famine: Ireland 1845–1849*, Penguin Books, Harmondsworth, 1992, pp. 54–5.

16 J. Gray, *False Dawn: The Delusions of Global Capitalism*, Granta Books, London, 1998, p. 207.

17 R. Bronk, *Progress and the Invisible Hand*, Warner Books, London, 1999, p. 239.

10   VALUE, DISTRIBUTION, AND GROWTH

1 A. Smith, *An Inquiry into the Nature and Causes of the Wealth of Nations*, Modern Library, New York, 1937 (1776), p. 20.

2 A. Smith, cited in T. Riddell, J. Shackleford and S. Samos, *Economics: A Tool for Understanding Society*, Addison-Wesley, Reading, Mass., 1987, p. 82.

3 T.R. Malthus, *Essay on the Principle of Population*, Dulton, New York, 1961 (1798); cited in D. Fusfeld, *The Age of the Economist*, Addison-Wesley, Boston, 2002, p. 40.

4 E.R. Canterbury, *The Literate Economist: A Brief History of Economics*, HarperCollins, New York, 1995, p. 68.

5 According to Smith, ten men making pins and dividing the sequential tasks between them might make 48 000 pins a day (averaging 4800 each). One man doing all the steps would make between one and twenty per day.

6 Smith, *op. cit.*, p. 340.

7 For a critique, see R. Gollan, *The Myth of the Level Playing Field*, Catalyst Press, Sydney, 1995. See also C. Hamilton, 'The case for fair trade', *Journal of Australian Political Economy*, no. 48, December 2001, pp. 60–72.

8 J.K. Galbraith, *Economics and the Public Purpose*, Houghton Mifflin, New York, 1973, p. 21.

9 T. Carlyle, cited in Canterbury, *op. cit.*, p. 74. It may also be noted that economics was 'dismal' to Carlyle because classical political economists like J.S. Mill advocated the abolition of the slave trade and thereby put the interests of 'subhuman' Africans above the interests of the English working class; see L.S. Moss, review of M.A. Lutz, *Economics for the Common Good*, in *Economic Journal*, vol. 111, no. 469, February 2001, pp. 129–36.

10 R. Heilbroner, *The Worldly Philosophers*, Simon & Schuster, New York, 1967, p. 117.

11 *Idem.*

12 Quoted in Heilbroner, *op. cit.*, p. 119.

13 *Ibid.*, p. 121.

11   CAPTURING THE ECONOMIC SURPLUS

1 For a brief introduction to the physiocrats, see R. Lekachman, *A History of Economic Ideas*, McGraw-Hill, New York, 1976, pp. 80–6.

2 D. Ricardo, *On the Principles of Political Economy and Taxation*, Dent, London, 1962 (1817) quoted in M. Dobb, *Theories of Value and Distribution*, Cambridge University Press, Cambridge, 1973, p. 72; see also R. Heilbroner, *The Worldly Philosophers*, Simon & Schuster, New York, 1967, pp. 87–90.

3 See F. Stilwell, 'Land, inequality and regional policy', *Urban Policy and Research*, vol. 17 no. 1, March 1999, pp. 17–24.

4 H. George, *Progress and Poverty*, Robert Schalkenback, New York, 1966 (1879), p. 224.

5 For an argument, and some supporting calculations, to suggest that land tax could indeed be a sufficient source of tax revenues, see P. Day, *Land: The Elusive Quest for Social Justice, Taxation Reform and a Sustainable Planetary Environment*, Australian Academic Press, Brisbane, 1995.

6 For further discussion of Georgist ideas, see C. Collier, 'Henry George's system of political economy', *History of Political Economy*, vol. 11, no. 1, Spring 1979, pp. 64–93; and M. Gaffney and F. Harrison, *The Corruption of Economics*, Shepheard-Walwyn, London, 1994.

7 George, *op. cit.*, p. 224.

8 D. Harvey, *The Urban Experience*, Basil Blackwell, Oxford, 1989, pp. 265–266.

12   CONTESTING CAPITALISM

1 Interviewed during 2000 for a BBC television series tracking the lives of young Russians, one fourteen-year-old girl spoke wryly of 'the transition from the socialism we never had to the capitalism that never seems to arrive'.

2 For discussion of the remarkable survival of Cuba, see T. Anderson, 'Island Socialism', *Journal of Australian Political Economy*, no. 49, June 2002, pp. 56–86.

3 Samuelson later expressed regret for this slur, admitting that the neglect of Marx in the teaching of orthodox economics had been 'a scandal'. His best-selling textbook continued to perpetuate the neglect, however.

4 J.K. Galbraith, 'The Age of Uncertainty', television series, BBC, London, 1977.

5 For a fuller discussion of these non-Marxist socialists and their influence, see D. Fusfeld, *The Age of the Economist*, 9th edn, Addison-Wesley, Reading, Mass., 2002, pp. 56–9; or E.K. Hunt, *Property and Prophets: The Evolution of Economic Institutions and Ideologies*, Harper & Row, New York, 1990, ch. 5.

6 The classic description of the living conditions is in F. Engels, *The Condition of the Working Class in England in 1844*, Macmillan, New York, 1958 (1845). See also F. Engels, *The Housing Question*, Progress Publishers, Moscow, 1975 (1873).

7 See, for example, F. Stilwell, *Changing Track: A New Political Economic Direction for Australia*, Pluto Press, Sydney, 2000, ch. 8.

8 K. Marx, *Critique of Political Economy*, New World Paperbacks, New York, 1970 (1859), p. 20.

9 Friedrich Engels, quoted in D. McLellan, *Karl Marx: His Life and Thought*, Harper & Row, New York, 1973, p. 14.

10 K. Marx, *The German Ideology*, cited in *Marx on Economics*, ed. R. Freedman, Penguin Books, Harmondsworth, 1961, p. 5.

11 K. Marx and F. Engels, *Manifesto of the Communist Party*, Foreign Languages Publishing House, Moscow, 1960 (1848), p. 45.

13   UNDERSTANDING CAPITAL

1 K. Marx, *The Critique of Political Economy*, reprinted in part in *Reader in Marxist Philosophy*, eds H. Selsam and H. Martels, International Publishers, New York, 1963, p. 186.

2 V. I. Lenin, *Marx-Engels-Marxism*, Progress Publishers, Moscow, 1968. 'Determine' is the contentious word here. As E.K. Hunt notes: 'To argue that Marx believed that the economic base determined, completely and rigidly, every aspect of the superstructure is grossly inaccurate (although it is often done). He did assert, however that the mode of production was the most important single aspect in determining not only the present social superstructure but also the direction of social change'; see *Property and Prophets: The Evolution of Economic Institutions and Ideologies*, Harper & Row, New York, 1990, p. 75.

3 For discussion of these contemporary concerns in the political economy of education, see S. Slaughter and L.L. Leslie, *Academic Capitalism: Politics, Policies and the Entrepreneurial University*, Johns Hopkins University Press, Baltimore, 1997; and S. Marginson and M. Considine, *The Enterprise University: Power, Governance and Reinvention in Australia*, Cambridge University Press, Cambridge, 2000.

4 K. Marx, *A Critique of the Gotha Programme*, cited in *Marx on Economics*, ed. R. Freedman, Penguin Books, Harmondsworth, 1962, p. 241.

5 For an excellent discussion of the cooperative movement and the alternative it offers to capitalism, see R. Mathews, *Jobs of Our Own: Building a Stakeholder Society*, Pluto Press, Sydney, 1999.

6 M. Dobb, *Studies in the Development of Capitalism*, Routledge & Kegan Paul, London, 1963, ch. 1.

7 *Ibid.*, p. 4.

8 M. Weber, cited in Dobb, *op. cit.*, p. 5.

14   LABOUR, VALUE, EXPLOITATION

1 E. Mandel, *An Introduction to Marxist Economic Theory*, Pathfinder Press, New York, 1970.

2 K. Marx, *Wage Labour and Capital*, Progress Publishers, Moscow, 1976 (1849), p. 26.

3 The significance of this problem for the coherence and applicability of Marxian theory is hotly debated. See, for example, A. Shaikh, 'Marx's theory of value and the transformation problem, in *The Subtle Anatomy of Capitalism*, ed. J. Schwartz, Goodyear, Santa Monica, 1977. For a more general critique of the value theory underpinning orthodox Marxism, see I. Steedman, *Marx after Sraffa*, New Left Books, London, 1977.

4 K. Marx, *Capital*, vol. 1, Progress Publishers, Moscow, 1974 (1867), p. 164. For further discussion of the concept of labour power, see K. Marx, *Wages, Price and Profit*, Foreign Languages Press, Peking, 1970 (1865), pp. 43–6.

5 This is partly why Marxian class analysis, in its modern forms, emphasises complexity rather than a simple binary opposition; see J.K. Gibson-Graham, S. Resnick and R. Wolff, 'Towards a post-structuralist political economy', in *Re/Presenting Class: Essays in Postmodern Marxism*, eds J.K. Gibson-Graham, S. Resnick and R. Wolff, Duke University Press, Durham, 2001. We return to this issue in chapter 36.

6 For further discussion of shorter working time initiatives, see A. Hayden, *Sharing the Work, Sparing the Planet*, Pluto Press, Sydney, 1999.

7 Joan Robinson, for example, took this view. In her words: 'We are told that it is impossible to account for exploitation except in terms of *value*, but why do we need *value* to show that profits can be made in industry by selling commodities for more than they cost to produce, or to explain the power of those who command finance to push around those who do not?', 'The labour theory of value', *Monthly Review*, no. 29, 1977, p. 51. See also her earlier sympathetic critique of Marxism: *An Essay on Marxian Economics*, 2nd edn, Macmillan, London, 1966.

8 H. Braverman, *Labor and Monopoly Capital: The Transformation of Work in the Twentieth Century*, Monthly Review Press, New York, 1974.

9 R. Edwards, *Contested Terrain: The Transformation of Work in the Twentieth Century*, Basic Books, New York, 1979. For an interim stocktake of debates on the labour process, see also P. Thompson, *The Nature of Work*, Macmillan, Basingstoke, 1983. The more recent book edited by Thompson in conjunction with C. Warhurst, *Workplaces of the Future*, Macmillan, Basingstoke, 1998, contains a compilation of articles on contemporary trends in work organisation and capital–labour relations.

10 E. Applebaum and R. Batt, *The New American Workplace: Transforming Work Systems in the United States*, ILR Press, Ithaca, 1994.

15   CAPITAL ACCUMULATION

1 See L. Sklair, *The Transnational Capitalist Class*, Blackwell, Oxford, 2001.

2 See K. Marx, *Capital*, vol. 1, Progress Publishers, Moscow, 1974 (1867), p. 579, n. 2. See also D. Bhattacharya, *Economic Development and Underdevelopment*, Australian Professional Publications, Sydney, 1987, p. 90.

3 For discussion of this concept of the reserve army of labour and its contemporary relevance, see J. Collins, 'Marx's reserve army of labour: Still relevant one hundred years on', *Journal of Australian Political Economy*, no. 16, March 1984, pp. 51–65.

4 See K. Marx, *Capital*, vol. 1, Progress Publishers, Moscow, 1974 (1867), p. 582.

5 For an example of this reasoning, see Collins, *op. cit., loc. cit.*

6 Marx, *op. cit.*, p. 588.

7 *Idem.*

8 See, for example, P. Baran and P. Sweezy, *Monopoly Capital: An Essay on the American Economic and Social Order*, Monthly Review Press, New York, 1966.

9 For a Marxian analysis of globalisation as a process that extends its competitive features world-wide, see R. Bryan and M. Rafferty, *The Global Economy in Australia: Global Integration and National Economic Policy*, Allen & Unwin, Sydney, 1999.

10 C. Rhodes, reported in the *Spectator* on 26 January 1885 and cited in D. Bhattacharya, *Economic Development and Underdevelopment*, Australian Professional Publications, Sydney, 1987, p. 157.

11 V.I. Lenin, *Imperialism: The Highest State of Capitalism*, Foreign Languages Press, Peking, 1970 (1917).

12 See E. Hobsbawm, *The New Century*, Little, Brown & Co., London, 1999, pp. 52–3.

13 H. Magdoff, *Imperialism: From the Colonial Age to the Present*, Monthly Review Press, New York, 1978, p. 117.

14 H. McQueen, *The Essence of Capitalism*, Sceptre, Sydney, 2001, p. x.

15 See B. Norton, 'Reading Marx for class', in *Re/Presenting Class: Essays in Postmodern Marxism*, eds J.K. Gibson-Graham, S. Resnick and R. Wolff, Duke University Press, Durham, 2001, pp. 45–8.

16 REPRODUCTION, GROWTH, CHANGE

1 For a non-technical discussion of this, see R. Heilbroner, *Beyond Boom and Crash*, Norton, New York, 1978; an extract from this book appears in *Economics as a Social Science: Readings in Political Economy*, eds G. Argyrous and F. Stilwell, Pluto Press, Sydney, 1997, pp. 63–8.

17 ECONOMIC CRISES

1 K. Marx and F. Engels, *Manifesto of the Communist Party*, Foreign Languages Publishing House, Moscow, 1960 (1848), p. 53.

2 A fuller exposition of these three theoretical strands is in P. Sweezy, *The Theory of Capitalist Development*, Monthly Review Press, New York, 1942.

3 One Australian study, for example, sought to apply this reasoning to explain the booms and slumps experienced in the twentieth century, showing that a rising organic composition of capital in the 1920s and early 1930s led to the Great Depression; then a rising rate of surplus value facilitated economic expansion through the 1950s and 1960s, then into the 1970s, when the rate of surplus value stopped rising and boom turned again to recession. See R. Kuhn and T. O'Lincoln, 'Profitability and economic crises', *Journal of Australian Political Economy*, no. 25, October 1989, pp. 44–69.

4 For a more general discussion of these views, see M. Bleaney, *Underconsumption Theories: A History and Critical Analysis*, Lawrence & Wishart, London, 1976.

5 Marx, quoted in P. Sweezy, *Theory of Capitalist Development*, p. 177.

6 P. Baran and P. Sweezy, *Monopoly Capital: An Essay on the American Economic and Social Order*, Monthly Review Press, New York, 1966. The term 'monopoly' here embraces oligopoly as well as single-firm industries, so it is a general description of big business. J.B. Foster, *The Theory of Monopoly Capitalism*, Monthly Review Press, New York, 1986, provides a critical appreciation of Baran and Sweezy's influential political economic contribution.

7 For examples, see E. Mandel, *Late Capitalism*, NLB, London, 1975; and E. Mandel, *The Second Slump*, Verso, London, 1980.

18 FREE-MARKET ECONOMICS

1 R. Dorfman, *Prices and Markets*, Prentice Hall, Englewood Cliffs, NJ, 1967, p. 146.

2 Hayek was joint-winner of the Nobel Prize in Economic Sciences in 1974 (with Gunnar Myrdal). Hayek's best known political tract is *The Road to Serfdom*, Routledge, London, 1944. For an evaluation of Hayek's work, which is sympathetic to his methodology but critical of the political inferences, see J. Mulberg, *Social Limits to Economic Theory*, Routledge, London, 1995. For a shorter sketch of Hayek's approach, see Y. Varoufakis, *Foundations of Economics: A Beginner's Companion*, Routledge, London, 1998, pp. 187–90.

3 For a brief discussion of Spencer and social Darwinism, see D. Fusfeld, *The Age of the Economist*, 9th edn, Addison-Wesley, Reading, Mass., 2002, pp. 76–8. See also R. Hofstadter, *Social Darwinism in American Thought*, Beacon Press, Boston, 1959.

4 Fusfeld, *op. cit.*, pp. 80–1. See also T. Arnold, *The Folklore of Capitalism*, Yale University Press, New Haven, 1937.

5 On a personal level, Walras was a reformer favouring a good deal of state intervention. The incoherence of his theoretical and practical positions is not unique among economists. In a similar vein it is pertinent to note that Vilfredo Pareto, originator of the liberal economic principle discussed in Chapter 23, became a supporter of facism in Italy.

6 C. Menger, *Principles of Economics*, trans. J. Dingwall and B. Hoselitz, Free Press, London, 1950, p. 120.

7 In a letter to another economist, he set out his views on maths in economics: '(1) Use mathematics as a short hand language, rather than an engine of inquiry. (2) Keep to them till you have done. (3) Translate into English. (4) Then illustrate by examples that are important in real life. (5) Burn the mathematics. (6) If you can't succeed in 4, burn 3'; see J.K. Whitaker (ed.), *The Correspondence of Alfred Marshall*, Cambridge University Press, Cambridge, 1996.

8 R. Lekachman, *A History of Economic Ideas*, McGraw-Hill, New York, 1976, p. 274.

9 R. Skidelsky, *John Maynard Keynes*, Vol. 1, 1883–1920, Macmillan, London, 1983, p. 48.

10 P.D. Groenewegen, *A Soaring Eagle: Alfred Marshall, 1842–1924*, Edward Elgar, Cheltenham, 1995.

11 See E.K. Hunt, *Property and Prophets: The Evolution of Economic Institutions and Ideologies*, Harper & Row, New York, 1990, p. 90.

12 And even to John Stuart Mill's political economy, which opened the door for income redistribution from rich to poor. From a particular class perspective, these were 'dangerous doctrines', too.

13 See Fusfeld, *op. cit.*, pp. 49–52.

14 B. Toohey, *Tumbling Dice: The Story of Modern Economic Policy*, William Heinemann, Port Melbourne, 1994, ch. 4.

15 A. Marshall, *Principles of Economics*, 8th edn, Macmillan, London, 1959, bk 5, ch. 3, s. 7, p. 290.

19 CONSUMERS

1 The term *Homo economicus* commonly has a somewhat tongue-in-cheek ring. For an example of its more serious usage, see J. Friedman, Introduction, in *The Rational Choice Controversy: Economic Models of Politics Reconsidered*, ed. J. Friedman, Yale University Press, New Haven, 1995, pp. 1–24. On the origin of the concept, with particular reference to J.S. Mill, see J. Persky, 'The ethology of *Homo economicus*', *Journal of Economic Perspectives*, vol. 9, no. 2, Spring 1995, pp. 221–31.

2 *The Rubaiyat of Omar Khayyam, The Astronomer-Poet of Persia*, ed. and trans. Edward Fitzgerald, Bernard Quaritch, London, 1859.

3 For discussion of what economics could learn from psychology, see M. Rabin, 'Psychology and economics', *Journal of Economic Literature*, vol. 36, no. 1, March 1998, pp. 11–46, and R.H. Thaler, 'Doing economics without *Homo economicus*', in *Foundations of Research in Economics: How Do Economists Do Economics?* eds S. Medema and W.J. Samuels, Edward Elgar, Cheltenham, 1996.

4 See the classic article by H. Leibenstein, 'Bandwagon, Snob and Veblen effects in the theory of consumers' demand', reprinted in *Micro-Economics: Selected Readings*, ed. E. Mansfield, W.W. Norton, New York, 1971, pp. 12–30.

5 For a geometrical demonstration of this link between indifference curve analysis and demand curves, see D. McTaggert, C. Findlay and M. Parkin, *Microeconomics*, Addison–Wesley, Reading, Mass., 1996, p. 176.

6 P. Samuelson, *Economics: An Introductory Analysis*, 6th edn, McGraw-Hill, New York, 1964, p. 56.

7 See, for example, G. Stigler, 'Can regulatory agencies protect the consumer?', *Economics as a Social Science: Readings in Political Economy*, eds G. Argyrous and F. Stilwell, Pluto Press, Sydney, 1997, pp. 87–90.

8 This observation that preferences are shaped by social experience tends to lead to a more institutionally focused economic analysis; see S. Bowles, 'Endogenous preferences: The cultural consequences of markets and other institutions', *Journal of Economic Literature*, vol. 36, no. 1, March 1998, pp. 75–111.

9 P. Baran and P. Sweezy, *Monopoly Capital: An Essay on the American Economic and Social Order*, Monthly Review Press, New York, 1966, p. 126.

10 This type of critique is developed by H. Gintis in 'Consumer behaviour and the concept of sovereignty: Explanations of social decay', in *Readings in Political Economy*, eds E.L. Wheelwright and F. Stilwell, vol. 2, ANZ Book Co., Sydney, 1976, pp. 15–28.

11 This reasoning derives from F. Hirsch, *Social Limits to Growth*, Routledge & Kegan Paul, London, 1977.

12 There have been attempts to reconstruct consumer theory on different lines. See, for example, Kelvin Lancaster's attempt to focus on how consumers might seek to attain particular characteristics (e.g. transport) rather than commodities per se (e.g. cars or bicycles); see K. Lancaster, 'A new approach to consumer theory', *Journal of Political Economy*, vol. 74, 1966, pp. 132–57. The theory of revealed preference, pioneered by Paul Samuelson, had earlier sought to do away with the indifference curve apparatus. However, within the neoclassical approach (as represented in the undergraduate textbooks), the emphasis on an individualistic, rational, maximising decision process remains hegemonic.

20   FIRMS

1 Marshall used this concept as a means of talking about the dynamic equilibrium of an industry, rather than as a deductive tool for a general theory of economic agents.

2 Critics have argued that it is fundamentally misleading. In the words of A.G. Papandreou (before he became prime minister of Greece): 'To extend, unwittingly or not, the analytical conclusions of a model best fitted for the study of shopkeeper society to present-day capitalism is probably the supreme form of ideological bias'. (*Paternalistic Capitalism*, University of Minnesota Press, Minneapolis, 1972, p. 40.)

3 S. Zamagni, *Microeconomic Theory: An Introduction*, Basil Blackwell, Oxford, 1987, p. 442.

4 This tradition of analysis derives from the pioneering article by R.H. Coase, 'The nature of the firm', *Economica*, vol. 4, 1937, pp. 386–405. Coase said, 'The distinctive characteristic of the firm is in its overcoming of the price mechanism.'

5 The view is expounded by J.K. Galbraith, *The New Industrial State*, Penguin, Harmondsworth, 1969, ch. 15.

6 This view is associated with the behavioural theory of the firm; see, for example, R.M. Cyert and J.G. March, *A Behavioral Theory of the Firm*, Prentice Hall, Englewood Cliffs, NJ, 1963.

7 See N. Lamoreaux, D. Raff and P. Temin (eds), *Learning by Doing in Markets, Firms and Countries*, National Bureau of Economic Research Conference Report Series, University of Chicago Press, Chicago, 1999.

8 This distinction between the short run and the long run is a distinctive legacy of Marshall's *Principles of Economics*. It seems to introduce a time dimension into the analysis but does not treat time as a continuous variable. As such, it is part of the problem rather than part of the solution in dealing with the temporal dimension of economic activity.

9 The principle of diminishing returns, it should be emphasised, was not a neoclassical innovation. It was a well-established principle in classical political economy. The diagrammatic exposition and its incorporation into a general theory of supply and demand are the distinctively neoclassical elements here.

10 As with the theory of the consumer, there are many variations on this core theory of the firm. Neoclassical economists have experimented, for example, by changing the assumed objective of short-run profit maximisation to sales revenue maximisation, by considering the effect of joint production, and by 'learning by doing' as a means by which firms acquire information to gain or maintain their competitive advantage in industry.

21   MARKET STRUCTURES

1 A standard model of this tendency to price rigidity under conditions of oligopoly is the 'kinked-demand-curve' model developed by, among others, Paul Sweezy, who was later to become renowned as a Marxist economist. See P.M. Sweezy, 'Demand under conditions of oligopoly', *Journal of Political Economy*, vol. 47, no. 4, August 1939, pp. 568–73. For a more recent contribution to oligopoly theory, see R.E. Keunne, *Price and Nonprice Rivalry in Oligopoly*, Macmillan, Basingstoke, 1998.

2 The Australian passenger airline industry in the 1990s provided a striking example. Every time a new airline challenged the market shares of existing airlines, vigorous price-cutting occurred. At the start of the 2000s, Virgin Blue established a firm foothold, but Ansett, hitherto one of the two major airlines, then folded.

3 Rupert Murdoch, quoted in the *Sydney Morning Herald* (a newspaper he does not own), 25 January 2001, p. 13.

4 On game theory, see R. Gibbons, 'An introduction to applicable game theory', *Journal of Economic Perspectives*, vol. 11, no. 1, Winter 1997, pp. 127–49; and X. Vives, *Oligopoly Pricing: Old Ideas and New Tools*, MIT Press, Cambridge, Mass., 2000.

5 The terminology 'monopoly capitalism' is particularly associated with P. Baran and P. Sweezy, *Monopoly Capital: An Essay on the American Economic and Social Order*, Monthly Review Press, New York, 1966. The foundations for theories of 'imperfect competition' were earlier laid by Joan Robinson, later renowned as a leading post-Keynesian economist, and by E.H. Chamberlin. Robinson's book was *The Economics of Imperfect Competition*, Macmillan, London, 1933; Chamberlin's was *The Theory of Monopolistic Competition*, Harvard University Press, Cambridge, Mass., 1933.

6 A classic exposition of the 'structure–conduct–performance' approach is R. Caves, *American Industry: Structure, Conduct, Performance*, Prentice Hall, London, 1964. See also F.M. Scherer, *Industrial Market Structure and Economic Performance*, Rand, McNally & Co., Chicago, 1970, figure 1.1. The influence of this approach can be discerned in D.W. Carlton and J.M. Perloff, *Modern Industrial Organisation*, 3rd edn, Pearson Education Australia, Sydney, 2000.

7 It is pertinent to note that there is a conservative critique of the view that perfect competition is 'ideal'. This points out that, because many firms have high fixed costs, marginal cost pricing could

generally cause losses, bankruptcies, and recession. To the extent that this view has any policy implications, it stresses the desirability of business self-regulation. See M. Perelman, *The End of Economics*, Routledge, London, 1996.

8 In the US Department of Justice's battle against Microsoft, the reasoning underlying the government's case also drew on game theory, involving strategic entry, deterrence, and raising the costs of business rivals. See W.A. Kovacic and C. Shapiro, 'Antitrust policy: A century of economic and legal thinking', *Journal of Economic Perspectives*, vol. 14, no. 1, Winter 2000, pp. 43–60.

9 J. Quiggin, 'Is competition policy crazy?', *Arena*, no. 55, October 2001, p. 56.

22   DISTRIBUTION

1 J.B. Clark, *The Distribution of Wealth*, Augusta M. Kelley, New York, 1965, p. v.

2 V. Pareto, quoted in E. Roll, *History of Economic Thought*, Faber, London, 1973, p. 453.

3 H. George, *Progress and Poverty*, Robert Schalkenback, New York, 1966 (1879), p. 224.

4 M. Friedman and R. Friedman, *Free to Choose*, Penguin, Harmondsworth, 1980, ch. 1.

5 For further discussion of this issue, see E. Nell, 'The revival of political economy', in *Economics as a Social Science: Readings in Political Economy*, eds G. Argyrous and F. Stilwell, Pluto Press, Sydney, 1996, pp. 154–62; or (rather more fully), G. Harcourt, *The Social Science Imperialists*, Routledge & Kegan Paul, London, 1982, pp. 223–328.

6 C. Ferguson, *The Neoclassical Theory of Production and Distribution*, Cambridge University Press, Cambridge, 1969.

7 See A. Okun, *Equality and Efficiency: The Big Trade-off*, Brookings Institution, Washington, 1975; R. Kuttner, *The Economic Illusion: False Choices Between Prosperity and Social Justice*, Houghton Mifflin, Boston, 1984; and P. Aghion, E. Caroli and C. Garcia-Penalosa, 'Inequality and economic growth: The perspective of the new growth theories', *Journal of Economic Literature*, vol. 37, no. 4, December 1999, pp. 1615–60.

23   ECONOMIC WELFARE AND NEO-LIBERALISM

1 As with everything in economics, there are exceptions. The so-called 'hog cycle' is an example of dynamic disequilibrium in neoclassical economics. Consumer demand for bacon rises; the price of bacon rises, so farmers rear more pigs; eventually there is excess supply, so the price plunges; this stimulates demand, but discourages farmers from keeping pigs. Continual oscillation of prices rather than stable equilibrium prevails in these market conditions.

2 A.C. Pigou, *The Economics of Welfare*, Macmillan, London, 1920.

3 For further discussion, see S.K. Nath, *A Perspective of Welfare Economics*, Macmillan, London, 1973; and A. Sen, *Choice, Welfare and Measurement*, Basil Blackwell, Oxford, 1982, introduction.

4 A more formal statement of the principle is R. Lipsey and K. Lancaster, 'The general theory of second best', *Review of Economic Studies*, vol. 24, 1956–57, pp. 11–32. For a more readable interpretation of the principle, see P. Ormerod, *The Death of Economics*, Faber & Faber, London, 1994, pp. 82–4.

5 There are other 'blind alleys' in welfare economics, too. Of particular note is the problem of constructing a 'social welfare function' to show the preference ordering for a whole community. One might think this could be done by the aggregation of individual preferences (utility functions). However, according to Kenneth Arrow's 'impossibility theorem', this cannot be done because, among other things, of the problem of intransitivity in preference ordering. According to Arrow, the only social welfare function that ranks outcomes consistently is that of a dictatorship. This conclusion, being unpalatable to liberals, has led to the abandonment of the notion of an identifiable 'social welfare function'. D.T. Slesnick, reviewing this and other problems in welfare theory,

concludes that 'this left a gap between what theorists felt was a suitable framework for applied welfare economics and what policy analysts needed to provide a complete and consistent assessment of policies'. Indeed it did. See D.T. Slesnick, 'Empirical approaches to the measurement of welfare', *Journal of Economic Literature*, vol. 36, no. 4, December 1998, p. 2139.

6 Quoted in M.A. Lutz, *Economics for the Common Good: Two Centuries of Economic Thought in the Humanist Tradition*, Routledge, London, 1999, p. 122.

7 'Neo-liberalism' is the most widely used term. 'Economic rationalism' is the term generally used in Australia, and 'economic fundamentalism' is the term used in New Zealand. For a general critique, written at the time when the influence of neo-liberalism was at its zenith in the UK and the USA, see E. Nell (ed.), *Free Market Conservatism: A Critique of Theory and Practice*, Allen & Unwin, London, 1984. On the dramatic New Zealand experiment, see J. Kelsey, *Economic Fundamentalism: The New Zealand Model*, Pluto Press, London, 1995.

8 J. Buchanan, *Liberty, Market and the State: Political Economy in the 1980s*, Wheatsheaf Books, Brighton, UK, 1986, p. 256.

9 For further discussion of this awkward link between welfare theory and neo-liberalism in practice, see P. Self, *Government by the Market*, Macmillan, London, 1993, and (by the same author) *Rolling Back the Market: Economic Dogma and Political Choice*, Macmillan, Basingstoke, 2000, ch. 3. See also L. Orchard and H. Stretton, *Public Goods, Public Enterprise, Public Choice*, St Martins Press, New York, 1994.

10 Recent articles questioning the basic assumptions of welfare economics, such as the presumption that higher incomes and more 'status' goods are conducive to happiness, include R.A. Esterlin, 'Income and happiness: Towards a unified theory', *Economic Journal*, vol. 111, no. 473, July 2001, pp. 465–86; and B. Cooper, C. Garcia-Penalosa and P. Funk, 'Status effects and negative utility growth', *Economic Journal*, vol. 111, no. 473, July 2001, pp. 642–65. See also G.F. De Martino, *Global Economy, Global Justice: Theoretical Objections and Policy Alternatives to Neoliberalism*, Routledge, London, 2000, chs 1 and 2.

24   ECONOMY AND SOCIETY

1 W. Lazonick, *Business Organisation and the Myth of the Market Economy*, Cambridge University Press, Cambridge, 1991, p. 8.

2 See, for example, N. Smelser and R. Swedberg (eds), *Handbook of Economic Sociology*, Princeton University Press, Princeton, 1994.

3 The professional association of institutional economists based in the USA is called the Association for Evolutionary Economics. On the character of evolutionary economics, see G. Hodgson, *Economics and Evolution: Bringing Life Back into Economics*, University of Michigan Press, Ann Arbor, 1993. For a dialogue between an institutionalist and a Marxist regarding how best to study economic evolution, see W.H. Dugger and H.J. Sherman, *Reclaiming Evolution*, Routledge, London, 2000.

4 See S. Berger and G. Dore (eds), *National Diversity and Global Capitalism*, Cornell University Press, Ithaca, NY, 1996; J.R. Hollingsworth and R. Boyer (eds), *Comparing Capitalisms: The Embeddedness of Institutions*, Cambridge University Press, Cambridge, 1997; and R.D. Whitley, *Divergent Capitalisms: The Social Structuring and Change of Business Systems*, Oxford University Press, Oxford, 1999.

5 See R. Swedberg, *Max Weber and the Idea of Economic Sociology*, Princeton University Press, Princeton, 1998; and J.N. Baron and M.T. Hannan, 'The impact of economics on contemporary sociology', *Journal of Economic Literature*, vol. 32, no. 3, September 1994, pp. 1111–46.

6 On the origins and history of institutional economics, see R. Lekachman, *A History of Economic Ideas*, McGraw-Hill, New York, 1976, chs 12 and 13.

7 See J.K. Galbraith, *The Age of Uncertainty*, BBC, London, 1977, ch. 2.

8 This theme is further explored in chapter 27. For further discussion of the nature and influence of Veblen's ideas, see R. Tilman, *The Intellectual Legacy of Thorstein Veblen: Unresolved Issues*, Greenwood Press, Westport, Conn., 1996.

25   A DISSIDENT TRADITION IN ECONOMICS

1 See D. Fusfeld, *The Age of the Economist*, Addison-Wesley, Reading, Mass., 1999, ch. 8.

2 The problem—from an institutionalist economic perspective—is that econometrics has become tied to particular economic theories. An obvious example is computerised general equilibrium models, based on the Walrasian conception of the market economy, as outlined in chapter 23. Contrary to Mitchell's empiricist inclination, the theory here determines what is measured, and the quantitative work tends to be largely a demonstration of the theory. Of course, such models may be appraised according to the accuracy of their predictions, but this process usually leads to minor modifications of the econometric model's specifications rather than to a rejection of the underlying theory. Mitchell will probably be turning in his grave. For some further reflections on the relationship between econometrics and political economy, see F. Stilwell, 'Barro and beyond', *Journal of Economic and Social Policy*, vol. 3, no. 2, Winter 1999, pp. 221–8.

3 See, for example, K. Cowling and R. Sugden, *Transnational Monopoly Capitalism*, Oxford University Press, Oxford, 1987. The authors argue that the traditional definition of the firm, according to ownership, is not appropriate in the circumstances of modern industry, where firms can exercise control over other, nominally independent, firms. A broadened definition of the firm based on 'effective strategic control' is advocated.

4 R.L. Heilbroner, *An Inquiry into the Human Prospect*, W.W. Norton, New York, 1974, p. 132.

5 For a summary of key themes in the theory of circular and cumulative causation, see G. Argyrous, 'Economic evolution and cumulative causation', in *Economics as a Social Science: Readings in Political Economy*, eds G. Argyrous and F. Stilwell, Pluto Press, Sydney, 1997, pp. 112–20. For a fuller exposition of its historical development, see P. Toner, *Main Currents in Cumulative Causation: The Dynamics of Growth and Development*, Macmillan, Basingstoke, 1999.

6 N. Kaldor, 'The irrelevance of equilibrium economics', *The Economic Journal*, December 1972, vol. 82, no. 328, pp. 1237–55.

7 G. Myrdal, *An American Dilemma*, Harper & Brothers, New York, 1944.

8 R. Nurske, 'Some aspects of capital accumulation in under-developed countries', commemoration lecture, Cairo, 1952.

9 G. Myrdal, *Economic Theory and Underdeveloped Regions*, Methuen, London, 1957, p. 27.

10 On urban bias, see M. Lipton, *Why Poor People Stay Poor: Urban Bias in World Development*, Maurice Temple-Smith, London, 1977.

11 Argyrous, *op. cit.*, p. 114.

12 G. Myrdal, *The Political Element in the Development of Economic Thought*, Simon & Schuster, New York, 1969, p. xii.

13 See G. Ramia, 'The downturn of the Swedish model: Inevitable?', *Journal of Australian Political Economy*, no. 38, December 1996, pp. 63–97.

14 P.J. O'Rourke, *Eat the Rich: A Treatise on Economics*, Pan Macmillan, Sydney, 1998, p. 56.

15 L.S. Moss, review of M.A. Lutz, *Economics for the Common Good*, in *The Economic Journal*, vol. 111, no. 469, February 2001, pp. 129–31.

16 Fusfeld, *op. cit.*, pp. 102–3.

17 For a pioneering contribution to developing an understanding of these issues, see I. Gough, *The Political Economy of the Welfare State*, Macmillan, London, 1979. A more recent work is N. Barr, *The Economics of the Welfare State*, 3rd edn, Oxford University Press, Oxford, 1998. A comprehensive compendium of key contributions to analysis of the welfare state is R.E. Goodwin and

D. Mitchell (eds), *The Foundations of the Welfare State*, 3 vols, Edward Elgar, Cheltenham, 2000. On recent reversals, see A.B. Atkinson, *The Economic Consequences of Rolling Back the Welfare State*, MIT Press, Cambridge, Mass., 1999.

18 J. O'Connor, *The Fiscal Crisis of the State*, St Martins Press, New York, 1973.

19 See, for example, O.E. Williamson, *The Economic Institutions of Capitalism*, Free Press, New York, 1985; and R. Langlois (ed.), *Economics as a Process: Essays in the New Institutional Economics*, Cambridge University Press, Cambridge, 1986.

20 O.E. Williamson, *Markets and Hierarchies: Analysis and Anti-trust Implications—A Study in the Economics of Internal Organisation*, Free Press, New York, 1975, p. 20.

21 G.M. Hodgson, 'The return of institutional economics', in *Handbook of Economic Sociology*, eds N. Smelser and R. Swedberg, Princeton University Press, Princeton, NJ, 1994, p. 70. On the critique of 'new' institutionalism, see also J. Mulberg, *Social Limits to Economic Theory*, Routledge, London, 1995, ch. 5.

22 On 'new growth theories', see P.M. Romer, 'The origins of endogenous growth theory', *Journal of Economic Perspectives*, vol. 8, no. 4, Winter 1994, pp. 3–22. For contributions to a more institutionalist interpretation of path dependence in the growth process, see P. Garrouste and S. Ionnides (eds), *Evolution and Path Dependence in Economic Ideas*, Edward Elgar, Cheltenham, 2001.

23 See J. Phillimore, 'Neo-Schumpeterian economics: Political possibilities and problems', *Journal of Australian Political Economy*, no. 42, December 1998, pp. 48–74. More generally, on the significance and influence of Schumpeter, see H. Hanusch (ed.), *The Legacy of Joseph A. Schumpeter*, Edward Elgar, Cheltenham, 1999.

26   ECONOMIC POWER

1 J.K. Galbraith, *The Anatomy of Power*, Corgi Books, London, 1985, p. 23.

2 *Ibid.*, p. 24.

3 *Idem.*

4 Galbraith's clearest statement of the 'imperatives of technology' is *The New Industrial State*, Penguin, Harmondsworth, 1972, ch. 2.

5 Galbraith, *The New Industrial State*, p. 31.

6 See, for example, H. Thompson, 'The social significance of technological change', *Journal of Australian Political Economy*, no. 8, July 1980, pp. 57–68.

7 Galbraith used this term in *Economics and the Public Purpose*, Andre Deutsch, London, 1974, p. 285, in a rather different way—to denote the case for more public control over both 'unduly weak industries and unduly strong ones'.

8 *The New Industrial State*, p. 86.

9 J.K. Galbraith, 'The good society: The economic dimension', in *Economics as a Social Science: Readings in Political Economy*, eds G. Argyrous and F. Stilwell, Pluto Press, Sydney, p. 272.

10 W.M. Dugger argues that the relative autonomy of the technostructure was characteristic of the 1950s and 1960s; but, squeezed by the creation of a 'market' for corporate control, power was effectively shifted back to the shareholders from the 1970s. See W.M. Dugger, 'The great retrenchment and the new industrial state', *Review of Social Economy*, vol. 50, Winter 1992, pp. 453–71.

11 J.K. Galbraith, *The Affluent Society*, Penguin, Harmondsworth, 1962, p. 107.

12 *Economics and the Public Purpose*, pt 3.

13 *The New Industrial State*, p. 216.

14 J.K. Galbraith, 'Economics as a system of belief', in *A Contemporary Guide to Economics, Peace and Laughter*, Andre Deutsch, London, 1971; extract in *Readings in Political Economy*, vol. 2, eds E.L. Wheelwright and F. Stilwell, ANZ Book Co., Sydney, 1976, pp. 32–43.

15 J.K. Galbraith, *The World Economy Since the Wars*, Sinclair-Stevenson, London, 1994 p. 1.

16 *The Affluent Society*, p. 206.

17 J.K. Galbraith, *American Capitalism: The Concept of Countervailing Power*, Penguin, Harmondsworth, 1952, ch. 9.

18 *Economics and the Public Purpose*, pt 5.

19 J.K. Galbraith, in Argyrous and Stilwell, *op. cit.*, p. 274.

20 *Ibid.*, p. 275.

21 *The New Industrial State*, ch. 25.

22 J.K. Galbraith, *The Culture of Contentment*, Houghton Mifflin, Boston, 1992.

23 C. Lasch, *The Revolt of the Elites and the Betrayal of Democracy*, W.W. Norton & Co., New York, 1995.

24 J.K. Galbraith, in Argyrous and Stilwell, *op. cit.*, p. 272.

25 *Ibid.*, p. 273.

26 *Idem.*

27 *Ibid.*, p. 274.

28 *Idem.*

29 *Ibid.*, p. 275.

30 *Economics and the Public Purpose*, p. 223.

31 *Ibid.*, pp. 277, 283.

27   CORPORATE GLOBALISATION

1 See, for example, K. Ohmai, *The End of the Nation State: The Rise of Regional Economies*, HarperCollins, London, 1995. A more carefully reasoned contribution, emphasising potentially progressive aspects of globalisation, is G. Kitching, *Seeking Social Justice Through Globalisation: Escaping a Nationalist Perspective*, University of Philadelphia Press, Philadelphia, 2001.

2 See, for example, P. Hirst and G. Thompson, *Globalisation in Question: The International Economy and the Possibilities of Governance*, Polity Press, Cambridge, 1996; and R. Went, *Globalisation: Neoliberal Challenge, Radical Responses*, Pluto Press, London, 2000.

3 The most substantial of these contributions is G.J. Crough and E.L. Wheelwright, *Australia: A Client State*, Penguin Books, Melbourne, 1982. Also with a focus on Australia is a useful collection of articles compiled in a book from the Evatt Foundation and the Public Sector Research Centre: C. Sheil (ed.), *Globalisation: Australian Impacts*, UNSW Press, Sydney, 2001. See also J. Wiseman, *Global Nation? Australia and the Politics of Globalisation*, Cambridge University Press, Cambridge, 1998.

4 See UNCTAD, *World Development Report 2001*, UNCTAD, New York and Geneva; and E.L. Wheelwright, 'The crisis of contemporary capitalism', in *Economics as a Social Science: Readings in Political Economy*, eds G. Argyrous and F. Stilwell, Pluto Press, Sydney, 1996, p. 6.

5 The use of 'market capitalisation' is a distinctively capitalistic criterion for this ranking, it should be noted. It values national economies according to the toal value of domestic equities traded on their stock exchanges. This valuation of national economies excludes publicly-owned assets, environmental assets and most residential real estate.

6 Crough and Wheelwright, *op. cit.*, ch. 2.

7 Crough and Wheelwright give a striking example: 'International Telephone & Telegraph Corporation, ITT, is often cited as the classic conglomerate: it is involved in hotels, insurance, finance, teleprinters, cosmetics, automotive parts, pipes, pumps, food, cellulose, timber, fire extinguishers, coal and land development, as well as major communication companies. It employs 348 000 people, nearly two-thirds of whom are employed outside North America, and as one of its annual reports said, "is constantly at work around the clock, in 67 nations on six continents, in activities extending from the Arctic to the Antarctic and quite literally from the bottom of the sea to the moon" ' (*op. cit.*, p. 12). ITT is now ATT, with even more extensive global operations.

8 TNCs accounted for two-thirds of US exports in 1996, of which 45 per cent was to the exporters' own affiliates or related companies; see H.J. Shatz and A.J.Venables, 'The geography of international investment', in *The Oxford Handbook of Economic Geography*, eds G.L. Clark, M.P. Feldman and M.S. Gertler, Oxford University Press, Oxford, 2000, pp. 125–45.

9 Crough and Wheelwright, *op. cit.*, p. 13.

10 On the 'footloose' character and destabilising effect of the transnationals, see H.P. Martin and H. Schumann, *The Global Trap: Globalisation and the Assault on Prosperity and Democracy*, Zed Books, London, 1997, ch. 4.

11 The classic reference on this topic is F. Froebel, J. Heinrichs and O. Kreye, *The New International Division of Labour*, Cambridge University Press, Cambridge, 1980.

12 See, for example, R. Fagan and M. Webber, *Global Restructuring*, Oxford University Press, Melbourne, 1994; and T. Bramble, Solidarity Versus Sectionalism: The Social Tariff Debate, *Journal of Australian Political Economy*, No. 48, December 2001, pp. 73—114.

13 On transfer pricing, see G.J. Crough and E.L. Wheelwright, *op.cit.*, pp. 143–7.

14 D. Peetz, *Trade Unions in a Contrary World: The Future of the Australian Trade Union Movement*, Cambridge University Press, Melbourne, 1998.

15 This view is particularly associated with British (transnational?) sociologist Leslie Sklair; see *The Transnational Capitalist Class*, Blackwell, Oxford, 2001.

16 Crough and Wheelwright, *op. cit., passim.*

17 N. Hertz, *The Silent Takeover: Global Capitalism and the Death of Democracy*, Heinemann, London, 2001, p. 7.

18 S. Holland, *The Global Economy: From Meso to Macroeconomics*, Weidenfeld & Nicolson, London, 1987, pp. xiii–xiv.

19 See, for example, R. Bryan and M. Rafferty, *The Global Economy in Australia: Global Integration and National Economic Policy*, Allen & Unwin, Sydney, 1999.

20 E.L. Wheelwright, *Capitalism, Socialism or Barbarism? The Australian Predicament. Essays in Contemporary Political Economy*, ANZ Book Co., Sydney, 1978.

21 The former interpretation is presented by R. Catley, *Globalising Australian Capitalism*, Cambridge University Press, Melbourne, 1996, p. 222.

22 See K.R. Cox (ed.), *Spaces of Globalisation: Reasserting the Power of the Local*, Guildford Press, New York, 1997; and J. Mander and E. Goldsmith (eds), *The Case Against the Global Economy and for a Turn Toward the Local*, Sierra Club Books, San Francisco, 1996.

23 A good example of an effective campaign, contesting the proposed Multilateral Agreement on Investment (MAI), is described in J. Goodman and P. Ranald (eds), *Stopping the Juggernaut*, Pluto Press, Sydney, 2000. For more general discussion of social movements contesting the globalisation of capital, see A. Starr, *Naming the Enemy: Anti-corporate Social Movements Confront Globalisation*, Zed Books, London, 2000 and J. Goodman (ed.), *Protest and Globalisation*, Pluto Press Australia, Sydney, 2002.

28   THE DISILLUSIONED DEFENCE OF CAPITALISM

1 This self-perpetuating character of unemployment is sometimes labelled *hysteresis*. It may be interpreted as one illustration of the principle of circular and cumulative causation discussed in chapter 25.

2 See J. Langmore and J. Quiggin, *Work for All*, Melbourne University Press, Melbourne, 1994, p. 30; P.N. Junankar and C.A. Kapuscinski, *The Costs of Unemployment in Australia*, Economic Planning Advisory Council Background Paper No. 24, AGPS, Canberra, 1992; and M. Watts and W. Mitchell, 'The costs of unemployment in Australia', *The Economics and Labour Relations Review*, vol. 11, no. 2, December 2000, pp. 180–97.

3 On the Great Depression, see J.K. Galbraith, *The Great Crash*, Houghton Mifflin, Boston, 1954; and T.E. Hall and J.D. Ferguson, *The Great Depression*, University of Michigan Press, Ann Arbor, 1998.

4   See J. Robinson, 'Marx, Marshall and Keynes: Three views of capitalism', in *Readings in Political Economy*, vol. 1, eds E.L. Wheelwright and F. Stilwell, ANZ Book Co., Sydney, 1976, pp. 147–59.

5   Critics of Keynes sometimes contend he simplified and/or misrepresented the prevailing economic orthodoxies; see S. Kates, *Say's Law and the Keynesian Revolution: How Macroeconomics Lost its Way*, Edward Elgar, Cheltenham, 1998. Of course, cutting through to the essence of the prevailing orthodoxies is usually a precondition for pushing them aside and moving on.

6   A.C. Pigou, *Theory of Unemployment*, Macmillan, London, 1933, p. 252.

7   It is pertinent to note that Keynes did not seek to establish a link between his 'macro' theory and the 'micro' theories of 'imperfect competition' being developed at Cambridge University (by Joan Robinson) at the same time. This kept the primary focus on the aggregate level of economic activity and its management—but at the expense of having a more comprehensive analysis of the capitalist economy.

8   J.M. Keynes, *The General Theory of Employment, Interest and Money*, Macmillan, London, 1936, p. 131.

9   D. Fusfeld, *The Age of the Economist*, Addison-Wesley, Reading, Mass., 1999, p. 127.

10 R. O'Donnell, 'Keynes's socialism: Conception, strategy and espousal', in *Keynes, Post-Keynesianism and Political Economy: Essays in Honour of Geoff Harcourt*, vol. 3, eds C. Sardoni and P. Kriesler, Routledge, London and New York, 1999, p. 165.

29   CONSTRUCTING A KEYNESIAN MODEL

1   For a political economic reinterpretation of the circular flow model, see E. Nell, 'Economics: The revival of political economy', in *Ideology in Social Science*, ed. R. Blackburn, Fontana, London, 1972, pp. 76–95; extract in *Economics as a Social Science: Readings in Political Economy*, eds G. Argyrous and F. Stilwell, Pluto Press, Sydney, 1996, pp. 154–62.

2   For an analysis of investors' confidence and the associated instability and cyclical patterns in the economy, drawing also on the ideas of Michal Kalecki, see J. Courvisanos, *Investment Cycles in Capitalist Economies*, Edward Elgar, Cheltenham, 1996.

30   INSTABILITY IN A MONETARY ECONOMY

1   In estimating the money supply and in formulating monetary policy, various definitions of money are used (e.g. M_1, M_2, M_3) according to which classes of liquid assets are included with cash. In this chapter, for ease of exposition, cash is taken to be synonymous with money (i.e. M_1).

2   This does not mean that *only* money can function as a means of exchange. Local Area Trading Schemes (LETS) have proliferated as a means of combating unemployment, fostering social reciprocity, and strengthening local communities. The problems of barter are avoided by the adoption of a common unit of value, without recourse to money in the form of notes and coin.

3   G. Argyrous, 'The economics of the general theory', in *Economics as a Social Science: Readings in Political Economy*, eds G. Argyrous and F. Stilwell, Pluto Press, Sydney, 1996, p. 125.

4   The use of the term 'speculators' should not necessarily be taken to imply a distinct class of people separate from ordinary citizens. Anyone seeking the best rate of return on his or her savings would wisely consider different types of financial assets and their likely changes in value. Of course, some people (and institutions) have very much more surplus funds to use for such purposes than others. Such people also usually have a higher propensity to switch assets based on day-to-day changes in market prices. They can reasonably be identified as being central to the processes of speculation.

5   There is a separate body of post-Keynesian economic analysis examining the possibility of *endogenous* money supply, that is, changes in the supply of money through the banking system in direct response to changes in the conditions of demand for money—depending on the level of investment.

6 There is one circumstance where this policy does not work. If virtually all savings are currently being held as cash (i.e. liquidity preference is high), an increase in the money supply may not cause the interest rate to fall. So there will be no stimulus to investment. This is the problem known as the 'liquidity trap', where interest rates have hit rock-bottom and investment remains stagnant. Monetary policy is usually said to be of no avail in these circumstances. However, a *public-sector-led* recovery is still possible. If the central bank provides low-interest loans to the government and the government then spends the money on job creation and public works, economic expansion can occur.

7 On this 'post-Keynesian' view of endogenous money, see R. Guttman, *How Credit Money Shapes the Economy: The US in a Global System*, Sharpe, London, 1994. The quotation by Galbraith comes from a review of this book in *Journal of Economic Literature*, vol. 33, no. 4, December 1995, p. 1989.

8 J. Hartley, reviewing D. Laidler, *Fabricating the Keynesian Revolution*, Cambridge University Press, Cambridge, 1999, in *Journal of Economic Literature*, vol. 37, no. 4, December 1999, p. 1799.

9 The LM curve in Box 30.1 becomes steeper to the right because more money is held for transactions and precautionary purposes as national income rises, so the equilibrium interest rate (needed to balance the supply and demand for money) must rise. The curve becomes vertical when the whole of the existing money supply is held for transactionary and precautionary purposes. This limit represents the highest level of real income which can be financed by the existing money supply. For a brief but insightful comment on the limitations of this IS/LM model, see D.E. Moggridge, *Keynes*, Macmillan, Basingstoke, 1986, Appendix, pp. 165–7.

10 Chapter 35 returns to these issues.

11 J.M. Keynes, *The General Theory of Employment, Interest and Money*, Macmillan, London, 1936, p. 159.

12 *Ibid.*, p. 376.

31   MACROECONOMIC POLICY

1 A comprehensive discussion of measures to address unemployment, explicitly linked to a social democratic perspective on the state, is provided by G. Dow, P. Boreham and M. Leet, *Room to Manoeuvre: Political Aspects of Full Employment*, Melbourne University Press, Melbourne, 1999.

2 J.K. Galbraith, *Economics and the Public Purpose*, Houghton Mifflin, New York, 1973, p. 21.

3 R. O'Donnell, 'Keynes's socialism: Conception, strategy and espousal', in *Keynes, Post-Keynesianism and Political Economy: Essays in Honour of Geoff Harcourt*, vol. 3, eds C. Sardoni and P. Kriesler, Routledge, London and New York, p. 169.

4 For discussion of this tendency in Australia , see J. Dullard and D. Hayward, 'The democratic paradox of public choice theory: The case of the Costello cuts', *Journal of Australian Political Economy*, no. 42, December 1998, pp. 16–47.

5 There are significant exceptions. Hugh Stretton advocates a general long-term policy of running the lowest achievable interest rates for this purpose; see H. Stretton, *Political Essays*, Georgian House, Melbourne, 1987, pp. 37–47. Others advocate linking monetary policy, specifically low-interest loans to the government from the central bank, to higher levels of government expenditure on job creation and infrastructure provision.

6 For discussion of how financial deregulation has worked out in the Australian context, see J. Spoehr, *From Lending Binge to Credit Squeeze: The Failure of Bank and Finance Sector Deregulation*, United Trades and Labour Council, Adelaide, 1990.

7 J.M. Keynes, *The General Theory of Employment, Interest and Money*, Macmillan, London, 1936, p. 372.

8 For discussion of the Accord, see the various contributions to K. Wilson, J. Bradford and M. Fitzpatrick (eds), *Australia in Accord*, South Pacific Publishing, Melbourne, 2000.

9 Keynes, *op. cit.*, p. 378.

10 For further discussion of the lessons from the Swedish experience, see G. Dow, 'The Swedish model and the Anglo-Saxon model: Reflections on the fate of social democracy in Australia', *Economic and Industrial Democracy*, vol. 12, no. 4, November 1991, pp. 515–26.

11 For further discussion of the proposed Tobin tax, see M. ul Huq, I. Kaul and I. Grunberg (eds), *The Tobin Tax: Coping with Financial Volatility*, Oxford University Press, Oxford, 1996; and H. Patomaki, *Democratising Globalisation: The Leverage of the Tobin Tax*, Zed Books, London, 2001.

32   THE KEYNESIAN LEGACY

1 J.M. Keynes in a letter to George Bernard Shaw dated 1 January 1935, quoted in M. Stewart, *Keynes and After*, Penguin, Harmondsworth, 1972, p. 12.

2 See R.M. Collins, *The Business Response to Keynes, 1929–1964*, Columbia University Press, New York, 1981.

3 J.K. Galbraith, *The Age of Uncertainty*, BBC, London, 1977, p. 221. The New Deal of President Franklin D. Roosevelt in the USA was a more positive example, putting people to work in socially beneficial jobs. Beginning in 1933, this was 'primal Keynesianism' before Keynes's theory was fully developed and published. Thus, 'in the end Keynesian economics was to justify policies already in vogue' (E.R. Canterbury, *The Literate Economist*, HarperCollins, New York, 1995, p. 158).

4 In the UK, a national health system was set up by the first Labour government after World War II. In Australia, the introduction of a universal public health system had to wait until the election of a Labor government in 1972. In the US, a national health system has never been introduced.

5 E. Jones, *Was the Post-War Keynesian?*, Working Paper No. 131, Department of Economics, University of Sydney, October, 1989.

6 See, for example, R. Sutcliffe, 'Keynesianism and the stabilisation of capitalist economies', in *Economics: An Anti-Text*, eds F. Green and P. Nore, Macmillan, London, 1977, pp. 163–81; extract in *Economics as a Social Science: Readings in Political Economy*, eds G. Argyrous and F. Stilwell, Pluto Press, Sydney, 1996, pp. 142–4.

7 M. Bleaney, *The Rise and Fall of Keynesian Economics*, Macmillan, London, 1985, pp. 131–54; see also R. Leeson, *The Eclipse of Keynesianism: The Political Economy of the Chicago Counter-Revolution*, Macmillan, Basingstoke, 2001

8 See W.J. Barber, 'Chile con Chicago: A review essay', *Journal of Economic Literature* vol. 23, no. 4, pp. 1941–8.

9 N.G. Mankiew, 'The inexorable and mysterious trade-off between inflation and unemployment", *The Economic Journal*, vol. 111, no. 471, May 2001, p. 59. See also David Laidler's review of the collected works of A.W. Phillips in the same journal (no. 472, June 2001, p. 526). Laidler notes that, by drawing a curve through the scatter, Phillips was 'unintentionally providing an empirically based functional relationship for others to interpret as a policy menu'. As a result, 'Phillips' name will forever be associated with damaging fine tuning policies whose many pitfalls his own work was designed to reveal and warn against'. Moreover, as P.J. Kurwin had earlier noted, Phillips recognised the existence of 'loops' causing the expansion and contraction paths to differ, so the dynamic instability in the unemployment–inflation trade-off was acknowledged from the start; see P.J. Kurwin, *Inflation*, Macmillan, London, 1976. A comprehensive compilation of contributions by Phillips is presented by R. Leeson (ed.), *A.W.H. Phillips: Collected Works in Contemporary Perspective*, Cambridge University Press, Cambridge, 2000.

10 M. Friedman, 'The methodology of positive economics', in *Essays in Positive Economics*, ed. M. Friedman, University of Chicago Press, Chicago, 1953, pp. 3–43.

11 On the evidence of 'crowding-out', see C. Kearney and K. Chowdhury, *Does Public Capital 'Crowd in' Private Capital? Evidence for Australia 1966–1988*, University of Western Sydney, Department of Economics and Finance Paper, January 1992; D. Aschaur, 'Does public capital crowd out private capital?', *Journal of Monetary Economics*, vol. 24, no. 2, 1989, pp. 171–88; and A.H. Munnell, 'Policy watch: Infrastructure investment and economic growth', *Journal of Economic Perspectives*, vol. 6, no. 4, 1992, pp. 189–98.

12 For discussion of the NAIRU, see the special symposium in *Journal of Economic Perspectives*, vol. 11, no. 1, Winter 1977, especially J.K. Galbraith (Jr), 'Time to ditch the NAIRU', pp. 93–108.

13 See, for example, Committee on Employment Opportunities, *Restoring Full Employment*, Green Paper on Employment Opportunities, AGPS, Canberra, 1993.

14 J.B. de Long, 'The triumph of monetarism?', *Journal of Economic Perspectives*, vol. 14, no. 1, Winter 2000, pp. 83–94. On de Long's reasoning, 'new Keynesian' economics is a misnomer: it is really 'new monetarism'.

15 See F. Stilwell, *Changing Track: A New Political Economic Direction for Australia*, Pluto Press, Sydney, 2000, ch. 6.

16 On 'rational expectations', see L. Thurow, *Dangerous Currents: The State of Economics*, Oxford University Press, Oxford, 1983, ch. 6.

17 See J.E. Hartley, *The Representative Agent in Macroeconomics*, Routledge, London, 1997; and T. Sargent, *Bounded Rationality in Macroeconomics*, Clarendon Press, Oxford, 1993. The work of Robert Lucas pushes this emphasis on the 'micro' foundations of macroeconomics to an (anti-Keynesian) extreme. In his own words, 'progress in economic thinking means getting better and better abstract analogue economic models, not better verbal observations about the world' ('Methods and problems in business cycle theory', *Journal of Money, Credit and Banking*, vol. 12, 1980, pp. 696–715, cited (approvingly) by V.V. Chari, 'Nobel Laureate Robert E. Lucas, Jr., architect of modern macroeconomics', *Journal of Economic Perspectives*, vol. 12, no. 1, Winter 1998, pp. 171–86).

18 For assessments of these policies in Australia, see J. Quiggin, *Great Expectations*, Allen & Unwin, Sydney, 1996; and T. Anderson, 'The meaning of deregulation', *Journal of Australian Political Economy*, no. 44, December 1999, pp. 5–21. For discussion of what policies could put the emphasis back on solving unemployment, see S. Bell (ed.), *The Unemployment Crisis in Australia: Which Way Out?* Cambridge University Press, Melbourne, 2000.

19 See, for example, W.F. Mitchell, 'Full employment abandoned: The macroeconomic story', in *Out of the Rut*, eds M. Carmen and I. Rogers, Allen & Unwin, Sydney 1999, pp. 17–48; and T. Aspromourgos, 'Is an employer-of-the-last-resort policy sustainable?', a review article, *Review of Political Economy*, vol. 12, no. 2, 2000, pp. 141–55.

20 P. Sraffa, *The Production of Commodities by Means of Commodities*, Cambridge University Press, Cambridge, 1960. For an introduction to this otherwise enigmatic theory, see Y. Varoufakis, *Foundations of Economics: A Beginner's Companion*, Routledge, London, 1998, pp. 191–200.

21 One book emphasising Sraffa's work as a superior analysis than either neoclassicism or Marxism is S. Keen, *Debunking Economics*, Pluto Press, Sydney, 2001.

22 M. Kalecki, 'Political aspects of full employment', in *Collected Works of Michal Kalecki*, vol. 1, ed. J. Osiatynski, Clarendon, Oxford, 1990; reprinted in Argyrous and Stilwell, *op. cit.*, pp. 146–9.

23 H. Minsky, *Stabilising an Unstable Economy*, Yale University Press, New Haven, 1986.

24 A. Eichner, *The Megacorp and Oligopoly*, Cambridge University Press, Cambridge, 1976.

25 See, for example, F. Lee, *Post Keynesian Price Theory*, Cambridge University Press, Cambridge, 1999.

26 For fuller discussion of post-Keynesian economics, see P. O'Hara (ed.), *Encyclopedia of Political Economy*, Routledge, London, 1999, pp. 880–7; J. King, *Conversations with Post Keynesians*, St Martins Press, New York, 1995; and P. Davidson, *Post-Keynesian Macroeconomic Theory*, Edward Elgar, Aldershot, 1994.

27 This characterisation of the Keynesarian state is by S. Holland, *The Global Economy*, Weidenfeld & Nicholson, London, 1987, p. 1.

33   A RADICAL REFORMULATION

1 There are some modern political economists who, continuing to operate within the analytical traditions we have considered, see no need for a synthesis of this sort. Marxist economists, such as those contributing to the journal *Monthly Review*, are generally of the view that what is required is the further development and application of Marxism in the context of contemporary

capitalism. On the other hand, some post-Keynesian and institutional economists prefer to have no truck with the Marxian analysis, seeing its basis in value theory as an obstacle to empirical study. The classic reference on this latter position is I. Steedman, *Marx after Sraffa*, New Left Books, London, 1977, which stimulated contributions to I. Steedman and P. Sweezy (eds), *The Value Controversy*, Verso, London, 1981. Some of the most interesting work in modern political economy is concerned with exploring fruitful interconnections between Marxian and non-Marxian perspectives; see, for example, S. Tsuru, *Institutional Economics Revisited*, Cambridge University Press, Cambridge 1993; and P.A. O'Hara, *Marx, Veblen and Contemporary Institutional Political Economy: Principles and Unstable Dynamics of Capitalism*, Edward Elgar, Cheltenham, 2000.

2 It even features in 'postmodern' Marxism; see J.K. Gibson-Graham, S. Resnick and R. Wolff (eds), *Re/Presenting Class: Essays in Postmodern Marxism*, Duke University Press, Durham, 2001.

3 For discussion of the contributions of Gorz and theorists of 'post-Fordism', see chapter 35.

4 See chapter 36.

34   ECONOMY AND ENVIRONMENT

1 D. Attenborough, 'The State of the Planet' (television series), BBC, 2000.

2 D. Meadows *et al.*, *The Limits to Growth*, Earth Island Limited, London, 1972.

3 An important publication, giving official international status to the concern over global environmental issues was The World Commission on Environment and Development, *Our Common Future*, Oxford University Press, Oxford, 1987.

4 See chapter 8, nn. 1 and 3.

5 For discussion of this concept, see M. Diesendorf and C. Hamilton (eds), *Human Ecology, Human Economy: Ideas for an Ecologically Sustainable Future*, Allen & Unwin, Sydney, 1997; H. Daly, *Beyond Growth: The Economics of Sustainable Development*, Beacon Press, Boston, 1996; S. Beder, *The Nature of Sustainable Development*, Scribe, Newham, 1993; D.W. Pearce and J.J. Warford, *World Without End: Economics, Environment and Sustainable Development*, Oxford University Press, Oxford, 1993; M. Jacobs, *Sustainable Development: Greening the Economy*, Fabian Society, London, 1990 and J. Bowers, *Sustainability and Environmental Economics: An Alternative Text*, Addison Wesley Longman, London, 1997.

6 These four categories are adapted from I. Lowe, 'Ecologically sustainable development', *Consuming Interest*, Australian Consumers Association, June/July 1991. See also Diesendorf and Hamilton, *op. cit.*, ch. 3.

7 From July 2000, the profit and loss statement became known as the 'statement of financial performance', and the balance sheet as the 'statement of financial position'.

8 See, for example, P. Hawken, *The Ecology of Commerce: A Declaration of Sustainability*, Phoenix, London, 1995.

9 See Diesendorf and Hamilton, *op. cit.*, ch. 12.

10 C. Hamilton, T. Hundloe and J. Quiggin, *Ecological Tax Reform in Australia*, Discussion Paper No. 10, Australia Institute, Canberra, April 1997.

11 For discussion of the influence of vested economic interests in transport, see one of the first reference books on environmental issues by a political economist: M. Edel, *Economies and the Environment*, Prentice Hall, Englewood Cliffs, NJ, 1973, ch. 6.

12 For discussion of claims and counter-claims about the LA experience, see B.C. Snell, 'American ground transport: A proposal for restructuring the automobile, truck, bus and rail industries', Part 4A, Appendix to Part 4, *Hearings Before the Sub Committee on Antitrust and Monopoly of the Committee on the Judiciary*, United States Senate, 1974; and P. Mees, *A Very Public Solution: Transport in the Dispersed City*, Melbourne University Press, Carlton South, 2000, pp. 42–5.

13 This need not be an absolute impediment to achieving a shift from private to public transport; see Mees, *op. cit.*, *passim*.

14 K. Boulding, Environmental Quality—Discussion, *Papers and Proceedings of the American Economic Association*, May 1971, p. 169.

15 This position is argued strongly by T. Trainer, *The Conserver Society: Alternatives for Sustainability*, Zed Books, London, 1995.

16 On the concept of common heritage capital, see A.F. Anderson, *Challenging Newt Gingrich*, Tom Paine Institute, Eugene, Oregon, 1996, pp. xvii–xx.

17 For an example of an attempt to move beyond conventional approaches to environmental economics and construct an ecological political economy, see F.P. Gale and R.M. M'Gonigle, *Nature, Production, Power: Towards on Ecological Political Economy*, Edward Elgar, Cheltenham, 2000.

35   TECHNOLOGY, INDUSTRY, WORK

1 E. Nell, *The General Theory of Transformational Growth: Keynes after Sraffa*, Cambridge University Press, Cambridge, 1998.

2 M. Castells, *The Information City*, Basil Blackwell, Oxford, 1989, and *The Rise of the Network Society*, Blackwell, Cambridge, Mass., 1997. For a more sceptical view on the 'new economy', see R. Boyer, 'Is a finance-led growth regime a viable alternative to Fordism?', *Economy and Society*, vol. 29, no. 1, February 2000, pp. 111–45. Critical assessments of how the potential of new technologies is distorted in practice are to be found in R.W. McChesney, E.M. Wood and J.B. Foster (eds), *Capitalism and the Information Age*, Monthly Review Press, New York, 2000.

3 L. Thurow, *The Future of Capitalism*, Nicholas Brealey, London, 1997.

4 This argument is put by G. Zappala, 'The economic and social dimensions of the new economy', *Australian Journal of Social Issues*, vol. 35, no. 4, November 2000, pp. 317–32.

5 D. Munro, 'The knowledge economy', *Journal of Australian Political Economy*, no. 45, June 2000, p. 9.

6 H. Braverman, *Labor and Monopoly Capital: The Degradation of Work in the Twentieth Century*, Monthly Review Press, New York, 1974. See also box 14.1, p. 118.

7 This distinction between a regime of accumulation and a mode of social regulation is characteristic of the 'regulation school' of political economy based in France. See R. Boyer, *The Regulation School: A Critical Introduction*, Columbia University Press, New York, 1990; and R. Boyer and Y. Saillard (eds), *Regulation Theory: The State of the Art*, Routledge, London, 2001. For further discussion, see also T.J. Barnes, *Logics of Dislocation: Models, Metaphors and the Meanings of Economic Space*, Guildford Press, New York, 1996, p. 34.

8 The classic exposition of this view is M.J. Piore and C. Sabel, *The Second Industrial Divide*, Basic Books, New York, 1984.

9 For a fuller description of these features of post-Fordism, see R. Murray, 'Fordism and post-Fordism', in *New Times*, eds S. Hall and M. Jacques, Lawrence & Wishart, London, 1990, pp. 38–53, an extract from which appears in *Economics as a Social Science: Readings in Political Economy*, eds G. Argyrous and F. Stilwell, Pluto Press, Sydney, 1996, pp. 264–8.

10 See, for example, D. Harvey, *The Condition of Post-Modernity*, Basil Blackwell, Oxford, 1989.

11 For a critical perspective on the various currents in explanations of post-Fordism and regional development, see A. Amin and K. Robbins, 'The mythical geography of flexible accumulation', *Environment and Planning: Society and Space*, vol. 8, 1990, pp. 7–34.

12 On new industrial spaces, see A.J. Scott, *New Industrial Spaces: Flexible Production, Organisation, and Regional Development in North America and Western Europe*, Pion, London, 1988; and B.T. Asheim, 'Industrial districts: The contributions of Marshall and beyond', in *The Oxford Handbook of Economic Geography*, eds G.L. Clark, M.P. Feldman and M.S. Gertler, Oxford University Press, Oxford, 2000, pp. 413–31.

13 A positive view of these possibilities is J. Mathews, *The Culture of Power*, Pluto Press, Sydney, 1988. Mathews replied to his critics in *Journal of Australian Political Economy*, no. 30, December, 1992, pp. 91–128.

14 See, for example, I. Campbell, 'The Australian trade union movement and post-Fordism', *Journal of Australian Political Economy*, vol. 26, 1990, pp. 1–26; and B. Harrison, *Lean and Mean: The Changing Landscape of Corporate Power in the Age of Flexibility*, Guildford Press, New York, 1994.

15 R. Reich, *The Work of Nations*, Alfred A. Knopf, New York, 1991.

16 H-P. Martin and H. Schumann, *The Global Trap: Globalisation and the Assault on Democracy and Prosperity*, Zed Books, London, 1997.

17 On developments in establishing shorter working weeks, see A. Hayden, *Sharing the Work, Sparing the Planet*, Zed Books, London, 1999, ch. 7.

18 C. Sanne, *The (Im)possibility of Sustainable Lifestyles: Can We Trust the Public Opinion and Plan for Reduced Consumption?* Working Paper No. 63, Urban Research Program, Australian National University, Canberra, August 1998.

19 Australia Institute, *Redistributing Work: Solutions to the Paradox of Overwork and Unemployment in Australia*, Discussion Paper No. 7, Australia Institute, Canberra, June 1996.

20 A. Gorz, *Paths to Paradise*, Pluto Press, London, 1985, and *Reclaiming Work: Beyond the Wage-Based Society*, Polity Press, London, 1999.

21 See F. Stilwell, 'Speculation or productive investment?', *Journal of Australian Political Economy*, no. 23, August 1988, pp. 25–44. The following arguments draw primarily from this source.

22 One estimate is that about one in seventy foreign exchange deals actually reflects needs arising from international trade and commerce; see D. Richardson, Client Memorandum, Department of Parliamentary Library, Information and Research Services, Canberra, 18.6.1999.

23 R. Bryan and M. Rafferty, *The Global Economy in Australia: Global Integration and National Economic Policy*, Allen and Unwin, Sydney, 1999.

24 S. Melman, *Profits Without Production*, Alfred A. Knopf, New York, 1983.

25 *Ibid.*, p. xiii.

26 D. Gordon, T. Weisskopf and S. Bowles, *The Imperilled Economy*, URPE, New York, 1987; extract in Argyrous and Stilwell, *op. cit.*, pp. 256–9.

27 D.M. Gordon, R. Edwards and M. Reich, *Segmented Work, Divided Workers: The Historical Transformation of Labor in the United States*, Cambridge University Press, 1982, pp. 13–17.

28 For a powerful indictment of what flexibility means in practice, see Harrison, *op. cit.*, ch. 9.

36   CLASS, GENDER, ETHNICITY

1 D. Ricardo, *On the Principles of Political Economy and Taxation*, Dent, London, 1962 (1817).

2 See A.K. Sen, *Inequality Reexamined*, Harvard University Press, Cambridge, Mass., 1992. On social aspects of the analysis of economic inequality, see the classic essay by R.H. Tawney, *Equality*, Unwin Books, London, 1964; and P.N. Troy (ed.), *A Just Society?* Allen & Unwin, Sydney, 1981. There are numerous books on contemporary trends in the distribution of income and wealth. On the Australian situation, see P. Saunders, *Welfare and Inequality: National and International Perspectives on the Australian Welfare State*, Cambridge University Press, Cambridge 1994; and R. Fincher and P. Saunders (eds) *Creating Unequal Futures: Rethinking Poverty, Inequality and Disadvantage*, Allen & Unwin, Sydney, 2001. For perspectives on economic inequality in the USA and its links to globalisation, see A. Fishlow and K. Parker (eds), *Growing Apart: The Causes and Consequences of Global Wage Inequality*, Council on Foreign Relations Press, New York, 1999; and J.K. Galbraith (Jnr) and M. Berner, *Inequality and Industrial Change: A Global View*, Cambridge University Press, Cambridge, 2000.

3 See, for example, A. Okun, *Equality and Efficiency: The Big Trade-Off*, Brookings Institution, Washington, 1975.

4 Marx developed a different position in *Theories of Surplus Value* (Lawrence & Wishart, London, 1951, ch. 17, p. 6) where he refers to 'the continual increase in numbers of the middle classes ...

situated midway between the workers on one side and the capitalists and landowners on the other'. On this point, see also T. Bottomore, *Theories of Modern Capitalism*, George Allen & Unwin, Boston, 1985. Bottomore seeks to reconcile the two views of Marx in terms of a distinction between the 'tendency' and 'counter-tendencies', akin to the Marxian analysis of the tendency of the rate of profit to fall and the counteracting forces to push in the opposite direction.

5 Some background on this issue is provided by B. Connell, 'The money measure: Social inequality of wealth and income', in *Inequality in Australia: Slicing the Cake*, ed. Social Justice Collective, Heinemann, Port Melbourne, 1991, pp. 129–49; see also F. Stilwell, 'Labour's capital: Individual or collective?', *Arena*, No. 57, February 2002, pp. 48–50.

6 For some evidence on these economic inequalities in Australia, see F. Stilwell, *Changing Track: A New Political Economic Direction for Australia*, Pluto Press, Sydney, 2000, ch. 7.

7 This analysis is adapted from E.O. Wright, *Class, Crisis and the State*, New Left Books, London, 1978, ch. 2. For other works by the same author, see *Classes*, Verso, London, 1985, and *Class Counts: Comparative Studies in Class Analysis*, Cambridge University Press, Cambridge, 1997; see also E.O. Wright *et al.*, *The Debate on Classes*, Verso, London, 1989.

8 A. Gramsci, *Selections from the Prison Notebooks of Antonio Gramsci*, ed. and trans. Q. Hoare and G. Smith, Lawrence & Wishart, London, 1971. See also D. Foracs (ed.), *A Gramsci Reader*, Lawrence & Wishart, London, 1988.

9 See R. Connell, *Ruling Class, Ruling Culture*, Cambridge University Press, Cambridge, 1977.

10 J.K. Gibson-Graham, S. Resnick and R. Wolff (eds), *Re/Presenting Class: Essays in Postmodern Marxism*, Duke University Press, Durham, 2001.

11 Some recent writings on political economy from a gender perspective include: J. Humphries (ed.), *Gender and Economics*, Edward Elgar, Aldershot, 1995; S. Hanson and G. Pratt, *Gender, Work and Space*, Routledge, London, 1995; J. Nelson, *Feminism, Objectivity and Economics*, Routledge, London, 1996; L. Adkins, *Gendered Work: Sexuality, Family and the Labour Market*, Oxford University Press, Buckingham, 1995; J. Gardiner, *Gender, Care and Economics*, Clarendon Press, Oxford, 1997; L. McDowell, 'Feminists rethink the economic', in *Handbook of Economic Geography*, eds G. Clark, M. Gertler and M.A. Feldman, Oxford University Press, Oxford, 2000; and M.A. Ferber and J.A. Nelson (eds), *Beyond Economic Man: Feminist Theory and Economics*, University of Chicago Press, Chicago, 1993.

12 On patriarchy, see S. Walby, *Theorising Patriarchy*, Blackwell, Oxford, 1989.

13 See F. Blau and R. Ehrenberg (eds), *Gender and Family Issues in the Workplace*, Russell Sage Foundation, New York, 1997, especially the chapter by Goldin; and L. Peattie and M. Rein, *Women's Claims: A Study in Political Economy*, Oxford University Press, Oxford, 1983, ch. 4. For a fuller discussion of social reproduction from a feminist perspective, see also N. Folbre, *Who Pays For the Kids? Gender and the Structure of Constraint*, Routledge, London, 1994.

14 One of the leading contributions to this type of analysis was A. Game and R. Pringle, 'Production and consumption, public versus private', in *Unfinished Business: Social Justice for Women in Australia*, ed. D.H. Broom, Allen & Unwin, Sydney, 1984, pp. 65–79. For contemporary discussion of the relationship between women's work in the two spheres, see N. Folbre and J.A. Nelson, 'For love or money—or both?', *Journal of Economic Perspectives*, vol. 14, no. 4, Fall 2000, pp. 123–40.

15 See M. Waring, *Counting for Nothing: What Men Value and What Women are Worth*, Allen & Unwin, Wellington, 1988; extract in *Economics as a Social Science: Readings in Political Economy*, eds G. Argyrous and F. Stilwell, Pluto Press, Sydney, 1996, pp. 184–8; and L. Beneria, Thou Shalt Not Live By Statistics Alone—But it Might Help, *Feminist Economics*, vol. 2, no. 3, 1996, pp. 139–42.

16 For a specific example of the bias against women's domestic contributions, see J. Smith and L. Ingham, 'Breastfeeding and the measurement of economic progress', *Journal of Australian Political Economy*, no. 47, June 2001, pp. 51–72.

17 See A. Summers, *Damned Whores and God's Police: The Colonisation of Women in Australia*, Penguin Books, Ringwood, Vic., 1975, ch. 12.

18 Important research on gender and work includes A. Game and R. Pringle, *Gender at Work*, George Allen & Unwin, Sydney, 1983; R. Pringle, *Secretaries Talk*, Verso, London, 1989; and R. Pringle, *Sex and Medicine*, Cambridge University Press, Cambridge, 1998.

19 See A. Hochschild, *The Managed Heart: The Commercialisation of Human Feeling*, University of California Press, Berkeley, 1983.

20 F. Stilwell, *Changing Track*, pp. 86–7.

21 See G. Meagher, 'Evaluating women's work: NSW nurses and professional rates', *Journal of Australian Political Economy*, no. 34, December 1994, pp. 77–102; and E. Sorensen, *Comparable Worth: Is It a Worthy Policy?* Princeton University Press, Princeton, 1994.

22 J.K. Galbraith, *Economics and the Public Purpose*, Houghton Mifflin, New York, 1973, p. 233.

23 A radical feminist perspective, by contrast, emphasises gender inequalities as a more pervasive feature of all patriarchal societies.

24 See J. Collins, 'The economics of racism or the racism of economics?', in Argyrous and Stilwell, *op. cit.*, pp. 41–5.

25 G. Becker, *The Economics of Discrimination*, University of Chicago Press, Chicago, 1957.

26 M. Friedman, *Capitalism and Freedom*, University of Chicago Press, Chicago, 1962, p. 108.

27 See M.N. Leiman, *Political Economy of Racism*, Westview Press, Boulder, 1993; and E.H. Tuma, *The Persistence of Economic Discrimination: Race, Ethnicity and Gender*, Pacific Books, Palo Alto, 1995. See also K.J. Arrow, 'What has economics to say about racial discrimination?', *Journal of Economic Perspectives*, vol. 12, no. 2, Spring 1998, pp. 91–100.

28 For an example of this opposition to 'reverse discrimination', see M. Friedman, 'A comment on SWEP' (the American Economic Association's Committee on the Status of Women in the Economics Profession), *Journal of Economic Perspectives*, vol. 12, no. 4, Fall 1998, pp. 197–9. See also B.R. Bergman, *In Defence of Affirmative Action*, HarperCollins, New York, 1996.

29 See C. Taylor, 'The politics of recognition', in A. Gutman (ed), *Multiculturalism*, Princeton University Press, New Jersey, 1994, pp. 23–73; and N. Fraser, 'From redistribution to recognition? Dilemmas of justice in a "post-socialist" age', *New Left Review*, no. 212, July/August 1995, pp. 68–93.

37   THE POLITICAL ECONOMY OF THE STATE

1 An example of this position is G. Dow, P. Boreham and M. Leet, *Room to Manoeuvre: Political Aspects of Full Employment*, Melbourne University Press, Melbourne, 1999.

2 A strong statement of this view is M. Friedman and R. Friedman, *Free to Choose*, Penguin, Harmondsworth, 1980; an extract appears in *Economics as a Social Science: Readings in Political Economy*, eds G. Argyrous and F. Stilwell, Pluto Press, Sydney, 1996, pp. 77–81.

3 See R. Alford and R. Friedland, *Powers of Theory: Capitalism, the State and Democracy*, Cambridge University Press, Cambridge, 1985.

4 The United States is somewhat exceptional in this regard.

5 J.K. Galbraith, *The Anatomy of Power*, Corgi Books, London, 1985, p. 42.

6 A. Okun, *Equality and Efficiency: The Big Trade-Off*, Brookings Institute, Washington, 1975, p. vii.

7 These phrases appear as the titles of two books: B. Jessop, *The Capitalist State: Marxist Theories and Methods*, Martin Robertson, Oxford, 1982; and R. Miliband, *The State in Capitalist Society*, Quartet Books, London, 1973.

8 List shared one experience with Karl Marx: he was expelled from his native Germany for perceived excessive forthrightness in his journalism. For discussion of List, see W.O. Henderson, *Friedrich List: Economist and Visionary*, Frank Cass, London, 1983.

9 For a brief introduction, see E. Jones, 'The neglected spirit of reform', in Argyrous and Stilwell, *op. cit.*, pp. 102–8.

10 For a little more on Fabianism, see B. Burkitt, *Radical Political Economy: An Introduction to Alternative Economics*, Wheatsheaf Books, Brighton, UK, 1984, ch. 6.

11 R.H. Tawney, *Equality*, Unwin Books, London, 1964. Tawney argued strongly for an assault on economic inequality notwithstanding the vested interests opposed to any such program of reform.

12 S. Holland, *The Socialist Challenge*, Quartet Books, London, 1975.

13 A. Gorz, *Reclaiming Work: Beyond the Wage-Based Society*, Polity Press, London, 1999, p. 8.

14 K. Marx and F. Engels, *Manifesto of the Communist Party*, Foreign Languages Publishing House, Moscow, 1960 (1848), p. 66–7.

15 The classic debate in the Marxist literature on the state was that between Nicos Poulantzas and Ralph Miliband; for a brief summary, see D. Gold, C. Lo and E.O. Wright, 'Recent developments in Marxist theories of the capitalist state', in *Readings in Political Economy*, vol 1, eds E.L. Wheelwright and F. Stilwell, ANZ Book Co, Sydney, 1976, pp. 260–5.

16 This relationship between capital accumulation and legitimisation is a major political-economic theme established by J. O'Connor, *The Fiscal Crisis of the State*, St Martins Press, New York, 1973.

17 A focus on the influence of freemasonry is not a normal feature of Marxist analysis. It is mentioned in this context as an example of an institutionalised process of preferment. For further discussion of how it works, see S. Knight *The Brotherhood: The Secret World of the Freemasons*, Granada, London, 1984; and M. Baigent and R. Leigh, *The Temple and the Lodge*, Guild Publishing, London, 1989.

18 See, for example, R. Bryan and M. Rafferty, *The Global Economy in Australia: Global Integration and National Economic Policy*, Allen & Unwin, Sydney, 1999.

19 G. Baldelli, *Social Anarchism*, Penguin, Harmondsworth, 1971, p. 19.

20 D.C. Mueller, *Public Choice*, Cambridge University Press, Cambridge, 1979, p. 105. See also G.D. Myles, *Public Economics*, Cambridge University Press, Cambridge, 1995; and D.C. Mueller (ed.), *The Economics of Politics*, Edward Elgar, Cheltenham, 2001.

21 See L. Orchard and H. Stretton, *Public Goods, Public Enterprise, Public Choice*, St Martins Press, New York, 1994; and P. Self, *Government by the Market*, Macmillan, London, 1993. For a less-than-riveting dialogue between a proponent of public choice theory and an advocate of a more substantial role for the state and public finance, see J.A. Buchanan and R.A. Musgrave, *Public Finance and Public Choice: Two Contrasting Views*, MIT Press, Cambridge, Mass., 2000.

22 Self, *op. cit.*, p. 209.

23 This point is strongly argued by E. Jones, 'Economics and the neglected spirit of reform', *Journal of Australian Political Economy*, no. 35, June, 1995, p. 84.

24 An example is the 'green bans' movement that saved Sydney from more environmentally damaging 'urban renewal' in the 1970s. See M. Burgmann and V. Burgmann, *Green Bans: Red Union*, University of NSW Press, Sydney, 1998; and J. Mundey, *Green Bans and Beyond*, Angus & Robertson, Sydney, 1981. The prospects for 'red–green' coalitions today is further discussed in F. Stilwell, *Changing Track: A New Political Economic Direction for Australia*, Pluto Press, Sydney, 2000, chs 12 and 13.

38   WHY DO ECONOMISTS DISAGREE?

1 This notion comes from K. Boulding, *The Image*, University of Michigan Press, Ann Arbor, 1956. See also E. Jones, 'Methodology in economics: An introduction', in *Readings in Political Economy*, vol. 1, eds E.L. Wheelwright and F. Stilwell, ANZ Book Co., Sydney, 1976, pp. 275–9.

2 A standard reference on these epistemological issues is A. Chalmers, *What Is This Thing Called Science?*, University of Queensland Press, St Lucia, 1976. See also A.S. Eichner (ed.), *Why Economics is Not Yet a Science*, M.E. Sharpe, New York, 1983.

3 W.S. Jevons, 1888, quoted in B. Toohey, *Tumbling Dice: The Making of Modern Economic Policy*, William Heinemann, Port Melbourne, 1994, p. 12.

4 E. Jones, 'Positive economics or what?', *Economic Record*, vol. 53, September 1957, pp. 350–63.

5 See, for example, R. Bhaskar, M. Archer, A. Collier, T. Lawson and A. Norrie (eds), *Critical Realism: Essential Readings*, Routledge, London, 1998; and S. Fleetwood, *Critical Realism in Economics: Development and Debate*, Routledge, London, 1998.

6   See M. Foucault, *Power/Knowledge: Selected Interviews and Other Writings, 1972–1977*, ed. and trans. Colin Gordon, Pantheon Books, New York, 1980.

7   A.J. Scott, 'Economic geography: The great half-century', in *The Oxford Handbook of Economic Geography*, eds G.L. Clark, M.P. Feldman and M. S. Gertler, Oxford University Press, Oxford, 2000, p. 34.

8   T. Barnes, *Logics of Dislocation: Models, Metaphors and the Meanings of Economic Space*, Guildford Press, New York, 1996, p. 95.

9   C. Mouffe, 'Rorty's pragmatic politics', *Economy and Society*, vol. 29, no. 3, August 2000, pp. 439–53. See also R. Rorty, *Truth and Progress*, Cambridge University Press, 1998, and *Philosophy and Social Hope*, Penguin, Harmondsworth, 1999.

10 See D. McCloskey, *The Rhetoric of Economics*, University of Wisconsin Press, Madison, 1985.

11 There are many currents in postmodernism, so generalisation is difficult. For further discussion of the status and influence of postmodernism, see P.M. Rosenau, *Post-Modernism and the Social Sciences*, Princeton University Press, Princeton, NJ, 1992.

12 For example, R.G. Lipsey, *An Introduction to Positive Economics*, Weidenfeld & Nicolson, London, 1979; and various subsequent editions and nation-specific adaptations, e.g. R.G. Lipsey and K.A. Chrystal, *Principles of Economics*, Oxford University Press, Oxford, 2000.

13 The classic exposition of this view is G. Myrdal, *The Political Element in the Development of Economic Theory*, Simon & Schuster, New York, 1969.

14 F.M. Watkins, *The Age of Ideology: Political Thought, 1750 to the Present*, Prentice Hall, Englewood Cliff, NJ, 1964. See also R. Bronk, *Progress and the Invisible Hand: The Philosophy and Economics of Human Advance*, Warner Books, London, 1998.

15 This position is argued by F. Stilwell, *Changing Track: A New Political Economic Direction for Australia*, Pluto Press, Sydney, 2000, ch. 3.

16 For a more comprehensive view, see R. Leach, *Political Ideologies: An Australian Introduction*, Macmillan, South Melbourne, 1993.

17 See P. Feyerabend, *Against Method: Outline of an Anarchistic Theory of Knowledge*, London, New Left Books, 1975.

39   A LEVEL PLAYING FIELD FOR ECONOMIC IDEAS?

1   An interesting example of something less than liberalism is the proclamation of the Texas State Board of Education: 'Textbook content shall promote citizenship and the understanding of the free enterprise system, emphasize patriotism and respect for recognised authority … Textbook content shall not encourage life-styles deviating from generally accepted standards of society' (quoted in J.K. Galbraith, *The Anatomy of Power*, Corgi Books, London 1985, p. 39.).

2   Personal communication with an academic economist at a British university.

3   See E. Jones and F. Stilwell, 'Political economy at the University of Sydney', in *Intellectual Suppression*, eds B. Martin, C. Baker, C. Manwell and C. Pugh, Angus & Robertson, Sydney, 1986.

4   See R.H. Frank, T.D. Gilovich and D.T. Regan, 'Does studying economics inhibit cooperation?', *Journal of Economic Perspectives*, vol. 7, no. 2, Spring 1997, pp. 159–71. It is also interesting to note that a survey of US economics graduate students (cited by A.J. Field, book review, *Journal of Economic Literature*, vol. 36, no. 1, March 1998, p. 229), reported only 3% of students as thinking it important for an economist to have knowledge about the real world.

5   M. Pusey, *Economic Rationalism in Canberra: A Nation-building State Changes Its Mind*, Cambridge University Press, Cambridge, 1991.

6   M. Pusey, 'The impact of economic ideas as public policy in Australia', in *Economics as a Social Science: Readings in Political Economy*, eds G. Argyrous and F. Stilwell, Pluto Press, Sydney, 1996, p. 229.

7   W. Parsons, *The Power of the Financial Press*, Rutgers University Press, New Brunswick, 1990, cited in B. Toohey, *Tumbling Dice: The Story of Modern Economic Policy*, William Heinemann, Melbourne, 1994, p. 216.

8   D. Hallin, *The Uncensored War: The Media and Vietnam*, University of California Press, Los Angeles, 1986, cited in Toohey, *op. cit.*, p. 218.

9   On bias in journalism, see also R.W. McChesney, 'Journalism, democracy and class struggle', *Monthly Review*, vol. 5, no. 6, November 2000, pp. 1–15.

10 R. Cockett, *Thinking the Unthinkable: Think-tanks and the Economic Counter-revolution, 1931–1983*, HarperCollins, London, 1995.

11 In Australia, the principal example is the Canberra-based Australia Institute, whose publications have been cited in previous chapters of this book.

12 See P. Sheldon and L. Thornthwaite, *Employer Associations and Industrial Relations Change*, Allen & Unwin, Sydney, 1999, for discussion of these institutions in Australia.

13 Their meetings also provide focal points for 'anti-globalisation' protests, such as those that occurred in Seattle, Prague, Melbourne, Quebec City, Gothenburg, and Genoa in 2000 and 2001 (see box 3.1, p. 20).

14 Even that is disputable. The argument of F. Hayek is that the real strength of a competitive market system is not its allocative efficiency or other equilibrium properties, but its anarchic character which fosters risk-taking and innovation. See Y. Varoufakis, *Foundations of Economics: A Beginner's Companion*, Routledge, London, 1998, pp. 189–90.

15 See C. Kaysen, 'The social significance of the modern corporation', *The American Economic Review*, May 1957, p. 314.

16 J.K. Galbraith, 'Power and the useful economist', *American Economic Review*, March 1973, p. 1.

40   W(H)ITHER CAPITALISM?

1   K. Marx and F. Engels, *Manifesto of the Communist Party*, Foreign Languages Publishing House, Moscow, 1960 (1848), p. 68.

2   R. Heilbroner, *An Inquiry into the Human Prospect*, W.W. Norton, New York, 1974, p. 76.

3   On the connection between happiness and material progress, see also R. Bronk, *Progress and the Invisible Hand: The Philosophy and Economics of Human Advance*, Warner Books, London, 1998, ch. 9; P. Saunders, *Capitalism: A Social Audit*, Open University Press, Buckingham, 1995, ch. 4; and R. Kuttner, *Everything for Sale: The Virtues and Limits of Markets*, Alfred A. Knopf, New York, 1998.

4   Marx and Engels, *op. cit.*, p. 67.

5   See F. Stilwell, *Changing Track: A New Political Economic Direction for Australia*, Pluto Press, Sydney, 2000, ch. 8.

6   R.A. Esterlin, *Growth Triumphant: The Twenty-first Century in Historical Perspective*, University of Michigan Press, Ann Arbor, 1996.

7   H. Minsky's analysis, briefly mentioned in chapter 32, is particularly relevant in this context.

8   Admittedly, this is a tricky distinction between redistributive and transformative activities. Most struggles have a local and specific focus but contain the potential for wider impacts. Treating struggles about production relations as more important than struggles about distribution is not necessarily implied. We all do what we can. For an article reasserting the strength of class consciousness, see P. Sweezy and H. Magdoff, 'Socialism: a time to retreat?', *Monthly Review*, vol. 52, no. 4, September 2000, pp. 1–7.

9   The view that the dispossessed comprise the principal source of challenge to the existing social order is not novel. It was one of the celebrated claims of philosopher Herbert Marcuse, in the penultimate paragraph of his book *One Dimensional Man*, Sphere Books, London, 1968, pp. 200–1.

10 For a defence of Marxism against this claim, see M.E. Gimenez, 'Does ecology need Marx?', *Monthly Review*, vol. 22, no. 8, January 2001, pp. 60–2.

11 The following analysis is partly reproduced from Stilwell, *op. cit.*, ch. 10, where it is more fully developed.

12 For debates about market socialism, see J. Roemer, *A Future for Socialism*, Verso, London, 1994; D. McNally, *Against the Market: Political Economy, Market Socialism and the Marxist Critique*, Verso, London, 1993; and P. Bardhan and J. Roemer, *Market Socialism*, Oxford University Press, Oxford, 1993.

13 See A. Tausch (ed.), *The Three Pillars of Wisdom: A Reader on Globalisation, World Bank Pension Models and Welfare Society*, Nova Science, New York, 2002; and B. Frankel, *When The Boat Comes In*, Pluto Press Australia, Sydney, 2001, ch. 5.

14 On the case for cooperatives, see R. Mathews, *Jobs of Our Own: Building a Stakeholder Society*, Pluto Press, Sydney, 1999.

15 This guideline was posited in F. Stilwell, *Economic Inequality: Who Gets What in Australia?*, Pluto Press, Sydney, 1993, ch. 10. The contrast between the guideline and the extent of economic inequality in 'actually existing capitalism' is even greater now.

Further Reading

GENERAL

A user-friendly introduction to political economy, including extracts from key articles, both classical and modern, is G. Argyrous and F. Stilwell (eds), *Economics as a Social Science: Readings in Political Economy* (Pluto Press, Sydney, originally published in 1996, 2nd edn, 2002). That is the obvious 'companion volume' to this book, suitable both for the general reader and for teachers seeking material around which supplementary tutorials can be structured. Other general reference books to which it is useful to have access are: P. O'Hara (ed.), *Encyclopedia of Political Economy* (Routledge, London, 1999) and P. Arestis and M. Sawyer (eds), *The Elgar Companion to Radical Political Economy* (Edward Elgar, Cheltenham, 1994).

On the competing currents flowing into modern political economy, see B. Clark, *Political Economy: A Comparative Approach* (Praeger, Westport, Conn., 1998); J. Caporoso and D. Levine, *Theories of Political Economy* (Cambridge University Press, Cambridge, 1992); and W.K. Tabb, *Reconstructing Political Economy: The Great Divide in Economic Thought* (Routledge, London, 1999). Well-established standard textbooks seeking to introduce students to the study of economics from a political economy perspective include E.K. Hunt and H.J. Sherman, *Economics: An Introduction to Traditional and Radical Views* (Harper & Row, New York, various edns); and S. Bowles and R. Edwards, *Understanding Capitalism* (Harper & Row, New York, 1985). These have been joined more recently by the massive work by Hugh Stretton, *Economics: A New Introduction* (UNSW Press, Sydney, 1999), which presents a view of how economic analysis can be developed and applied for progressive social purposes.

There are numerous books on the evolution of economic ideas. R. Heilbroner, *The Worldly Philosophers* (Simon & Schuster, New York, 1968) is a classic exposition of the ideas of the key figures in the development of economic thought and is still the liveliest introduction to the subject. E. Ray Canterbury, *A Brief History of Economics* (World Scientific, New Jersey, 2001) is a modern equivalent. D. Fusfeld, *The Age of the Economist* (Addison–Wesley, Boston, various edns) and E.K. Hunt, *Property and Prophets* (Harper & Row, New York, various edns) are succinct introductions, showing the political element in the development of economic ideas. W.J. Barber, *History of Economic Thought* (Penguin Books, Harmondsworth, various edns) is a standard, easily accessible short work, too. Among the many more voluminous tomes for the serious scholar of the history of economic thought are E.K. Hunt, *History of Economic Thought* (HarperCollins, New York, 1992); M. Blaug, *Economic Theory in Retrospect* (Cambridge University Press, Cambridge, 5th edn, 1997); and J.K. Galbraith, *Economics in Perspective* (Houghton Mifflin, Boston, 1987).

PART I: ECONOMIC PROCESSES AND PROBLEMS

Some of the best books on political economic trends in the last decade have been written by economic geographers, e.g. P. Dicken, *Global Shift: Industrial Change in a Turbulent World* (Paul Chapman, London, 3rd edn, 1998); P. Knox and J. Agnew, *The Geography of the World Economy* (Arnold, London, 1994); and J. Allen and C. Hamnett (eds), *A Shrinking World?* (Oxford University Press, Oxford, 1995). Other useful sources tend to be journal articles rather than books, given the time lags normally involved in producing the latter. Journals such as *Monthly Review, Capital and Class, Economy and Society* and *New Left Review* have an international orientation. Other journals tend to be more nation-specific, e.g. the *Journal of Australian Political Economy* and the Canadian *Studies in Political Economy*. Yet others combine a concern about contemporary issues with more academic concerns; see, for example, *Cambridge Journal of Economics, Review of Radical Political Economics, Journal of Post-Keynesian Economics, Review of Political Economy* and *New Political Economy*. The magazine *New Internationalist* provides a more popular treatment of contemporary political economic, social, and environmental concerns.

PART II: ECONOMIC SYSTEMS

On the nature of capitalism, see R. Heilbroner, *The Nature and Logic of Capital* (Norton, New York, 1985). How the economic history of capitalism is intertwined with the development of economic thought is the central concern of R. Backhouse, *Economists and the Economy: The Evolution of Economic Ideas* (Transaction Publishers, New Jersey, 1994). A similar theme is pursued more entertainingly and with a more explicitly radical political economic perspective by D. Dowd, *Capitalism and its Economics: A Critical History* (Pluto Press, London, 2000). The ideas and influence of the great political economic thinkers, such as Smith, Marx and Mill, are discussed in M. Cohen, *Political Philosophy: From Plato to Mao,* (Pluto Press, London, 2001).

PART III: BACK TO BASICS

The various books on the history of economic thought recommended earlier under 'General' all contain sections on classical political economy. Reading some of the classics in the original is useful to get the 'flavour' of the authors' concerns, a feel for their breadth of analysis and the authors' personal values; see particularly A. Smith, *An Inquiry into the Nature and Significance of the Wealth of Nations*, and D. Ricardo, *Principles of Political Economy and Taxation* (various edns). D.P. O'Brien, *The Classical Economists* (Clarendon Press, Oxford, 1975), and G. Routh, *The Origin of Economic Ideas* (Macmillan, London, 1975) consider the significance of other important classical contributors, too. R. Heilbroner and W. Milberg, *The Making of Economic Society,* (Prentice Hall, New Jersey, 11th edn, 2002) sets the historical context in which the ideas were developed.

PART IV: THE CRITIQUE OF CAPITALISM

There is an enormous range of books on Marxist economics. Some are brief introductions, such as G. Hands, *Marx: A Beginner's Guide* (Hodder & Stoughton, London, 2000); E. Reiss, *Marx: A Clear Guide* (Pluto Press, London, 1997); E. Mandel, *An Introduction to Marxist Economic Theory* (Pathfinder, New York, various edns); P. Jaleé, *How Capitalism Works* (Monthly Review Press, New York, 1977); B. Fine, *Marx's Capital* (Macmillan, London, 1975); and J.G. Gurley, *Challengers to Capitalism,* (Addison-Wesley, Reading, Mass., 1988), chs 1–3. Fuller expositions include P. Sweezy, *The Theory of Capitalist Development* (Monthly Review Press, New York, 1942); E. Mandel, *Marxist Economic Theory* (Merlin, London, 1968); J. Gouveneur, *Contemporary Capitalism and Marxist Economics* (Martin Robinson, Oxford, 1983); G. Kay, *The Economic Theory of the Working Class* (Macmillan, London, 1979); J. Weeks, *Capital and Exploitation* (Edward Arnold, London, 1981); B. Fine and L. Harris, *Rereading Capital* (Macmillan, London, 1979); and A. Brewer, *A Guide to Marx's Capital* (Cambridge University Press, Cambridge, 1984).

Going back to the original works, the polemical pamphlet by Marx and Engels, *Manifesto of the Communist Party* is the obvious place to start. At the other extreme is *Capital,* Marx's massive three-volume *magnum opus,* and Marx's *Contribution to the Critique of Political Economy* (and Engels' preface thereto). Pamphlets by Marx include *Wage Labour and Capital,* and *Wages, Price and Profit* (various edns).

Key extracts from Marx's voluminous work are compiled in E. Kamenka (ed.), *The Portable Karl Marx* (Penguin Books, New York, 1983). Assessments of Marxism include F. Parkin, *Marxism: A Bourgeois Critique* (Tavistock, London, 1979), R. Heilbroner, *Marxism: For and Against* (W.W. Norton, New York, 1980), G. Dow and G. Lafferty (eds), *Everlasting Uncertainty: Interrogating the Communist Manifesto, 1848–1998* (Pluto Press, Sydney, 1998); and R. Munck, *Marx@2000* (Zed Books, London, 2002).

PART V: THE IDEOLOGY OF THE MARKET

There are more textbooks on neoclassical economics than you could poke a stick at! Here is a striking example of the neoclassical economists' own theory of monopolistic competition—endless variations on the same basic theme. See, for example, D. McTaggert, C. Findlay and M. Parkin, *Microeconomics* (Addison-Wesley, Reading, Mass., 1996); and J.M. Perloff, *Microeconomics* (Addison-Wesley, Boston, 2nd edn, 2001). A book that explains the theory but also encourages a critical perspective is Y. Varoufakis, *Foundations of Economics: A Beginner's Companion* (Routledge, London, 1998).

Going back to the roots, Alfred Marshall's *Principles of Economics* (London, Macmillan, 1890 and subsequent edns) is the classic reference. A.C. Pigou's *The Economics of Welfare* (London, Macmillan, 1920) is also interesting because it, modestly if somewhat laboriously, sets orthodox economic concerns in a broader social setting. The more contemporary neoclassical tendency is towards an invasion of other social sciences; see G. Becker, 'The economic way of looking at behaviour', Nobel lecture, *Journal of Political Economy*, vol. 103, no. 3, pp. 385–409, or G. Stigler, 'Economics —the imperial science', *Scandinavian Journal of Economics*, vol. 86, pp. 301–13. For a critical evaluation of this tendency, see G. Harcourt, *The Social Science Imperialists* (Routledge & Kegan Paul, London, 1982), pp. 377–93; or M Zafirovski, 'Extending the rational choice model from economy to society', *Economy and Society*, vol. 29, no. 2, May 2000, pp. 181–206.

More generally on the critique of neoclassicism and its dominance in modern economics, see S. Keen, *Debunking Economics* (Pluto Press, Sydney, 2001); P. Ormerod, *The Death of Economics* (Faber & Faber, London, 1994); B. Toohey, *Tumbling Dice: The Making of Economic Policy* (William Heinemann, Melbourne, 1994); and L. Thurow, *Dangerous Currents: The State of Economics* (Oxford University Press, Oxford, 1983).

PART VI: EVOLUTION AND REFORM

For brief introductions to the institutional tradition in economics, see G. Hodgson, 'The approach of institutional economics', *Journal of Economic Literature*, vol. 36, no. 1, March 1998, pp. 166–92; M. Rutherford, 'Institutional economics: Then and now', *Journal of Economic Perspectives*, vol. 15, no. 3, Summer 2001, pp. 173–94; or J. Elliot, 'The institutional school in political economy', in *What is Political Economy?*, ed. D.K. Whynes (Basil Blackwell, Oxford, 1984), ch. 3. For fuller treatments, see A. Gruchy, *Contemporary Economic Thought: The Contribution of Neo-Institutional Economics* (Macmillan, London, 1972); G. Hodgson, *Evolution and Institutions: On Evolutionary Economics and the Evolution of Economics* (Edward Elgar, Cheltenham, 1999); and F. Louca and M. Perelman (eds), *Is Economics an Evolutionary Science?* (Edward Elgar, Cheltenham, 2000). The leading journal for ongoing contributions to institutional economics is the *Journal of Economic Issues*.

PART VII: STABILISING THE ECONOMY

Reading J.M. Keynes, *The General Theory of Employment, Interest and Money* (Macmillan, London, first published 1936) is a tall order for anyone coming anew to the study of political economy. A handy short introduction is G. Argyrous, 'The economics of the *General Theory*', in *Economics as a Social Science: Readings in Political Economy*, eds G. Argyrous and F. Stilwell (Pluto Press, Sydney, 1996). Among the numerous works on Keynes and his economics, two succinct ones are D.E. Moggridge, *Keynes* (Fontana, Glasgow, 1976) and M. Stewart, *Keynes and After* (Penguin Books, Harmondsworth, 1967). M. Blaug, 'Recent biographies of Keynes', *Journal of Economic Literature*, vol. 32, no. 3, September 1994, pp. 1204–15 surveys subsequent more substantial studies. R. O'Donnell, *Keynes: Philosophy, Economics and Politics* (Macmillan, London, 1989) combines philosophy and political economy—as did Keynes.

On the influence of Keynesian economics, see M. Bleaney, *The Rise and Fall of Keynesian Economics* (Macmillan, Basingstoke, 1985); H.L. Wattel (ed.), *The Policy Consequences of John Maynard Keynes* (Macmillan, Basingstoke, 1986); and L. Pasinetti and B. Schefold (eds), *The Impact of Keynes on Economics in the Twentieth Century* (Edward Elgar, Cheltenham, 1999). Specifically on the influence of Keynesianism in Australia, and the subsequent backlash, is T. Battin, *Abandoning Keynes* (Macmillan, Basingstoke, 1997). On post-Keynesian economics, the *Journal of Post-Keynesian Economics* contains ongoing contributions.

PART VIII: CONTEMPORARY CHALLENGES

Critical contributions to ongoing debates in modern political economy include J. Mulburg, *Social Limits to Economic Theory* (Routledge, London, 1995); and A. Sayer, *Radical Political Economy: A Critique* (Blackwell, Oxford, 1995). On the diverse ideas of individual political economists, see P. Arestis and M. Sawyer (eds), *A Bibliographical Dictionary of Dissenting Economists* (Edward Elgar, Cheltenham, 2001). Some of these views are further developed in C.J. Whalen (ed.), *Political Economy for the Twenty-First Century: Contemporary Views on the Trend in Economics* (Sharpe, New York, 1996).

PART IX: WHITHER POLITICAL ECONOMY?

References on the nature of economic inquiry and its philosophical status include M. Hollis and E. Nell, *Rational Economic Man* (Cambridge University Press, London, 1975); S. Hargraves Heap, *Rationality in Economics* (Basil Blackwell, Oxford, 1989); R. Backhouse, *Truth and Progress in Economic Knowledge* (Edward Elgar, Cheltenham, 1997); H. Katouzian, *Ideology and Method in Economics* (New York University Press, New York, 1980); and K. Cole, *Economy, Environment, Development, Knowledge* (Routledge, London, 1999), which provides a taxonomy of competing viewpoints in these interconnected fields, paving the way for further progress in social science.

For different views on the prospects for capitalism, see A. McEwan, *Neo-liberalism or Democracy: Economic Strategy, Markets and Alternatives for the 21st Century* (Zed Books, London and Pluto Press, Sydney, 1999); Lester Thurow, *The Future of Capitalism* (Nicholas Brealey, London, 1997); and D. Corten, *The Post-Corporate World: Life After Capitalism* (Pluto Press, Sydney, 2000). For a social democratic critique of neo-liberalism see also P. Self, *Rolling Back the Market: Economic Dogma and Political Choice* (Macmillan, Basingstoke, 2000). Finally, for a stocktaking of political economic developments, problems, and possible policies for future directions, with particular reference to Australia, the interested reader might consider looking at F. Stilwell, *Changing Track: Towards a New Political Economic Direction for Australia* (Pluto Press, Sydney, 2000) on B. Frankel, *When the Boat Comes In: Transforming Australia in the Age of Globalisation*, Pluto Press Australia, Sydney, 2001.

Index

Entries in *italics* refer to glossary; entries in **bold** refer to text boxes.